306.09
Had

132208

Hadley.
A free order.

Learning Resources Center
Nazareth College of Rochester, N. Y.

A FREE ORDER

National Goal and World Goal

A FREE ORDER

National Goal and World Goal

by Hamilton Hadley

GREENWOOD PRESS, PUBLISHERS
WESTPORT, CONNECTICUT

LEARNING RESOURCES CENTER
NAZARETH COLLEGE

The Library of Congress has catalogued this publication as follows:

Library of Congress Cataloging in Publication Data

Hadley, Hamilton.
    A free order.

    Reprint of the 1963 ed.
    1. Social history. 2. Social conflict. 3. Politi-
cal psychology. 4. Power (Social sciences) 5. Toleration. I. Title.
[HM136.H2 1973]   301.24   72-9542
ISBN 0-8371-6582-2

Copyright © 1963 by Hamilton Hadley

All rights reserved

Originally published in 1963
by Dodd, Mead & Company, New York

Reprinted with the permission
of Dodd, Mead & Company

Reprinted from an original copy in the collections
of the University of Illinois Library

First Greenwood Reprinting 1973

Library of Congress Catalogue Card Number 72-9542

ISBN 0-8371-6582-2

Printed in the United States of America

306.09
112d

To

E. M. H.

Contents

PART III. THE RULE OF A FREE ORDER

Chapter 21. Truth to Fact   410

Chapter 22. Truth to Fact and Political Institutions   420

Chapter 23. Current Institutions and Principles of Reform   431

Chapter 24. Equity   446

Chapter 25. Towards a Free Order on the World Scene   455

Chapter 26. Friends and Enemies on the World Scene   473

Chapter 27. Rule as Role   480

Concluding Remarks   497

A FREE ORDER

National Goal and World Goal

Introduction: Motives of Reform

EVERY man wishes to better his condition. As he does not live alone but is a member of one or more kinds of group or community, small or large, his attempts at betterment take place as such a member. Within any large community serving a general interest, such as that of defense of the whole or the maintenance of sufficient peace to permit orderly life of all, lesser groups—interior communities—are invariably present. These are small or great in numbers and extent, and less or more closely knit, depending on the particular interests which they serve and the ideas and techniques of the time and place. Examples of such interior groups within the large community are ethnic groups, families, clans, guilds, corporations, professional associations, artistic, literary, scholarly and scientific societies, sports clubs, labor unions, stock exchanges, cities, churches. Indeed, the groups that can be named are coextensive with the interests or activities that have seemed essential or worthwhile to men and women.

In the Introduction to this book we point out, in a summary way only and without any attempt at detail or analysis, important motives underlying the efforts of communities and groups and their leaders to promote their own advantage. The efforts of a group to promote its own advantage can take the shape of pushing ahead with a reform. Or it can take the shape of resistance to reforms advocated by others, that appear to be to its disadvantage. That is to say, the same motives which make for change and reform can, and often do, make use of a tactic of resistance which may for the time being be the most conspicuous feature of the activity of the group.

In this Introduction the illustrations of the motives of reform will be plain, many on the simplest level and already familiar to most of us, and will serve to indicate briefly the significant motives making for political change on the domestic scene and world scene alike.

We then go on to the main parts of the book. First we examine these same motives of reform as they take politically harmful turns and work out in various forms of *divided community* both on the domestic and world scene, often in the complex circumstances of contemporary events. Next we inquire into the *origins of right* in order to see how men acquire those ideas of what is right for them which have so great an influence on the course in fact taken by the motives of reform—their outlet in action in the political community. In the concluding part of the book we describe the kind of political actions, habits, institutions, and aims which offer a prospect of the reconciliation of the motives within a free order—*the rule of a free order*—again on the domestic and world scenes.

1. SATISFACTION OF MATERIAL NEEDS

Summary Illustrations of Association to Promote Economic Interests

The assurance of enough food and shelter, the desire for more creature comforts and easier living conditions, have always occupied a major part of the time and attention of mankind. The groups and associations formed in connection with these economic interests have been important in the life of the state—which is the community viewed in its political relationships of government and governed— and have greatly influenced its form and function.

Those engaged in producing the food for a highly differentiated community like the United States have interests to protect and promote which are different from those of the producers of manufactured goods. There is thus an agricultural grouping, on a wide and not closely knit organizational basis, which wishes to better its position. There is also an industrial grouping which likewise wishes to better its position. Within the wide agricultural grouping, there are to be found smaller groups with more particularized interests, let us say the wheat growers or the dairy farmers. And similarly in the industrial grouping may be found the manufacturers of automobiles or miners of ores. All alike have the desire to better themselves.

In a particular business enterprise producing a specific article— say sheet metal—there are the varying interests of owner and employed or of management and labor, and here again the members of each group will seek to bring about changes which will strengthen their relative position. They may recognize a common interest with those of similar situation or occupation in other business enterprises, and join them in an organization to promote this mutual interest.

Saint Luke, in his account of the Acts of the Apostles, describes a small-scale but informative instance of economic motivation of resistance to reform. The leader of a group of craftsmen incites his followers to opposition to an economic threat, and also adopts the ancient and modern technique of making use of a mob to back his opposition.

A silversmith named Demetrius was making large profits for his workmen by the manufacture of silver shrines of Artemis. He got the workmen in that and similar trades together, and said to them,

"Men, you know that this business is the source of our prosperity, and you see and hear that not only in Ephesus but almost all over Asia, this man Paul has persuaded and drawn away numbers of people, telling them that gods made by human hands are not gods at all. There is danger, therefore, not only that this business of ours will be discredited, but also that the temple of the great goddess Artemis will be neglected and the magnificence of her whom all Asia and the world worship will be a thing of the past!"

When they heard this, they became very angry, and cried,

"Great Artemis of Ephesus!"

So the commotion spread all over the city, and by a common impulse the people rushed to the theater, dragging with them two Macedonians, Gaius and Aristarchus, Paul's traveling companions. Paul wanted to go before the people himself, but the disciples would not allow it. Some of the religious authorities also, who were friends of his, sent to him and begged him not to go into the theater. Meanwhile the people were shouting, some one thing and some another, for the meeting was in confusion, and most of them had no idea why they had come together. Some of the crowd called upon Alexander, as the Jews had pushed him to the front, and he made a gesture with his hand and was going to speak in defense of them to the people. But when they saw that he was a Jew, a great shout went up from them all, and they cried for two hours: "Great Artemis of Ephesus!"

Divisions of interest within the community may rest on a territorial basis, depending on access to some natural resource of vital importance. Thus the citizens of the states watered by the Colorado River have differing interests in its waters, so that those downstream, if there is a shortage of water, may come into conflict with those upstream, as each group seeks to better its position, and to secure itself with the water supply it needs for today and for the future.

The effective pressure exerted by any group for economic reform of things as they are, depends on many factors. One is the amount of deprivation which the group feels taken together with the prospect which its leaders see of curing the deprivation. When there is enough to go around, when men see no insuperable obstacles to the fulfillment of their desire for a fair share, when there appear to be only curable man-made interferences with a greater degree of satisfaction for some group within the community, the group and its leaders are likely to exhibit hope, alert activity in their own behalf, and an effective pressure for reform. Thus in the United States, in the business depression in the early nineteen-thirties, when industrial machines were operating far below capacity and there seemed to be no substantive necessity for the want and unemployment which existed, the unemployed groups were vocal in demands for reform and were alertly and hopefully led.

In these hopeful situations, the efforts towards reform are frequently addressed not only to obtaining a greater share of what is or might be available currently in the community, but also towards the provision of a substantive increase by way of better techniques and skills and a more rational use of plant or of land.

On the other hand in a situation where there may be a far greater degree of misery and want and a greater actual need for people to improve their condition, if there is an actual substantive shortage of food or of goods, and a cure of the shortage is difficult to foresee, there is likely to be much less effective pressure for reform. There is apathy on the part of those suffering the deprivation and their leaders. Such has been the case in times and places when there has not been enough to go around and no reasonable prospect of providing enough, as in regions too heavily populated in relation to their resources or available techniques of production. In such circumstances leaders may seek a personal religious escape from the hardships of existence, rather than attempt to cure the horribly difficult conditions in which their community finds itself.

The size of the reforming group and its contacts with the rest of the community are significant. When a great number of people in a large area have an interest to promote, political leaders must pay attention to this interest. Thus the farmers in the Ukraine, if overreached for the benefit of the city-dwellers and industrial workers of Russia, will exert a constant pressure on the ruling regime for reform of their position and correction of their injury.

Everyone within a community obviously has a vital interest that the community produce the necessary minimum needed to satisfy essential wants for food, clothing, and shelter. In the presence of political or economic disorganization sufficient to threaten this minimum production, the various groups within the community and their leaders may accept any ruler or government—however unpalatable in other respects—which gives promise of curing the disorganization and providing the required essentials. For example, when the relative prosperity in Germany from 1924 to 1928 failed, the almost dormant Nazi party awoke to new life and new reforming strength as a potential savior of a discouraged people.

The closeness and effectiveness of the organization, the degree of discipline within the reforming group, also influence the course of reform. There may be very able and competent groups of men who would be benefited by one and the same political reform, but who have such divergencies of interest along other lines that they are not effectively organized for reform. Thus in the United States associations of manufacturers, chambers of commerce, and public debtholders such as churches, charitable and educational institutions are competent groups all interested in a stable financial structure and the political reforms which might aid such a structure, but these groups are insufficiently organized and led as far as political action on any united basis is concerned.

A similar case was to be seen before the French Revolution, when professional men, businessmen, and the producers of food all alike had a common interest in reform of the inefficiencies of the old regime and the removal of irrational local tax burdens on the movement of food and goods. But they were in separate walks of life and had no common program or organization to take effective steps towards orderly reform.

Workingmen with a relatively simple interest to pursue—higher wages—may often be readily organized and led, because not subject to divergence of interests, or at least not aware of such divergences as may in fact exist. Such organizations of workers are effective in political reform movements, particularly in a state where there is universal free suffrage. The mere numbers of workers and their votes are so useful to political candidates who aspire to gain or hold office that the candidates will support—or promise to support—the programs of the organization of workers. This has happened in both England and the United States due to the numerical power of workmen at the ballot box.

The feasibility of organization of workingmen for political ends is related to their present economic condition as well as to their freedom. When the workers are in real subjection—like the slaves in earlier American history, or the workers in some of the ancient mines—and almost completely illiterate, they may participate in events and periods of violence but scarcely in any effective scheme of reform. That is to say, the more abject the condition of a particular group within the community, the less is the likelihood for leaders to achieve any reform through the efforts of that group itself. In a country with a coercive tradition, the present-day Russia, as long as the government remains able to maintain coercion, the relative position of the groups of workers will improve or deteriorate, depending on the wisdom and aims of the ruling group—the political government. Both in the free and in the coercive systems the substantive burden of a war effort—as in the late stages of a losing war—may make real, as opposed to relative, improvement of position impossible.

Effect of Changing Circumstances

The effect of change of circumstances or of altered techniques has a marked effect both on desires for reform and on the prospects for reform; and this is true of all times, both ancient and modern.

When in the middle of the fourteenth century the Black Death killed from a third to a half of the people of England, a slowly changing society underwent a rapidly accelerated reform. The shortage of ploughmen resulted in the multiplication of sheep runs and the growth of cloth manufacture. Free laborers found their services in such demand that despite statutory efforts to fix wages, their economic position was greatly improved. The unfree laborers, the villeins, supposedly bound to the soil, found that if they fled far from home they would be accepted as free laborers by landholders critically short of working hands. As the author of *The Vision of Piers Plowman* put it at the time:

> Laborers with no land but only their hands work
> Deigned not to dine on day old vegetables;
> No penny a gallon did for them nor a piece of bacon
> But pork, fish or fresh flesh, fried or baked
> And that *chaud, plus chaud* for the chill of their maw
> And but he has high wages else will he chide
> And bewail the day he ever became a workingman;
> Curses the king with a will and all his parliament
> That make such laws to keep the laborer down.

Change in techniques of work produces new groupings of interests. The development of steam power and of manufacturing machinery established a new set of conditions both for those who controlled the industrial establishments and those who worked in them. Both the need and the opportunity for reform accompanied these changes.

Technical improvements in communications have made possible organization of groups on an ever wider territorial basis, because orders can be transmitted, sentiment formed, and people in person enabled to interchange their views in a way entirely impossible when travel was slow and quick transmission of thought impossible. When to this possibility of organization there is added a need for a huge effort in production—as, for example, in the manufacture of equipment for modern war—the relative position of workingmen will change. Their bargaining power exerted through well-organized nationwide unions is powerful in a way that would have been impossible in a day of slower communication.

Motives for Economic Reforms on the World Scene

So far we have pointed out some of the motives of economic reform within the political state—a community integrated in its political aspects, with its own laws and its own more or less effective organs of government exercising authority throughout the territorial extent of the community. The same motives are at work on the world scene, where the competing groups are the separate political communities—the independent states of the world. These separate states are trying to improve their respective positions in the world community, which has never yet been integrated as a political unit and is little organized to serve any common interest of its inhabitants.

A community growing in population in a territory with assets inadequate for its increasing size needs to cure this substantive economic shortage. The choice of method would seem to be between a reduction of population or the acquisition of more resources, the latter method being pursued either peacefully or with the aid of violence. As a matter of history the way of violence has been a usual but by no means invariable method by which a community has improved its economic position within the world community.

An ancient example of community attempts to improve position in the world community is seen in the recurring efforts to gain control of the fertile river basins of Mesopotamia. Such attempts were made from time to time by those living in the mountains to the east or in the almost desert lands to the west and south. A recent example was seen in the effort of Japan to improve its position by gaining control of the material resources of Southeast Asia.

To him that already hath, his having may create a need for more. For example, a community may have discovered or learned the use of industrial processes which require a large supply of raw materials if the community is to succeed in operating these processes for the creation of greater wealth. If these raw materials are not within the community territory, either at home or abroad, there arises the need for assuring a supply elsewhere. This need has made colonial empires seem desirable to those communities which have not had as free access to resources as they would like, as in the case of nineteenth-century Germany, which envied others who had got ahead of her in the possession of colonies. It has also made desirable possession of strategic bases for the protection of trade either with such colonies or with other communities, as in the case of nineteenth-century Britain. In these cases, as well as in those of more acute shortage of assets, the economic urge has been a factor for attempted reform of the world community.

The time when a reform by way of conquest in aid of cure of hard circumstances is most likely to appeal to the capable leaders of a community is when the need is acute, but has not existed long enough to have already sapped the energy and strength of the community. Illustrations of this principle at work were seen in the cases of Germany and Japan before the Second World War.

The frequency with which people have tried to move into areas offering better prospects of comfort and security for them, is evidenced by the mixtures of differing physical types of mankind to be found in areas where the prospects are relatively pleasing—such areas, let us say, as Germany or France or the United States. Conversely, it is in those places where life has been relatively hard that we might expect to find remaining racially purer stocks, as for example in Scandinavia.

The need or desire of a community to improve its economic position on the world scene by means of the possession and possible use of military power may be an effective factor for internal reform.

Japan in the early twentieth century, with population growing too great for Japanese resources, was the scene of internal reforms increasing the power of the military, with the purpose of curing the hard circumstances by external conquest.

Russia today, with an uncertain food supply largely because she has too little rain and a short growing season due to too much cold, offers a picture of a community needing to improve its position in the world in the vital area of control of a sufficient food supply. For this reason among others Russia is the scene of internal reforms in the direction of enhanced prestige of the groups—executive, military, and industrial—necessary for such improvement of world position.

2. DOCTRINAL BELIEFS

Beliefs about what is the right way to view certain important aspects of life, or what is the right manner of conduct of certain important affairs, are the source of groupings which have a great influence on the state and which represent potent factors of reform in the life of the community.

Religious Doctrine

One of the relationships which has always been significant to men is their relation to the ultimate powers of the universe, their place, their security, in an overwhelmingly puzzling and baffling world. A socially organized belief about this relation—a belief manifested through an appropriate institution—constitutes a religion.

Religious groups are frequent mainsprings of reform in the community. The leaders of such groups, thinking that their view is the right and necessary view for the welfare—perhaps even the salvation from destruction—of their own community, and often of other communities as well, engage in a ceaseless effort to convert others to their belief. One historical method is for the leaders of a religious group to make agreements with the political ruler in order to advance and strengthen the position of their cult. Examples may be found in ancient and modern times. The agreement of the Christian leaders with Constantine resulting on the one side in the privileging of Christianity in the Roman Empire and on the other side the benefits to the political ruler that accrue from a state church, represents one such effort of a religious group towards reform to strengthen its position. In 1941 the Orthodox Church in the U.S.S.R. reached an accord with the political government in order to protect the former from persecution and to gain for the latter the acquiescence of the clergy.

In the efforts of religious groups to effect reform, the mixing of motives characteristic of reform movements is well exemplified. Thus Queen Elizabeth in her controversy—as a representative of religious Protestantism—with the Pope and the Jesuits was aided by a growing sense of island interests in the secular leaders. The pressure for religious reform went hand in hand with the growth of insular confidence and desires for local autonomy in secular as well as church matters.

Ethical and Aesthetic Influences

A sentiment of ill-defined unrest and of discontent with things as they are is not to be disregarded as a source of reform, since such a sentiment if widespread represents potential support for those groups which have definite programs of reform.

Any community, any human regime, is certain to present plenty of blemishes, if only the excesses of qualities for the most part good and useful. The moral rigidities of puritanism in New England gave rise to this kind of discontent amongst those in whom the demands of aesthetic enjoyment were not readily stilled. So, too, the vulgarization of standards which proceeds from the excessive commercialism of much of American business practice today raises feelings of dissatisfaction in those with a reasonably sound literary, artistic, or aesthetic sense. This dissatisfaction, and its feelings of frustration and hope that any change might be for the better, provides support for those who may have serious programs for radical political reform. Although the support may be irrational and for the most part neither ready nor able to consider whether the proposed cure is worse than the disease, it is none the less a factor of significance in the effective pressures for reform.

These sentiments of discontent are doctrinal factors of reform, because they are founded in convictions or prejudices—correct or wrong —concerning what is the right way for people to conduct themselves, and what are proper standards of moral or aesthetic seemliness.

Doctrine in the Economic Field

We have mentioned the differences of interest amongst those groups performing different economic functions in the community—for example—the competition for greater wealth and greater control of wealth that takes place between those engaged in agricultural and those in industrial functions. Arising from these differences, there sometimes develops a politically more potent division of interests characterized by adherence to inconsistent doctrines as to how the economic phases of the community life ought to be organized and controlled.

A doctrinal belief about the right methods of economic control originates in the effort to overcome disabilities, interferences, and restraints upon the economic aims of those who are both ambitious and intelligent. As a result of these disabilities, and addressed to their cure, a movement for reform appears. Such a reform movement is radical if it insists on measures inconsistent with the principal tenets or bases of the traditionally accepted economic system. It is in addition doctrinal, if its proponents regard it as more than a change of convenience in the direction of a better-ordered economic mechanism, and rather as a change essential for justice and necessary to save the community in its social, political, and moral relationships from wrongs regarded as inherent in the accepted economic system. Communism is a contemporary example of just such a doctrinal reform movement.

The salvation promised by an economic doctrine is likely to be along lines determined by the conspicuously evident faults in the traditional system. If those who are in the positions of power and influence in the traditional economic arrangement are believed to be exercising their power and utilizing their influence excessively in their own behalf at the expense of the rest of the community, this belief is a source of a doctrine of reform which stresses equality. Those in the community who wish to better their position contrast the old fault and the new doctrine, pushing the latter and the reform it calls for.

For example, the economic life of eighteenth-century France was characterized by much irrational privilege of persons and places, unsystematic and inequitable tax exemptions, and local burdens by way of excises and demands for services in kind on the production and transportation of goods and food. All this was in large part due to the remnants of feudalism. Hand in hand with the economic inequalities was an exasperating social discrimination and assumption of superiority by the nobility, especially the hereditary nobility. As a result of this conspicuous fault of privilege in the traditional French scheme, the tracts of the reformers of the time are filled with slogans of equality, hopes for return to simplicity, and the elimination of artificial distinctions between persons.

In the United States, in the nineteen-twenties, those in control of the credit mechanism of the community, including the principal officers of New York City banks, lost their sense of vocation and their obligation to maintain a sound credit structure. They took part in unsound loans by their banks to themselves or to corporations which they controlled for the purpose of making gains on the sales of shares in business ventures whose worth was enormously overrated. Similarly, those whose economic function consisted in effecting purchases and sales on the markets for securities and raw materials—brokers on the stock and commodity exchanges—became members of trading syndicates and prostituted their brokerage function to the making of money at the expense of the public in an artificially stimulated and maintained fever of public speculation. When the speculative and credit bubble burst, there followed a substantive business maladjustment with very great unemployment. The resulting reform movement was of an equalitarian nature—a "New Deal" on behalf of the "forgotten man," characterized by bureaucratic regulation of the economy, especially in those phases where abuse had been conspicuously evident. This was the form which was taken by the reform efforts of those who had been injured by the credit spree and by the subsequent business collapse and who felt that governmental control of the financial community ought to be established in the wake of its demonstrated failure of self-control.

A doctrinal reform and the political parties and alignments in which it is embodied are likely to last long beyond the period and events which shaped the reform movement.

In England, which was the earliest country to become industrialized, the industrialization was marked by fearful conditions of work—the "dark Satanic mills"—by miserable housing for the workers in the growing industrial cities, and by a heedlessness of these conditions on the part of owners of the industries and also on the part of the English landowning class. The hardship gave rise to a determinedly led labor movement (soon professing the socialistic doctrine of ownership and control by the community of the instruments of production) in the interest of improving the position and condition of the workers and of their leaders. The nineteenth century was a period of unprecedented prosperity for Britain, so conditions were favorable for a curative reform as the means were in fact available to provide better working conditions and housing. Accordingly this reform labor movement was hopefully and energetically led and the political party by which it was eventually implemented became powerful.

When the main economic problems of England became fundamentally altered, when her need in the early twentieth century was for improved techniques and better machinery, and when her need after the First World War and conspicuously after the Second World War was the development of means of producing goods which could compete in the world market on even terms with those produced elsewhere— it was still the political parties formed on the basis of the nineteenth-century issues that had to address themselves to the solution of the new problems.

An extremely inefficient and burdensome government is likely to give rise to a doctrinal reform along economic lines. The form of the government is not specially significant. It may be a monarchy, a republic, or a despotism.

Thus in eighteenth-century France, the King's government was an integral part of the system of irrational privilege which we have already mentioned, and the governmental system somehow seemed to combine the maximum inefficiencies of bureaucracy, in those aspects where it was centralized, with the maximum inefficiencies of local authority in those aspects where it was decentralized. The need was to free the initiative of those who were capable of initiative, and a corresponding slogan was *laissez faire*—let people do or make what they choose, without the burden of government interference.

In England, at the same period, similar sentiments of reform in the direction of greater freedom from government restriction were being voiced by Adam Smith. But in an economic sense and particularly in the field of a more rational and equitable tax burden—England shone by comparison with France. This fact and the excesses evident in the course of the French Revolution dampened any pressure for radical reform in England.

In twentieth-century Germany in the period between the two world wars, as the result of various factors which we do not need to consider at the moment, there was economic disorganization with which the parliamentary government seemed unable to cope. The need was for order. The corresponding slogans of reform rang the changes on the idea of order—the "Leader Principle," authority, responsibility, obedience.

In twentieth-century Russia, the support given to Lenin by capable people outside the ranks of professional revolutionaries was explicable, not by their reasoned hopes that Communism provided even a temporary solution for the economic problems of Russia, so much as by the hopeless prospect—whether in farm or city—which lay in any return to the economic derangements and governmental and social intolerance of prerevolutionary days. The Czarist regime had withstood efforts at liberal reform in the preceding century and in the early years of the twentieth, and then had demonstrated its complete incapacity to serve or to lead in the crises of the First World War.

Today, the economic burden of Russian government lies in the inefficiencies of an overcentralized bureaucracy and the doctrinaire ideals to which the rational requirements of production and distribution must give way. When a competent Russian manufacturer sees a market for a useful and needed article which his plant could supply if it were only left free to do so, and when similarly caused shortages become evident to many citizens in many instances there is of course a powerful desire for reform. The slogans of such a reform—if expression were permitted or dared—would be akin to those of *laissez faire.*

In connection with these doctrinal economic reforms concerned with how the economy ought to be ordered, it is noteworthy that the reforms are proposed with respect to every type of political or economic organization. In the examples we have given, the governments have been monarchical, republican, authoritarian, and democratic, and the methods of ownership individualistic and socialistic. This suggests that the difficulties to which the reforms are addressed lie deeper than the form of government or form of economic control.

Relatively few people have the capacity for organizing a complex economic effort. If the task is to be well performed, these few are the people who must have the lead. Accordingly the political and economic order should be such that these few are free of too much hindrance in what they are trying to do. Reformers, in their efforts to modify or overthrow a current economic system on account of its defects, often do not address themselves to this substantive factor in the solution of their problem. It thus happens that the upshot of reform often proves unsatisfactory. A right reform requires either luck or an unlikely understanding of, and will to deal with, the real needs of the time and place.

Doctrinal beliefs—which we have characterized as those having a strong connotation of how some phase of life *ought* to be ordered, of what is emotionally felt to be *right*—are frequent accompaniments of the effort of a political community to improve its position amongst other political communities in the world scene.

An illustration of this principle at work today may be seen in the case of Russia who, along with other efforts to improve her relative position amongst the several world powers, is forwarding as far as she can, not only within her own borders but externally, Communism according to the gospel of Marxism-Leninism.

Just as doctrinal beliefs may cut across group lines within an organized state, leading to new alignments, of short or long duration, so they may cut across national or state lines within the world community, effecting similar changes of alignment. The growth of Protestantism in England and Scotland in the sixteenth century drew these two hostile countries together, the process being largely stimulated by fear of the religious and political power of Roman Catholicism.

Some Characteristics of Doctrinal Reform

Certain features of doctrinal reform are repeated again and again, and are important in the development and course of this kind of reform.

Where there is no longer the possibility of a first-class role for the able and magnanimous in the current tradition, the stage is thereby set for the appearance of some new doctrine or positive belief and an accompanying reform.

In the Roman Empire after the Antonines there was a lackluster prospect. Economic burdens on the capable were great. The arts had sunk to such a low state that the novel and the bizarre, rather than the solid and beautiful, excited admiration. Religious belief was almost absent, and even a Stoic determination to make the best out of a brief life found little nourishment in the bleak and discouraging deterioration of Roman aims and standards. The scene was thus set for the entry of some vigorous kind of belief. The doctrinal reform which moved into this Roman vacuum was Christianity. It flourished as a result of the decadence of the old hopes and ideals as well as by its own merits.

In the case of the economic doctrinal reforms of Lenin in Russia, we have already described the scene of confusion and disorganization which set the stage for the appearance of a new and positive economic belief and an accompanying reform. Again the practical success of the reform was due as much to the old inefficiencies as to the new zeal.

The consciousness of right is usually strong in the believers in a positive doctrinal reform. They find a scope and a role in furthering their doctrine. Unlike those who are simply discontented with the current tradition, they take what they are doing to heart, think they have discovered the way things ought to be ordered, and are notably given to excess and to lack of any sense of restraint or of ordinary equity. This confidence that a man has got hold of the right principle, the one best way to govern some important aspect of life, is the trademark of the doctrinal reformer; and it explains much historical intemperance and bitterness about procedures that to an earlier or a later period might seem indifferent.

Religious and moral radicals or religious and moral conservatives, alike confident in their rightness and desiring to mold or re-form the whole community in their own image, hound their foes with relentless zeal. Witness the harsh intolerance of the Roman Catholic Inquisition, of the early New England settlements, or of the Anti-Saloon League in the United States.

The confidence of right held by doctrinal reformers and the fact that they find scope for their energies and a satisfying role within the reform movement give rise to an intense loyalty to the reform and to the leader who is its personal embodiment. When the content of the reform is in fact harmful, this loyalty is socially destructive. For example, the attitude of his German followers towards Hitler—their devotion to this fanatic and his narrow-minded, cruel ideals—illustrates the power of a doctrine and its leader for reform within the community, irrespective of the good or evil content of the reform.

3. GREATER RECOGNITION IN THE COMMUNITY

In any large community, some groups feel that they have a good role within the community and that they are generally recognized as important and respected; other groups feel that they have much less recognition than they deserve, that the part they play is a poor one, and that they are objects of disdain.

The effort to gain greater recognition and respect may be an effective source of reform. It is frequently associated with other factors, particularly with the effort to improve economic position; because it is often, although not always, the case that a group which is held in disdain by those who are dominant in the community is denied fair economic opportunity.

Ethnic Differences

Ethnic differences are a common cause of discrimination which in turn gives rise to an effort to reform the community in the interest of a racial group which feels that it has less recognition and position than it deserves.

Groups within a community sometimes differ from one another markedly in the physical appearance of their members, and along with this difference there are likely to be differences of custom, of attitude, and sometimes of ability. As a matter of history, such ethnic differences in a community are often the legacy of conquest of the people in a territory by some alien group or the result of immigration into the community of alien elements, as adventurers, traders, laborers, or slaves. It is usually the case that of these differing groups in a community, some will be in a position of dominance, others in a position keenly aware of political or social discrimination, in need of improving their position, and ready to do so if possible.

In South Africa in the early nineteenth century, England acquired political control of the Cape Colony and its Dutch settlers. The latter, dissatisfied with English rule and policies—which included restriction of native slavery—wanted new lands and freedom. About 10,000 Dutch accordingly took part in a "Great Trek," one division of which set up a South African republic beyond the Vaal River—the Transvaal, whose independence was recognized by the British in 1852, repudiated in 1877, and again imperfectly recognized in 1881. Towards the close of the century the richest gold deposits yet found in the world were discovered in the Transvaal. A gold rush followed, and this Dutch republic was soon inundated with foreign adventurers, the *uitlanders,* who soon outnumbered the Dutch both in heads and in ounces of gold; but the Dutch refused them citizenship. Then the *uitlanders,* sparked by their British core, determined to gain political power consonant with their numbers, activity, and economic position. Here we see an illustration of a so-called racial grouping—under the prick of an economic urge—as a source of reform in its own interest.

Language differences sometimes set off and accentuate the efforts for reform of an ethnic group. The revolt of 1830 in the Netherlands which resulted in the birth of the Belgian state was partly attributable to the fact that when Dutch was the sole official language, the Walloon populations were for the most part excluded from public life and the important civil and military offices were a near monopoly of the Dutchmen.

The retention by the Poles of their language despite many years of Russian, Austrian, or German domination has been a significant element in their preservation as a group.

It may be that the predominant racial group in a community is itself for some reason afflicted with a sense of insecurity or of uncertainty as to its position. This may have come about as a result of defeat in war with some outside community, or as a result of being regarded as a black sheep amongst the various states in the world. An internal reform of such a community may take the form of oppression of some minority, by which oppression the predominant group seeks to shift the blame of its own shortcomings, and to fortify itself against its own doubts. Such an ethnic pressure for reform of the community and specious enhancement of the position and recognition of the majority by a harsh worsening of the position of a minority is to be seen in the treatment of the Jewish minority by the Germans of the Third Reich. The world will long remember Hitler's whipping up of the intolerant force of extreme racial pride in his followers. In ranting about the German *Volk* ideal he said that "a folkish State primarily will have to lift marriage out of the level of a permanent race degradation in order to give it the consecration of that institution which is called upon to beget images of the Lord and not deformities half man and half ape." The Germans not only tried to acquire a feeling of group superiority at the expense of the Jews, but they also wished to oust the latter from positions of importance in the economic life of the community. Thus economic motives were mixed with ethnic motives in the effective pressure for this oppressive movement of reform.

In the European colonial empires of the nineteenth and twentieth centuries, the exploitation in many instances of the vast majority of native colonials by the tiny minority of conquering colonists has often given rise to unrest and desires for reform on the part of the natives. In these cases, despite the poor organization and lack of leadership of the natives, due to the huge disparity by which they outnumber the European residents, the likelihood of a more or less effective reform through violence by the natives, or fear of it by the Europeans, is ever present. With the lapse of time the hand of native leadership may grow stronger, as the capable natives learn for better or worse from observation of and acquaintance with the ways of the European minority.

Religious differences are commonly compounded with ethnic differences as sources of reform. Thus the partition of Palestine between Arab and Jew in 1949 exemplified effective pressures for reform of these two factors of reform working side by side.

It may be that the religious doctrine, especially in matters of rigorous observances of ritual and the strict preservation of religious practices, is consciously used as a means of holding the ethnic group together and preserving it from dissolution. The teaching of Ezekiel in the exile of the Jews was addressed to this end, and present-day observation of certain of the practices of Judaism is similarly motivated and similarly successful.

If an ethnic group which has a minority status in the community is also extremely small in numbers relative even to other minority groups of the community, its prospect for effecting substantial reforms in its favor is not great. Thus the Gypsies in Western Europe have endured centuries of disdain and discrimination, carrying on their half-nomadic culture as a small alien ill-assimilated group; but creating no major political problem for the community, and having no substantial hope of a better recognition for themselves. So also the American Indians in their reservations in the United States are today of no influence for reform of the ways of the larger community. The same observation would be true also of Chinatown in New York City.

If there are a great many such small, ill-assimilated ethnic groups in a community, they may represent a factor for reform in that they have a common interest in a change of things as they are, in the hope that any major change might improve their position in the community. Thus in a state with universal franchise, such groups might well be an influence in the turning of a conservative party out of office.

The abilities of an ethnic group holding an inferior position affect their opportunity of exerting effective pressure for reform, but here again, if their numbers are relatively small and they have no basis of ready cooperation with other depressed groups, the prospect of effective reform in their favor is not great. In ancient Athens, there were many able resident aliens who carried on a large part of the trade and commerce of the community, but they were of many different origins, and never appeared to have exercised any effective pressure for a position of increased political power or a cure of their political disqualification.

On the other hand, when a depressed ethnic group is large in numbers, especially where it is living in the land of its own old history and traditions, it may for generations represent a potential factor of reform of the greatest importance. Parents, teachers, priests, despite the efforts of a dominant minority to shut them up or cut them off, may keep alive a memory of old glories and old power such that the group is ready to rally with effective support to a hope of liberation. The nationalities of central Europe were thus ready to cast off the yoke of their German, or Austrian, or Russian conquerors, and after the

First World War, when the principle of political self-determination was adopted as a formula, a batch of new political communities—new states—testified to the long preservation of these ethnic forces for reform.

When the status of a depressed ethnic group has been fixed for a long, long time, it comes to be taken for granted, and this situation has a self-perpetuating nature, so that the prospect for effective reform is for the time being slight. Particular instances of race prejudice, as well as race prejudice generally, have a long history.

Desires for More Recognition on the World Scene

If we turn from the domestic scene to the world scene, we find that here also desires for greater recognition are a source of reform in the interest of one state or nation amongst the other states and nations of the world. Operating usually alongside other motives for reform in attempted improvement of the position of one community amongst others is the desire of its members for greater recognition of their community and greater respect for it.

The National Socialists in Germany emphasized the concept of the German *Volk,* stressed its superiority to other peoples, and concluded that it therefore ought to occupy a position of supremacy in the world —in short, that it was a *Herrenvolk,* a sacred, self-conscious, masterful community. The fact that such ideas—whether or not based on the truth—are stimulators of attempted reform of the world community indicates their influence among the sources of reform.

Other slogans affording a glimpse of the presence of this factor of reform in the case of old and new communities trying to improve their position in the world are the "manifest destiny" of the United States, the "white man's burden" of Britain, the "chosen people" of Israel. We are beyond all others best, and our worth should be recognized and rewarded.

4. AMBITIONS FOR CONTROL

The ambition of a group leader for greater control of the life of the community is most readily furthered by enhancing the position and power of his group. He tries to increase the numbers and strength of his following and to make alliances with leaders of other groups so long as that offers a prospect of aiding him in the realization of his ambitions.

In the United States the military services—the Army, the Navy, and the Air Force—are supposedly merely agencies for the defense of the whole community. They have no intrinsic function of promoting each the betterment of its own membership at the expense of the others. Yet once these defense groups have been organized, the familiar picture appears of the heads of the respective services jockeying for the position of kingpin and greatest control in the whole defense picture. The leaders of a particular service persuade themselves that their service is the most important. If two of the service groups can improve their position by a temporary alliance with one another at the expense of the third, such an alliance is forthcoming.

In the military anarchy in Rome, the nominees of the various legions for the emperorship fought one another with the same vigor with which they fell upon the external enemies of Rome. Here also was to be seen the result of ambitions of leaders of units within a military service attempting to effect reform each in his own interest.

A characteristic of the ambition for power and control is its ability to convince the men possessed of the ambition that what furthers their ambition is what is right for the community.

Thus in the United States it has been the usual rule that the leaders of the party in federal office at any given time—the federal executive —believe that an increased use of federal power is for the good of the whole community. The leaders of the party out of federal office believe that states' rights and powers are to be preserved and enhanced. Now it is true that at a given time in history one of these doctrinal positions is probably more correct than the other; but the significant fact in the consideration of ambition as a factor of reform is that the ambition tends to shape the idea of what is right, rather than the idea of what is right to shape the ambition.

The ambitions of a family or of a clan have often been important factors of reform. In England, in the Wars of the Roses, the houses of Lancaster and of York fought with one another for control of the government. The general populace was not much affected, so the upshot was that two groups of nobles—with too little to do now that the Hundred Years' War had lapsed—killed one another off. But who can fail to see that, had there been present in England some imminent factor of deep social cleavage, these ambitious adventurers would have seized the opportunity of obtaining popular followings, and instead of a picturesque war for succession to power, there would have been serious and thoroughgoing effort at political reform which would have involved the whole community.

Another illustration of clan ambition in the competitive effort to gain control of the government was to be seen in the rivalry in Japan in which the Tokugawa shoguns were successful in their struggles with the shoguns of other clans.

From time to time in history, patriots or political adventurers enter a scene of confusion and, fired with an ambition—sometimes admirable in aim, sometimes not—effect spectacular reforms. Saint Joan, obedient to her voices, deeply patriotic, suddenly unified a French leadership split by years of faction and of fighting with one another to the advantage of the enemies of France, and brought to life the power latent in the French community when the small-mindedness of its leaders was overcome. Through this reform the English political power in France was overthrown.

Personal ambition may make for reform that results in an increase of confusion in the community. The extraordinary career of Bishop Cannon, that energetic and fanatical leader of a crusade against alcoholic beverages in the United States, demonstrates the power of personal ambition to promote a major reform. The main long-term result of this reform was as we know the organization and financing of a criminal underworld.

Even when a group of some kind has been so successful in the propagation of its views as to become coterminous with the whole community, there is still present the effort of the inner group which constitutes its leadership to push their power at the expense of leaders of other phases of the community life. For example, in the early fourteenth century the doctrines of Catholic Christianity were substantially accepted by the whole Western European community, so that Christianity was no longer one doctrinal group struggling with others for the place of dominance but was rather the whole community viewed in its religious aspect. And yet the leadership of the Church was still ambitious to reform the community in the direction of even greater control for the Church leaders, as opposed to leaders of other aspects of the life of the community or of leaders of groups with particularized interests within the Christian community:

"We are told by the word of the Gospel that in this His fold are two swords—a spiritual, namely, and a temporal. . . . Surely he who denies that the temporal sword is in the power of Peter wrongly interprets the word of the Lord when He says, 'Put up thy sword in its scabbard.' Both swords, the spiritual and the material, therefore, are in the power of the Church; the one, indeed, to be wielded for the

Church, the other by the Church; the one by the hand of the priest, the other by the hands of kings and knights, but at the will and sufferance of the priest. One sword, moreover, ought to be under the other, and the temporal authority to be subjected to the spiritual. . . . Indeed, we declare, announce, and define that it is altogether necessary to salvation for every creature to be subject to the Roman pontiff." These words of the bull *Unam Sanctam* of Boniface VIII, illustrate ambition both as a factor of reform and as the producer of reasons in support of the view that what furthers the ambition is what is right for the community.

The chief executive of a country and his executive department are like any other group in the community in their desire to push their own position of power and to effect reform in their own interest. This was true, for example of the King and the court circle in the old regime in France. It is equally true of the executive branch of the federal government in the United States, which is furthered in its efforts to extend its political power by its ability to spend huge amounts of public funds raised by revenue measures enacted by the federal legislature. It is in turn the hope of the individual legislators that the expenditure by the federal executive of these funds in their local districts will, by its influence on the local voters, increase their own prospects of being returned to office.

Promises Made by Ambitious Leaders

When an ambitious political leader is trying to increase his following, a usual method is by promises of what he will do for discontented groups in his constituency who want to improve their position. The more urgently the need for this improvement is felt by a group, the more effective the promises made to it are likely to prove. Usually there is no consistency in the promises made to the various discontented groups on the part of those who are trying to set themselves up as protectors of the discontented. This is true, irrespective of the form of government.

In the United States, a candidate for presidential office will promise higher prices to the farmers, higher wages to workers in industry, a reduction in the national debt, and a lowering of the burden of taxation—irrespective of whether circumstances are such that any man both intelligent and honest could make such promises. In a country like the United States, which has a system of free universal suffrage, these promises are made for the purpose of getting votes. An attempt to carry out the promises may be a powerful factor of reform, but the actual results of the reform will be determined by the circumstances of the time and place and not by the promises. For example, the results may include an increasing bureaucratization of the government, or a lowering of the position in the community of pensioners or of teachers and others with relatively fixed income or salaries the purchasing power of which will be hurt by the depreciation of money involved in attempts to carry out the promises.

The reform leader who sees real injustices in the community often asks the right questions about the community and points to ills which need to be cured. But if he gives the wrong answers to the questions, he will initiate cures no better than the old ills.

In Germany on the eve of Hitler's coming to power, the substantive disorganization was such that many groups were in acute need of improving their position, and all alike felt an urge to undo what seemed to them an unjust foreign control of their destinies. Hitler played upon the discontents, provided scapegoats, and promised to cure the situation. He succeeded in gaining power. In carrying out his promises by his methods, in the actual world circumstances then existing, the long-term result of his reforms was the undoing of contemporary Germany.

The ambitious reformer is aided by the willingness of those in trouble to jump to reform without considering—often without having the means intelligently to consider—whether what they are likely to get will be any better than what they have already. The medieval baron, in trouble with some temporal overlord that he knows all about, thinks he will be better off as a henchman of the Pope. Or the labor leader of a group of factory workers, keenly aware of his troubles with some great corporate employer, thinks he will be better off with a labor government as an employer.

It is clear enough that ambitious political leaders are often either honestly mistaken or cynically dishonest in their promises of reform, and also that their promises often have little relation to what they can deliver. All this does not alter the fact that the ambitions of such leaders are a potent source of reform, but it does mean that the reform which actually eventuates in such cases may not be relevant to the real needs of the community.

Ambitions of Leaders on the World Scene

The personal ambition of the leaders of one of the countries in the world community may be a source of reform of the relations in the latter. Just as in the case of the leaders of an internal group within the state, the leaders of an organized state will do everything to enhance their own power by enhancing that of their state relative to that of other states on the world scene. This may take the form of measures for increasing the state's military or economic power, or the form of alliances or agreements with other states for mutual temporary improvement of position. The purpose of all such expedients is the reform of the existing international situation in favor of the particular state so as to better enable it to satisfy its interests and fulfill the ambitions of its leaders.

The overambitious do not like to recognize limits imposed by reality upon realization of their ambition. So an Alexander may create an empire under such conditions that its maintenance is impossible. Or a Napoleon may undertake campaigns too great for the powers of the community which he leads. Or a Hitler, successful in the arbitrary exercise of judgment within his individual community, may rely on a similar arbitrary exercise of judgment with the aim of overreaching other communities in the world community, in an ill-destined effort of reform in favor of himself and his country. The ambition effects a major reform, but it is a reform far different from that intended.

5. SPREAD OF REFORM SENTIMENT

When inequities do not bear directly on a strong group, when by reason of illiteracy, or oppression, or long-continued social custom, the people who are unduly burdened have no adequate leadership of their own, and no sufficient support to be found in other parts of the community, there is no likelihood of immediate reform. This may be the case even though the numbers of oppressed are relatively large, differing in that respect from the difficulty of reform in the case of small ethnic minorities.

In the slave insurrections and plots for such insurrections in the United States in the eighteenth and nineteenth centuries, the planning was ineffective and betrayal of plans frequent. No self-propelled reform by the slave group was capable of achieving any result beyond an intermittent unrest, and perhaps a feeling of disquiet and uneasiness in the southern atmosphere.

The natives of Egypt were subject in the Ptolemaic period to the rule of Macedonian foreigners and thereafter to the rule of Roman foreigners—rulers recognized by the Egyptian gods through the acquiescence of a subservient priesthood. The natives had to work for the gods and the rulers, in tilling the soil, in the making of clothes or of oil, or in other productive activities. The gods and the rulers often demanded too much of the natives, who, ill-organized and unarmed, could only avail themselves of passive resistance, "strikes" in which they retired to a temple by way of protest until their wrong was righted or they were forced to return to work, as the case might be. As these natives were without support at any level of potential power in the community, the prospect for reform in their behalf was substantially nil.

When in contrast to this kind of situation there comes to be a general recognition amongst the capable in the community that a serious inequity exists, that it is harming the strength or efficiency of the community, and that it is caused by curable defects in the institutions or man-made arrangements of the community, the prospect for reform is likely.

The fact that the grievance is thought to be due to human causes is important. Job cursing the day and the night is not as significant a factor of reform as John Jones cursing the government. The relative hardship of men at sea in a lifeboat and of the workers in a Manchester mill has been compared by a historian. The former are much worse off than the latter; but they have no "grievance" and no human institution to blame.

When the cause of a wrong or inequity is human and curable, independent-minded people all along the line who are not directly concerned in the immediate issue or dispute become convinced that reform is necessary. This general support of the abused group or groups often indicates the imminence of reform. When the workers in the "dark Satanic mills" are in fact overreached as well as thinking that they are, they obtain the aid of the Thomas Carlyles, and formers of public opinion. Reform prospers. When everyone in Russia who can think at all sees the rottenness of the Czarist regime and the needless inequities and inefficiencies which it maintains, reform is in the offing. The Nazi reform movement in Germany, more or less in abeyance in the relative prosperity of 1924 to 1928, springs into new life with failure of the economic institutions at the close of the decade.

Discontent among some groups of workers may be present in any community at any time. But when their hardship is man-made, and when there is at the same time a middle class wanting freedom of the press, more voice in the government, better education, and a liberal constitution, a reform movement is in the making. Such was the situation in 1848 in France.

For reasons which we shall consider later, there are within every community a number of able people interested in the good of the whole community. Such people frequently have a considerable degree of effective organization in professional and other associations. In cases of curable economic hardship and bad government these people are likely to become allies of whatever groups are pushing in their own interest for reforms and a better position. They can become an exceedingly powerful influence for reform. Such were the *philosophes* in France in the late eighteenth century. Such were the journalists and writers, and leaders in the arts and the professions, after the Wall Street excesses in the United States of the nineteen-twenties.

The attitude of the bulk of the capable in the community—the leaders of the middle class in England in the nineteenth century, for example—when aware of real inequities is a major factor in the likelihood of productive reform. This is in contrast to the situation which we have already mentioned of fruitless disorder even in acute forms, like the private brawls between energetic British nobles which constituted the Wars of the Roses at an earlier day.

Feeling may be less intense on the outer fringes of support as the sentiment for reform becomes more widespread. But this wide sympathetic support for the still intense "core" of the reform makes the reform more feasible. For example, today, when there is an absence of popular weapons and all effective armament is controlled by the ruler through the army or the police, it is principally by such a widespread conviction of the need of reform that ambitious leaders within the government—within the "palace"—would be fortified in the effort to accomplish a *coup d'état*. It is on account of this consensus of opinion that they would be able to find support at high levels in the army or the police.

6. EFFECTS OF OUTSIDE PRESSURE

When the threat or the actuality of attempted conquest by an external enemy subjects a political community—a state—to outside pressure, internal reform is promoted. The historical instances of this kind of reform show many kindred features—a recurrence of similar changes in the power and prestige of the various groups within the community which finds that it has to defend itself.

Short-term Results of Outside Pressure

The more dangerous the outside pressure appears, the clearer it becomes to the intelligent members of the community that there is need of an internal government which can act rapidly and the need of a powerful army. Accordingly changes are promoted which strengthen the relative power in the community of the executive branch of the government (the "ruler") and also of the military group and those groups essential to military effectiveness. Who these last may be varies with the techniques of the time. Today, for instance, they include most of the organized and unorganized groups in heavy and medium industry.

In the midsummer of 1793 the hostile forces arrayed against revolutionary France presented an excuse if not a necessity for the extremists at the moment in power in Paris to consolidate further their power. They took advantage of the atmosphere of uncertainty and fear, when everyone felt better for quick and drastic action, and were ready to condone extreme measures in the interest of the government which would hardly have been stomached in more normal times.

The National Assembly of 1919 in Germany was controlled for most purposes by the Social Democrats, a group of the moderate left. But they offered to the country small hope of cure of the humiliations heaped on Germany by outsiders—cessions of territory, disarmament, the trial of war criminals, reparations, the vengefulness of France. It was felt that the Weimar Republic would not prove able to deal with these problems, and reform was promoted in the direction of a radical and thoroughgoing attempt to make a strong government.

If major internal reforms are already in process in a country, the pressure of an outside enemy may cause a change of direction in these reforms. On the whole the wisest of the French leaders in the early days of the great Revolution were aiming at a limited monarchy, and the sentiment of the country itself was overwhelming in favor of the institution of the monarchy. But the outside enemies of France, Austria and Prussia, made assurance doubly sure that such a reform would fail by their deliberate and ill-advised stimulation of a general French fear that the King would align himself with these foreign monarchs in a successful effort to restore the old regime, with its arbitrariness, inefficiencies, and privilege.

The proclamation of July 25, 1792, of the Duke of Brunswick:

His Majesty the King of Prussia, united with his Imperial Majesty by the bonds of a strict defensive alliance and himself a preponderant member of the Germanic body, would have felt it inexcusable to refuse to march to the help of his ally and fellow-member of the empire. . . .

The proclamation continues:

To these important interests should be added another aim equally important and very close to the hearts of the two sovereigns—namely, to put an end to the anarchy in the interior of France, to check the attacks upon the throne and the altar, to reestablish the legal power, to restore to the King the security and the liberty of which he is now deprived and to place him in a position to exercise once more the legitimate authority which belongs to him. . . .

Their said Majesties declare, on their word of honor as emperor and king, that if the chateau of the Tuileries is entered by force or attacked, if the least violence be offered to their Majesties the King, Queen, and royal family, and if their safety and their liberty be not immediately assured, they will inflict an ever memorable vengeance by delivering over the city of Paris to military execution and complete destruction, and the rebels guilty of the said outrages to the punishment that they merit. . . .

Aside from the likelihood that such language as this could gain its end only if addressed to those who were convinced that the speakers were in fact able to deliver the goods—which was not the case in this instance—the thing to note for our present purposes is that by this proclamation his Majesty the emperor and his Majesty the king of Prussia by their threat put the weight of their pressure behind that very development of reform—the overthrow of the monarchy—of which they were afraid, and which without their acts might never have taken place.

The centralization of political authority, a reform in favor of the executive arm of the government, is an almost invariable tendency in cases of outside pressure, both ancient and modern, because this permits the machinery of the government to act without the hindrances and restraints provided by tradition or by constitutional limitations. The successive temporary dictatorships in the Roman republic, and the war powers exercised by the executive in both Britain and the United States in World Wars I and II, illustrate this principle of internal reform, under widely different technical conditions.

If the external pressure is removed soon enough, and the old peacetime form of government has been reasonably satisfactory, a substantial return may be made to it. This was the case, for example, in the United States after the First World War.

Similarly, in the great years of the Roman republic, temporary dictatorships to meet recurring emergencies came and went, but return was made to the traditional processes of civil government when the particular emergency passed.

A dramatic effect of severe outside pressure is to be noted in those cases where reform desires and needs were extremely acute before the advent of the outside pressure. Here the reform tendency in favor of the current regime may appear at first; but the internal differences and the needs for thoroughgoing reform are too great and the government correspondingly too insecure to maintain its authority. Thoroughgoing internal reform may be effected if the consequences of defeat in war do not prevent it.

In Austria-Hungary, after two years of the First World War, there reappeared the old national conflicts represented in the efforts of the racial groups—Czechs, Poles, Rumanians, Slavs—to better their status, and the old economic differences of agrarian Hungary and mercantile Austria. In this case the results of defeat in war forestalled the possibility of self-achieved reform of Austria-Hungary as a going concern.

Outside pressure on Russia in 1917, by revealing the rottenness of the current regime and government, afforded the opportunity to internal reformers for displacing the old and discredited system and its leadership. On March 12 of that year the government simply collapsed. Troops called upon to suppress a bread riot in Petrograd, instead of putting down the disturbance, fraternized with the disturbers. It appeared that no one was willing to shed the blood of a fellow-countryman in behalf of the Czarist regime, which was put aside almost without a struggle.

Long-term Results of Outside Pressure

If outside pressure on the community is perennial, the reforms promoted in the direction of strengthening the government and enhancing the military tend to become permanent.

The continual presence of strong enemies on the frontier requires the maintenance at all times of a powerful army to meet the threat. Sooner or later the leaders of the army—the generals—will recognize that their power in the state can be made superior to that of the civil authorities. This recognition may take a long time, especially when the internal tradition has been on the whole satisfactory and the customary form of government is taken for granted. It was not until two centuries after the time of Augustus that the old formula of the Roman state as founded on the *Senatus Populusque Romanus* lost its hold and, along with the extension of citizenship to the inhabitants of the cities of the Empire, the social power of the upper classes in Rome vanished. The political power was usurped by the generals, and Rome was subjected to seventy years of first military monarchy and then military anarchy—the successive aspects shown by this permanent reform in the direction of government by the military. The relative position of a particular group—the military—improved, but the absolute position of all groups deteriorated.

Negative evidence of the effects of outside pressure in enhancing the position of the military as against that of the remainder of the body politic is afforded by the relative political unimportance of the military in the United States through most of its history, where critical outside pressure was largely absent. This is in contrast to the relative importance of the military in the countries of Europe where the political communities were literally as well as figuratively at swords' points through much of recent history.

7. EFFECTS OF CONTROL OF A USEFUL TECHNIQUE

If some group within the community is in a position to exercise control over, or to monopolize, an instrumentality of great importance in the life of the community, this is a factor for reform in favor of that group.

When, in the Middle Ages, only the clerics could read and write, this monopoly of a highly useful means of communication meant that any secular ruler must as a matter of course rely on churchmen for the carrying on of his administration. These churchmen belonged to a coherent, well-organized group with a definite doctrine to promote —that of the Church. Their presence at key positions in every court and every bureaucracy was a continuing powerful factor in reform in the direction of increasing influence of the Church in the community.

With the powerful political position resulting from this clerical combination of technique and doctrine we might contrast the position of the engineers and technical experts in the United States today. They are in a key position as far as custodianship of an essential type of knowledge and skill is concerned, but are not members of a coherent group and are without a social doctrine of any kind.

The leaders of a group which is in a good situation for utilizing in its own interest some important discovery or development in means of exercising economic control may get a fortuitous access of power at the expense of other groups in the community. For example, the development of paper money and of credit mechanisms—taken together with the improvement in communications already mentioned—has given great power in economic affairs to those who have been in a position to manage the monetary and credit mechanism. Financial management in the United States until recently lay in the hands of the banking profession, but today is increasingly coming into the hands of the political ruling group—the government—with a corresponding shift of power to the government. A government group, like any other group in the community, wishes to strengthen its own place and sway, and this control of credit and the financial mechanism allows it to do so.

The particular stage of scientific development at a given time and place may furnish a kind of equipment to some group which enhances its power. For example, the monopoly by a government today of heavy and rapidly mobile armaments is not only, as we have already noted, a deterrent to popular uprising against an unjust regime, but is also a potential factor of reform in the further interest of the government leaders or the leaders of whatever group may gain control of the army and the police of the community.

When the longbow and gunpowder made practicable attack upon the knights in armor and their castles, the prospect became much brighter for reform of those inequities in the social order which were bolstered by the fact of the invincibility of the knights and their castles. It is as though today or tomorrow some light and relatively inexpensive types of equipment were devised which could jam the detonating mechanism of any type of explosive located within a radius of five hundred miles. Such an invention would deprive the executive power in contemporary governments of the advantage they now have of the invincibility and mobility of heavy weapons.

In the world community as in the national community, the possession by a competing group—in this case one of the separate states of the world—of a better technique than that of its neighbors is a significant factor in aid of reform.

In the case of nineteenth-century England, the possession of coal and iron and a growing knowledge of the industrial processes brought about great internal reforms in the economic and social field. So also in the world community, the relatively advanced phase of England's industrial development was an effective factor of reform in her favor of the international relations of the world community, enhancing her position and power.

A recent instance of monopoly of a potent technique was that of the sole possession by the United States of nuclear weapons in the period from 1945 to 1949. Had this technique been a monopoly of Nazi Germany during the preceding four years, it might well have served as the power base for a reformation of world control along Nazi lines and in Nazi hands. Had it been a monopoly of Soviet Russia in the same four years of 1945 to 1949, it might have served a similar function in aid of the expansion of the Russian despotism. It is perhaps fortunate for the world that the monopoly was that of the United States. It would have been still more fortunate had there been such an exceptionally high degree of intelligence and ingenuity in our political and diplomatic leadership as to devise and establish an effective world-wide control of nuclear weapons and their manufacture, and thereby provide a future period of respite at home and abroad from the fear of war with nuclear weapons. The actual course of events was otherwise.

8. THE POLITICAL AIM

The motives of reform are at work in every community. They are what constitute the ever-present desire of men and women and of groups and group leaders to improve their position. The absence of efforts at reform would mean either that the motives of the leaders and members of the various groups in the community were finding full scope and full satisfaction in the current tradition, or that all hope of scope and satisfaction had been abandoned. Neither of these conditions has ever existed in any human society.

What we want to know as a practical matter is why these ever-present and ever-active motives of reform are sometimes reconciled in an orderly, peaceful manner in an improving and rightly developing community, and why sometimes such a reconciliation fails, and these very same motives of reform eventuate in discord and perhaps in violence. If the reasons for this difference in the actual course of events can be identified, then we want to know to what extent it is possible to realize the conditions, dispositions, political habits and institutions which will promote the good event and avoid the bad. We want to attain this just result both in the case of our own political community of the United States of America and, if possible, in the assemblage of political communities on the world scene—the presently ill-organized world community of separate states.

PART I. THE DIVIDED COMMUNITY

I. Discord: Holding to an Unjustifiable Position

INSTITUTIONS—the organized ways in which a community carries on its activities—are always susceptible of improvement. Often the institutions are so much out of keeping with the real needs of the community that a change in the institutions is essential. In such cases many individuals and groups will be pushing for reform, but very likely not in the same directions because, as we have seen, the different groups, due to their differing interests, have different ideas of what changes are desirable.

The various reform efforts within the community often end in un-adjusted discord—usually in the form of imposed, unjust order, sometimes in the form of overt disorder—rather than in an orderly development to a better reconciliation of the interests of the several competing groups. To find out why in any specific case this discordant result occurs, a first line of inquiry is to look at the motives and acts of those group leaders who have the greatest opportunity to bring about a reconciliation and see what causes their failure to do so.

We shall note the attempts of groups both on the traditional and on the reforming sides to make use of the power of already existing institutions, including the government, as well as the attempt of the leaders of the government group itself to improve their own individual and group position.

The aspects of government in which we are most interested are those which ordinarily and popularly are associated with the idea of government. These include the control of the police and the armed forces, the determination of policies at home and in foreign relations, lawmaking and law enforcement, and taxing and spending; and in modern times control over money and credit. In some governments— as in that of the United States today—these powers have been separated so that there have been a number of groups exercising governmental powers within the inclusive government group. In other governments —as in that of the totalitarian states today—the powers have been concentrated in a few hands, as in a monarch or in the leader of a single recognized political party and his immediate circle.

1. GERMAN FAILURE IN THE NINETEENTH CENTURY TO ACHIEVE GOVERNMENT WITH CONSENT OF THE GOVERNED

The leaders of a privileged group in the community in the effort to maintain and enhance their power may cling too long to a political system to which they are accustomed. They know the ropes, and would stay with a ship of state ill-fitted to the needs of the actual voyage that must be taken rather than embark on a less familiar vessel.

In the second quarter of the nineteenth century, Central Europe was loosely organized in a Germanic Confederation—a mainly defensive alliance of German states formerly within the Holy Roman Empire, maintaining at Frankfurt-am-Main a permanent conference of delegates from thirty-eight participating governments. The purpose of the Confederation was the preservation of peace and independence within and between these various German states, and as against their foreign adversaries. The most powerful of the participating states were the two principal German powers—Austria and Prussia—each of which belonged to the Confederation by virtue of that part of their territories which had been within the Holy Roman Empire, the balance being excluded. Thus East Prussia and neighboring parts of West Prussia and Posen were not within the Confederation; nor were Hungary and the other non-Germanic parts of the Austrian Empire. Thus, as to the Confederation, Austria and Prussia were both members and also strangers.

At a period when other European nations were making great strides in the improvement of their political and economic position in the world community this atomized Germany was not. Within the separate German states themselves the capacities of the able people were unduly fettered by the several local governments, overcontrol of economic affairs by government bureaus, and especially by censorship of the press in the interest of the current unsatisfactory political arrangements. In those parts of Prussia roughly east of the Elbe River, the social picture to a great extent consisted of a small landowning class and a subservient peasantry.

Political clubs, largely centered in the universities, were active in advocating liberal reforms; but by the middle of the eighteen-thirties these had been generally prohibited from any above-ground meetings. The attitude of the principal governments towards these societies and towards expression of political ideas had been stated as early as 1819, in the Carlsbad Resolutions, ratified by the diet of the Germanic Confederation:

As to teachers: "The confederated governments mutually pledge themselves to remove from the universities or other public educational institutions all teachers who, by obvious deviation from their duty, or by exceeding the limits of their functions, or by the abuse of their legitimate influence over the youthful minds, or by propagating harmful doctrines hostile to public order or subversive of existing governmental institutions, shall have unmistakably proved their unfitness for the important office entrusted to them. . . ."

As to societies of students: "Those laws which have for a long period been directed against secret and unauthorized societies in the universities shall be strictly enforced. These laws apply especially to that association established some years since under the name 'Universal Students' Union,' since the very conception of the society implies the utterly unallowable plan of permanent fellowship and constant communication between the various universities."

As to printed matter: "So long as this decree shall remain in force no publication which appears in the form of daily issues or as a serial not exceeding twenty sheets of printed matter, shall go to press in any state of the union without the previous knowledge and approval of the state officials.

"The Diet shall have the right, moreover, to suppress on its own authority, without being petitioned, such writings . . . as, in the opinion of a commission appointed by it, are inimical to the honor of the union, the safety of individual states, or the maintenance of peace and quiet in Germany. There shall be no appeal from such decisions, and the governments involved are bound to see that they are put into execution. . . ."

In early 1848 a rash of revolutionary disturbances broke out over much of Europe, symptomatic of constitutional inadequacies in the

European states. The events in Germany in February and March and the content of the demands for reform in the several German states indicate that professional and middle-class groups, students, and indeed all those who were not specially favored by the current regimes, felt keenly the need of political changes to bring about a Germany more liberal at home, as well as stronger on the world scene. There were many mass meetings and petitions to the local rulers, most of which called for freedom of the press and of assembly, a national parliament through which there might be a more general participation in influence on the government, which should in one of its main aspects be a government of a united Germany. There were demands for civil rights, trial by jury, and freedom of religion. The tendency of these reform demands indicated the felt deficiencies of the current regime.

The local rulers were universally frightened by these demonstrations of public sentiment. The memory of the not too far distant excesses of the French Revolution was present in their minds; and in the first flush and excitement of the 1848 uprisings, the German rulers almost everywhere—even in the absence of major violence against their authority—promised local constitutional reforms, removed unpopular ministers from office, and spoke out in favor of a political federation more satisfactory than that of the existing Germanic Confederation. But as events were to prove, these promises went against the grain of many of the promisers, and as time passed and the nerve of the rulers was recovered, the promises were not kept.

In the interval, while the reforming fervor was still high and the existing governments still frightened and conciliatory, the diet of the old German Confederation, after various preliminary committee meetings, invited the several governments to send representatives to a pre-parliament which in turn provided for the elections of representatives to a national assembly. In May 1848, this assembly—the Frankfort Parliament—opened its deliberations on a new constitution for the German states.

The Frankfort Parliament then started to debate the basic civil rights of Germans and to formulate the provisions of a constitution, a task made difficult by the differing aims of the reformers, which ranged all the way from an imperial constitution preserving separate and autonomous state governments, through the middle position of a greater weight of authority for the central monarchical government and a definite subordination of the several states to this federal state, to the more extreme position of a strongly centralized republic and the abolition of monarchy.

While the Parliament was thus debating a new order, the old traditional local governments, particularly and significantly those of Prussia and of Austria, were recuperating from the shock of the early revolutionary disturbances.

As time passed it became clear that Austria, where the revolution had lost momentum and been overcome by the end of 1848, was going to stand by her old empire if she could, and that she would not enter a German federation which excluded her eastern and southern appendages, as that might cause her eventually to play a second fiddle to Prussia's first.

The Frankfort Parliament was without any military force and had to rely even for the preservation of order in Frankfort itself on Austrian and Prussian troops. This lack of power was emphasized in a matter vital to national sentiment. Prussia, in the name of the Germanic Confederation, had undertaken a military conflict with Denmark over the control of Schleswig-Holstein; but made such an ignominious and halfhearted effort that a truce was proposed which was a grievous humiliation to the German position. Yet it had to be accepted by the Frankfort Parliament.

Nevertheless, and despite its great difficulties, the Frankfort Parliament produced a constitution that looked as though it offered a real prospect of a Germany—minus Austria for the time being—united on a much stronger basis than the old, and a basis with promise of development along free and liberal lines. That it might be possible for Prussian leadership to come into line with middle-class ideas had been suggested by the success of the Customs Union (Zollverein) which by the middle of the century had shown that the greater part of Germany was at least capable of becoming an economic entity—a free trade area. The practical hope now lay in the prospect of getting Prussian strength and discipline aligned with the ideas of the liberal German leadership in a regime which should be both powerful and based on the consent of the governed. The central imperial government was to control the entire military force of Germany and to speak for the whole of Germany in matters of war and peace; and all of Germany was to be one economic area regulated by the federal government. The head of the federation was a hereditary "Emperor of the Germans," having a suspensive veto upon acts of the national legislature. His ministers were answerable to the legislature which consisted of two bodies—an upper house chosen half by the several state governments and half by the lower houses of the state legislatures, and a lower house elected by universal male franchise in single-member constituencies.

At the end of March in 1849 the Frankfort Parliament elected the King of Prussia as the new hereditary German Emperor, and on April 3rd offered him the crown. The King put off the necessity of a final decision by saying that the new constitution must have the assent of the German princes and the Free Cities. When it appeared that this assent was forthcoming not only from the lesser princes, but from the four kings—of Bavaria, Saxony, Hanover, and Württemberg—so that all Germany except Austria agreed to the new constitution, the King of Prussia stated that he, a king by divine right, could not receive a crown at the hands of a popular assembly.

Why did Prussia decline the headship of the German nation? The answer is because it was not a headship on her own terms and sufficiently absolute. Other considerations, such as fear of the hostility of Russia to a united Germany, or fear of possible Austrian resentment, exerted a minor but not controlling influence. The ultimate cause lay in the fact that the capabilities of the leaders in Prussia did not lie along the lines that were necessary for participation in a government structure that required give and take on the part of Prussia.

In the nineteenth century Prussian control of the army and the government lay in representatives of the eastern landowning group, the Junkers. The Junkers were descendants of those sons of the nobility, junge Herren, originally chosen for their fighting prowess and discipline. They were to be capable of successfully pushing out against the pagan Slavic natives who represented a threat to the German Christians in the twelfth and thirteenth centuries. The Junkers regarded as unworthy any occupations other than fighting, hunting, managing their land, or serving as government officials. Possessed of a sense of austere discipline, inbred through cousin and in-group marriages, these autocratic and intolerant leaders were pleased rather than dissatisfied with the breakdown of a scheme like the Frankfort Constitution. They were doing too well in the system they knew. They would not risk their position by taking part in a liberal regime which opened up channels for middle-class abilities and in which the aptitudes of the Junkers might not keep them at the top. They might lose the power of maintaining laws and administration specially favoring their interests as landowners. Whatever the need of Germany as a whole, the Junkers preferred to hold tight rather than chance the hazards of a reform scheme where they could not be sure of their political power. Their motives of desire for political control and for economic advantage dictated their resistance to the proposed reforms. This was a hardheaded group of men who were in control of Prussia; but their talents and their hopes were not fitted to meet the apparent current need of the time and place, which required that they participate in a political regime set up on terms that were not exclusively their own.

2. EVENTS LEADING TO THE PROTESTANT REFORMATION

Political Power of the Church

Sometimes the leaders of a religious organization hold a place of great power in the political community, and exercise dominant influence in economic and governmental affairs as well as in the affairs of the Church. Such was the case in Western Europe for many years preceding the Protestant Reformation and the Roman Catholic Counter-Reformation.

When the Emperor Henry IV had succeeded in 1075 in putting down an uprising among his Saxon subjects, he proceeded to punish those leaders of Church and state who had opposed him. In his efforts to strengthen his own position he asserted the right not only to confirm bishops in their possessions and temporal rights, but also to appoint them to the bishopric and confirm them in their spiritual rights and office—investiture with ring and staff as well as with scepter. Pope Gregory VII was determined that the investiture of bishops by a lay ruler must cease. He then proceeded to excommunicate certain of the Emperor's council on the ground that they had obtained the church offices which they held by buying the offices.

This interference in what he regarded as his own political affairs was not acceptable to the Emperor, and he thus vilified the Pope:

By craft abhorrent to the profession of monk, thou hast acquired wealth; by wealth, influence; by influence, arms; by arms, a throne of peace. And from the throne of peace thou hast destroyed peace; thou hast turned subjects against their governors, for thou, who wert not called of God, hast taught that our bishops, truly so called, should be despised. . . .

Let another assume the seat of St. Peter, who will not practice violence under the cloak of religion, but will teach St. Peter's wholesome doctrine. I Henry, king by the grace of God, together with all our bishops, say unto thee: "Come down, come down, to be damned throughout all eternity."

The Pope retaliated by decreeing the deposition of Henry, by forbidding anyone to serve him as king, and by cutting him off from the community of Christians—excommunication:

O St. Peter, chief of the apostles, . . . Thou and my Lady, the Mother of God, and thy brother, St. Paul, are witnesses for me among all the saints that thy Holy Roman Church placed me in control against my will; that I had no thought of violence in ascending to thy chair, and that I should rather have ended my life as a pilgrim than by worldly means to have gained thy throne for the sake of earthly glory. . . .

To me, in particular, as thy representative and the recipient of thy favor, has God granted the power of binding and loosing in heaven and earth. In this confidence, therefore, for the honor and security of thy Church, in the name of Almighty God—Father, Son and Holy Ghost— by thy power and authority, I withdraw from Henry the king, . . . a rebel of incredible insolence against thy Church, his right to rule over the whole kingdom of the Germans and over Italy. And I absolve all Christians from the bonds of the oath which they have taken to him or which they shall in future take; and I forbid anyone to serve him as king.

For it is fitting that he who strives to lessen the honor of thy Church should himself lose the honor which seems to belong to him. And since he has scorned to obey as a Christian, and has not returned to God whom he has deserted, but has had intercourse with the excommunicated; practiced manifold iniquities; spurned the counsels which, as thou art witness, I sent to him for his own salvation; separated himself from thy Church and endeavored to rend it asunder; I bind him, in thy stead, with the chain of the anathema. Relying upon thee, I bind him, that the people may know and prove that thou art Peter, and upon thy rock the Son of the living God hath built his Church, and the gates of hell shall not prevail against it.

As a result of the Pope's action, the King's adherents began to fall away from him, and in just a year he made humble submission to the Pope. The ban of anathema and excommunication was thereupon revoked.

The practical power of the head of the Church had been shown to extend to the deposition of an emperor and the release of his subjects from the obligation of their oath to him.

Philip Augustus, one of the most powerful and famous kings of France, had as his second wife Ingeborg of Denmark. Shortly after marriage he took a distaste to her, put her in a convent, and persuaded a French ecclesiastical council to dissolve the marriage. Thereafter he married Agnes of Meran. Ingeborg appealed to Pope Innocent III, who threatened to put France under the interdict, suspending religious services in the kingdom, unless the king should submit the case to Rome. The King refused, and the Pope imposed the interdict, excommunicating the king. In less than a year, the dissatisfaction of his people compelled the King to submit to the Pope in order to get the interdict removed. To be sure, he kept Ingeborg isolated from him for some years more; but he was compelled to put Agnes aside and to recognize Ingeborg as his lawful wife.

In the course of extending the papal power this same Innocent ran into embroilment with other rulers than Philip Augustus. There was a dispute in the reign of King John of England over who should be Archbishop of Canterbury. Certain of the monks secretly elected one Reginald and sent him along with some of their number to Rome to secure his confirmation from the Pope. After Reginald's departure for Rome the monks made another election, of King John's candidate, the Bishop of Norwich. Innocent refused to recognize the election of either of these candidates, and induced the Canterbury monks who had come to Rome to select a candidate who was the Pope's own choice, one Stephen Langton, an English expatriate. This was in the year 1207.

King John refused to let Langton come to Canterbury and he exiled the Canterbury monks. In 1208 Innocent imposed the interdict on England. In 1209 he excommunicated King John, and thereafter released John's subjects from their oaths of loyalty and John's allies from their treaty obligations.

All of these measures of Pope against king were not enough to bring the king to heel. So in a move of power politics the Pope deposed John as king and offered the English throne to Philip Augustus! In the face of threatened invasion and the failing support of his own subjects, John yielded in the matter of Langton, surrendered his kingdom to the Pope, and received it back as a vassal of the Pope, agreeing to an annual payment of 1,000 pounds to Rome.

Other European states acknowledging vassalship to Innocent were Aragon, Bulgaria, Denmark, Hungary, Poland, Portugal, and Serbia. The extent of the papal claim is illustrated in the terms of the oaths of one of the rulers, Peter of Aragon:

I, Peter, King of Aragon, confess and swear that I will ever be the obedient vassal of my Lord, Pope Innocent, and his Catholic successors, and of the Roman Church. I will faithfully keep my realm in his obedience, will defend the Catholic Faith, and will persecute heresy. I will respect the liberties and immunities of the Church, and will make others observe its rights. I will strive to establish peace and justice in all the territory subject to my control. I swear it by God's name and on these holy Gospels.

I confess from the heart and with my mouth that the Roman pontiff, successor to St. Peter, takes the place of Him who governs earthly realms, and confers them upon whom it seems good to him. I, Peter, by the grace of God, King of Aragon, Count of Barcelona, and Lord of Montpellier, desiring above all else the protection of God, of the Apostle, and of the Holy See, declare that I offer my kingdom to thee, admirable father and lord, sovereign pontiff Innocent, and to thy successors, and through thee to the most sacred Church of Rome. And I make my kingdom tributary to Rome at the rate of 250 gold pieces which my treasury shall pay every year to the Apostolic See. And I swear for myself and my successors that we will remain thy faithful vassals and obedient subjects.

Such was the power of the Church in the affairs of temporal rulers. What was the organization which made possible such political effectiveness and what were the main reasons for its influence?

The fundamental basis of the power of the Church was the general belief amongst men of every rank and every occupation that the priest had the ability to confer or to withhold salvation, that God forgave only those whom the priest forgave—all the unforgiven being condemned to everlasting torment. The parish priests were in general nominated by a local patron—lay or cleric—of the parish church, but the appointment required the approval of the bishop as well as ordination by him.

The priests were subject to the supervisory control of their bishop, who in addition to being a spiritual authority in the Church was also likely to be a powerful feudal lord with the power of a local prince or noble in affairs of the world. This temporal power was usually utilized in behalf of the aggrandizement of the Church, as it was to the interest of a bishop as against lay rulers and princes that the position of the Church be paramount and superior to that of purely secular governments. It is said that when a legate of Pope Innocent demanded from King Richard the Lion-Hearted the release from prison of the Bishop of Beauvais, the King replied that the prisoner had not been captured as a bishop, but as a layman, an armored knight, a robber, tyrant, and incendiary who wasted Richard's lands. Such was the secular activity of a bishop.

The clergy were not subject to the ordinary courts of justice but to special Church tribunals and this special jurisdiction was a great protection of the independence and special privilege of the Church position.

By the time when the power of the Church had reached its height the clergy were required to be celibate. Despite the fact that concubinage was rife, a celibate clergy were none the less free of family ties in the usual sense, and this tended to produce an undivided loyalty to the advancement of whatever the Church cause might be.

Of significance to the maintenance of Church dominance was an element of freedom not elsewhere illustrated in medieval society—the fact that a Church career was open to talent irrespective of the social level into which a man happened to have been born. Famous Popes in fact came from families where the father might be baker, carpenter, cobbler, or shepherd.

As we have already noted, the Church had what was close to a monopoly of reading and writing. This meant that a lay ruler virtually had to have churchmen in his immediate governing group as a matter of mechanics in carrying on his government. It also meant a preponderant influence by the Church in contemporary education, such as it was.

The Pope was at the head of the hierarchy. He usually had his office at Rome, being Bishop of Rome; but for the greater part of the fourteenth century was established at Avignon. A central administrative organization afforded the necessary means through which the Pope exercised his authority. There was a College of Cardinals, functioning as an advisory cabinet, its membership also supplying the presiding officers of the various administrative bodies. There were the several tribunals in charge of disciplinary matters such as excommunication, and of violations of canon law and appeals from episcopal courts. There were executive offices in charge of matters relating to appointment to benefices, the necessary administration of papal property, collection of revenue, and education. The totality of this bureaucracy assisting the Pope in the government of the Church went by the name of the *curia,* in theory exercising powers delegated by the Pope.

The papal administration was represented also by legates sent into the several territorial jurisdictions of the Church. To the legate was delegated a greater or lesser degree of the papal authority in accord with the tasks committed to him, which might be of carrying out some particular local purpose of the Pope, or of inspection and reporting.

Within a particular locality there might well be jealousy between a bishop on the one hand and the head of some monastery who would resent what he thought was undue interference by a bishop with his affairs. Such a conflict would tend to enhance the power of the Pope, as each disputant would look for papal friendship. Similarly, the Orders of itinerant preachers, the friars, would rely on the Pope for protection against the resistance they might meet from locally established clergy.

The degree of centralization of Church authority in the *curia* was conspicuous shortly before the Reformation. Despite the place of power in worldly affairs held by prelates within their own jurisdictions they exhibited a striking lack of independence and referred even trivial matters of policy or action to the Pope.

The papal bureaucracy was financed by a complex system of taxation consisting of shares in the income collected locally in the parishes, payments of proportions of income of the beneficed clergy, for example, bishops and abbots, and payments for the right to succeed to a benefice when it should fall vacant. There were also payments of various fees in connection with resort to the tribunals for the administration of papal justice. Another source of income, relied upon especially in the case of various particular purposes such as the financing of a crusade, or the building of St. Peter's, was monetary offerings made on the occasion of receiving an indulgence, that is to say, the remission of punishment—on earth or in Purgatory—due to those sins of which the guilt has been forgiven by God at the instigation of ecclesiastical authority.

Flaws in the Church Viewed as a Secular Institution

Such were the main features of the organization through which the Church exercised its political power. Unfortunately for the Church, the abuses and dysfunctions within this organization were so notorious and harmful as to produce, after the failure of efforts at internal reform, the discord which resulted in reformation by way of schism— the Protestant Reformation.

The need of the Pope and of his *curia* for funds to carry out their temporal ambitions, as well as the greed of the Pope or of those in the curial circle, led to the sale of benefices as a means of procuring revenue over and above what would be produced by the ordinary levies. The ability of a candidate to pay for his office did not mean that he was qualified to hold it, and when a bishopric or abbotship went to the highest bidder, this might result in the appointment of those conspicuous for their lack of understanding of their office. The sale of supposedly holy office enormously injured the Church in the eyes of sincere men. The poet Dante recounts how he stood in Hell beside Pope Nicholas III who was buried head down, the soles of his extending feet eternally on fire. The Pope becomes aware of the poet's presence and mistakes him for Pope Boniface VIII, who is also destined for like torment. In the course of their conversation it appears that Pope Clement V is also going to be punished in the same way. Boniface and Clement were both still living when Dante wrote, so he adopted the literary device of prophetic vision by Nicholas to consign the two of them to Hell. All three Popes sold church offices, the sin of simony. The attitude of a contemporary loyal Catholic is shown in Dante's scathing words to Nicholas:

> I do not know if I was now too bold,
>   but I answered him in this strain:
>   "Alas, now tell me, how much treasure
>
> did our Lord ask of St. Peter
>   before he put the keys in his hands?
>   Surely he demanded only, "Follow me!"
>
> Nor did Peter and the others ask Matthias
>   for gold or silver when he was chosen
>   for the place the guilty soul had lost.
>
> Therefore, stay there, for you are well punished,
>   and keep securely the ill-got money
>   which made you so bold against Charles.
>
> And if I were still not prevented
>   by reverence for the holy keys
>   which you kept in the happy life,
>
> I would use words still heavier,
>   for your avarice afflicts the world,
>   crushing the good and lifting up the bad.
>
> The Evangelist had shepherds like you in mind
>   when she that sitteth upon many waters
>   was seen by him fornicating with kings. . . .

> You have made a god of gold and silver,
> > and how do you differ from the idolater,
> > > except that he worships one thing of gold, and you a
> > > > hundred? . . .
>
> While I sang these notes to him,
> > whether anger or conscience stung him,
> > > he kicked hard with both his feet.

An abuse traceable to greed was that of appointing an officeholder to such a multiplicity of offices that, although he could collect the income, he could not perform the functions of the offices. It is said that the Cardinal Giuliano della Rovere, later Pope Julius II, was not only made a cardinal by his uncle, Pope Sixtus IV, but also was designated to the archbishopric of Avignon, the bishoprics of Bologna, Coutances, Lausanne, Munde, Ostia, Velletri, and Viviers, and the abbacies of Grottaferrata and Nonantola.

Another income-producing papal abuse was the creation and sale of offices in the papal bureaucracy. For example, Pope Leo X is reported to have appointed 60 chamberlains and 140 squires, against a payment to him of 90,000 ducats by the former and 112,000 ducats by the latter.

Pope Alexander VI, to obtain funds for his son Cesare Borgia, created 21 cardinals at a total sale price of 250,000 ducats.

It is no wonder that in connection with a general practice of the sale of benefices or of expectations to them, there might on occasion occur conflicting claims that gave rise to litigation requiring recourse to the judicial side of the *curia*, which, as in the case of any dealings with the papal institutions, was expensive. Representatives of the French Church in Council at Bourges in 1438 complained of the number of such suits, of the greed for plural appointments caused by the mercenary practices of the Pope, of the drain on French resources, and of the reduction to poverty of those having recourse to the papal courts, where rightful claims gave way to fraud in favor of those who could make the largest payments.

As to how papal exactions affected those from whom they were exacted, the following written by a critical cleric at Avignon is instructive.

For carrying on these exactions and gathering the gains into the *camera,* or Charybdis, as we may better call it, the popes appoint their collectors in every province—those, namely, whom they know to be most skillful in extracting money, owing to peculiar energy, diligence, or harshness of temper, those, in short, who will neither spare nor except but would squeeze gold from a stone. To these the popes grant, moreover, the power of anathematizing anyone, even prelates, and of expelling from the communion of the faithful everyone who does not within a fixed period satisfy their demands for money. What ills these collectors have caused, and the extent to which poor churches and people have been oppressed, are questions best omitted, as we could never hope to do the matter justice. From this source come the laments of the unhappy ministers of the Church, which reach our ears, as they faint under the insupportable yoke—yea, perish of hunger. Hence come suspensions from divine service, interdicts from entering a church, and anathemas. . . .

In this mercenary atmosphere and in the pursuit of worldly power the Popes were playing politics on the grand scale, allying their interests now with this, now with that prince, as seemed advisable to further their temporal ambitions. But this is a game which two can play, and in the course of the game princes might succeed in utilizing Popes for advancement of the princes' schemes. But whether it was prince or Pope who happened to be prime mover in some particular political conflict, the reputation and authority of the Church as a moral and spiritual institution suffered irreparable injury in these conflicts of worldly ambition.

When Philip the Fair of France, at the close of the thirteenth century, needed funds to further his territorial schemes, he tried taxation of the clergy, thereby precipitating a quarrel with Pope Boniface VIII. The Pope forbade (in the bull *Clericos Laicos*) any churchman to pay taxes to any prince without the express permission of the Pope. The King retaliated by forbidding the export of money or valuables from France so as to cut off a source of papal income. Then further quarrels over rights of Church and state arose. The King imprisoned a papal legate. As the controversy continued unreconciled, the bull *Unam Sanctam* was issued asserting, as we have seen, the superiority of the papal power over that of kings and secular rulers. In this atmosphere of no compromise on the Pope's part, the King sent a representative to Italy, who with the aid of a powerful Italian family temporarily captured the Pope. Shortly therafter the Pope died. Two years later the Archbishop of Bordeaux was elected Pope. Largely as a result of the contemporary disorder in Italy this Pope, Clement V, who never went to Italy at all, established his residence at Avignon, a papal enclave in France, and there for seventy years the papal *curia* was established.

The *curia* at Avignon consisting as it did of Popes who were Frenchmen, and of a College of Cardinals with an apparently controlling French membership, was suspected of being under undue French national influence, and this stimulated anti-papal tendencies amongst rulers of other lands.

The Great Schism

The papal court resided in Avignon for seventy years, and then towards the close of his life, Pope Gregory XI returned to Rome. This seemed to be a good development, offering hope of a cure both of the corruption of the papacy, so rife at Avignon, and also of the undue influence on Popes of French political aims. But what in fact transpired was the election of an Italian Pope and then of a French Pope, representing a cleavage in the College of Cardinals between those with mainly French interests, and those oriented away from France. For forty years thereafter the Church was thus divided into two hostile wings, each with the support of learned theologians, and for six years towards the close of this period Church coherence was further threatened by a third Pope, resident at Pisa.

No thoughtful Catholic could view such disputes and such division at the center of his Church without recognizing a weakening of the moral authority of the papacy. Conflicts of ambition were diverting the central government of the Church from its proper duty of spiritual leadership. Respect for the papacy as an institution suffered a severe setback.

Deterioration at the Local Level

At the local level too the clergy were not what they should have been. Of course it is always the case that in any large institution, even though on the whole it is carrying out its functions well, there will be a number of its officers and employees who are derelict from right standards. This is only normal. But in the pre-Reformation Church the departure from right standards was too conspicuous and too prevalent.

The greed which characterized the papal *curia* was also present in the lower clergy. Dietrich Vrie, writing in the early fifteenth century in his history of the Council of Constance, describes some aspects of this:

The supreme pontiffs, as I know, are elected through avarice and simony, and likewise the other bishops are ordained for gold. These in turn will not ordain those below them—the priests, deacons, subdeacons, and acolytes—except a strict agreement be first drawn up. Of the mammon of unrighteousness the bishops, the real rulers, and chapters each receives a part.

The once accepted maxim, "Freely give, for freely ye have received," is now most vilely perverted: "Freely I have not received, nor will I freely give, for I bought my bishopric for a great price and must indemnify myself impiously for my untoward outlay. I will not ordain you as a priest except for money. I purchased the sacrament of ordination when I became a bishop, and I propose to sell you the same sign and seal of ordination. By beseeching for gold I obtained my office, and for beseeching and gold do I sell you your place. Refuse the amount I demand and you shall not become a priest."

In the twelfth century a Lateran Council decreed that marriages of clergy were not true marriages. This became the official position of the Church and the rule was enforced. One result was the profitable toleration of concubinage—prelates collecting fees from priests who kept concubines. In its effect on the public attitude towards the clergy, it may well be that the recognition of marriages would have been a sounder policy. We have noted that celibacy was probably useful as a device for attaching the main interests of the clergy to the Church rather than to their own families and children. But this advantage may have been more than offset by the effect on contemporary opinion of the nonmarital liaisons of clergy.

Attempts within the Church for Reform and Their Failure

The two main lines of attempted reform within the Church organization followed from the two main forms of abuse which we have just sketched—first, the excessive claims of the Pope to a right to interfere in secular affairs, and the related burden on the ecclesiastical organization as a whole of an overcentralized and extravagant papal *curia;* and second, the prevalence of bad standards and corruption within the clergy.

With respect to the Church's own attempts to reform the papacy, outside factors played a part. The secular princes in trying to improve their own position wanted to cut down the pretensions of the papacy. This aim at times fell in line with the reform efforts of those within the clergy who were genuinely alarmed by the absence of ade-

quate controls over Popes dedicated to the pursuit of arbitrary power and increased wealth. Princes also might find themselves in alliance with some faction of the clergy engaged for the time being in conflict with the Pope then in office.

A few years after the conflict between Boniface VIII and Philip the Fair, a serious dispute arose between the Frenchman Pope John XXII and Lewis of Bavaria, who after military victory over an Austrian rival had declared himself German King and proposed to exercise his rights as Holy Roman Emperor in Italy. The Pope went through the standard procedure of excommunicating Lewis and his supporters, and placing the interdict upon territories loyal to Lewis. Lewis set up an antipope in Italy to further the imperial cause there. In this confused picture one thing seems more or less clear: although the conflict in superficial appearance was between Church and state, it was in truth a conflict between the ambitions of Frenchmen and of Germans. Italians sided with the position of Pope or of Emperor as might be best for the particular community to which they owed allegiance in Italy.

Unfortunately for the Pope, he chose the time of this struggle to offend the Franciscan order by condemning as heretical their tenet of evangelical poverty. He thereby brought into the controversy—more against himself than in favor of his opponent—a powerful and intelligent attack. In the course of this attack there was ably developed and presented the twofold thesis that the Pope ought not to be able to compel obedience to his dictates by secular or ecclesiastical penalties unless sanctioned by the whole body of the Church, and that the Pope ought to be subject to the whole body of the Church as represented in a general council. The effort to reform the papacy became centered in this conciliar movement. The conciliar leaders held that when a Pope abused his office, then the necessities of the case required that he be controlled in the interests of the whole Church.

Then, as the seventy years of papal residence at Avignon was succeeded by the forty more years of the Great Schism with its two competing Popes—and on occasion three—it became more than ever evident that the essential lawlessness of the Popes and their rivalries needed to be controlled.

The Great Schism was finally healed in the selection by the Council of Constance in 1417 of a Pope who made good his claim, and so once more there was a single Pope. But this Pope turned on the Council which had chosen him and immediately set about the restoration of the untrammeled power of Pope and papal *curia*. In another twenty years the Popes had re-established their independence of Councils, and the old financial and moral abuses reappeared.

In 1492—Columbus' famous year—Rodrigo Borgia ascended the papal throne under the name of Alexander VI. The means used by Alexander to destroy the power of Italian princes, his appropriation of their property to improve his own and his family's finances, the scandal of the bribery by which he bought his elevation to the papacy, the notoriety of his sex life and his devotion to his children's schemes at the financial expense of the Church, the packing of the College of Cardinals with his personal supporters, demonstrated in dramatic form that the conciliar movement had failed to establish good standards or adequate controls for the papal institution.

Force and Fraud in Support of Orthodoxy

The leaders of the fifteenth-century Church were holding too tight in a system which gave them great economic and political power. Like the nineteenth-century German leaders, they did not benefit from criticism but instead suppressed those reforming elements hostile to the received system. The orthodox regime was to be untouched because those who administered it did so well by themselves in a worldly sense. As Capito put it at the turn of the sitxeenth century:

Simple, pious folk meekly follow the beck and nod of our counterfeit Church. The more thoughtful have had their spirit quenched by its tyranny. As for us, the theologians, who loudly proclaim our special sanctity and knowledge of Christ, we constantly compromise his cause by our arrogance. We take advantage of all the abuses in religion and under the guise of piety we decently guard our own interests.

The Church's system of sacraments—baptism, confirmation, partaking of the body and blood of Christ under the appearance of bread and wine, penance, last anointing, holy orders, and matrimony—mainly rested on the belief in original sin—a state of sin in which each individual was involved by virtue of his descent from Adam who by disobedience to God had rejected God's gift of a supernatural life. Adam's sin became the sin of human nature, inhering as habitual in all sharing that nature. Even after baptism, which remitted original sin and the punishment which was its due, the tendency to sin and the physical disability of death remained.

The office of the Church and its justification as an institution re-

LEARNING RESOURCES CENTER
NAZARETH COLLEGE

volved around its function of saving man from sin. The Church came
to acquire an economic interest in its version of sinfulness, for if
sin as defined by the Church did not have the force and effect im-
puted to it by the Church dogma, or if the escape from the effect of
sin might take place as well without as within the Church organization, if the priest were not an essential mediator between God and
man, or if the sacraments were not essential to the welfare of a man's
spirit and his salvation, then the monopoly of the Church in the field
of salvation would be gone. The loss of monopoly would threaten the
Church's revenues.

Regimes both ancient and modern which have based their authority
on a doctrine which is not to be questioned, have to find a method of
dealing with questioners. When the doctrine itself does not prove
sufficient through persuasion and argument to command men's willing
assent, force is threatened or used to compel compliance. The authority of such a regime is also often bolstered by fraudulent claims
in support of its legitimacy or position.

Questioners, doubters of the rightness of the Church position from
time to time arose and kept arising.

An early and important heresy was that of Pelagianism, with which
Saint Augustine engaged in controversy for many years. Pelagius held
that children were born innocent, not tainted by original sin; that
death of the body was the lot of all animal life, including man, and
hence that human sickness and death were not due to Adam's disobedience. He held that God's grace had given man the attributes, in
free will and reason, which might lead him to God and enable him to
reach for God's further grace and assistance. Human nature, he
thought, was not necessarily vile, because in his view sin was not inherited. This was a huge heresy, as it rendered the sacrament of baptism unnecessary to save the soul of a new-born infant, as such a
soul was innocent and saved anyway. He even went so far as to think
that virtuous pagans, living before the coming of Christ, might go to
heaven rather than hell. Pelagianism disappeared as an organized
heresy in about the year 600, but its theories remained a topic of theological discussion for a thousand years thereafter. Even today it is
not unlikely that some Catholics would feel a spontaneous sympathy
with the tenets of this humane heretic.

A famous reform group which started in the thirteenth century
mainly as a reaction against luxury and a move to return to gospel
simplicity was the Waldenses. But as the years passed and as clerical

worldliness flourished, the Waldensian leaders began to take positions threatening to the orthodox powers of the clergy. They came to hold that an evil priest could not minister validly. They denied the doctrine of Purgatory. Now since some priests were evil, and since much of the Church power over laymen arose from the ability of clerics to mediate the remission of punishment—as by material fire—in Purgatory, tenets such as these of the Waldenses were so dangerously radical as to constitute heresy.

The medieval church held that where a heretic could not be won over by persuasion, he should be won over by force. An effective instrument of persuasion backed by force was the Inquisition, by the use of which the property of persistent heretics was confiscated. As a means of gaining support of the secular rulers the Church was willing to have the confiscated property go largely to these rulers. This was obviously the kind of procedure subject to abuse, and it was abused, particularly in its unfair rules of evidence and in its use of terror as an inducement to the profession of true belief. But for our present purposes what is significant is the forceful suppression by the Church of interior criticism, and the condemnation as heretics of those who were sincerely unwilling to assent in practice to the ministrations of a corrupt clergy and—as they believed—to a mistaken and injurious orthodoxy.

The life of the English churchman, John Wyclif, fell within the period of the papal residence at Avignon and the opening years of the Great Schism with its duplication of Popes. Wyclif's career shows the effect on a philosophically minded reformer of the political division in the Church and the notorious worldliness of the Popes and the higher clergy. Although in the beginning loyal to the institution of the papal *curia* and to the Pope as head of the Church, his actual observation of and participation in contemporary events led him to the position that an ecclesiastic had a right to the temporalities—the property and income—of his office only as long as he was not abusing his office. The Popes being what in fact they were, he castigated them.

Before Wyclif had lived out his days as the Roman Catholic rector at Lutterworth, he had fully developed the views that were later so important in the reform movement led by the Czech, John Huss. Thirty years after Wyclif's death, the Council of Constance, frightened by the Hussite heresy, turned over Huss to be burned at the stake and decreed that the dead Wyclif be dug up from his grave and burned.

In addition to the use of force to maintain its system of belief against critics, the Church also used fraud. Well-known examples of this fraud were the Donation of Constantine, and the False Decretals. The former was a forged document purporting to grant the papacy temporal power in Italy and Western Europe. The latter was a series of forgeries which was designed mainly to support the rights of bishops against secular rulers.

3. REFORM BY REVOLT

A contribution of money may be made to a priest and accepted by him, on his undertaking to offer the sacrifice of Christ's body—i.e., to celebrate the Mass—for some specific purpose. Such a contribution is not the price of a Mass (if it were, it would be the sin of simony) but a contribution for the priest's support.

It is also lawful to make an offering of money on the occasion of receiving an indulgence, which is the remission before God of the temporal punishment otherwise owing on account of sins of which the guilt has been forgiven. In the absence of an indulgence, the punishment has to be worked off in this world or else it must be exacted in full in the hereafter in Purgatory.

It was the abuse of the grant of indulgences for money offerings that precipitated the Protestant Reformation.

The Archbishop Albert of Magdeburg in 1514 obtained the see of Mainz. To pay the Pope for this office and to cover his other expenses in connection therewith, he had borrowed money from the banking house of Fuggers. In order to obtain funds to repay the loan, he got permission to conduct the disposition of indulgences in his two archbishoprics of Mainz and Magdeburg, half the contributions to go to Albert and half to the rebuilding of St. Peter's at Rome.

The official instructions for collection set the character of the enterprise in a revealing light as primarily a money-raising scheme. Certainly a huckster spirit was later manifested in the conduct of the actual dispensation of indulgences.

In the instructions certain specific graces arising from the indulgences are listed. "The first grace is the remission of all sins." With respect to the first grace, which is for the benefit of living people:

Respecting, now, the contribution to the chest, for the building of the said church of the chief of the apostles, the penitentiaries and confessors, after they have explained to those making confession the full remission and privileges, shall ask of them how much money they would conscientiously go without for the said most complete remission and privileges;

and this shall be done in order that hereafter they may be brought the more easily to contribute. And because the conditions and occupations of men are so manifold and diverse that we cannot consider them individually and impose specific rates accordingly, we have therefore concluded that the rates should be determined according to the recognized classes of persons. [Here follows a table of rates for "classes of persons" ranging from kings and queens to tradespeople and artisans and others.]

The fourth distinctive grace is for those souls which are in purgatory, and is the complete remission of all sins, which remission the pope brings to pass through his intercession, to the advantage of said souls, in this wise—that the same contribution shall be placed in the chest by a living person as one would make for himself. . . .

It is furthermore not necessary that the persons who place their contributions in the chest for the dead should be contrite in heart and have orally confessed, since this grace is based simply on the state of grace in which the dead departed, and on the contribution of the living, as is evident from the text of the bull. Moreover preachers shall exert themselves to give this grace the widest publicity, since through the same, help will surely come to departed souls, and the construction of the church of St. Peter will be abundantly promoted at the same time. . . .

One John Tetzel, an experienced orator of indulgences, was appointed general sub-commissioner for this particular collection. He was accompanied by a representative of the Fugger banking house which had loaned Albert the sums to be repaid from the proceeds of the contributions of the faithful. Tetzel struck his keynote clearly: "As soon as the coin clinks in the chest, the soul is freed from purgatory!" This was even quicker in effect than one of our modern drugs, whose advertisers motivated by the like desire to sell their product and collect their cash, claim only that it is "ready to go to work in two seconds."

An Augustinian monk at Wittenberg, in Germany, was distressed by what was going on; and in accordance with practice at the university he posted on the door of the castle church 95 theses to be debated:

In the desire and with the purpose of elucidating the truth, a disputation will be held on the underwritten propositions at Wittenberg, under the presidency of the Reverend Father Martin Luther, monk of the order of St. Augustine, Master of Arts and of Sacred Theology, and ordinary lecturer in the same at that place. He therefore asks those who cannot be present and discuss the subject with us orally to do so by letter in their absence. In the name of our Lord Jesus Christ. Amen.

20. The pope, when he speaks of the plenary remission of all penalties, does not mean really of all, but only of those imposed by himself.

21. Thus those preachers of indulgences are in error who say that by the indulgences of the pope a man is freed and saved from all punishment.

23. If any entire remission of all penalties can be granted to anyone, it is certain that it is granted to none but the most perfect—that is, to very few.

27. They preach man (i.e., man's rather than God's teaching) who say that the soul flies out of purgatory as soon as the money clinks in the chest.

28. It is certain that when money clinks in the chest avarice and gain may be increased, but the effect of the intercession of the Church depends on the will of God alone.

50. Christians should be taught that if the pope were acquainted with the exactions of the preachers of pardons, he would prefer that the basilica of St. Peter should be burned to ashes rather than that it should be built up with the skin, flesh, and bones of his sheep.

81. This license in the preaching of pardons makes it no easy thing, even for learned men, to protect the reverence due to the pope against the calumnies, or in any event the keen questionings, of the laity.

82. As, for instance: Why does not the pope empty purgatory for the sake of his most holy charity and of the supreme necessity of souls—this being the most just of all reasons—if he redeems an infinite number of souls for the sake of that most fatal thing, money, to be spent on building a basilica—this being a very slight reason.

90. To repress these scruples and arguments of the laity by force alone, and not to solve them by giving reasons, is to expose the Church and the pope to the ridicule of their enemies and to make Christian men unhappy.

91. If these pardons were preached according to the spirit and wish of the pope, all these questions would be solved with ease; nay, would not exist.

Tetzel accused Luther of heresy. Johann Maier of Eck, an able theologian and professor of theology at Ingolstadt, became an extremely formidable opponent of Luther's positions, and also accused him of heresy. Luther was cited to appear at Rome as a heretic and rebel. Then the citation was changed to appearance before a papal legate at Augsburg. Luther refused to retract unless he was proved from scripture to be in error. This was a potentially serious challenge to Church authority, as no one could safely know how far Church practice had departed from scriptural precept.

Then, as Luther in defense of his position engaged in controversy with Eck and others, he developed doctrines radically in conflict with the accepted teaching of the Church. So it was that the financial abuses of the Church had precipitated an open revolt against its most fundamental doctrines. Both the alleged effects of the sacraments and the monopoly of the priesthood as mediator between God and man were put under attack. Personal faith was declared to be more effective than Church-defined good works for the salvation of men.

Luther was condemned as a heretic in the papal bull *Exsurge Domine* for his errors in regard to penance, indulgences, the authority of the Holy See, the Church and councils, good works, and Purgatory. Luther publicly burned the bull.

4. SOME POLITICAL ACCOMPANIMENTS OF THE REFORMATION

German leaders had felt that the French Popes at Avignon were furthering French ambitions at the expense of Germans. In a like way there was anti-Italian feeling amongst Englishmen, Spaniards, and Frenchmen with regard to the Italian Popes. In every case this kind of feeling was strengthened in the economic sphere by the drain of resources out of the various communities to the foreign land where the Pope held court. Nationalism was promoted by way of dislike of the foreigner and his financial exactions. The local rulers were eager to stop the loss of revenue; and if protection of heretics and the furtherance of revolt against the Church were helpful means to this end, they were adopted. In the great days of the Church the local rulers would have been afraid to support heretics; but now, as the Bishop of Torcello had remarked, the Church had forfeited its moral power and alienated the respect of the sincere and straightforward.

In the course of the conflict between Popes and Councils, the Popes had been afraid of the councils on account of the strong backing of the councils by secular rulers who wanted to bring the Popes to heel. As a means to deal with this threat and to deprive the councils of powerful princely support, the Popes made agreements with the princes, granting concessions to the latter which in effect gave the princes a large amount of control in local church affairs. Thus the Popes themselves had pointed the way towards that establishment of national churches which occurred in Protestant countries.

The Popes too, as a means of keeping the Holy Roman Emperor weak, had tried to build up the power of the rulers of lesser communities, component parts of the Empire. This policy had been particularly successful in Germany, where there was a plethora of independent local rulers. But now the success of the policy struck back at its creators. When some particular local ruler, usually himself a Roman Catholic but with political interests in conflict with traditional religious authority—for example the Elector Frederick of Saxony—felt inclined to take under his protection a particular heretic—in Frederick's case Luther—there was no effective secular authority in Germany upon whom the Pope could call to prevent such action. In countries other than Germany the decay of the Holy Roman Empire had tended towards a strengthening of nationalism as a means of political development. But in Germany the atomization of political rule had been so great that the fading of the Emperor was accompanied by a lack of any effective general authority. So it was that successful organized resistance to Luther's followers failed to materialize.

The lure of seizing the wealth of the Church was illustrated in the case of England. The orders of monks and friars were suppressed, their monasteries and land confiscated and sold. The purchasers obviously had an economic interest in seeing that the land should not be returned to the Church.

In England too, a personal motive of the ruler was significant. The wish of Henry VIII to marry Anne Boleyn despite the refusal of the Pope to declare his existing marriage invalid, played a part in the overthrow of papal power in that country.

If we ask the basic reason why in the course of a few years there were so many permanent wanderings from the Roman Catholic flock, we are brought back to the Church's own abuse of its position and function in the life of Europe. It lost its power because it was not doing its right religious work in the light of the needs and the ideas of the time. And it was not doing its right work largely because arrogance, greed, and other forms of worldliness had interfered with its intellectual candor and moral integrity. It no longer saw its right place in the scheme of things. Some of its leaders—a man like Erasmus is an example—did see what was right for the Church. But there were not enough such leaders.

5. THE SHAPE OF REFORMATION AND COUNTER-REFORMATION

The main religious consequence of the Reformation was the overthrow of the power of the clergy. Priests were eliminated as an essential medium between man and God. The sacraments became evidences that a man had received divine grace; they were no longer in and of themselves, *ex opere operato,* the means of grace. But a baby had still to be saved from original sin, and an adult from the consequences of his own sin. This remained the field of effort of the Protestant churches.

Biblical truth was substituted for Roman Catholic truth as the datum of reasoning. Each Protestant sect diligently searched—and still searches today—the Bible for those passages which support its own particular position. But the Bible is full of inconsistencies, as it is a collection of writings addressed to all sorts of varying occasions with their several different circumstances requiring the stress now of one consideration now of others. So each differing group within any church whose basic document is the Bible can use it successfully to bolster its own position. Each sect falls upon and stresses those passages favorable to its own particular views.

The new Protestant churches continued in the old methods of intolerance. It was due to Calvin that Servetus, discoverer of pulmonary circulation, was condemned to death for questioning the doctrine of the Trinity. It should be said in mitigation of Calvin's intolerance that he wanted Servetus beheaded, whereas in fact he was burned at the stake. Erasmus, dismayed by the fanatical reformers, wrote to Melanchthon: "Is it for this that we have shaken off bishops and popes, that we may come under the yoke of such madmen as Otto and Farel?" A century later in England the English poet Milton wrote: "New Presbyter is but old Priest writ large."

How did it fare with the Roman Catholic Church? What steps did that Church take to meet the threat of the Reformation spirit?

In the first place, the Roman Catholic Church succeeded in purging itself from the corruption which had brought about Luther's revolt and precipitated the Reformation. This Catholic Reform uprooted perhaps the worst feature in Church life, the sale of offices irrespective of the capacity of the candidate—cash down as the main test of qualification of a bishop or priest. High educational standards were set and observed in the selection of the clergy. These reforms were carried out in pursuance of one part of the work of the Council of Trent, which met in three periods between 1545 and 1563. One Pope in this period, Paul IV (1555 to 1559) achieved the reform of the Papal Court itself by purging it of the luxurious and worldly atmosphere which had characterized it in pre-Reformation days. All in all, on the side of practical morality, the Catholic Reform was signally successful.

On the doctrinal side, the Council of Trent also did a thorough-going piece of work. It had such effective committees that the twenty-five solemn one-day sessions of the Council succeeded not only in setting up the principles for the practical reforms which we have just described, but also dealt authoritatively with every feature of the Church dogma and belief. This work set the Church doctrinal system from that day to this in an essentially medieval form, adhering strictly to the old sacramental system. The teaching of the fathers was the test of truth. The way to God was through the daily repeated sacrifice of Christ's body. The power of the old and the familiar rule had reasserted itself.

Thus the Council of Trent: "He who is gifted with the heavenly knowledge of faith is free from an inquisitive curiosity; for when God commands us to believe, he does not propose to have us search into his divine judgments, nor to inquire their reasons and causes, but demands an immutable faith. . . . Faith, therefore, excludes not only all doubt, but even the desire of subjecting its truth to demonstration."

6. THE GERMAN NATIONAL SOCIALISTS IN THE TWENTIETH CENTURY

As causes of discord we have now considered the case of a dominant group within the community holding too tight to a particular position in the economic and governmental province and also a case of holding too tight in the religious province. We now turn to a case of a dominant cultural faction holding too tight in a preferred position and to the discord resulting therefrom.

When Germany lost the First World War she was plunged from a position of world power to one of submission to and dependency on foreign countries. Her internal affairs were in confusion, and her external relations showed her to be powerless. At this juncture, there was a need for the restoration of a due measure of German self-respect, and a buckling down to work to restore the impaired German productivity. There was also a legitimate need for increased German strength, if overreaching of the fatherland by its recent enemies was to be avoided.

Events had demonstrated the deficiencies of recent German policies and ambitions; but many Germans hated to look at things as they were. As events developed, these people found compensation for their failures in an absurdly high opinion of themselves, irrespective of what the facts might indicate.

To these Germans, the National Socialists offered "a world outlook" and a program which soothed their pride, explained away their defeats, and offered hope of restoration to power. The key feature in this program on the emotional side was the idea of the German *Volk,* superior to all other kinds of people, and the rightful claimant to political power and glory.

We have seen in the introductory sections of this book that a group set apart from others by way of life or a religion or by racial distinctions has often felt a powerful ambition to assert its own superiority and improve its own position as against other groups. The German Nazi leaders attempted to take advantage of this kind of motivation by setting up the main human components of the current German fatherland as such a self-conscious cultural group—the *Volk.*

The task was not easy, because the Germans were as hybrid a people as any other in Europe or America. But the Nazi sociologists listed the relative proportions of the five preponderant recognizable strains in the German population, which they called the "German Races"—their estimates apparently meaning that if an "average" German were to be found, Nordic Race factors would constitute 50 per cent of his make-up, Eastern Race 20 per cent, Dinaric Race 15 per cent, East Baltic Race 8 per cent, Phalic Race 5 per cent, and Western Race 2 per cent. "The principal ingredient of our people is, therefore, the Nordic Race. That is not to say that half of our people are pure Nordics. All the aforementioned races, in fact, appear in mixtures in all parts of our fatherland. The circumstance, however, that the great part of our people is of Nordic descent justifies us in taking a Nordic standpoint when evaluating character and spirit, bodily structure and physical beauty. It also gives us the right to shape our legislation and to fashion our state according to the outlook on life of the Nordic man."

That is to say, in setting up this spurious ideal of acceptable German manhood and womanhood, the Nazi scientists took a look at who in fact happened to occupy the fatherland. That mixture of peoples was none other than the superior and gifted German *Volk.* The Germans set up their ideal in their own image. This type of scientific method had been described two thousand five hundred years previously by the Greek philosopher Xenophanes when he pointed out that the "Ethiopians make their gods black and snub-nosed; Thracians give theirs blue eyes and red hair." The Germans of 1935 A.D. made theirs 50 per cent Nordic, 20 per cent Eastern, 15 per cent Dinaric, 8 per cent East Baltic, 5 per cent Phalic, and 2 per cent Western! It is almost too ludicrous to be true—ludicrous when one thinks of Hitler's Nordic soul in Hitler's hybrid body, or of Goering's Nordic spirit in his fat non-Nordic carcass. "The Nordic man grows tall and slender. He has, according to our discoveries, limbs which are large in proportion to the body. That suits our sense of beauty."

Having got this idea of German "blood" safely defined, the Nazis then proceeded to use the idea to fortify their schemes for world political power by getting rid of elements in the population who were bound to oppose such schemes. They ousted from positions of importance in Germany those who were not of this specious German *Volk,* and found in these "foreigners" a scapegoat for the failures and tragedies of the First World War. This was less humbling than to admit the truth that they had been Germanic failures, failures of the *Volk* and its own folkish leaders.

The Jews were made the principal scapegoat for the faults and failures of the German leaders, there thus being visited upon them in a horrible and cynical fashion as a modern group, a process picturesquely described and symbolized in their own scriptural presentation of the religious concepts of an earlier day. In the case of the original scapegoat, the people, conscious of their own errors, ritualistically laid them upon a live goat which was then led out to perish in the desert along with his burdens of the sins of the people. In the case of the Germans, the Nazi leaders pretended that their own errors were the fault of the scapegoat, and the Jews were unjustly compelled to suffer and die for faults falsely attributed to them.

It was necessary for the Nazi reconstruction of German pride to have a whipping boy, and if the Jews had not been conveniently available, some other minority would have had to serve. But the Jews were available.

The German People have direct contact only with one type of foreign people: with the Jews. So for us fostering race is one and the same thing as a defensive warfare against mind and blood contamination by the Jews. The extent to which Germans and Jews cross each other's paths scarcely needs to be presented today. The Jewish hegemony in the cultural and intellectual life of the last few decades has brought the disrupting and disturbing character of this people to the attention of all Germans.

The first opposition measures of the National Socialists must, therefore, aim to remove the Jews from the cultural and economic life of our folk. Numerous laws have laid the bases for this. All these laws cannot be enumerated here. Only the most important will be noted: The "law for the restoration of the civil service" of April 7, 1933, is the first to contain the Aryan clause and exclude the Jews from the German civil service. From here on the cleansing process has quickly extended to all other spheres of life, to economic and cultural organizations, the professions, motion pictures, theatre and press. . . . The Inheritance law of September 29, 1933, excludes the Jews from German soil by stipulation that "a peasant can only be one who is of German blood." That the Military Defense law of May 21, 1935, and the Labor Service law of October 15, 1935, exclude the Jews from active service to the nation is self-evident. Finally, the Citizenship law of October 15, 1935, deprives the Jews of their citizenship.

This official recital of statutes, while it shows a clean sweep made of the Jews from every kind of profession and public office, gives no inkling of the ever-increasing violence and brutality with which the property and lives of Jews were destroyed. In all history there can have been no political leaders more evil than these Nazis motivated by overweening self-esteem and lust for domination over others.

II. Discord: Radical Reformers Push Too Hard for Reform

THE same motivation which makes the leaders of an established regime strive to enhance an already preferred position, makes the leaders of some radical reform groups push too hard for reform, to a degree that is not in the cards and that cannot be realized in the existing state of facts. Here again motives are mixed, sometimes the economic motive being dominant, sometimes motives of doctrine, or of desires for control, or of greater recognition in the community, or the spread of reform sentiment to groups sympathetic with the reform.

1. RECONSTRUCTION IN THE AMERICAN SOUTHERN STATES FOLLOWING THE CIVIL WAR

In the southern United States immediately after the Civil War, the old institutions of the South had been overthrown. The planter aristocracy, with its wealth based on slave labor, was no more; the labor system was demolished; transport was crippled, railways and bridges ruined; banks were insolvent; Confederate paper money and securities and state securities were worthless; live stock was reduced by more than one half; and starvation was close for those planters who did not have sons surviving the war who could work the land. Disorderly, wandering, and idle Negroes without means of livelihood were in a desperate state. Not so desperate was the state of those who had continued to work for their old masters.

To remedy this condition of disorganization, it was necessary that governments be established and control put in the hands of those capable of exercising control. President Lincoln, as early as December 1863, while the war was still in progress, had set out a temperate plan for restoration of orderly government in the South. The first provision of this plan was that any southerner upon taking an oath of loyalty to the United States and its constitution, the terms of the oath accepting the acts of Congress passed during the rebellion with relation to slavery, would receive pardon and amnesty, with restoration of all rights of property, except property in slaves. Excluded from the benefits of these provisions were higher officers of the Confederate government, army, and navy. There followed provisions for the mechanics of re-establishing government:

And I do further proclaim, declare, and make known that whenever, in any of the States of Arkansas, Texas, Louisiana, Mississippi, Tennessee, Alabama, Georgia, Florida, South Carolina and North Carolina, a number of persons, not less than one-tenth in number of the votes cast in such State at the Presidential election of the year A.D. 1860, each having taken oath aforesaid, and not having since violated it, and being a qualified voter by the election law of the State existing immediately before the so-called act of secession, and excluding all others, shall re-establish a State government which shall be republican and in nowise contravening said oath, such shall be recognized as the true government of the State, and the State shall receive thereunder the benefits of the constitutional provision which declares that "the United States shall guarantee to every State in this Union a republican form of government and shall protect each of them against invasion, and, on application of the legislature, or the executive (when the legislature can not be convened), against domestic violence."

And I do further proclaim, declare and make known that any provision which may be adopted by such State government in relation to the freed people of such State which shall recognize and declare their permanent freedom, provide for their education, and which may yet be consistent as a temporary arrangement with their present condition as a laboring, landless, and homeless class, will not be objected to by the National Executive.

After the assassination of President Lincoln, his successor, President Johnson, tried to follow the general lines of this Lincoln scheme, with the important modification that in Johnson's proclamation of May 29, 1865, there were excepted from the pardon and amnesty "all persons who have voluntarily participated in said rebellion and the estimated value of whose taxable property is over $20,000." This additional provision had the practical effect of excluding from participation in setting up the reorganized government any large property holder and gave a preponderant influence to the poor whites.

By the opening of the year 1866 governments had been established under either Lincoln's or Johnson's plan in all of the erstwhile rebellious states except Texas.

During the course of this presidential re-establishment of southern state governments, a determined and powerful opposition to the presidential plan was gathering strength. A much more radical plan for the reform of southern government was being formulated by the leadership of the Radical Republicans in Congress. This group, due partly to lack of sufficient organization of more moderate groups, gained control of Congress in the elections of 1866.

The motives of these radical northern reformers of the South, who pushed much too far in their reform schemes, were a mixture of vengefulness, self-righteousness, personal prestige, and a shrewd calculation of economic benefit and the maintenance of their own control in national politics. They believed they could gain popular support amongst those who had held slavery in abhorrence and who were ready to go far immediately in schemes that appeared to benefit the Negro.

The desire of some northern politicians to wreak vengeance on the South overrode their willingness and perhaps also their ability to judge what kind of reconstruction would bring the South most quickly into restored productivity as part of the Union. Thaddeus Stevens, United States Representative from Pennsylvania, was a leader of this vengeful sentiment. Even before the end of the war he had been a leader in the enactment of legislation aimed at the confiscation of property of individual southerners. Near the close of the war he was in favor of having the North treat the southern states as "conquered provinces" and "settle them with new men and exterminate or drive out the present rebels as exiles." For any constitutional restraints on the arbitrary treatment of citizens he had no respect. Like Kaiser Wilhelm II, who regarded the treaty guaranteeing the neutrality of Belgium as a mere "scrap of paper," Stevens referred to the U. S. Constitution as "a bit of worthless parchment." Of the leaders of the South, he said: "I have never desired bloody punishments to any great extent. But there are punishments quite as appalling, and longer remembered, than death. They are more advisable, because they would reach a greater number. Strip a proud nobility of their bloated estates; reduce them to a level with plain republicans; send them forth to labor, and teach their children to enter the workshops or handle a plow, and you will thus humble the proud traitors."

The aims of a man like Stevens were abetted by the unrealistic view of some of the abolitionists concerning the ability of the Negroes at that time and in their then condition of ignorance to play an intelligent political part in the reconstruction of the South. Gerrit Smith, a New York philanthropist interested among other things in strict Sunday observance and prohibition of alcoholic beverages, asserted:

that our black allies in the South—those saviors of our nation—shall share with their poor white neighbors in the subdivisions of the large landed estates of the South. Let the only other condition be that the rebel masses shall not, for say, a dozen years, be allowed access to the ballot-box, or be eligible to office: and that the like restrictions be for life on their political and military leaders. . . . The mass of the Southern blacks fall, in point of intelligence, but little, if any, behind the mass of the Southern whites. . . . In reference to the qualifications of the voter, men make too much account of the head and too little of the heart. The ballot-box, like God, says: "Give me your heart." The best-hearted men are the best qualified to vote; and, in this light, the blacks, with their characteristic gentleness, patience, and affectionateness, are peculiarly entitled to vote. We cannot wonder at Swedenborg's belief that the celestial people will be found in the interior of Africa; nor hardly can we wonder at the legend that the gods came down every year to sup with their favorite Africans.

This combination of northern vindictiveness against the southern planter whites and northern sentiment in regard to the virtue and ability of southern blacks proved to be politically effective. The course of radical reform of the South by the North was also promoted by certain attitudes and actions of southerners, to which we now turn.

The state governments set up under the presidential plan had to deal, as one of their first problems, with the status of the recently freed Negroes. The various states enacted statutes regulating such matters as property rights, ability to sue and to be sued, to act as witnesses, penalties for crime, conditions of labor and labor contracts, and marital relations. The system of relations based on slavery had been overthrown, and it was necessary to have legislation in aid of the new order if social disintegration was to be avoided. The statutes in a general way attempted to provide an assurance of steady labor essential for the production of the main southern crops. Racial intermarriage was proscribed. The statutes also tried to legalize slave marriages and slave liaisons—for example, as far as practicable, to have only one wife for one husband. Apprentice laws were adopted to cover the living out of poverty-struck youth and orphans, sometimes giving the first claim to former owners. Generally speaking, the greater the proportion of blacks to whites in a given community the stricter was the regulation of the blacks, so that in a state like Mississippi, where blacks outnumbered whites, the new laws appeared highly restrictive.

What seemed to many southerners essential measures for the preservation of order seemed to some northerners attempts to fix the erstwhile slaves in a new condition of serfdom approximating slavery. This latter view was vigorously promoted by the Radical Republicans. Northern newspapers sympathetic to the interests of the Radical Republicans engaged in a campaign both of outright misrepresentation of southern aims and of playing up occurrences of racial friction in accounts which attributed the blackest motives to the whites and the whitest motives to the blacks.

The war had of course left a legacy of bitterness in the South against the North. As General Wade Hampton wrote to President Johnson: "The South unequivocally 'accepts the situation' in which she is placed. Everything that she has done has been done in perfect faith, and in the true and highest sense of the word, she is loyal. By this I mean that she intends to abide by the laws of the land honestly, to fulfill all her obligations faithfully and to keep her word sacredly, and I assert that the North has no right to demand more of her. You have no right to ask, or expect that she will at once profess unbounded love to that Union from which for four years she tried to escape at the cost of her best blood and all her treasures." No northerner could take exception to such sentiments as those; but unfortunately for the South, many southerners showed a petty and spiteful hatred for their northern conquerors. Great harm was done to the South and aid given to the party of vengefulness in the North by the intemperate compensatory expressions of contempt by many southerners towards the northern victors. Especially mischievous was the conduct of southern women in this regard. Their supercilious attitude towards the "Yankee" irritated the latter and helped prepare the way for northern extremism in southern reconstruction.

The spirit of vengeance among northern radical reconstructionists and impractical idealization of the Negro by certain northern abolitionists, in the absence of other factors, would probably not have sufficed to upset the moderate presidential plans for reconstruction. Economic factors and those of political ambition also took part.

In the last presidential election before the Civil War, that of 1860, the Republicans, a young political party, had carried the election largely on the issue of opposition to the extension of slavery, being helped to victory by a split in the Democratic party. In the election of 1864 the Democrats still showed great strength, but many of its most capable leaders had rallied to the support of President Lincoln in the conduct of the war. Thus Lincoln's victory in the 1864 election was due to the union of War Democrats with the Republicans in a Union party, which had for its nominees for President and Vice-President a Republican, Lincoln, and a Democrat, Andrew Johnson.

After the war there was great fear in the minds of the Republican leaders, whose dependable following was mainly in the northeast, that the War Democrats would go back to their old party affiliations. They feared that if the representatives of a Democratic South were to come back into national politics, a Democratic party representing the predominantly agricultural interests of the South and West would gain control of the national legislature and perhaps of the executive department as well. This the leaders of the Republicans were determined to prevent by fair means or foul, and in fact by the use of both fair and foul means they made their determination prevail.

To this desire of the Republicans to hold control of Congress as against a possible combination of western and southern opposition was added the Congressional ambition to dominate the executive, President Johnson, the War Democrat who had succeeded to the presidency on Lincoln's assassination. Their aim was to insure that southern reconstruction should be carried out under legislative rather than executive direction.

President Johnson himself played a great part in the success of his Congressional opponents. He was subject to intemperate loss of judgment and a vituperation of his foes which did them no harm but did alienate his own moderate supporters. In the campaign for the Congressional elections of 1866, Johnson made a speechmaking tour, in the course of which, under heckling from his listeners, he habitually lost his temper, and with it his effectiveness as a campaign orator.

The upshot of the clash between President and the Congressional Republicans was the victory of the latter, the overthrow of the Lincoln-Johnson plans for reconstruction of the South, and a scheme of Congressional reconstruction which brought about in the southern United States the worst period of misgovernment in any English-speaking community in recent times.

As early as March 1866 Congress adopted a concurrent resolution to the effect that no southern state should be recognized for admission to the union until Congress declared it entitled to recognition. This not only showed the legislative intent to have the last word on the process of reconstruction. It also signified an intent that Republican control of Congress was not to be jeopardized by the presence in Congress of southern representatives. The aim was that no southern representatives were to be recognized until such time as southern representatives of a kind that would vote Republican were forthcoming from the southern states.

In June 1866 Congress proposed to the legislatures of the several states what is now the Fourteenth Amendment to the United States Constitution. The second section of this amendment contained an ingenious provision which dodged the issue of Negro suffrage by declaring that when the right to vote was denied by a state to any male inhabitant twenty-one years of age, the basis of representation of the state in Congress should be reduced in the proportion which such males bore to the whole number of males twenty-one years of age in the state. Such a provision could obviously have a very different result in the southern states with their heavy Negro population from what it could have in the northern states. The third section in effect disqualified from officeholding under the United States or any state those southerners who had taken part in the Civil War after having held important office either federal or state. This provision meant that politically experienced southerners were ineligible to serve in their state governments or as members of state constitutional conventions. This Fourteenth Amendment was rejected by the legislatures of all the secession states except Tennessee. These were the legislatures which had been chosen under the reconstruction programs of Presidents Lincoln and Johnson.

The Radical Republican leaders in Congress now proceeded not only to deny admission to the Union of these southern states, but to overthrow the new governments even as local governments. This was done despite the fact that the new governments were functioning *de facto* and providing a degree of law and order in the South far superior to what was about to be provided under the reconstruction scheme shortly to be hatched by Congress.

Declaring that no "legal" state governments or adequate protection for life or property presently existed in the rebel states of Virginia, North Carolina, South Carolina, Georgia, Mississippi, Alabama, Louisiana, Florida, Texas, and Arkansas, and that "it is necessary that peace and good order should be enforced in said States until loyal and republican State governments can be legally established," the First

Reconstruction Act (March 2, 1867) of Congress divided these states into five military districts under military command. The Congressional statute contemplated the election, by the "male citizens" white and black "except such as may be disfranchised for participation in the rebellion or for felony at common law," of delegates to a constitutional convention. This convention was to adopt a constitution which must provide for universal male suffrage of those twenty-one years old and upward. Then, to make certain of Congressional control of the process of reconstruction and the exclusion from authority in the new governments of any who had been leaders in the South, the Act stated that "when such constitution shall be ratified by a majority of the persons voting on the question of ratification who are qualified as electors for delegates, and when such constitution shall have been submitted to Congress for examination and approval, and Congress shall have approved the same, and when said State, by a vote of its legislature elected under said constitution, shall have adopted the amendment to the Constitution of the United States proposed by the Thirty-ninth Congress, and known as article fourteen, and when said article shall have become a part of the Constitution of the United States said State shall be declared entitled to representation in Congress, and senators and representatives shall be admitted therefrom on their taking the oath prescribed by law, and then and thereafter the preceding sections of this act (those relating to military government) shall be inoperative in said State: *Provided,* that no person excluded from the privilege of holding office by said proposed amendment to the Constitution of the United States, shall be eligible to election as a member of the convention to frame a constitution for any of said rebel States, nor shall any such person vote for members of such convention." This last clause guaranteed that the proposed constitutional conventions would not include any southerner of previous political or judicial experience.

When it looked as though the South might rather remain under military rule than register voters and form a government under the Congressional requirements, this statute was followed in the same month by a Second Reconstruction Act to provide the military governors with machinery for calling elections to the constitutional conventions.

The President vetoed both the First and Second Reconstruction Acts on the grounds that they set up arbitrary governments without the consent of the governed and irresponsible to the governed, and on the further ground that existing constitutions and existing governments were already formed and functioning in the southern states. Both statutes were then passed over the presidential veto by a two-thirds vote of House and Senate.

The five military districts under their military commanders were then set up. Pending the establishment of the new state governments under the Congressional scheme, it was necessary as a practical matter to make use for the time being of the officers of the existing *de facto* state governments. But by a Third Reconstruction Act in July 1867 the military district commander was given power to suspend or remove any civilian officer of these governments and to appoint to fill the vacancy. This power was importantly exercised—for example, five governors of southern states were removed from office. The appointments to the vacancies were likely to be of a northerner who had come South to take part in the reconstruction—a so-called "carpetbagger" from the fact that southerners believed the whole property of such a northerner could be carried in one of the usual traveling bags of the period—or of a southern radical who had opposed and taken no part in the rebellion, or perhaps of a northern army officer.

The Attorney-General of the United States in Washington endeavored to include in the process of reconstruction some southerners of the majority southern point of view. This he did by ruling that the disfranchisement of southern whites was a punitive measure, and therefore must be strictly construed by registration boards in favor of the potential voter and against his disfranchisement.

To prevent any such liberality towards the South, the Third Reconstruction Act struck down this restraint on the Radical Republicanization of the whole region by providing (Section 10) "that no district commander or member of the board of registration, or any of the officers or appointees acting under them, shall be bound in his action by any opinion of any civil officer of the United States."

It was in this atmosphere that the registration of voters in the South proceeded. The motive of the boards was to insure an electorate favorable to the cause of the Radical Republicans. At the close of the registration in the autumn of 1867, 703,000 blacks and 627,000 whites had been registered. The elections to the constitutional conventions resulted in a radical reform majority in every convention. In two states there were Negro majorities in the delegations. Negroes and carpetbaggers outnumbered the native whites in the conventions of every state except two.

The value to the Republicans of this southern Negro vote was shown in the popular figures in the presidential election a year later. Six of the reconstructed states had been readmitted to the Union and were eligible to take part in the national election of 1868. Over the United States as a whole the vote was Grant, 3,012,000; Seymour, the Democratic candidate, 2,703,000—a lead of slightly over 300,000 and no lead at all as far as white voters were concerned. A sidelight on the cynicism of the northern enfranchisement of Negroes as Republican voters in the South is provided by the fact that at the time of this election the Negroes had no vote in eight of the northern states. The Republican campaign platform of 1868 took the stand that Negro suffrage was for the northern states a local question, though for the southern states a matter of federal compulsion.

The reconstruction governments provided for by the constitutional conventions were, when set up and in operation, oppressive, incompetent, corrupt, and maintainable only by force. This outcome was bound to follow as a result of the important place occupied by illiterate Negroes under the direction of vindictive northern enthusiasts and Radical Republicans bent on maintaining their national party supremacy.

The organization of the southern Negroes for northern political purposes was accomplished by various methods. The most important of these was the Union League movement, which successfully enrolled the Negroes into local lodges of the Union League of America. Prior to the defeat of the South the local Union Leagues in the North had been important in election of officials devoted to the war cause and the Union. After the war ended, these northern units tended to become social clubs. In the South, the first activities of League agents were welcomed by the upland non-planter whites, some of whom had been unionists before the war, and almost all of whom were opposed to the control of the South by the lowland planter aristocracy. But this upland white membership fell away as the organization of the Negroes into local lodges grew and became the main object of the carpetbaggers, because, though the upland whites did not like the planters, they liked the Negroes still less.

Night meetings, mummery and flummery—similar in purpose and effect to the ritualistic paraphernalia and atmosphere later adopted by the German National Socialist leadership to control their following— and a skillful appeal to Negro superstition were the methods used to impress the blacks, together with a threat of violence against any black with Democratic leanings. Influential in the leadership of these Union

Leagues were army followers, some northern teachers and missionaries, and agents of the Freedmen's Bureau.

The Freedmen's Bureau was a federal agency set up in March 1865 and continued with enlarged powers in 1866 over the veto of President Johnson. The purposes of the Bureau were beneficial, and had its powers not been abused by its officials, might have been wholly useful in southern reconstruction. The Bureau was charged with relief work, food, and hospitalization—amongst refugee whites as well as freedmen; with the regulation of contracts involving black labor; with the protection of civil rights of Negroes and proper administration of justice in cases involving them; with allocations of abandoned and confiscated property; and with the establishment and support of schools for freedmen. The Bureau accomplished much in the field of relief, food, and hospitalization. In regard to its other functions it did not do itself credit. In actual practice it tended to become an agency for the schooling and indoctrination of the blacks in partisan Republican interests, and openly hostile to the leaders of white opinion.

To rebuild the devastated physical equipment of the south and to achieve a governmental structure which would have provided justly for the interests of the newly freed Negroes and of both upland and lowland whites called for an exhibition of political virtues and social and economic abilities of a high order. These virtues and abilities did not appear. The value of the actual reconstruction governments to a study of politics lies in their failures and in their illustration of narrow-minded reform efforts pushed too far along wrong lines. The South—which theretofore had furnished to the United States more than its proportionate share of statesmen, teachers, and men of letters—was for many years blighted and forced into a defensive narrowness of its own.

The following figures have been reported of the South Carolina reform legislature: It consisted of 155 members. Of these only 22 could read and write; all but 11 were Radical Republicans; 98 were Negro. The Radical majority of 144 paid an aggregate annual tax of $340. The Governor was a carpetbagger. The state treasurer was black, as also the secretary. Many trial justices could not read. The population of South Carolina at this time was slightly over 700,000, of whom about 60 per cent were Negro.

This poverty-struck, illiterate group was an extreme case of the type of legislature and government foisted on the southern states by northern reformers using the methods which we have described. Such a legislature, as might be expected, enacted laws which were a travesty of suitable legislation for a country requiring the full services of every competent man for the necessary task of restoration. The reform legislatures did not address themselves to this problem of substantive restoration—indeed they were not capable of doing so.

In some states rival factions arose among the carpetbaggers for control of the Negro vote. This factionalism resulted in two rival governments coexisting side by side in three of the southern states, thereby further adding to the inefficiency and wastefulness of the Radical Republican reforms.

Throughout the history of the South before the Civil War there had been a divergence of interest amongst the whites, the lowland planters on the one hand and the more numerous uplanders on the other. Many of the latter had been against secession. For example, in 1851 there had been a unionist governor in Mississippi, one of the predominantly black states, and majority white sentiment was probably loyal to the Union. It was in this upland unionist population that shortly after the Civil War white supporters of the northern-sponsored reforms were to be found. Their motive was their old aim of wresting control from the lowland planters, their fear being that the lowland planters would control the new Negro vote on behalf of the planter interests against the uplander interests. At first these southern white radicals outnumbered the carpetbaggers in the reform movement. But the northerners succeeded in gaining control of the Negroes and no longer needed the support of the southern whites. As the latter saw any hope of their own control of southern politics vanishing before northern ambition and became acutely aware of the disreputable and oppressive character of the reconstructed governments, all respectable southern white support of the Republican party was withdrawn. A solidly united white opposition appeared instead. The picture now was one of black and carpetbag governments under carpetbag control—governments entirely without the consent of those amongst the governed who were most capable of providing the constructive leadership so desperately needed.

Needless to say, these reformed state governments would not have been allowed to survive if any choice had been left to the competent people of the South. The source of their authority and of their continuance in office was northern military power—in some states supplemented by a Negro militia—acting under the control of the Radical Republicans in the United States Congress.

2. SPAIN BETWEEN THE FIRST TWO WORLD WARS

A moderate group trying to achieve the reforms really needed by a state may have its efforts rendered useless by other powerful groups themselves pushing for reform on lines such that if successful an oppressive order results.

Spain towards the close of the third decade of the twentieth century found herself with an inheritance of internal historical, regional, social, and economic animosities and conflicts. This had been due in part to difficulties in communication, rising from the east to west trend of her mountain ridges, and the presence of deep river gorges and nonnavigable rivers. Over the short term there had also been technical economic problems arising from an abrupt falling off of exports after the First World War and a hard situation both internally and with regard to exports in the world-wide economic depression setting in around 1930. But Spain's troubles arose mostly from human failings, for despite her difficulties of internal communication, shortage of rainfall in her high central area, and temporary problems of foreign trade, the fact was that relative to the other countries of Western Europe, Spain had a reasonably good economic base.

Close to one half the people of Spain were illiterate. The Church, which was a main influence in such education as there was, had a particularly intolerant tradition and was deeply involved in politics. It also had an extensive position as a landowner, owner of industry, and moneylender.

About one-fifth of the population was engaged in trade and industry. One phase of industry, mining, was largely financed by foreign capital and a large part of its product taken abroad. In all Spanish industry, frequent and violent strikes of workers were characteristic.

Spanish agriculture was backward. In the southern half of the country large estates predominated, worked by hired labor dependent on absentee landlords and their local agents. The poor standards of cultivation on these estates aggravated difficulties of dryness. Pasturage had been unduly fostered, to the harm of farming. The poverty and illiteracy of the peasants goes far to excuse their hatred of landowners and of any government associated with the landowners.

An overofficered and inefficient army, which had suffered ignominious disaster in Morocco in 1921, was the weak prop of the monarchy, and, until it broke with him, of the military dictator and Prime Minister Primo de Rivera. The latter fell from power in 1930 after a decade of rule as the head of a directorate to which was delegated the King's executive authority.

Despite the fact that Spain was united in religion, strong movements for local autonomy were on foot on economic, regional, linguistic, and even racial lines, in the north amongst the Galicians and the Basques, and in the northeast amongst the relatively industrialized Catalonians. Among the Basques the regional solidarity was sufficiently strong so that even the clergy there took a position in favor of reform, and in the revolutionary events which were to transpire were found generally on the side of the republicans.

The Real Needs of the Situation

Certain obvious needs stood out in this Spanish situation. If these needs were not met, Spain would remain in continuing discord.

An improvement of farm methods including irrigation was required both to increase the internal food supplies and to put the farmers in a position to have something to exchange for the products of industry, and to avoid the presence in Spain of a poverty-struck labor supply. Reform of land ownership was also indicated, although this was substantively important mainly as it bore on the matter of modernization of farm methods. Industry needed to be stimulated for internal use, so as not to continue, for example, mining almost entirely for export. It is true that a deficiency in fuels necessitated some export to provide means for the purchase of fuel. Transportation required new roads and railroads. Above all, illiteracy had to be overcome and a system of education provided which might bring to the fore what talents existed in the variegated Spanish population. On the side of government institutions, it looked as though some form of federal structure might reconcile the local feeling of regional groups with an economically integrated Spain.

The basic difficulty in meeting these needs arose from the fact that there was no large body of united opinion in Spain, no constructive leadership with sufficient following to overcome the extremists of the right and of the left. On the right, the clerics, the landowners, and the few industrialists above all wanted to hold tight to their respective preferred positions in the current social scheme, unsatisfactory as that might be. On the left, some extremist groups were prone to violence and strikes as their chief political method, disliking any firm government; others wanted an immediate and complete breaking of the power of the Church; and many wanted the displacement of private ownership of farm and industry, whether small or large, and instead ownership by a government controlled by class-conscious labor leaders.

Attempt and Failure to Meet Spain's Needs

Town and provincial elections were held in Spain in April 1931. The rural districts largely voted for conservative monarchical candidates. The voters in the large towns elected the candidates of those reform parties who aimed at the establishment of republican institutions. Following the elections and the unexpected showing of strong republican sentiment in the cities, the King left the country, the semi-dictatorship which had been functioning in the royal name fell, and a provisional government of republicans assumed power for the time being.

Elections for a national assembly—this assembly (or Cortes) to draw a new constitution—were held in June. In these elections the candidates of those parties which favored republican institutions, although greatly divided in their detailed aims, prevailed.

The constitution adopted by the Cortes at the close of 1931 provided for suffrage of all men and women over twenty-three, a single chamber legislature (the Cortes), a tribunal of constitutional guarantees to test the constitutionality of laws and to protect civil rights, self-government of provinces subject to necessary federal powers of the Spanish republic, procedures for establishing within the Spanish republic partly autonomous regions of adjacent provinces, religious freedom, nationalization of church property, secularization of education, and powers for the taking of private property. An indication of republican fears of reaction appeared in the clauses relating to selection of the President, the titular head of the new government, who might not be a military officer in active service, a clergyman, or a member of any royal family.

This new constitution might have been adequate for a country which had a sufficient leadership in many independent lines with a political habit of give and take. But in Spain this was not the case. The provisions of the constitution had to be put to work under conditions of pressure from intolerant extremists of the right or left, and by a government appealing ultimately for its constitutional power to an electorate of men and women who were largely illiterate, poverty-struck, and without benefit of a good political tradition. The reforming republican parties were greatly at odds in their aims. Those who were more moderate aimed to build up a competent middle class, to promote widespread independent property ownership, and not to interfere drastically, beyond correction of obvious abuses, with the clerical influence in Spanish affairs. Those who were more radical had as their goal political control by manual workers and their leaders, socialization of property, and the termination of Church power.

In 1932 and 1933 the Cortes by its legislation indicated the main lines which it intended its reforms to take with regard to the Church and the religious orders, education, land reform, a federal solution of the problems of regional autonomy, and army reorganization.

Pursuant to the new constitution all Church property was declared the property of the nation, but the clergy continued to live in the buildings and to carry on their clerical work. A law passed in 1932 by a majority of 140 out of the 470 members of the Cortes provided that after November 1933 the clergy should receive no subsidy from the government.

Early in 1932 a law was enacted for the dissolution of the Jesuit order, the confiscation of its property, and the distribution thereof for purposes of social welfare. In May 1933 a Law of Confessions and Congregations subjected religious orders to the authority of the Ministry of Justice, forbade them to buy property except for shelter and the practice of religion, prohibited them from engaging in industry or trade, prohibited them from conducting educational establishments and terminated as of the closing months of 1933 any teaching by members of religious orders in the primary and secondary schools of Spain. This action called forth the papal encyclical *Delectissimi nobis* and the warning that those responsible were excommunicated under the canon law.

The ending of primary and secondary teaching by the monks and nuns of Spain who numbered about 80,000 would leave a gap in the ranks of teachers which was to be filled by a training program to be directed by the government.

An agrarian reform bill was adopted in the late summer of 1932 authorizing the taking of lands owned by the nobility for distribution to landless laborers and small landowners. About 52,000,000 acres were affected. Although the value of the land was great, the government saw to it that the taking would be inexpensive by allowing no compensation except for recent improvements the cost of which had not yet been recovered. The implementing of land legislation of this kind was made difficult by the fact that the various parties in the reforming republican group, while in agreement that the inefficient large estates ought to be broken up, were themselves divided as to whether the land should be socialized and owned by the state or whether those to whom possession was given for working the land should own it.

A start was made under the constitutional provisions towards the federal solution of Spain's problems of regionalism by a statute under which the four provinces of Catalonia became an autonomous Region within the Spanish State, with extensive powers of legislation and administration in the fields of taxation, education, and local economic and social matters.

An effort was made to deal with the inefficiency of the army and with the meddling of army officers in Spanish politics, by a reorganization which retired half the officers and prohibited political activity.

While this republican legislation of 1932 and 1933 was being enacted, there occurred violent disturbances and agitation by those on the right who thought reform was proceeding too far and too fast and those on the left who thought it was not far-reaching enough and too slow.

In the late summer of 1932 General Sanjurjo seized Seville in a royalist uprising. This was quickly suppressed by troops loyal to the new republic, and the property of the rebel leaders was confiscated.

In January 1933 there were strikes and rioting in Barcelona under sponsorship of extreme left-wing anarchist and Syndicalist leaders. Similar disturbances took place in other cities. These uprisings were suppressed by the government which claimed to have found 5,000 bombs ready for use by rioters in Barcelona alone and 4,000 in other cities.

Three sets of elections in 1933 showed an increasing trend to the right in their results—the municipal elections in rural areas in April, elections for the Tribunal of Constitutional Guarantees in September, and first regular elections under the new constitution for the national Cortes in November. These last elections, in which all men and women over twenty-three were entitled to vote, returned a Cortes of 473, in which 207 members belonged to five distinctly conservative and rightist parties, 167 members to six moderate and center parties, and 99 members only to the nine leftist parties. This result in the Cortes elections was partly due to a failure of the leftist parties to agree on slates of candidates in the various constituencies. It may also have represented in part a protest against reform measures of too radical a character, or against the disorderliness and violence of extreme left elements. Some think it represented the influence of women voting for the first time in the election of a national assembly. Another factor in the result was presumably a voting against the current bad times and poverty in Spain, and in favor of a desire to turn out those who happened to be in authority. This is a common basis for swings of voting sentiment in countries with the democratic franchise. For example, in the United States, the voters in the presidential elections of 1924 and 1928, in a period of apparent economic prosperity, gave popular majorities to the candidate of the Republican party; but in 1932, the voters cast their ballots against the current economic depression and in favor of turning out of office those who were in authority, and thereby gave a popular majority to the Democratic candidate.

This national Cortes elected in November 1933 was slightly over two-fifths rightist. The extreme right was definitely opposed to the republic and the balance of the right opposed to the land reforms and Church reforms as they had been adopted by the preceding Cortes. Slightly less than two-fifths of the Cortes had center views, also for the most part to the right of the opinion which had prevailed in the preceding Cortes. Almost exactly one-fifth of the Cortes was leftist, representing at the extreme left those who had thought the preceding Cortes had been too conservative in its measures. This lineup of the parties indicated that there would have to be coalition government of some kind as there was no real majority viewpoint in the assembly. It indicated that there would be a delay in carrying out necessary and wise reforms as well as those which had been too far-going for the practical good of Spain. Such proved to be the fact, as a series of coalition ministries appeared unable to advance any sound republican program.

Leftist groups in Spain were alarmed at the rightist complexion of the new Cortes, and the close of 1933 and early months of 1934 saw organized violence in some Spanish districts, notably in the city of Barcelona, the center of syndicalism and anarchism. These uprisings were suppressed, and a general strike called by the Syndicalist leaders proved ineffective.

The temper of the left was shown in February when a cabinet minister in the preceding Cortes called on the parties of the left to seize power in Spain, establish a proletarian government, and confiscate private property in land.

The spirit of regionalism caused trouble for the government in 1934, when the legislature of Catalonia passed a statute providing that farm tenants could after twelve years become the owners of the land they cultivated. The statute was declared unconstitutional by the Tribunal of Constitutional Guarantees. The Spanish Premier took the position that the local Catalonian legislature had no power of land legislation, that being within the jurisdiction of the national Cortes. The Catalonian legislature re-enacted its statute and the President of Catalonia defied the national authority.

At this juncture a new coalition ministry was formed. Included in its number were three members of the Catholic Popular Action party, the fourth largest party in the Cortes, with sixty-two delegates, extremely rightist, monarchical, and clerical. This ministry was formed on the fourth of October.

On the fifth of October the leaders of the leftist parties called a general strike in Spain. On the next day the President of Catalonia declared the independence of Catalonia. In the Asturias there was an insurrection of miners and the proclamation of a Communist regime. Churches and convents were burned by anti-Catholic extremists. In the crisis the army stood with the government. Martial law was declared throughout Spain. The rebellion in Catalonia was suppressed after the shelling of Barcelona. The rebellion in the Asturias was suppressed by the use of troops and aircraft, and for some months thereafter harsh methods of persecution were used against its sympathizers. Strikers went back to work, and insecure order was again restored in Spain.

The year 1935 was a year of governmental confusion, sporadic outbreaks of violence, and inability of a succession of ministries to discover a way out of continual political and economic distress. Due to the failure to develop either in the Cortes or among Spanish leaders any dominant body of opinion as to the main outlines of essential reform, it now looked more and more as though the ultimate decision between right and left was going to be made by force rather than by any orderly processes of the young republic. As to who would have command of predominant force when the time came, the year 1935 furnished a likely clue. The War Minister in the shifting cabinets was most of the time the leader of the Catholic Popular Action party, and the general to whom he entrusted the reorganization of an enlarged Spanish army saw to it that as far as possible its loyalties would be to a rightist leadership.

In January 1936 the Cortes was dissolved and in mid-February elections for a new Cortes held. All the parties which believed that a republic was the best form of government for Spain and those parties to their left who above all feared a rightist rule by force gathered their strength for these elections. They were alarmed by the anti-republican trend in neighboring European countries, notably Germany and Italy where the Fascist leaders had established their totalitarian governments. The result of the elections was a vote that, though fairly evenly divided between right and left sentiment on an over-all popular basis, nevertheless in its manner of distribution returned a Cortes that was strongly republican and leftist—the left parties having 263 delegates, the center 62, the right 148.

The bane of orderly Spanish republican reform again put in its appearance at once, and extremest elements of the left committed acts of violence against rightist sympathizers, took part in jail deliveries of political prisoners imprisoned on account of the leftist rebellions during the regime of the preceding Cortes, made assaults on landowners and their buildings and especially on religious houses, and did not shrink from bloodshed.

In July, revolution broke out in Morocco and on the Spanish peninsula. Sponsored by officers of the army, monarchists, the higher clergy, and leaders of extreme rightist opinion, the revolutionaries had the support of most, though not all, of the army and navy, and of the troops in Morocco, consisting of Spaniards, foreign volunteers, and natives. In addition they were supported by semi-military groups of volunteers which had been organized by rightist parties on the German model, such as the Spanish Falange.

Facing such a line-up of force the Republicans nevertheless at first held their own in Madrid, in Barcelona, in the southeast fringe of the peninsula, and in the extreme northern Asturian, Cantabrian, and Basque regions, areas where sentiment was strongly opposed to the right; and it seemed likely that with the lapse of time their position would have improved and their cause perhaps have prevailed. But following Italian and German intervention on the rebel side and do-nothingness of Britain and France who, if they had felt conviction and expressed it in a diplomacy backed up by control of the sea, might have stood in the way of Italian and German access to Spain, the republic fell.

3. AN ANCIENT RADICAL REFORMER: IKHNATON

A doctrinal reformer who pushed too hard for a reform which was not possible in the light of contemporary traditions and ideas was the

Egyptian king Ikhnaton in the fourteenth century before Christ.

Sun-worship had always been an important element in Egyptian religion, and principal Egyptian gods among their other aspects and attributes were likely to have solar aspects, like the gods Horus, Ra, and Amon. Indeed a sun-god was likely to be the chief god in a hierarchy of lesser gods. A good many gods, of varying degrees of power and usefulness, existed side by side. In the reign of Ikhnaton's father, Amenhotep III, the most significant god was Amon, the deity of Thebes, his name indeed being incorporated in that of the pharaoh Amenhotep. But Amenhotep III, for reasons perhaps as much political as religious, saw an advantage in having a more powerful and more universal god than the local Egyptian gods. He fostered a conception of the supreme power of the sun-god whom he designated by the name of the physical sun, Aton.

Amenhotep III's son at his accession was also named Amenhotep. This younger Amenhotep apparently underwent a religious conversion, and became convinced that the sun-god Aton was the only god and that there was no other god beside him. Aton's rays filled existence with life-giving light, the source of all good. Amenhotep changed his name to Ikhnaton—Aton is satisfied—and the better to establish the new religion as the sole religion set up a new capital Akhetaton. Critical of the artistic conventions of Egypt, perhaps because they did not show enough honor to the sun, the king encouraged a new and more naturalistic school of art representing more accurately the real and living objects produced through the beneficent influences of the sun.

It is possible that Ikhnaton may have had the support of a priesthood of some other sun-god such as Ra in a bid for power at the expense of the priesthood of Amon, the traditional state god at Thebes, whose chief priest was the top figure amongst the various Egyptian priesthoods. Certainly there is an element of sycophancy and self-interest in some of the inscriptions of Ikhnaton's immediate following —the master of the king's horse saying: "He doubles to me my favors in silver and gold"; and another official saying: "He hath doubled to me my favors like the numbers of the sand. I am the head of the officials, at the head of the people; my lord has advanced me because I have carried out his teaching, and I hear his word without ceasing. My eyes behold thy beauty every day, O my lord, wise like Aton, satisfied with truth. How prosperous is he who hears the teaching of thy life."

A loyal henchman of Hitler or of Stalin could hardly have done any better than that by his master and the source of his bread supply.

As for Ikhnaton himself, there was a real beauty and a true feeling in his faith and it shines through the hymns to Aton:

> Thy heart created all, this teeming earth,
> Its people, herds, creatures that go afoot,
> Creatures that fly in air, both land and sea,
> Thou didst create them all within thy heart.
> Men and their fates are thine, in all their stations,
> Their many languages, their many colors,
> All thine, and we who from the midst of peoples
> Thou madest different, Master of the Choice.
> And lo, I find thee also in my heart,
> I, Khu en Aten, find thee and adore.
> O thou, whose dawn is life, whose setting, death,
> In the great dawn then lift me up, thy son.

So great was Ikhnaton's fanatical devotion to his Aton that he proceeded to deface all works of art in which Amon's name appeared, including monuments with his father's name, of which Amon's name was a part. He tried to break the power of the priestly groups in the service of the old gods, and he deeply offended all conservative religious sentiment, attached to the old polytheistic notions. Particularly hard on popular opinion must have been the banishment of the resurrected Osiris, god of the afterworld, through whose rites and by whose favor immortality was believed attainable.

Inheriting a great empire, Ikhnaton failed to hand it on to his successors because his preoccupation with religious ideas was so exclusive that he neglected his kingly functions and the government of the provinces of his realm. Nor did he hand on his new religion either, for in his zealous pushing for reform, he had pushed too hard, and wakened an opposition which after his death overthrew his cult of Aton. The old priesthoods and the vested religious interests of Egypt re-established the old polytheism. Contemporary opinion had not been receptive to Ikhnaton's reforming ideas.

4. PERSONAL AMBITIONS AND PUSHING TOO HARD

Where reformers are pushing too hard for reform, the personal ambitions of the reform leaders are specially likely, through intemperateness and inequity, to be a factor in the failure of reconciliation and the perpetuation of discord. In some instances attempted political reform takes place almost entirely as a result of personal desire of a leadership for power. In the Wars of the Roses in England, or in many instances of palace revolutions where an ambitious coterie succeeds in seizing the place of power, there is no attempted change in the form of government or society but simply a contest between rival factions to gain the seat of authority.

Exhibitions of unalloyed ambition for power put us on warning that ambition for power will make an appearance in the more complex course of attempted substantive reform, and may have a great effect on its progress in the way of hindering a peaceable and orderly adjustment of the differences. This will occur not only in large-scale events like those of American southern reconstruction and Spanish factionalism, but in small-scale events such as the Herrin Massacre in Illinois in 1928. There, as a means to power, the ambitious labor leadership whipped up hatred in its following.

As any human community exhibits many injustices, it is easy for a reform leader to point these out and to arouse a following in the interest of their correction. Pointing the finger at some individual or group as the true or alleged source of the injustices will always be a method available to any leader, capable or merely demagogical. But this is no guarantee that the proposed reform will be any more free of abuse or injustice than the old system it seeks to supplant. Thus in Russia, the Ukraine as a relatively productive component of the Soviet Union was from time to time overreached by the Soviet leaders on behalf of other parts of Russia, and too much was taken from the Ukraine. This was seen by Ukrainian leaders who perennially tried to resist and were perennially purged for doing so. Some of these leaders no doubt believed that the problem of how best to liberate the creative abilities of the Russian people, wherever to be found, can never be solved by a system of complete economic and political power lodged in an overcentralized bureaucracy. Yet, suppose that a Ukrainian-led reform were to be successful. No one can say whether the cure of the specific unfairness to which the Ukraine has been subject would be accompanied by a new Russian regime that would be really satisfactory. Such an outcome requires more luck or more wisdom than historical fact usually allots to reform leadership. So it is that a reform when put into effect may prove itself just as much or more in need of further reform as the old form which it supplanted. The true curative idea has not been at hand, or if at hand has not been sufficiently recognized and implemented.

III. Discord: Inefficiency or Mistake of Fact Intensifies Discord

HAVING looked at some cases of discord produced by important groups in the community pushing too hard to enhance an already privileged position or pushing too hard for a particular kind of radical reform, we now turn to discord in which government mistakes, confusion, and inefficiency have been conspicuous. The government has seemed incapable of seeing where the potential strength of the community lies, so that it has not only failed to promote the development of that strength, but has actually set obstacles in the way of such a development.

1. FAILURE OF GOVERNMENT TO SEE REAL NEEDS OF TIME AND PLACE

Events Leading to the French Revolution: The General Picture

France, on the eve of the French Revolution, was mainly an agricultural country, having land of such quality as should have assured her of adequate food. But in fact there were recurrences of famine and starvation. Tolls and local prohibitions on dealing in farm products, export and import duties on goods passing from one province to another, resulted in great variations in price in the different provinces, and furthered the chance of scarcity in one section although there might be plenty in another. Monopolies enjoyed by some dealers and government contractors, together with an arbitrary regulation of markets, discouraged production. Cultivation was depressed and its methods antiquated.

Despite an increase in both internal and external trade in the years before the Revolution, this trade was still but a small superstructure on the large agricultural base. The trade of the cities—except port cities like Bordeaux and Rouen—was confined mainly to what was necessary for the maintenance of their own inhabitants. Too large a part of the inhabitants of Paris consisted of impoverished workers, domestic and other, living under the threat of famine.

As a result of dues, tolls, and market restrictions, and the impediment of an archaic system of rights in land, the price of bread was forced too high and the supply rendered uncertain. Unnecessary bread famines occurred in 1785 and 1789.

Salt in many districts was the monopoly of those who collected the tax on salt, and the high price charged by these monopolists placed needless hardship upon those who must buy the salt from them. To take an extreme contrast: in a province where salt was free, the price might vary from 2 to 9 livres the hundredweight; but where it was a monopoly of the Tax Contractors, the consumer might have to pay 62 livres the hundredweight.

In a land where water was unfit to drink, wine and cider were necessities of life; and sales of wine and cider were subjected to an excise tax.

A basis for discontent—of country worker and city worker alike—lay in this scheme of artificial restraints on the production and distribution of the necessities of life in what was then potentially the country in Europe best able to supply such necessities in abundance.

The owners and workers of farms—other than certain noble owners—paid to the royal government taxes either on their land or their income from it. These taxes, standing alone, would have been by no means unbearable. But they were only one item in a complex and inefficient scheme of taxes—direct and indirect—inequitably laid and collected. In addition to the taxes there were requirements of labor in kind on the roads, which might be demanded at times inconsistent with the needs of farming.

The nobility were privileged to ride and hunt over the farm land. Fencing, however essential to the production of crops, might not interfere with the hunt. Nor could the farmers kill the game that wasted the crops. The privileges of the hunt were to the peasant a legalized wasting of his land.

The nobles of an earlier day had fought in defense of the people who lived on their estates. In return for this protection they received dues and services and exemptions in order to facilitate the performance of their military duties. In earlier days it had been necessary to hunt and destroy wild animals that wasted fields and injured men. The common good required that the hunters ride where the pursuit led. But those days were long since passed; and now, no longer defending the people against either man or beast, the nobles still claimed their exemptions, their dues and services, still exercised the right of the hunt.

At the top of the French social structure, in terms of honor and prestige, were such of the landowning nobility as were sufficiently rich—by one means or another—to maintain a position of influence at the King's court. In contrast, the poverty-struck nobility were not to be envied. They perhaps found some sort of satisfaction in the memories of their ancestors, but lived a penurious and hard life, clinging stubbornly to the privileges that inhered in their noble heritage. Many of them held commissions in the much overofficered French army. The entire nobility—rich and poor alike, and whether hereditary or newcomers—stood fast for their tax exemptions and their customary rights. This nobility, which constituted only about one-half of 1 per cent of the French population—perhaps 140,000 out of a total of 26,000,000—were owners of about one-sixth of the land of France.

The attitude of holding to any sort of preferred position irrespective of the good or the need of the whole community was not confined to the nobility. Trades were organized into corporations or guilds which made every effort to see that competition was stifled, and that mastership in the trade should be open only to those who were socially acceptable—by blood relationship, marriage, or otherwise—to the already established masters. As one of the needs of France was increased trade and the liberation of the abilities latent in the French people, this fact of restriction, repeated in every branch of endeavor, was something that both stimulated and baffled reform.

Such commoners as were exceptionally well-to-do—many of them lawyers, some manufacturers—bought tax exemption, either by direct bribery or by buying their way into either offices or marriage ties which carried a status of nobility. With all its many faults it cannot be said that the system of the old regime closed the ranks of the nobility to newcomers or froze the social structure of France into closed classes. But venality was so widespread that the rich newcomer was often able to buy tax exemption, so the taxes of France continued to bear most heavily on those who could least afford to pay them.

The economically well-to-do and privileged groups in any country have always been relatively small in number, and this smallness—while a favorite theme of equalitarian reformers—is of much less importance than the way in which these people are using their favorable position and how they are exerting their influence. In pre-Revolutionary France the position and influence of the privileged were obstructing the development of French potentialities and the growth of French wealth.

The problem to be solved for the good of France was how to get rid of the various kinds of privilege that were interfering with the welfare of the whole community. A solution of the problem would require that the privileged give up such of their privileges as were indefensible, and a wise government would have bent every effort to achieve this result peacefully—by act and persuasion in aid of reform and by allying itself clearheadedly with those who saw the need for reform. Exactly the opposite occurred. It was the privileged people themselves—especially the court nobility—who wielded the greatest influence in the government. And this nobility effectively resisted the necessary changes. The descendants and the successors of the old elite of France still clung to the privileges of that elite, although they were no longer doing its work. The higher clergy—drawn from the ranks of the nobility—also resisted necessary reform.

The picture that emerges is one of a France substantively strong, well able to feed and supply her people, well able to maintain in the future as in the past her powerful military establishment, well able to increase her trade and build her industry. But this potential strength of France is seen to be hampered by the irrational system of internal dues, tolls, services, taxes, and a tenacious grasping of privilege by anyone who has been lucky enough to have acquired by birth or by shrewdness a position of privilege.

The financial upshot of the mess of internal dues and tolls, inequitable taxation, and irrational exemptions, was bankruptcy of the government. The political upshot was the conviction in the mind of the intelligent that reform was essential. The government house must be set in order as a step to setting the social house in order. This conviction was strengthened by the awareness of a restless popular discontent, alike of peasant in the countryside and worker in the city.

Reform was necessary. But the King, as head of the government, most of the court circle and the central bureaucracy, and most of the local governments were too much drawn from that identical privileged nobility, the removal of whose privileges was the most-needed single element of reform. Too blind to see that there were arrayed against them both the intelligent leadership and the popular force of France, the nobility—with some conspicuous exceptions who took notable part in the leadership of the Revolution—stood fast for privilege and resisted reform.

The Opportunity of King and Government

The aims of the government of Louis XVI were no different from those of other governments of the time. One aim: to head a powerful state in the family of states. A second: to head a state internally sound and growing in strength. A third: to maintain itself in office.

Of these three aims, the first had been achieved by the French government. Although the ability of France to act effectively was being put in jeopardy by the threat of bankruptcy, there is no doubt that France was powerful among its contemporaries.

The third aim of the government—what is ordinarily the strongest motive of officeholders—to keep in power and stay in office, depended in the long run on achievement of the first and second aims. In the case of the government of Louis XVI, the third aim was not achieved, due to failure in the second aim. The state was not internally sound; and the government, while sometimes perceiving the causes, was never able—despite adequate opportunity—to eliminate them and effect a cure.

POSITION OF THE KING

The power of the King and his Council was absolute, as a result of six centuries of development of the royal government at the expense and diminution of the political power of the nobles. The mechanics of the royal rule was through a small ministry and a council of about forty—subdivided into lesser councils to deal with the respective affairs of state. The local agents of the crown were the Intendants, about thirty in number, in charge respectively of the government of their territories, the généralités. The actual operation of this government we will discuss shortly, in analyzing the opportunity which lay before it and its failure.

It is true to say that the King, certainly in the early years of his reign, and perhaps up to the moment of his attempted flight to the enemies of the Revolution, had a practical chance to bring about in an orderly way the reforms required by France, and to have completely avoided the excesses of the Revolution. As we shall see, the

King was generally regarded as the focus of political power and the different groups of people of France were loyal to the monarchy. This being the case, each group in furthering its own interests would try to rely upon and make use of the royal power. In short, the historical position of the crown was such that it had an extraordinary opportunity to influence and to control the political development of France.

CENTRAL GOVERNMENT AND LOCAL GOVERNMENTS

The government, taken in its central and its local aspects, exhibited a paradoxical combination of unhealthy centralization and of unhealthy decentralization.

France was emerging, but had not yet emerged, from feudal methods of local rule and regulation. A significant feature of feudalism is the result of the prolonged absence of a widespread general governmental authority. The several localities, functioning largely on their own under their respective local leaders, develop almost as many separate customs of rights and duties, services and claims, as there are separate localities under the protection of local leaders. While the local leader himself owes obligations to his superiors—especially obligations of a military nature, as the supply of a certain armed force for the needs and purposes of a wider territorial power—these obligations do nothing to hinder the growth of innumerable local diversities and privileges. This local diversity is a striking social characteristic of feudalism.

Despite the growth of the royal power in France and the decline in the political power of the nobles, there still remained throughout France a large and active residue of the old feudal claims, rights, dues, and customs. Upon these had been superimposed the royal bureaucracy, which we have mentioned—the system of government by the Council and the Intendants.

Some of the legacies of feudalism in economic life were the local barriers and dues on the movement of products, especially food; the rivalry of town with town, taking the easy and harmful form of the one trying to injure the other and hamper its trade; the organization of local business and trade into guilds, jealous of their rights and monopolistic if possible; detailed local regulation of trade practices.

The influence of the increasing power of the King on this method of control and organization of economic life had not been in the direction of greater freedom. On the contrary, the Intendants naturally tended to work through the already existing channels of control—

by supervision of the guilds and their regulations, by exercising authority in the most minor matters of economic life and practice. What had developed was a superposition of bureaucratic royal control on top of the atomized feudal control. An inefficient central control was imposed on an already quaint and antiquated local organization.

France was, as we have said, mainly an agricultural country, at least four-fifths of her population being engaged in farming of one kind or another. In a very rough approximation, about half the land was owned in equal proportions by the crown, the clergy, and the nobility; the other half owned by commoners. There were a relatively few large farms which were held on lease in terms of money rent. Generally, rent was in the form of a proportionate part of the crop. There might also be payments in animals—let us say chickens—as established by terms of lease or of custom. And, in the case of most farms, the legacy of the feudal system had resulted in the farmer, whether tenant or owner, being obligated for a set of services and liabilities—inefficient, annoying, and ancient—some days of unpaid labor, the obligation to send grain or wine to the lord's mill or wine press for a fee, local tolls for the lord's benefit, payments to the lord on the sale of land, and the subjection to the destructive activity of protected game animals, such as deer and rabbits, and the destruction caused by hunting of the game.

In short, in the countryside, feudalism had ceased to be a rational system of local military protection for which services were rendered, and had instead degenerated into a relic of local vexation, harassment, and inefficiency.

The influence of the increasing power of the King on those engaged in farming—other than in matters of taxation which we will consider later—was felt in the interference of the Intendants in the administration of village life. Permission of the Royal Council through the Intendant was often required for the undertaking of matters needful to the local community. For instance, it is said that a village which wanted to cut some of its own wood to obtain lumber for the repair of its church, so as to protect the worshipers from the weather, had to wait more than four years for the required permission.

It was not only in village government that the local authorities were subject to the interference and control of the Intendant and the royal power. The same thing was the case in the towns. Municipal business and contracts as well as public works were within the jurisdiction of the Council through the Intendants. In the government of

the provinces a similar arrangement was in general to be found—
except that in those provinces which historically had preserved their
medieval Parliaments—their Estates—there was a relatively greater
degree of self-government.

The administration of justice exhibited a like mixture of local confusion with royal inefficiency and interference. The local confusion
consisted in a multiplicity of local courts—those of the lords, for example—and perhaps even more in a multiplicity of local laws, so
that something a man was doing was legally right in one place but
legally wrong in another. Even in a court of the highest jurisdiction—
from which no appeal lay—one of the thirteen *Parlements,* there
might be many different bodies of law applicable to its cases. The
Intendant claimed the right of sitting in any court of law within his
district. The Royal Council asserted its authority to call cases out of
the regular courts, even from a *Parlement.* This might be done as a
matter of favoritism to a particular suitor desiring to evade the normal
result of justice.

As an example of the arbitrary spirit of the monarchy in the administration of justice was the issuance of orders of arrest under the
King's hand and that of a minister, the *lettres de cachet.* Such orders,
issued as a matter of discretion, resulted in arrest and imprisonment
for an indeterminate period. They were used in the cases of authors of
disapproved books, unruly children whose families wished to punish
them, fallen cabinet ministers, and personal enemies of those in court
favor. Like much else in the government of France at the time, arbitrary imprisonment was thoroughly unsystematic and irregular—and
so not comparable to the concentration camps of Germany or of Russia one hundred fifty years later, which were used as a systematic instrument of policy. In France it was a capricious abuse and denial of
justice.

TAXATION

Anomalies, exceptions, complications, irregularities, discrimina-
tions—these are the characteristics of French pre-Revolutionary government which we have so far noted. Nowhere were these characteristics more evident or more harmful than in the methods of taxation.
The direct tax of the royal government largest in amount of revenue
was named the *taille*—a graphic term, indicating the *cut* taken from
a man's means. In some provinces this was a tax on real estate, in
others on income. The amount of this tax for the respective districts

of France was fixed by the Royal Council. It was locally assessed in various ways—sometimes by the royal officials, sometimes by the Estates of those provinces which had them, and then by officials of lesser political subdivisions. The clergy was exempt. So also for the most part was the nobility. Liability for the tax in the governmental unit where it was collected was joint, so that in a given parish if one man failed to pay, another was called on for the delinquent's share. This made for concealment of assets and a fear of appearing prosperous—which in turn resulted in discouragement of thrift and industry. For example, when an Intendant, intending to encourage the production of honey, called for statistics on the number of hives in his province, the result was that the farmers—fearful that a basis for tax assessment was in the making—forthwith destroyed their hives.

Some villages were assessed much more lightly than others, without regard to justice or fairness. The collectors were made personally responsible for the collection of the tax, so that a man of means hesitated to be a collector, despite the percentage of the tax allowed to him as compensation.

Another direct tax—second in amount collected—was the *twentieths,* laid on income. During most of the reign of Louis XVI, the rate was a little over two-twentieths, but participation in aid of the American Revolution brought about the imposition of a third twentieth. The clergy was exempt from this tax, the nobility not. But here as elsewhere, there appears to have been favoritism and unfair discrimination in the estimates of income of those subject to the tax.

A third direct tax of importance was the *capitation,* on the head of each household. For the purpose of this tax, the people of France were divided into numerous classes, according to assumed ability to pay. In some districts the tax was proportioned to that of the *taille;* in others, different bases of classification were used. Everywhere, the rules were complicated. In 1709 the clergy by a down payment had bought exemption from this tax for eighty years.

A further disorderliness in connection with the direct taxes lay in the fact that some provinces and some towns, as a result of bargains with the crown, had agreed on amounts to be collected by themselves for the tax. At different times and places, the differing skill of the bargainers and the differing immediate needs of the crown resulted in unequal tax burdens.

The major part of the indirect taxes in France were farmed—that is to say, let out on contract to companies formed for the purpose of their collection, against a payment to the royal treasury of a fixed sum and of part of what profits the farmers might make.

In the sale of some products subject to tax, the tax Farmers were granted a monopoly by the government. In these cases the burden on the taxpayer took the form of paying more than the product was worth. Conspicuous among these taxes was the Salt Tax. Here again was to be found the familiar irregularity in French administration. In certain provinces there was no monopoly, and sales of salt were free. In others it was a complete monopoly of a Farm. There thus arose a situation such that salt cost thirty times as much in one province as in another. One result of this inequality of price was the encouragement of profitable smuggling.

Tobacco was also a monopoly of a similar kind.

Taxes on wine and cider were laid on sales and presumed sales. This was a vexatious tax, because potable water in France was in short supply and therefore wine and cider were necessaries of life. From these taxes also some localities had purchased whole or partial exemption; so that here again there was unevenness in the weight of the tax.

The taxes we have so far considered were those for the benefit of the royal government. In addition to these, and likewise requiring simplification and regularization, there were other taxes, such as the corvées—service in kind on the roads. Such service was owed to local lords. It was also owed to the royal government, this service including transportation of the baggage of soldiers. Various local dues on goods in transit were demanded by towns, or the Church, or by the nobles; and these made an effective hindrance on trade.

The Englishman, Arthur Young, a famous agricultural authority, at one time Secretary of the Board of Agriculture, traveled extensively in France in 1787 to 1789. He and other observers at the time thought that taxes in England were heavier and more productive of revenue than those in France, but all agreed that the taxes in England were more easily borne because more fairly distributed.

MANY FRENCHMEN SAW THE NEEDS OF THE TIME

With the benefit of hindsight, it seems that tax reform would have avoided the bankruptcy of France, and that a central administration less given to regulation of the minutiae of local activity, less arbitrary, and more aware of the damage done to the community by irrational forms of privilege, would have been a powerful aid in the orderly growth of French welfare.

What is unusual in the period preceding the French Revolution is that this opportunity was also plain enough at the time, and clearly seen not just by a few but very generally by the leaders of all classes in France. This can be demonstrated by means of the *cahiers,* documents of instruction for the deputies sent to the Estates-General of 1789. This assembly of the three estates (clergy, nobility, commoners) had been called in the hope of dealing with the imminent bankruptcy of the French Government.

The *cahiers* of the clergy and of the nobility were drawn in local assemblies, which were numerically constituted so as to represent more the views of the lesser nobility and of the lesser clergy. In the case of the assemblies of the nobiilty, all members of the order of twenty-five years of age or over were summoned. In the case of the assemblies of the clergy, all the beneficed secular clergy were summoned, while regular establishments and chapters sent representatives on a basis resulting in a smaller representation than that of the parish priests, all of whom were in theory entitled to attend the assembly.

The *cahiers* of the Third Estate were consolidations made in district assemblies of local *cahiers* drawn in earlier, primary assemblies in the different towns and parishes and sent up to the district assembly by deputy. The voting franchise in the Third Estate was wide, including all men on the tax rolls twenty-five years of age, neither cleric nor noble.

AREAS OF AGREEMENT OF LEADERS OF CLERGY, NOBILITY, AND COMMONERS

It might be expected that these documents, the *cahiers,* representing the views of the three classes in France in regard to their grievances and their hopes of reform, would be in substantial disagreement in vital matters. So it is surprising to find that they did in fact exhibit agreement in such a large area as to indicate the practicability of a useful reform of relations between local and royal authority.

With regard to the executive power in France, loyalty to the King, to the institution of the monarchy, was unanimous. And this was in 1789, after fifteen years of the vacillation of Louis XVI. Indeed in February 1790, the address of the National Assembly to the French people, reviewing its work, still shows this strong recognition of the King as rightful head of the government.

All three classes wanted to be rid of the arbitrariness and irregularities in French administration, and stated that the King and his ministers should be subject to law, and that provincial, town, and village administration should have more local autonomy—for example, the Provincial Estates should have increased authority in administration, notably in regard to taxes. In the field of taxation for support of the royal government, there appears to have been almost unanimity for a more equitable tax burden, and a reform of the methods of assessment and collection. Since the King himself stood in need of tax reform if his government were to avoid bankruptcy, it seemed that here there was an agreement of all concerned, which augured well for reform.

There was really little question in the minds of those who drew the *cahiers* of the substance of the most-needed reforms. The problem was how to bring about the gradual increase of a healthy decentralization in administration with a useful and needed degree of central authority. And it was just here that the great opportunity of the King and his circle lay: everyone was reconciled to the need of the reform and at the same time everyone recognized the authority of the King, and so could have been expected to follow his lead if given in the needed direction.

In regard to the reform of administration of justice, the *cahiers* generally ask that this be simplified, and especially again that the arbitrariness and privilege be abolished. The *lettres de cachet*—the arbitrary orders for imprisonment—are to be abolished.

With regard to legislation affecting France generally, again particularly in the fields of taxation and the authority of the ministers, the Estates-General are seen as a national legislature, to meet regularly and to be the ultimate lawmaking authority.

Private property was taken for granted, and until a period much later than that of the *cahiers,* it was generally assumed that feudal claims were to be recompensed in those cases where they were to be relinquished.

To be sure there were also areas of disagreement in the *cahiers* of the three estates and some of them on matters of importance.

The lesser nobility did not want to give up its local feudal rights, some of which, as we have seen, were harmful. Those of the hunt, for example, were injurious to crops as well as vexatious to people. Yet even here there was perhaps more recognition of the real needs of France than appears on the surface. The general abandonment by the nobility of its privileges in the National Assembly on the night of August 4, 1789—although this abandonment was precipitated by news of rioting and burning of buildings in many parts of France—suggests by its unanimity that the representatives of the nobility recognized the indefensibility of their old legacy of now unearned privilege.

In matters of freedom of the press and of speech, which was generally favored by nobles and commoners, the clergy was generally opposed.

There was a serious dispute as to whether voting in the Estates-General was to be by head or by order. Since the representatives were a few more than 300 clergy, a few less than 300 nobles, and approximately 600 commoners, the decision of whether vote was to be by head—in which case the commoners would be preponderant—or by order—in which case the weight of each of the three orders would be equal—was a decision of the utmost importance.

With respect to trade and commerce, there was no definite uniform trend in the views of the *cahiers,* unless it was in a recognition that there were in fact too many restrictions both on the conduct of trade and on the movement of goods.

It is not remarkable that there were great differences in the *cahiers.* That was to be expected of the views of leaders of three different social groups with differing particular interests. What is remarkable is the agreement on the main features of essential reform of the relations of the central government to the local government in the fields of administration, taxation, justice, and legislation. There was agreement on the substance of a long first step in the direction of orderly reform—for change by way of growth rather than by way of violence.

The Failure of King and Government

The King of France, coming to the throne in 1774 at the age of twenty, was a well-meaning but weak-willed man, so that he never pushed on resolutely in any course whatever. He was jealous of authority, so that it was hard for him to follow consistently the advice of an able and powerful minister. At the same time his weakness of will made him at any given moment amenable to firm advice. The result was vacillation, short periods of following one line, short periods of following another. His brother, the Comte de Provence, is reported to have said that when you could keep a number of oiled ivory balls together, you might do something with the King. When Turgot was Controller-General there was a critical occasion on which he wrote the King: "Do not forget, sire, that it was weakness which put the head of Charles I on the block; it was weakness which formed the League under Henry III; which made crowned slaves of Louis XIII and of the present king of Portugal; it was weakness which caused all the misfortunes of the late reign." The King, the head of the administration which sorely needed reform, was thus essentially unreliable and undetermined. He was not even a good weathervane, as he did not know in which direction the political winds of France were beginning to blow.

It is characteristic of a government circle—as it is of any group known to one another and working together—that the members of the circle favor one another and their own personal friends. This is natural. But if this kind of favoritism is not to prove injurious to the community, it is necessary that those favored are exerting their efforts along lines useful to the community, that the favoritism is not to those who are positively harmful and whose ideas are out of keeping with the needs of the time.

The court circle in France were thoroughly out of sympathy with the needs of the time. Their friendships were not with those who represented the strength or hope of France. Various facts indicate the attitude of the King and the court nobility towards commoners: an attitude of an assumed inferiority of the commoners, yet tempered with the unavoidable necessity of utilizing and placating them.

In connection with commissions in the army, this compromise between snobbishness and realism can be seen. After 1781, commissions were limited to those who could show four generations of nobility on the father's side, with the exception—the compromise with real need —of the two branches where intelligence was most required, the engineers and the artillery, where lower commissions were open to the commoners.

That favoritism to the nobility was permitted to interfere with substantive defense is shown in the proportion of numbers of officers to those of enlisted men. It has been estimated that there was a little more than one general for every 160 privates, and one staff officer for every 80.

Although it was the influence of the court nobility which had the final say in the King's employment and dismissal of his ministers, and although it was the great noble families who were the permanent fixtures in the court circle—still it was necessary to make use of the brains of some commoners, and so men like Turgot and Necker are found in the highest positions in the ministry—but expelled when their measures proved distasteful to the nobles.

There is always intrigue and jockeying for the places of influence and power in any court or government circle. In France this intrigue occupied the courtiers to the exclusion of their doing their useful work. The Queen Marie Antoinette was here a harmful influence. Young, high-spirited, self-willed, dull-husbanded, extravagant, courageous, devoted to the interests of her favorites, she was more concerned with the game at court and friendship for Austria than with the needs of France.

What were the results that arose from the fact that this king and this court circle were the repositories of political power and therefore a main factor in any attempted orderly reform of a governmental system generally recognized as needing reform and in circumstances such that reform appeared practicable?

Certain effective measures of reform were put into practice in the administration of two provinces, and this was done early in the reign of Louis XVI. A local administrative assembly—half nobles and clergy, half commoners—was established in each of these provinces, being charged among other duties with the highly important assessment of taxes. Although not free of supervision by the Intendant, such an assembly, operating subject to law and consisting of local members, resulted in a more orderly and just administration.

On the very eve of the Revolution, a somewhat similar type of provincial assembly was provided for the provinces generally, but these new assemblies had no time to prove their worth. They seemed sound in theory, as giving a prospect of better local administration and better protection of local interests from arbitrary government interference.

These attempts at administrative reform, even though too late, were bright spots in a story of failure by the King and his administration to meet the opportunity of working out a better set of relations between central and local government, and of modifying the more harmful of the class privileges and the trade restrictions and regulations which were so injurious to France.

There was an able man, Turgot, who had made an extraordinary record as Intendant of Limoges, where he had improved the assessment and collection of taxes, abolished services in kind on the roads, encouraged agriculture by the distribution of seeds and by measures against pests—from wolves to moths—increased the facilities for grain trading, introduced the manufacture of pottery, promoted freedom in the practice of professions, and increased the opportunities for education.

Shortly after Louis XVI came to the throne, Turgot became Controller of the Finances in the King's ministry. He immediately made such improvements and economies, largely by way of abolition of useless offices, that he was able to refund at 4 per cent a loan of 60 million livres previously borrowed at 12 per cent.

Turgot started on tax reform by abolition of the joint liability for the *taille* in the communes. As in Limoges, he replaced service in kind in the building and repair of roads by a money charge. He started to reduce taxes on the necessaries of life.

As steps to the liberation of the energies of the competent and the promotion of trade, Turgot then did away with the governmental restrictions and price regulations on trade in grain and in wine. Except in certain cases where regulation was made easier by the existence of monopoly—as, for example, in the business of apothecaries—Turgot abolished the trade guilds, the corporations which monopolized manufacture and trade where such monopoly was feasible. This reform widened the opportunity to go into business.

Bad luck, in the form of temporarily hard circumstances, now hurt the prospects of needed reform. Scant harvests in 1774 and 1775, coinciding with Turgot's efforts to free the grain trade from restrictive regulations, enabled the vested interests of the old regime to discredit his intelligent and necessary measures, as well as to get rid of Turgot himself.

Here the court ring played its part. The Queen, the King's brothers, the courtiers who did not like economy, those whose useless offices were threatened, those who feared for their feudal privileges—backed by those outside the court who had been hurt by Turgot's reforms—descended on the King. "Only M. Turgot and I love the people," commented the King—and dismissed Turgot.

The need for reorganization of the finances, already critical in Turgot's period, became more acute as time went on. Bankruptcy appeared imminent. The expenses of aid to the American revolutionaries was a factor in this worsening of the French finances.

Of the two obvious ways to meet the financial crisis—economy and tax reform—Turgot had tried both, and had been forsaken by the court in his efforts. The extravagance of the Queen, her losses in gambling, her increase of useless and costly offices, can stand as a symbol of some of the reasons for failure of the government along the needed lines of remedy. There was an unwillingness to do what had to be done, sometimes even blindness to see what had to be done, due to an affectionate clinging to old habits and customary privileges. One result of the fiscal incapacity of the King's government was to reconcile holders of the government debt—a group normally conservative and in favor of existing order—to the idea of the necessity of thorough-going reform.

It is hard to say when the opportunity to take the lead in reform finally passed out of the King's power. But certain significant failures accompanied the passing of this opportunity.

Malouet, Intendant of Toulon, later a delegate to the Estates-General, says that he advised the King's chief ministers that they should take the lead in starting the reforms necessary for France and the commoners. This they should do by attempting to give direction to the *cahiers* of instruction which were to be drawn in connection with the calling of the Estates-General. They should sponsor a program and stand behind candidates who would promote it. The advice was not taken.

The threat of bankruptcy was the reason for calling the Estates-General. Because the productive strength of France lay in the diligence and industry of the commoners, the consent of the latter to a tax program was seen to be important. The King and his ministry accordingly provided for a representation of 600 commoners, 300 clergy, and 300 nobility in the Estates-General. Then, although it was the vital factor in whether this representation was to be made effective, King and ministers could not muster the determination to take a position that the Estates should vote by head rather than by order. The refusal to give a lead in this crucial matter promoted disorder in the assembly, and provoked the first revolutionary assumption of authority. This occurred when the representatives of the Third Estate declared themselves the National Assembly, inviting the other orders to join them.

A few months later, still evidencing the failure of the King and his circle to come to grips with the facts of what was taking place, was their refusal in October 1789 to take Mirabeau's written advice. Mirabeau pointed to the loss of public confidence in the work of the Assembly and to the King's opportunity to lead his people in a peaceful revolution to save the kingdom. Prophetically he warned the King—long before the King had attempted flight to join the émigrés or the Revolution had deteriorated into terror—of what would be the result of his attempting to take refuge with the émigrés, the extreme reactionary nobility:

A king, who is the only safeguard of his people, does not fly before his people. . . . Who can say to what a state of frenzy the French nation might be aroused if it saw its king abandoning it in order to join a group of exiles, and become one of them himself, or how it would prepare for resistance. . . . To join the nobility would be worse than for the king to throw himself into a foreign and hostile army. He has to choose between a great nation and a few individuals, between peace and civil war carried on upon exceedingly unequal terms. . . . It is certain . . . that a great revolution is necessary to save the kingdom . . . and that there is no safety for the king and for the state except in the closest alliance between the monarch and his people.

But the advice was lost on the King, because the group he understood, with whom he sympathized, and with whom his long-standing associations lay, was a blind court nobility and the worldly, power-minded higher clergy that had played the court game.

2. PREOCCUPATION OF GOVERNMENT WITH ONE REAL NEED WHILE NEGLECTING OTHER REAL NEEDS

Sometimes the government inefficiency which intensifies discord takes its rise in paying too much attention to one particular need of the community while equally vital needs are neglected. It may happen that in this process there will also occur a failure in meeting even the one need that is more or less clearly seen.

Good Years of the Early Roman Empire

In the first two centuries of the Christian era the Roman Empire appeared to be doing well in an economic sense. Throughout the provinces there were flourishing municipalities, largely autonomous administrative centers of their own town life and that of the rural territory around them. There were signs of growing trade, although this was mostly on a local scale. There were a few industries producing for a large market—notably in pottery, metalware, glass, and brick. Such industries arose only where specially favorable environment supplied useful raw materials, or where some unusually able organizer established an efficient factory. In Rome itself, and also in the provinces, there was a well-developed art and industry of construction, as evidenced by the monumental buildings of the time, the skillful use of aqueducts and pipes to bring water to large cities, and the excellent paved roads, better than any built thereafter until the times of Telford and McAdam early in the nineteenth century. Companies of shareholders were engaged in construction of public works. The predominant wealth and activity in Italy and the empire was agricultural; but beginnings were being made in other lines, as is witnessed by the existence of prosperous cities at intersections of trade routes or on navigable rivers or at seaports.

The growth of towns and the spectacular building that took place throughout the provinces, as well as in Italy, were evidence of the existence of surplus wealth in the hands of at least some people. Gifts of buildings and gardens were made by prominent municipal citizens to their towns and cities. There were also gifts of those great gladiatorial contests which showed the callous general attitude both in Rome and the provinces—except Greece—towards death as a form of public amusement. There was a local pride and spirit in the various municipalities. It looked as though there might be a future of indefinitely increasing economic strength under the direction of the municipal leaders, in whom the energy and ability of the empire was largely concentrated.

Imperial taxes for the support of the central government and other imposts for imperial revenue were light, varying in different parts of the empire, depending largely on the historical circumstances of the several provinces and the arrangements that had been set up on their incorporation into the empire.

In Egypt, where the Ptolemies had come close to being the all-inclusive landlord, the Roman emperor, after the conquest of Egypt, so to speak, stood in the shoes of the traditional king. The form of revenues derived by the imperial government reflected that fact. Thus there were rentals of wheat lands, one to three bushels per acre being taken, dependent on the productivity of the soil. With regard to oil-producing crops, the government bought the oil, manufactured the edible products in its own factories, and then supervised the sale of the product. Most staples were similarly the subject of government ownership and control: flax, hides, salt, honey, brick, and timber, for examples.

The revenue situation in other provinces would be quite unlike that in Egypt. The ordinary basic tax on a provincial was a tithe, intended to be equivalent to about 10 per cent of his annual produce. Garden produce and fruit might be subject to a double tithe—as was the case in Sicily, where the relatively lighter tax on grain may have resulted in overdevotion to raising the latter and injury to the land. The taxes—after the termination of abuses of the public companies which in the earlier republican period had bid for and bought the right to collect the tithe—were generally honestly assessed and honestly collected, the municipality being the agent for collection. The amount assessed was determined by imperial officials and the municipality.

In any province, as well as in Italy, revenues might be derived from government-owned mines, rented lands belonging to the emperor, or a monopoly like that of salt.

Roman citizens—except as they might become subject to tax by owing provincial tithe land, or become subject to ad valorem port dues by engaging in trade or incur taxes on particular transactions like the sale or freeing of a slave—got off easily from imperial taxes. Augustus instituted an inheritance tax of 5 per cent on citizens, and within Italy a general sales tax of 1 per cent.

In return for the relatively light taxes which they paid to the central government, the inhabitants of the empire received protection of transportation both by sea and land, and defense from external enemies, so that orderly development of the many self-governing municipalities was rendered possible.

Later Neglect of Needs Other Than Military

This form of Roman life which appeared to hold so much promise for the future—the prosperous independent self-governing units within a beneficent imperial structure—disappeared in the third century.

On the long frontier of the empire, there was almost constant external warfare. Due to the superior Roman military organization and techniques, enemies could be held off by forces of a size which the empire was capable of supporting as long as there was orderly maintenance of a sufficiently strong economy within the empire.

As early as the second century there were indications that all was not well within the empire. There was a lack of inventiveness along new lines. There was no more great literature, and no improvement in art. In the predominantly agricultural society no new methods to increase farm productivity were developed. A plague, brought back by the troops of Verus after a three-year campaign from 162 to 165 against the Parthians, swept through the empire as well as the army, and took a harsh toll of life in Italy.

By the beginning of the third century the legions consisted largely of provincials drawn from the small farms rather than from the towns. The leaders of this army realized that the ultimate voice in political power had come to rest with the armed forces as represented in themselves. The support of their officers and soldiery was essential to the generals if they were to retain their commands. The generals accordingly, in addition to maintaining the legions in good fighting condition—which was entirely good and essential to the safety of the empire—were forced to give great attention to the demands of their legions. These demands were for more pay and bigger shares in booty—demands which bore no relation whatever to the real needs of the empire for a further development of trade and a greater increase in the independence and prosperity of the municipalities.

The close of the second century and the opening years of the third saw a demonstration of what was now wrong with the empire and what was soon to wreck its economic organization and its strength.

In the year 193 the British legions proclaimed Albinus as emperor, the Pannonian legions Septimius Severus, and the Syrian legions Niger. It took four years for Septimius Severus to defeat his rivals, which he accomplished by 197. In 197 and 198 there was war with the Parthians, in which Severus was victorious and after which he reorganized the Province of Mesopotamia. In 205 to 211, at the other end of the empire, the Caledonians were invading the province of Britain and succeeded in forcing the Romans to give up the land between Antoninus' Wall (running from the Clyde to the Firth of Forth) and Hadrian's Wall (from Solway Firth to Tynemouth). Severus strengthened the latter wall. He died at York in the year 211.

This pattern of wars of succession between rival candidates for emperor and wars against the external enemies of the empire was repeated throughout the third century, and the combination was more than the empire could stand. The successive emperors understood well enough the need for defense against outside enemies. This put their attention mainly on the legions. Then, as the legions proved to be the means to gain the office of emperor, their importance in the Roman scheme of things was re-emphasized.

The focusing of attention on the legions and their demands resulted first in breaking down the resources and independence of the municipalities, and thereafter even the ability of the legions to hold off the pressure of the outside enemies.

The taxes which had been imposed in the first and second centuries were no longer able to sustain the requirements of constant civil war and constant external war. New taxes—property, poll, occupation, and sales—were devised for the cities. There were also some heavy irregular impositions. The so-called crown-gold, in theory a free gift to the emperor upon his inaugural, became too frequent a levy, when, as in the years between 235 and 283, there were 13 emperors, all of whom met violent death at the hands of troops of rival candidates except one who was taken off by the plague. The requirement of rousing and feeding armies in transit became more burdensome as the regular commissaries broke down in the growing disorganization. In the early days of the empire services such as these had been paid for by the government, but now the process was more like looting by an army of strangers.

In the early empire the municipal officials had been agents for the collection of taxes. Now they were made personally liable for arrears of taxes in their districts. They were required to take up abandoned farms and cultivate them in the hope of restoring the base for the increased needs for revenue. Finally, as the municipal offices became nothing but grief, they were rendered hereditary.

Needless to say, this kind of process killed off the energies and spirit of the municipalities. As the demands for revenue grew, the wealth from which revenue could be collected shrank. In the last analysis the burdens came to bear mostly on farmers, as the economic life of the empire was predominantly agricultural. It is ironical that the legions, drawn from the agricultural population and owing the impoverishment of their families to the ambitions and inefficiencies of the emperors, never saw where the trouble lay. The farmers petitioned the emperors for redress against the townsmen, perhaps because the latter were the tax collectors. But townsman and farmer alike were the victims of the emperors; and the emperors themselves the victims of the ignorant legions, the effective electorate of that day.

As the revenues diminished under the increasing inefficiency of administration, more and more collections came to be made in kind. The complex and fair arrangements of the early empire gave way to something simpler, primitive, and unjust. The autocratic solution of force was the only answer the emperors knew for their problems. By the close of the third century workers were compelled to stay in their jobs, the guilds of workers were compelled to supply food and services for the government, and farmers were bound to their soil. Concurrently with this deprivation of liberty went a decreasing productivity, and the hopes and enterprise of people disappeared. An apathy of spirit prevailed as a result of man-made unnecessary hardship—an apathy not unlike that caused in some countries in our own times of today by substantive hardship in the form of the existence of too great a population in a land of too meager resources.

At the turn into the fourth century the emperor Diocletian by a series of decrees froze this economic disintegration and governmental oppressiveness into a permanent system. The days of freedom in the empire, of the self-governing districts and flourishing economy, were at an end, never to be restored under Roman rule.

3. SLIGHTING A REAL NEED

The American Legislature at the Opening of the Second World War

Government officials though aware of a vital need of the community may through fear of unpopularity and possible loss of office fail to take the measures which the need requires.

In the two years preceding the entry of the United States into the Second World War our country had repeated warnings of the danger to itself in the aggressive acts of Germany and to a lesser extent of Italy and Japan.

The majority view in the United States in the spring of 1939 was that there would be no war. This opinion was demonstrated to have been wrong by the outbreak of war in the opening of September. Gradually the true state of affairs shook the country free of some of its false prevalent beliefs. One such false belief was that agreeing not to fight (as in the Kellogg Pact) would stop someone who was out for world conquest. Another was that neutrality and embargoes on sales of arms would protect us from war, whereas their actual effect was only to penalize those foreign countries which had been peace-minded and slow in preparing for conflict, and to reward those which had been war-minded and quick to prepare, like Germany, Italy, and Japan. By November 1939, after the conquest of Poland by Germany, Congress repealed the arms embargo but still forbade American vessels to enter combat areas.

After the British withdrawal from the European continent at Dunkirk in the opening week of June 1940, and the losses and abandonment of arms which it entailed, it was evident that Britain needed what help it could get from the United States and that it was to the United States' interest to give such help. But the President was rightly afraid of what position might be taken by Congress on deliveries of arms by the government to a foreign country, and a subterfuge was adopted by which the government sold a substantial supply of rifles and machine guns to the U. S. Steel Export Corporation, which thereupon resold them to the British.

On June 22, 1940, France surrendered to Germany.

On June 28, Congress passed a bill to the effect that no matériel belonging to the United States government should be delivered to foreign armed forces unless the Army Chief of Staff or the Chief of Naval Operations certified it to be surplus matériel. The President in August, in view of the heavy losses sustained by the British destroyer fleet (10 sunk and 75 more laid up for repairs, representing nearly half their destroyers) and Britain's acute need for more of these vessels, made an agreement for the transfer of 50 American destroyers to the British in exchange for the right to establish military bases on British possessions in the Atlantic. The Chief of Naval Operations thought the value of the bases so great as to justify his certification. The President acted with secrecy, and some destroyers were on their way before the transfer was made known in the United States.

There was thus being built up as a result of the ineffectiveness of Congress in a critical juncture a disregard of Congress by the executive.

The fall of France had a jolting effect on the leaders of American public opinion, and in time also on Congress, which adopted a conscription law in mid-September 1940 providing for a twelve-month period of training for those conscripted. The twelve-month term of service was subject to extension whenever Congress should declare the national interest imperiled. This last clause was inserted to preserve the power of Congress as opposed to that of the executive. Without some such provision the United States Congress would presumably not have adopted a conscription law.

In the campaign for the November 1940 election of a President of the United States, the candidates of the two principal parties each promised that American boys would not fight in Europe, although each candidate was amply intelligent enough to have seen that such fighting was at least likely.

The German submarine drive against British shipping rose sharply in the opening months of 1941. In May of that year, 658,000 tons were sent to the bottom, far beyond the combined replacement capacity of American and British yards. To counter this, although the United States was not at war, the President in March seized German and Italian ships in American ports with a view to their use by England. The United States took over the protection of British shipping routes in the Pacific, landed Marines in Greenland and Iceland, and established patrols along the western convoy routes, thereby freeing the English to concentrate in the eastern Atlantic, particularly off Ireland.

It was at this critical juncture in affairs that there came up in August 1941—about four months before the Japanese attack on Pearl Harbor—the question of extending the twelve-month service of those draftees whose year of training was soon to be completed. Many congressmen now sorely regretted that Congress had left the authority up to itself. In briefest terms the question was: Should Congress in the dangerous days now threatening the United States permit the dis-banding of almost the whole of its trained army? The leaders of Congress were nearly unanimous in their opinion that a bill to extend the term of service would not be adopted. Fortunately they were just barely wrong, as the bill passed the House of Representatives by a majority of one, the vote being 203 to 202.

Thus Congress scarcely allowed the United States to protect itself. The representatives must have been intelligent enough to see the real need; but they were afraid that their constituents, the mothers and fathers of the soldiers, might vote them out of office if they kept the boys in the army. As a result of this fear, the representatives came within one vote of disorganizing American capacity for offensive or defensive military operation on land.

4. HOW LONG CAN AN INEFFICIENT REGIME DRIFT?

An inefficient government together with the state which it governs can stay in existence for a long time if no crisis comes to test it. As long as the inherited techniques of the inefficiently governed community remain better than those of outside enemies, it can drift on.

In the case of the late Roman Empire it was many years after the confusions of the third century became permanent that the outside pressure of enemies from north, east, and south finally both broke the control of the emperors over Mediterranean Sea communications and overwhelmed the western half of the empire.

The community, as distinct from its government, may through the appearance of strong leadership get rid of its inefficient government, and if during this process it has the strength or the luck not to be conquered by its enemies, it may go on to a great future. There have been instances of this in history.

France, despite the disorders and violence of the French Revolution, kept the military strength to hold off its external enemies. Then under the leadership of Napoleon, order was re-established. This order, itself relatively short-lived, was even more absolute in its rule than that of the monarchs of the old regime but was more in tune with contemporary conditions and needs.

The Roman Republic, due to a falling off in the abilities of its predominantly landowning senate and to the intransigency of its popular reforming leaders, had fallen in its closing years into disorder and a series of civil wars. The republican government failed to cope either with the domestic problems of Italy or the provincial problems of the territories which it had conquered. The confusion and inefficiencies of the period were ended by the leadership of Augustus, who set up an imperial structure under which Rome and the provinces blossomed for two hundred years until, as we have seen, new inefficiencies created new burdens and a discord which was never cured.

The United States, despite its governmental inefficiencies in the failure to prepare for either the First or the Second World War, drifted along without results fatal either to the independent political existence of the community or its form of constitutional government. Outside pressure was held off by European buffers, particularly Britain, until the threat of events was made so clear that the executive branch of the government and capable leaders of industry and of public opinion were, in the case of the crisis posed by each of the two wars, enabled to frame a temporary and mainly constitutional dictatorship to deal with the threat. The community itself, its leaders freely consenting to this ordering of their efforts, had ample strength in each case to meet and overcome the immediate crisis.

While inefficiency in government is not always fatal to the political independence of the community, it is always dangerous.

IV. Force Does Not Cure Discord

1. FORCE IN A BREAKDOWN OF ORDER

When there is an acute breakdown of order and the rule of traditional authority is lost, there is likely to ensue a violent conflict between competing groups each of whose leaders are trying to establish order and their own authority by means of force. Sooner or later this use of force succeeds in establishing authority and a restoration of some degree of order, but it does not cure the discord in the community.

Force Fails to Solve Substantive Problems: Violence in the French Revolution

We have described earlier the election of the Estates-General in France in 1789, and the events through which its members became a National Assembly which was to produce a reformed constitution. Despite the enactment of much good legislation, as well as the new constitution which provided for a limited monarchy, and the celebrated Declaration of the Rights of Man, the achievements of the Assembly looked better on paper than they worked in practice. The Assembly failed to devise and set in operation the minimum administrative necessities for orderly government.

Thereafter began an accelerated drift into disorder which ended in an excessive use of force and violence. There was no longer any accustomed rule by which the leaders of different factions felt bound. Each faction was suspicious of every other, each thought it was the country's best hope, each feared its own eclipse as a factor in the government of France. We will briefly examine some aspects of this deterioration.

Many Revolutionary leaders feared a reaction in favor of the *Ancien Régime*. In July 1789 a party of Paris insurrectionists had forced the surrender of the Bastille, hated prison and symbol of the Old Order. Its seven prisoners were released and the governor who had surrendered himself and his small force to the insurrectionists was murdered. Shortly thereafter one of the King's brothers and other well-known members of the nobility had left France to seek foreign refuge and aid. Other waves of like emigration followed, and these émigrés successfully provoked moves towards foreign intervention in favor of the Old Order.

The reform legislation of the National Assembly had included a civil constitution of the clergy which provided for popular election of priests and bishops by voters of the districts and departments respectively. This measure set the clergy, lesser as well as higher, against the entire reform movement, and thereby blocked the chance of reform based on the consent of the leaders of all three estates. Those who feared reaction had good reason to fear that the injured clergy would provide a powerful aid and support to any counterrevolutionary moves that promised to right the wrong which had been done to the clergy.

Nor could the Assembly as a whole free itself from suspicion of such of its leaders—Mirabeau, for instance—who saw the need of strong executive power and who believed that a constitutional monarch was in the actual circumstances the right form of such an executive. So the Assembly provided that no deputy might accept a position from the executive, closing one practicable door to the re-establishment of workable relations between executive and the reforming Assembly.

Though there was much talk of fraternity, the action certainly was not suited to the word. The actual relationships of the political groups were those of distrust and suspicion.

When the National Assembly removed from Versailles to Paris in October 1789, some of the deputies from the distant provinces thought it would be a convenience to have a place near the Assembly where they could meet to discuss matters which were to come before the Assembly. Space in the convent of the Jacobins was leased for 200 francs a year, a committee appointed to make regulations, and a society formed which styled itself the Friends of the Constitution. Thus originated the club of the Jacobins, whose subsequent history provided models for revolutionary cells and organizations in many later times and in many countries other than France.

In December some of the leading inhabitants of the provinces were introduced at the society. It was decided that the establishment of similar societies in the chief cities would be a useful means of organization of those opposed to the interests of the old nobility. Within a year and a half there were over 400 of these affiliated clubs in the provinces.

Another Paris political club, a continuation of a group in one of the districts formed for the elections of the Third Estate, was the Society of the Friends of the Rights of Man and of the Citizen, called from its meeting place the Cordeliers, to which Danton and other Revolutionary leaders belonged.

As outbreaks of disorder continued to increase in Paris, as the volunteer soldiers, now police, proved more and more derelict in the enforcement of order either amongst themselves or others, and as the National Assembly attempted to counter riot, pillaging, and murder with proclamations and deputations requesting that criminals desist from their crimes, the time was approaching when someone would have to exert organized authority by way of force.

In the spring of 1791 Mirabeau died. In June the King and his family confirmed the fears of reaction by their unsuccessful attempt to flee to the northeast frontier to the protection of monarchist troops and émigrés friends. They were captured at Varennes and brought back under guard. In September the National Assembly dissolved, after providing that none of its members should be eligible for the next Assembly, thereby insuring the continuance of the complete parliamentary and legislative inexperience that had already proved the bane of the dissolved Assembly.

The new Legislative Assembly was for a time under the leadership of a group of relatively moderate republicans from the neighborhood of Bordeaux in the Gironde. The Girondists believed that sentiment against the return of the monarchy would be made strong by war against foreign monarchists, supporters of the émigrés; so they precipitated war with Austria and Prussia, who, believing France to be an easy victim, were themselves not unwilling. At first the judgment of Austria and Prussia seemed justified by a series of French reverses.

The orators of the Legislative Assembly were unable to deal with such a crisis by speeches. The Assembly in effect abdicated its powers. A provisional government headed by Danton, an official of the Paris municipality, and leaders of the political clubs and of the Paris municipality permitted the arrest and massacre in prison of those they suspected of being their political enemies. They convoked a

National Convention expected to proclaim a French republic.

The reforms in France, originally set on foot by essentially moderate middle-class people hoping for the elimination of inefficiencies and arbitrariness in government and the attainment of greater freedom, had passed out of the hands of the moderate reformers due in large measure to the political inexperience of their representatives. The reform movement was now under the control of leaders prone to violence, many of them not even members of the Assembly.

Force was invoked as the political means of unifying France; terrorism appeared as the method of government. The problems posed by war, disorder, hunger, royalist discontent, émigrés, and the nonjuring priests were to be solved by knife, gun, and scaffold as the essential instruments of policy and political solidarity.

Force having been called upon as the method of gaining and holding office, it was important to the contesting factions to gain the control of soldiers and police, as practical control at the right times and places would be likely to determine which faction would come out on top of the heap.

Generally speaking, the least fanatical were those who were least deliberate in organizing force and using it. While the King was still an important political factor, he had been as diffident and hesitant in his use of soldiery—for example, the loyal Swiss Guard—as he had been diffident and hesitant in every other matter of political importance.

The French army was politically unreliable from the point of view of any domestic group, and no faction ever felt secure in counting on its support. It will be remembered that the higher officers were nobles, and that except for engineers and artillery all officers, prior to the Revolution, were from the noble order. But amongst the ranks revolutionary ideas began to spread early under the influence and direction of Jacobin committees. The flight of the King to Varennes dramatized the differences between nobles and commoners, and resulted in a situation where the officers felt their duty to the King, in accordance with their oath, whereas the soldiers were in sympathy with the Revolutionary government. Many officers deserted. War ministers were continually changed due to suspicions of the influences that they might be bringing to bear in behalf of their own interests or those of reaction. No one wanted the army at home. It was easier to count on the loyalty of some other kind of force, politically more predictable. Late in 1792 when it looked as though the war with

Austria and Prussia might spread to war with Holland, perhaps with the involvement of England, a French emissary in London, Maret, said candidly to a British representative: "Peace is out of the question. We have 300,000 men in arms. We must make them march as far as their legs will carry them, or they will return and cut our throats!"

But if the army was not politically reliable, perhaps reliance might be placed on less regular police groups. Thus the municipal government in Paris, the Commune, late in 1791 manufactured and supplied pikes to recruits from the slums of Paris. They would be useful for intimidating expressions of moderate opinion. Another part of the policy of intimidation was to exert mob pressure on the Assembly by use of vociferous galleries. This kind of pressure had been facilitated by the move of the Assembly to Paris in October 1789.

When elections were to be held in the summer of 1792 for the National Convention, highly practical means of political persuasion were adopted both in Paris and in the provinces. The Paris Commune subjected the city to a search of homes for muskets, and on the eve of the elections had the jails packed with leaders of moderate views. Similar methods of influence brought to bear on the electorate in other parts of France resulted in the fact that of about 7,500,000 primary electors, approximately 600,000 registered. In Paris, the radical leadership provided that the primary election in the meetings of the *Sections* should be by voice vote. If this might not be sufficient intimidation, the knowledge that moderate leaders were in prison was no doubt influential.

A few days before the secondary election in Paris, which would actually choose the Paris deputies to the National Convention, there was murder of imprisoned moderates—the "September massacres"—to the number of over a thousand—a hint as to how it was expedient to vote.

From now on more and more violence—largely motivated by the fear of counterviolence and suspicions of reaction—came into use. Violent episodes included the execution of the King, the threatening use of mobs, the temporary organization for use as political pressure in Paris of provincial recruits who were eventually to be sent to the front in the foreign wars. It was more and more the extremists who organized successfully this political pressure by violence.

A late attempt to use force in the hope of a justifiable result was by Danton and the Committee of Public Safety in June of 1793. Danton had visited the armies in the spring. He was convinced that orderly and strong government was necessary for successful defense of France and for at least a minimum of domestic order. He was therefore prepared to join for the time being with the extremists of the Commune and the extremists of the Jacobins to terrorize the moderate party in the Convention into withdrawing from it. In achieving this aim, Danton was successful. But now began a triangular struggle between the leaders of the Commune motivated by the desire for political power and what they could get out of it, the extremist Jacobins, similarly motivated, and those leaders like Danton who, though willing to use violence, were still subject to the restraints of national political aims and a patriotism that in the last analysis weighed heavily with them.

During this period of use of force as the means of gaining or holding political power, little was happening towards the solution of the substantive problems of France and the meeting of her substantive needs.

The loss of the familiar administrative machinery in France was accompanied by an inability to collect taxes. During the period of use of force to get and hold office, no solution was made of this fiscal disorder. The issuance of paper money, the *assignats,* was adopted as the revolutionary method of finance. The fanatical and the violent who were coming to power as political survival depended more and more on control of force, did not have sufficient capacity of truth to fact to meet the fiscal challenge successfully. Their abilities lay elsewhere. They tried to make bad money good by decreeing that imprisonment—first short, then long—and subsequently death should be the penalty for tendering or receiving *assignats* at less than their face value. The use of coin and the refusal of *assignats* were made punishable by death. Violence and terror were the legislative panacea, and they did not work. Trade became disorganized and local famine increased.

The elimination of inequities amongst the orders of France was not achieved. The persecution of the nonjuring priests, the proscription of the nobility (who, it will be remembered, had in August 1789 consented to the abolition of their feudal rights), the confiscation of their property, the terrorizing of the moderates in Paris and elsewhere, the devastation and depopulation of districts resisting the revolutionary regime, all were accompaniments of the attempt to hold office by violence. All were also a treatment which worsened the ills of France. The reign of disorder was of no aid to the scope of able commoners to serve their country. The abilities of clergy and nobility, needed for a sound reconstruction of France, were thrown overboard.

The efficiency of government was undermined by suspicion and the pressure to get rid of anyone who was suspected of reactionary sentiment or of hostility to the violently ambitious revolutionary leaders.

It was a lucky thing for France that her foreign enemies were so divided and at cross-purposes in their own aims. Because otherwise the taking on of unnecessary wars—like that against England—and the inefficiencies of the revolutionary armies, especially in matters of supply, would have proved fatal, and France would have passed under alien control. But perhaps because warfare was a matter of violence, the violent were capable of understanding the minimum essentials for waging war. In any event, the terrorists kept in office special military members of the Committee of Public Safety who proved capable of dealing with discipline and supply. It was a near thing, but this was the one important substantive matter where the violent saw to the meeting of a real need.

The Terror began building up to its climax in the autumn of 1793, when military success against the foreigner and against counter-revolutionary insurrections within France were not yet certain. But that this uncertainty was not the sole motivation of the Terror was demonstrated by events in 1794, after the uncertainty had disappeared and France was militarily secure.

In the month of October 1793 the principal revolutionary Committees of Public Safety and General Security were controlled by the leaders of the Paris Commune. This month saw the trial and execution of Marie Antoinette, the trial and execution of those members of the relatively moderate Girondin party who had not fled. The executions continued into 1794.

The leaders of the Commune were atheists. In November they closed the churches of Paris as churches of Christ and reopened them as Temples of Reason. This insult to Roman Catholic Paris paved the way for the doom of the municipal leaders, because it permitted that astute terrorist Robespierre, the Jacobin, to rally the strong and popular Danton to his side in a struggle against the supremacy of the atheistical Commune—a successful struggle in which Robespierre and Danton gained control of the Committee of Public Safety.

In March 1794 the leaders of the Commune were executed.

Robespierre now felt strong enough to turn on Danton and other relative moderates. On March 30, on the basis of a report of Robespierre's henchman St.-Just read to the Committees of Public Safety and General Security, the Dantonists were arrested. Their arrest was confirmed a few days later by a frightened Convention. Execution took place on April 6.

On May 8 Antoine Lavoisier, light of French science and a builder of the foundations of modern chemistry, was guillotined. Aside from his brilliance in chemistry, Lavoisier had given distinguished service to his country in the fields of economics, improved methods of agriculture, and as director of the government powder mills. During the revolutionary period he served as a member of various committees, one of which devised the metric system. He had also been one of the contractors for collection of revenues during the *ancien régime*. It was for membership in this group that he was made an object of revolutionary suspicion and hatred and suffered the death penalty of the Terror.

Robespierre now came to exhibit a combination of religiosity and extreme bloodthirstiness. The latter was perhaps motivated by his desire to save his skin from every potential enemy. On June 8 he presided at a festival of the Supreme Being, in an effort to put across a new religion in France. On June 10 he procured from the Convention the law which gave the Terror its legal climax. Every citizen was authorized to denounce conspirators; in addition to the two principal committees, the Convention and various officials were empowered to deliver accused persons to the Revolutionary Tribunal; and last but not least, the Convention surrendered the immunity to arrest of its own members. Forthwith several hundred opponents of the Robespierre regime were executed.

But Robespierre had now gone too far in the effort to save his own skin from conspirators imagined and real. His terrified opponents, united at least in personal hatred and dread of Robespierre, arrested him and his immediate followers on July 27, and by order of the Convention this group was severally beheaded on the following day.

It is evident that the use of force and the maneuvering by rival leaders for the control of force did not solve the problems of France. The force was addressed to another end altogether—that of gaining and keeping office; and later, as the force went to extremes, simply to the end of self-preservation of those in office. No governmental framework was provided within which France could realize her potentialities. No good citizen was secure or free to do his work under a government to which he could consent. The real needs of the nation could only be met by a regime which provided order and justice. But these can be provided only by leaders who see facts as they truly are.

Jacobins and Bolsheviks

A general breakdown of order is likely to be more the result of weakness in the government than of strength of any reform group. The disorder is characterized by such a loss of a rule to go by that no one can conduct his life or his business with any sense of security. There is absent even the minimum framework of law and authority which permits ordinary people, however docile and obedient they would be ready to be to their rulers, to do their work, engage in trade, go about unmolested, and be at peace in their homes.

Unless somewhere on the scene there is a disciplined well-led group with a program, a rule, to which its leaders adhere and which contains the minimum practical means of establishing and enforcing order, disorder may continue for a prolonged period, as in the French Revolution.

A contrast to the course of events in France in 1789 and after is provided by the course of events in Russia in 1917 and after. After the fall of the Czarist regime in 1917, which had been precipitated by its failures and inefficiencies in the First World War, the provisional government of Kerensky was presiding over a situation verging upon a general breakdown of order. The authority of officers in the army vanished with the disappearance of the old regime. Desertion was rife. In the countryside the peasants, like the rioting peasantry of the French Revolution, seized land and disregarded existing property rights. Industrial workers and their leaders demanded control of industrial production. Not only were they prepared to drive off the old owners of the factories, but also any managers or superintendents who might be necessary to the efficient functioning of industry. The liberal Kerensky government was unable in the circumstances to wield the law and authority needed to establish order.

It was in this disorderly situation that the Bolshevik revolution of November 1917 was successful. In Petrograd the well-organized Bolsheviks took over with a minimum of violence the place of the provisional government, capturing the Winter Palace, the seat of the ministers of the provisional government. In some of the other cities of Russia, notably Moscow, there was violence and fighting in the streets. Authority passed into the hands of the Bolsheviks, whose leaders were accomplished in the technique of revolutionary organization and believed in force as the chief instrument of politics.

In the breakdown of order in the French Revolution there was no disciplined organized group on the French scene, corresponding to the Bolsheviks on the Russian scene, to fill the governmental vacuum created by the loss of the familiar governmental and administrative rule. Neither the Jacobins nor the other organizations of competing revolutionary leaders produced a group both disciplined and with a definite practicable program for the restoration of an orderly going concern. In Russia the Bolsheviks did have a program, a discipline, and a rule to go by, and they were able to establish their version of order, however harsh, arbitrary, and unjust it might be.

2. FORCE TO GAIN THE SEAT OF AUTHORITY

The Strike in Vital Areas

In our own times we have seen occurrences of well-prepared breakdown of order, the deliberate effort to produce the kind of disorganization in the community which in earlier cases, like that of the French Revolution, had appeared accidentally as a result of ineffectiveness and mistaken fact. The purpose of the prepared breakdown of order is the creation of a situation in which the leader of some group which is seeking government power may seize the power on the pretext that he and his group and his ideas are the only means capable of restoring order.

The revolutionary use of a strike of workers in activities essential to the continued life of a complex state is a case of this kind of prepared breakdown of order. A great city is dependent, if its inhabitants are to live, on organized transportation for its food supply and on functioning aqueducts for its water. Scarcely less important is the continuous supply of electric power for light, for the operation of mechanical burners to produce heat, and for movement within the city itself. A strike in these areas, crippling the necessary services, especially if the strikers have the sympathy of the police officials and army officers so that compulsion will not be brought to bear to break the strike, can produce the breakdown of order that gives the revolutionary leader his chance to seize power on the ground that he alone can re-establish the necessary public services.

The use of this particular revolutionary technique was made possible for the Bolsheviks by their control of industrial workers, and aided their seizure of power in Russia in 1917. The fact that the revolutionaries were hostile to the managers most capable of operating the industries—as we have just seen—did not hinder the disorganization which rendered the seizure of power possible. It simply illustrated that the use of force to gain control of power is not addressed to the task of a substantively good performance in industry, but only to the task of getting to the top of the political heap, the position of governmental authority.

In the troubled course of events in Spain in the nineteen-thirties we saw that strikes were used to contribute to disorder in the interests of the ambitions of leftist group leaders. But the leftist leaders were unable to hold control. After the Republic lost what little effectiveness it ever had, power passed to another group of extremists on the extreme right—an army-church-landowner group—whose leaders came to the top of the heap by the use of force and violence. Here again, no solution was reached of the critical Spanish problems of intelligent use of land, rational organization of industry, and improved transportation. Once again it was seen that force, while a potent political weapon, is more adapted to seizing office than it is to performing rightly the functions of office.

Thirty Years of Czechoslovak History

The thirty years of Czechoslovak history from 1919 to 1948 show a newly organized state beset by many political problems, perhaps for twenty years on a way to solution by methods of give and take, but eventually dealt with by force and intolerance used on behalf of one group or another. The result was that more new problems were created than old ones solved, the use of force only deciding what faction was to be in the saddle and uneasily ride the rest of the community.

LAND AND PEOPLE

Of the territorial components of Czechoslovakia at its creation as a new state at the close of the First World War, Bohemia was the most important. A Slavic wedge between the German peoples of Silesia on the northeast and of Austria on the southwest, Bohemia's former existence as an independent state had ended in 1620 by its absorption into the Austrian state. Mountainous frontiers on southwest, northwest, and northeast were a natural protection for Bohemia and may have accounted for the fact that the basin of Bohemia within this circle of mountains was not occupied by German peoples. But the frontier territory itself adjacent to the mountains did have a large German-speaking population—German immigrants and Germanized natives. In the growth of industry in the nineteenth century this German settlement, where water power, coal, and minerals were found, became the industrialized part of Bohemia. In the new Czechoslovakia, Czechs numbered about 6,000,000 and Germans and Germanized about 3,000,000.

Bohemia had been a prominent participant in the events of the Protestant Reformation, and at the beginning of the seventeenth century most Bohemians were Protestants. By 1918 this situation had been reversed, and there were only about 1,000,000 Protestants. But there was no unanimity amongst the Roman Catholics, as shown by the fact that in the first years of the new Czechoslovak state about 1,000,000 Czechs left the Roman Catholic Church (about half of them then uniting in what they called the Czechoslovak National Church) with a program for celebrating Mass in the Czech language, and the abolition of the celibacy of the priesthood. There was also a division within the Roman Catholic clergy over the proper influence to be allowed to clergy of Czech speech, that being the language of the great majority of the lesser clergy.

Moravia, to the southeast of Bohemia and not separated from it by any difficult physical barrier, was in culture and language closely akin to Bohemia, and for our present purposes can be regarded as a unit—Bohemia-Moravia. As in Bohemia, the hilly northern margin of Moravia, adjacent to German Silesia, had a heavy German population, as did also the city of Brno, the Moravian capital, one of the important textile centers of Europe.

A small strip of Silesia, to the north of Moravia, with a population of roughly 600,000, contained a German minority of a little more than two-fifths.

Slovakia, for a thousand years subject to the Hungarian monarchy, was much less well developed than Bohemia-Moravia, and at the close of the First World War would have been incapable of independent statehood. It is likely that the Slovakians were better satisfied with their integration (agreed upon by both Czech and Slovak leaders and favored by an influential body of Slovak immigrants in the United States of America) as part of the new state of Czechoslovakia than they would have been by any other disposition on the breakup of the Austro-Hungarian empire. Although in race and language close to the Czechs, the Slovakians as a result of a different religious and cultural inheritance and their 1,000-year control by Hungary, were not a group easily assimilable in the new state. In religion a majority of the Slovakians were highly devout Roman Catholics. Slovakian economic ties were mainly with Hungary, and Slovakian roads and communications were disposed north-south towards Hungary, rather than east-west towards Bohemia. The location of the boundaries of Czechoslovakia was such as to include within Slovakia about 3,000,000 Slovaks and something in the neighborhood of 1,000,000 Hungarians. Slovakia in its economics was mainly pastoral and agricultural, with a significant mining industry as well.

At the eastern tip of the new state and added to it for strategic reasons was Ruthenia, the Carpathian Ukraine. The Ruthenians, about half a million in number, were mainly an agricultural and pastoral people. In their economic life they were ridden by poverty, in their religious by superstition. Their religious allegiance was so-called Uniate, an Eastern rite acknowledging the supremacy of the Roman Pope.

CZECHOSLOVAK HISTORY AFTER 1919

In favor of the prospects for success of the new country of Czechoslovakia was the fact that it had the possibility of a well-balanced economy—its industries, most importantly in the Germanized fringe of Bohemia, being complemented by its agriculture and its pasture. It had interior transportation problems, wanting a sufficiency of roads and railroads between its eastern and western parts. Being landlocked, its rights of egress northerly by way of the Elbe to German ports, and southerly by way of rail to the Adriatic, were at the mercy of outside governments, as was also its traffic by way of the Danube, on which it had an important port in Bratislava, the capital city of Slovakia. Whatever may have been the deficiencies of the departed Austro-Hungarian Empire, it had provided 700 miles of navigation along the Danube under one governmental jurisdiction—a jurisdiction fractured by the setting-up of new governments after the First World War.

Despite the relatively favorable economic basis of the new state, other kinds of difficulties were to wreck it twenty years after its inception, and then once again three years after the re-establishment of the Czechoslovakian state following the Second World War. These difficulties were the racial, cultural, and doctrinal differences within its people, and the influence of outside states competing with one another for control over its physical and human resources, especially those of Bohemia. Instead of a peaceful and orderly reconciliation of the interests of the different groups, force was twice invoked to gain political rule, and the needs of the people and of their state in each instance disregarded.

For a time it looked as though the new state might furnish the world with an example of how even deep-going differences between the various powerful groups in the community could be brought into a working accord by peaceful means.

On the economic side, despite postwar tariff barriers, Czechoslovakian manufactures found a foreign market sufficient to pay for the import of needed raw materials. With regard to food, the country was itself approximately self-sufficient. Until the world-wide depression of the nineteen-thirties, Czechoslovakian economic enterprise shone amidst that of her neighbor states.

Great strides were made in education. On the whole the predominantly Czech government at Prague gave fair-minded attention to the rights of minorities, especially those of the German fringe, both with regard to the use of their own language in schools and the preservation of their particular cultural customs and interests.

Nevertheless it was hard for the German minority, which in prewar years had exercised much more political influence than the Czech majority, to accept a reversal of this role, and to find the Czech influence now predominant in legislation.

Land reform with a view to farmers—the peasantry—becoming landowners rather than tenants of a few large owners was put into effect. The old owners, other than the monarchy, received compensation for the land taken from them. Some of the great landholders were German. The Church as a landowner was opposed to this reform, and it will be remembered that Slovakia was devoutly Roman Catholic. The land reform intensified the friction between the rather anticlerical group in the government at Prague and the Church leadership in Slovakia. There was also within Slovakia not only a group of Hungarians but a considerable number of Slovakians as well who, despite the close racial affinities of the latter to the Czechs, would by virtue of old interests and ties, economic as well as religious, have preferred Hungarian rule to that of the new predominantly Czech regime. But the Slovakian farmers themselves could not but be partial to a land reform offering so much promise for the betterment of their standing and voice in the community.

In foreign policy Czechoslovakia leaned towards France and away from Germany. This was to be expected in the case of a country owing its independence to the defeat of Germany and the victory of France in the First World War. This direction of foreign policy was another item distressing to some of the German minority. But here again, as long as economic conditions were improving there were two views within the German minority. Those wishing to take a whole-hearted part in the success of the Czechoslovakian experiment were at least as strong as the dissenters.

Such was the condition of affairs in Czechoslovakia when two sets of events in the early nineteen-thirties paved the way for the undoing of that country just before the Second World War. The first was an economic worsening—the repercussion on Bohemian industry of the great international economic depression, and the second was an ethnic push—the pan-German pressure and propaganda emanating from Adolf Hitler's Berlin.

Industry in Czechoslovakia was mainly located in the German fringe of Bohemia, these Germans for convenience being referred to as Sudeten Germans, by virtue of the fact that the Sudeten mountains extended along about 180 miles of this German-populated frontier area. Both owners and employees of this industry were seriously hurt by the shrinkage of foreign trade which accompanied the world-wide economic depression of the nineteen-thirties. Central European trade and finance suffered a further local disorganization after the financial crash in Vienna in the spring of 1931. In Czechoslovakia as a whole, unemployment figures had increased from 53,000 in January 1929 to 839,000 in January 1934. Thus economic hardship was added to such causes of dissent and discontent as were already affecting the Sudeten as a political, racial, and cultural minority.

In these troubled waters German extremists began hopefully to fish. In the course of 1933 the ideas of Hitler's National Socialist party in regard to the German *Volk* and its reunion wherever possible in a greater Germany made great headway amongst the Sudeten. They formed social and political organizations, sporting clubs, and youth groups for the propagation of these German notions. Some went to the length of promoting a political separation which from the point of view of the Czechoslovak state was treasonable, and certain Sudeten leaders were accused of treason. In October 1933 the Sudeten National Socialist party dissolved in the face of an impending order outlawing it. Shortly thereafter the leader, Konrad Henlein, organized a Sudeten German party which in its official program did not expressly call for secession of the Sudeten from the Czechoslovak state. The election results in May 1935 showed that this party had won to its standard the great majority of those in the German fringe. With 44 out of the 300 seats in the national Chamber of Deputies, it was the second largest of the 14 parties represented.

Those who live in countries like the United States or Great Britain, which at the present moment have only two major parties, do not generally recognize the difficulty which a representative democratic government has in establishing any definite policy of action in a country with many parties, such as Czechoslovakia in 1935. A tabulation of the composition of the Czechoslovak Chamber of Deputies, even with no further description of the divergent party programs than is indicated by the party names, suggests the problem:

Czechoslovak Agrarian	45
Sudeten German	44
Czechoslovak Social Democratic	38
Communist	30
Czechoslovak Socialist	28
Czechoslovak People's Catholic	22
Slovak People's	22
Czechoslovak Trades	17
National Union	17
German Social Democratic	11
Sudeten German Wahlblock	9
Fascist	6
German Christian Socialist	6
German Agrarian League	5
	300

In this fractioned political scene Konrad Henlein's party steadily pursued a more extreme course in favor of Germany and against Czechoslovakia—both in its internal and foreign policies. On the German side of the fence Dr. Goebbels, the Nazi Minister of Propaganda, brought repeated accusations against Czechoslovakia of allowing Soviet aviation bases within its borders.

Towards the close of 1937 the Czech police suppressed a meeting of the Sudeten German party in Teplice in the German fringe. Henlein thereupon demanded complete autonomy for the Germans in Czechoslovakia. Shortly thereafter the Sudeten German deputies walked out of parliament.

Then followed the crisis of 1938. Under threat of military intervention by Germany, and forsaken by her ally, France, contrary to the direct treaty obligation of the latter, and under the urging of a Britain ill-prepared for war and perhaps still doubtful as to the intentions of Nazi Germany against herself, Czechoslovakia was forced to agree to the surrender to Germany of 10,000 square miles of Czech territory inhabited by about 2,000,000 Germans and 700,000 Czechs. This ceded area was the industrial heart of Czechoslovakia. It also contained her key frontier fortresses.

Czechoslovakia was now a helpless rump state. Her neighbor Poland proceeded to occupy the important Teschen coal mine area, which had about a quarter of a million population, considerably less than half of whom were Poles. Hungary, with the consent of Germany and Italy, took a slice of southern Slovakia populated by about one million.

The remainder of Slovakia, under the leadership of Father Joseph Tiso, long an agitator against the Czech government on religious grounds and a noted pro-Fascist and anti-Semite, became an autonomous region of the rump state.

Then, a week before the spring equinox of 1939, the armed forces of Hitlerian Germany occupied Prague and declared Bohemia-Moravia a German protectorate, part of the German Empire. Slovakia was recognized as an independent state, which in practice meant a German puppet under the despotic local rule of Father Tiso. Ruthenia was occupied by Hungary.

Thus Czechoslovakia after twenty years of effort to work out her destiny along free lines was first dismembered and rendered economically and militarily impotent, and then obliterated as an independent state.

CZECHOSLOVAKIA IN 1948

Germany after her defeat in the Second World War was deprived of Bohemia-Moravia. Czechoslovakia was restored as a state. The borders were substantially as in the former Czechoslovakia except that Ruthenia became a part of the Ukrainian Soviet Socialist Republic.

The liberation of the country from German domination was by Russian troops in the spring of 1945. The government-in-exile, which during the war had maintained its headquarters in London, returned home with the Russian forces. This group believed that Czechoslovakia would be best served by a parliamentary representative government. This was agreed to by the victorious allies, and the new Czechoslovak state started out on that basis, with a mainly socialized economic structure, the banks and most heavy industry being slated for ownership by the state. Free elections for a constituent National Assembly were held in May 1946. The Communists emerged as the largest party with slightly less than two-fifths of the vote. If representatives were to be roughly classified in accordance with whether their opinions were leftist or rightist, the Assembly's 300 members consisted of just over half left, with 114 Communists solidly aligned and 37 Czech Social Democrats, with a good deal of divergence as to the degree of their leftness, making up this half. The cabinet of 26 members appointed by President Beneš consisted of 24 representatives of six different political parties and of 2 nonparty members. The largest single party representation in the cabinet was 6 Communists. The prime minister was a Communist.

Czechoslovakia needed in her industry all the skill available, and it happened that her main source of skilled workers were the Germans. But the Germans had proved so politically intractable in the first Czechoslovakia, that following approval of a new population policy at the 1945 Potsdam Conference of the victorious allied powers, about 3,000,000 Germans were expelled. This may have been the lesser of two evils—the alternative evil being the presence in the community of an intransigent minority. None the less this loss of skilled and intelligent people was an unsatisfactory solution of the problem of a country which critically needed their skill. Hope of reconciliation was abandoned with the expulsion of the German minority.

In determining the distribution of ministries in the 1946 Czechoslovakian cabinet, the Communists insisted that the Ministry of the Interior, with its control of police forces, be put into the hands of a member of their party. This was done, and this appointment of a Communist Minister of the Interior was the first step towards the downfall of the system of freely chosen governments.

The Minister of the Interior forthwith entered upon the practical policy of making sure that police commands were in Communist hands. Throughout Czechoslovakia there was unavoidably considerable disorganization following the overthrow of the German government. As a practical means of dealing with this situation there were established various local committees, which like the national cabinet were designed to be as representative as possible of the several Czechoslovakian parties. But in practice the Communists, understanding the requirements for political survival in times of turmoil, took pains to see that on the local scene the officials in charge of security and police should be loyal Communists. Thus at the local level, just as in Prague at the national level, the control of force was in Communist hands.

Early in 1948 the Minister of the Interior removed from office certain district superintendents of police, replacing them with completely reliable Communists. By now all the other political parties—even the leftist Social Democrats—were alarmed at the increasing concentration of police control under the Interior Minister. So the entire non-Communist membership of the cabinet demanded that the Interior Minister suspend his new police appointments. This he did not do.

In the next six days, from the 20th to the 25th of February, events moved quickly.

Twelve cabinet ministers, representing parties with two-fifths of the popular vote of the country, resigned on account of the disobedience of the Interior Minister to the instructions of the cabinet. The premier denounced the resigned ministers as enemies of the people, and demanded that President Beneš accept their resignations and fill their places with those who would follow the Communist dictate. But Beneš still insisted on a representative cabinet, still believed in representative government and did not wish his country to follow the single party totalitarian model.

At this juncture the Communist Ministry of Information refused radio time to the Minister of Food, a leftist Social Democrat who had not resigned from the cabinet, but who may have believed in representative government. During the crisis the radio did all possible to influence the public against the resigned ministers.

The threat of a general strike was brought by delegates at a meeting of the Communist-controlled General Federation of Labor, in order to bring pressure upon the President to accede to the Premier's demands. This meeting also demanded complete nationalization of all industry employing over fifty people, nationalization of all wholesale trade, of retail department stores, and of all publications and printing offices.

The Premier now went into action with carefully prepared measures for the use of force to seize authority. Small armed bands, "action committees," took over the offices of the non-Communist ministries, replacing the ministers with temporary appointees of force. They occupied the headquarters of the Socialist party, the second largest party in Czechoslovakia on the basis of popular vote, alleging that this party was conspiring for armed revolt against the state.

Doubtful of the allegiance of the Social Democrats, without whom any pretense of a parliamentary majority for the Communist program was impossible, police made an effective gesture of intimidation by searching the headquarters of the Social Democratic party also.

Action committees occupied independent newspaper plants.

Student demonstrations for the republic of Masaryk and Beneš were suppressed.

The General Confederation of Labor announced a general strike unless Beneš acceded to the Communist demands.

Five days after the resignation of the twelve ministers, President Beneš accepted their resignation and appointed new ministers satisfactory to the Communist Premier, saying that he did this as the alternative to general chaos. Thus representative government disappeared from Czechoslovakia. Force took control. A new constitution on the Russian soviet model was adopted. The state became a single party state.

Force had seized the seat of authority. The real needs of the community were disregarded. Czechoslovakia needed relations with both east and west. But just as in 1938 one group of extremists had forced a solution in which the good of the country was sacrificed to the interests of Germany, so now in 1948 another group of extremists forced a solution in which the good of the country was sacrificed to Russian interests. The misfortune of Czechoslovakia was what should have been her blessing—her factories capable of turning out armaments, precision instruments, steel piping, steel rails, textiles, glass, wood products, and her material resources, coal, iron, silver, copper, lead, uranium. These were needed by her acquisitive neighbors, who by turns saw to it that the efforts of successive free governments to reconcile and harmonize the various groups within the country should fail. It was a difficult task at best—that of bringing together the many kinds of difference that existed within Czechoslovakia. But it did not appear to be impossible, except as made so by the efforts of first Germany and then Russia to emphasize the differences, to whip up extreme fanaticism, and to support partisan leaders unfaithful to the whole needs of the country.

In the *coup d'état* of 1948, the utility of small armed groups of doctrinaire fanatics was thoroughly demonstrated. It was by means of these, the action committees, that the principal offices and machinery of government were taken over. As for the population at large, even those parts of it capable of leadership, so great is the need of a rule to go by and so great the fear of disorganization, there is little that they are likely to do in such a crisis except follow along and put up as well as they can with whatever clique gains control of the place of government and wields the predominant force. Everybody can see the need of elementary order—for purposes of distribution of food, prevention of looting, maintenance of muncipal services necessary to health and life. So, when an organized band gets control of the government offices and armed force, people will tend to obey them for the sake of rule and order, however unjust and unsatisfactory the regime and however prevalent the factors of discord for the time being. Otherwise the people who make up the public would be completely at a loss and in maximum uncertainty in their lives and their businesses. The more highly differentiated the functions in a country, the more is this sure to be true, as the failure of order means disease and starvation.

3. FORCE TO MAINTAIN ORDER

Force the Sign of Discord

The actual course of events in these specific cases of the use of force in acute disorder or in attempts to seize authority shows that force does not solve the long-term problems of the community. The use of force in these cases is not aimed at the cure of discord; it is aimed either at the suppression of disorder or the decision of who is going to come out on top of the political heap and rule the community.

But how does the matter stand with the use of force to maintain order that has not yet broken down or that has been for the time being restored, force to sustain a going concern? Is such a use of force able to prevent or to cure discord?

The answer to these questions has already been indicated for us in the facts of the several cases of discord we have already described, where there has been a failure to reconcile reform efforts tolerantly. All those cases demonstrated that force does not prevent or cure discord. On the contrary it was evident that the degree of discord in the community is closely paralleled by the degree of force used or threatened for the purpose of maintaining order. This correlation of force and discord is notably evident in our own times today, so that what has been amply indicated by earlier history is proved before our own eyes—that force does not cure discord, but is instead the sign of discord.

Repressive Government

In the police states we have witnessed in our own times, like that of Stalin in Russia, the reason for existence of the undercover political police is to prevent dissenters who are abused by the regime and dissatisfied with it from getting a following sufficient to compel a change in the government. The presence of such a punitive and repressive agency—as in the earlier case of the Inquisition and its informers—is a confession that the ruler has failed to gain the consent of his subjects, and that dissent and heresy would break out unless forcibly suppressed.

The denial by the Russian government to the people of the Ukraine of enough of their own produce for their own well-being meant continual dissent in the Ukraine, evidenced by recurrent purges of Ukrainian leaders.

The rising of the Ku Klux Klan in the period of Reconstruction of the southern United States and the need of the northern government to suppress it was evidence of continuing discord in the South and of the failure of the North to find a means of ruling the South by a just rule that would gain the consent of the South.

Lutheran and Roman Catholic opposition to the bigoted racial doctrines of Hitler's National Socialists was met by harsh repression. This use of force was again a confession that the Nazi government was unable to obtain the willing consent to its policies of a large part of its subjects. As in the case of Stalin, or the Inquisition, or the United States' carpetbaggers, the reliance on force was itself the proof of the presence of discord and of the failure of the ruler to find the right substantive solution of the current governmental problem.

We have looked at these repressive governments mainly from the point of view of their unfortunate subjects. But from the point of view of the government the situation is also entirely unsatisfactory. The repressive government as a practical matter does not know how many of its subjects are obeying a hated regime only because of fear that disobedience will mean starvation, imprisonment, or death. The government does not know the size of the groups who will turn against it when they see the chance. In its constant fear of those to whom it has given cause for hatred and dissent, the government resorts to its purges, inquisitions, St. Bartholomew's Day massacres, all in the name of maintaining order. The certain result is the perpetuation of discord.

A repressive ruler has always to fear for his life. Tyrannicide—the assassination of a ruler who has in fact been oppressively unjust and against whom there has been no other practicable remedy—has frequently been practiced and almost universally approved. As this is well known to unpopular rulers, they are under a compulsion of fear to strike back in advance, which in turn augments the already dangerous fear and hatred against the ruler. Tyrannicide was illustrated by the assassination of Huey Long, the fear of tyrannicide by the periodic purges carried out by Stalin.

Far from curing discord, the prolonged use of force promotes further discord. Hatred is created in the families and friends of those who are imprisoned or killed. What wholehearted support of his government can be expected from a citizen who when speaking his own views to a friend has simultaneously to keep up a constant noise by tapping with his pencil on his telephone instrument for fear that listening devices are in the room and that his conversation may be overheard by the security police? Perhaps from the point of view of the government these police are a source of security; but to the unfortunate citizens they are the source of insecurity, providing a maximum invasion of privacy and a maximum presence of fear.

The type case of discord is not the case of acute disturbance and the effort to cure it by violence to gain the seat of authority and restore order. To be sure, such cases are, as we have seen, common enough. But the type case, as we have also seen, is that of the prolongation of an unjust order, too much human force and organization arrayed against needed reform—as in Germany in the nineteenth century, in the pre-Reformation days of the Roman Catholic Church in Europe, in third-century Rome, in Nazi Germany, in Soviet Russia. In the sequence of events in these cases—with the possible exception of third-century Rome—violent disorder has been relatively absent or sporadic. But discord, the continual presence of suppressed civil discontent and protest, has been profound. The independent-minded have been unable for the time being to break out of their bondage.

4. DISORDER MAY HAVE A MORE HOPEFUL PROGNOSIS THAN UNJUST ORDER

When disorder threatens to interfere with the continuing production and distribution of articles and services necessary to the life of members of the community, or when disorder is so violent that it threatens life directly, the use of force to restore order is justified. This is so whether the disorder is on a large scale and widespread, or in some limited but vital sector, such as transportation, or the supply of water or heat and power.

Before you can quarrel about how shares in product are to be divided, you have got to see that the necessary product is first provided. There is a common interest that what is needful be produced and distributed, a divergent interest in the sharing or the control of the distribution. When disorder is seriously interfering with the essential production and distribution, the common interest requires that the disorder be suppressed, by force if necessary.

It may be a shorter or a longer time before order is restored. In Germany in the Ruhr in 1919 a general strike disrupted production. After negotiation and apparent agreement between the strikers and representatives of the government, the agreement failed to be carried out, and a state of insurrection against the authority of the government followed. This the government suppressed by armed force. The interference with the common interest in production was short-lived in this instance. Similarly Bolshevik control was established in Russia in 1917 in a relatively short period. But if neither party to the dispute possesses the requisite predominance of force, disorder may be long-lived as in the Spanish Civil War of 1936 to 1939, in which the republican government was eventually overthrown by the authoritarian leader Franco.

Needless to say, discord as well as disorder exists in these cases of solution of disorder by force. But the picture may not be entirely black. That depends on who is going to come out on top in the struggle, and what kind of governmental and social ideas this victor represents.

With all the great disorder of the French Revolution, the prognosis for a country which had so many leaders who believed in the essential decency of human nature was far from bad. Even if the disorder should be eventually resolved, as it was, under the influence of a military leader of great personal power, still the temper of French leadership was such that there could be great prospect of a hopeful, energetic, and enlightened France.

By contrast to this case of the acute disorder of the French Revolution, there was relatively small disorder in the Germany in which Hitler came to power. But the ideas of the German leadership were cynical and narrow-minded. These successful revolutionaries believed in the essential depravity and cowardice of men. The prognosis here, in the country of Rosenberg, was far different and far worse than in the country of Rousseau, where the belief was impractically at the opposite extreme.

A violent crisis may be resolved in a reasonably just order. After the period of violence which signalized the collapse of the Roman republic, the reform ideas represented by Augustus resulted in a freeing of productive energies throughout the Empire. Augustus established his order on a foundation of scope to capable people whose abilities could not function in the disorganization which the republican leaders had seemed powerless to cure. Something of the gratitude and relief that was felt by good citizens of Rome at their removal from a nightmare of political disorder comes clearly through today to a reader of the great, good-humored, and tolerant poet Horace, himself in his younger days a republican opponent of the emperor, but later converted to a follower by the fact of Augustus' rescue of the Roman state from disorder.

The lack of a violent crisis in discord does not mean that the order which is maintained is a just order. In the eighteenth century, when France had her Revolution, Germany and Spain each escaped any similarly violent upheaval. And yet it is questionable whether Germany and Spain were not each thereby the losers, as each stood in need of a reorganization and liberalizing of a social order more backward than that of pre-Revolutionary France. Indeed it was in part this very backwardness of ideas in Germany and Spain and the lack of widespread reform sentiment at the leadership level, that permitted the governments to keep the clamps on their respective subjects.

Even when it is using force against a violent and intractable group —as, for example, in the case of the Spanish republican government against extremists of both left and right—the government and all other leaders, as well as foreign observers, ought to recognize that this force of itself is not going to produce a substantively good community. That will depend on persuasion and consent. Consent will only be forthcoming if the program of the government in fact comes somewhere near meeting the needs of the time and the place. The program of Augustus in Rome did meet the needs and did gain the consent of the governed. The program of Lincoln for the reconstruction of the South in the United States would have met the needs and would have gained southern consent had Lincoln lived to put his program into effect.

The sooner the government can put into effect a rule that meets the needs and the sooner it can drop its use of force, the better. When force is still being used a long time after violent disorder has been cured, and when willing consent to the regime has failed to make its appearance—as in the discord cases we have reviewed—then the government leadership needs to turn an inward eye upon itself and its program, as that is where the difficulty is likely to lie.

The community in disorder is like Plato's temporarily blinded man, confused and unable to see his circumstances clearly. This confusion may be because he is on his way from dark to light, or on his way from light to dark. The degree of confusion, as noted long ago by the philosopher, may be much the same in either case. But when the man is on his way from dark to light, he soon will see more clearly. When on his way from light to dark, he will soon be in complete obscurity. So for political disorder—the question is, Are you coming out from it into a good and just regime or into a period of repressive discord? In the eighteenth-century French Revolution, the French were moving towards the light; in the twentieth-century German, the Germans towards the dark.

After the period of acute disorder has ended and the necessary minimum of order been re-established, the problem of those who are in control of the community—the government—now becomes the same as that of a government of a community where no serious breakdown of order has occurred. In each case the government has to set about gaining or holding the consent of the governed, so that the people and their leaders will not be kicking against the pricks but can put their time and effort to constructive pursuits useful to themselves and to others, so that all will prosper in a strong and peaceful order.

To the extent that the government fails to achieve this end and does not gain the consent of the governed, the community is once more caught in the familiar picture of discord, its government—and perhaps other groups also—pushing too hard, holding too tight, or being too inefficient and burdensome, and manifesting the threats of force and the overuse of force which we have reviewed in cases of those several kinds.

V. Why Force Cannot Cure Discord

IF might made right, there would be no political problems. The wielders of superior force in the community would by decree establish what was right and that would be the end of the matter. But every case of discord we have described demonstrates that that is not the end of the matter at all. Far from it. Despite the bolstering that might receives from the obvious advantages of order and everyone's need of a rule to go by and everyone's recognition of the dangers of disorder to well-being and even life, still if might has imposed an injurious rule there are continuing efforts for reform. People caught in discord which is backed by might still look for the solution of their troubles. Might has most certainly not made right in actual fact.

Since force has often augmented and has never cured discord, it is likely that there are discoverable factors in the use of force which will show why this has been the case and will indicate what are the prospects for a good community in future cases of reliance on force.

1. CHARACTERISTICS OF RULERS RELYING MAINLY ON FORCE

In a military organization quick obedience is essential if a workmanlike military result is to be obtained. The purpose of an army is extremely narrow—the application of force successfully to defeat a counterforce. Quick obedience in behalf of a narrow purpose of this kind is not compatible with a whole mass of differing views as to how to go about reaching the object. If officers hold radically independent ideas and are allowed to try them out in action, the army will be beaten.

Absolute obedience is mainly valuable in an organization which has a particular limited objective. An entire great community—except in war with an outside enemy—never has a particular limited objective. The leaders of a whole society do not know and cannot know except in a general and indefinite way where its welfare lies or what precise institutions are going to be most useful for it. This complexity of the aims of a society is one of the reasons why military rule, or rule by force, is unlikely to prove satisfactory for it. The needs of the situation are too difficult to be grasped by a small leadership group. When this group gets on the wrong track and demands implicit obedience from its followers, it is likely to stay on the wrong track indefinitely.

The kind of narrow-minded stubbornness shown by Hitler in the policy laid down for his generals before Stalingrad was tragic enough even in the limited military field. But the narrow-mindedness of the same leader when applied to the infinitely more difficult problems of the whole German state in its relation to the rest of the world completely wrecked that state.

An argument can be made in favor of concentrating authority in self-perpetuating leaderships in fields where the purpose is a narrow one. For example, in actual practice in the United States today a corporate management of a company manufacturing bricks, or the corporate management of any other company, designates its own successors. Only in the event of abject failure of the management is it—or its self-appointed succession—rejected by the stockholders. When the management of a specific company of this kind gets too set in its ways, no great harm is done to the community at large, if the current economic organization is such as to allow the company to lose its business to more efficient competitors.

But as the field of endeavor gets broader, when the purposes become as indeterminate as those of a whole country, then the self-perpetuating leadership pursuing mistaken ways becomes a menace to the welfare of its subjects, and if it possesses the force to maintain itself and enforce obedience to its orders, the menace will be realized. This very sequence of events we saw in third-century Rome, in the pre-Reformation Roman Catholic Church, and in the Germany of the National Socialists.

The capacity to deal wisely with events, to see what they mean for the community, or what ought to be done about them, is rare. The mathematical chances are against this capacity being found in any particular spot, such as in any particular ruler or government group. There is, however, an excellent chance that those outside the ruling group will include amongst their far greater numbers a few who can foresee or happen upon the right course, set the pace, and establish the new standards. A wise government can recognize the new trend.

But this cannot happen in a country where the government vigorously maintains its own rule by force. In such a case the community is limited in its chances of right development by the capacity of the ruler. And the chance that the ruler will be a George Washington or an Augustus is too slender. It is more likely that events will turn up someone who is long on ruthlessness in the use of force—a Robespierre, a Hitler, a Stalin, a Franco—but short on political wisdom.

History leaves no doubt that force and terror vigorously applied by the narrow-minded fanatic can get him to the top of the heap at the expense of those wiser and more moderate. Robespierre, whom we just mentioned, is a good example. But that is only another way of saying that force as a political method is likely to result in those who cannot fulfill the functions of good government getting power at the expense of those who can.

There seem to be some who love force and violence just for the sake of force and violence. The great stress in Hitler's *Mein Kampf* on terror as a sovereign political method indicates a temperament of this kind in his particular case. But the problems of the community require for their solution a much greater range of ability than mere proneness to use force. There needs to be patience and wisdom and understanding and willingness to use force only when necessary and with the recognition that of itself it solves few political problems except that of who is to be the boss.

Wisdom, patience, knowledge, honesty, determination, and as much tolerance as the circumstances allow, are needed in a leader if he is to solve the internal problems of a community. This combination of characteristics is such that he is less quick on the trigger than the narrow-minded leader who regards force as the sovereign method. Thus there exists a recurring predicament of politics: those most prone to use force are likely to get to the top of the political heap; those most prone to use force are likely to be ill fitted to discover the real needs of the community and their way of satisfaction.

The good of a great community today is dependent on a highly differentiated organization of people with specialized skills, knowledges, techniques, and tendencies to experiment. The crude use of decree and force is not suited to be the regulator of any such complex scheme. The authoritarian ruler, if he is to rely on the quick application of force for the control of specific activities and ideas, requires a more primitive and simpler organization in which decentralized discretion is at a minimum. Unfortunately the fact that an unjust authoritarian state may be effective in the narrow and limited purpose of preparing for war and waging war means that such a state—whatever its internal discord and inequities—is an intense danger to its more tolerant, fairer, and more just neighbors.

2. L'ÉTAT C'EST MOI

The state is the community in its political aspects—the going concern viewed in its relations of government and governed. The government is the power-wielding agency of the state. Historically the government constantly makes the error of confusing itself and its aims with those of the state and the community. The *l'état c'est moi*, attributed to Louis XIV of France, is a succinct statement of the error. Translated into today's ordinary terms it means "The government is the state."

This error of identification of the aims of the political community with the aims of the ruler is not confined to absolute monarchs. The same error is made by the government of a representative democracy when it takes the view that the will of the majority as expressed through its representatives must be obeyed—as in the case of the prohibition of alcoholic beverages in the United States. The same error is made by the ruler of a totalitarian state when, like Stalin or Hitler, he requires implicit obedience to his own will of the moment.

There is an ancient eastern idea that so long as a ruler (who may or may not have gained office in the first place by force) fulfills his principal function in meeting the real needs of his people he has, as a ruler, the Mandate of Heaven. When he fails in this function, he loses the mandate, and is no longer entitled to office. This view, although it would of course be stated much differently in modern western terms, is substantially correct today as well as in ancient times and is the opposite of the *l'état c'est moi* view. The authority of government is insecurely founded on force unless it is meeting the needs of the community—when it scarcely requires great force. The just powers of government are derived from the consent of the governed.

The *l'état c'est moi* error, in its overemphasis of the importance of the government in the home community, falls victim to a like overestimate of its importance in the general scheme of things and attributes enormously greater significance to the acts and words of the ruler than they can possibly possess. Our same Louis XIV said *"Il n'y a plus de Pyrénées,"* thinking that the circumstance of the accession of his grandson to the throne of Spain was capable of obliterating the political effect of the great geographical fact of the Pyrenees Mountains. In the 1940's there was a widespread American notion that President F. D. Roosevelt, by means of personal ingratiation with Stalin, might alter Russian foreign policies. But those policies were largely determined by a perennial shortage of rainfall in Russia. Like the Pyrenees Mountains, the Russian droughts had political effects not easily amenable to good personal relationships of heads of state.

The *l'état c'est moi* error may not do much harm to the community in practice when things happen to be going well. It is otherwise when times are difficult, and the government is baffled and confused. Then this error as to the place and significance of the government leads to a reliance on force and fiat to deal with obstinate dissenting elements in the community and with intractable dissenting ideas. The arbitrary government leaders—the Thaddeus Stevenses in the United States, the pre-Reformation Popes, can serve as types—may set themselves against the underlying forces in men's needs and motives, against the tides of hope and courage, as King Canute is said to have set himself against the rising tide of the Atlantic, bidding it recede.

3. RELATION OF FRAUD TO FORCE

No one will ever visualize as part of his own willing, worthwhile, and accepted role his knuckling under to a compulsion to do things he hates. Yet unless his government can somehow persuade the individual subject that its aims are correct, this yielding to compulsion is the necessity with which he is faced when he is ruled by a government that is maintaining an imposed order and perpetuating discord with the aid of force.

There are some typical methods by which governments attempt to persuade the governed that all is well, and to cover up the fact that the government is in fact failing to meet the needs of the time and place. The greater the degree of the substantive failure, the greater the need for the government, if it is to stay in office, to bolster itself with fraudulent claims of competence and success.

Even the Nazi leaders, with their overreliance on force and terror as normal political methods, saw the need of getting as much willing consent as they could. Their effort to gain the consent of their subjects took the form of promises to the discontented which they could not fulfill, and of a program appealing to powerful motives of self-esteem in the German people.

One aid to the temporary success of this kind of fraud is that people like to believe promises that they are going to be relieved of their fears or satisfied in their wants. Hitler knew the fear that his industrial leaders and his financiers had of communistic and leftist trends. So he promised them protection and privileges. He knew that his farmers disliked and feared the program and designs of organized labor. So he promised the farmers a sure place of honor and power in a regime especially honoring blood and the soil. He knew that workmen and laborers had been disappointed in their efforts to gain security by means of their organization or their strikes—as after all a strike does not produce plenty where in fact there are shortages. So he promised the laborers food and housing and recreation in a program honoring and recognizing their place in German life. Army leaders were distressed by Germany's powerlessness in a world of armed enemies. So he promised the military men a return of German military power. Each discontented group wanted to believe the promise addressed to its particular predicament and hope, and was mesmerized to become for the time being a follower of the promiser.

People like and need to follow a leader, as they thereby gain a sense of security and a rule to go by. As the leader is aware both of this and of the tendency to believe bright promises, he can make unscrupulous use of the combination. We have already noted that it is the common case—seen often in the young—that a man, impressed with the real injustices he sees around him, jumps to the wholly unwarranted conclusion that some particular reform scheme (which he eagerly identifies as the embodiment of his hopes and ideals) will be a step towards greater justice. He just doesn't have the intelligence or the experience to see whether or not this really will be so in fact.

Another aid to the temporary success of fraud in covering up the failure of a government to hit upon the substantive answers to the problems of the community is sought in appeals to the pride and self-esteem of the governed. This may result in their closing their eyes for the time being to the actual situation in which they find themselves. To see yourself in the clear light of truth as one of a group eating too meager meals is much less satisfactory than to see yourself as one of a glorious group eating too meager meals but only against the day when your just claims will be recognized by all and you will eat square meals. The need of a good self-estimate is so powerful that it can be persuaded to seize on almost any kind of alleged superiority, irrespective of the real facts or real possibilities.

Here again, the Nazi leaders utilized this powerful motive—the need for self-esteem—to try to make their subjects satisfied with the Nazi government. They deluded their followers into the belief that the latter were by nature a superior and master people, a *Herrenvolk,* entitled for the good of themselves and the world to oppress and boss everyone else. At home in Germany this view encouraged a cruel savagery towards racial minorities, and abroad created a fear and hatred that eventually brought physical destruction upon German cities and industry and the political dismemberment of the fatherland.

Had the Nazis won dominion over Europe and put into practice their *Herrenvolk* ideal and their political method of terror, the peoples of Europe would have been subjected to an arbitrary harsh rule that while fearful to contemplate might at least have had the advantage of demonstrating for future ages the failures and miseries of a government by force and fraud. Historians have sometimes spoken of the Middle Ages as a long period of convalescence—with many relapses —from the worst catastrophe of the Western World. Had the Nazis conquered Europe, there would have been another great catastrophe and the need perhaps for another period of convalescence after the Nazi disease had been thrown off. The earlier catastrophe was one of political fragmentation and disorder; the second would have been one of evil and discordant order.

Another method used for gaining consent of the governed to the aims of the ruler is through the organization and activities of youth movements, in which those who are young and impressionable, both boys and girls, are indoctrinated with the ideals decided upon by the government. The drills, songs, and lessons of the Hitler Youth were designed to inculcate implicit obedience to the leader and conviction of the superiority of the Germans as a master people. The movement was successful in turning out an unusually harsh, intolerant, unpleasant, and smug lot of youngsters, short on independence and self-reliance.

War with an outsider or the fear of such a war is sometimes used by a government as an excuse for suppressing those who see the need for internal reform. We noted this in connection with some of the extreme measures in Paris during the French Revolution. The same excuse was certainly utilized by Hitler in Germany and by Stalin in Russia to justify the suppression of political critics. It is tempting for a government or a group promoting a particular program to discredit its critics by identifying them with unpopular foreign views—which they very likely do not in reality represent—and then denouncing them or subjecting them to public obloquy.

When a government is failing to meet the needs of its subjects, it is aware that there will be potential leaders of opinion who will want to put forward new political ideas, new theories of government, all with a view to practical changes in the unsatisfactory current regime. To cut down the spread of these ideas which threaten its continuance in power, the regime relies on censorship of the press, of lectures, and of other means of communication of ideas, such as the radio and television. Such censorship is accompanied by the positive control of as many media as possible for propagating the approved ideas of the government. This method of suppression of reform ideas and sentiment we pointed out in nineteenth-century Germany, in the pre-Reformation Church, in Czechoslovakia in the nineteen-forties, and in Hitlerian Germany. It is a usual feature of efforts to bolster the use of force in situations where willing consent of large portions of the governed is wanting.

Today the concealment of facts and ideas as a prop to government is conspicuously seen in the Union of Soviet Socialist Republics. The government is fearful of the effect on its subjects of possible free inquiry and discussion, or of a factual comparison of conditions at home with those abroad. The regime therefore maintains the so-called iron curtain, a censorship to exclude from any part of the Union data about the outside world—data which might permit dissenting leaders to point out the relative misery of living conditions and lack of freedom within the Soviet Republics as compared with those of other countries, especially in Western Europe and the Americas.

4. GOVERNMENT BY BLAME AND PRESTIGE

None of these fraudulent aids to force—whether on the positive side of promoting specious aims and misrepresenting facts or the negative side of suppression of ideas and concealment of facts—is addressed, any more than the force itself, to a real solution of the ills of the community. These ills remain uncured. The unfulfilled promises of the government prove insufficient to gain the consent of the governed. So the government finds itself obliged to turn to some method of shifting from itself the blame for its failures and for the continued discord in the community.

This method consists of an assertion that the head of the central government is without error or mistake, but that agents of his government or various local governments in direct daily contact with the discontented subjects are at fault either by way of failure to carry out properly the correct aims and orders of the central government or by way of deliberate sympathy for unorthodox ideas or action, including those of foreign nations. Or as a variant, some particular group—like the Jews in Nazi Germany—is denounced as the malicious source of the troubles of the community.

The object of this method is to maintain the prestige of the head of the government and his immediate circle by loud assertions of virtue and infallibility, and to concentrate blame for mistakes on someone else who is not in fact at fault.

This form of deceiving the public is of course of no value in correcting the ills of the community. Even in the minds of those who use the method—although they may sometimes deceive themselves as well as the public—its purpose is to assign blame.

In our discussion of the troubles of the late Roman Empire we saw the method of government by blame and prestige at work. The inhabitants of the municipalities were induced to believe that their hardships were due to the municipal officials, although the real but unrecognized cause of the extremely heavy servitudes and taxes was the policies of the emperor. Petitions were made by the inhabitants to the emperor for relief from the acts of the local officials who were in truth nothing but helpless intermediaries for the transmission to the governed of the burdens resulting from the mistakes of the imperial government.

The conspicuous modern example of blame and prestige as methods of propping up government is to be found in the top Russian leadership. When something goes fundamentally wrong in some part of the soviet system or among the border puppet states, this leadership promptly selects for denunciation and punishment some prominent local leader, attributing to his alleged errors or disloyalty the blame for a failure in fact due to the mistaken policies of the heads of the regime.

After the Communist coup in Czechoslovakia which we described in connection with the use of force to seize authority, the Russian government became the dominant influence in Czechoslovakian affairs, much as the German government had earlier wielded major influence in the Sudeten area. In the pushing of its own military needs and in the effort to cure its own perennial shortages, Russia took out from Czechoslovakia in manufactured goods and raw materials much more than she put back in any form whatever. The Czechoslovak economy, as we saw, while potentially reasonably well balanced was suffering from a loss of much of its skilled personnel and from the disruption of its normal external trade. The added Russian demands could only spell hardship and increasing poverty. This would naturally be attributed by the inhabitants to the new Communist regime and the combined influences of Communism and control by Soviet Russia. So the blame and prestige formula was called upon by the leaders in Moscow to save their names and that of Communism. In September 1951 the Moscow trainee Slansky, presumably a good loyal Communist doing his best, was deposed from his position as the General Secretary of the Communist party in Czechoslovakia. In January 1952, things still going badly, Minister for National Security Kopriva went the same way. The substantive troubles in Czechoslovakia were attributed to the lack of socialist vigilance of these local officials, rather than to the true causes, the burdensome demands of Russia and the inadequacies of totalitarian policy and control.

Governmental use of the formula of blame and prestige affords no more satisfactory solution of discord in the community than is afforded by any other of the fraudulent aids of force, because no more than they is it addressed to the substantive ills from which the community is suffering.

5. FRAUDULENT AIDS TO FORCE ARE A SIGN OF DISCORD

The use by a government of these fraudulent aids to force, like the use or the threat of the force itself, affords a sure indication to observers that there is discord within the community. That is to say, censorship of the press and other forms of communication or prohibition of popular or student meetings, or the isolation of citizens from outside data and contacts, or the use of any other of the devices we have described as aids to bolster governmental force, wherever we find them extensively relied upon, lead us to the conclusion that serious discord is present.

6. LOSS OF TALENTS

Within any actual historical community there is only a given amount of ability available, only a certain number of talented and creative people. This is a biological limiting factor on what that particular community can achieve. Each community needs to use all available talent. Otherwise it will fail in the realization of what it can achieve, adding a man-made limitation to that already imposed by nature.

Force as the principal means of maintaining order insures the loss of talents needed by the community. The very object of the force is the suppression of capable people. Instead of winning them over to the service of the community, the government eliminates them and their talents.

In the late seventeenth century the French government, by a series of harassing practices such as billeting rowdy soldiers in the homes of the Protestant Huguenots, and allowing abuses against their persons and property, succeeded in getting rid of this minority group in the French body politic. But the loss of the Huguenot talents was an immense loss to France. These people in numbers reaching the hundreds of thousands fled abroad and greatly contributed to the communities where they took up residence, as in England, Switzerland, the Netherlands, and in the eastern seaboard of America, furnishing invaluable contributions to the civic, business, intellectual, and artistic life of their new homelands. In the United States alone those with Huguenot ancestry have occupied the presidency five times, among them Washington and the Adamses; have been prominent in government, as Jay and Hamilton; in art and in science; and also in literature, as the poet Longfellow.

In our own time, in the matter of competence in making war, the German and Italian governments by the expulsion from their harsh regimes of leading but independent-minded and nonconforming mathematicians and scientists, harmed themselves and aided the United States in the development of new and powerful weapons.

Unfortunately today, as the methods of government by force have become more cruel, the loss of talents has been too often not only to the home community but to the world. The Fascist way with talented dissent was all too likely to be death, both in Germany and then in other countries which as allies of the Nazis came under their control. When the victorious Americans came into Rome towards the close of the Second World War, they had an opportunity to study and document the Nazi instigated murder of able young Italian leaders—the dispatch from this life of the good, the capable, and the independent.

The elimination by totalitarian governments of dissenting talent is a process of negative selection, weeding out from their ranks not the weeds, but superior stock.

Elements of greatness and strength shown by the United States in its first hundred years were in large part due to the independent-mindedness and determination of political and religious dissidents and refugees who chose to go their own way in a new land rather than continue to put up with unfair and unjust rule in their homelands. Yet it is precisely this type of individual—so useful to the community in whatever he sets his hand to—that the authoritarian ruler eliminates in the interest of maintaining his own regime.

Fortunately for the ultimate prospects of the community, it is hard for a despot to succeed in gaining permanent uniformity and docility in the community. Courage and curiosity keep being born anew. The curious man questions the validity of what he is being told. The courageous man risks punishment and death to overcome the obstacles between him and the goal he sees. It is not only the wise and the good whom the authoritarian has to fear. There are in every community a considerable number of people who by reason of their upbringing, or innate temperament, tend to be cranky and contrary to established authority. Some of these people will be intelligent—perhaps Rousseau was such a man. When the ruler happens to be wrong in his aims and methods—which, as we have seen, is often the case with rulers who mainly rely on force and fraud—these dissentients, with the truth behind them, may well be an effective reform force.

The dissenting individuals and groups that keep rising into being are too disintegrating an influence to be tolerated in the rigid authoritarian system, where the government rules by an imposed rule. So the ruler is involved in an endless task of suppression. He feels his vulnerability to people and to facts that do not accord with his regime. He must continue to shout his infallibility and shoot his opponents.

The government trying to cure discord by force, not only suffers the loss of the talents of those whom it suppresses, exiles, or kills, but also wastes the energies of its own leadership in suspicions of rivals, plots, and counterplots. Where the rule is by force and not by custom or law, each holder or contestant for office is compelled to direct a great part of his time and energy to protect himself against the plots of rivals and in the laying of schemes which will enable him either to get or to keep office.

This misapplication of energy which ought to be applied to the substantive problems of the community but is instead applied to problems of how to become boss or stay boss or be in the good graces of the boss is specially characteristic of regimes based on force and is an additional reason why such regimes are ill suited to effect a cure of discord. The fact of this kind of misapplication of energy in plots and suspicions was demonstrated in the disorder of the French Revolution. We have also seen it in our own times in the course of seizure of authority by force, in Spain, in Czechoslovakia, and in some Latin American states. We have also seen it in the cases of maintaining authority by force in the Soviet Union and in Nazi Germany. In the meantime the complex real requirements of the social, economic, religious, scientific, literary, and artistic life of the community have been neglected. The only real need—and it is an important one—likely to be carefully tended to by an arbitrary government is the need of national defense. The control of force at home goes hand in hand with the maintenance of powerful force on the international scene, in the possible hope of making up by conquest for failures in productivity at home.

If an arbitrary government succeeds in holding power for a long time and continues to discourage independent decentralized local leadership, a lack of self-reliance may result that can take a long time to cure. The condition of the Balkan peoples after centuries of arbitrary Turkish rule is an instance of this kind of legacy from a long period of unresolved discord under a government which relied on force as its method for curing discord, and so never in fact succeeded in effecting a cure.

VI. The Essence of Discord

EACH group—as well as each individual—in the community needs the law or a rule, because for the purpose of coherent community life people have to know where they stand in relation to one another and to be able to count upon the meaning of one another's acts and words. A community without rules would, with the best of intentions and the best of good will, be completely disorganized and unable to do its work.

An example of a rule willingly accepted for the sake of getting things done is to be found in contract law. You and I agree to rules of law controlling our business relations, because then we know what we can do in reliance on one another's words and what the words mean in their business context. We do not misunderstand each other's rights and duties. We are then free each to do our part of the bargain. I do not have to worry about taking moves to get ahead of you or to forestall you lest you do the same to me. We have a rule which we have agreed upon, and to interpret and enforce which we have set up courts. Each of us is freed for untrammeled effort by virtue of the rule of law which we have accepted and by which we are bound. The rule has been instituted by us or by those with like problems and interests, for the governing of this kind of relation.

We consent to rules for the enforcement of our promised performance or for damages in case of a breach of contract. This is not because either of us expects or wants to break our word, but because sad experience has taught that there is a small minority of fraudulent contractors, and because even when we both wish to be completely honest—the usual case—it is a practical support to our intentions and our reliance on each other to have them fortified by this kind of rule. The supremacy of law in addition to providing the certainty of a rule to go by is a protector of each of us against our own unjust suspicions and their consequence in unfair acts of overreaching one another.

What is true of contract law is true of the law generally. The law is a set of rules which helps people know where they stand, what is expected of them, and what they can expect of others. The rule of law willingly accepted is a positive advantage to every member of the community in that it frees him for constructive effort and saves him from unnecessary conflicts and misunderstandings with his fellows. A man willingly accepts the rule of law as long as he feels that he has fair scope for his talents and his energies within the rule and that his scope is on the whole greater within the rule than it would be without it.

Needs for reform and change may be recognized, even when there is active and willing consent to the general scheme and the basic law and rules of the community. This, as we saw in the Introduction, is the usual and normal situation. There is no insuperable discord present as long as there is a good prospect of effecting needed reforms within the constitutional and legal tradition of the state.

1. A DEFINITION OF DISCORD

In contrast to the willing acceptance of the rule of law, which is characteristic of a free community, we can see that in all the cases of failure to reconcile reform efforts which we have described, there has been no willing consent to the rule of the regime, and there has been no reasonable prospect of bringing about needed reform through the traditional and permitted political methods. Those who dissent from the regime are held in line only because they see no chance of trying any practical way out. This is discord.

The leaders in various lines of activity in the community find that their activities are no longer mainly self-determined. Instead of free willing effort there is unwilling effort under imposed control and direction by the government or other ruling group. This is discord.

Consider again the situation of distress which existed in the United States of America in the great economic depression of the nineteen-thirties which had been precipitated by the abuses of the credit structure under the banking mismanagement of the late twenties. This situation of distress could be attacked in the political area by traditional constitutional methods. Leaders of independent opinion could get a following sufficient to turn the current government out of office and elect one pledged to reform. The capable and misused citizens saw that they had available a practical and peaceful way out of the distress. As long as means are present within the current constitutional order for attempting substantial reform, there is no incurable discord.

In every community there is always need for reform and re-reform for the better. If that can be attempted in a peaceable manner with recognition of the important needs of the various groups in the community, there is no discord.

2. A PROBLEM OF POLITICS

In contrast to a rule willingly accepted, and also in contrast to the absence of any known rule in acute disorder, an orderly discord is marked in the typical case by a rule known all too well and resented if not feared and hated. People know where they're at and don't like it. There is imposed unjust order, repression, and arbitrary rule. There is an undue and overlong perpetuation of the need for reform. This is discord.

If in any actual community it were true that there were a significant number of capable people who by character and disposition were unable to agree in practice on the basic rules for the conduct of community life, that community could not be set up on a free basis with a constitution permitting individual liberty. Freedom would simply mean constant conflict. The community would, for the sake of establishment of the necessary minimum order, find itself engaged in struggles for power until such time as an authoritarian regime succeeded in establishing an imposed order.

A basic question of politics is whether one can believe in freedom and self-control as the best political method, or on the other hand must conclude that in the long run and in most communities force must be the main political method. The answer is determined by whether one believes that enough people in the community are good enough—both on grounds of intelligence and of disposition—to give a lead in the way of tolerance, honesty, equity, and truth to fact such that government by consent can work. The possibility of a free order depends on the presence of give and take in the leaders all along the line, and a willingness to abide by rules as long as they remain on the whole fair and reasonable.

Otherwise, no matter how good the government might be in trying to fulfill its proper functions and meet the real needs of the time and place, there would constantly arise ambitious leaders of discontented followers, incapable of finding the right substantive answers for the community. As these leaders could not be dealt with by persuasion, they would have to be dealt with by force.

As we shall see later in this book, there have been historically enough periods of freedom in the government of communities to let us avoid the conclusion that force is destined to be the universal political method in the constitution and maintenance of the state. One problem of politics which we are trying to solve is to determine what are the characteristics which leaders of the various lines of activity within the community must have if government by way of consent of the governed and a free flow of the constructive energies of the governed is to be possible. So far we have been inquiring into situations of discord, where government by way of consent has been absent or has failed and where the free flow of constructive energies within the community has been interfered with by a rule of force or of fraud. The purpose of this inquiry has been to get clear in our minds the kinds of situations, motives, temperaments, and dispositions which lead into severe discord, in the hope that we will thereby be aided in discovering the kind of situations, motives, temperaments, and dispositions which might produce a free order with a maximum of self-rule and a minimum of imposed rule.

VII. Kinds of Discord to Which Specific Governments Are Prone

1. SOME CLUES TO THE TYPE OF DISCORD

In the cases of discord which we have investigated there are useful clues to the kind of discord to which any specific contemporary state today is particularly liable, and the kind of government likely to be associated with a particular kind of claim to office.

One of these clues is to be found in the desires and ideas of those on whom the government officials depend for getting and keeping office. Who is the effective electorate and for what do they stand? For example, Britain in the late eighteenth and early nineteenth centuries had a representative government with a limited franchise heavily weighted in favor of landowners and the rising industrialists, both characterized by an overstrict valuation of the rights of their own property. The resulting discord was an overreaching of the labor force, the period of "the dark, Satanic mills," and an unconscionable exploitation of child labor. At a much earlier date we saw that the aims and the policies of the late Roman emperors were limited by the fact that their effective electorate consisted of the legions—an ignorant lot of provincials interested mainly in their own pay and with no idea of where the hope and strength of the Empire lay. The emperors, reflecting this character of those on whom they depended for office and without being aware of the fatal effects of their own actions, crushed the creative and constructive elements in the empire under a burden of ill-devised services and ill-laid taxes.

Another clue to the likely kind of discord—a clue closely related to that found in the characteristics of the effective electorate—is to be found in the qualities needed for getting and holding office in a particular state, because this determines the quality of its officeholders and their probable dominant abilities. We saw examples of this principle in states where, after the traditional government had proved unsatisfactory and unable to meet its problems, there was in the resulting confusion a premium on the use of force in coming to the top. Such cases were those of Spain in the nineteen-thirties or Czechoslovakia in the nineteen-forties or France in the seventeen-nineties. The qualities needed to get and keep office were ruthlessness and speed on the trigger, and the corresponding type of discord consisted of suppression of independent views and abilities and the extermination of political opponents, with the predictable failure to solve the substantive problems of the community. The qualities needed for getting and keeping office were irrelevant to the underlying needs of the community.

A third clue to the probable direction of discord lies in the main interests and ideas of the time and place, because this determines the likely line along which the errors of a bad government will be pushed, the aspect which the particular discord will show. For example, when religious interests and beliefs occupied a greater share of people's and governments' attention than they happen to do today, monarchs fortified themselves with one or another aspect of the doctrine of the divine right of kings. In this way the monarch and his government circle tried to enhance their own power and prestige as against other claimants to political power in the community. We recall the conflicts of Church and Monarch in the Middle Ages. The kingship, as well as the priesthood, was divinely instituted. As Philip the Fair put it in the course of his controversy with Pope Boniface VIII: "Before there were any priests, the King of France had the care of his kingdom and could make laws for it."

Sometimes, when the king was not of an old line, but he or his family had come to power recently—the ancient counterpart of a Stalin or a Hitler—the theory was that the office itself of the king was divinely appointed, so that whoever held the royal office derived his authority directly from God. At another time, when the king's party thought they could trace the current king's lineage to an ancient royal ancestor—as James VI of Scotland and James I of England claiming descent from William the Conqueror—the doctrine might be strengthened by the claim that the particular king in his own person derived authority from God by way of inheritance from some earlier king whose divine authority was assumed to have been valid—the theory of hereditary divine right.

In these cases of the divine right of the king himself or of his office the consent of the governed or the ability and fitness of the king to rule were beside the point. Discord in the community was characterized by a pushing of arbitrary royal authority under the alleged sponsorship of God's will and guidance. *L'état c'est moi* error was compounded by the *Moi, je suis le bon Dieu* error.

2. LIKELY ERRORS OF SELF-PERPETUATING GOVERNMENTS

In Russia today there is a government by a self-perpetuating clique, relying—like Hitler's government—on a tight discipline amongst the top leaders of a relatively small party for its maintenance in power. As there is no freedom of discussion or the prospect that goes with it of rallying a political opposition, the fear of being turned out of office arises elsewhere. It arises from secret plots by ambitious members of this same leadership group just below the top and within close reach of it or from secret plots by some group of dissatisfied regional leaders within the Soviet Union. With regard to popular support, such as it is, the government looks to the cities and the industrial workers, as the leadership regards the building of heavy industry as a key Russian need. The main interests of the time in Russia are an increased production of war equipment, and eventually an increased production of consumer goods.

Even from this oversimplified abstraction of Russian governmental facts, the likely errors and direction of discord can be seen; and these are in fact the errors which have characterized Russian government in the mid-twentieth century. In the first place there is the *l'état c'est moi* error—the overestimate of what the government can achieve by decree and regulation. There flows from this the economic inefficiency resulting from overcontrol by political leaders who have been selected for office by reason of their ruthlessness, or of their devotion to the party tenets, or to their shrewdness of maneuver in the "court circle." None of these qualities—however necessary for getting or keeping office in such a regime—bear any significant relation to competence in managing industry, or transport, or agriculture, on a realistic or efficient basis. There is an overreaching of the farmers and of the farming areas of the country in the interests of the city and of the industrial workers. By centering attention on war preparation a formidable military establishment can be created, but at the expense of severe strains elsewhere in the overcentralized economic structure.

As the leadership is antireligious and with no god except that of power, art and literature under the rigid government censorship are utilitarian and directed to the practical furtherance of the political aims of the regime. As such a regime relies on imposed central rule rather than individual and local self-rule, it continues to require the services of a secret political police for the location and suppression of the dissent which has always arisen in a state of this autocratic type. In Russia the location of this potential dissent is notably in the farming regions. It will also be likely to turn up amongst capable industrialists who see how much more effectively they could do both in their own behalf and in that of the public generally if they could rid themselves of the cumbersome interferences of government officials and bureaus. There are also certain to continue to be many individuals who will see clearly enough the defects of the regime.

As long as the political police is able to imprison, banish to outlying regions, or shoot active dissenters, reform will be held in abeyance and severe discord will continue. The very purpose of such a political police is to forestall the coming into existence of any "effective electorate" wider than that of the party leadership and its party members carefully tested for fanatical loyalty and devotion to the regime and its tenets.

Despite Russia's internal stresses and the likelihood of severe continuing discord, the Soviet Union has a great military power. There is more than a sufficiency of natural resources—with the important exception of food—resources which even inefficient transportation can bring to the building of a great war machine. This military might constitutes a dangerous threat to other states in the world. It is specially dangerous to those who may either themselves suffer from internal discord and indecision, or else be asleep to the danger of a power-seeking, food-seeking state.

3. LIKELY ERRORS OF REPRESENTATIVE DEMOCRACIES

States which have a representative form of government and a universal secret franchise, so that all inhabitants of age are entitled to vote for their political representatives, have their own characteristic tendencies to discord. One of these discord factors lies in the liability of such a state to a multiplicity of political parties representing many divergent groups whose social and political aims are at cross-purposes.

In France today there are a number of divergent political parties, each with representatives in the legislature who reflect the various shades of opinion of their constituencies. After the Second World War this multiplicity of parties paralyzed French administration. Under the constitution of the Fourth Republic the executive government—the ministry—could be turned out of office by a majority vote in the National Assembly. On the eve of the fall of the Fourth Republic—in 1958—the approximately 600 members of the Assembly were divided into a dozen parties, plus or minus one or two, depending on how affiliations are counted. Of these parties the Communists, with 142 representatives, were the largest. A ministry was obviously dependent for its tenure of office on a coalition of multiparty support. Party alignments kept changing in the jockeying of the various party leaders for power and ministerial office. As a result the executive government kept being overthrown as their coalition majorities in the Assembly failed. Coherent governmental policy in these circumstances of rapidly changing governments was extremely difficult and sometimes impossible to achieve, as French governmental vacillation and weakness in both domestic and foreign affairs showed.

The constitutional reforms of General De Gaulle put great powers in the President of the Fifth Republic, including the possibility of dictatorial power in emergency. The President appointed the "government"—the Prime Minister and Ministers. Provisions which made more difficult the forced resignation of ministries rendered the government much less vulnerable to parliamentary overturn. The fiscal and debt-incurring powers of the legislature were cut down.

Whether these reforms will result in the necessary degree of order and coherence in French politics remains to be seen. There may be a future shift towards even greater executive strength at the expense of the Assembly, or on the other hand towards a temporary cutting down of the executive power. If the latter, France, in the absence of thoroughgoing reform of her system of multiparty representation, will return to political instability.

A state with a free and secret universal franchise may, like any other state, have a fundamental cleavage of leadership opinion in a matter vital to the functioning of the community. In such a state the government may still be able to govern effectively, despite the basic cleavage of opinion, if there is no multiplicity of parties on whom the executive is dependent for office and if there is a habit of political orderliness and tolerance so that the minority is willing at least for the time being to follow the lead of the majority. Such a state is England today. The cleavage of opinion is between those who believe in state ownership—government management and control—of heavy industry and public utilities and those who believe in private ownership—decentralized independent management and control. There are only two major political parties, and these represent the two sides of this cleavage. Whichever group is for the time being in the minority, its representatives then out of executive government office, is in basic opposition to the policies of the majority and the government. There is bound to be an uncertainty about the organization of industry in the future which has a hampering effect on some lines of long-term economic endeavor. Nevertheless the tradition of orderly processes is strong, and England has not yet seen in recent times any seizures of political power or overturning of her usual political procedures by extremist leaders and followings of either the right or the left.

It is for the future to disclose whether such an atmosphere of political tolerance can be maintained, despite a basic cleavage of opinion, long enough for a peaceful solution of the differences in an economic doctrine and political rule acceptable to all.

The United States today happens not to have any basic cleavage of opinion represented by political parties of great size and strength. The leaders of the two main parties, the Democrats and the Republicans, profess to believe in private ownership and control of the instruments of production. Nor is there any acute religious difference reflected in political party lines. The economic and social differences between North and South which brought about the Civil War and then resulted in the severe discord of the period of southern reconstruction, while still leaving a legacy of bitterness in the "Solid South," no longer threaten the vital functioning of the whole community. Differences between agrarian and industrial interests are not such as to seem insoluble by the normal methods of traditional American politics and a spirit of mutual give and take.

Despite this freedom from a multiplicity of parties and also from bitter partisan conflict, the United States shows certain tendencies towards possible discord which may be inherent in the universal franchise as such, and need to be guarded against.

As in England, so in the United States but not to such a great degree, there has been a strong trend towards economic equalitarianism and the leveling of incomes by means of a graduated income tax with increasing rates in the higher brackets of income. The kind of likely discord in this procedure is that of restiveness and possible radical reform attempts on the part of capable individuals who believe that they could do better both by themselves and by the community if allowed to retain their income and apply it to building their own businesses or pursuing their own interests in accordance with their own ideas. As yet this danger seems remote, because the government has not imposed either tax burdens so great or inefficient centralized controls so great as to prevent the constructive and productive efforts of the able and ambitious.

The tendency towards equalitarianism in the United States was much speeded as a sequel to the financial crash and crisis of credit in the late nineteen-twenties and the great economic depression in the early nineteen-thirties. This economic breakdown was largely caused by the fact that the leading positions in the financial field had fallen into the hands of those who allowed their greed to overmaster their discretion. The business leaders had shown themselves incapable of controlling or modifying the traditional business institutions so as to avoid a widespread public hardship which was entirely unnecessary as far as the substantive wealth of the country was concerned. This was an undoubted evil that the electorate had actually experienced and they were justified in condemning the leaders and institutional practices which had brought it about.

A principal object of good government is to have the community so organized that the best abilities wherever they exist in the community can come to the fore and function to the greatest benefit of the community. If this is achieved, the thwarting of abilities which is a common cause of discord is likely to be reduced to a minimum. One danger of equality as an overriding political aim lies in its tendency to hamper or to actually strike down the possessors of these best abilities when they occur in the economic field. This is because everyone appreciates and wants a big share of economic goods, and because it is easy to make the error that one way to get this result is to take from those who have much and distribute to those who have little— a piece of verbal oversimplification that apparently satisfies a large part of some democratic electorates.

Equality of opportunity is an excellent aim and one that is necessary if the community is to succeed in finding and utilizing those who are most talented. Equality of opportunity is denied by poverty, and so requires the elimination of poverty. Equality in fair and just treatment is due from man to his fellows and avoids bitterness and hatred in social relations. Equality before the law—fair and impartial application to all of the current rules of the time and place—is necessary both to aid equality of opportunity and to avoid that kind of discord arising from anger and frustration at human favoritism and injustice.

Equality of condition is a nonconstructive aim. It is the inequalities, the exceptional abilities, which need to be given their freedom to produce the instruments and the institutional devices that improve opportunity for everyone. Even equality of opportunity is drastically limited in actual life and fact by those natural inequalities of talent and of health which have been in the past and still appear to be a part of nature's scheme, perhaps someday to be lessened through discoveries in genetics—discoveries which if they are made will be made by the exceptionally capable, those endowed with more than their equal share of intelligence and persistence.

Some candidates for office in a universal franchise state advocate equality of condition as an aim. It is an aim agreeable to many voters who are envious of their minority of better-situated neighbors. The office seeker seeks these votes. They may be his effective electorate. The situation is reminiscent of that in Rome when the aims of aspirants for the office of emperor tended to gravitate to the level of aims satisfactory to and understood by their effective electorate, the legions.

The long-term avoidance of discord in free, democratic states as well as in authoritarian states is dependent on the establishment of political habits and institutions which maximize the opportunity of the able, the intelligent, and the good to come to the fore in their various lines of endeavor.

4. THE PERENNIAL CHANGE OF UNSATISFACTORY GOVERNMENTS

Our study of political discord has shown that in the course of human events one major occupation of the capable has been the reform or overthrow of unsatisfactory governments. The usual percursor of basic political change or political decline within the state has been an undue cramping of the opportunities of too many of the capable members of the community. The new governments have in their turn sooner or later become unsatisfactory and burdensome, their power being abused or misapplied, and they themselves have been reformed or overthrown. It is from this cycle of ever unsatisfactory governments that we wish to escape.

The main long-term result of the reform of a method of government has sometimes been obscured by the many details of the specific historical instances. It may now be useful to state in general terms, abstracted from the many facts we have discussed in detail, the upshot of the reform process in some of the cases we have discussed.

The abuses, misapplications of power, and mistakes of a great autocracy have resulted in its disintegration into a system of local rule by local lords—the feudal system and lack of system.

The capable have built up and used the power of a king in order to break the abused and misapplied power of the feudal nobles.

The capable by a widened franchise have built up and used the power of an electorate to break the abused and misapplied power of a king.

Today in some states the capable have before them the problem of how to break the abuses and misapplications of power of the electorate as expressed through its political representatives.

In some communities a totalitarian, single-party scheme of government has been tried as a means of gaining the support of opinion of the whole community and of avoiding the conflicts and inefficiencies of many bitterly divergent parties. But these totalitarian single-party states have themselves been conspicuous examples of abuses and misapplications of power, particularly along the very lines which are precursors of change or decline, the suppression of too many of the capable members of the community.

The movement in the eighteenth century known as the Enlightenment, a rational spirit of enquiry and criticism, was a great factor in the successful effort to break away from arbitrary royal government. Yet the upshot of the Enlightenment, by way of the French Revolution, was only a new European despotism, that of Napoleon.

Nationalism—the presence of a strong self-conscious state with a sense of its own destiny—has been used to break the abuses of some wider power. Nationalism was used at the time of the Reformation to help break the Roman Catholic power. Nationalism was used to help break the power of Napoleon. Yet nationalism, so useful in the protection of local liberties, has sometimes become a powerful instrument for building up despotic totalitarian power in government leaders in the name of measures for defense of the community against neighboring states.

Mankind is engaged in a never-ending quest to find good government. From time to time various institutions are invented or rediscovered and utilized to beat down the hindrances of some particular bad government. Then the new arrangement proves unsatisfactory, and again people look around for some effective means to get rid of the unsatisfactory rule.

This cycle of perennially unsatisfactory governments suggests that important as political form may be—democracy or monarchy or dictatorship, rule by the few or rule by the many—the answer to the problem does not lie solely or even mainly in the field of political form. The character, ideas, and intelligence of the government are as important as the formal means by which it has come to office, holds its power, and is recognized. The answer is at least as likely to lie along lines of political attitudes and habits as along lines of political form. The political form and the institutions of a state are of course of great importance as an aid or hindrance to right and useful political attitudes and habits of the government leaders and of the leaders among the governed.

VIII. Secession

THE motives which produce discord within a community may produce attempted secession by one part of the community from the rest with a view to setting up an independent political community—a new state—under its own government. This attempt is likely when the basic division of interests in the community more or less coincides with economically self-sufficient geographical regions, so that the region wishing to secede is capable of self-maintenance.

1. ATTEMPTED SECESSION OF THE SOUTHERN STATES FROM THE UNITED STATES

In the United States of America, in the fifty years before the Civil War of 1861 to 1865, a basic cleavage of interests had come to exist between the South with its agricultural, mainly cotton-producing, plantation society dependent upon the institution of Negro slavery, and the North with a mixed agricultural, commercial, and industrial economy and a system of free labor. The northern states were prospering in an economic sense more than the southern, and this growth in economic strength of the North was accompanied by a corresponding decline of the power of the southern leaders in the affairs of the nation.

The institution of Negro slavery was standing in the way of southern industrial and social progress and was really rendering the entire South—whites and Negroes alike—slave to the demands of a one-crop, one-method economy. And yet the southern leadership seemed to lack the ingenuity to reform the institution. The capital of the South was too much tied up in slaves. This fact, in view of the comparative inefficiency of slave labor in most lines, impeded industrial development. The large cotton planters, though relatively few in number, had the wealth and constituted the ruling group in the South. Like many of the ruling groups in the *discord* cases, they held too tight for too long to the system they knew, although it was a system injurious to their own South and to the South's place in the United States.

From the earliest days of the American union the question of recognition and extension of slavery had posed a difficult problem. In order to get South Carolina and Georgia to come into the union at its inception, it had been necessary to protect for twenty years the right to import slaves from abroad. And to offset the fact that the southern slaves were chattels and not citizens, the relative strength of the South in the national legislature was protected by apportioning representatives on a basis of population computed by adding three-fifths of the number of slaves to the entire number of free persons.

As time went on, the population of the North increased more rapidly than that of the South—perhaps in part because immigrants were unwilling to settle in the South where they would be faced with the competition of slave labor—so that the North acquired a relatively greater representation in the national House of Representatives. But the number of states, and hence of Senators—two to a state—was evenly balanced. It seemed evident that as new states were added to the union from time to time, the influence of the South in national politics would be directly related to whether these states were slave states, and so tending by economic interest to be aligned with the southern point of view, or free states and aligned with the North. A variant of this same issue was that of whether federal territories not yet admitted to statehood be slave or free. Although several compromises were tried, no solution of the issue of extension of slavery was ever devised which proved satisfactory to North and South alike.

The conflict of interest between the sections over slavery was aggravated by other differences which bore a more or less direct relation to slavery and the southern agricultural system. The southern economy was dependent on the export of cotton and the import of goods bought with the proceeds of the cotton. The South as a section would therefore be injured by a tariff on imports enacted by the national legislature to protect northern industries, as this would raise the price to the South of manufactured goods they must buy. The fear of such a tariff was one of the reasons why the South was apprehensive about possible northern control of the United States Senate.

On the northern side, so great was the bogey of increased southern political power through extension of slavery that many northern leaders saw in the 1845 annexation of Texas to the United States and in the Mexican War of 1846–48 nothing so much as steps in a deliberate southern plot to extend slavery at the expense of the North.

The southern justification of their "peculiar institution" was stiff-
ened and reform rendered more difficult as a result of southern resentment against northern publicists who pressed with every device of
propaganda, truthful and untruthful, for the immediate abolition of
slavery, painting a picture of it in terms of exaggerated cruelty and
horror. The northern abolition movement was marred by a mixture
of extreme intolerance and extreme self-righteousness, perhaps representing in part a defense mechanism—notably in Massachusetts—
against self-condemnation on account of the facts that the slave trade
had been vastly profitable to the maritime states of the Northeast and
that conditions of free northern labor in factories and mills were too
often oppressive and degrading.

In any event the South was stimulated to a vigorous defense of slavery and to vigorous exposition of the hardships of free labor, the southern publicists copying the intemperateness of their northern counterparts. George Fitzhugh, of Virginia, put it picturesquely in 1857:

We are, all, North and South, engaged in the White Slave Trade, and he
who succeeds best, is esteemed most respectable. It is far more cruel than
the Black Slave Trade, because it exacts more of its slaves, and neither
protects nor governs them. We boast that it exacts more, when we say,
"that the *profits* made from employing free labor are greater than those
from slave labor." The profits made from free labor, are the amount of the
products of such labor, which the employer, by means of the command
which capital or skill gives him, takes away, exacts, or "exploitates" from
the free laborer. [Fitzhugh sounds like an American Karl Marx, and like
the latter fails to state all the facts. But he is none the less effective.] The
profits of slave labor are that portion of the products of such labor which
the power of the master enables him to appropriate. These profits are less,
because the master allows the slave to retain a larger share of the results
of his own labor, than do the employers of free labor. But we not only
boast that the White Slave Trade is more exacting and fraudulent (in fact,
though not in intention,) than Black Slavery; but we also boast that it is
more cruel, in leaving the laborer to take care of himself and family out of
the pittance which skill or capital have allowed him to retain. When the
day's labor is ended, he is free, but is overburdened with the cares of
family and household, which makes his freedom an empty and delusive
mockery. But his employer is really free, and may enjoy the profits made
by others' labor, without a care or trouble as to their well-being. The Negro
slave is free, too, when the labors of the day are over, and free in mind
as well as body; for the master provides food, raiment, house, fuel, and
everything else necessary to the physical well-being of himself and family.

The master's labors commence just when the slave's end. No wonder men should prefer white slavery to capital, to Negro slavery, since it is more profitable, and is free from all the cares and labors of black slave-holding.

Church leaders in the South rallied to the cause of slavery, justifying it on the grounds of Biblical practice and authority. In 1845 the Methodist Episcopal Church, South, was organized as a result of the difference with their northern brethren on this issue. This church, which bitterly opposed dancing and card playing and which in later years was to be prohibitionist and archaically literal and fundamentalist in the interpretation of the Holy Scriptures, thought slavery a beneficent institution.

In November 1860 Abraham Lincoln was elected President of the United States, having a plurality but far less than a majority of the popular vote. The Republican party platform of 1860, upon which he campaigned, declared in its eighth paragraph:

That the normal condition of all the territory of the United States is that of freedom; That as our Republican fathers, when they had abolished slavery in all our national territory, ordained that "no person should be deprived of life, liberty, or property, without due process of law," it becomes our duty, by legislation, whenever such legislation is necessary, to maintain this provision of the Constitution against all attempts to violate it; and we deny the authority of Congress, of a territorial legislature, or of any individuals, to give legal existence to Slavery in any Territory of the United States.

That this Republican position was directly contrary to the interpretation of the Constitution which had been adopted by the Supreme Court of the United States simply increased the southern fears that the position of slavery in the Union and its extension into new territory would alike be doomed by a government committed to abolition. Although Lincoln himself made it clear that he did not intend to interfere with slavery in the slave states, he also was explicit that his position was against its extension. In December 1860 in a letter to Alexander H. Stephens of Georgia, he wrote:

Do the people of the South really entertain fears that a Republican administration would, *directly,* or *indirectly,* interfere with the slaves, or with them, about their slaves? If they do, I wish to assure you, as once a friend, and still I hope, not an enemy, that there is no cause for such fears—
The South would be in no more danger in this respect, than it was in

the days of Washington. I suppose, however, this does not meet the case—
You think slavery is right and ought to be extended; while we think it is
wrong and ought to be restricted— That I suppose is the rub— It certainly
is the only substantial difference between us—

Linked as it was with the question whether southern leadership and
power were to be eclipsed in the affairs of the United States, the difference was substantial enough to produce attempted secession by the
South.

The fears of the southern planter leadership were displayed in an
editorial in the *Charleston Mercury* of October 11, 1860, shortly before the election of Lincoln, urging that in the event of his election
the southern states secede from the Union before he took office:

The first effect of the submission of the South, to the installation of
Abolitionists in the offices of President and Vice-President of the United
States, must be a powerful consolidation of the strength of the Abolition
party at the North. Success generally strengthens. If, after all the threats
of resistance and disunion, made in Congress and out of Congress, the
Southern States sink down into acquiescence, the demoralization of the
South will be complete. Add the patronage resulting from the control of
ninety-four thousand offices, and the expenditure of eighty millions of
money annually, and they must be irresistible in controlling the General
Government. . . .

With the control of the government of the United States, and an organized and triumphant North to sustain them, the Abolitionists will renew
their operations upon the South with increased courage. The thousands in
every country, who look up to power, and make gain out of the future,
will come out in support of the Abolition Government. . . . They will
have an Abolition Party in the South, of Southern men. The contest for
slavery will no longer be one between the North and the South. It will be
in the South, between the people of South. . . .

Already there is uneasiness throughout the South, as to the stability of
its institution of slavery. But with a submission to the rule of Abolitionists
at Washington, thousands of slaveholders will despair of the institution.
While the condition of things in the Frontier States will force their slaves
on the markets of the Cotton States, the timid in the Cotton States will also
sell their slaves. The consequence must be, slave property must be greatly
depreciated. We see advertisements for the sale of slaves in some of the
Cotton States, for the simple object of getting rid of them; and we know
that standing orders for the purchase of slaves in this market have been
withdrawn, on account of an anticipated decline of value from the political
condition of the country. . . .

Slave property is the foundation of all property in the South. When security in this is shaken, all other property partakes of its instability. Banks, stocks, bonds, must be influenced. Timid men will sell out and leave the South. Confusion, distrust and pressure must reign. . . .

The ruin of the South, by the emancipation of her slaves, is not like the ruin of any other people. It is not a mere loss of liberty, like the Italians under the Bourbons. It is not heavy taxation, which must still leave the means of living, or otherwise taxation defeats itself. But it is the loss of liberty, property, home, country—everything that makes life worth having.

Early in February 1861 in Montgomery, Alabama, delegates from six southern states—South Carolina, Georgia, Florida, Alabama, Mississippi, and Louisiana—which had seceded from the United States adopted a temporary constitution for the provisional government of the "Confederate States of America," and in the next month, with the addition of the recently seceded Texas, adopted a permanent constitution, shortly ratified by the seceded states. In effect the states continued their existence just as before, but with a transfer of the federal allegiance from the United States Government at Washington, to the new Confederate States Government, which in June 1861 was moved to Richmond, Virginia.

Shooting war between the North and South began in April 1861 with a southern attack on Fort Sumter, in Charleston Harbor, to forestall the relief of the federal garrison in that federal fort by an expedition which President Lincoln had sent by sea.

The question now was, were the southern states to be allowed to go their own way in their new Confederacy or were they to be compelled to remain in the United States by force of northern arms? President Lincoln stated the issue and the upshot in his second inaugural four years later:

Both parties deprecated war, but one of them would *make* war rather than let the nation survive, and the other would *accept* war rather than let it perish, and the war came.

The Confederate government from the very start imposed upon the community committed to its care a task that could not be borne. A state with a small population and a small industrial capacity undertook to fight a state where both were large. The South with its five and a half million free (plus three and a half million slaves) and its unbalanced agricultural system was pitted against the North with its twenty-two million, and a balanced agricultural, industrial, and commercial strength. The South, without a navy and in need of trans-atlantic trade, was set against a state with a navy and the means of making it rapidly more powerful; so that the South, to which imports were vital, did not have them, and the North, to which imports were useful but not vital, did have them.

For any hope of success in circumstances like these it is essential that the state of inferior strength be provided with some sort of advantage at the start, in the way of accumulation of materials of war, and the provision of a trained soldiery. Only in that way can the weaker state have a reasonable prospect of success. But no such temporary advantage or head start was made available to the Confederacy. Any rational ground for belief in victory was limited to mistaken hopes for foreign aid.

It was too one-sided. The war exhausted and impoverished the people of the South. Much of their land was laid waste in the campaigns, and the produce of the rest declined. Their resources were consumed. Their livestock perished. Their trade disappeared. Their railroads fell into ruin. Too many of their brave and capable were killed in battle.

When the South was finally defeated, more than the government went down. The result of the conflict was not only the disappearance of the Confederate government and state, but the disappearance of the southern social forms, the distinctive southern society with its slave-based economic order and the traditional organization of its cotton kingdom.

2. SUCCESSFUL SECESSION—THE AMERICAN REVOLUTION

The American Revolution affords an illustration of secession by a part of the state from the old whole in circumstances where the old government and the group it represented were holding too tight to a privileged position and in doing so were interfering with the development of the American colonies. The relations of the revolutionary and traditional parties was just the reverse of that in the United States Civil War where, as we have seen, it was the southern leadership holding too tight to its slave economy that brought about attempted secession from the rapidly developing greater state of which the South formed a part.

The government of George III of England was an oligarchy standing for the extension of the royal power at home. The oligarchy consisted of the King himself, and such lords of Church and state as considered it in their interest to extend the King's authority against that of the House of Commons. Mistakenly believing in the unlimited extent of the power of their government overseas as well as at home, the oligarchy undertook a series of enactments and decrees designed to keep the British colonies in America in a condition of subjection to the British crown, and to render them a docile source of commercial advantage to the mother country.

There was no fundamental difference of aspiration between colonists and mother country. There was no division between class and class, no circumstances of unavoidable internal disorder. There was simply an intolerant failure on the part of the home government to recognize the colonists' need of a reasonable measure of control of their own affairs, a self-respecting autonomy.

The King's government thought that the American colonists should bear part of the expense of the Seven Years' War, which Britain and Prussia had fought against France. Nor was this in itself unreasonable, as the outcome of the war had greatly increased the security of the colonists. The King's government also thought it advisable to tax the colonists for the support of the royal troops maintained in America, again not in itself an unreasonable aim. But the colonists were not represented in Parliament, which was the taxing body, and the colonial leaders affirmed that they would submit to no taxation without representation.

The geographical position of the colonies and their situation in regard to local assets and resources was such that they were capable of being a self-contained, self-supporting autonomous group which could exist as a separate political community, an independent state. In these circumstances a limit lay in fact upon the legislative and taxing power of Parliament and the King's government, a limit imposed by the colonists' desire for self-rule coupled with their likely physical power to make good their desire. If the leaders of a local community want self-rule and do not want to be subservient to the central government of the greater state of which their local community forms a political part, and if in addition to wanting self-rule they are capable in fact of overthrowing the power of those who deny it to them, it is impossible for the central government to make such a denial stick.

Nevertheless the King's government saw fit to obstruct local colonial legislation and to enact and to enforce vexatious measures regulating, restricting, and monopolizing colonial trade in the interests of the mother country, declaring the King's power of disposal of lands to the west of the seaboard colonies, asserting the legislative supremacy of the government in London, and imposing the unpopular taxes. When the colonial legislatures objected or petitioned for redress, they were dissolved by the royal governors. A determination to resist swept the colonies. Violent incidents occurred. The King's government adopted punitive measures. Revolution was precipitated.

The American Declaration of Independence stated the case of the colonies against the King:

He has made judges dependent on his will alone, for the tenure of their offices, and the amount and payment of their salaries. He has erected a multitude of new offices, and sent hither swarms of officers to harass our people, and eat out their substance. . . . He has affected to render the military independent of and superior to the civil power. He has combined with others to subject us to a jurisdiction foreign to our constitution and unacknowledged by our laws; giving his assent to their acts of pretended legislation: For quartering large bodies of armed troops among us: For protecting them, by a mock trial, from punishment for any murders which they should commit on the inhabitants of these States: For cutting off our trade with all parts of the world: For imposing taxes on us without our consent: For depriving us, in many cases, of the benefits of trial by jury: For transporting us beyond seas to be tried for pretended offenses: . . . For suspending our own legislatures, and declaring themselves invested with power to legislate for us in all cases whatsoever.

The British government tardily recognized their governmental mistake and in 1778 British commissioners of conciliation offered the Americans everything they had ever asked in the past, as none of it was in fundamental opposition to any real need of Britain or a wise colonial policy. But by 1778 it was too late for conciliation—the British General Burgoyne had been defeated in a major battle; the colonies had made an alliance with France, in which both parties had promised no separate peace; and the spirit of complete independence had taken hold throughout the land.

Thus it came about that the result of mistaken "acts of pretended legislation," and the thwarting of the legitimate needs of the colonists, was not compliance on the part of the colonists, but revolution and independence.

3. SECESSION AND POLITICAL FEDERATION

In the cases of *Discord*, a discontented social group within the community cannot be its own master and go its own way because independent political existence of the group is impossible. Somehow or other the various groups have to find their peace within the state, and reconcile themselves to the rule of those who have succeeded in getting the position of power. There is no basis of geographical self-sufficiency upon which a class division or an internal social conflict can be resolved by way of secession.

The *secession* cases, where separate political existence is seen to be feasible, show that a social group will if it can assert its independence of those who differ with it. Relatively simple differences, as in the case of the American colonists and Britain, suffice to bring about secession.

The facts of the secession cases refute the theory that federal union prevents wars which would otherwise occur. Since the formation of the American union, the great American Civil War has taken place. This is to be compared with the prolonged absence of war between the United States and Canada, two independent bordering states. The explanation of the war in the one case, and the absence of it in the other, plainly must be outside the field of influence of federal union as a cause of peace. In the main it is not law or union that has kept New York from fighting Pennsylvania. The principal reason is that the leaders and people within each state have felt reasonable scope within the United States' organization and have become accustomed to the unified going concern which allowed them this scope. It is obviously not the paper terms of the federal union which explain why the United States Civil War was fought between North and South rather than between East and Middle West.

Secession has often occurred after the death of a highly competent ruler, especially if he has ruled over a relatively new state where no traditional institutions have come down over a long period. The disintegration of Charlemagne's empire into separate parts, and the breakdown of Alexander the Great's new empire, both afford illustrations.

In communities without rapid communications and without means of bringing armed force quickly to bear at a particular point, the result of inefficient or burdensome government at the center was likely to be secession of those parts capable of separate existence. If in turn these lesser parts were inefficiently governed, some form of still smaller local governments, like those of the various feudal lords, put in an appearance. These little governments would be dependent or independent of rule above them as some more powerful territorial ruler or king might fail or succeed in establishing a wider overlordship over the little local rulers. Thus feudalism or a close equivalent has been common in many parts of the world from time to time, being characteristic of the breakdown of central government, bad communications, and little trade. Even though a powerful king—as in Norman England—might utilize the feudal order that lay to hand for his administration, the fact remains that a main feature of feudalism is the overassertion of local claims and rights.

In any existing state at a time and place when communications are rapid and it is possible to bring powerful armament to bear quickly at a given point, the result of inefficient and burdensome central government is more likely to be continuing distress and discord in the various local regions subject to it, as secession is harder to organize on an independent local basis. To this extent it may be true that federal union can preserve by force an unjust central government which in earlier days would have broken down by way of secession and civil war.

Were the political leaders of the world to succeed in devising a method of avoiding large-scale war, including wars of attempted secession, the problems of discord, of imposed, arbitrary rule, and of unjust government and the maintenance of unjust governments in office would remain at least as difficult as in the past.

IX. Separation

DISCORD arises when groups—including the government group—within a state, in trying to maintain or improve their respective positions, do so in such a way that there is a failure to come to a peaceful and substantially satisfactory reconciliation of their conflicts.

Secession occurs when a group politically integrated on a regional basis tries to maintain or improve its position by breaking away from the state of which it has been a part.

There is another type of divided community. This is the community on the world scene, the community of mankind, which however it may be organized from time to time in terms of trade and communication is scarcely organized at all politically. This kind of division—which I call *separation*—arises as a result of the several separate states of the world trying to maintain or improve their respective positions in ways injurious to one another.

As far as the welfare of their inhabitants is concerned, different portions of the world provide very different conditions. The rainfall necessary to an adequate food supply is lacking in great areas. Temperatures in many places, while allowing man's existence, are too hot or too cold for him to make his most productive effort. Mineral and fuel resources are plentiful in some regions, scarce in others. In some regions the population is much too great for the available resources, so that most of the people live in poverty and want. In others the population may be pressing on the resources, so that while the community is relatively well off at the moment, it foresees a time of shortage. In still other regions the land and the resources could sustain an increased population in comparative plenty.

These unequally endowed portions of the earth have come historically into the possession of separate political communities which in the course of time have each devloped distinctive customs and sentiments, their own constitutional and legal systems, and differing economic rules and structures, religions, and languages. Accompanying these differences in culture there also are often variations in physical make-up, notably in facial appearances and in color of skin.

The usual motives of reform—the desires of groups to improve their position along the lines described in the first part of this book—are at work in the relations between these various differentiated political communities, the separate states of the world.

1. MOTIVES OF REFORM LEADING TO WAR

The community of the island empire Japan in the nineteen-thirties was pressing very hard on the assets of the region in which it lived. Although possessed of good climates and good agricultural land, the latter was relatively small in extent in the predominantly mountainous terrain of the islands. Ready access to the sea helped offset the deficiency in food-producing land, so that in the Japanese diet the consumption of fish was more than twenty times that of meat. Coal supplies locally obtainable, while not of the best grade, were currently just about sufficient for needs. Great reliance was placed on hydroelectric power, about four-fifths of Japanese electricity being produced by falling water. Petroleum resources were meager. So were those of iron ore. All in all, the population was on the verge of becoming critically too large for its available assets and was already heavily dependent on imports for its supplies of oil and iron. The standard of living showed a slowly declining trend.

The population of Japan was too big to be usefully employed on the too scanty agricultural lands. Emigration to the relatively uncrowded and bountiful areas of the earth—as, for example, the North American continent—was restricted by the laws and regulations of the states already occupying those areas. Industrialization at home would offer possible gainful occupation to the excess people; but such industrialization required large imports, especially of iron, from abroad; and the Japanese means of purchase of such imports were hampered by foreign restrictions and foreign tariff barriers against her exports. Such foreign investment as the Japanese made in producing areas was insufficient in amount and lacked the protection of local political control to render adequate for the future her access to the needed resources. The collapse of Japanese foreign trade in the worldwide depression in the early nineteen-thirties made her leaders hesitate to rely on foreign trade as a main means to industrial expansion. Territorial gains made in the first quarter of the twentieth century at the expense of China, Russia, and Korea were not sufficiently productive to solve Japan's problem.

The Japanese were intensely proud of their culture and in recent years had become particularly insistent on their special divine sponsorship. The goddess Amaterasu-Omikami—the Heaven Shining Great August Goddess—was the ancestress of the emperor, he being direct descendant of her own grandson whom she had long ago sent to rule the state which she had herself established. The Japanese state was of divine origin; the Japanese people under their goddess ruler were someday destined to bring justice and order to the whole world under the dominion of the Japanese emperor.

Such being the Japanese capability and the Japanese destiny, what was to be done about the Japanese population which was growing beyond the resources of the empire? The course taken was to encourage an even greater population. The culture of Japan was so significant that it must not be lost. A declining population in a world that might elsewhere be expanding might mean the setting or the eclipse of the Japanese sun.

But where, with the world organized as it was, could this greater Japanese population live and prosper? How was a declining standard of living to be reversed if the same meager assets had to supply an ever larger number of mouths and bodies?

Japan's great mainland neighbor to the west, China, itself too heavily populated for its assets, was politically ill-organized. Perhaps Japan could gain some sort of control of the China seacoast areas, with a view to its future development in a way most advantageous to the Japanese people.

The lands of southeast Asia, and the islands of the adjacent southwest Pacific, could they be brought under Japanese control, might serve as part of a great new political and economic sphere under Japanese leadership. Precision industry in Japan itself, heavy industry in Manchuria, perhaps light industrialization in China, and the provision of food and raw materials to the maximum extent from a rationally organized Greater East Asia might offer a way out of the Japanese population predicament and a future worthy of the Japanese character and destiny.

Seen from the point of view of China, or from the point of view of a France or a Britain with colonies in East Asia from which they themselves drew raw materials or from the point of view of a United States of America drawing from East Asia substantially all of its tin, rubber, silk, Manila fiber, and quinine, these Japanese plans had a threatening aspect. China's control of her own affairs might be endangered. The western countries might be excluded from their vital Asiatic trade. To these countries the Japanese plans looked like a Japan pushing much too hard for reform on the international scene.

From the Japanese viewpoint, on the other hand, the position of the western countries with their imperial and economic interests in East Asia, controlled for the main benefit of the western countries—Japan fitting in the picture only to the extent the westerners saw fit—looked very different. It was a case of the westerners holding too tight to their privileged position on the international scene.

Here too the differences in skin color, which we noted in the first chapter of this book as often a factor in reform, played a part. As put by Hidejiro Nagata in Tokyo in 1939:

Today the world's population is two billion, of which the colored races are two-thirds, double the number of the white race. But the white races hold nine-tenths of the earth's surface and the colored races only one-tenth. This is certainly unjust.

Or by Teiichi Muto in the previous year:

How many of the colored races have been sacrificed for the advantage of the white men who have fenced in the world! It is beyond telling. Just as they spread the idea that the Japanese population growth is an international crime, they regard the very existence of the subjugated peoples as a crime. Although India may be called the treasure house of the world from the viewpoint of the British who have seized it, what benefit do the Indians themselves get from it? They are happy to barely escape death from starvation. And the world's paradise, America, blessed with natural resources, with an average income five times the Japanese, aren't the Negroes, its aborigines, notoriously the poorest people in the world?

The Hawaiian natives were taught by the tools of white imperialism, the missionaries, to worship heaven, and while they were looking up to heaven the ground was stolen from under their feet. The subjugated peoples of the earth have all been brought to their present miserable condition by such tricks. Meeting these international plunderers, sometimes pickpockets and sometimes highwaymen as well, the colored races were looted of everything while completely helpless.

As to China clinging to her inefficient organization and backwardness of development—so it seemed to Japan—here again was a state holding too tight to an outworn regimen, out of keeping with the real needs of the East Asian picture as they appeared to Japan.

When differences arise between separate states, as in the Japanese case which we have outlined, they are likely to be even harder to reconcile peaceably than are similar differences occurring within a particular historical state, difficult of reconciliation as these have often proved. War of attempted conqest on the one hand and of attempted defense on the other may well result. Such was the event in the case of Japan.

Within a particular state there is usually well-known and understood political machinery through which an attempt can be made to reconcile group differences. Before the United States Civil War there was always a chance that a working compromise would be reached between North and South under the federal Constitution. The Union, for which many leaders in both sections felt real devotion, might prove to have within itself the means of peaceable solution of the American differences. A method of give and take had worked reconciliation in the case of differences less serious than that of slavery. Yet even here, with the available machinery of the American Constitution, the hope for tolerance and peace failed.

Between the separate states of the world there is not and never has been any generally accepted means for the reconciliation of differences. On the contrary each state has specialized out its own way of doing things and each is suspicious of the methods and intentions of others. There has been no necessity for a tolerant rule of give and take between these states which have gone their own ways as far as possible. There is no custom of honesty between the separate states, such as has usually developed to a greater or lesser extent between the groups within a particular state. Each state feels that the promises of others has been made solely for the temporary opportunistic benefit of the promiser, and that the promises will not be kept in difficult circumstances—for example the promises of France to aid and protect Czechoslovakian independence in the period before the Second World War.

Each state wants to rely on its own methods and the rule with which it has become familiar. When a particular political philosophy, the source at one time of severe internal dissension, has come to dominate the life of a particular state—as Bolshevism in the case of Russia—then on the world scene this same idea again appears as a dissentient factor. The political community—the state—now committed to the idea seeks to push and promote it, partly for the sake of the idea but mainly because the idea has now become a convenient tool in pushing and promoting the position of the particular community amongst the other communities—the separate states—of the world.

Even within a single large community hostile groups have often been willing to let those who stand in their way starve or freeze. For example, consider the railroad and coal strikes in the United States in 1946. As between hostile states themselves this attitude is on the whole the typical attitude. The fact that individuals within the hostile states may be good friends and have warm feelings for one another or that at times of natural catastrophe succor flows freely across state lines to aid the victims of flood or fire or earthquake, appears to have little or no influence on the hostility between the states. The fact that David Hume was admired, fêted, and sincerely liked by many leaders in Paris, and himself reciprocated this feeling, or the fact of Voltaire's admiration of English institutions, was entirely compatible with bitter hostility between France and England in the late eighteenth century. Even if the American President F. D. Roosevelt had succeeded in his aim of cordial personal relations with Stalin, that could do nothing to cure hostility between the Russian and American communities with their alien systems of economics and politics; and of course could do nothing to cure basic causes of Russian restlessness, such as shortage of rainfall and too much cold in too great a part of that country.

The friendly individuals of another country may be entirely well disposed towards me as an individual. Yet as an organized group, a political community, a separate state, they may seem to be threatening or thwarting the ambitions of my country.

In the *discord* cases we saw that extremism, lack of fairness and tolerance, was likely to be characteristic of the leader of a reform movement. This was so because his very virtue of taking things to heart enough to want to push for radical reform was likely to override any feelings of fairness and tolerance. We also saw that confusion in the state, the breakdown or failure of the accepted rule and the customary regime, gave this extremist and ambitious leader of a radical group his chance at reform by violence.

In the cases of *separation* which we are now considering this opportunity of the extremist reformer is at a maximum just because there is no accepted international rule to go by or customary and understood method of resolving differences. In the *discord* cases the rule has for some reason broken down; in the *separation* cases the rule has been missing from the start. It is easy for a Hitler to whip up sentiment against the foreigner, because the divergencies which make for reform are at a maximum between the separate states, and because there is no machinery for curing real inequities or even for getting the truth established as to the absence of fictitious inequities. A Stalin always has at hand a situation of fundamental international misunderstanding.

We saw that within a particular community a movement for reform was likely to arise if a group in want, but not helplessly so, needed to improve its position, and also if a group even though already pretty well off desired changes which they could see would make their position better still. Now consider the upshot of these same two factors in the world community. Take the case of a separately organized state with leaders of ability feeling the need to improve its position in a world where there is no practical established way of getting the improvement peaceably. Resort may be had to violence.

When profound differences arise between states along any of the lines of the main motives of reform—as in the Japanese case which we have cited as an illustrative example—a peaceful resolution has not been too likely, and attempted resolution by war all too likely.

2. WAR'S EFFECTS ON WORLD POLITICAL SCENE

War usually fails to produce any constructive result or improvement in the world political scene. From the point of view of the world community there is no gain to offset the evils of war's destruction of men's lives and works.

Effects of Aggressive War

The common reasons for making aggressive war themselves indicate why aggressive war when pushed to a victorious conclusion is not likely to make any change for the better in the organization or harmonious functioning of the world community.

Surplus wealth over and above the mere means for continued existence is necessary if any significant part of a community is to be freed either for any leisure or for effort in the arts or literature or the advancement of science. But surplus wealth is conditioned on a sufficient food supply, a good climate, and useful resources. From the earliest times to the most recent, wars have been waged to gain control of these conditions of wealth. The Medes and the Mongols, the Nazis and the Bolsheviks, alike have sought control of the fertile crescents, the warm water ports, the mineral assets. But there is nothing in this aim of a particular community to improve its own position that is addressed to the problem of a more harmonious entire community of the world's peoples. The avowed aim of the maker of aggressive war is his own place in the sun, his own opportunity to work out his own national fortunes, the fulfillment of his own manifest destiny. When victorious, he displaces some other top dog in the international dog fight. There is for the time being a new top dog. But there is nothing in the achieved aim of one dog to be top dog that changes greatly for the better the life scheme of the whole community of dogs. Had the Japanese succeeded in the nineteen-forties in their aim of dictating peace terms in Washington, there was nothing in the Japanese purposes or character to indicate that a Japanese overlord would have resulted in a happy and harmonious mankind.

In the *discord* cases we saw how characteristic of religious and other doctrinal leaders was their attitude of intolerance. When transferred to the international scene, these doctrinal differences and their mutual intolerances have been responsible for some of the most destructive warfare in history, with harsh and cruel incidents rife. The Nazis with their doctrine of the German Master Race, the *Herrenvolk,* and their violent bias against other peoples, in their eyes mostly mongrel races, and particularly their phobia against the Jews, offer a modern instance of this intolerance at its worst. To the extent that this kind of doctrine was part of the Nazi motivation for making war, it was obviously not addressed to the making of a better world for the peoples of any of the separate states other than that of the Nazis themselves. A victorious Nazidom would not have resulted in any cure of the frictions and inequities amongst the separate states of the world community.

An ideal that is useful at home under some circumstances may lose its usefulness on a wider scene and become extremely harmful in new circumstances. The concept of the German *Herrenvolk* illustrates this deterioration of an originally valuable doctrine. In the torn Germany of the nineteenth century the idea of a German *Volk,* a people with interests which could be better pursued in unity than in political fragmentation, might be a useful instrument in trying to overcome the internal German frictions. But later, on the world scene and subjected to the twentieth-century exaggerations of the Nazis, this idea of a German People became that of a German Master People—the Master Race—hateful to every non-German and therefore entirely nonconstructive in the field of better world relations.

In the first part of this book we remarked on the powerful reform motive represented by sentiments of like interests, like appearances, like ways, and like language. On the world scene, the various separate nations demonstrate this motive at work. The strength and the stubbornness of these feelings of historical identity were shown internally in the efforts of Henlein's Sudeten Germans in Czechoslovakia to disrupt the Czechoslovak state in the interests of Hitler's Germany. The transfer today of intransigent racial minorities out of their homes so as to get them out of the jurisdiction to which they arc hostile and within a jurisdiction to which they are friendly, evidences how stubborn is this factor of nationality within a particular state. But what concerns us now about these transfers, and these conflicting sentiments which bring them about, is their effect on the world scene of the separate states. It may prove beneficial for the short term to a particular state to get rid of a hated and hateful minority. But it certainly makes no good prognosis for peaceful world relations to have these bitterly hostile peoples aligned against one another in politically isolated nations, the separate states of the world. The apparent gain to a particular state in the cutting away of a political minority sore spot, is offset by the apparent harm to the world community in the resultant drawing together into sharply separated states of these conflicting national sentiments. When one of these states makes war upon another with a view to its own aggrandizement, what hope can there be that out of such a war motivated by ambition and stimulated by hate will come an improvement in the peace and harmony of the world?

Nationalism today is exhibited in the form of many competing nation-states in conflict with one another over the apparently limited assets of the planet. But the motivating spirit of nationalism is exceedingly old—the feeling for kith and kin, the conviction that the methods of one's own group and the temperament, abilities and disposition of one's own kind are superior to those of others. When Ikhnaton tried to effect his religious reforms in Egypt and to establish a religion of an equitable God fair to all mankind, he was trying to break away from a nationalistic Egyptian spirit which had already existed for more than a millennium. The Roman Republic was as jingoistic and nationalistic as could be. But when the Republic and the early Empire succeeded in becoming ruler of the other nationalities of Western Europe and around the Mediterranean, for a long time thereafter there was no independent nationalism glaringly apparent in the modern sense. In the terms of this book, *discord* rather than *separation* was the form of political unrest.

The number of sentiments for which organized groups of people have been willing to kill one another is considerable. For many years religious differences were regarded in the western world as of vital significance, and western people—like some easterners today—were prepared to go to war with one another over divergent ideas of the means of salvation. Today historical national alignments seem to us more vital than religious doctrines, although doctrinal differences about divergent methods of controlling land and labor and the instruments of production play a potent contributing part even in today's predominantly nationalistic cleavages.

The transfer of minorities, or the partition of states along racial and nationalistic lines as in Palestine or in India, amounts to a practical confession of the difficulties that stand in the way of an equitable world order. It is an admission of belief that in those particular cases people of different historical background cannot get on together in a workable way of life.

Perhaps in the old days more than in the modern the pure spirit of adventurous ambition served as a motive for war. The conquests of Alexander the Great or those of the Normans can serve as illustrations. The same spirit is not totally absent in some of the more modern aggressors, notably Napoleon and Hitler. In the case of the last-named, the spirit of adventure was much overlaid by second-rate theory and conscious self-adulation. In every such case it is clear that there is nothing in the overweening ambition of a military leader that is primarily addressed to the making of a better world community.

It is nevertheless true that in some of these military adventures the leader has fortuitously represented a better civilized community than those which he has conquered, and benefit to the wider community has in fact resulted. The Hellenism of Alexander, the political ideas of the Normans, did produce benefits wherever they went. But how much better it would be if today—with our mightily destructive weapons— good political ideas could be spread by peaceable means and by way of orderly growth in a peaceful world climate.

In the *discord* cases we saw that the temperament of a set of leaders might make it difficult for them to play a co-operative part in the community, due to a failure of any ability of compromise or give and take. If they can, they try to run things exclusively in their own way and for their own benefit. The Junkers in nineteenth-century Germany offered a marked instance of this failing. Transferred to the international scene, this same temperament exerted itself in ways incompatible with a better-ordered world. For Germany in the twentieth century it would have been possible to be certain of adequate supplies of food and raw materials as a co-operative partner in the western world of states. It also would have been possible to attain the same result on an independent basis if Germany were to conquer and rule Central Europe and European Russia. The latter alternative made more appeal to the frame of mind of the German leadership. It appeared to the Germans that such a conquest, if it were to be safely attempted, required first a military neutralization of possible attack on Germany's western flank by France or Britain. Twice in the first half of the century Germany tried to gain this safety through the defeat of France and Britain. Twice she failed, due to aid to these countries by the United States, herself alarmed by the prospect of an overpowerful, militant Germany. Had Germany been successful in her plans, there is nothing either in the nature of these plans or of the German characteristics and temperament to indicate that German victory would have resulted in a harmonious world community. Germany's aim was her own aggrandizement. The bettering of the world community was, as in the usual case of aggressive war, simply beside the point, overlooked, not a significant item.

When Carthage and Rome struggled for control of the Mediterranean and its commerce, neither was aiming at a result which would be fair and equitable to all concerned. Each on the contrary was aiming at the increase of its own power and its own wealth. As in the internal *discord* cases, the conflict was over who was to come out on top as the boss of the situation, and no part of anyone's effort was directed towards the creation of a wholly better kind of situation.

As a matter of practice the aggressor in war is entirely unprincipled in his efforts to reach victory. He adopts means directly in contradiction of the needs for which he is professing that he maintains his war. Hitler preaching an anti-Bolshevik crusade on behalf of Western Europe engages as a preliminary step in war against France and England, two key components of the Western Europe he is purporting to save. Japan in a crusade against the westerner in behalf of justice for the Asiatic races engages as a preliminary step in an invasion of China who should be the principal of the proposed beneficiaries of the Japanese scheme! The truth is that the aggressor's real aim is his own benefit and aggrandizement. Any lofty other aims which he may propose are for the purpose of hiding from others—and perhaps also from himself—the exclusively selfish motives by which he is driven.

Effects of Defensive War

If it is true that the common reasons for aggressive war explain why aggressive war does not make any improvement in the world community, it is equally true that the common reasons for a war of defense also explain why defensive wars, even when successfully fought and won, do not have any more constructive world result than the aggressive wars.

A war of defense is fought to ward off some dangerous threat to the security or independence of the state. When the defensive war has been successfully won, the victor historically sits back until such time as a new threat develops. The victor does not try to use its victory and its power for any purpose wider than the preservation of its own apparent security, and makes no determined or well-conceived attempt to make its victory a step in the better ordering of the world community.

The United States of America took part in the First World War on the ground that a Germany dominant in Western and Central Europe would make too dangerous a transatlantic neighbor for the safety of the United States. It looked as though Germany would, in the absence of American intervention, succeed in defeating France, and thereafter perhaps Britain. In the outcome, the United States and its allies were successful in warding off for the time being German military and political predominance in Europe. As soon as this result was achieved, the United States disarmed, hoped for the best, took no steps rationally calculated to produce a more peaceable and orderly world, and simply carried on business as before, ignoring the political likelihood that new troubles would arise.

When alliances or coalitions are formed to beat a military threat, there is no principle involved other than that of merely beating the threat. It follows from this that as soon as the threat is beaten the coalition falls apart, some of its members very likely joining the old enemy against its erstwhile friends, who now perhaps appear too strong in the international scene. Such shifts may take place with rapidity.

After the abdication of Napoleon in April 1814, the big four victorious powers, Austria, Russia, Prussia, and Britain, took the "initiative" in September 1814 at the Congress of Vienna in determining the provisions of a prospective peace settlement. But Russian desire for Poland and Prussian desire for Saxony alarmed the English and the

Austrians, who seeing that France was likely to take their side as against Russia and Prussia, succeeded in having the big "four" expanded to include France, so as to become the big "five." The "five" then proceeded to settle the question of frontiers. Meanwhile a committee of "eight" (which included Spain, Portugal, and Sweden) proceeded to deal with less thorny questions.

But the dispute over Poland and Saxony, like many real differences, was too stubborn to be settled by talk. Prussia threatened war. So it actually transpired that in January 1815 England and Austria signed a secret treaty of defensive alliance with their recent enemy France, to resist the aims of Russia and Prussia, their recent allies! It was only two months later that Napoleon, by his escape from Elba and his triumphal entry into France, once more forced his old enemies into cohesion, Austria, England, Prussia, and Russia concluding a new alliance against Napoleon on March 25, 1815.

Obviously there is nothing in this kind of offensive and defensive political maneuvering that is designed to produce a better and more livable world community. The coalition victors are so afraid of one another as not to risk any chance that one might become so strong as to be the boss. Attention is solely centered by each state on its own security. The failure to make a real effort to establish a well-ordered world community has insured that no such community has ever come into being. The security won by a particular state has been temporary and illusory.

Each separate state pushes what looks like its immediate advantage against its momentary enemy. Russia in 1940 is for Greece and against Bulgaria, because the enemy of the moment is Germany with which Bulgaria is for the time being aligned. Russia in 1950 is for Bulgaria and against Greece because the enemies of the moment are England and the United States with which Greece is for the time being aligned.

Portugal in the nineteen-thirties was afraid of the Spanish Left, fearing that if victorious in Spain it might go on and try to absorb Portugal. Therefore she favored the Fascists—German and Italian. But when within a few years Germany appeared to be definitely failing, Portugal recognized an old alliance with England and allowed the Azores to be used as an anti-Fascist naval and air base.

These situations are analogous to one we have already noted in the case of the Roman Church. In the fifteenth century the Church sided with strong national rulers to suppress dangers which the Church thought might lie in increases of popular rule. In the twentieth century the Church sided with the democracies to suppress the dangers which the Church saw in strong national rulers. The motive for these shifts was obviously the desire to increase the security of the Church organization. The shifts were wholly independent of any question of improving the religion itself.

The leaders of a state at war may be so preoccupied with one threat that they altogether fail to see another of equal or greater danger in the making.

After the First World War the victorious allies were intent on weakening the German central authority. In carrying out this intent, they deprived the German government of sufficient force to maintain law and order. Thereby they paved the way for the establishment of private armies—powerful gangster groups—loyal to the most ruthless of the German leaders. So it was that in the effort to forestall strong central authority in Germany the allies in fact brought about in the end something directly contrary to their purpose—a central authority unprincipled and ruthless as well as strong.

At a much earlier period in history the Greek city-states were so intent on the threat one posed for another, and fought so protractedly with one another, that they weakened and impoverished themselves and laid themselves open to conquest by the Macedonian rulers. Today it may well be that England in her successful wars of the twentieth century has similarly weakened and impoverished herself.

In the European phase of World War II, the United States and England were so concentrated on the danger from Germany and on measures for its defeat, that they failed to take ordinary diplomatic, military, and economic precautions against an at least equally great threat in the making. It will be useful to take a brief look at this sequence of events.

It seems clear enough from Hitler's *Mein Kampf* that Hitler's policy was primarily aimed at gaining control of territory and resources in European Russia. To achieve this aim it was first necessary to consolidate his position in Central Europe. This he accomplished by union with Austria, conquest of Czechoslovakia, and alliance with Italy. Poland was the next essential step on the way to the coveted land. But the conquest of Poland by Hitler, especially if followed by a like conquest of Russia, would have made Hitler much too strong a European power for the safety of either England or France. So Britain and France tried to stop Hitler by a guarantee of military aid to Poland.

This did not alter Hitler's need for Poland; but did mean that if England and France honored their guarantee, it would require Hitler to render his flank against England and France secure, before proceeding against Russia. To free himself to deal with this possible threat of England and France, Hitler made the August 1939 nonaggression pact with Russia; and forthwith proceeded to gobble up Poland. (From Russia's point of view the pact was sensible, as it gave Russia a brief period for intensive preparation for war; and if all went as favorably as possible might even mean that Germany on the one hand and France and England on the other would exhaust themselves in conflict, leaving Russia untouched.) Upon Hitler's attack on Poland, France and England honored their guarantee and declared war on Germany. Hitler then proceeded to secure his flank against Britain and France. He thought he had accomplished this aim by his quick defeat of the British and French forces in Europe, and by the conquest of France and the latter's collapse, even though he had not succeeded in an actual conquest of Britain. Then Hitler, thinking his flank sufficiently secure, went ahead with his original plan of attempted conquest of European Russia.

Fortunately for England and for conquered France, the United States was brought into the war by the attack of Japan on Pearl Harbor in the Hawaiian Islands on December 7, 1941, and the declaration of war upon the United States by Germany four days later. The United States had already furnished billions of dollars of credit and material aid to England and Russia; but the American efforts were hugely intensified as a result of her enforced entry into the war.

So it came about that Hitler, for failure to have secured his flank against Britain, was defeated by Britain, the United States, and Russia. Yet Britain and the United States at the end of the war in 1945 found themselves no better off than they were at its start in 1939. Their preoccupation with the Nazi menace, and their military, material, and diplomatic aid to Russia had brought about a situation in which they had substitued for the threat of a Germany predominant in Europe the threat of a Russia predominant in Europe.

After the defeat of Germany the United States concentrated all her might against Japan, forcing surrender by that nation. The United States was so preoccupied with this problem and so keen to obtain the unnecessary help of Russia, that she agreed to permit Russian expansion, at the ultimate expense of China, in Japanese-occupied Manchuria. The upshot of American policy was to substitute for the threat of a Japan predominant in Asia the threat of a Russia predominant in Asia.

The results on American policy of the increased power of Russia both in Europe and in Asia were reminiscent of the rapid shifts of alliance at the time of the Congress of Vienna. The United States promptly lined up with the interests of its recent enemies Germany and Japan against those of its recent ally Russia!

Quite aside from the horror and destructiveness of any great war, it seems plain that even a victorious defensive war which leaves the victor and the world no better off than before is entirely nonconstructive. Yet such in our own time seems to be the pattern of United States warfare and its aftermath. We may be destined to have more defensive wars on our hands as our traditional geographical boundaries of ocean become less effective as barriers against those desiring to gain control of our land with its good climate and resources. Even were we to be successful in defense and even were we for the time being to destroy the industrial power and the manpower of an enemy within his own borders and avoid a like destruction of our own industry and people, yet we will not thereby have made any better or more just world community for the future.

Effects of Unsuccessful War

One of the separate states of the world may fight an unsuccessful aggressive or defensive war, so that it fails to carry out its aim of aggression or defense to the extent it planned or hoped. What effect for better or worse does this have on the world community, and on the part such a state, or what may be left of it as an independent organization, continues to play on the world scene?

The answer is that the nature of the world scene is very little changed. The state which has fought the unsuccessful war and yet has not disappeared as a going concern loses at least for the time being its relative strength amongst the competing states. It is likely to become the object of aggressive designs of its neighbors, or to become a means utilized by them in the international struggle between the more successful states.

France in the eighteen-seventies thought she could protect herself against the threat posed by the growing power of Bismarck's Prussia, by making war on Prussia. In this preventive defensive war she was defeated. Germany became unified under Prussian domination, the very thing which France feared and Prussia desired. France was required to cede Alsace and most of Lorraine to the new Germany. Germany could not at the time swallow up France within German rule. To do so would have incorporated within the recently created and discordant Germany additional discordant and undigestible elements. It might also have precipitated war between Germany and other European nations unwilling to see the recently unified and highly militaristic Germany of Bismarck become too strong. England especially, as a means for her security, was committed to the maintenance of a more or less even balance of power among the states of continental Europe. By aligning her power with that of any other European state in such a power-balanced Europe, England believed that she could make her own and the latter's position so strong that no one would dare to challenge it by war. So France remained as an independent state on the international scene, seeking to rebuild her strength, befriended by those afraid of Germany.

Germany had two main aims in the First World War. One was to gain political and economic control of Central Europe. This aim brought Germany into conflict with Russian interests in the largely Slavic Balkan countries, and with Russia's hope of gaining someday a warm water port at Constantinople. The other main aim was to gain political and economic control of colonies which would be sources of raw materials for German manufacture and as possible outlets for German emigration to areas which would be under the German flag, part of the German Empire. This second aim required as a corollary that Germany have a powerful navy, so in the early nineteen hundreds she started to build one. The colonial aim with its naval corollary brought Germany into conflict with France and Britain who saw that the greatest possibility of German colonial expansion lay at their expense with the wresting from them of their colonial possessions. A powerful German navy also constituted a threat to the British control of the seas on which depended, in Britain's view, her control of her supplies of raw materials, food, and outlets for her manufactures.

The First World War, fought on these basic issues, brought in the United States as a partner of Britain and France, as we have just noted, on account of American fears of a possibly victorious Germany too militantly strong for the safety of the United States.

Not long after her defeat in this war, Germany was befriended by England, because the latter, viewing Europe in accordance with her traditional policy of no predominantly strong single power in continental Europe, saw in her recent ally France the most likely contender for this position of too great power. No greater error of judgment could have been made by the British. Events proved that both Russia, though recently torn by revolution, and Germany, though defeated in war, were capable of better organization and stronger unity than the multiparty France with its many divergent political views and lack of adequate central executive authority.

Thus defeated Germany's unenviable position in the postwar game of power politics speedily took a turn for the better as she was allowed to rebuild her strength under the now generally friendly eyes of the British political leadership.

In the Second World War France was liberated by Britain, Russia, and the United States after she had been conquered by the militarily rejuvenated Germany of the Nazis. But she still continued to exhibit her plurality of opinions and deeply divided views about economic and political power within her hardly saved independence. On the world scene her attitude was that of a defeated and no longer great power, being alternately swayed by fears and hopes about the course of Russian and American international ambitions, rather than dependent upon any power of her own. Yet her intrinsic wealth, climate, and natural advantages seemed such as under competent and less divided leadership to have assured her of her own independent strength amongst the competing states of the world.

The defeated and dismembered Germany in the years immediately following the Second World War serves as a warning of what may come about as the result of unsuccessful aggressive war. Her houses and her industrial plants were destroyed by the bombing of her great cities. Her efforts to reconstruct her political and ordinary police power were subject to foreign control in a territory now politically cut in two. Such were among the misfortunes of the defeat into which Germany was led by an arrogant leadership without sufficient intelligence to have seen facts as they were.

Failure to Better World Community

It is plain that these recent wars, whether waged successfully or unsuccessfully, have not resulted in any betterment of the world community as a whole. The same bitter conflict of the separate states continues as before. The several competitors undergo shifts in their relative power, but it is still a world where the law of claw and tooth prevails—turned by man's ingenuity from its primitive phases into a new phase of enormously high explosive, blast, fire, and poison, but still the same old law of claw and tooth.

International conferences, institutions like the Concert of Europe or the League of Nations or the United Nations, have served rather more as instruments in the jockeying of the competing states for improved position in the international race than as instruments for an improved world order. This is inevitable as long as the main interests of the leaders in the different parts of the world are in the aggrandizement each of his own country, with no real attention paid to what would constitute a more equitable world or to the conditions on which the possibility of such a world is dependent.

Just as in *discord* the leaders of the separate groups within the state bring the groups into conflict with one another in struggles for power and who is to come out on top, so in *separation* the leaders of the separate states of the world similarly bring their states into conflict with one another over like struggles for power and dominion. In neither case is any effort directed towards the making of a better whole community. The matter of real improvement in the relations between states being thus left unattended and to chance, it is no wonder that real improvement seldom takes place.

3. DISCORD AND SECESSION INSTEAD OF SEPARATION

It would be easy at this point, in view of the undeniable evils of *separation,* to jump to the conclusion that the organization of a single world state would cure these evils. Indeed, there is an old school of thought, which has many contemporary and vocal adherents, that the evils of political separation can in fact be cured by some form of federal union of the competing states, and that this is the sovereign remedy to prevent warfare in the future. But of course the truth is that such a union in so far as it might be actually and effectively established, with force to support its decisions, simply changes the nature of the struggle between the competing groups and regions, into situations of *discord* and of *secession.* What formerly was international strife becomes internal strife. Rebellion either of the palace revolution or French Revolution type and struggles for the seat of power will still take place, for the same reasons and in the same manner as we have described in the many instances of acute *discord,* both yesterday and today, in ancient times and modern. The breakdown of the world state will take place in the manner and for the reasons that we have described especially in the *secession* cases. Simply to call competing groups and regions by the name of one state and give the new state a government and a constitution will not prevent desires and apparent needs for regional independence, such as we saw bring about the American Revolution and the United States Civil War, or in earlier days the fragmentation of the civilized one world which took place on the disintegration of the Roman Empire following its long-drawn-out time of *discord*.

Those nations which in our own times have had designs for a world state have planned for an imposed, arbitrary order without reference to the consent of the governed. The Nazi order was of such a type. The Bolshevik vision of a Communist world order under Russian dominion is of such a type.

4. SEPARATION ON WORLD SCENE AGGRAVATES LOCAL DISCORD

With today's techniques of possible delivery of weapons of huge destructive power against an enemy, one organized state is able to devastate or to threaten to devastate another with a suddenness that has not been possible in earlier periods of history. The hostile pressures exerted in the past were relatively slow in their results. The case is not the same today. The leaders of a country with an industry proficient in weapons production can bring immense striking power to bear rapidly from a great distance.

It follows from this that in states which hope to be or to remain independent on the world scene, that type of reform is taking place in which the factors contributing to military might become of greater importance. A greater part of the productive effort of each separate state is directed into military channels. This increase in the importance of arms and armies in turn produces that type of internal discord characteristic of overmilitarized communities. Such discord arises from the neglect of other problems than the military, and the sacrifice of other interests to the all-too-apparent military necessities of the moment. We saw the internal harm of this kind of discord in third-century Rome, in eighteenth-century France, in twentieth-century Germany, and may see it today, notably in the Soviet Union.

Discordant elements in the population of a state have to be suppressed in the interest of unity against the outside enemy. This, as we have seen, simply perpetuates the latent discord, which becomes more and more serious as nothing is done to cure its substantive causes. Consider as instances the political concentration camps, the force, and the fraud of the Nazi regime in Germany before the Second World War or in the Soviet Union today—means for outlawing and silencing those with real grievances, rather than working a substantive cure for the grievances.

Periods of freedom from overwhelming foreign menace like that of the United States in the greater part of the nineteenth century, or of the British Isles living her great centuries of development of parliamentary government, are absent today. No longer do natural defensive barriers to hostile outside pressure allow an escape from excessive attention to defense. In the nineteenth century a country with natural geographical barriers was not under compulsion to become overmilitarized. No immediate necessities of defense afforded an excuse for the suppression, and perpetuation by suppression, of discontented groups. Under these favorable circumstances, it proved possible to work out a tolerant compromise of different points of view and to develop a political and social system with a great degree of active consent of the governed.

When some particular separate state of the world has aggressive designs against another, or fears aggression by that other, it is the course of prudence for it to try to create internal weakness within the community of the prospective enemy. If the effort succeeds, an increase of local discord results.

When Hitler's Germany had aggressive designs against France, German agents and their following in France did everything possible to stress and intensify the existing bases of discord in France. The distrust of French property owners for French workers, already sufficiently acute, was stimulated. The multiplicity of factions in French politics, so disastrous for continuity of policy or stable executive government, were encouraged to greater factionalism by editorial, magazine article, and book. Workers' antagonism against employers was whipped up ostensibly in the interests of the workers but actually in the interests of the German enemies of France. It is hard to say how much part this externally inspired discord played in rendering French discord so great that some French industrialists and landowners welcomed German order rather than the increasing French disorder. It is sufficient for our purpose to note that the condition of political separation, with its competition for power between states, brings about more or less successful attempts to increase local discord.

We saw this process of domestic discord stimulated by outside agents in the case of German influence on Henlein's followers in

Czechoslovakia and in the case of Russian-trained leaders of the Communist coup in the same country in the nineteen-forties. In Austria in the nineteen-thirties strife between the Heimwehren Fascists and the Socialists, the only two groups capable of organizing a defense for Austria, laid that country open to the effects of Nazi agitation stimulating and encouraging the strife. Austria was rendered incapable of retaining control of her own development and destiny.

It is too far back in history to know the answer, but it would be interesting to learn about the activities of agents of Cyrus in the sixth century B.C. in stimulating amongst the priests of Marduk in Babylon distrust of the religious reforms proposed by the last Chaldean emperor Nabonidus. It appears that these priests took the side of the invader Cyrus and helped his forces enter Babylon. Similarly, it would be interesting to know how much, if anything, the agents of Mahomet II had to do with intensifying those theological quarrels amongst the defenders of Constantinople which in 1453 weakened its spirit of defense against his successful attempt to capture the city.

In going about the task of stimulating discord in some particular community, an accurate appraisal is needed of the factors of discontent already present there. The object of the enemy agent or propagandist is to prevent discontented groups from finding a peaceable reconciliation one with another, and instead to intensify the differences existing between the various groups in the community. The groups are encouraged to push their several interests in a spirit of hostility and irreconcilability.

For example, if foreign agents had been assigned the duty of promoting discord in the United States in 1932, the method would have been to stress some unquestionable facts, such as the failure of the leaders of the financial and business community to keep the wheels of production turning, and to point out especially that the financial leaders had through their excessive greed wrecked the credit structure of the country. These were the facts which were successfully stressed by the New Deal reformers in the political campaigns which put them in office. But the enemy of the country would go further. He would not only sow all the hatred he could for the financial and business leaders, but he would also be untruthful with facts in the effort to demonstrate that this irresponsibility of business leaders was an essential part of the American system of private ownership, that only the ruthless could get to the top, that private capitalism was a system of legalized and organized brigandage, supportable only by overreaching and impoverishing the great majority. If, in addition to this, an enemy leader could get his sympathizers within the United States to instill in any substantial number of writers, teachers, and various group leaders the idea that a system of control of business by private individuals was ethically wrong, the propaganda campaign would be much furthered.

As long as the subversive effort to create discord is based only on economic differences of relative wealth and relative poverty, the whole people of a country will still rally in war to the defense of the scheme with which they are familiar. But if in addition to the economic differences a doctrinal difference can be created, so that dissentients feel the American system is basically wrong in morals and ethics as well as in economic functioning as in 1932, then a lasting disbelief in American institutions can be created in some people. If enough of them are at the opinion-setting level, there may be the possibility of forming within the country disciplined cells of disloyalty which will actively side with the foreign enemy even in the crisis of war. It is this kind of doctrinal discord which is sought to be spread in the United States by followers of the Communist line and doctrine.

If a foreign enemy of Russia were to try to intensify discord within that country today, the same main principle would be followed of determining what and where the existing factors of discord lie, and then proceeding to intensify them by any available means. Difficult though the means may be, due to the existence of a secret political police in Russia, presumably something effective could be done by way of radio and by undercover distribution of leaflets and pamphlets. Knowledge could be kept before the people of the Ukraine that they are overreached for the benefit of the city proletariat elsewhere in Russia. The fact that extensive secret political police activity has to be maintained should be continually stressed, as it, like the forced labor of those in concentration camps, speaks eloquently of the injustice and harshness of the Russian regime. The low standard of living of the Russian population should be emphasized and demonstrated. The soldiers must be reminded that their mothers and fathers and sisters live in rags so that the government can maintain enough army and police to try to protect its own regime and power. Then in addition to these facts of economic hardship, there must be stimulated in as many Russian minds as possible the doctrinal belief that this kind of oppression is necessarily involved in a Communist and totalitarian political system, that the system is ethically and morally wrong and incompatible with a right manhood, that it is the new slavery and inherently bound to remain so.

These two examples of methods of externally inspired propaganda suitable for use in the United States in 1932 and in Russia today are set out in order to illustrate for American readers the kind of propaganda activity that was in fact carried out in Europe in the period between the two world wars, and which did in fact intensify internal discord in the countries of Europe. The point is that in a world organized in the present form of separate states competing for power and self-aggrandizement, internal discord within the states themselves will be promoted in every way possible by those neighbor separate states who feel the need either of aggrandizement or of defense.

5. PERSISTENCE OF FACTORS OF SEPARATION

Every political state in time disappears from the world scene, so that it is no longer an independent self-governing community. In our own days we have seen some small states thus lose their own political identity, and have seen some great states—notably France—miss the same fate by only a slight margin. Survival of an independent France was due to facts of rivalry in the relations between her neighbor states more than to her own strength and efforts.

Though the political organization of a community as a separate state may disappear, many of the aspects of the community life remain unless the people themselves should be wiped out. Usually the majority of the people of a community which has lost its political independence remain in their old geographical location. The old geographical features of the nature of the land, its climate, its desirability and relative advantages and disadvantages in usefulness to its inhabitants remain as before. Political history scarcely has been long enough to take note of those vast changes over thousands of years which turn hot lands into cold, and cold into hot, or cover temperate zones with a sheet of ice.

Speaking in the relatively short terms of political life and history, it is remarkable how long old ethnic and geographical factors of separation leave their traces, so that even today the same kind of separation conflicts repeat themselves in much the same places and with much the same basic factors at work as could have been seen a thousand years ago, and still powerfully influenced by factors of two thousand years ago. Nor is it necessary to go to those relatively static locations with severe geographical limitations such as Egypt to see this kind of repetition. On the contrary, an example lies in Europe.

The secure Roman imperial boundary in the early centuries A.D. lay in Western Europe along the Rhine. Even the temporary conquests of the mighty Attila, the "Scourge of God" and his Mongoloid Huns, in the middle of the fifth century, did not push beyond this Rhine frontier. To the west of this boundary the Germanic peoples—notably the Franks—became thoroughly Romanized. Such Germans from further east as from time to time under pressure from eastern foes crossed into this area also adopted Roman ways and ideas. On the other hand, the Germanic peoples who inhabited the territory to the east of the Rhine and north of the Alps never came under any prolonged influence of the Roman civilization.

These eastern Germans were for centuries in conflict with Slavic language peoples still further to their east. In the three hundred years between the early sixth century and the close of the eighth century they were gradually pushed westward from the neighborhood of the Vistula River (which flows from the south through what is today Warsaw and thence somewhat east of north to the Baltic Sea) to the line of the Elbe and Saale rivers. It was about the year 800 that this western Slavic flow began to ebb, and for the next thousand years there was a gradual Germanic flow eastward, which was not seriously set back until the times of the German rulers Wilhelm II and Hitler.

Hitler, whose professed aim was the establishment of a new order under German domination to last for a future thousand years, in fact came much closer to undoing an old German order which had been in the process of growth for the past thousand years. This can be seen in the geographical dividing line which lay between eastern and western power in Europe after the Second World War. On the eastern side lay the Russian zones of occupied Germany and Austria and the states politically aligned with Russia. On the western side lay the American, British, and French zones and the states politically aligned with the West. This dividing line approximated the line of furthest Slavic expansion westward as it was to be seen in about the year 800.

X. Hint of the Cure for the Divided Community

EVEN in physical circumstances of climate, resources, and health favorable to a good community life, communities under every institutional form of government—whether monarchy, democracy, federal republic, feudal organization, despotism, or any other—have suffered from both acute and chronic discord, been threatened with secession, and taken part in the conflicts and wars of separation. This fact indicates that the primary causes of these various kinds of political division are to be found in something other than the form of political organization. Discord, secession, and separation are not mainly to be avoided by mechanical means, as by federation, or by self-determination of nations, or by the provisions of written constitutions. This is not to say that political forms are insignificant and unimportant. They are both significant and important. But their significance and importance are secondary and lie in the fact that one form of government may in the actual existing circumstances do more than another to promote the primary factors of division or harmony. Or a particular form of government may in the actual existing circumstances reflect the presence or absence in the community, especially in the leaders of its main lines of activity, of these more significant primary factors.

In the course of our survey of political division we have observed in operation the primary causes of discord, secession, and separation, the attitudes and dispositions of mind, often abetted by institutions not suited to the time and place, which have led political groups to hold too tight, push too hard, become too inefficient or too mistaken— the usual routes towards a seriously divided community. We now briefly summarize these factors in general terms and indicate, also in general terms to be later substantiated, the lines along which discord, secession, and separation might be avoided.

1. THE CAUSES OF THE DISEASE

In *discord* the main political faults—the attitudes that caused the trouble and prevented the reconciliation of the various motives of reform—were intolerance, inequity, dishonesty, mistake of fact, and indifference. These principal political faults, with varying relative significance in the specific historical cases, played the major parts in the several types of discord. These types of discord we characterized by their conspicuous features, such as holding too tight against change, pushing too hard for change, inefficiency of the traditional regime and government, and the bungling of attempted reform.

In the holding too tight type of discord, intolerance was exhibited as a principal feature. The powers that were in political control suppressed views and acts which appeared to them to question or threaten the going concern with which they were familiar and which seemed advantageous to them. Reformers, whether along economic or doctrinal lines or along the line of more recognition for hitherto neglected groups, were opposed by a stone wall of resistance and a blanket of repression. Associated with this intolerance was dishonesty, by which the aims of reformers were misrepresented, and by which the attempt was made to keep the following of the traditional leaders from finding out the errors of the leaders or correctly attributing their troubles to the ideas and acts of those leaders. In addition to intolerance and dishonesty there was also usually on exhibit the fault of inequity, or unfairness, in that the leaders of the regime put false values on the several groups in the community, denying to some their due place and influence, while seeing in themselves the sole rightful authority.

In the pushing too hard type of discord, there was intolerance against those who opposed the reforms and in addition to this intolerance usually a conspicuous mistake of fact as to what reform was actually possible in the existing circumstances, so that the reformers were pushing for something contrary to the make-up and sentiments of the people—especially at the leadership levels—in the community.

In both the holding too tight and pushing too hard types of discord it was normal that intolerance should be such an outstanding feature, because those who are holding too tight or pushing too hard alike have no use for the forces at work in a free community. They fear the fragmentation which may come from leaving leaders of independent groups and local leaders to their own devices with their own power and followings. In consequence they have intolerantly tried to cram all reform into their own mold and along their own direction.

In the inefficiency type of discord, where the state suffered from administrative confusion, the conspicuous political fault was mistake of fact, and a close second was indifference.

Mistake of fact, the failure to see the political forces at work in their true relative strength, the failure to grasp political cause and effect, was the basic factor behind the inefficiencies and government burdens which broke down states whose governments focused attention on certain important problems, like defense, and neglected others equally but less obviously important to the welfare of the community.

Sometimes as a result of these government burdens an apathy and indifference set in amongst the capable people of the community so that inefficiency spread throughout the community with a failure of achievement and productive effort all along the line. In other cases inefficiency arose from lack of belief on the part of the leaders in any worthwhile aim for the community and the want of loyalty to any cause other than the immediate material gain of the competing individuals and groups in the community. In such cases the government was without any coherent purpose, and the community exhibited drift and confusion.

Occasionally the discord of inefficiency and confusion was produced less from political fault than as a result of outside pressure and hard circumstances so formidable as to produce apathy, discouragement, and outright privation.

In those cases where needed reform was attempted but the attempt was so bungled that instead of the intended reform acute discord and disorder occurred, the principal political fault at work was again mistake of fact. The leaders through ignorance adopted measures and means not adapted to the realities of the situation, or abolished familiar administrative machinery without putting anything adequate in its place. A breakdown of authority—loss of any rule to go by—was the result.

We saw many cases in which force was relied upon to cure discord, whether in a breakdown of order, or in an effort to gain the seat of authority, or in maintaining an unsatisfactory regime in power. This use of force was accompanied and evidenced by intolerance, inequity, and dishonesty. Also present was mistake of fact about the real needs of the community, due to the exclusive focus at the leadership level on the tasks of getting and keeping power. While the force was in many cases necessary to cure actual disorder, the intolerance, inequity, dishonesty, and usually mistake of fact, accompanying the use of force, prevented any cure of the discord and instead served to perpetuate and intensify it. We noted that when the stage of violence or acute conflict was reached, intolerance for the time being was no longer a political fault. Instead it became necessary for survival when the issue of basic differences had actually been joined and attempt at peaceable reconciliation of the motives of reform had been abandoned by some really powerful partisan group in the community. Intolerance in these circumstances, though no longer a political fault or error, was still a potent political evil with its consequences of suppression and choking off of talents needed by the community and its perpetuation of discord.

The main political faults in the *secession* cases were intolerance and inequity, along with mistake of fact. The reason that these faults resulted in attempted secession rather than in continued discord was geographical, in that the discontented groups were so situated that existence as a separate state, a new political community, seemed practicable to the seceders. They tried by force to break loose from the traditional and hated government. If unsuccessful, the bitterness aroused in the strife and warfare of the attempt perpetuated and intensified the intolerance and inequity that had formerly existed. The community, though still held together by force in the form of the old state, showed discord more virulently than ever.

If the attempt at secession was successful, a new separate state came into being to take its part in the drama of *separation* on the world scene.

In the cases of *separation,* which is the situation existing amongst the separate states of the world, the political faults appeared at their maximum. The very fact of separation meant the absence of familiar customs and modes of adjustment between the competing groups. The usual relationship was one of conflict or anticipated conflict rather than of any genuine effort to cure differences on an equitable basis. Intolerance, inequity, and dishonesty, often compounded by mistake of fact, were the rule of the game.

2. POSSIBLE LINES OF CURE

As the divided community is characterized by disorder or unfree order and by change through conflict, it would seem likely that any real cure would lie along the lines of political attitudes and political methods conducive to a free order changing by way of growth to a better free order. At this point we shall simply state in the most general terms what may be these likely lines of cure, deriving some hints of the nature of a free order changing by way of growth out of the study we have made of the characteristics of its opposite—an unfree order changing by way of conflict.

If a man consents to the political order within which he lives, if he does willingly within it what he does, and if his consent is associated with an open and unfettered flow of truthful information, politically speaking he is free. He regards himself as a participant in a good scheme of activity and thinks that the rules of the activity are approximately right. He is like the player in a game who believes that he is playing according to the good rules of a good game.

For protection against the development of discord by way of arbitrary rule by an overpowerful government representing too limited an idea of the good of the community, it is necessary for a free order to have many loci of social and political power—independent individuals, associations, and groups with their own command of means and their own followings. To keep these independent groups and people from working at cross purposes or engaging in a competitive strife which results in such discord or disorder that an arbitrary rule becomes necessary, these independent individuals, associations, and groups in their relations with one another have to be subject to underlying rules, appropriate to a free order, which they accept as good and observe in practice.

These are the two principal ingredients of a free order: the independent individuals and groups with access to full and truthful information on the one hand, and their willing acceptance of the rules of the order on the other. Each group pushes its own way and in its own interest along the lines of the several motives of reform, but all this is within and subject to a scheme which each group either takes for granted as obviously right or sees as desirable and good.

If any kind of order—including a free one—is to accomplish anything worthwhile on a community basis, its leaders need to have loyalty to causes along which its energies are directed, and to have the courage of their convictions. Without this there is hardly the motive power for real achievement. The Roman sense of a just law, the Puritan standards of the colonists in New England, the Mormon belief in diligence, the religious fervor of the Hebrew prophets, are illustrations of the power that stems from loyalty to a cause. It was failure of loyalty to worthwhile causes and failure of courage which went hand in hand with the small-mindedness and indifference of France before World War II, the drifting along with no object in view over and above that of material personal gain.

If a free order is to change by way of growth, rather than to fall into discord and change by way of conflict and violence, the objects of the loyalty of its leaders have to be in fact good and right. More is necessary than energy, courage, and loyalty. Many followers of the *ancien régime,* or of Hitler, or of Stalin were energetic, courageous, and loyal. The *discord* cases showed that loyalty is often to bad purposes and bad leaders. The leaders in the community must not only believe that they are participants in a good order with good rules, but the order and the rules must be in fact good in the sense that they tally with the real needs of the community.

A free order, by the very fact of being a free order, is one in which the capable people will think they are performing correctly their functions in the community and will believe in the political framework within which they are doing this. Change by way of growth requires more, namely, that this performance of functions in the current institutions is in fact along lines that mean the continuing development of the order towards the increase of free order. Change by way of growth means that the free order and its methods and objectives are such that the free order is maintained and perfected. Then the political scheme is in fact good as well as appearing so to its participants.

From our study of the characteristics of the divided community we have knowledge of harmful political attitudes, beliefs and methods. We also fortunately have some hints of other attitudes, beliefs, and methods, such as might be expected to promote a free order in the first place, and then bring about its change by way of growth.

Tolerance consists in the willingness of one who has positive views of his own to concede that there may be good and usefulness in the contrary views of others and a willingness to let those views be presented in an effort to gain adherents. Tolerance is necessary to a free order and to change by way of growth to a better free order. Without tolerance there is no freedom for those who are trying to reform the traditional community practices, and the situation is accordingly typical of discord by way of holding too tight rather than of free order. The principal political fault which appeared in the divided community as a denial of tolerance was its opposite, intolerance, the suppression of dissent and of criticism of the traditional regime or the party line. Tolerance is, as we have seen, not invariably a political virtue. When irreconcilable division has taken place between powerful groups in the community and the free order has for that reason ceased to exist, an intolerant group—and very likely one committed to intolerance as a permanent political method—has prevailed over those who have tried to remain too long tolerant of it. Tolerance is conditioned on mutuality. It tolerates contrary views when peacefully promoted, but not when violently promoted.

Honesty means that one's statements and actions are in actual correspondence with one's belief and intent, and faithfully represent that belief and intent to other people. Honesty is necessary to a free order and to its change by way of growth. If a man or a group cannot trust the honesty of others but must instead fear that others are lying, then that man or group is unable to go ahead with constructive action in reliance on the word of others. Energy that between those of honest intent could be freely put into confident activity, has instead to be diverted to precautions against the dishonesty of others. Dishonesty towards another acknowledges that other as an enemy.

As a matter of course one deceives one's enemies in time of conflict and this is perhaps necessary in order to come out on top in the struggle. All is fair in war. Like tolerance, honesty between rivals is a doubtful virtue when the issue has been once joined in violence. But dishonesty though no longer a political fault is still a political and social evil, destructive in its consequences to freedom and to free relations between people and groups. Our study of separation showed that dishonesty was usual between nations even in times of nominal peace, and even between nations nominally allied with one another. We saw that each separate nation tended to take lightly its own obligations and promises in international relations when it seemed likely to be hurt by keeping its word. No free world order has been possible on such a basis, because no nation has felt secure in relying on the word of another. For example, agreements for disarmament have been regarded as worthless unless the agreeing states should be allowed to inspect one another against the dishonest cheating which would take place in the absence of inspection.

Equity, or fairness, means that one recognizes the due and just place and opportunity in the community which are owed to others as well as to oneself and one's own group. Equity is necessary to a free order and to its change by way of growth. Inequity was the political fault which in the internal affairs of England permitted the "dark Satanic mills" and the merciless overreaching of labor associated with them. Inequity was the political fault exhibited by the financial leaders of the United States in the events leading to the credit fiasco of 1929. Each had been solely out for himself, and the devil take the credit structure and the people of the country—which the devil proceeded to do. Inequity was the political fault in Hitler's doctrine of the rights and virtues of the German Master People. It was the political fault of other leaders who have regarded themselves as chosen to be the masters, but never the servants, of others.

Truth to fact means that one sees events as they actually are, makes a correct judgment about political cause and effect, and estimates properly the strength of the various forces at work in the community. Truth to fact is a virtue which requires intelligence and discipline. It is greatly aided by tolerance and equity, since these avoid bias which interferes with a clear view of things as they are. Truth to fact is necessary to a free order. It is necessary for defense against enemies within and without. In the vital American Congressional voting in August 1941, on the eve of Japanese war against the United States, truth to fact would have provided for extension of the term of selective service and the maintenance of an adequate army in being by a margin of more than one vote in the House of Representatives. Truth to fact gives right direction to tolerance and equity by enabling them to see the groups of the community in true colors and perspective. It is by truth to fact that the tolerant leader knows when the political situation has deteriorated beyond the time for continued tolerance and has instead reached that point where its continuance would only mean its overthrow by a party committed to permanent intolerance.

Truth to fact is necessary to change by way of growth to a better free order. Aside from luck—which is unpredictable—it is only through truth to fact that there is hope of escape from the mistakes, confusions, and inefficiencies which lead to and compound internal discord. Only through truth to fact is there a prospect of seeing the needs of the separate states of the world with sufficient accuracy so that tolerance, honesty, and equity will in their turn be enabled to work towards bringing a free order out of the present disorder of separation.

It might well be that the practice of tolerance, honesty, equity, and truth to fact, in an institutional framework conducive to these virtues, would prove to be the means of channeling in the direction of a free order the energies and loyalties which without these virtues have brought about discord and secession, and have perpetuated separation.

If tolerance, honesty, equity, and truth to fact are in accord with basic needs in the make-up of individual men and women, it would mean that these virtues were something that we might reasonably hope to attain and maintain by right education and the aid of appropriate institutions, both on the local scene and on the world scene.

PART II. SOURCES OF RIGHT

XI. Need of a Rule and Need of a Role

1. A RULE ON WHICH TO RELY

In the cases of discord, secession, and separation, the members of each group or party looked upon their own particular rule of action as right. This was true whether the group was one that was conservative, trying to preserve and maintain the customary tradition—like the old regime in pre-Revolutionary France or the southern planter aristocracy in the United States before the Civil War—or whether it was radical and reforming—like the commoners who were pushing for the abolition of the economic and political relics of feudalism in that same old regime France, or like the northern reconstructionists of the American South following the Civil War.

The reason for this is that any individual or group in order to accomplish anything, even to have a basis for coherent action, must have a working rule in which it believes. Without such a rule a man is lost, unable to move or act effectively. To push aside any deep-going doubt about the rule is necessary for self-protection and the maintenance of a confident basis for life's activity.

Those theologians who believe in an infallible Church are diligent and ingenious in their demonstration that the papal condemnation of Galileo's support of the Copernican theory that the earth moved around the sun was not a formal *ex cathedra* and infallible pronouncement of the Pope, but only a disciplinary measure. Of course from the point of view of Galileo the real difficulty was that the measure was disciplinary. But for the theologians, whose position, prestige, and certainty are today dependent upon the rightness of their views about infallibility, it is a necessity of self-protection that the Pope makes no error when speaking from the throne. That is the rule on which they rely;

and it has to be right. Otherwise they are adrift on a sea of doubt. Hence, when the Pope has made what now looks like an error, it must be that he was speaking only in a disciplinary line, not at all in a matter of faith and from the throne.

So today in the matter of scientific investigation and publication of its results in the Soviet Union. Any deduction drawn from observed facts must conform in its political inferences and tendencies to the requirements of Marxism-Leninism, the Soviet political line. The science of statistics must exhibit no bourgeois leanings. The science of genetics must believe in the inheritance of acquired characters, because if change in human nature cannot thus be brought about, there is danger that the Soviet theories of society and economic control cannot be brought into perfect realization. It may be that some of the views of this Soviet science which hews close to the party line will turn out to be right. But it will be an accident and have nothing to do with a good scientific method. It is fortunate for the military power of the Soviet Union that the physical theories underlying nuclear weaponry are so recondite that no Soviet politician can tell whether or not they conflict with Marxist-Leninist science.

The Tennessee fundamentalists believe in a literal interpretation of a particular English translation of the Bible. They forbid the teaching in schools of inferences drawn from geological observation which might run counter to this literal interpretation. The reason is the same as in the other cases: the fundamentalists cannot afford to lose their certainty and with it their hopes of salvation and personal survival. It is too devastating. They must push the apparent facts to one side, close their eyes, and refuse to look.

Curiosity is a powerful and characteristic trait of man as it is of many other mammals—consider the dog. For man it finds much of its usefulness in dispelling uncertainty and in helping him to know where he stands and in helping him to discover his reliable working rule. Curiosity also creates uncertainty because of its questioning of any current political or economic scheme. Those who are in a preferred position in the going concern—the nobility in the old regime, the Prussian Junkers in their heyday, the Wall Streeters of 1929—do not like critical curiosity about political and economic organization because it disturbs their certainty and is unsettling to the traditional rule which has done well by them and which they consequently regard as right. On the other hand those who feel in need of improving their position in the community approve curiosity and inquisitiveness about the shortcomings and the failures of the going concern, because they are looking for a new certainty that will be better for them, a new working rule that will seem right, and curiosity is a good tool for upsetting the old rule that is wrong for them. The curiosity that is dispelling uncertainty for one group is creating it for the other. As the former tend to think curiosity is a good part of their working rule and attitude, so the latter are likely to regard it as irreverent and dangerous.

In an industrialized country like the United States there is from time to time and in some segments of industry bitter hostility between laborers and their employers. Yet such is the value of a familiar rule, that if conflict occurs between the United States and a foreign country, ranks of employer and employee draw together, and distrust and fear of the outsider about whom little is known override any distrust and fear of the hostile domestic group about which a great deal is known.

The occasional exception to this exhibition of domestic solidarity in time of external conflict itself demonstrates the importance of the rule on which to rely as a factor in the working rule of what is right. As we saw in the discord cases, when there is within the community a deeply convinced, dissentient radical minority group which has cast aside both belief and hope in the domestic rule and its improvement by orderly means, such a group adopts its own dissentient rule to which it clings and which it regards as right. Then such a group, in the hope or wish that somewhere else there exists a better society exemplifying this rule and able to further and support it, attributes to the strange and foreign community about which it knows very little the excellences and virtues which it feels must exist somewhere in an ideal functioning of its own radical rule. Until there was convincing documentation of the harshness and severity of political rule within Soviet Russia, many radical reforming intellectuals in the United States thus projected their hopes upon Russia, and looked upon it as a place of greater political virtue and happiness. It is the time-honored wish to believe in a Golden Age embodying the political virtues conspicuously absent here and now.

To the extent that a reformer can avoid upsetting the mechanical rules with which people are familiar, he can lessen discontent with his reform. When Augustus reformed the Roman republican institutions and set up the principate, he preserved as much as possible old forms and old names. He did not abolish the ineffective Senate but sought to reinvigorate it. The British habit of observing the custom of the land, of a government by established law rather than by arbitrary fiat of the ruler, has given them stability through recent periods of reform. British leaders all along the line have carried on under the familiar processes of law and parliamentary procedure, and honored the tradition of peaceful reconciliation of differences.

One main source of strength of any political leader is that he gives his followers a rule to go by, so they know where they stand and what they can do next. Yet often a leader, due to hostile political pressure, is not sufficiently confident to maintain a constant rule. He changes the party line too frequently. And this by rendering his rule unpredictable to his followers, increases the ruler's as well as the followers' insecurity. One sees this fact clearly in the memoirs of some of Hitler's contemporaries. Injury was done to the German community and to the German army by overmuch personal rule by the unpredictable individual Hitler. In such cases the followers do not have any rule that is right, other than obedience to the shifting dictates of the ruler or the ruling group, and with this failure of certainty of the rules to go by, goes a corresponding failure of conviction both of what is reliable and what is right. Since an element in the composition of right is this very factor of reliability of the rule by which a man must operate, when that reliability becomes doubtful, the rule itself begins to lose in people's hearts and minds the quality of rightness.

Even in relatively minor matters, such as observance of the ordinary conventions in personal manners, his particular group tradition not only controls a man's actions, but he is unhappy, uncertain, and ill at ease in departing from the accepted code of behavior. People feel they are doing better to abide by the currently approved rules of sociability, whatever they may happen to be at the moment. There is a good market for books of etiquette which set forth correct manners of greeting guests or seating them at table, or the right rules of grammar or the traditionally proper use of the words *shall* or *will* quite irrespective of any relationship these may have to the accurate and clear expression of ideas. How the thing has been done in the past by leaders of the community is the right way to continue to do it. While this may be a relatively trivial field, it provides evidence of our need of a rule on which to rely.

The administration of justice in the courts is aided and developed by the invention of legal fictions the purpose of which is to bring cases within some familiar well-established rule of law. The lawyers and judges alike feel safer and more secure if they can bring a cause of action within the time-honored right framework of their old rules. For example, the law will make a man return money taken from me by force, on the ground that there is an implied promise to return on the part of the taker, a promise brought into being by the act of wrongful taking. Of course in fact any such promise is probably the furthest thing from the actual mind of the wrongful taker. But the lawyers, like the rest of us, function more securely in a set of familiar rules felt to be right by reason of their familiarity. Laws in any community must be subject to growth and change if justice is to be done in changing circumstances; but there is comfort and security in the idea of a fixed right rule—like the laws of the Medes and the Persians, which altered not.

The convenience of the known rule is such that one is not surprised when the substantive habits of eating and sleeping of an urban community are altered by an hour through the device of changing the hands of the clocks an hour. When the hands are set forward everyone gets out of bed, dresses, goes to work, takes their meals, and goes to bed again, an hour earlier than before. One smiles at the ease with which the change is brought about. But to some farmers who have adjusted their hours of work with animals and crops to such things as when the ground is dry in the mornings or the needs of their animals, this shifting of the clock seems actually wrong. They have to rise and eat at untraditional hours of the clock. The old rules of clock behavior to which they had accustomed themselves were the right rules.

When a child happens to have arranged his building blocks in a satisfactory manner, he is indignant when someone in an untactful manner tries to make some other arrangement the next day. The old way was the customary and the right way. In this feeling the child is father to the man.

When a child comes into a roomful of strangers, he is likely to be uncertain and ill at ease. He has for the time being lost his rule to go by, doesn't know where he stands, or what he is expected to do next. In this type of uncertainty in the absence of a rule on which to rely, the child is father to the man.

The motive which makes a man try to find a course of action, a way of life, that seems to him worthwhile also has a direct influence on the content of the rule he relies on and regards as right. If he can hit upon a working rule that aids him in fulfilling his ambition, then he tends to regard that rule as right. We saw an instance of this in the case of political leaders of the party out of federal office in the United States. The ambition of these leaders was furthered by a belief in states' rights as opposed to an increase of the power and rights of the federal government. Thus a program in support of states' rights was also a program which helped to satisfy the ambition of these politicians out of federal power, and so became their working rule of political action which looked to them as right. This states' rights attitude was adopted by the Democratic party when it was out of federal office in the years preceding and the years following the First World War. It was similarly adopted by the Republican party when that party was in its turn out of office in the twenty years following the great economic crisis of 1932.

A man needs his rule to go by, and if his rule is proving anywhere near satisfactory to him, he asserts its rightness as a matter of self-protection and preservation of his confidence and effectiveness.

2. A ROLE THAT IS WORTHWHILE

A group within the community, or a community within the larger community, likewise regards the particular part it is playing, its own attempted achievement, its own political role, as right. A man needs to have a sense of self-worth; he needs to think that what he is doing is worthwhile. Otherwise he looks upon himself with discontent. But, as we have seen, almost everything a man does is as a member of a group with which he has identified himself and his interests. Accordingly he feels an urge to believe that what his group does is worthwhile and right. This tendency to regard the role of his group as worthy and right is again a matter of his own self-defense and the preservation of his own effectiveness and confidence. It is like the case of his regarding as right his working rule that gives him his needed sense of security, of knowing where he stands and what to expect.

The sedentary people of lower Egypt and the neighboring Arabs of the desert are racially closely allied with similar hereditary mixture and intermixture. Yet the agriculturally minded and relatively static Egyptian looks down upon the nomadic-minded and wandering Arab, and the latter in his turn looks down upon the former. Each regards his own role as the right role. This is an old feeling in this part of the world:

Then Joseph said to his brothers and his father's household, "I will go and tell the Pharaoh that my brothers and my father's household have come to me from Canaan, and that the men are shepherds, for they have been breeding cattle, and that they have brought their flocks and herds and all they possess. When the Pharaoh summons you and asks what is your occupation, say to him, 'Your servants have bred cattle ever since we were young, both we and our fathers.' In this way you will get the district of Goshen to live in, for all shepherds are an abomination to the Egyptians."

In the Southern United States before the Civil War the poor whites, although suffering much from the competition of slavery because it rendered their labor almost worthless, nevertheless were vociferous supporters of slavery, because they derived a *standing* from its existence. Slavery made the place, the role, of the poor whites look more worthwhile in their own eyes.

When the followers and successors of Marius were pushing the Gracchan reforms—in favor of redistribution of land and of more popular government as opposed to the traditional senatorial control—the new Roman citizens who had been enfranchised as a result of the Social War were on the reforming side, which appeared likely to promote their position. Sulla was opposing these reforms, and within his following were many of the economically impoverished peasants and landless city poor of the old Roman stock, along with freedmen citizens, not of the old stock, but also not "new" citizens. As followers of Sulla they all no doubt hoped for preferential treatment in the event of eventual Sullan victory. Historians have nevertheless expressed surprise that these indigent citizens who might have been expected to line up with the reformers pushing for redistribution of land and more popular government were instead found in the camp of the aristocratic Sulla. The explanation has been put forward that as old citizens they felt their standing was threatened by any increase of political power or prestige of the new citizens. This seems a likely explanation and one in accord with the general principle of jealous protection which people give to their own sense of self-worth.

Adam Heinrich Müller in the early nineteenth century had this to say of his German compatriots and their worthiness:

The great federation of European peoples which will come someday as sure as we live, will also bear German lines, for everything great, fundamental, and external in all European institutions is certainly German. . . . The seed of German life has indeed, in these recent folk-tumults, only been extended ever further and further over the ground of our continent; it will proceed in its rampant growth and from quite unpretentious beginnings will gradually advance to mighty effects; let its growth be left to eternal nature.

Ludwig Woltmann, a century later, is even more certain of the German worth: "It is susceptible of anthropological proof that all European civilization, even in the Slavonic and Latin lands, is a product of the German race." "The Germanic race is called to fetter the earth in its domination, to exploit the treasures of nature and the physical forces of man."

Sentiments similar to these and similarly demonstrating the strength of the need for a sense of self-worth were put forward by many Japanese writers who stressed the essential excellence and rightness of the Japanese people and their arms in the period before the Second World War. We reviewed some of these statements in our discussion of political *separation*.

Political leaders everywhere seem to find themselves at the head of a group of people plainly chosen for some specially valuable purpose. In 1845 an American editor John L. O'Sullivan wrote of "our manifest destiny to overspread the continent allotted by Providence for the free development of our yearly multiplying millions." No doubt but we were the people. This manifest destiny of Americans helped to justify the annexation of Hawaii, when those islands were taken over by the United States in the course of its westward push of empire.

Sometimes man feels the kinship of mankind as contrasted with all the rest of the world, and he feels, despite the continual divisions within the community of mankind, a degree of common superiority. In this mood the need for a sense of self-worth, a favorable self-estimate, a role that seems worthwhile, leads man to refer to himself as the summit of creation, and he looks upon it as right that he should occupy this exalted role.

One's own role can often be made to seem more worthwhile in one's own eyes by depreciating the role of someone else. As this is an easy course to adopt, requiring no constructive effort, and as it serves to give some kind of satisfaction to the need for a favorable self-estimate, it is a widespread form of behavior. Prejudice affords some examples of this course. The man who is an object of oppressive prejudice might in fair competition beat out his oppressor, and the prejudice and oppression are a good way for the latter to avoid running this risk. The bigot who is absolutely convinced of the rightness of himself and of his role and equally convinced of the wrongness and inferiority of someone else and a different role is a familiar figure, and represents the need of a sense of self-worth gone to excess.

Another method for satisfying the sense of self-worth is daydreams.

These may be harmless, and if not too removed from reality may even have their usefulness as encouragement for constructive activity. Our interest in them here is solely in the evidence they offer of the urge towards a good self-regard, a gratifying self-appraisal. The esteem of other people is in actual life an important factor in helping one gain his needed sense of self-worth. In daydreams this esteem of others is imaginary. The gratifying self-regard is real enough.

The fact that flattery often proves successful in practice as a means of creating good will is another demonstration of the need for a sense of self-worth. One has a favorable idea of oneself—perhaps not too well sustained by any objective facts—and this idea the flatterer confirms.

The need for a good self-estimate may work in gruesome ways, destructive of the satisfaction of the need, but nonetheless illustrative of its power. A man unable to accomplish what he has set his heart upon, perhaps by some reason of temperament or lack of some necessary quality, and so failing to see himself in his worthwhile role, may try to gain forgetfulness of this failure through the drugging action of alcohol.

These various instances both from political life and social life demonstrate the presence in men and women of the need for a worthwhile role.

The motives springing from love, as of love of parent for a child, can in the case of normal people override considerations of ordinary rule and role. A man will help at all costs those whom he loves. The dictate of love determines for the time being what is right and establishes its own immediate role. It goes without saying that such a powerful force also plays a most significant part in the formation of the usual rule and role which it is capable of superseding. The relations between love and affection and the content of rule and role are such that they go far to determine the idea of what is right, as we shall shortly see.

Yet there are some people whose established rule becomes their whole worthwhile role, held so strongly that it overrides even powerful human impulses. The test of a fanatic in his role of fanaticism consists of his overcoming any competing claim to his loyalty, however powerful the claim may be. For example, when at a time of personal or family crisis the hard-core Communist puts the dictate of the party ahead of family love or other profound human impulse, he is thereby demonstrated to be a reliable party member. It is as if, to be specific, he deserts a sick and helpless child at the behest of the party that he undertake some insignificant chore taking him away from home at the critical time. The party rule has for him become his worthwhile role in life. Like the Tennessee fundamentalist he dare not face the prospect of losing the rule which has become his innermost value. Such harsh fanaticism is, in its own excessive way, testimony to the strength of the needs for rule and role.

3. WHAT DETERMINES THE CONTENT OF RULE AND ROLE?

In the following pages of this part of the book we look at how a man comes to acquire his ideas of a right rule and a right role. In making our inquiry we shall not go beyond what we can readily see and verify. We shall be content to describe what actually takes place, and shall not attempt to account for this actual behavior by any psychological theory. The reasons for this are twofold: first, a statement of theory is not particularly germane to our inquiry, which is concerned with observable acts and attitudes and observable sequences of cause and effect; and second, to the extent psychological theory might be germane, the science of psychology is as yet in a stage of development such that its theories and explanations, while often illuminating and useful, are no more than tentative.

XII. Imitative Response
and Impersonation

1. IMITATIVE RESPONSE

Imitative response is the involuntary tendency in each of us to re-enact the motions, manners, or feelings of another, whose state of mind and body gives for the moment a partial lead to our own, his feeling and manner setting up in us an echo, a replica, of themselves.

A familiar example of this primitive responsiveness is seen in the case of those who make up a crowd in panic, as in a theater threatened by fire. Even those who resist the impulse feel powerfully the urge to echo those who have given way to fear. When the panic takes hold, the echoing nature of response is evident, except that unlike an echo of sound in which the effects diminish as the original sound is reflected back and forth, in this psychic echo the effects of response increase and strengthen, each person becoming more and more involved in a common intensified feeling.

Sometimes a medium in a trance, with her own conscious personality in abeyance, will echo so completely the personality of her client or consultant that she will speak out the thoughts and hopes and fears of the client, appear to know intimate details of the life of the latter, as the pet name for a husband or a wife, and will produce in detail a story of what is supposed to be happening to some loved one of the client who may be on a journey of which the medium is entirely ignorant except as she is reflecting ideas and notions in the conscious or unconscious mind of her client. This is an extreme instance under unusual conditions of imitative responsiveness, the tendency to echo, but it sheds light on a process taking place in each of us all the time to a less marked degree.

Another less well-authenticated and much rarer, but apparently

truthfully reported, description of this primitive imitative response—
again in unusual and extreme conditions—is found in those cases
where human infants have been reported to have been brought up for
some years by a wolf foster mother in the wolf family. The accounts
of the behavior of such children, as in their feeding habits and in their
eerie periodic howling are, if true, a revealing illustration of the adoption of a rule and a role of sorts through primitive response.

It is not necessary for our present purposes that the physical mechanism of response should be understood. We are concerned with the
process by which rule and role are acquired, and if imitative response
is adequately identified as an important feature of this process, that is
sufficient. Perhaps physical tissue changes accompanying the acts of
response will someday be charted and described. How localized in the
brain or elsewhere these structural or physical accompaniments of
response will prove to be is an interesting question. A child could presumably not learn to speak without the power of response, the involuntary tendency towards mimicry and echo. That such response
takes place is a fact. How it takes place is at least for the time being
among the many more things unknown than known.

Alongside one's structure of instincts, and alongside one's specific
powers like those of seeing, hearing, eating, moving about, each complex and appropriate for meeting or helping to meet life's needs, there
exists this general tendency of imitative responsiveness, this tendency
of the bodily and emotional set of one person to communicate itself
and produce its replica or echo in another. It is difficult to visualize
the nature of the mechanics of a tendency which is spread over so
many different areas of behavior; but it would be more difficult still
in the absence of such a tendency to visualize the possibility of human
learning as we see it every day.

If I am possessed strongly by some feeling, under the sway of some
sentiment, and my friend to whom I respond has at the same time a
different strong feeling—then I am subject to the two inconsistent
feelings, until one succeeds in supplanting the other. I am out of tune
with him. This form of emotional discomfort is due to the unavoidable
echo of response, and to get rid of the discomfort I must either give up
my own sentiment or seek the company of someone whose feeling is
the same as my own. The desire to get rid of disharmony in feeling is
recognized in popular sayings, such as "misery loves company." If
my own feeling and sentiment is at the moment more or less neutral
and not at all strongly set then I take on easily the feeling and senti-

ment of someone else. In the presence of happiness I will then feel happy. Emerson noted that "All mankind love a lover." When my friend is sad I too will be sad.

A shrewd, calculating, narrow, and selfish man, with a well-set character along these lines, none the less is still endowed with a quota of primitive response. Such a man is baffled by one who is magnanimous. By means of response the former is intuitively aware of a confidence in the latter which he himself lacks. He feels the superior confidence of the other, but his experience is such as to prevent his having any understanding of why the difference exists. In such circumstances the need of a favorable self-estimate is likely to take itself out in the form of a verbal belittlement of the magnanimous by the shrewd and narrow.

Affection

Love and affection greatly reinforce the part played by response in the formation of rule and role. The parent is a major part of the child's sentimental system of what is lovable. As the child responds to the parent's ways, he find in those ways his rule to go by, his ideas of what is right. To the ordinary action of response is added the effect of love in making the ways of the one attractive to the other. Just as the youngster who falls in love for the first time seems uncritically to construct a sentimental system in which his girl stands for all that is good, beautiful, and right, so also is the natural tendency of a child's feeling about father or mother—a tendency capable of withstanding much abuse, and never wholly eradicated. Even in the case of the most arbitrary and harsh parent the child is torn between the demands of love and response on the one hand and hate and his own needs for autonomy on the other.

It is easy to see the primitive nature of response in a child. The child's ways are not yet set. Everything is new and undetermined, and the uncritical adoption of the attitude of a parent is consequently plain and undisguised. The little boy has never seen or heard a thunderstorm. As the sky darkens and the lightning flashes and the roll of thunder is heard, he watches his mother who is watching the storm approach. His own attitude is not yet taken. Now the mother shows alarm. The boy instantly responds, and bursts into tears. He has started to acquire a rule to go by in the case of thunderstorms.

If a child's parents unfortunately happen to belong in a despised minority group in a community, the action of response, which no one can escape, tends to make them take on some of the opinion of the community about their own group. This feeling, if they are sufficiently capable and resourceful, they may overcome. But to the extent that it lingers and to the extent that they have a keen feeling of distress at their lack of standing, this feeling will be communicated to their children by response.

The affection of close friendship similarly makes for the uncritical adoption of someone else's ways as my own. How my friend thinks and acts gains added attraction, and to the primitive suggestion of response is added an impulse to accept and adopt my friend's views and behavior just because he is my friend, and my sentiment is therefore such as to predispose me favorably towards his attitudes.

Each of us, as we have seen, stands in need of a rule to go by and of a role which seems worthwhile. The absence of such a rule and role is unbearable—a vacuum requiring to be filled as promptly as possible. Here in a trusted and loved one—especially a loved one like the father or mother who has had the answer to one's needs in the most vital and meaningful matters—is a near and immediate model of both rule and role. Response to such a one is specially resonant and imitative.

Near Attachment and Near Threat

Response to one's immediate group and desire to preserve the standing of that group and one's own role within it are so powerful as to focus the fear of the group and its members on whatever is the apparent nearest threat to the group and its ways, and to override any intelligent consideration of wider interests and more distant dangers.

At the time of the Thirty Years' War the Lutheran fear of Calvinism as a near immediate threat to the power and prestige of the Lutheran leaders led the Lutherans of Saxony to join the Roman Catholics of Bohemia in the aim of the Catholics to gain control of Bohemia. The response of the Lutheran leaders to their own close group was so intense as to override any considerations of the need for Protestant unity.

In the struggles between England and Germany in the twentieth century, the internal response of each group led to each regarding the other with fear and hatred as the nearest immediate threat to itself and its interests, and closed the eyes of each to the need for western European unity in the face of the power and ambitions of Soviet Russia.

The situation is reminiscent of the mercilessness with which a group of children will treat a newcomer who is a little different in dress or manner from the rest. The need of the members of the original group for a favorable self-regard and a good self-estimate bolsters the force of their response to one another and hinders response to the newcomer from taking normal effect. The familiar response that is comfortable and habitual outweighs a response that might make for insecurity and discomfort. It is as though the children were afraid to let themselves be friendly to the slightly different newcomer.

Perhaps this is the childish prototype of the destructive adult attitudes towards those just outside the immediate group and the nearest threat to the immediate group's good, as in the case of the antagonism of Lutheran and Calvinist, or the other near group antagonisms productive of discord within the larger community. One that we had occasion to note was the antagonism between owner and worker in industry, leading to a political alliance in the twentieth-century United States between the industrial workers and the farmers as opposed to the industrial owners, although the economic interest of industrial worker and owner is rationally closer than that of industrial worker and farmer.

Institutional efforts have sometimes been made to obliterate the possibility of close response when its likely results were regarded as injurious to the interests and accomplishment of the aims of the institution. Thus the Roman Catholic Church has attempted to prevent an imagined interference of close family ties and close family response with the functions of its clergy and their sole devotion to the cause of the Church. The Church has enforced a rule of celibacy on the clergy. Similarly, and for a like reason, in the third century in China, an effort was initiated to establish primary loyalty of court officials to the court and government rather than to their families. The method adopted was recourse to eunuchs as court officials. This arrangement, while even more successful than clerical celibacy in preventing the results of primitive response to mate and children, did not prevent response to other close groupings inimical to the interests of good Chinese government.

2. IMPERSONATION

Impersonation is the primitive tendency to put oneself in the place of some other person, or in the place of some thing, or to see oneself as an actor in some aspect of one's surroundings. Impersonation is used as a means of understanding the significance of the person or thing or situation with respect to which the impersonation occurs. The impulse to impersonate is primitive in everyone and either takes place spontaneously or is easily stimulated. As people vary in capacities, temperament, and acquired character and knowledge, the extent and the results of impersonation vary with each individual impersonator.

Impersonation in the Place of People

When, in the absence so far as is possible of any question of discipline, parents persuade a child to be fair to some other child, let us say to share toys with him—to observe the golden rule and act towards the other as he would like to have the other act towards him—two influences are availed of. One is the established parental relation, as a result of which the child wants the esteem of his parents and to stand well in their sight and judgment. The second is his *impersonating* the other child—putting himself in the place of the other child—by means of which he sees how the other child feels and looks at the situation. He pictures, because he himself is now in the place of the other, the other's sharing with him or depriving him of a toy and what his own feelings and reactions would be in that case. The result may likely be an awareness of the practical need for mutuality, and an actual observance of the golden rule. In a case of this kind, where there is direct personal contact between two children—or adults—primitive response is also involved along with the impersonation.

The impersonation of a pet animal obviously results in an improved rule of action towards him. I appeal to a little girl to stop jerking the leash attached to the collar around Dash's neck. How would she like to have someone jerk a collar that was around her neck? I am helped by the fact that she likes Dash to begin with, and this sentiment is in my favor. But even if she bore him a grudge, the appeal would be likely to take effect.

The desire for equity in distribution of material things, which has historically been an important cause of political reform or discord, is, as we saw, related in part to actual hardship and in part to the need for a good standing. A serf says it isn't fair for his landlord to have ease and fine clothes while he has labor and rags. Impersonation on the part of the landlord would result in a recognition of the attitude of the serf. Willingness and ability on the part of the former to do something to soften the disparity would be one way of avoiding what we have called the "holding too tight" kind of discord.

In the Book of Deuteronomy, as a sanction for enacting and observing equitable laws for the treatment of slaves and aliens within the Hebrew community, the sanction is this: "Remember you were once a slave yourself in the land of Egypt."

Impersonation in the Place of Things

There is no possibility of imitative response to creatures whose physical and mental structure is so different from our own that there is no biological basis whereby an echo of their condition or activity could be set up within our own structure. The nature of the experiences of such creatures is to us a closed book. Yet we cannot escape impersonation of such creatures. Though the bees have no queen, and the ants no industry, a man is none the less understood by other men when he talks about the queen bee, or says "Go to the ant, thou sluggard."

When a child impersonates his mother, and puts himself in his mother's place as a means of understanding how she feels towards him, he is aided greatly by primitive response. Not so when he impersonates a tree, to which he biologically does not respond. A child puts himself or someone of whom he has had experience into the place of a tree and thinks of the tree as a good or bad person, depending perhaps on whether it has given him cool shade or a painful bump when he ran his head into it. A savage impersonates the tree by putting a spirit in it, and takes steps to placate the spirit so that the tree will produce fruit. He thinks the spirit acts and feels like himself, as indeed it must, being the creature of his impersonation.

A man may see hints in nature of good luck or misfortune coming to him, when in fact the natural events may be quite impersonal. A man knows that he himself might wish to have some way of giving information to a friend. For such a purpose he might well work out a code or method of signals that would be understood by the friend. Now this man carries over the same kind of code or signal-giving tendency to nature, and thinks that some spiritual power is giving him signals by means of ordinary daily events. The black cat crosses his road, and he thinks it a signal of misfortune. A man impersonates— puts his person into—these insignificant events of his daily world and imposes upon them his own sentiments of the moment—his cheerfulness or foreboding, his love or hate—and comes out with a corresponding set of interpretations of the events, as if nature were a person communicating with him.

A famine might have been caused because a community leader had broken his oath and had been so cruel as to offend God—that is to say, God as impersonated by the successors of the cruel leader. The period of the famine might somewhat inconsistently be extended because the bones of the same cruel leader had not been properly buried and because the expiation for the cruelty had itself been cruelly overdone. Such an impersonative interpretation of the cause and subsequent cure of a famine is set out in the Bible in the 21st chapter of the Second Book of Samuel:

For three years during the reign of David a famine came, year after year. When David consulted the oracle of the Eternal, the Eternal said, "The guilt of blood lies on Saul and his house, for having slain the Gibeonites" (the Gibeonites did not belong to Israel but to the survivors of the Amorites; still, the Israelites had sworn an oath to them, though Saul had tried to kill them in his zeal for the Israelites and for the Judahites). So the king summoned the Gibeonites and asked them, "What am I to do for you? How am I to make some expiation, that you may bring a blessing upon the Eternal's heritage?" The Gibeonites said to him, "There is no question of silver or gold between us and either Saul or his house. And it is not for us to have any man in Israel put to death." "Then what do you think I should do for you?" he said. So they said to the king, "The man who consumed us and planned to exterminate us from all the territory of Israel —let seven of his sons be handed over to us, and we will hang them up before the Eternal at Gibeon on the hill of the Eternal." The king replied, "I will let you have them."

(Then the king handed over seven, including two sons of Rizpah, Aiah's daughter.)

These he handed over to the Gibeonites, who hung them on the hill before the Eternal. The seven of them perished together, put to death in the early days of harvest.

Then Rizpah, Aiah's daughter, spread sackcloth on the rocks for herself to lie upon, from the early days of the harvest till the rains fell from the sky upon the bodies; she would not let the wild birds settle on them by day, nor the wild beasts by night. When David was told what Rizpah, Aiah's daughter, a concubine of Saul, had done, he went and took the bones of Saul and his son Jonathan from the citizens of Jabesh-Gilead, who had stolen them from the citizens of Beth-shan, where the Philistines had hung them on the day the Philistines killed Saul at Gilboa; he took away the bones of Saul and his son Jonathan, along with the bones of the seven who had been hanged, burying the bones of Saul and his son Jonathan, along with the bones of the seven who had been hanged, in the grave of Saul's father Kish at Zeba within the territory of Benjamin. All these orders of the king were carried out, and after that God was propitiated over the land.

Impressed by the power of a thunderstorm many peoples have impersonated the storm putting into it a spirit—a god in their own image. The Norse god Thor was such a spirit. A people like the Hebrews who tended to monotheism impersonated the storm by putting into it the God whom they had already impersonated into the scheme of things as its creator. So in the 29th Psalm we hear Yahweh thundering:

> Praise the Eternal, O ye angels,
> praise the Eternal for his might and glory!
> Praise the Eternal for his open glory,
> worship the Eternal in festal attire.

> The voice of the Eternal peals across the waters—
> it is the God of glory thundering,
> the Eternal pealing over the mighty waters,
> the mighty voice of the Eternal,
> the majestic voice of the Eternal.
> The voice of the Eternal shatters cedars,
> the Eternal shatters Lebanon's cedars,
> till like a calf Lebanon leaps,
> and Sirion like an antelope.
> The voice of the Eternal splits the rocks,
> splits them with flashes of fire;
> the voice of the Eternal whirls the sand,
> the Eternal whirls the desert of Kadesh.
> The voice of the Eternal twists the trees,
> the voice of the Eternal strips the forest—
> while in has palace all are chanting, "Glory!"

> At the Flood the Eternal was enthroned as King,
> and King he sits for evermore,
> bestowing strength upon his people,
> blessing his people with peace.

It may or may not be true that man is made in God's image; but it is certainly true that God is made in man's image. This is an unavoidable result of the part impersonation plays in our attempts to explain the world around us. It is so because a man can think only by means of the mental equipment with which he is endowed, and his thoughts are marked all over with the characteristics of that equipment.

Among that group of modern philosophers, the existentialists, many are alike in that they have felt keenly their loss of values and have found themselves without an adequate rudder in their voyage through life. When they come to describe the world about them, they impersonate it, and come out with an alien universe, entirely meaningless in human terms. From that point some go on to one solution of their distress, perhaps by way of religious faith, others to another, perhaps by way of skepticism and defiance.

The content of impersonation appears to be one aspect of the fact that no thought can escape the limitations of the thinker. The unavoidable putting of oneself into the place of people and things in the effort to explain them is simply the crudest and most easily observed instance of a necessity of any mental process—namely, that it must use what qualities and abilities have been vouchsafed to the mind. No process of thought can escape the defects and inadequacies of the mind itself.

As it is vain to attempt to escape from the natural limitations of the mind's possible range of perceptions, an impersonative mirroring of the thinker is seen in even his most abstruse thoughts. David Hume pointed out two centuries ago that no one had ever been able to demonstrate a necessary connection between cause and effect. And no one has been able to do so since. Indeed some modern exponents of theories of probability maintain that in a long enough sequence of repetition of an identical cause, the identical effect would not invariably follow. The idea of necessary connection between cause and effect is a combination of observation of uniformity of sequences plus an impersonative carrying over into the observed sequences of the ideas of compulsion which we have experienced in our own personal lives. Probability itself is no more than a humanly limited interpretation or description of incompletely perceived events.

Even with all his limitations of perception, man's thought has enough correspondence with reality so that he is able to make useful descriptions of the behavior of phenomena, and thereby produce useful results. The engineer, the physicist, and the mathematician design bridges that will stand, subatomic weapons that will explode, and equations whose statements find a correspondence in observable fact. Yet the mathematician and his equations are subject to the constitution of his mental structure, so that his equations represent the necessities of his thought processes as much as they do the incompletely understood phenomena they describe. The facts are seen through the human spectacles or not at all, and are colored by the native tints in those spectacles. In the efforts of even the most talented of mankind, the quality and limitations of the thinker are necessarily impersonated upon his thought, and only in a being of unlimited perceptions could it be otherwise.

Impersonation in Situations

Everyone is his own playwright. Imagination sets up the scenes or situation in which the action is to take place, and impersonation determines the way in which the people in the scenes, including the impersonator himself, conduct themselves. To have a notion about something to be done, or something possible to do, is to have an accompanying impulse—although the impulse may be slight and at a low level of consciousness—to act the thing out. Such an impulse is usually overborne by contrary considerations or circumstances, such as other more significant matters at hand. Yet such an impulse is necessary to account for the possibility of acting on one's ideas. Without impersonation there would be no mechanism for anything other than purely instinctive actions.

Looking at a mountain suggests the notion of being at the top of it, what it might be like, what one might see from the top, and other related ideas; and then the imaginative and impersonative ideas of how an expedition might get there, and then a greater or less urge to put the ideas into effect.

If one impersonates starving children in Poland under severe war conditions, there is an impulse to do something to remedy the situation, attaining a greater or less intensity, depending on the ease or difficulty of practical action and the qualities of the impersonator—the vividness of his impersonation and the temperamental vigor of his urge.

A man at least momentarily sees himself as doing what he hears about someone else doing in a given situation even though the action may be one that he disapproves and that is out of keeping with his own character and habit. Such an impersonative thought is involved in his process of understanding what it is the someone else is doing, and has as one of its components a bodily and mental set, even though slight, in the direction of the described action. In this potentiality lies the basis on which, as we shall see, impersonation takes a main share in the building of rule and role.

Unconscious Impersonation

In most of the cases of impersonation we have so far considered, the impersonator has been aware of his impersonation, has known that he was interpreting the actions of others by attributing to them his qualities or the qualities of friends or enemies in his past experience. These supposed qualities of friends or enemies themselves result from previous impersonation as well as previous experience, so that they reflect to a great extent the impersonator's own frame of mind about the qualities rather than what the qualities really are.

But in impersonation we not only attribute to others feelings and ideas which we ourselves knowingly possess, we likewise project upon them our dimly felt and unconscious leanings. It is said that a wife wanting to be unfaithful and well aware of that fact may as a result of impersonation of a neighbor's wife accuse the neighbor's wife of infidelity. So also may a wife unaware of her desire to be unfaithful—perhaps because the notion is too shocking to her conscience—project upon the neighbor's wife this unknown desire of her own, and likewise accuse the neighbor's wife of infidelity.

The projection of one's own unwanted and disowned desires upon someone else is a special, but significant, kind of impersonation. It is significant because it demonstrates the fact that impersonation is more than a conscious device. When a man doesn't like to face in himself a fault of which he may be only dimly aware or not aware at all, a fault calling for self-condemnation, he projects the fault upon someone else —impersonates himself and his own fault into that other—and then can be as righteously indignant about it as he feels inclined.

Qualities which we wish other people had—perhaps because our lives would thereby be rendered easier or because the world would thereby be a place more in accord with our desires—we try to induce them to have by various devices of persuasion. One of these devices is to hold before them a model exemplifying these qualities, a model into whom we impersonate the desired qualities. This is often a partly unconscious process. One of my close friends in college was in his days at preparatory school a great leader in the school, with the normal schoolboy attitudes about school discipline and the normal leaning to pranks. A few years after graduation from college this young man died, and I attended a memorial address delivered by the headmaster of his former school. The headmaster described him as meekly law-abiding, obediently trustful of the wisdom of the rules set by his teachers, and as saying to his classmates that "our headmaster always knows best." As a portrait of my friend the characterization could not have been more inaccurate, misrepresenting a spontaneous and active youngster as a prig. But as an impersonative performance on the part of the headmaster, in which he wished upon his former pupil those qualities which—if more generally possessed by his schoolboys— would make that particular headmaster's life easier, it was an instructive address.

Ministers of the Christian churches in their sermons commonly impersonate into Jesus characteristics which they wish their parishioners might have. Especially in dealing with children, the minister sets up his own notion of what constitutes good behavior, ascribes it to Jesus, and exhorts the children to follow the example of Jesus, "to do what Jesus would do." As in the case of the headmaster, and the schoolboy, these impersonative ascriptions of character are worthless for any portrait of Jesus, but may be close to accurate reflections of the state of mind and ideals of the minister.

Like the ever-recurrent ideas of the "good old times" or of the golden age, people feel that somewhere, somehow, there must have existed in the past, or that there must come to exist in the future, or must exist somewhere else than where they are today, a world more nearly in accord with their hearts' desire. In the spring of 1944 a Japanese broadcast warned the Japanese people that "our brilliant history is about to be smeared by devils, the United States and Britain" and that they must be prepared to "die brilliantly to serve our nation." The exhortation went on:

We are at the crossroads of life and death, where the rise or fall of our nation will be determined. This is a most serious time. If we should prove to be a people of dead history, we should be ashamed before our ancestors.

Here the Japanese leaders impersonate standards of bravery, worth, and heroism upon the ancestors, in the hope that the leaders themselves as well as the people will be stirred to follow this impersonative example and avoid shame before their illustrious ancestors.

It is said that part of a man's mind will sometimes impersonate itself into a figure in his dreams, and will speak as a separate person to the man, perhaps trying to disclose to him needs of his own of which he has been consciously unaware. A particularly harsh businessman may have habitually suppressed the demands of his own primitive response and oppressed his subordinates and overreached his rivals; he may have been equally hard on himself and his family by pushing aside his and their normal needs for affection and attention. Perhaps the submerged part of his nature will appear to him in a dream as a person, and in language veiled—because even in sleep the customarily dominant part of his personality will try to shove aside such promptings and refuse to listen to them—but still capable of being interpreted, tell him of his own neglected needs.

It is a relatively common experience for one's mind, when consciousness is either in abeyance in sleep or directed to some immediate activity requiring attention, to solve one's problems or order one's ideas for one. Many people wake from sleep with a course of action clear to them about which they had been in much confusion. This creative, ordering part of the mind outside the conscious attention will sometimes impersonate, as when Joan of Arc heard the voices of her saints giving her excellent and practical advice about action to be taken at a military or political crisis.

It may well be true that a skilled fencer is more likely to be upset by a complete novice than by a semiskilled fencer. The skilled fencer correctly impersonates the semiskilled and knows what his motions mean, correctly interpreting his intent. With the novice, on the other hand, the skilled fencer may make errors of interpretation, because when by impersonation he puts himself in the place of the novice, he attributes to the novice skills and ideas which the latter simply does not have at all.

A historian writing about some people far removed in place and time and customs is under constant likelihood of making impersonative errors when he puts himself in the place of those who are the subjects of his study. How should a Victorian student in nineteenth-century England accurately impersonate a political insurrectionist in Palestine in the first century before Christ?

The content of their own primitive and uncritical impersonation is frequently not guarded against by political leaders and statesmen. Thus an American politician will attribute to the politicians of some other country substantially his own frame of mind and will thereby make misinterpretations and false inferences about what the foreigner is thinking and the meaning of his actions. For example, in a country short of food where the leaders are temperamentally given to violence as the method of settling controversy, neither verbal threats nor verbal fair promises are of any special significance except as incidental moves pending the real business of appeal to violence to determine who will be the boss and who will get the big share of the scanty supplies. When the politicians of such a country make threats or fair promises to some other country—one with plenty of food and a tradition of tolerance and give and take—the politicians of the latter take both threats and fair promises much too seriously, as if they had been made in their own easygoing and peaceably inclined community.

Painful Impersonation

Sometimes and with some temperaments impersonation produces such distress that it results in radical changes in basic living habits. The impersonation of animals killed for human food supply has turned some people into vegetarians. The more usual outcome of this kind of impersonation—which presumably takes place at some level in all of us—is to continue to put the slaughterhouse out of mind, to forget it in the interests of a correct diet.

When a group of frantic fanatics take part in a pogrom it is obvious that for the time being they have pushed out of mind the normal impulses which must arise from the impersonation of their victims.

All of us constantly see others in painful and embarrassing situations. The commonest protection against the discomfort of such situations is laughter, and release of the tension which might otherwise be quite uncomfortable. So if someone who is poverty-struck and unable to sustain a loss of any kind slips and falls against a painted wall, ruining his clothes and spraining his wrist, most of the spectators get off easily from their impersonation by a good hearty laugh. It is well for mankind that this is so. Laughter, and some of its quieter equivalents in a saving sense of humor or even a sense of powerlessness and irresponsibility, can be a comfort in a world awry.

Impersonation and the Near and Dear

Impersonation is a principal means—of equal importance with response and functioning alongside it—by which the rule and role of others are adopted as one's own rule and role. This is plain enough in the everyday learning of more effective ways in which to carry on one's ordinary activities. If you are an amateur gardener you may see some better gardener pruning a shrub in a more efficient manner than your own. By impersonation you put yourself in his place. Then you adopt his method if it seems desirable and effective. Unless either by response or impersonation you thus participated in his action and then subsequently impersonatively visualized yourself in the situation of carrying out the action yourself, there would be no means or possibility for you deliberately to copy the action of someone else.

The work of impersonation in establishing rule and role goes still deeper than the deliberate and calculating copying of effective ways of doing things; and this is particularly the case where the impersonator has affection, love, or admiration for the person whom he impersonates.

Love and affection remove resistances to the suggestions from impersonation. This comes about from one of the universally experienced results of the sentiment of love—the fact that love makes all things which are identified with the loved one seem good and desirable. So when the child impersonates a loved parent, or a loved teacher, the sentiment of love makes what the parent or teacher does, his ways of looking at things, his virtues and even his vices, seem part of a desirable and good scheme of things. Then the child's impersonation is followed unthinkingly by adoption of the ways and the attitudes of the parent or teacher as part of the child's own rule and role. There is thus a powerful early set towards good or bad, useful or harmful ways through impersonation of those who are near and dear.

3. THE INHERENT TREND OF RESPONSE AND IMPERSONATION

It is recorded in more than one instance in the early history of North American colonization that after months of savage Indian attacks upon some tiny group of colonists, when these same colonists were almost wiped out by starvation, their Indian enemies brought them food, saving them from extinction.

If a great natural disaster occurs today in the form of an earthquake in some Japanese city, aid and succor will at once be forthcoming from Americans to help the Japanese sufferers in their time of hardship, notwithstanding that only a relatively short time ago our airmen were dropping devastating atomic nuclear bombs upon other Japanese cities with the intent of destroying them and their inhabitants.

When one sees or hears of another who is in grievous trouble, response or impersonation makes his situation felt and understood, suggests appropriate action for the cure of the trouble, and if no other contrary motive or consideration intervenes the helpful action is taken.

It is possible that there is a specific motive of helpfulness, as when one removes the thorn from a dog's foot or hastens to rescue the man hanging from the ledge. It is certain that response or impersonation is necessary to pave the way for such a motive to take effect. Without the response or impersonation the situation would not be clear and the need of the sufferer would not be understood.

If imitative response alone were involved in the case of my seeing a man in peril, I could escape the distress arising from response by the act of running away and leaving the scene. But as impersonation and memory are also unavoidably involved, running away will not turn the trick for me in the same way as carrying out the line of aid suggested as a result of impersonation.

Why is it that when a boy rescues a frog from a snake, or interrupts the stealthy approach of the cat upon a bird, he impersonates the prey more vividly than the predator? Why does he make himself uncomfortable by putting himself in the disastrous situation of the hunted rather than in the much more satisfactory situation of the hungry hunter about to be fed?

The answer may lie in the dramatic fact that something irrevocable is happening in the case of the victim, and that one's impersonation is seized by the awareness of this and gives full attention to it. For the snake and for the cat, only an ordinary incident in the workaday life of either is taking place. But in the lives of the frog and of the bird the incident is singular, perilous, and terminal. Or the answer may lie in childhood experiences and of an acquired dislike of snakes and of liking for birds. In the case of frog and snake, no primitive response is likely to either. In the case of bird and cat, primitive response to the cat would seem more likely than to the bird. But in both cases impersonation seems to run more strongly towards the victim.

All mankind unites to overcome disease; and this is not only from a selfish calculation about the fact that each one of us might become subject to the disease—as in the case of one that is communicable—but also from a benevolent impulse, whether existing in its own right or as a result of the processes of response and impersonation.

For our present purposes we exclude from consideration the powerful impulses towards benevolence and protection which arise from the instincts necessary for the preservation of the life of infants, the devotion of mother to offspring throughout the mammalian realm. This desire to protect and cherish perhaps spills over to other young, who are not the natural specific objects of the impulse—as in the accounts of the rearing of human young by wolves—but this gives no basis for an inference that the motive applies in totally different kinds of situations, where no protection of young by adults is involved. The case of the wolf mother nursing the human child is perhaps more analogous to the spilling over of the powerful sexual impulse in a nonspecific way in those cases of sexual intercourse of men with animals.

If outside the parent-child relation there is a specific motive of helpfulness or benevolence for which impersonation and response pave the way, or if impersonation and response themselves in their own action tend towards benevolence, this motive or tendency is in either case one that is easily countered and overcome by other factors.

For example, consider the mercilessness of children to a newcomer to their group, or the way in which one child if he is strong enough grabs the toy of another. Think of the wars between nations in which instead of rescuing those in distress we artificially heap more distress upon them, or where instead of uniting to defeat disease we lay plans for germ warfare. Think of the brutalities and cruelty practiced upon man by man, of the pleasure of the populace in gladiatorial combat. It is evident that the capacity for cruelty is just as much a part of one's native endowment as is that for friendliness or mercy.

Yet if we are right as to the unavoidable mechanism by which response echoes the states and feelings of others and by which impersonation puts one in the place of others, we can see that bitterness, harshness, and cruelty cannot be wholly satisfactory. The spontaneous sympathy cannot be altogether stilled; so discomfort and dissatisfaction remain, and the need for finding a better way than harshness and brutality to deal with opposition. The natural impulses towards benevolence have to be suppressed in the course of a pogrom or in dropping a nuclear bomb upon the inhabitants of an enemy city. At some level of our being the cruelty is registered as wrong for us, contrary to an urge that ought to be fulfilled.

Our impersonation of animals is spontaneous but is not nearly so strong as in the case of impersonation of people. It is not so fortified by primitive response, as we do not have the physical and psychic likeness to animals that we have to people, and so there is less liability to echo their condition. The involuntary shudder at seeing a dog run over by an automobile is probably more impersonative than responsive. In any event we have no difficulty in eating other animals to nourish ourselves. It is of course true that some people have customarily eaten their kind, someimes under the mistaken notion that they thereby acquired the virtues of the eaten. Cannibalism again shows that what I have called the inherent trend of impersonation can be readily turned from its course in the case of some kinds of people in some stages of development.

It is likely that there are different native capacities for allowing the inherent trend of response and impersonation to take its natural course. Positive affection and friendship are more easily triggered in some than in others, just as one man or woman has more capacity for love than another. Similarly it is reasonable to suppose that some native temperaments are more easily triggered to suspicion and hostility than are others.

All mankind needs to learn to avoid those dispositions which lead to political division, the harmful attitudes of intolerance, dishonesty, and unfairness, shown in the earlier part of this book to be conspicuously identified with discord, secession, and separation. In attempting to rid ourselves and our children of these divisive attitudes and dispositions, we would find ourselves up against an almost hopeless task if the inherent trend of impersonation and response were towards hostility rather than benevolence.

In the case of impersonation of and response to the helpless in acute distress, the impersonation and response do appear to be followed by an urge towards giving aid. This may very likely be because those who are helpless and in acute distress offer no threat in ordinary circumstances to any of our own interests, so that the tendency of impersonation and response is allowed unhindered scope to take its naturally benevolent course.

In our effort to devise means of avoiding discord and division, it is fortunate that we do not have to run up against an inherent trend towards hostility and intolerance in the basic primitive mechanisms of response and impersonation. The inherent trend, weak though it may be, is benevolent and in our favor.

XIII. What Is Built Upon Response and Impersonation

IN Chapter 12, in our preliminary identification of some of the main features of imitative response and impersonation, we noted the effect produced in the case of each of them by the presence of affection and of trust. That effect is to give a free scope to the promptings of response and impersonation. The echoing action of response is increased; the impersonator willingly copies the ways of the person in whose place he puts himself. The process is cumulative, the response and impersonation reinforcing the affection, and the affection reinforcing the response and impersonation. The interests of those who are near and dear become one's own interests, and altruism comes into being. The fear-ridden thrall of an oppressive regime, reconciled to his own hardship, may still strike the blow for the freedom of his son or his friend that he will not strike for himself.

How, in the relations between man and man and between group and group, is the cycle of the interaction of response and impersonation with friendship to be more widely attained so that response and impersonation will strengthen friendship between more people and groups of people? How are we to minimize the chance that individuals and groups, by erroneous impersonation or by misinterpretation of response, will read into the aims and actions of others a hostility that may not be there, or will regard an actual hostility as permanent or unavoidable when in fact it could be dissipated?

1. HOME AND THE LOCAL GROUP

A child's character is at first formed on the bases of his native endowment of ability and temperament by those near to him to whom he responds most freely and impersonates most readily. To the extent that he likes and trusts them he starts to adopt their ways as his and to acquire his rule and role from theirs. Indeed so great in his need of rule and role that even in a case where his feelings are mixed—as in feelings towards a harsh parent—he will still largely take his ways from his parent. Simply the physical nearness of the parent makes the parent the principal object for response and impersonation. It is the parents that in the first instance determine what aspects of the child's character are being enhanced by impersonation and response, how the child sees himself as doing things, the child's developing rule and role.

This control of the parent over the fundamental trends in his child's character, always within the limitations and conditions set by natural endowment, is cause for both encouragement and discouragement in the prospect for gaining traits of character that will be useful in avoiding political discord and division—encouragement, because it is likely that if parents come to possess the habits of tolerance, honesty, equity, and truth to fact, these will be adopted by their children; discouragement, in that parents so generally are conspicuously lacking in these virtues, and given instead to the habits of mind and attitude productive of discord.

Little is definitely known about the effect of some very early events that may go into the development of a hostile or fearful character, such events, for example, as thwarting in the case of infant feeding or other early experiences of distress or grave uncertainty. When the effects—if there are any of importance—of such factors are demonstrated to be facts, the facts must be included in the instruction of prospective parents. Whether the effect, if any, of such a situation upon a child's character and attitude towards people is produced by way of extremely early and primitive impersonation or by way of a direct distrust of all events—people included—is a speculation with which we do not need to concern ourselves here. Such an experience would be but one of many early experiences, and it seems likely that the whole range of experiences would be more determinative of the child's attitude than a single particular experience.

We do little in our formal education at present to teach the young what the family can and should do in bringing up better citizens, so that when the students become themselves parents—and some of them will be parents of highly capable potential leaders—they will have a conscious realization of the power that is in their hands. They should be taught to know that through the mechanisms of the child's impersonation and response, and subject only to the child's constitutional predisposition and capacity, there falls upon them the setting of their child's character along lines that are likely never to be wholly displaced. The hand that rocks the cradle can indeed do much to rule the world; and hopefully by a rule better than the defective one disclosed by the political facts of discord, secession, and separation.

Virtues like fairness and tolerance, which are essential for a community if it is not to fall into discord, can be taught early by example better than by precept, though precept too is useful. For this reason too, mother and father have an opportunity at home that is of basic importance for the good of the state.

It is not only parents that provide children with rule and role. There are other immediate standard setters for the young in this process of gaining attitudes and habits of mind that may stick to them for life. The schoolteacher is such a standard setter. Since impersonation and response work at a primitive level and so in the first instance make for an automatic imitation, it is most important with a view to a harmonious and orderly community that teachers of the very young have a socially useful character—especially in habits of mind and attitude. Imitative response is by its nature uncritical and unthinking. Impersonation although spontaneous is a more subjective and conscious process. Yet when the child puts himself in the place of another, it is for him and for the time being he the impersonator who is doing what that other is doing. The impersonator's interpretation of the action or attitude may not be identical with that of the person in whose place he has put himself, but none the less he is picking up from the impersonation some kind of suggested pattern for future actions and attitudes of his own.

The child, like the adult, needs a reasonably good self-estimate, the sense of worthwhile role. The views of others, their condemnation and approval of what we do, are, through our response and impersonation, factors in our own self-estimate. So for the growth of good character and useful virtues in the young, the judgments and opinions of teachers need to flow from a right character and sound frame of mind. The primitive responsive and impersonative processes of the pupil pay attention and give effect both to the frame of mind of the teacher and to his judgments and opinions.

The Nazi regime in Germany distrusted the influence of parents because the Nazis thought parents might tend to produce an individuality in children contrary to the kind of blind obedience useful to the Nazi political leadership. So if a child in school repeated views of his father or mother hostile to the regime, this was duly reported by the teachers to the Nazi party, with possibly disastrous results to the parents. Such a process of course destroyed the free confidence within the child's family, as the parents must be continually guarded in their speech. The transmission from parent to child of a confident and self-reliant character in so far as it is not due to inborn temperament depends on impersonation and response, and this fact in turn requires that the parent be confident and self-reliant, since response—and impersonation too—copy what is below the surface of the mind with as much facility as what is on the surface. The Nazi leaders were unwittingly setting themselves against what every community needs for its maximum creativeness and usefulness—self-reliant individuals going about their work confidently. By the reporting of childish statements about parents, as a means to discover and eliminate dissentient views, the Nazis undermined the greatest educational tool available —the unrestrained confidence within a family—for the creation of outgoing character. What this Nazi technique could at most produce —and did in fact produce—was an undue number of ill-natured subservient henchmen with no faith in their own individuality.

The acquiring of standards by response and impersonation does not end with youth. Those engaged in the various lines of activity in the community copy the successful leaders in those lines. In circumstances where the successful leaders happen to be ruled by standards harmful to the community, their followers pick up the harmful standards. In discussing *discord,* we saw that when the financial and business leaders of Wall Street were mainly motivated by the desire to feather their own nests—with no attention given to the good of the community in the form of a sound financial credit structure—this attitude spread to the subordinates in their offices, and to the rising leaders there, like an infectious disease. We can now see why this was so, and that response and impersonation were the explanation for adoption of the standards of the current Wall Street leaders. There is an element of truth in the cynical jest that a practical businessman is a man who practices the business errors of his contemporaries. The mechanisms of response and impersonation indicate that this is likely always to be the case, and that errors of leadership tend to perpetuate themselves until changed by some major pressure. The effect on Wall Street practices of the reforms which followed the financial disaster of the late nineteen-twenties and early thirties was an effect of such a major pressure.

Good practices too have this self-perpetuating tendency, also through the copying action of response and impersonation, and may prevail until a change in circumstance unfortunately renders them no longer good or useful. This sequence we saw in the case of the Junkers, whose tradition was useful in conditions of frontier warfare, but harmful in the nineteenth-century attempts of the Germans to become unified on a basis of tolerance and the free consent of the governed.

Standards for action are probably most often set by those who have a reputation in their community for sound and successful carrying on of their own affairs. Such local leaders might be the owner of the general store in the village, the farmer who has taken his animals to market at the right time or who has planted in past years the crops that did well and were needed, the local minister whose judgment of his neighbors has proved correct. Like the president of the bank, or the industrialist of demonstrated competence, what these people do serves as a model of action for their neighbors. It would be interesting to know what is the effect on individual action of such wide-reaching agencies as the radio commentators and newspaper and magazine editorials. It seems likely that their greatest effect on actual conduct would be by way of their persuasiveness to these various local leaders. Public opinion and especially actual action—let us say in such a matter as voting for a candidate for public office—by any large numbers of the public very likely result from the lead given by these local leaders rather than directly as a result of the radio broadcasts, newspaper editorials, or other far-spreading forms of expression of opinion. If the publicists succeed in influencing those who have for one reason or another come to be looked upon as local leaders, these in turn set the actual pattern of action in the community. It is only on some such basis as this that the formation of a positive and intelligent public opinion in a political community of seventy million adults can be regarded as at all likely.

2. EXTENSION TO WIDER GROUPS

As a local community grows and comes into relations of trade or exchange of ideas with geographically neighboring communities, an increase of impersonation by the members of one community into those of the other necessarily takes place. Each sees through his own eyes and with his own interpretation the other's interests and aims and how they accord with his own. With this impersonation a greater understanding each of the other is achieved. The impersonative interpretation becomes more accurate and useful. The familiar cycle which we saw at work in the near groups of home and neighborhood has got under way in a wider range—the cycle of increased understanding and more accurate impersonation. So on the local scene this may lead to an attitude of friendliness and the recognition of another's interests as one's own or as consonant with one's own. This is the normal process of attaining a larger community of interests along with the formation of a greater political community or state which serves the common interests. The contemporary end result—end result for the time being—of this historical process is shown in some great political community existing today which, despite the presence within it of local special interests and possibilities of discord, nevertheless recognizes common interests. Such a community is the United States of America, which consists of many individuals in local groups and local participating communities, all of whom to a greater or lesser degree recognize the bond of common interests, common sentiments, and common aims which brought into being, accompany, and sustain the fact of United States citizenship. Without the recognition by impersonation of the common interests, common sentiments, and common aims, the political structure—the United States—would fall into discord.

When the wider community of interests has once been recognized to the extent of the formation of a politically organized state, the citizens tend to follow and take as their own the standards of the conspicuous leaders of the state. If the leader and idol of a nation happens to be a Hitler, that is too bad; just as it was too bad for the young man in 1929 Wall Street if his office leader happened to be the unsocial-minded president of one of the great banks.

Heroes in the Past

In the effort to form the character of children along patriotic lines, we rightly hold up as objects for their impersonation heroes in the past history of our own country—like the young Nathan Hale whose only regret was that he had but one life to give for his country. In going in this way to a hero of past years, we can abstract his conspicuous patriotism and free it from our own contemporary quarrels and differences, and so set up and impersonate a hero representing the pure idea of patriotism. We are no longer confused by whether or not Nathan Hale stood for ideas which in his own time—or were he living in our own time—might have made us dislike and fear him. We forget that half of us might have been loyalists and half revolutionaries, and at bitter odds with one another. But now there is no threat in Nathan Hale's patriotism and we can all see its excellence, and he can rightly serve as a model for all our young.

As we look into the past, we gain a perspective and a disinterestedness which lets us see people in those days for what they were trying to accomplish, and as we put ourselves in their places by impersonation, select models whom we admire, and teach our children about those models, hoping that our children will impersonate and copy them. We idealize a Robin Hood for his quick sympathy and his aid to those in need, for his skill in archery and his personal courage. We succeed in overlooking his lawlessness and that he was the head of a robber band. Were he our contemporary, threatening some of our own interests, we would find admiration harder.

Socrates in our minds stands for an unswerving effort to uncover fact and truth and is accordingly a hero in the realm of mind and spirit. We find it hard to sympathize with the jury of Athenian citizens who condemned him to death for corrupting the morals of Athenian youth.

Distance in time seems to help us impersonate great figures in a friendly way, so that we estimate them in the light of their own aim and the need of their own group. Even a conqueror like Genghis Khan we admire for skill in ordering his troops, and his ability through superior organization to defeat greater numbers of European opponents.

In our attitude towards these heroes of the past, our impersonation for the most part follows what we have called its inherent trend, making for appreciation of the situation of the person impersonated and a feeling towards him that is free of hostility. As in other cases of impersonation, the hero is interpreted in the light of his impersonator's character and experience, and in turn exerts a formative influence on the impersonator's character and becomes an additional part of the impersonator's experience. It is for this reason that the ideal heroes and heroines admired by young boys and girls are of such significance in the development of the character of these young people. A part of the art of education at school and college levels consists in the teacher's success in firing his pupils with enthusiasm for the heroes and heroines of history.

Impersonation of the Foreigner

As soon as ideas of hostility have arisen towards a contemporary present group with which some great man of the past may be identified, then our friendly impersonation of such a man becomes subject to interference. For example, when the United States and Germany were enemies in the First World War, many American audiences did not want to hear the music of German composers. American critics were tempted to view classical German music which had been distinguished for its orderliness as pedantic, and the music of romantic German composers which had been distinguished for its poignancy and excitement as intemperate and uncontrolled.

When circumstances are such that the members of two groups see a possible clash of interests, and even more after conflict has actually set in between two groups, the resulting fear, hostility, and suspicion on each side towards the other makes an accurate impersonation extremely difficult. I see him and he sees me as a threat or a foreign devil, and we each implant upon the other intentions and traits of character drawn from our own hostile potentialities. This of course renders reasonable compromise on a basis of fair give and take most unlikely.

When we look at groups other than our own, we should get as accurate information as possible about their actual needs and what they are trying to do—looked at as much as we can from their point of view. This would as a rule result in a friendly disposition towards them. After the establishment of such a disposition there is plenty of opportunity to see the various crossings of interests that may exist between us and them. But the original friendly disposition increases the chances of a reconciliation rather than a fight.

When you don't see what the other fellow is up to, you are uncertain and have no rule to go by. At best you are suspended in suspicion; at worst you make a mistaken impersonation. Until you have the facts, your impersonation is almost sure to be mistaken. But when you understand his problems and what he is trying to do to solve them, you then more accurately impersonate him. Unless what he is doing is in fact deliberately hostile to you, which may well be the case—and perhaps even then—you think of ways of working out his problem as well as your own.

In the specific case of a foreign nation in the contemporary world, teach people—young and old but especially the young—about what the foreign nation is legitimately trying to do, before you make people afraid of it as an enemy and a menace. Give the inherent trend of impersonation a chance to produce its naturally tolerant result before establishing an acquired hostility. Of course the facts of danger and hostility, where they actually exist, cannot be disregarded. Hostility may have to be met with hostility. But the discovery of a sound basis of reconciliation of the hostility is more likely if there is understanding on one side rather than on neither. If reconciliation is not possible, accurate impersonation and understanding mean a more intelligently directed and successful hostility.

We saw in our discussion of political separation that a world scene consisting of independent hostile nations is a bad scene. Unfortunately we saw in our discussion of secession that no cure is necessarily brought about by bringing different regions within a single political state. There will still be regional conflicts such as those which brought on the American Civil War and other wars of secession. The creation of a world-wide neighborhood may well be marked by world-wide neighborhood feuds. Nevertheless, as communications and transport improve, and physical closeness of peoples to one another becomes a fact, it seems inevitable that the solution to the problem of a just and orderly world has to be sought along the lines of a larger neighborhood. If there is to be hope for success, the young who are to become political leaders will have to be started off friendly to alien groups. In any such world neighborhood there will be bound to be—and for a good life there ought to be—particularized regions with their own special interests. Such parts of the whole can likely get along together on a reasonably co-operative basis only if they have tolerance and fairness towards one another.

The Nazi method of trying to evade the golden rule and dodge the natural tendency of impersonation was to play up excessively the German need for a sense of self-worth and to teach the German people that other nations were in a different and inferior category, so that the Germans ought rightfully to be their bosses. This kind of sense of role—involving as it does an offensive assertion of superiority to foreigners—provides no basis for getting on with foreigners—especially when the assumptions are incorrect. A much better method is to use impersonation so as to point up the common problems of ourselves and the rest of mankind. We are all in the same boat, all on the same kind of unsought adventure of life. Impersonate strangers for what they are—people trying by their own lights to work out their own worthwhile role.

3. BAD STRUCTURES AND GOOD ARE ALIKE BUILT ON THE BASE OF RESPONSE AND IMPERSONATION

The Nazi Germans, opposed to the growth of merciful sentiments in the young, made a deliberate attempt to create sympathy only with the strong and to avoid response to and impersonation of the weak. Such indoctrination started early with the *Pimpf*—the Little Ones— aged from six to ten, still too young to be *Jungvolk*—ten to fourteen— or *Hitler Jugend*—fourteen to eighteen. A poem was composed for these Little Ones to repeat in class in unison, reciting the natural prey-ing of the strong upon the weak:

> "Please," begged the victim, "let me go,
> For I am such a little foe."
> "No," said the victor, "not at all,
> For I am big, and you are small!"

There sometimes are valid reasons for refusing mercy, but the Nazi reason—*because I am big and you are small*—is not one of them.

Fear is a powerful factor in the perpetuation of error. When the Canaanites had become dominated by a religion whose god was vin-dictive and terrible, the fear of this god produced the most extravagant means of placating him, of winning his favor and averting his arbitrary wrath, or of assuring him of the loyalty of his people and the faithful observance of their vows. First-born children were sometimes fed to this god—were passed through the fire to Moloch. The process per-haps involved placing the children on the inclined arms of a figure of Moloch, whence they rolled down into a fire roaring in the belly of this particular image of God.

How did the parents of a child fed to Moloch feel about the sac-rifice? They were part of a group struck with fear of the god. They had been taught from childhood what the god sometimes required. By imitative response and impersonation they had taken over the fears and false science of their elders and leaders. So above their sorrow and horror, we can imagine a solacing conviction that in doing something to save their group from the wrath of God their course was right, as well as a feeling of certainty that it was expedient and neces-sary.

But such a religious requirement of passing a child through the fire to the god is an inherently unstable requirement, because as soon as a prophet comes along with the vision and courage to see the uselessness and the wrong of such a practice, he has on his side the natural forces of affection, and of primitive response to and impersonation of the child. This is a hard line-up for even superstition and fear to prevail against, and in the long run the priests will lose out in their effort to maintain the ancient ritual and their role as its ministers.

> How shall I enter the Eternal's presence,
> and bow before the God of heaven?
> Shall I come to him with sacrifices,
> with yearling calves to offer?
> Would the Eternal care for rams in thousands,
> or for oil flowing in myriad streams?
> Shall I offer my first-born son for my sin,
> fruit of my body for guilt of my soul?
> O man, he has told you what is good;
> What does the Eternal ask from you
> but to be just and kind
> and live in quiet fellowship with your God.

When people are crazed by exhaustion, they are no longer wholly human, in that many of the normal requirements of a normal disposition are temporarily suppressed, and actions are taken which would never gain the consent of the whole man. In some of the police states today there is a use of brutality, exhaustion, and fear which reduces the objects of the enmity of the state to such a subhuman condition that they will do anything to escape their distress. They will confess to crimes they did not commit. In a semistupor they will accept the reiterated suggestions of their oppressors. No longer being free agents to accept or reject the promptings of response, in these cases they respond without any further resistance to the ideas of their inquisitors. In a haze of confusion and misery they take the role laid down for them, their impersonative powers under the sway of duress, exhaustion, and emotional upheaval.

A group of political prisoners broken in spirit through abuse and brutality may see one of their number who is still somewhat himself acting in defiance of authority—what they all would want to do if really themselves and under their own control. But now, in mortal fear that his defiance will bring punishment on the whole group, their only wish is that he would keep in line. Their fright has overwhelmed any judgment of right or wrong. They do as they are told and feel foreboding and terror if any one of their number by a rash act threatens their meager remnant of security from brutality.

Today some totalitarian leaders have learned deliberately to bring about a warping of mind and spirit of their followers. They have scored an advance over the priests who required people to take part in the fiery sacrifice of their first-born sons to Moloch. The priests were not as callously deliberate as these modern leaders. The men of old were caught in emotions they did not understand, and did not know what they were doing. Today men know better, and produce by design their own modern instances of horrible inhumanity.

The prophets and reformers who got rid of human sacrifice had on their side the natural sentiments of parents, the love for their children, and the promptings of their impersonation and response to parents cruelly deprived by this fatal rite. The successors of these prophets and reformers who are today trying to get rid of war have upon their side the same natural sentiments. Instead of now passing a few children through the fires of Moloch to placate that god so as to avert calamity, we now pass a great many children through the fires of Mars, the war god, in the hope of averting the calamity of being conquered by our neighbors. There is this to be said in favor of our present practice. We sometimes succeed in gaining our end in that we do in fact escape conquest by an enemy, whereas it is doubtful whether passing the children through the fire to Moloch escaped or gained anything for the practitioners of that sacrifice. Yet even if we grant that the sacrifices in the destructive wars of today are in some cases better than to have yielded to violence and live in ignominy and misery under an unjust rule, still it is true that the process of passing our children through the fires of Mars is evil. We need a new method of constructive achievement on the world scene. We need to use impersonation and response to produce a world of tolerance and fairness instead of our familiar world of intolerance and injustice with its consequent violent discord, secession, and separation.

The reforms that get rid of Mars will be harder to effectuate than those that got rid of Moloch, because they will require either that the leaders of the powerful separate nations of the world are brought to a sufficient disposition of fairness and tolerance, or that some one of the separate nations becomes both so just and at the same time so overwhelmingly strong as to produce a rule and role that will eventually gain the consent of the world's peoples. A prerequisite for either of these results is that impersonation and response are used to build dispositions of friendliness and fair-mindedness, tolerance, honesty, and truth to fact at every possible opportunity. This is one great task ahead of education today, and one which it unfortunately largely neglects.

It may be too much to hope that any of us will come to feel positive love for the people of an alien group—the kind of thing of which St. Bernard spoke when he said, "Love takes its name from loving, not from honoring. Let him who is struck with fear or astonishment or dread or admiration be satisfied with honoring, for all these feelings are absent in him who loves. Love is filled with itself, and where it has come it overcomes and transforms all other dispositions."

But liking and friendship may be within our reach. They increase the naturally benevolent trend of impersonation and response, which in turn increases the liking and friendship, in the beneficent circle we have described. We must use impersonation and response to awake good will and its sentiments rather than hostility and its sentiments. Our aim is to avoid attitudes that make for discord, secession, and separation and to gain attitudes that make for harmony. Hostility makes for intolerance, dishonesty, and unfairness. Good will makes us tolerant, honest, and fair.

XIV. Physical Conditions as Influences in Determination of Rule and Role

1. CURRENT ENVIRONMENT AND CURRENT TECHNIQUES AND IDEAS

The physical conditions and the geographical environment in which any group finds itself, influence the rule and role that are acquired through response and impersonation. This is obvious in extreme instances, as in the differences that must exist between the cultural traditions of those living in a snowbound land, those living in a semi-arid hot desert, and those living in a rain-drenched tropical island. The varied conditions of life in these different places impose sharp limitations on the rule and role of the inhabitants.

In ancient times it was observed that whatever changes might take place in the cultures of the other lands around the Mediterranean, Egypt was "always the same," her way of life determined by its dependence on the River Nile, without which Egypt would have been a desert. The annual habit of the Nile of overflow every autumn from its shallow bed gave the possibility of life and even abundance to the inhabitants, but only if they faithfully observed the requirements and opportunities represented by this behavior of the river.

Students of climate have pointed out that window glass is one of the most significant inventions of mankind, permitting unrestricted winter activity in climates, let us say like that of northern New York, where without window glass activity would, prior to the invention of electric light, have been reduced in those seasons to something like the mere maintenance of existence. With window glass, on the other hand, life in those places with harsh winters becomes easy, and the rigors of the weather may be a stimulus rather than a handicap.

It is said that Cyrus feared that the conquest of fertile areas would turn his soldiers into softer men. And it is true that the successive communities inhabiting the fertile crescent of Mesopotamia suffered political overthrow, as conquerors either from the desert on one side or the mountains on the other gained control of the fertile crescent, were softened by its influence, and then in their own turn were conquered by a new invader.

In our discussion of the likelihood of reform when social conditions required it, we noted that any benefits from reform, or even the undertaking of reform, might be rendered unlikely if physical conditions were so hard as to make the community leaders apathetic or hopeless, and without the initiative or energy that is the prerequisite of any positive achievement, good or bad. We pointed out what happened when the population was so big that it could not be rightly sustained by the resources of the country. Poverty, bad diet, malnutrition, ill health, and inertia resulted, and there really seemed no prospect of a substantially good rule or role. In overcrowded conditions such as those in parts of India and China, there is a real question whether marked social inequalities may not be of benefit to the community, as it is likely that for any reasonable prospect at all for future reform it is better for a few to be adequately clothed and fed and sufficiently energetic to address themselves to the problems at hand, than for all to share equally in the deficient assets and all alike be ill-clothed, ill-housed, ill-fed, and unwell.

When conditions are such that a need cannot be satisfied, an aspiration cannot be fulfilled, one tries to disparage the need or forget the aspiration. This kind of resignation does not produce happiness. The need still remains, and one is still unsatisfied even if he forgets the need. He may be better off forgetting the unsatisfied need than remembering it. But his choice is a choice between evils. And it is just this choice between evils that is imposed upon the people of any area on which they have to rely for their sources of supply, where the numbers of the people have overrun the contemporary capacity of the area to supply their needs.

Tolerance, so important in the successive generations of leaders of a community if discord is to be avoided, is acquired by response to and impersonation of their elders and leaders by those who are rising up from youth to take over the positions of responsibility in the community. In an area where assets are short and the numbers of people long, tolerance is rendered extremely difficult, as also is honesty, since conditions impose such a severe necessity on everyone to grasp what he can for himself. In such an area the rising leadership is brought up and educated within the harsh tradition and viewpoint that it is possible for only a few to be well off and that the great majority must of necessity be in misery.

It is true that the presence of plenty of elbow room and access to plenty of resources, as in the case of the United States in the nineteenth century, is a great aid to political tolerance. Able people who didn't fit too well into the scheme of things at home in the East could move West and work out their energies in subduing the land and organizing new communities. The dispossessed and down and out at home were likely to be without able leadership, because anyone with the ability to lead a group could do well on his own in pastures new. Not so when the unoccupied frontier has disappeared. Thereafter those discontented with the home scene are found, if they are of sufficient ability, as leaders of dissident groups of one kind or another.

Important as a frontier is, its influence can be exaggerated. There are those who, impressed by the influence of the American frontier on American life, have gone on to attribute the growth of political liberalism in Europe to the new resources of the West and the increase of food and other material supplies which that made available to Europe. But the main increase in European material wealth and the nineteenth-century zoom of population to consume it, and the resulting problems and their attempted solutions, were due to mechanization and invention applied to resources which were not American. The new political ideas of value in the French Revolution—the constructive ideas of freedom and opportunity as contrasted with its oppressive and backward excesses—long antedated any significant material exports from the New World, as did also the critical steps in the development of parliamentary power in England. It is true that the example of the young American community, with its notions of liberty and equality that were owing in part to frontier conditions, had a direct influence on political theory and political leadership in Europe, but the main trends in politics in Europe and the growth of liberalism and then of socialism, were European developments due to European factors.

A frontier in itself is of small aid in the political development of its inhabitants, unless they have the techniques and the ideas to utilize the frontier. The American Indians had plenty of frontier in the year 1600; Europeans had plenty of frontier in the year 1000. But it was useless frontier in the absence of suitable techniques and ideas.

There are thus two aspects of the relationship of geographical environment to rule and role: the environmental conditions provide both opportunities for and limitations on the possible development of rule and role; the rule and role which the community has already attained at any particular time affect for better or worse the utilizable extent of the opportunities and the deterrent extent of the limitations.

2. CHANGES IN THE GEOGRAPHICAL ENVIRONMENT

As the recorded memory of man is both short and incomplete, we do not know what effects on his life may have been attributable to climatic changes in the past. It is plain on theoretical grounds that if the water supply of an area fails, people have to leave the area. But we do not have the historical records to know what influence a diminished rainfall may have had on the people of Greece, and how much if any of the decline of Grecian achievements since its great days twenty-five hundred years ago can perhaps be accounted for by a deficiency of fresh water.

The failing of crops and of animal life in a country which had formerly been plentifully supplied would produce the same results on the inhabitants as we can see before our eyes today in those countries in which the population is pressing too hard on their food-producing capacity. Such a country would suffer a decline of energy and achievement, unless prior to the weakening effect of the shortages its leaders and people succeeded in gaining access to the production of other areas. Russia today is very likely at a critical period when her population is beginning to press hard on her food supply, but not yet to such a degree as to have permanently weakened her. If this is the fact, it provides one reason why it is hard for Russia to be internally tolerant or externally honest with her neighbors. The same kind of critical period might come upon the United States, even without a great increase in population, were our climate to suffer a change for the worse so that we could no longer produce an adequate abundance of food.

Of the effect on rule and role of changes beyond the recorded memory of man we know nothing except legend, like the widespread legends of a flood destroying much of mankind. We can see in records in the earth that in relatively recent geological times parts of the eastern seaboard of what is now the United States were under water, and parts which were under water are now dry land. It was only a few thousand years ago—scarcely beyond the memory of man—that the site of Hartford, Connecticut, reappeared from beneath a cap of ice. It can be no more than a speculation as to what would be the effect on mankind, and on man's notions of rule and role, should severe climatic conditions such as those of ice cover or of flooding return to the presently habitable parts of the earth and man be then present to witness and endure them.

3. CHANGES IN CURRENT KNOWLEDGE AND TECHNIQUES

At any period in history the then current body of scientific and other beliefs and the techniques and skills available at the time have a significant effect on men's notions of what is right and the content of their rule to go by and their worthwhile role.

In ancient Syria when the winter rains had ceased and the spring verdure failed as the ground lost its water and the long drought set in until autumn, the vegetation dried up and the source of food and nourishment appeared to be dead. The scientific and religious view at the time was that this was due to the fact that Death had slain the god who was responsible for rainy weather and vegetation. The rains returned in the autumn because the god was brought back to life by some of those who had been his friends, among them the Goddess of Fertility. When restored to life the god had sexual intercourse with the goddess, and this union was responsible for the outburst of spring's green growth. Had the god and the goddess failed to get together in this way, the consequences would have been general starvation. Anything that might further their intercourse was accordingly right. So the institution of sacred harlotry became part of the religious rule, as copulation of the worshipers with temple prostitutes would not only remind the god and goddess of their highly desirable union but also celebrate the union.

When conditions of time and place were such that the most important skill and technique of a people were their ability in maintaining their flocks, the dog had a place of extraordinary value in their lives and it was right that the welfare of the dog should be carefully protected. So it is that we find in the sacred scriptures of such a people a recitation of one's duty to the dog.

Ahura Mazda is speaking to Zarathustra:

"Whosoever small smite either a shepherd's dog, or a house-dog, or a Vohunazga dog, or a trained dog, his soul when passing to the other world shall fly howling louder and more sorely grieved than the sheep does in the lofty forest where the wolf ranges. No soul will come and meet his departing soul and help it, howling and grieved in the other world; nor will the dogs that keep the Chinvad bridge help his departing soul howling and grieved in the other world."

"O Maker of the material world, thou Holy One! If a bitch be near her time, which is the worshipper of Mazda that shall support her?"

Ahura Mazda answered: "He whose house stands nearest, the care of supporting her is his; so long shall he support her, until the whelps be born. If he shall not support her, so that the whelps come to grief for want of proper support, he shall pay for it the penalty for wilful murder . . .

"It lies with the faithful to look in the same way after every pregnant female, either two-footed or four-footed, two-footed woman or four-footed bitch."

When modern states make war upon one another, they use whatever weapons will be most effective to win. But in the extent of the use of the weapons they have to pay some attention to neutrals lest in injuring these unduly they will make new enemies. They also have to pay some attention to their treatment of noncombatants, lest they offend the opinion of those states which have not yet become actively engaged in the war. So rules of international law come into being for the mitigation of the effects of war on neutrals and noncombatants, and these rules have the support of men of good will even within the ranks of the warring states. But these rules for the mitigation of war have not gone so far as seriously to interfere with the available means of warmaking, and as new weapons and new techniques of combat are discovered, the rules have adjusted themselves to the weapons rather than the weapons to the rules. The new weapons and techniques have changed the current ideas of rule to go by.

In the days prior to the invention of the submarine, the destruction of neutral ships on the high seas by a belligerent was absolutely forbidden, and only in case of military necessity was the destruction of an enemy merchant ship permitted, and then only if passengers and crews were first removed to safety. The normal rule was that when one of the belligerents captured an enemy merchant ship, the prize was to be taken to port for adjudication by a prize court of the status of the ship and of the property she carried, which might be found to belong to a neutral rather than to an enemy. The invention of the submarine and the fact that if she attempted to bring a prize into port the attempt would almost certainly result in the detection and destruction of the submarine at sea, changed the rule for the treatment of cargo ships so as to allow in actual practice the destruction by the submarine of the cargo ship and the drowning of her crew and passengers.

It was for long a principle underlying the laws of war that only the armed services of a belligerent nation fought, while the remainder of the nation remained at peace. The distinction between combatants and noncombatants was fundamental, and war was not to be waged against the peaceful inhabitants of enemy territory. But the invention of the airplane and the efficacy of bombing as a technique of warfare brought noncombatants, though far removed from the scene of land operations between opposing armies, within the classification of those subject to destruction. The impracticability of separating out the many noncombatants from the few combatants within a bombed city, and the fact that many noncombatants were engaged in activities useful to the war effort of the enemy simply overrode the old rules designed for the protection of noncombatants. Now that a plane or a missile can carry a single warhead of such power as to destroy an entire great metropolitan area, the old distinction between combatants and non-combatants has vanished.

In the nineteenth century the invention of new uses and new kinds of machinery powered by steam had striking effects on not only the manner of life of Europeans but also on where they lived and under what conditions of crowding. The concentrations of population followed the geological distribution of the available coal deposits. The machines and the fuel that raised the steam were changing the rule and role of the people.

The development of steamships changed the principal trade routes of the world's peoples. The inland German cities ceased to be the centers of German trade. The Italian cities which had been located centrally on the important land routes went into a decline. North American resources and trade developed. England and the west coast of Europe were now centrally situated on the main trade routes. Changes in the rule and role of the people in these various places were brought about by the changing location of geographical advantage which resulted from the change in techniques.

4. THE PRESSURE OF NEEDS

Changes in the rule and role of people that are brought about by changes in their environment are but a special case, one manifestation of the determining power of environment over the forms and activities of life. Things are in the saddle and ride not only mankind but all the rest of living creatures as well.

If a reptile was to carry on life successfully in the sea, it needed to swim efficiently. So the reptile, under this need determined by the environment, developed fins and a tail and a streamlined body, an ichthyosaur—the reptile like a fish. When a mammal today is a dweller in the sea, it likewise takes on the streamlined form and the means of locomotion appropriate to its watery environment. So the mammalian porpoise of today in its outward aspects looks not unlike the reptilian ichthyosaur of long ago. Still another order of animals, the fishes, have developed the same form of streamlined body. So it is that under the persuasion of environment the reptile ichthyosaur in superficial appearance has a much closer resemblance to the shark than to its own much nearer relative the rattlesnake; and the porpoise has a closer resemblance to the shark than to its own much nearer relative the man. These different orders of life—reptile, mammal, and fish—with different histories and heritages, none the less in a like environment exhibit like forms well suited to that environment.

Certainly one of the fundamental forces in human life is the pressure of needs, the requirements of an individual's constitution and structure in the presence of the actual environment in which he finds himself. This pressure of needs, driving a man towards an attempt to satisfy them all along the line, is the basic force responsible for the successes of his civilization and its failures—his mistaken attempts— as well. Growth lies in the direction of a better satisfaction of the needs. Decay lies in a less good satisfaction.

Whether a suppression of the needs—as advocated, for instance, in a book like *The Imitation of Christ*—represents growth or decay is arguable. It seems likely that most of us today would say that it was better to get our whole range of needs in perspective and to try to reach a harmonious satisfaction of them, than it was to try to eliminate real needs—a task that like the creation of such needs probably has to be left to long reaches of time.

XV. Ability and Disposition in Relation to Political Patterns

1. EFFECTS OF NATIVE ABILITY ON RULE AND ROLE

The variation in different individuals of what is built on response and impersonation is in part due to the native differences in temperament of different people. They may be biologically predisposed to differing rules and roles. One can only educate what is there to begin with. A sow's ear never made a silk purse.

Tolerance, a habit of give and take, appears to be a virtue that is mainly acquired from imitative response to tolerant parents, friends or associates and impersonation of them. It is, as we have seen, favored by physical circumstances in which there are adequate resources and plenty of elbow room for the members of a community which is not too numerous in relation to the available assets. It is not something innate; a man learns tolerance. Nevertheless there are very likely innate characteristics in some people that make a tolerant attitude easier for them to acquire than for others. To admit this much we do not have to go the length of some of the students of the correlations between constitution and character, who would list tolerance as a temperamental counterpart of a certain trend of body structure. Tolerance, they would say, goes with that structure which shows a tendency to roundness throughout the body and a massiveness of the digestive viscera—the so-called endomorphic structure—because they believe these viscera to be derived from the inner germ layer, the endoderm of the embryo.

In certain easily observed areas, such as that of children's awareness to sensations of various kinds, there are marked native differences between one child and another, as in accurate perception of colors, or in critical awareness of kinds of sounds. There are also innate differences in the powers of visual imagination. These various native differences in talent have a direct bearing on what will prove to be satisfactory roles later in life, since a man functions more happily and constructively along lines that are within the field of his own particular abilities.

If there are native differences between people in their tendencies towards friendliness and tolerance, so that, other things being equal, impersonation and response will result for some more than others in friendly and tolerant character, this fact would have a direct bearing on the prospect for tolerance in a particular community. In a community where a large proportion of the capable people were endowed with a native temperament conducive to tolerance, there would be a greater chance, than in a community where only a few were so endowed, of avoiding those types of political division which we have seen to be promoted by intolerance.

A defect in our practical political knowledge is that we do not know the influence of native endowment on the acquisition of such political virtues as tolerance, honesty, and equity. It follows that we are a long way off from any prospect of increasing, by intelligently directed mating, the likelihood of these virtues in any state, or of decreasing the likelihood of the intolerance, dishonesty, and unfairness characteristic of discord, secession, and separation.

If the needs of one vital part of a person's physiological constitution were inconsistent with the needs of another vital part, it is plain that he could never become a wholly healthy person, because what resulted in health for one part would result in disease or wrong functioning for another. It is as if some component of diet were necessary for the proper strength and functioning of his bones and joints, and at the same time the same component of diet impaired his vision or some other important function of his bodily structure. Fortunately there is enough flexibility and latitude in the ways of satisfying physiological needs so that a dilemma of this kind very likely does not arise in the case of most people.

In our discussion of rule and role we have seen that a man's needs for a rule that lets him know what to do and expect and for a role that seems worthwhile are satisfied or denied in a social setting. He is involved in relations with other people. Their views and interests are by way of response and impersonation important factors in the determination of his rule and role. If one's needs as a member of the group, such as needs for a good standing and requirements either to conform to the group ways or else to be outlawed, were inconsistent with one's individual needs, such as those for sex satisfaction or an unusual degree of ambition for power or material gain, a dilemma would arise for the individual. He could never hope for a real satisfaction of his needs all along the line. The best he could get would be a working compromise that would on balance do him the most good and the least harm. He would be as badly off as the man who had a diet good for his joints but bad for his eyes. He would be subject to permanent dissatisfaction.

If there were in the leaders of the various lines of activity in the community an irreconcilable inconsistency of this kind between their needs as individuals and as members of the group, the consequences for the form of organization of the community and its government would be along lines of restriction of individual freedom. We would have the type of discord described in the cases of a political order which did not have a willing consent of the governed but relied instead upon force for gaining obedience. If people were by native endowment made with such intensity of temperament or such powerful ambitions that they could not control their desire or curb their ambitions to such an extent as to be peacefully absorbed in a society of give-and-take, tolerance, and equity, it would be necessary to have recourse to a despotic government and a regimented community to obtain the order needed by everyone but which was unattainable on a basis of willing consent.

Fortunately history affords examples of communities existing for significant lengths of time on the basis of a free order. So we can say that at least in the case of some groups under some conditions, there has not been such an irreconcilable difference between the needs of the capable as individuals and as members of the community as to render a free order impossible. To ask whether this might always be the case under right influences of education and tradition, and a right use of impersonation and response in the forming of rule and role, is to ask whether a free order can become possible throughout the world.

The circumstances in which the people of a community are living become opportunities for achievement of a constructive kind only if enough of the people are capable of discovering and utilizing the opportunities. We noted the influence upon Britain of the favorable location of the British Isles upon the Atlantic trade routes. This undoubtedly played a major part in the development of her wealth and strength. Yet for this development to have taken place at all it was necessary that enough of the British were capable of seamanship along with sufficient energy and intelligence to avail themselves of the opportunity represented by the sea and their location with respect to it.

Why was it that the Phoenicians, rather than some other of the peoples around the Mediterranean margin, emerged as a group of successful seamen and traders and held that position for at least five hundred years, so that by the first quarter of the first millennium B.C. they had dotted their colonies all about the islands and shores of that sea, and pushed their navigation even beyond the Mediterranean? It is likely that the answer lay in their having a greater adaptability to the conditions of a seafaring life, as well as a relatively high order of ability in other lines. It is significant that in addition to their commercial success, they played a major part in the development of a phonetic alphabet of practical, easily used letters.

If the temperament and abilities of a people are not such as to let them avail themselves of what the circumstances might offer to those more suitably disposed, for them the opportunities are nonexistent.

It is said that the Huns, able though they were in a military way at the time of their great westerly migrations and possessed of a horsemanship superior to that of anyone else, were unable or unwilling to give up their nomadic way of life when they came into country suitable for agriculture. By the fifth century A.D., having swept across Asia, pushing before them the Germanic peoples who in turn pushed west and south into the heart of the Roman Empire, the Huns reached the grasslands of the Hungarian plain. From here they made great raids, living off the land as they raided into Gaul and into Italy. But the Hungarian plain with its grasslands was as far west a territory as they could bring under a long-term rule, unless they were to give up their pastoral nomadic life and have recourse to agriculture. Some historians have speculated about what would have been the results on Roman civilization in Europe had the Huns been possessed of a more westerly base than Hungary from which a leader like their Attila could have launched his depredations. But such a westerly base was geographically impossible unless they were to adopt agriculture. Had they adopted agriculture, their military superiority—dependent on their mobility and horsemanship—would likely have disappeared. However that may be, it looks as though the hold upon them of the traditional rule and role of their nomadic way of life and a possible temperamental or other inability and unwillingness to settle down, closed off for them opportunities that might otherwise have been available in the physical circumstances of Western Europe.

The hold of a traditional rule and role with its own particular set of interests can for the time being be just as effective as a native lack of capacity in preventing a group and its leaders from availing themselves of an opportunity. We have already noted an example of this in the case of the other worldly orientation of the Church leadership in the Dark and Middle Ages. This orientation of interest accompanied, if it did not bring about, a situation in which the engineers of the time did not have sufficient knowledge and skill to keep the Roman aqueducts functioning.

At times a group of people will turn up with an ability and a leadership that is very striking along some particular line. We saw such a case in connection with the organizing ability of the Normans, in England and in Sicily especially. Another specialized line of ability, maintained for many generations, was that shown by the Jews in the religious field. They developed monotheistic religious ideas that have since proved satisfactory—sometimes with modifications and softenings of the simple and severe Jewish doctrine—to great numbers of diverse peoples. The tenacity of the Jews, even under rigorous trials and persecutions, in adhering to their ideas is a story known to everyone, and for the most part an admirable story.

We have seen that where the relations of individuals and groups within a community are marked by intolerance, dishonesty, unfairness, and lack of truth to fact, the community exhibits some form of political division, whether discord, secession, or separation. In such cases the leaders of the community have for some reason failed to discover and utilize in the total circumstances of the community opportunities such as to permit the realization of a free order changing by way of growth, an order characterized by tolerance, honesty, equity, and truth to fact. As in the case of purely physical circumstances, the opportunities only exist for those who are capable of discovering and using them.

What are the prospects in the discordant and separated communities of the world of finding a kind of leadership and a kind of following that will be capable of discovering in the actual divisive circumstances the hidden opportunities to bring into realization anywhere— and possibly in time everywhere—a community characterized by the political virtues so that it will be a free community and one that will make its political changes by orderly growth rather than by violence?

Are we up against a situation where people and their leaders are so constituted that we might as well give up hope over the long term of just and fair government in a just and fair community, or is there a prospect that people and leaders will be capable of attaining the political virutes of tolerance, honesty, equity, and truth to fact? We have seen that without these virtues the community—on the local, national, or world scene—will be either in discord or disorder or ruled by an unjust order.

In asking these questions, we are addressing ourselves to the possibility of an eventual free political order.

For the time being we pass over questions of the relative importance of the specific political virtues under different specific conditions. For example, we saw in the *discord* and other cases that tolerance has to be laid aside after violent division has appeared. If one party practices tolerance towards a party committed to violent intolerance—both being of about equal strength in other respects—this simply brings about the defeat of the tolerant by the intolerant. This fact is recognized by the intelligence in the exercise of the virtue of truth to fact, and in these particular circumstances truth to fact is obviously a more important virtue than tolerance, which is at this particular juncture a political weakness rather than a virtue. Nevertheless the fact remains that for the attainment of a free order changing by way of growth, tolerance is a necessary virtue in the leaders of the several lines of community activity. The capacity to practice tolerance is therefore a condition of such an order.

Some light can be shed on the likelihood of getting leaders and a following capable of forming a relatively free community. We will examine a specific historical instance of the acquisition by a people of a new political rule and role, the organization of a new state, in circumstances that at the time made it seem doubtful whether a free order was possible.

2. THE MAKERS OF THE UNITED STATES

Whether the colonies established on the eastern seaboard of North America in the seventeenth century were founded for purposes of trade, at least a factor in the case of all of them, or as a refuge from political and religious persecution, or to forestall the spread of Spanish power, or from a restless desire for change which characterized a few of the adventurer leaders, there were certain features in common that accounted for an exceptional degree of resourcefulness and determination amongst the colonists as compared with those they had left behind. This was true not only of those who had come as leaders of their groups, or as independent freemen. It was also true of most—although not all—of those who had come as indentured servants, men whose time and labor for a term of years could be commanded or sold by those to whom they were bound, perhaps to pay off a debt or perhaps to the master of the voyage in return for food, clothing, and transportation.

They had been willing to give up the kind of life with which they were familiar; they had undertaken the dangers of a prolonged and perilous sea voyage; they had undergone the risks of attack by the native savages; all who had survived the early days and remained in the colonies had shown physical and spiritual endurance. All, simply if they were to maintain themselves in the new surroundings, had to deal realistically and inventively with the conditions imposed by a terrain and climate unfamiliar to them.

Qualities such as these characterized the early settlers, and were likely handed down to their descendants of the time of the Revolutionary War. Those who had migrated to the colonies in the intervening century still came to a land distant and strange, still—with the exception of the relatively few who were kidnaped or deported as paupers or convicts—possessed the venturesomeness to attempt a new kind of life in still unsettled conditions.

The Northern Colonials

The northern colonies—New England—were predominantly of English stock, about 700,000 strong, at the time of the Revolution. The century and a half of their existence had been marked by the leadership and influence of the clergy, and by a concern of all in matters of religion and religious form. The Massachusetts Bay Company, within about two years after its establishment in March 1629 as a trading and colonizing group of merchants, had become a church-dominated community. The Company was composed originally of twenty-six Anglican Puritan and Nonconformist members. Before emigration of any of its members to America, control of the Company passed into the hands of dissentient Puritans who felt there was not sufficient prospect in England of Puritan reform of the Church of England. Some of these "Freemen" of the Company, having obtained a company vote in favor of removing Company and charter to New England, migrated thither in the spring of 1630, and under their company charter set up a theocracy. The charter provided for a government made up of governor, deputy governor, and eighteen assistants to be "elected and chosen out of the Freemen of the saide Company" and provided that the governor and such of the assistants and Freemen as should be assembled in a general assembly or court might have power to establish laws for the conduct of the Company. The charter provided for a monthly "Courte or Assemblie" at which any seven or more of the assistants—the governor or deputy governor being assembled with them—should be a sufficient court for certain specified purposes, among them the important one of appointing "soe many others as they shall thinke fitt" to be new Freemen "to be free of the said Company and Body, and them into the same to admitt." Under this provision of the charter, no one was in fact admitted as a freeman to the Company and its general court or assembly unless his religious views were in line with those of the radical Puritans in control of the colony.

Certain wealthy Puritans in England in 1636 thought of migrating to this new Massachusetts Bay Colony, but wished to be assured in advance that their wealth would give them and their families a place of influence in its affairs. The colonial reply to their inquiries made it clear that the Massachusetts theocracy was glad to welcome newcomers of worth and honor but that rightness of religious view was essential to a voice in the rule of the colony. A part of this reply summarizes the position, and fortifies the argument by reference to Scripture:

Now, if it be a divine truth, that none are to be trusted with public permanent authority but godly men, who are fit materials for church fellowship, then from the same grounds, it will appear, that none are so fit to be trusted with the liberties of the commonwealth as church members. For, the liberties of the freemen of this commonwealth are such, as requires men of faithful integrity to God and the state, to preserve the same. Their liberties, among others, are chiefly these. 1. To chuse all magistrates, and to call them to account at their general courts. 2. To chuse such burgesses, every general court, as with the magistrates shall make or repeal all laws. Now both these liberties are such, as carry along much power with them, either to establish or subvert the commonwealth, and therewith the church, which power, if it be committed to men not according to their godliness, which makith them fit for church fellowship, but according to their wealth, which, as such, makes them no better than worldly men, then, in case worldly men should prove the major part, as soon they might do, they would as readily set over us magistrates like themselves, such as might hate us according to the curse, Levit. XXVI, 17, and turn the edge of all authority and laws against the church and the members thereof, the maintenance of whose peace is the chief end which God aimed at in the institution of Magistracy. I Timothy, II: 1, 2.

During the decade 1630 to 1640—in the middle of which the foregoing statement of theocratic principle was written—lines were forming in England both in religious conflict and in the parallel struggle for power between Parliament and Crown. Religious persecution of the Puritans was severe, and one answer to it was the migration of more Puritans to Massachusetts Bay, which by the opening of the sixteen-forties probably numbered not far from 20,000 people, half of them concentrated in the area about Boston, the balance in independent Congregational communities.

The intolerance of the Massachusetts Puritan clergy proved to be as unpalatable to some of the inhabitants as the Anglican intolerance in England had been to the Puritans. Of the vigor of the intolerance there is no doubt. In the middle of the seventeenth century any Quakers coming to Massachusetts were to be whipped and transported. (Plymouth and Connecticut felt the same way about Quakers.) Earlier, Roger Williams had been banished by the General Court of Massachusetts Bay for denying the authority of the civil magistrates in matters of conscience. He had then founded a colony at Providence, Providence Plantations, the first colonial settlement in Rhode Island. In this settlement, almost alone in New England, a degree of religious toleration was observed, with a real separation of civil and religious authority.

Thomas Hooker, prominent in the early history of Connecticut, was another divine who was restive under the theological rule of the Massachusetts oligarchy. In 1636 he took his flock with him to what is now Hartford, and settled them there on the site of a Dutch trading post.

Anne Hutchinson, born in Lincolnshire near the end of the sixteenth century, migrated with her husband and family to Massachusetts Bay in 1634. Here she soon acquired a following for her religious ideas. She emphasized that, through divine grace, faith without good conduct was a sufficient basis for salvation. She believed that the Puritan insistence on good works as an evidence that faith had been achieved, minimized the all-important place of faith. She was sentenced by the General Court in 1637 to banishment for antinomianism—that is to say, as one who regarded the moral law as without essential significance for those redeemed by Christ, and good works or good conduct unnecessary as evidence of salvation. She was declared to have traduced the ministers. Some of her followers went with her. She took part with them in the founding of the second settlement in Rhode Island, at Portsmouth. There she continued to have religious differences with her fellow colonists. She removed to Long Island in 1642, and in the following year, along with all but one of her family, was killed by Indians in what is now the outskirts of New York City. Such was the stormy life of one individual who took to heart her religious convictions.

In later colonial days the religion of the Puritan fathers ceased to be the sole qualification for political power in Massachusetts. The colony, as its inhabitants spread over more territory, early elected delegates to a general assembly. These delegates from the towns gained experience in parliamentary government in the course of representing various sectarian and economic interests of their supporters. Toward the end of the seventeenth century, at the time of the Glorious Revolution which brought William and Mary to the English throne, Massachusetts became a royal province with a governor appointed by the Crown. The new royal charter did not permit the franchise to be limited to those of one religious viewpoint. The conditions and techniques of the time made for small settlements necessarily relying much on themselves in all things, as the settlements were distributed over a wide area with bad communications. Such circumstances led to a lessening of doctrinal religious interest and of church affiliation along with a falling off from the strict views of the old leadership. Yet even after the exclusive power of the Puritan theocracy had been broken, the ministers were still leaders of opinion. Throughout the colonial period the leaders of Massachusetts, like those of the rest of New England, which had been largely settled by migrations from Massachusetts, remained strong in the persuasion of a church without a bishop.

Radicals who from time to time arose with religious and political views strongly dissenting from those of the ruling group were not lost to the American scene. They pulled up their Massachusetts roots and established new settlements of their own elsewhere. They had been banished, not suppressed or killed. Today, in some of our modern communities the abilities of vigorous dissenters are extinguished, as, for example, in the Soviet Union, where if a man does not conform to the regime he may be imprisoned or killed. The Russian rulers are ridden by a fear and insecurity unknown to our Massachusetts forebears.

They regard dissenters as sources of revenge or of aid to an enemy state so long as alive and free. Thus the abilities of these dissenters are lost not only to Russia but to the whole world community.

A factor tending to make for an individualistic point of view in secular matters—and thence, as we have just suggested, for independence from theocracy as well—was the fact that the terrain and climate were not such as to make for production of large crops on great areas with a considerable labor force. Farms were small and run by their several owners independently. The growing season in New England was short, and in the winter farmers needed to occupy themselves with projects other than those of strict farming. Conditions were thus right for the rise of handcrafts, and small manufacturing early developed for local use. In the backward condition of land transportation, with its bad roads and worse bridges as the means of travel through a wild and rough country with but few spots of settlement, organization of inland trade on a large scale was out of the question; but the Yankee peddlers of Yankee notions became known throughout all the colonies.

In the later colonial years exports by sea from New England became significant in trade both with other colonies and abroad. Relatively early exports had been made of timber, fish, and corn. Subsequently trade enlarged, not all of it of a kind of which we are today proud. Large New England fortunes were built on a triangular trade in which American products—in a given voyage very likely rum, iron bars, flour, tar, and miscellaneous provisions—were taken to Africa and there exchanged for slaves and perhaps some gold dust and spices, which were in turn carried to the West Indies and there sold for molasses and sugar and bills of exchange drawn on London, thence homeward. In the port towns merchants had to be resourceful and not too law-abiding if they were to overcome restrictions on trade provided by the attempts of the British to control colonial trade in ways thought to be for British benefit—an item of harassment which we mentioned in connection with the secession of the American colonies. This resourcefulness was another likely factor in the individualistic and self-reliant disposition of New Englanders.

Middle Colonials

The territory granted to William Penn in 1681 had prior to that date been the scene of trading posts established by Swedes, Dutch, and English. The territory had come under control of the English when

New Netherland to the north had fallen to the English in 1664, the name of New Amsterdam being changed to New York. Penn was a very great Quaker leader, and an eloquent advocate of religious liberty. It was in Philadelphia and its neighborhood that the Pennsylvania Quakers were mainly settled. They were industrious and prosperous. Later, at the time of the American Revolution, their strong influence as pacifists was not sufficient to keep Pennsylvania out of the forefront of the Revolutionary movement. The Declaration of Independence and the Constitution were written in Philadelphia, and it was there that the Continental Congress met during the war.

The Glorious Revolution of William and Mary took place in 1688, not long after the founding of Penn's colony. In the approximate century between that date and the American Revolution, a period during which the population of New England was growing mainly by natural increase, Pennsylvania was host to immigrants who were of the greatest importance in the development both of that colony and of the frontier movement pushing towards the Alleghenies.

In the first half of the eighteenth century there was a heavy immigration from southern Germany into the mid-colonies, especially Pennsylvania. In 1766 Benjamin Franklin estimated that one-third of the Pennsylvania population was German. Of the six newspapers published in the colony at mid-century three were in the German language. These German immigrants were of various Protestant sects for whom life at home was rendered miserable by economic hardship and dangers of religious persecution due to the half-religious half-political warfare plaguing Germans in the seventeenth and eighteenth centuries. In Pennsylvania, as elsewhere in the colonies, there was a great shortage of labor, and Pennsylvania was well advertised by those wishing immigrants for labor. The tolerance of Pennsylvania for those of varied religious views was in marked contrast with New England, where, as we have noted, Quakers were whipped out of town, and where German newcomers such as those welcomed in Pennsylvania would not have been tolerated.

Those Germans who came indentured soon worked out their freedom. The same spirit of taking a chance which had led them to leave Germany inspired some to leave the American seaboard and push on west and southwest. Many of these Germans settled in the Shenandoah Valley. In 1748, when George Washington as a youth of sixteen was surveying claims of Lord Fairfax in the Shenandoah Valley, he wrote of the German immigrants there. He regarded them as ignorant as the

Indians, perhaps on account of a language barrier. He seems to have had his troubles in communicating with them, remarking that "they would never speak English but when spoken to speak all Dutch!" John Wesley, subsequently the founder of Methodism, when on a three-year missionary journey in America in 1735 to 1738, was much influenced by his contact with a little group of German Moravian colonists, then just settled in Georgia but shortly to remove to Pennsylvania, where they were later joined by more immigrants of their sect.

Another group of immigrants, again largely coming in through the mid-colonies although Baltimore in Maryland was also a main port of entry, were the so-called Scotch-Irish. These were Scottish Presbyterians whose fathers or grandfathers, in the reign of James I of England and after, had left Scotland for what they hoped would be greater religious freedom in northern Ireland. But there both economic and religious conditions were adverse. Absentee English landlords were grasping, British statutes forbade the export of wool from their Irish sheep, and at the turn into the eighteenth century, Presbyterians were excluded from civil and military office while at the same time being taxed to support the Church of England. Restive under this discrimination, increasing numbers migrated to America. It is estimated that at least 200,000 of them were in the colonies at the time of the Revolution.

These Scotch-Irish had motives and traits in common with some of the New Englanders, a desire to live their own religious life and an unwillingness to be pushed around by others. From their ranks in each generation appeared determined and able leaders. It is in keeping with their twice demonstrated spirit of independence, which had brought them to leave first Scotland and then Ireland, that many of them moved through the seaboard to the American frontier. Here independence from man-made institutions was at a maximum, however absolute the need to meet nature's conditions and the onslaught of savages.

Still other settlers in America who left Europe for religious reasons were the French and Walloon Protestants. The Walloons came from the part of northeast France which is now Belgium. Walloons were early settlers in various parts of New Netherland, in what are now Manhattan, Brooklyn, and Albany. The French Protestants were the Huguenots (the term Huguenot has for long been applied to Walloon Protestants also) whom we have already mentioned in connection with their persecution in France. What was lost to France as a result of intolerance was gained by America. In Revolutionary times among those of Huguenot ancestry were Washington, Adams, Jay, and Laurens, president of the Continental Congress. The relatively small Huguenot leaven in the more numerous nationalities represented in the American colonies was of disproportionately large political usefulness. Once again the developing American political community was fortunate in newcomers who had had the fortitude to cling to their religious convictions through the bitterest kind of violent persecution.

The fact of people of different religious conviction being able to get on with one another in the ordinary relations of community life and activities was something experienced almost from the start in the mid-colonies. It was something not lost on the colonial leaders—even those from New England, where religious intolerance had earlier been so harsh—when the time came for the formation of the United States.

As in the case of New England, there was a seagoing trade from the mid-colonies with the West Indies. Philadelphia was the principal port. The West Indies in this way got lumber and provisions such as meat and grain cheaper than they could have been obtained otherwise. What the New Englanders and Pennsylvanians and New Yorkers in turn obtained from these sugar islands enabled them to buy more English manufactures than they could have paid for in any other way. Nevertheless the English Parliament did not like to see the French or other foreign-controlled West Indies islands competing with trade of the British West Indies. In 1733, burdensome duties were imposed on imports of foreign molasses, sugar, and rum into the American colonies subject to Britain. The evasion of these duties by the colonials and their violation of the law was an item, in the mid-colonies and in New England alike, in the building of an attitude of disrespect towards British rule.

The Southern Colonials

The early colonists in Virginia, like those in New England, had a middle-class English leadership. But the Virginians were not dissenters from the Church of England, and did not have the religious preoccupation of the Pilgrims and the Puritans. They were mainly motivated by hope of gain, perhaps persuaded by the imaginative accounts of every manner of animal, vegetable, and mineral wealth to be expected in America, about which Sir George Peckham wrote in 1583.

In addition to hopes for wealth through prosperous trade and commerce, there was also a political reason for the founding of Virginia. A colony there might well check Spanish power in the New World. Spain had indeterminate claims in the southwestern part of North America based on Ponce de León's discovery of the mainland of North America in 1513, where he had landed in early April very likely near the mouth of the St. Johns River. It was near Easter, *Pascua florida,* and he found spring flowers. He named the land La Florida.

The early years of Virginia colonization proved very difficult. Attacks of fever and attacks by Indians alike cut down the colonists. At first the colonists were not allowed to work for themselves but for a common store. This experiment failed after a few years. Captain John Smith said:

When our people were fed out of the common store, and laboured jointly together, glad was he could slip from his labour, or slumber over his taske, he cared not how, nay the most honest among them would hardly take so much true paines in a weeke, as now for themselves they will doe in a day: neither cared they for the increase, presuming that howsoever the harvest prospered the generall store must maintaine them, so that wee reaped not so much Corne from the labours of thirtie as now three or four do provide for themselves.

The colonists also had absentee government trouble from London. They had not started out with the assurance of local control that was present in Massachusetts Bay, despite the fact that in 1619 the first representative assembly in the colonies was established in Virginia. Sir Thomas Smith, a great merchant and first governor of the East India Company, was treasurer of the Virginia Company from 1609 to 1620. He resigned under charges of unjustifiable self-enrichment. What some of the colonists thought of him appears in the following declaration of the "Generall Assembly in Virginia" in 1624:

In those 12 yeers of Sir Tho. Smith his government, we averr that the colony for the most parte remayned in great want and misery under most severe and Crewell lawes sent over in printe, and contrary to the expresse Letter of the Kinge in his most gracious Charter, and as mercylessly executed, often tymes whithout tryall or Judgment. The allowance in those tymes for a man was only eight ounces of meale and half a pinte of pease for a daye, the one and the other mouldy, rotten, full of Cobwebs and Maggots loathsome to man and not fytt for beasts, which forced many to flee for reliefe to the Savage Enemy, who being taken againe were putt to sundry deaths as by hanginge, shooting and breakinge upon the wheele and others were forced by famine to filch for their bellies, of whom one for steelinge of 2 or 3 pints of oatemeale had a bodkinge thrust through his tounge and was tyed with a chaine to a tree untill he starved, yf a man through his sicknes had not been able to worke, he had noe allowance at all, and soe consequently perished. Many through these extremities, being weery of life, digged holes in the earth and there hidd themselves till they famished.

Wee cannott for this our scarsitie blame our Comanders heere, in respect that our sustenance was to come from England, for had they at that time (not) given us better allowance we had perished in generall, soe lamentable was our scarsitie that we were constrayned to eate Doggs, Catts, ratts, Snakes, Toadstooles, horse hides and what nott, one man out of the mysery that he endured, killinge his wiefe powdered her upp to eate her, for which he was burned. Many besides fedd on the Corps of dead men, and one who had gotten unsatiable, out of custome to that foode could not be restrayned, untill such tyme as he was executed for it, and indeede so miserable was our estate, that this happyest day that ever some of them hoped to see, was when the Indyans had killed a mare, they wishinge whilst she was a boylinge that Sir Tho. Smith were uppon her backe in the kettle.

Even if allowance is made for bitter feelings and partisanship, this declaration paints a picture of colonial hardship and harshness for the first families of Virginia.

By the year 1700 the geography of the tidewater region had already decisively influenced the political and social life of Virginia. The land and climate were right for the growing of tobacco as a staple crop for export. The long inlets and leisurely gradient of streams east of the fall line permitted navigation to each planter's door, so there was no need for a seaport of substantial size. A plantation was its own sufficient seaport. The most advantageous economic pursuit was growth of tobacco. There was no development of manufacturing in Virginia. Manufactured articles were brought in from abroad and bought with the proceeds of tobacco sales.

So it came about that large landholdings in a uniform countryside were characteristic of Virginia, rather than the compact townships which developed in the smaller and more separated fertile spots of New England. As wealth lay in landownership along the streams, economic power fell to those who got control of great stretches of this land; and then political power followed economic power. One royal governor, with the support of the planters, was able for sixteen years after 1660 to keep in office the same legislature, submissive to the views of the planters.

Although in 1700 the population of Virginia was only about 70,000, of whom 20,000 were black slaves, already some of the younger sons of the seaboard families and other ambitious whites felt held down by the close ownership of land and an inequitable land grant system, and had started settling above the fall line. These frontiersmen thought the seaboard authorities did not give them sufficient protection against Indians. They were restive also because not represented in the legislature proportionately to their numbers.

At this time, when slavery had not yet become so well established as to fasten the South in fetters anything like those of the cotton plantation system which came after 1800, the tobacco growers were an intelligent aristocracy. They had the money to tutor their children at home and to send them to England to school, and for advanced education to England or the northern colleges, or to their own William and Mary. There was resourcefulness in the Virginia leaders, as demonstrated by their outstanding part in the Revolutionary War and the formation of the American union. Great though the differences in the life of North and South may have been as a result of the factors of climate and terrain, both regions were alike in a spirit of individual self-reliance unlike anything to be found in the old conditions of England or Europe.

Tobacco growing lent itself to the employment of stereotyped labor, and as a result importation of Negro slaves increased rapidly between 1700 and 1750. In 1740 it is estimated that blacks outnumbered whites in Virginia, a situation that was shortly reversed as a result of the arrival of foreigners in the "Valley." It is estimated that in 1756 of a total population of 290,000 in Virginia, 120,000 were blacks. Manual labor as a consequence of slavery became something that a free white did not want to undertake and at which he could not make a living. The status of a white man without much property had greatly deteriorated. This resulted in the movement westward of non-landowning whites who had any ambition. We have already mentioned the coming of Scotch-Irish and southern Germans into the Shenandoah Valley. Political friction grew between the upcountry and the tidewater, a friction that was increased by the fact that upcountry religion tended to be evangelical and missionary in nature, whereas the tidewater clergy of the established and government-supported Church of England had become rather lax and were regarded by the upcountry as not worthy of their hire. There was in the older property and slave-owning eastern counties a distrust and fear of growing democratic radicalism to their west, a sentiment which may have influenced the Virginia leadership towards support of a federal government with strong recognition of rights in property.

The Frontier

As the establishment of the seaboard colonies as going concerns had been achieved by adventuresome and chance-taking people, it is not surprising that when friction arose between government and governed, or when some found themselves not doing as well as their neighbors or foreclosed from the acquisition of desirable land, a secondary migration inland got under way.

The migration of Thomas Hooker and his flock from the rule of Massachusetts Bay to the Connecticut River valley in 1636 was an early step in this process of shifting towards the west by those ambitious for more scope and freedom for their own way of regulating their lives. The same motive was at work in those who left tidewater Virginia for the upland back country. This westward moving fringe of settlement was, as we have seen, reinforced by other than seaboard colonial emigration and from sources not stemming back to England, as, for example, the Germans and the Scots.

The men and women who at any given time were in the western edge of settlement were dependent on their own household for most of their vital family needs, except that for attack or defense against Indians they would require a base in a common fort with a good water supply and proper enclosure for protection of people and their animals. These pioneer communities, removed as they were by poor communications from effective discipline of the established colonial governments, tended to become a law unto themselves. The cooperation of these westerly populations could be gained only through their own consent. They were aggressive and tough, and demanded greater representation in the government of the colonies with which their ties had not been completely severed. They complained of inadequate support in their struggles with the Indians.

The frontiersmen and the economically poorer families who had stayed at home on the seaboard had at least one political characteristic in common, and that was a certain amount of hostility and distrust for the well-to-do and well-established families of the seaboard. There was in this a faint foreshadowing of the much later political alliance between western farmers and industrial workers of the East in opposition to the financiers, merchants, and industrialists, and the wealth symbolized by the name of Wall Street.

In the course of fighting Indians and French in the eighteenth century, the colonists, and especially those at the scene of the fighting, could not help but be struck by the frequent conspicuous blunders made by British military officers. This may have been a factor which worked along with others of greater significance towards an attitude of colonial independence.

The frontier colonists felt resentment against England for measures taken by her with the best of intentions at the close of the French and Indian War. The Proclamation of 1763, in order to prevent Indian disturbances and "frauds and abuses" against the Indians, made an Indian reservation of the land west of the Appalachian watershed— "all the land and territories lying to the westward of the sources of the rivers which fall into the sea from the west and northwest. . . ." This Proclamation appeared to close to the colonists the lands won from France as a result of the French and Indian War. The handful of pioneers who at this date had settled themselves west of the watershed were required "forthwith to remove themselves from such settlements."

When the time came to form the American union, the task was scarcely at all one to be dealt with by frontiersmen, who, as we have seen, neither had much respect for distant government nor much of an immediate governmental problem. But the frontiersmen nevertheless had a great influence on the kind of legal structure that was finally adopted for the union. One line of influence we have already mentioned: the fear in eastern conservatives of radical tendencies and disrespect for debt in the westerner. An important and formative influence was the fact that when the colonial leaders were framing a constitution, the framers were aware that the laws of a union and the union government would not be agreed to or obeyed unless freely consented to. Means of enforcement were just simply lacking for a law unpopular at the frontier, so that to have an effective union its constitution had to be drawn with recognition of local rule in matters of local interest. The situation was not at all what it is today when communications are so good that a distant government can at once shoot or imprison refractory local leaders and thus at least for the short term impose an arbitrary rule.

Colonial Assemblies and Attempts at Confederation

A British contribution to the formation of the American union was the experience allowed to the colonials in the practice of representative government. On the eve of the Revolution eight of the twelve colonies were royal provinces; two—Maryland and Pennsylvania, from the latter of which Delaware had not yet been separated—were proprietary colonies; and two—Connecticut and Rhode Island—were self-governing. Whichever form of government obtained—royal, proprietary, or self-governing—each colony had an elected representative assembly. In the royal and proprietary colonies a usual but not invariable pattern was that in addition to the elected assembly there was an appointed governor—by Crown or proprietor—and an appointed council which served as a second legislative body. In all the colonies the elected representatives claimed control of the purse. There were differences in practice as to who was qualified to vote in the election of representatives. In all the English colonies the colonials themselves had a major voice in their own government, a situation which did not exist in the French and Spanish colonies in America.

By the eve of the Revolution, all the elected representative bodies of the colonies had engaged in controversy with England over British parliamentary power and control in matters of American trade and commerce. The colonies thus had experience not only in self-government but in the assertion of colonial demands for independence from regulation of their commerce for the benefit of others than themselves.

Prior to the Revolution, the colonies as a whole had never united under anything that resembled a general government. But there had been experience with limited confederation of some of the colonies and suggestions of wider union.

In 1643 articles of confederation were agreed to "between the Plantations under the Government of Massachusetts, the Plantations under the Government of New Plymouth, the Plantations under the Government of Connecticut, and the Government of New Haven with the Plantations in Combination therewith," the confederation to be called by the name of the United Colonies of New England. For managing the affairs of the confederation there were eight commissioners, two from each of the jurisdictions. The purposes of the confederation of these four colonies of Puritan persuasion were more effective offense and defense against Indians, "free and speedy passage of justice in every Jurisdiction" so that those moving from one to another would be fairly treated, and the return of fugitive servants and prisoners.

In 1754, on advice of the British government, a meeting of colonial delegates was held in order to arrange for obtaining the friendship and support of the Iroquois Indians against France. After the colonials had met with a group of Indian chiefs and the latter had taken their departure, the delegates turned their attention to possibilities of colonial union. Under the leadership of Benjamin Franklin, a plan was adopted to petition for an Act of Parliament for the establishment of a general government in the colonies. Each colony was to retain its own constitution, unmodified except as might be required for the act of general government to be effective according to its provisions. The provisions of the act were in the main to provide for an executive, the President-General, to be appointed and paid by the Crown, and a Grand Council of forty-eight members to be chosen by the assemblies of the eleven colonies, the largest and smallest colonial representations being seven in the cases of Massachusetts Bay and Virginia, and two in the cases of New Hampshire and Rhode Island. The Council was never to be enlarged, but the representation of the several colonies was to be reapportioned from time to time in accord with the amounts of money raised from the respective colonies for the general treasury. The maximum number of representatives of any one colony was to remain seven, the minimum two. The purposes of the general government were exclusive jurisdiction of Indian relations, including war, peace, regulation of trade, and purchases of land; new settlements of land and laws regulating them until the Crown should establish them as "particular governments"; the raising and pay of soldiers and sailors, the building of forts for defense, and equipping of vessels to guard the coasts and protect trade on ocean, lake, and river. There was no power to draft soldiers or sailors in any colony without the consent of the legislature of that colony. The document by its terms seems to provide for the levy of taxes directly by the general government on the people of the colonies, and goes on to state that "they"— apparently the President General, with the advice of the Grand Council—"may appoint a General Treasurer and Particular Treasurer in each government when necessary; and, from time to time, may order the sums in the treasuries of each government into the general treasury; or draw on them for special payments, as they find most convenient." This plan, stronger in the vital phase of raising revenue than the later Articles of Confederation, was unpalatable to the colonies as cutting down their independence, and to the British government as cutting down its power, and was rejected.

The States in the Revolution

During the Revolutionary War there was a potent loyalist minority within each state. Nevertheless, the predominant opinion of the leadership was for independence from England and was sufficiently strong so that this war aim brought about the needed unity in an otherwise shaky alliance of the states.

The predominant opinion for independence was slow in its growth. The original intercolonial congress which assembled in Philadelphia in the late summer of 1774 was an emergency council. The meeting of this First Continental Congress had been prompted by the enactment of British statutes retaliating against Massachusetts for her resistance to British regulation and taxation of foreign commerce, and by the obvious British intention to stiffen the assertion of the authority of the British government over the colonies. Opinion had not yet solidified for independence in the early fall of 1774, when a plan for "a proposed union between Great Britain and the Colonies" was defeated only by the margin of the vote of one colony. This plan, submitted by Joseph Galloway of Pennsylvania, proposed that "within and under" a new intercolonial government "each colony shall retain its present constitution and powers of regulating and governing its own internal police in all cases whatsoever"; that the intercolonial government "be administered by a President General, to be appointed by the King, and a grand council to be chosen by the Representatives of the people of the several Colonies in their respective assemblies"; and further

That the President General, by and with the advice and consent of the grand council, hold and exercise all the legislative rights, powers, and authorities, necessary for regulating and administering all the general police and affairs of the colonies, in which Great Britain and the colonies, or any of them, the colonies in general, or more than one colony, are in any manner concerned, as well civil and criminal as commercial. That the said President General and grand council, be an inferior and distinct branch of the British legislature, united and incorporated with it for the aforesaid general purposes; and that any of the said general regulations may originate, and be formed and digested, either in the Parliament of Great Britain, or in the said grand council; and being prepared, transmitted to the other for their approbation or dissent; and that the assent of both shall be requisite to the validity of all such general acts and statutes.

Actual fighting broke out in the spring of 1775, when British troops who had been ordered out from Boston to destroy military stores at Concord shot down some colonials at Lexington. After going on to Concord and burning stores there, the Britishers had to return under colonial fire first to Lexington and then to Boston. The total casualties on both sides were 366; 49 Americans and 73 Britishers were killed. The provincial irregulars had discovered that they were a match for the British regulars. The British had set on fire more than military stores; they had set alight the flame of revolution. Even then it took a full year more of British stupidity combined with colonial propaganda, which we described in connection with our discussion of political separation, before the colonies, assembled in the Continental Congress, declared themselves *free and independent States.*

The Continental Congress had no effective means of raising either troops or the money with which to equip and pay them. States sent and took back troops as they or the troop commanders chose. General Washington stated that the militia would "come in you cannot tell how, go you cannot tell when, and act you cannot tell where, consume your provisions, exhaust your stores, and leave you at last at a critical moment."

In March 1781, on their signing by Maryland, Articles of Confederation and perpetual union which had been proposed three and a half years earlier, became effective. The Continental Congress thenceforward functioned under these Articles, each state retaining "its sovereignty, freedom and independence, and every Power, Jurisdiction and right, which is not by this confederation expressly delegated to the United States, in Congress assembled."

Under the Articles of Confederation, as before, the federal government had no direct taxing power, no direct source of revenue of its own. The states were obligated to pay the bills of the federal government; but no machinery to compel performance of the obligation was provided.

The jealousy of the states towards one another, which was shown in the reluctance of each one to let taxing power pass even in part to the coalition of the states, had earlier broken out in intercolonial strife, and this strife continued between states even during the Revolution against Britain. Rivalry for control of lands to the west was a natural source of conflict between states, each pushing its own interest. In 1769 to 1771 military skirmishing took place between Connecticut and Pennsylvania over the rivalry of Connecticut and Pennsylvania settlers in the Wyoming Valley of the upper Susquehanna River. Violence again broke out in 1775, when the settlement was unsuccessfully invaded by 700 Pennsylvania militiamen. There were about 2,000 Connecticut taxpayers in the settlement. During the Revolutionary War these settlers provided many soldiers of the Connecticut

Line to the continental army, thereby weakening the possibility of valley defense, so that in July 1778, the valley garrison of about 300 men was overwhelmed by a joint loyalist and Indian attack. Colonial opinion was enraged by a subsequent massacre of the wounded. This was a factor in the unifying of Revolutionary sentiment against England.

The Connecticut claims to the Wyoming Valley were based on the terms of her 1662 charter, and so were prior to those of Pennsylvania, which stemmed from the 1681 charter of William Penn. But the inhabited territory of Pennsylvania was contiguous with the settlement, and that of Connecticut was not. Near the close of 1782 a committee of the Continental Congress awarded title of the disputed valley to Pennsylvania. In the following year militia action was once again authorized against the valley, this time by the Pennsylvania assembly. But the effort to oust the Connecticut settlers by further violence was unpalatable to equitable-minded Pennsylvanians, and after a period of uncertainty, the controversy was settled. Pennsylvania statute confirmed title to the settlers in seventeen Connecticut townships in the valley, who became for the future useful citizens of Pennsylvania.

Post-Revolutionary Troubles

After the Revolutionary War had been won by the Americans, Congress in April 1783—just eight years after the Battle of Lexington—proclaimed the end of the war. Thereupon the separatist tendencies of the states, the weaknesses of the federal government, and discord within the particular states resulted in a situation which was too difficult for the American Congress.

Control of the states to make them live up to the agreements of the United States was sometimes impossible. The treaty of peace which closed the Revolutionary War contained promises that private debts from and to American and British debtors and creditors would be valid. But the American states put obstacles in the way of English creditors and made collection of their claims impossible. This breach of treaty resulted in Britain's refusing to give up certain fortifications and garrisons in western United States territory. The British motive perhaps was an economic one, as control of the western fur trade may have resulted from the location of these garrisons. In any case the British position was: no observance of the treaty provisions about English creditors, no evacuation of the British garrisons.

Ratification by nine states acting individually as sovereign states was required to make a treaty valid under the Articles of Confederation. Furthermore, every foreign power was aware that a single dissenting state was under no compulsion to comply with a treaty it did not like. In these circumstances it was difficult to get agreement on treaties. Treaties which were so free of controversy as to have no opposition whatever in the several states might be feasible; for example, such a treaty as one for the suppression of piracy at sea.

Eight of the American states in the year 1785 adopted their own statutes with regard to regulation, duties, and tariffs on foreign commerce. In the same year the British truthfully pointed out to American representatives abroad that there was no use entering into a commercial treaty with the United States unless separate confirmation was obtained from the individual states.

The states did not act to meet the legitimate requisitions of the national government for its support. An $8,000,000 requisition made during the war in the autumn of 1781 had been less than one quarter met by the opening of 1784; and in 1785 Rhode Island refused outright to pay the current requisition of Congress. Bills which had been issued by Congress to finance the war were virtually worthless—witness the saying "not worth a continental"—and the United States government had no taxing power to get the means to pay its debts.

James Madison, writing in 1787 of the weakness of the government, said:

A sanction is essential to the idea of law, as coercion is to that of government. The federal system being destitute of both, wants the great vital principles of a political constitution. It is in fact nothing more than a treaty of amity of commerce and of alliance, between independent and sovereign states.

The reasons why such a weak government had been contrived can also be summarily stated, and were so stated by Jedidiah Morse, the "father of American geography," three or four years later than the statement just quoted from Madison. Morse pointed out that the Articles of Confederation

were framed during the rage of war, when a principle of common safety supplied the place of a coercive power in governments; by men who could have had no experience in the art of governing an extensive country, and under circumstances the most critical and embarrassing. To have offered to the people, at that time, a system of government armed with the powers necessary to regulate and controul the contending interest of thirteen states, and the possessions of millions of people, might have raised a jealousy between the states, or in the minds of the people at large, that would have weakened the operations of war, and perhaps have rendered a union impracticable. Hence the numerous defects of the confederation.

At the local state level there was economic hardship. There was an unfavorable trade balance in 1784 and 1785, when imports from Britain much exceeded exports to her. Shipping charges were not enough to close the gap, and there was an outflow of specie. Wartime paper money that had become worthless had disappeared from circulation. There was an acute scarcity of money. Debtors were unable to pay their debts, and taxpayers their taxes. Foreclosures and legal process on behalf of unpaid creditors were depriving farmers and other debtors of clothing, furniture, and the tools necessary to the conduct of their business. To relieve the money shortage, seven of the states in 1785 and 1786 resorted to paper money issues of doubtful soundness. Issues of money against the security of land was the favored device. North Carolina in effect monetized tobacco by purchasing it at twice its hard-money value in new paper money. Creditors hid themselves in order to escape having to accept this depreciating money in payment of their claims.

Jedidiah Morse, making no pretense of nonpartisanship and no attempt to conceal his own bias or his own prejudices of right and wrong, described the situation in one of the states:

Rhode Island exhibits a melancholy proof of that licentiousness and anarchy which always follows a relaxation of the moral principles. In a rage for supplying the state with money, and filling every man's pocket without obliging him to earn it by his diligence, the legislature passed an act for making one hundred thousand pounds in bills: a sum much more than sufficient for a medium of trade in that state, even without any specie. The merchants in Newport and Providence opposed the act with firmness; their opposition added fresh vigor to the assembly, and induced them to enforce the scheme by a legal tender of a most extraordinary nature. They passed an act, ordaining that if any creditor should refuse to take their bills, for any debt whatever, the debtor might lodge the sum due, with a justice of the peace, who should give notice of it in the public papers; and if the creditor did not appear and receive the money within six months from the first notice, his debt should be forfeited. This act astonished all honest men; and even the promoters of paper-money-making in other states, and on other principles, reprobated this act of Rhode-Island, as wicked and oppressive. But the state was governed by faction. During the cry for paper money, a number of boisterous ignorant men were elected into the legislature from the smaller towns in the state. Finding themselves united with a majority in opinion, they formed and executed any plan their inclination suggested; they opposed every measure that was agreeable to the mercantile interest; they not only made bad laws to suit their own wicked purposes, but appointed their own corrupt creatures to fill the judicial and executive departments. Their money depreciated sufficiently to answer all their vile purposes in the discharge of debts—business almost totally ceased, all confidence was lost, the state was thrown into confusion at home, and was execrated abroad.

What if a state government did not resort to issues of fiat money or ease the lot of debtors? Take the case of Massachusetts. In that state, hard-hit by the depression, the legislature in 1786 resisted demands for paper money or for a moratorium on foreclosures of farms and homes, and took a summer adjournment without providing relief for the hard-pressed. The result was a series of events not unlike what took place a few years later in the preliminary tremors of peasant violence and rioting in the early days of the French Revolution.

At first the demands for reform were orderly and made by way of town meetings or the assembly of delegates from many towns. Demands were for reform of the taxes—which in fact bore relatively hard on those of less wealth—for reform of court procedures and costs in the interest of relief of debtors—at that time imprisonment for debt was general—and for issues of paper money to relieve the shortage of currency.

Then in August and September, armed bands prevented and broke up the sitting of the courts in Northampton and Worcester respectively. Similar mob action followed in other towns. The most serious disturbances took place near Springfield, where in September the Supreme Court was forced to adjourn, and in January 1787, an armed clash took place between militia under General William Shepherd and two forces of insurrectionists attempting to capture the federal arsenal at Springfield. The larger of these two forces of insurrectionists consisted of about 1,200 men under command of Daniel Shays, a veteran Revolutionary officer. The insurrection was put down. But the next session of the legislature adopted statutes easing the objectionable taxes and exempting tools of trade, clothing, and household furniture from debt process.

Shays' Rebellion was not an isolated event. Violence on a less well-organized basis took place in other states. Conservative leaders throughout the states were thoroughly alarmed. General Washington wrote:

There are combustibles in every state which a spark might set fire to. I feel infinitely more than I can express for the disorders which have arisen. Good God! Who besides a Tory could have foreseen, or a Briton have predicted them?

Thus prospects did not look promising either at the national level for an effective union of all the states which might overcome the rivalries and jealousies between the states, or at the local level for an orderly reconciliation between the conflicting and discordant groups within the several states.

A Solution Is Found

The leaders in the several states had the wisdom and the tolerance —the necessary give-and-take—to find a peaceful solution of their difficulties. They were able to put aside the intolerance which had been necessary during the war, when the property of loyalists was confiscated, loyalist leaders exiled, and upwards of 100,000 loyalists returned to England. They found a satisfactory harness in which the northern manufacturer or merchant and the southern planter could pull together along with the frontiersmen and the doctrinaire lovers of liberty to whom control by an American federal government looked almost as obnoxious as one by a royal British government.

The troubles within the states and the forewarnings of an approach to economic disorder through want of a reliable medium of exchange were utilized for the good that was in them as stimuli to a better ordering of affairs. The bad in them as opportunities for adventurers to fight or intrigue their way to political power did not prevail. There were enough Madisons and Adamses, and not too many Aaron Burrs or Benedict Arnolds.

The amount of give-and-take exhibited by the leaders was remarkable. States with western land claims ceded them to the union in order to make union palatable to states without such claims. The small states' fear of the overgreat influence of large states was overcome by the arrangement whereby in the federal Senate the representation of states would be equal, although in the federal House based on population. Another compromise which made agreement on union possible was the provision accepted by the northern states that the union government would leave the slave trade alone until 1808, in return for which the southern states were willing to allow the union government the power to regulate interstate and foreign commerce. The difficulties with the varying state currencies paved the way for agreement on federal power to coin money and regulate its value. And the weakness of the old confederation due to no federal taxing power was cured by the first paragraph of the section of the Constitution granting powers to Congress.

The adoption of this Constitution, whatever else may be said about it, at least demonstrated that enough of the leaders of the American people and enough of the people themselves had the wisdom and the discipline to produce an orderly and good result out of the acute problems posed by their postrevolutionary discord. They did not follow the usual model of ancient and modern times, which, as we have seen, is to work out of discord into an unjust order by way of violence or compulsion. There was no seizure of power by someone with a strong arm, no rule by force or fraud.

It seems likely that one reason for the success in the forming and adoption of the American Constitution lay in the highly selected quality of the American leadership. The colonists had been men and women willing to take a chance in new and difficult country. Many of them had torn up their home ties on account of their loyalty to religious principle. A highly capable minority of the stock of England and northern Europe, having a leadership equipped with the best governmental and philosophical ideas of the time, had come into a wilderness, where they and their immediate descendants had the opportunity and the necessity of creating a political order of some kind. Though intolerant at times, they seemed to be for the most part creative and self-reliant, motivated by a relatively large proportion of the desire to get ahead rather than by a relatively large proportion of envy of their neighbors, which had been the bane of much of European politics.

In the upper, the middle, and the lower classes in an old Western European country there is presumably a supply of latent talent in the great numbers of people—at least a thin sprinkling of the unusually capable. If some selective process could be brought to bear that would bring this talent to the fore, it would likely come up with a group of superior ability. Perhaps this is just what happened in the case of the American colonies, where the appeal of America—whether for freedom or ambition or adventure—could only be taken advantage of by those Europeans willing to undergo the hardships and uncertainties involved in taking their chance on a life in America.

The Americans were the same kind of people as the English, the Germans, the French, and the Scotch. But a selective process had in fact been at work in their case. The early Americans had of necessity been hardy and adventurous. Their leaders had been loyal to principle and willing to undergo tribulation for its sake. Their near-term descendants proved to have the necessary temperament and disposition, along with the hardheadedness and sense of the real needs of the situation, that permitted an orderly and constructive way out of their political discord. They cured the errors in their past experience rather than perpetuating them.

3. BARBARIANS IN THE WESTERN ROMAN EMPIRE

The American Constitution and the formation of the United States of America was the outcome of two centuries of the history of the European colonists and their descendants in North America. Their leaders—selected, as we have seen, for ability and adherence to principle—were equipped with the most advanced political ideas of the time. They had come into a wilderness thinly inhabited by savages with ideas and customs far more primitive than their own. They worked out the solution of their governmental problems in a land without any prior political institutions to which they had to accommodate themselves.

A far different result of the arrival of newcomers on an existing scene occurred when the barbarian tribes came into the Western Roman Empire in the fourth and fifth centuries of our era. In that case the newcomers and their leaders were migrating tribes selected by hardihood in warfare. Such political ideas as they had were backward for their day and age. Instead of coming into a wilderness, they came into the remains of a splendid civilization breaking down, whose leaders and people had lost the key to their own earlier greatness. The outcome of two centuries of this historical development was a disintegrating Western Europe about to enter five hundred years of the so-called Dark Ages.

Rome as It Looked in the Fourth Century

In our discussion of *discord* we described the loss of freedom of the creative local municipal leaders and the increasing burdens which had come to be imposed on them by the imperial government throughout the Roman Empire at the turn into the fourth century. This cramping and burdensome situation continued and worsened throughout the century.

Taxes so heavy that the capable were prevented from producing what the people of the Empire needed were one form taken by governmental intolerance. Another was the requisitioning in kind of services and supplies. The municipal leaders—the *curiales*—were made personally liable for the collection of the assessed imperial taxes, and severe decrees were enacted to punish anyone who sheltered a fugitive *curialis* who sought to escape burdens which had become too heavy to bear. Such industry as existed was either state-owned or closely controlled by the state.

The necessities of military defense, made evident in the barbarian invasions of the third century, in combination with the deteriorating effectiveness of the army, resulted in the fortification of the theretofore pleasant, open and spreading provincial towns. The later prevalent practice of using beautiful buildings as rock quarries for various utilitarian structures likely got its start at this time. The earlier pagan intolerance of Christians had given way with the rising strength of the Church to a severe and bitter Christian intolerance of pagans.

Dishonesty required men to turn their attention from constructive activity to protecting themselves and their property from the designs of their neighbors. Brigandage had become a vocation both of erstwhile farmers and city folk alike. In the cumbersome bureaucracy, bribery became rife, especially bribery of those who were charged with the apportionment of taxes.

In the Roman Empire of the fourth century corrupt officials in a province were far removed by time and distance from any prompt disciplinary action by an honest emperor or his aides. Plunder in the government service offered an attractive opportunity for economic advancement. The decrees of the emperors could not check the evil.

Although the municipal leaders in the provinces, who had been the backbone of the economic strength of the earlier empire, were now so burdened as to have lost their productiveness, there still remained a class of people in the Empire who were in a position of economic power. These people were the owners of great landed estates, proprietors of the senatorial class—who in the good days of the empire had furnished to it their share of soldiers and statesmen. The Roman senators in the days of the republic had been an able group recruited from the ex-magistrates.

The Roman landowners in the late Empire had got themselves into a politically privileged position, being exempt from the tax liabilities which were crushing the municipal leaders and from certain other taxes and services which bore upon small landowners. The great estates were worked for their owners by slaves, and by *coloni,* who were legally freemen with rights which slaves did not have—for example, they could own property or get married. Many, perhaps most, *coloni* were by this time bound to the estates on which they were born, and even the landlord could not free them from their servitude to the land. They were subject to an imperial poll tax and owed various services in kind to the state, such as road labor and transport services, as well as an obligation to cultivate a part of the landlord's estate. How the system of cultivation by *coloni* came into being is not known. By the late fourth century the system was widespread in Italy and the provinces. Perhaps the necessities of producing food led the emperors to copy what they had found in the eastern provinces. In Egypt, for example, grain was produced by a system of labor by peasants bound to their districts.

To have restored the comparative freedom of the early Empire to this degenerating and overburdened fourth-century Empire would have required constructive statesmanship of the highest order. Such statesmanship was not to be found in the ranks of the powerful landlords. These great landlords, like their counterparts in some other times and places, were holding too tightly to their privileges. Fugitive *curiales* and other bankrupt free settlers were adding to the ranks of the *coloni.* The landlords took no steps to rearrange more justly the social order. They failed in the sense of equity, making no effort to see where they and others might most rightly and fairly fit in the social and political picture in the light of the needs of the time.

One important test of a good community is, as we have seen, the degree to which the energies and constructive abilities within its people have been tapped, so that the community gets the benefit of what they achieve and what they produce. The fourth-century Empire never found the formula for releasing and liberating the energies of its subjects along lines of material productiveness. A good part of the energy and intelligence of the times was going into the growth of the Christian Church. The orientation of the Church leaders was otherworldly— witness the great development of monasteries and monastic life at this period—and did not produce any effective political reorganization of the state or sound economic development. The Church and its organizers were not to the purpose in salvaging the political and economic wreck, because their interests were otherwise focused. No cure was to be found here for the decline in municipal autonomy and wealth which had been taking place in the third century under the rule of the rapidly changing emperors who sprang from the army. The Church in the West was vigorous enough to assert its independence and its own ecclesiastical ideas against the East, yet in the political field no kind of useful western innovation was made. The Church leaders did not put their finger on what was sapping the Empire's strength.

In the badly organized agriculture of the fourth century, coupled, some think, with a deterioration of the soil in Italy and perhaps in the European provinces, shortages and famines occurred. These the Christians regarded as punishment for pagan impiety, and the pagans regarded as punishment for Christian disregard of the old gods and the old piety.

The leadership of the Western Empire did not have a sufficient power of truth to fact to diagnose the troubles or to cure them. There was no vision of political development by way of growth, no spirit of ability to revivify what had been good in the old order or to take what was good in it and go on from there. The Empire was coasting, its creative political ideas were gone.

Barbarian Leaders on the Roman Scene

By the fourth century the Western Empire was thoroughly familiar with the presence of barbarians. Ever since the first century they had been employed as soldiers—this being true in the case of the Franks as far back as Julius Caesar's days, before the turn into the Christian Era. Throughout the third and fourth centuries, as successive barbarian invasions were defeated by the Roman armies, themselves now increasingly barbarian in manpower, more barbarians were taken within the Roman orbit and assimilated to the Roman scheme. The barbarians within the Empire were no more of a novelty than central European immigrants and their descendants were a novelty in the United States in the early twentieth century. In a province such as Gaul—roughly comprising the area that is France today—the infiltration of barbarians was one factor in the way of life becoming gradually less like the old Roman order of the great days of the second century. The barbarians on the borders of the Empire were different in custom and habit from their ancestors described in Tacitus' *Germania* in the early days of Roman and barbarian contact. For instance, by the end of the fourth century many of the Germanic tribes had been converted to Christianity (of the heretical, nontrinitarian Arian variety) before they came into the Empire in large numbers and to stay.

That there was no disabling prejudice against barbarians in the life of the state is shown by the fact that some of them held the highest positions in the Empire, as military generals and as consuls of Rome. Stilicho, the Vandal, at the close of the fourth century and the opening of the fifth, was the greatest Roman general of his time, inflicting defeats on the Visigoths and other barbarian invaders of the Empire. He was a keen statesman as well as a general and a greater man than most if not all of the "old Romans" who were his contemporaries. What was true of Stilicho was true of other barbarians within the Empire—they were among its most brilliant and cultured leaders. The career of Stilicho calls attention to another fact which was evident: the barbarians were as likely to fight both as officers and soldiers either within the Roman ranks or as Roman allies as they were to fight as enemies of the Empire.

Although, as we have said, there was no special selection of the barbarians who were coming into the Empire—as there was in the case of the colonists who came into North America—yet the general ability of the stock was presumably good, if we are to judge by the achievements of their descendants in Western Europe in late medieval days and thereafter. Their most conspicuous long-term political failure is that they have never to this day succeeded in producing in Western Europe a peace comparable to that of the early Roman Empire in the same area.

Whatever the latent ability of these newcomers, the actual historical events which followed their arrival showed that there were not enough leaders either among their ranks or those of the old inhabitants of the Empire with sufficient political knowledge or adequate political virtues to prevent the steady deterioration of the political and social scene. The old leadership had thinned out too much and the new was not capable of filling the vacuum. The incoming barbarians adopted the old administrative forms; they did not have ideas of their own as to how the Roman order could be improved upon. Like Ataulf, the Visigothic king from 410 to 415, their best hope was to maintain the Roman civilization by the barbarian sword. Orosius, a contemporary of Ataulf, has him say:

To begin with I ardently desired to efface the very name of the Romans and to transform the Roman Empire into a Gothic Empire. *Romania,* as it is popularly called, would have become *Gothia;* Ataulf would have replaced Caesar Augustus. But long experience taught me that the unruly barbarism of the Goths was incompatible with the laws. Now without laws there is no commonwealth. I therefore decided rather to aspire to the glory of restoring the fame of Rome in all its integrity, and of increasing it by means of the Gothic strength. I hope to go down to posterity as the restorer of Rome, since it is not possible that I should be its supplanter.

The impressiveness of the empire, even in its disintegrated condition, was great. Athanaric, another Gothic leader, on visiting Constantinople, the capital of the Eastern Empire, somewhere around the year 390, is reported (by the Gothic historian Jordanes a century and a half later) as saying:

"Lo, now I see what I have often heard of with unbelieving ears," meaning the great and famous city. Turning his eyes here and there, he marvelled as he saw the circumstances of the city, the coming and going of the ships, the splendid walls and the people of divers nations gathered like a flood of waters streaming from different regions into one basis. So, too, when he saw the army in array, he said: "Truly the emperor is a god on earth and whoso raises a hand against him is guilty of his own blood."

The influence of the Eastern Empire as a going concern far beyond anything the barbarians themselves had ever created had a powerful and continuous effect on the barbarians in Western Europe and their ideals of political order.

The course of the fifth century saw the trends of the fourth carried on without respite: constantly more barbarians constantly less well assimilated to a constantly worsening order. The West had become a melting pot where the old elements and the new did not provide the right mixture to produce a good political result. The barbarians were by now setting up their own kingdoms, but were still nominally allies of the western or of the eastern emperor. The state of the law became further confused by the increase of numbers of barbarians living under their own personal law side by side with the Romans under theirs. The public law was still the Roman, and still largely administered for barbarian kings by Romans.

Until 476, there was still nominally a western emperor, and perhaps one of the things that kept this diminished office so long in existence was the need of all—Romans and barbarians alike—to beat off Attila, the Scourge of God, and his Huns, whose terrible inroads into Western Europe started to recede after his defeat in 451 at Châlons by the Roman general Aetius commanding Romans, Visigoths, Franks, and Burgundians.

The relations of barbarians with the old Romanized and Romans had perforce become closer, and there continues to be no deep-seated antipathy between the two. In 455, the old leaders of Gaul got together with the Visigothic king—whose headquarters was Toulouse—to put Avitus on the throne and thereby to control the western emperor in the interests of Gallic autonomy. Certainly in this playing of politics by the old Romanized Celts of Gaul they have no feeling against the Goths as long as the latter can help further their ambitions.

The western emperor was by now more and more an instrument utilized for the most part by this or that barbarian leader for his own purposes and ambitions. So the fact that it was a leader of revolting Germanic troops (Odovakar and his Heruls) that threw out the last western emperor is a truthful symbol of what had happened in substance already.

The Decay of Roman Politics

When Caesar conquered Gaul at about the turn into the Christian Era, Roman customs, Roman law, Roman religion, Roman language soon supplanted the old institutions. When the Goths conquered Gaul in the fourth and fifth centuries, their own institutions supplanted nothing. They took as well as they could the institutions they found among the conquered, and their own contributions only served to debase further the already declining Roman civilization.

We have said that the fifth century saw a continuation of the trends of the fourth. In fact the trends ran so much more strongly that the change which took place almost became one of kind rather than degree. At the close of the fourth century, about the year 400, the Roman political organization in the West was in appearance intact. The administrative divisions were still as they had been. There were already many capable barbarians who had been assimilated to the Roman scene and were in positions of the highest importance, and esteemed by the Romans of Western Europe. The Romans and the barbarians within the empire and in its military service could still defeat—although not always, as witness Adrianople in 378—the new barbarian invaders. But by the year 500, a change was evident. There had been a series of failures in the fifth century to withstand the new barbarian invaders so as to be able to take them into the empire on any pretense of Roman imperial terms. The result was that there were now a series of more or less independent kingdoms throughout the West, Visigothic and Frankish struggling for supremacy in Gaul,

Vandal in North Africa, Ostrogothic in Italy, Burgundian north of Italy, and Visigothic in Spain. The political situation around the Mediterranean was just as disintegrated as it is today, a millennium and a half later.

The creative mind in Roman politics had disappeared by the year 300. By the year 500, the body politic was broken too. The fragmented Mediterranean community was about to go to school and for a long time with a Church which had its own message of salvation, but scarcely any understanding of the civilization that was vanishing and no understanding of a free political order.

Another two centuries and even this fragmented Mediterranean community was to be brought to an end by the Moslem conquests and the long slow years of growth of a more northerly centered European civilization to get under way.

From the experience of the breakdown of the Western Roman Empire it looks as though a deteriorating civilization could not be restored by the entry of new and vigorous people who themselves lack a good civilization. The declining empire had lost its tolerance, its honesty, its equity, and its truth to fact; and the newcomers, the invading barbarians, could themselves provide none of these virtues except perhaps a greater honesty. Even though the quality of the newcomers and the old residents taken together was such that they had within them the potentiality for leadership that was to produce a good result —given centuries of shaking down—still the prognosis for the immediate political future was bad. Political skills and political virtues were lacking in old resident and newcomer alike.

4. PRESENT QUESTIONS FOR FUTURE ANSWERS

The need for a favorable self-estimate leads people to attribute the difficult circumstances in which they sometimes find themselves to some cause other than their own shortcomings and deficiencies. A common cause that is often thus selected as an explanation for the troubles of a community is the presence within the community of an ill-assimilated minority. A recent example was the Nazi designation of the Jews as the cause of the troubles of Hitlerian and pre-Hitlerian Germany. The same process of pointing the finger of scorn and calumny takes place in most societies in periods of stress or dissatisfaction. The spokesmen of group sentiment hit upon a minority scapegoat.

The satirist Juvenal at the opening of the second century explains a deterioration in the morals of Rome by attributing it to an influx of easterners; *the Orontes has flowed into the Tiber:*

> A Grecian capital in Italy!
> Grecian? O, No! with this vast sewer compared
> The dregs of Greece are scarcely worth regard.
> Long since, the stream that wanton Syria laves
> Has disembogued its filth in Tiber's waves,
> Its language, arts; o'erwhelmed us with the scum
> Of Antioch's streets, its minstrel, harp and drum.

Speech or writing which disparages wops, foreigners, commies, yanquis, or kikes is a common way by which groups and their leaders preserve their own self-esteem, and the disparagement is not to be taken at face value. Whatever the truth of the matter may be, it requires dispassionate inquiry to find it out. Derogatory remarks by the representatives of one group about the stranger within or without their gates are always suspect.

Quite irrespective of any questions of factual superiority of one group to another, or of one group's way of doing things to that of another, we have seen that when people of different religion, or of different physical appearance, or of different traditions of carrying on business find themselves parts of one political community there is likely to be ill feeling and misunderstanding. The historical cases which we reviewed in discussing the divided community made this plain. The difficulties of late Roman Western Europe that we considered in the last section and its failures to produce a good political result out of the mixture of barbarian and Roman elements are illustrative on a grand scale of the difficulty of mixing people of different traditions when there is no powerful and predominant good culture to which all can adjust themselves.

Although disparaging statements by one group about another are to be discounted, it is still of basic importance to a community that the facts be known as to the effects on the welfare and growth of the body politic of the abilities and customs of different groups within the community. It is wise to be aware of whether one group is more capable or useful than another and in what its superiority or inferiority consists, and what is the result for the community of mixing a more capable or more educable group with a less capable or less educable.

It has happened in the course of history that a fortuitous set of circumstances has selected out a more than usually capable group with a more than usual endowment of useful characteristics. This has taken place in the case of some nomadic groups, the conditions of whose life have made a combination of self-reliance with a strong sense of group discipline necessary to their survival. It has taken place in the case of some religious groups whose tenacity under persecution and adherence to their religious ideals has been the condition of the maintenance and preservation of the religion and its bearers. It has taken place when a group has had to face and overcome the obstacles of a harsh or desert environment, when out of loyalty to principle they have gone into exile and have had to have the stamina and determination and technical competence to make the desert bloom.

The question arises as to whether it is a good thing or a bad thing for such a fortuitously selected capable group to undergo a random mixture with people less capable along either cultural lines or lines of native temperament. Consider the specific case of communities whose members have undergone selection on account of loyalty to religious ideals. What is the effect on the future of the community when the good elements of the Puritan cultural and biological inheritance are watered down? Should the Mormons willingly forgo the inheritance of ability and of temperament capable of undergoing hardship for an ideal? Should the Jew allow to be dissipated the extraordinary talents that in his case seem to have been associated with tenacity of purpose under persecution?

The best solution for the future of a group that by historical accident has emerged as an able group would seem to involve their taking into their group as newcomers as far as possible only those who in temperament, mind, and constitution are endowed with the capacity to take what is good in the ways of the group.

If a melting pot is to produce a good alloy, it needs to contain the appropriate elements for a good alloy.

In considering the degree of political excellence or the political superiority or inferiority of a community historically carrying on at a given time and place, one important question concerns the relative frequency with which the members of the community produce capable individuals. The idea of what is a politically capable individual needs definition. Capability may in part be a matter of temperament—it is possible, for instance, that there is in some people more than in others a native predisposition making easier or more likely the acquisition of politically good qualities like tolerance, honesty, equity, and truth to fact. Political capability also implies the possession of certain active qualities which are morally neutral in their aim—neutral in the sense that they can be applied to good or bad ends—but qualities so necessary that without them no constructive end at all, good or bad, is likely to be achieved. Such qualities include courage, vigor, intelligence, and a due quota of aggressiveness. These qualities are good in and for themselves, but they can be applied in the service of bad ends.

A superior group or a superior community for political purposes would be one which contained a high enough proportion of these capable individuals to allow the organization and maintenance of a free order. As this is an area in which the necessary facts are wanting, we are obliged to assume some arbitrary figures which may or may not be of the right order of magnitude: Let us say that a politically superior group were one that per 100,000 adults contained 4 out of 100, or 4,000, capable of intermediate leadership in a free order; and a politically inferior group were one that per 100,000 adults contained one out of 100, or 1,000, capable of such intermediate leadership.

Both inborn native ability and the effectiveness of education play a part in the production of the necessary numbers of intermediate leaders. To take again the arbitrary assumption we have just made as to the needed proportion of capable for the functioning of a free order: in a country with a population of 100,000,000 adults, our assumption would call for the presence of 4,000,000 who in understanding and in action were capable of tolerance, honesty, truth to fact, and equity. Our assumption is that these would be sufficient to set the standard and give the lead to the rest. If the educational system of the country were effective in reaching most of those with the necessary native ability and temperament, the country would not require as high a proportionate rate of births of the potentially capable as if the educational system were missing and failing to reach considerable numbers of those with the necessary native ability.

There is also to be considered the much rarer occurrence in a population of the very few leaders of real genius in the various lines of human endeavor—the Newtons in science, the Shakespeares in literature, the Lincolns in politics. It is a fortunate community that can boast one of these among its members. But the achievements of these very great men can be understood and put to use by others of exceptional ability, so that their supreme accomplishments benefit the whole world and are available for the good everywhere of those able to make use of them.

We have raised questions to which, though the questions are important and the answers are needed, the factual answers are unfortunately not available. At present not enough is known about the frequency with which different groups give birth to potentially capable individuals or the effect on this frequency of mixing the groups in general relations of intermarriage. Also to the extent that a predisposition favorable to the acquisition of politically useful traits is heritable, not enough is known as to the effect of group intermarriage on the relative numbers, in subsequent generations, of those who would have such a favorable predisposition and those who would lack it.

Beneficial conditions of selection might occur in the case of an erstwhile inferior group, so that its relatively fewer capable people were for some reason segregated out and favored and as a result produced either in a new territory or in the old relatively greater numbers than before. Or harmful conditions of selection might occur in the case of an erstwhile superior group so that the relatively incapable became produced in greater proportions, and the relatively capable in smaller proportions. Thus the groups might come to change their standing, and the formerly inferior, or an offshoot from it, surpass the formerly superior.

This is an area in which the facts are not known. Yet they are facts which may have been and may yet be of critical significance in the formation, preservation, and growth of a good political community.

We have certainly not come up with any definite answers to questions about the prospects for long-term maintenance of a community made up of the kind of people capable of a continuing free order. The two specific cases we examined to try to get light on the subject—the European colonization of North America and the infiltration and then irruption of newcomers into the Western Roman Empire—were suggestive but not conclusive.

The influence of the right kind of political ideas was obvious. The colonial leaders in North America were equipped with the best political information of their times; the newcomers into the Western Roman Empire were without any useful political knowledge at all, and the old inhabitants had lost the key to what had made their community formerly great.

A good following was significant—a large enough intermediate leadership capable of enough tolerance, honesty, truth to fact, and equity so that the good political ideas had a practical means through which to function on a basis of the consent of the governed.

It seems to be true that the likelihood of realizing a free order and political institutions and a government suitable to it is increased by factors of inheritance and education which enlarge the proportionate numbers of those of an appropriate native temperament and acquired disposition to the degree that tolerance, honesty, truth to fact, and equity can prevail in the community.

When we survey our world today, with its separate states in conflict with one another, and see in addition the discord within most of these states themselves, there is brought home to us the staggering problems before the leaders and peoples. Where are there to be found and how are there to be nurtured the good standards of a free order and the political virtues to which the powerful must adhere if there is to be a just world? Are the resources and climate on the world scene sufficient to allow a free order? Are there in the teeming millions of the world a sufficient proportion of those with temperament, disposition, and ability apt for a free world community?

XVI. Political Character

1. PERSISTENCE OF GOOD AND BAD ATTITUDES

An attitude once firmly set is, like any other habit, likely to persist. This is why people can count on the character of others who are well known to them. If a man has in the past been tolerant and fair-minded, it can be predicted that he will face a new situation tolerantly and fair-mindedly. If he has always been honest in his dealings, honesty will continue to characterize him. The intolerant man remains intolerant, and the greedy man greedy. We say that we do not believe a report of someone, because what has been reported is completely *out of character.*

It is part of nature's economy and a condition of man's effectiveness that what he has learned to do and what he has from time to time repeated should become a pattern of more or less unthinking habit. The rule and role he has acquired through impersonation and response come to be taken for granted and followed without hesitation. The solving of new problems would be hampered or prevented if too much of one's time had to be taken up in forming the appropriate attitude for each situation *de novo,* as if one had no working rules to go by. It is habit that saves our ability to get things done. If habit has taken over, if ways and attitudes have become what is called *second nature,* a man is freed to put his time and attention on an expanding horizon of activities.

When we discussed the need of a rule to go by, we showed the powerful psychic urge to want a rule and to regard customary familiar rule as right. Now we see that as part of nature's economy there is also this powerful urge of habit to adhere unthinkingly to the customary rule. In addition to the need for a rule, a man is endowed with the tendency to continue to obey and follow a rule once adopted.

In the case of a relatively uncomplicated virtue such as honesty, even if a man did not have as a result of his upbringing or otherwise a leaning towards honesty, he might learn to act as though he had it and might recognize honesty as the best policy for him in some particular transaction. But such honesty is unreliable. On the other hand, a man who has been brought up with an attitude of honesty, who has an honest habit and present honest disposition, does not think the thing out in terms of his advantage in each new situation. His neighbors can confidently count on his character and his word and go about their own constructive affairs without having to spend time and effort in protecting themselves against the possibiilty of his falsehood.

Habits of attitude are not only characteristic of individuals and persistent in individuals. When enough individuals at the standard setting and leadership levels of a community adopt an attitude, it is copied by others through response and impersonation and becomes characteristic of the community. Thus the British have for years been noted for a spirit of fair play and of a tolerant give-and-take in their political procedures, as compared with their more discordant European neighbors. Americans too have on the whole exhibited these same characteristics.

We have seen that the processes of response and impersonation in the young result in powerful sentimental attachments to what is near, dear, and familiar. These attachments, these loyalties, also are persistent. Patriotism is such an attachment—the love of country, the attitude "My country, may she ever be in the right, but my country, right or wrong." The child's parents and friends have come to equate the country with what is good and right for them and the child takes over the attitude as his own, finds security in it, knows where he stands, grows up in the same persuasion, and hands the attitude on in turn to his own children.

The theocratic society of ancient Egypt was characterized by centuries of relative stability—almost stagnation—with a populace for the most part uninventive and obedient to the traditional ways. Perhaps a reason for this stability was that under the all-pervasive influence of the priests traditional ideals of order were driven home young with the sanctions of religion and the heavenly powers, and thenceforward taken for granted as the right and unchanging social rule and role. We saw that when an individual ruler, Ikhnaton, tried to change the tradition he could not succeed over the long term. The old attitudes were too persistent for him to overthrow them.

The attitudes which community leaders have once acquired stick with them even when a truthful survey of the situation would indicate that the habits are destructive. The leaders of France at the opening of the Second World War were sufficiently patriotic to weep when France went down before the German invader. But their patriotism had proven of no avail in the face of the persistent attitude characteristic of French leadership. That attitude was each group and each group leader pushing his short-term immediate advantage with no consideration whatever to the good of the whole. Twenty years of this grasping spirit—instead of equity and observance of the rights and needs of others—this persistent attitude of practical unfairness coupled with (or perhaps the reverse side of) a persistent moral indifference, had undermined the strength of France.

The Nazi leaders came into national leadership already confirmed in attitudes of bluster and intolerance and with a genuine prejudice that they were representatives of a Master German Race. The Master Race idea lent itself all too well to use as a popular slogan for building a jingoistic German unity. It furnished a satisfaction for the need for self-esteem. The effect of repetition of such a slogan was to deepen the prejudice of the leaders themselves and harden them further in their disastrous political attitudes. They fell victim to their attitudes. There followed an egregious failure of truth to fact on the part of the Nazi leadership. They believed they could successfully take on in combat their powerful neighbors in the attempt to realize the ideal that the Germans were a master race entitled to lord it over others in an intolerant German world rule. The mistaken political attitude of Hitler and his henchmen had proven sufficiently strong and persistent to blind them to the facts. They continued to be triggered by their old habits and slogans long after the time had come when even cynical calculation would have indicated that their bluster, intolerance, and insolence were holding them to a self-destructive course.

It is common experience how hard it is for a man to break up a bad habit, even though he has come to recognize it as harmful and is fortified in the attempt to break it up by the needs of a good self-estimate and of a character in accord with his standards. If it is difficult for a man to break up a harmful habit of which he disapproves, it is hardly to be expected that a man should break up a harmful habit of which he is actually proud, such as the intolerance and tribal prejudice of the Nazi. He has no conscious motive to try to change his ill-conceived rule and role—his injurious attitude—doubly fortified by habit and a mistaken self-esteem.

We have already mentioned the reported distaste of the nineteenth-century Hungarian leadership for commerce and trade and its possible result in turning over the control of much of Hungarian business life to aliens. If this is a true statement of the Hungarian attitude and of what in fact took place, it would illustrate two things. One is the harmful result of a persistent attitude of distaste for a line of activity which truth to fact would have indicated to be useful and necessary. The other is that an attitude of which one is proud, which serves one's self-esteem, is likely to be specially persistent and hard to change, because it supplies not only a rule to go by, but a role that appears—even though speciously—to be worthwhile. A leader proud of his distaste for commerce may not be as virulently dangerous as a leader proud of his racial master qualities. But each attitude of vainglory is alike in the support it receives from its owner's sense of self-esteem, and each is alike persistent.

In our discussion of discord, secession, and separation we summarily described the characteristics of a divided community in terms of pushing too hard, holding too tight, inefficiency, and mistake. These several failings were mainly due to the overlong persistence of harmful political attitudes, the intolerance, dishonesty, failures of truth to fact, and inequity which were invariably associated with the actual histories of discord, secession, and separation.

Habits of Attitude as Guides for the Motives

Why is it that political attitudes, good or bad, and their persistence are determinative of the character of political life, capable of producing either discord or unjust order on the one hand or a free order on the other? It is the fact that those attitudes, those habits, are what guide or fortify or curb the energies and the motives that are the sources of all reform, right or wrong.

When we examined the sources of reform and the motives for political change, we saw the various competing groups in the community each trying to benefit and promote its own relative position. It is the habitual political attitudes—the political virtues or faults—that guide this process in orderly and constructive courses, or in discordant and violent.

No noteworthy political result can be achieved without the ambitions and energies of leaders and the hopes of their followers. Without courage and strength no great aim—good or bad—can be realized. But these excellent and indispensable qualities, the energies and the courage, are morally neutral in politics. They can be applied, as we have seen, by sordid political leaders and in the service of infamous political ends, as well as by good leaders and for good ends. Courage is no monopoly of the righteous. Satan himself was well endowed with it.

Since no worthwhile goal is likely to be attained without courage, courage is an essential political quality, and to the extent that it is teachable and can be learned, rather than a matter of native temperament, it should be taught and learned. The paralyses and interferences wrought by unreasonable fear have to be overcome, or men and communities alike falter. But for all the excellence of courage, it is like other powers in that it does harm if directed along wrong lines.

The motive forces of life, the range of powerful physical and psychic urges, are good in themselves in the sense that without them the world would stagnate. Whether they are to be regarded as originally tending to good or as originally sinful is a question which, despite its popularity in doctrinal disputes, is fruitless to argue, as these energies and urges are plainly the source of almost all that is good as well as a large part of what is evil. The question is, What is the course they are in fact taking?

If the motives are wrongly directed as they push for reform, they produce discord, unjust order, and violence rather than a free order. In the organized life of a political community, direction of the motives —their steering, prompting, and curbing—is accomplished, for better or worse, by the political virtues or faults—the habits of attitude with which we are now concerned.

2. EDUCATION OF USEFUL ATTITUDES AND STANDARDS

We have seen that a deteriorating community may for many years coast along smoothly enough on the strength of what has been left over from its past in the way of good political traditions and attitudes, even after it no longer has a positive understanding of them or a convinced belief in them. But in such a state of affairs the key to the good community has really been lost. When a change of internal circumstances for the worse or great outside pressure turns up, the community then, as we have seen, declines for want of the political virutes and falls into discord.

If it was clearly understood why certain attitudes were useful—why the political virutes of tolerance, honesty, truth to fact, and equity were necessary for a continuing free order—there might be a deliberate and successful effort to maintain and hand them on. The key to a good community would then not be lost and the community could count on the political virtues over the long term. This would avoid the usual deterioration into discord.

What we have seen of the operation of impersonation and response —how they are the building blocks of everyone's rule and role—would lead us to hope that parents and schools and community leaders who had come to understand the value of the political virtues and to practice them, could by deliberate effort and example bring up amongst the standard setters in each rising generation a preponderance who would continue to practice the right and useful political attitudes as a part of their second nature, along with a conscious understanding of them and loyalty to them as well.

Unfortunately, a nation whose leaders in recent years made a deliberate effort to teach political attitudes and made the inculcation of such attitudes a main objective of formal education was Hitler's Third Reich. The leaders were the Nazi leaders and the attitudes they taught were, to put it mildly, mistaken—the Nazi Master Race attitude, the bitter prejudice against the Jews, and the respect for violence and intolerance. But perhaps we can bring good out of this evil example by remembering that the Nazis did have marked success in the propagation in the young of their erroneous beliefs—the Nazi political vices —and by seeing that a much more useful and good success could be achieved in the conscious and designed effort to inculcate right beliefs and attitudes—the political virtues of tolerance, honesty, equity, and truth to fact. The aims of the Nazi education of attitudes were horrible and the attitudes they taught were wrong; but their concentration on education of attitudes was sound. When Satan uses effective and right means in the service of bad ends, we ought not to reject the effective and right means, when our own observation and our own experience could lead us to make use of them for good ends. We should not turn our back on the use of good means for good ends, because Satan once used, and abused, them for bad ends.

An aspect of youthfulness is that the young have not yet settled upon habitually fixed patterns for the expression of their motives. Their attitudes are in the process of forming and are still undergoing major development all along the line. They are still a long way from either a good maturity characterized by attitudes in accord with the meeting of their real needs or a bad maturity characterized by attitudes out of keeping with what is right for them. The way is open for the development of attitudes that will be good and useful, such as the political virtues in which our present interest lies.

A child cannot discover the virtues for himself. They are neither self-evident nor native. The child is not a noble little savage; he is an energetic and inquiring little savage, with potentialities for putting his energies to good or bad use. He can be brought up in habits of fairness and tolerance and the personal qualities associated with them, such as a constructive emulation of what is possible for him. Or he can be brought up in habits of unfairness and intolerance and their associated personal qualities like greed, or the compensatory sentiments of resentment and envy which take the place of constructive achievement.

Not even an extraordinarily bright young child could possibly have any intelligent grasp of what are right notions of duty and why they are right, except in the simplest kind of personal relations. But every child is capable through impersonation and response of a sentimental set towards what those near and dear to him regard as right. Correct tendencies, the beginning of right and useful habits of attitude, derived through correct upbringing, will obviously be much better than incorrect tendencies fallen upon by someone for himself or as the result of erroneous upbringing. Incorrect political tendencies are those that lead to the political failings which we have identified as the characteristics of discord, secession, and separation—the political faults of intolerance, dishonesty, inequity, and want of truth to fact.

The acquiring of loyalty to the political virtues depends in the first instance on a boy's parents, his teachers, and those near and dear to him and on how they feel about the virtues and on how they act them out. The Greek historian Polybius, in his painstaking assessment of all the facts he could find bearing on the rise and power of the Roman republic in the time of the Scipios, noted that the oath of a Roman could be relied upon, that of a Greek could not. He was impressed by the Roman efforts to create "virtuous aspirations" in the young. As to the results:

Again the Roman customs and principles regarding money transactions are better than those of the Carthaginians. In the view of the latter nothing is disgraceful that makes for gain; with the former nothing is more disgraceful than to receive bribes and to make profit by improper means. For they regard wealth obtained from unlawful transactions to be as much a subject of reproach as a fair profit from the most unquestioned source is commendation. . . .

Greek statesmen, if entrusted with a single talent, though protected by ten checking-clerks, as many seals, and twice as many witnesses, yet cannot be induced to keep faith; whereas among the Romans, in their magistracies and embassies, men have the handling of a great amount of money, and yet from pure respect to their oath keep their faith intact. And again, in other nations it is a rare thing to find a man who keeps his hands out of the public purse, and is entirely pure in such matters; but among the Romans it is a rare thing to detect a man in the act of committing such a crime.

The political virtues may be harder to inculcate than narrower ideals like those of blind obedience, or of patriotism, or of Hitler's Master Race. These narrower attitudes can be tied more directly to some particular powerful motive. They provide a simple rule to go by. They have a hypnotic effect and let a man feel suffused with a glowing self-estimate as one of a great and worthy group. His sense of self-worth is directly gratified. He thinks he has found a worthwhile role.

The company of the tolerant or of the honest or of the equitable is not quite so easily joined as is a flag-waving, band-blaring group of your neighbors—good, bad, and indifferent. There is a rational element in tolerance, or honesty, or equity, and each may sometimes be felt as a curb as well as an urge.

Still the rule of virtue can be taught as right and as second nature, and pride taken in following it and shame felt in departing from it. The pattern of tolerant or equitable or honest behavior can become as strong and persistent as any habit needs to be to be counted upon and dependable. We know that in actual practice the tolerant, fair, and true to fact continue to stay and act that way.

3. A NEGLECT IN AMERICAN EDUCATION

A neglect in American education is its failure to make any deliberate, well-conceived effort to teach the political virutes. We all know that notwithstanding their intelligence, many intelligent people are bad citizens, for want of tolerance, or honesty, or equity, or a desire for truth to fact. One of the reasons that the need for such teaching has not been clearly seen by educational leaders lies in the fact that in the early history of the country we had, as we have seen, a population that whatever their other differences had leaders who were intensely interested in moral and political principles. We have been able to coast on an inheritance of political institutions which reflect the fact that those who set up our United States were aware of the need for institutional protection of the political virtues. Witness such writings of theirs as the Declaration of Independence, the *Federalist Papers,* and the Constitution itself, with its contemporaneous Bill of Rights in the first ten amendments. But no community leadership can coast over-long on institutions made for one set of conditions, for as the conditions change, so must the institutions. And if the principal key has been lost to the nature and test of good political institutions, which is the presence in them and through them of the political virtues, then the changing political order and its new institutions will begin to show the signs of discord.

It is easier to impart factual knowledge and technical data than it is to impart character. Temperamental differences in the pupils make the teaching of good character an art calling for a wide range of accurate responsiveness and impersonation on the part of the teachers themselves. Even where the native endowment of pupils may be favorable and receptive, the mistakes or the character deficiencies of the teacher will render him more of a hindrance than a help to the practical teaching of right attitudes. So the teaching of character is left to the home. But many parents, having themselves been brought up without either understanding or actual practice of the political virtues, are incapable of imparting them to their children either by precept or example.

We make attempts in the schools to teach the young to make a reasonably happy adjustment to their surroundings as they find them. We are aware of their needs for winning friends and influencing people. This is good. But as to what are the right kinds of useful qualities in either ourselves or our friends or in those we are supposed to influence, there is a blank. Our goal is how to get on in a scheme of things as we find it, without any attention to whether it is good or bad or to its improvement.

We spend time and energy in disputing the relative amounts of teaching effort which should be put at both school and college levels into utilitarian and vocational courses as against liberal courses in history, literature, and the arts, and the allied and obscure question of whether there is a dividing line between what is liberal and what is utilitarian. But neither kind of course can save the body politic from discord unless along with it or as a part of it there is acquired a leaning towards the practice of the political virtues.

In a school or college community—let us say that of an American high school either public or independent, or the undergraduate body of a state or independent university—there will always be amongst the students themselves certain young leaders and standard setters. Every possible intelligent effort should be made to see that those young leaders and standard setters gain the spirit of tolerance, honesty, equity, and a desire for truth to fact. This is not only for their own future usefulness, but for that of their fellows as well. In school as elsewhere most individuals follow the leaders and try to fall in with the ways that are expected of them, and in that find their working sense of rule and role.

In our discussion of discord, secession, and separation we took note of the significance of the quantitative aspects of the political virtues and faults. The question was whether there were too many leaders, too large a proportion of the community at top and intermediate standard-setting levels, who were intolerant rather than tolerant, fraudulent rather than honest, pushing too hard or holding too tight rather than equitable, seeing things distorted by the light of their ambitions and desires rather than true to fact. When such was the case, the community was divided and we found discord, secession, and separation. It would seem a reasonable inference that if we want a free order changing by way of growth to a greater free order, we will have to bend every effort towards producing enough standard setters who are tolerant, honest, equitable, and true to fact.

4. TAKEN-FOR-GRANTED STANDARDS

The standards of right conduct which a man takes for granted, the origins of which he has forgotten or all but forgotten, constitute a major part of what is called his conscience and exert a powerful effect on what he does. These taken-for-granted standards operate almost outside his conscious attention. Conscience is an irrational standard in the sense that the man no longer thinks about it critically. It is felt as an immediate urge to do or to refrain.

As an illustration of the operation of conscience, we can take its control and direction of acquisitiveness. A small child is without any native honesty of a sort to prevent him from taking what he wants when he is able to. But by response to the examples and attitudes of those near and dear to him, and by appeals to his primitive impersonation of others—how would he feel or be able to accomplish anything if people made away with his toys or tools or stock in trade?—he acquires a standard that he ought not to steal. This standard of conscience comes to be so habitual and to operate so immediately and unthinkingly that henceforth he never even feels a desire to steal—a desire which may none the less be present, but, as we say, pushed out of mind.

Sometimes, and to a greater extent in some cultures than in others, physical punishment or the threat of it is used to enforce the teachings of impersonation and response. This may be sound, provided the punishment is not brutal and the child—or adult—is already wholly convinced in his own mind that what he is being punished for is wrong and understands why. A standard of conscience that once was, or that still is fortified by the conscious approval of the person has one more foundation than one based solely on unreasoning fear and an arbitrary command, even though the origin of the standard is in each case alike forgotten and the standard taken for granted. There is also freedom from open or hidden or repressed resentment.

In Sophocles' tragedy *Antigone* two nephews of Creon, King of Thebes, had been killed, one of them, Eteocles, in defending the city, the other, Polynices, in unsuccessfully attacking it. Creon ordered a state funeral for Eteocles and issued a decree that Polynices, the enemy of his country, should remain unburied, "a corpse for birds and dogs to eat, a ghastly sight of shame." A guard was set to enforce the decree and the penalty of death imposed upon anyone who should violate it. Antigone, the sister of Polynices, stole out from Thebes and scattered earth on her brother's body as a symbolic burial. She escaped the attention of the guards, who had removed themselves far off from the scene in order to escape the stench of the unburied body. Creon ordered that the earth be removed and that the guards capture the offender or be themslves hung up alive to die. On a second attempt to give her brother burial, Antigone was captured by the guards. She was brought before Creon.

CREON: Well, what do you say—you hiding your head there—do you
    admit or do you deny the deed?
ANTIGONE: I do admit it. I do not deny it.
CREON: Now tell me, in as few words as you can, did you know the order
    forbidding such an act?
ANTIGONE: I knew it, naturally. It was plain enough.
CREON: And yet you dared to contravene it?
ANTIGONE: Yes.
    That order did not come from God. Justice,
    That dwells with the gods below, knows no such law.
    I did not think your edicts strong enough

> To overrule the unwritten unalterable laws
> Of God and heaven, you being only a man.
> They are not of yesterday or today, but everlasting,
> Though where they came from, none of us can tell.
> Guilty of their transgression before God
> I cannot be, for any man on earth.
> I knew that I should have to die, of course,
> With or without your order. If it be soon,
> So much the better. Living in daily torment
> As I do, who would not be glad to die?
> This punishment will not be any pain.
> Only if I had let my mother's son
> Lie there unburied, then I could not have borne it.
> This I can bear. Does that seem foolish to you?
> Or is it you that are foolish to judge me so?

This is a justly famous description of conscience and its deep and forgotten origins.

In the series of wars that are being waged in our own time there are many examples of men following their taken-for-granted standards of right, no matter what the cost to themselves. A medical corpsman, himself seriously wounded, still continues to go to the aid of wounded infantrymen until he is no longer able to crawl. Then he props himself against a rock and carries on his treatment of wounded brought to him by litter bearers, and when no longer strong enough to render aid himself, instructs others how to do so—and goes to his own death in this course of obedience to duty.

The urges of conscience are by no means always good or useful. On the contrary, they are frequently harmful.

There are countries in the world where some article of wholesome food is available, but where for traditional reasons, very likely those of religious tradition, the food is taboo and people will not eat it. though to fail to do so is to subject themselves and their children to starvation and disease. Fish may be too sacred or too unsacred to eat, so that it is better to starve than to partake of it. In a case of this kind, the voice of conscience, the taken-for-granted standard, is wrong for the individual and the community. But like other habits of attitude, it is persistent and it is hard to bring about an eye-opening and a fresh perspective that will change the attitude.

In the mid-nineteenth century, the Sepoy Rebellion of the native soldiers in the Bengal forces of the East India Company was precipitated by the issue of greased cartridges for use in the rifles of these sepoys. They believed the grease was beef grease and that handling such grease was a violation of Hindu obligation. The shock to their conscience was a spark that set alight the flame of mutiny.

In one of the great religious communities of today's world, bowls of water are used in common in the temples for washing the hands of the faithful. This sacred water spreads eye, skin, and other diseases. The urge of conscience to wash in these bowls is an injurious urge.

A reason that prejudice is so intractable is that its inception often lies so far back and at such early levels in the childhood impersonation and response to parents and teachers and those near and dear.

What is important for us in our present inquiry is to see that in fact the conscience does have a great control on conduct. Even the most powerful motives like hunger—as in some of the examples we have just given—are directed, controlled, and curbed by conscience in their manner of outlet and satisfaction. Even the urge of sex can be repressed by conscience to such a degree that it has to find surprising forms of expression that dodge the specific inhibition of conscience which an individual may have acquired.

The success that professional moralists have from time to time had in beating down ordinary motives of enjoyment for enjoyment's sake really offer hope for what should be an easier and more natural development of a rightly ordered conscience which will aid and direct the energies and motives along mainly useful and constructive lines. If the conscience is capable of stopping us in our tracks or of directing us to do something highly harmful to ourselves, it would seem possible for it, if properly educated, to direct our energies in the ways of tolerance, honesty, equity, and a desire for truth to fact, all so beneficial to the community and to ourselves as members of the community.

As the conscience, the taken-for-granted standard, is so potent, it seems that ordinary good sense would lead us to bend our best educational effort towards the construction of a right conscience rather than a mistaken one. Parents, neighbors, and school, by way of response and impersonation, utilizing all means available to them by example, by literature, by the arts, by the sciences, and in the teaching of vocations, should unflaggingly educate taken-for-granted standards that are in actual accord with the real needs of those who are going to be controlled by the standards.

Effects of Departure from Standards

Although the urge and the curb of the taken-for-granted standards act immediately and without any rational thought, they make their presence felt in the awareness of the conscious mind in the form of satisfaction if the standards are followed, and of discomfort if they are forsaken. The standards are part of the role that is felt to be worthwhile, and in departing from them a man looks upon himself as in the wrong.

This discomfort, or sense of guilt or wrongdoing, on departure from the standards is one manifestation of the need for a favorable self-estimate which we have already seen to be so important in the formation of our ideas of what is right. We have seen that we try to justify what we have done and to look upon it as right if we can. Now we see another side of the same picture: when we have once adopted a course of action as right to the extent that it has become a part of our taken-for-granted standards, we try to keep ourselves in line with that right course, and when we see ourselves departing from it, we feel a small or great degree of guilt, depending on how significant a part of our right role the standard has become.

Let us take a case of discomfort in our self-regard on the departure from a norm that would ordinarily not be regarded as a matter of conscience at all, yet one which illustrates the principle that we hate to look upon ourselves in an unfavorable light. Consider a man's feelings if he thinks he is not doing as well as his neighbors, that he is not keeping up with the Joneses, an acknowledgment of inferiority of some kind, where no moral judgment is involved. The author of Piers Plowman stated it well enough six hundred years ago:

> Many other men have much to suffer
> From hunger and from thirst; they turn the fair side outward
> For they are abashed to beg, lest it should be acknowledged
> At their neighbors what they need at noon and at even.

Our sense of standing well is hurt. By response and impersonation we know how the other fellow feels, and we do not like his condescension. But most of all, we just don't ourselves like being too far off our standard.

Or take another case of the discomfort arising from an unfavorable self-regard, this time coming a little closer to a violation of the taken-for-granted standard of conscience. It is the case of an American newspaper correspondent having to go along with the general retreat at the time of the threatened German break-through in the Battle of the Bulge in the winter at the close of 1944:

I noticed in myself a feeling that I had not had for some years. It was the feeling of guilt that seems to come over you whenever you retreat. You don't like to look anyone in the eyes. It seems as if you have done something wrong. I perceived this feeling in others too.

The sentiment of remorse shows very clearly the self-regarding nature of the feelings of guilt on departure from a taken-for-granted standard of right. If a man in a fit of drunkenness had let his children starve, he would suffer remorse, as being derelict both from what he truly wants and from his standards of right, as well as for the injury done to those he loved.

The sense of honor is a recognition of a code in which certain kinds of behavior are taken for granted as good and worthwhile and better than others. The feeling that it is right and good to abide by the rules of the game is akin to the sense of honor. In the discord cases the leaders had harmful rules of the game, a wrong code to which they felt allegiance. In a rightly functioning community, on the other hand, enough of the leaders all along the line take for granted certain useful rules of the game which are not to be violated—rules that happen to be conditions of the harmony and strength of the community. These rules of the game, this useful code, are the political virtues of tolerance, honesty, equity, and truth to fact.

The fact that men feel self-driven to observe their standards and feel discomfort or guilt on departure from them is a factor supplementing the need of a rule to go by as a source of order and near-term predictability in the life of the community.

If further demonstration is needed of the importance we ascribe to obedience to the standards of conscience, the practical recognition we give to a favorable self-estimate, it can be found in the rules of our criminal law. If a man has committed an act injurious to someone else and constituting a breach of the peace, common law does not find him guilty of crime in the eyes of the law unless he has had a criminal intent. The reason may be that when we impersonate the man and are aware of his absence of feeling of wrong or guilt, we do not punish him because in the like circumstances we should think it inequitable were we ourselves to be punished. This indicates that in practice we not only recognize the process of self-regard and self-estimate, but let the content of the process in an offender determine our attitude towards his punishment. We subordinate the question of whether a man who has killed his neighbor under the influence of irresistible impulse is a lesser—or greater—menace to the community than one who, perhaps more grossly wronged by his neighbor, killed with deliberate intent. We hold the former not guilty, the latter guilty.

The need for a good self-regard operating alongside the taken-for-granted standards can produce distressing effects. A boy may have acquired an erroneous taken-for-granted standard that he should never be afraid. If this is powerful enough, he cannot bring himself to admit that he is afraid, even in circumstances where he should rightfully be shaking in his boots. Such a boy may in the stress of battle, if he is constitutionally so disposed as to make it possible, develop a paralyzed leg. The fear which he would not recognize has paralyzed his leg. He does not know that fear has accomplished this. He has kept his fear hidden, thus obeying his taken-for-granted standards of conscience and meeting his need for a favorable self-estimate.

We cannot escape the conclusion that since one's taken-for-granted standards are so powerful a practical influence on behavior, the resources of formal and informal teaching should be brought to bear on the education of standards that are useful and right in fact.

5. MODIFICATION OF TAKEN-FOR-GRANTED STANDARDS

In the introductory part of this book we described the principal motives making for political change and reform; in the next part we showed groups and communities under the influence of these motives working themselves into situations of discord, secession, and separation, and we identified some harmful political attitudes that seemed to accompany and account for these unfortunate results. In this present part of the book, the Sources of Right, we are trying to find out what might be the prospect of teaching good and useful political attitudes so that the community could have and perpetuate a free order, rather than the disorder or the unjust orders of discord, secession, and separation.

In all of this inquiry we have had to abstract from the whole range and variety of energies, motives, and capacities those which seemed pertinent to the production of political results and of order or disorder in the life of an organized community. We have focused our attention to such a degree on the motives of political reform and the attitudes controlling their course that we may forget the much larger setting, the huge variety and vitality of energies, the whole range of motives and needs that make the world of human activity, including the segment of political activity that we have separated out for investigation.

For the sake of our perspective and in order to make sure that we do not try to reach for political habits and institutions that are contrary to conditions set by nature, we should take a summary look at some of the more significant needs and motives of ourselves and our neighbors. As each man is a whole man, he maintains some kind of working reconciliation of these his many motives. Although some of them obviously have a more direct influence than others on the formation of his politically useful or harmful attitudes and standards, yet just because he is a whole and inseparable being there is not one of his motives that is completely without such influence. For instance, the thwarting of any powerful motive produces discontent and anger which are likely accompaniments of intolerance and unfairness in the organized life of the community.

If there is an underlying life force or elemental energy, it is something we cannot see directly. What we do see is men and women acting in accord with various motives. The motives on the subjective side consist of urges, aversions, likes and dislikes; on the objective side, of things and situations giving rise to these. There are many degrees of intensity and duration and many possible combinations of motives.

For the purpose of a quick perspective of the variety of motives, it is useful to classify them in a way that indicates some of the principal ends they severally serve, even while we acknowledge that the classification is arbitrary in that the motive in fact has a wider scope and significance than that attributed to it in any scheme of classification.

Some of the motives are directly concerned with the survival of mankind, in the sense that the presence of the motives explains his survival, so that it would be likely that if these motives did not exist there would be no problems, political or otherwise, as there would be no people. If men had no motive of activity, no need to be on the move, there would be no mankind. A man is hungry and thirsty, or otherwise he would cease to be. He needs sexual satisfaction and to mate. He needs to give and to receive affection. He is aggressive. He must be capable of anger and violence if crossed. He has to get and to hold, so as to have the wherewithal to keep going and doing. He must be able to be afraid, so as to escape mortal peril. He must be able to feel disgust and revulsion. He needs a sense of humor; he laughs. He needs rest and comfort. He has a religious need, for things to make sense in human terms. He needs a rule to go by, some certainty, some security.

Motives necessary to survival have to be powerful in nature's scheme. Yet they are not so instinctively specific but what they wander out of their appropriate channels. It is certain that they are liable to excess and abuse and that their operation is beset with psychic and spiritual pitfalls. Greed, cruelty, destructiveness, lecherousness, superstition, and anxiety are some of the familiar excesses and misdirections of these motives.

There are certain of his motives that work in the direction of a man's personal freedom, so that he is restive if subjected to too much restraint or control. He needs to assert and express himself; he doesn't want to be pushed around by others. He is curious; he explores. He reflects, thinks things over, and chooses. He is skillful, inventive, creative. He competes, beats down obstruction, and tries to realize his aims. He needs a worthwhile role.

Some motives, while perhaps making for his survival and freedom, seem mainly to make for a man's enjoyment. He likes variety and excitement. He delights in beauty, color, motion, sound. He has a sense of time, rhythm, form, proportion, balance.

If the useful attitudes and standards, the political virtues of tolerance, honesty, equity, and truth to fact are to be successfully taught, conditions will have to be such that those virtues will not run positively counter to too-powerful motives in the whole array of motives. For example, we have already pointed out the influence of physical conditions on one's moral standards. It might be wrong as well as difficult to teach a taken-for-granted standard or attitude of tolerance to a man, if that meant that he would have to starve in the actual conditions of his community.

An influence is exerted on the expression of the motives by rationally adopted standards, of whose origin we are likely to be aware, as well as by the taken-for-granted standards of forgotten origin. As these rationally adopted standards become habitual, they tend to become a part of the body of taken-for-granted standards. To illustrate in a simple area the difference between a taken-for-granted standard —a matter of conscience—and a rational standard—the application of current judgment and intelligence to conduct—we can turn again to the satisfaction of the motive of hunger. From religious training in childhood a man may have acquired a taken-for-granted standard that forbids him to eat some particular article of wholesome food, either always or on special occasions. On the other hand, current experience that he well remembers may have led him to a rational standard that forbids him to eat some article of food that puts him in a state of collapse or shock if he eats it. As he habitually avoids such food, its avoidance itself may become a part of his unthinking and taken-for-granted standards.

We have discussed the education of right standards in the young. But as it is the adults who are managing or mismanaging affairs today and who will both train and set an example for those of today's youth who are to be tomorrow's leaders, we are equally concerned with what can be done for adult standards here and now.

A man's intelligence works in the interests of his motives. This involves him in a rational criticism and a possible modification of his taken-for-granted standards, if they are thwarting his interests, as well as a clarification of his own motives in his own eyes. His intelligence serves to let him see better what it is he wants and needs. This is true in his individual and personal life. It is equally true in his political life, as a member of an organized political community.

The intelligence mainly serves as an instrument of the motives, and is a secondary factor in the formation of attitudes as compared with impersonation and response. But it is the factor that gives the chance for alteration for the better of attitudes that are already established. We wish to be free of discord and in aid of this desire, this interest, we call on our intelligence to help us identify the causes of discord and discover a way to eliminate or lessen them, all in the actual circumstances of time and place in which we find ourselves.

6. ASSIMILATION TO RIGHT POLITICAL STANDARDS

Immigration into the growing United States was so rapid that 13 per cent of the entire white population in 1920 had been born abroad, and 34 per cent—more than one in every three persons—were either foreign-born or of foreign or mixed parentage. Such large numbers of foreigners and their children, quite irrespective of any question of their native ability and assuming them all to have been of capable stock, obviously presented America in the thirty years to mid-century with an immense educational task of trying to teach them a working understanding of American political standards. To the extent that the natives born of native parentage had themselves lost the key to what was good and strong in the American tradition, the task was rendered just that much more difficult. If at the leadership level America had too much lost the sense of equity and tolerance, and instead was governed too much by prejudices and intolerance, then obviously the chances would be lessened for creating in the newcomer the attitudes of equity and tolerance needed in our American community for a free order changing by way of growth.

The writing of a prescription for tolerance into a government constitutional document does not mean that the people are or will be in fact tolerant. But such provisions do indicate that the authors of the constitutional document were themselves aware of the need of tolerance, and were trying to protect tolerance. Where such a constitution with such provisions was effectively adopted for a large political community, it shows that at the time the leaders of the community were aware of the need of tolerance. Such a constitutional document is the American Bill of Rights, with its restraints against intolerant acts by the federal government—for example, interferences with free speech or the control of religious beliefs through governmentally established churches.

It is reported that a survey of 250,000 people conducted by a western American university in the middle of the twentieth century indicated that only 12 per cent of Americans had a reasonably accurate knowledge of the Bill of Rights. This gives rise to a fair inference that our contemporary leaders were not convinced of the importance of the political virtue of tolerance. Otherwise they would scarcely have failed to teach the reasons for it and to explain the attempt to secure it in our political life by provisions in our written constitution.

The reasons for the political virtues need to be taught. They are not self-evident, and in historical communities where they have been present they have sooner or later been lost, as we learned in our description of discord and secession. In the United States we are going through great technical developments in the field of communications which make it possible for this or that group to propagandize for particular purposes, and to use slogans for the rapid arousing of an uncritical public emotion. How can we make sure that in the presence of these developments we can promote the political virtues?

Changes in political attitudes in our own history have sometimes been for the better rather than for the worse. This is so despite the unpalatable truth that we backslid into the intolerances, inequities, and failures of truth to fact that resulted in our Civil War and the harsh period of Reconstruction which followed it. We know on the good side of the account that we modified the fierce intolerances, inequities, and prejudices of the colonial period and of our post-Revolutionary war years into sufficient attitudes of give-and-take and of truth to fact to allow the United States to be brought into being on a sound and fair foundation.

It is relatively easy to adopt a change in the mechanical method of attacking a particular problem. In our political life we shift our views about the right way to control, let us say, the credit structure of the country, or our views about what is the right amount, if any, of tariff protection for particular industries, established or new. Followings in great numbers can be got for a new political leader with bright promises of what his new economic and monetary methods will do for the welfare of the people. But what really counts for a free order changing by way of growth is the political virtues of tolerance, honesty, equity, and truth to fact in the leaders all along the line. To bring these into being in a community where their opposites hold sway is hard.

When harmful political attitudes hold the field, the start in changing them, though the process is slow, has to be first made in the field of conscious conviction, and thereafter by persuasion, reasoning, practice, and example in the field of habit and attitude. We have an adequate motive, in that we want to live in a good order that gives us the means and the opportunity to do what it is within us to do. We have the need, because our lives are rendered unhappy and our opportunities are cut down by political discord. We have the experience and the lessons of experience, because we can demonstrate that failures of the political virtues produce and accompany discord and unjust order. Reflection, thought, and testing will invariably come up with the answer that if the community is to improve rather than to deteriorate, it must not stray too far from the political virtues toward the political faults. It is certain that if too many at the leadership level have the wrong political standards the community is in for discord.

The obstinacy with which people cling to their prejudices is a cloud which has its silver lining. The obstinate prejudice itself suggests that they are uncertain and are protecting themselves from a real inquiry by maintaining their prejudice in a dogmatic manner. Perhaps facts can be got in edgewise that in time will shake the prejudice.

We are concerned with basic attitudes more than with day-to-day programs, though the latter are also important, particularly as they relate to the basic attitudes. We are trying to establish at the standard-setting levels right ideas of the game and of the rules of the game. If that is done, then the community will be in a fair way to attain a free order changing by way of growth. We want to be sure that whether public opinion is formed by the local leader from the cracker barrel in the local general store—as used often to be the case—or by means of a few hundred thousand copies of a pictorial booklet or comic strip, or by radio or television exhortation or spectacle, the shapers of opinion are themselves tolerant, honest, fair, and true to fact.

Community leaders should acknowledge and observe as second nature standards that are in fact right both for the political life of the community and for themselves as members of the community—standards right in the sense that they avoid discord and produce a free order. The right standards of tolerance, honesty, equity, and truth to fact can be derived from an examination of our real needs for ourselves and as members of the community, and can be shown to be the means of avoiding discord and maintaining a free order.

XVII. Religion and Ideas of Right

1. THE CHURCH AS A SOURCE OF IDEAS OF RIGHT

In our American community the institution of organized religion consists mainly of the several sects of the Christian Church. In other times and places it has also consisted of organizations of believers and their leadership of priests or ministers—over the length and breadth of history, for the most part not Christian.

The priests and ministers are charged with the administration of the practices and rituals of the religion. These practices and rituals have grown up about the core of beliefs concerning a man's, or a group's, place in the ultimate scheme of things and his relation to a power or powers believed to be external to him and in control of his lot and life in this world and the world beyond it. The object of the practices and rituals is to permit men to appeal to such an external power or to gain contact with it—to call upon God or to be in communion with God. The priests and ministers are thus the formal and organizational custodians of the means of coming before God.

Earlier in this book we have discussed a man's need to know where he stands—to be free from crippling uncertainty, doubt, and fear—and his need for a worthwhile role—to see himself having a good part to play. Religion concerns itself with the answer to these needs in their most basic aspect; it tries to strike through to a discovery that God's order is good and that men have a meaningful place in it. This is certainly a principal field of religion, however many other areas it may also busy itself with, such as interceding with the external powers for human goods of various kinds.

To the extent that the religious beliefs can be rationally grasped or stated, they reflect the knowledge and circumstances prevailing at the time of their original formulation or subsequent modification. At the basis of the beliefs, there usually lies the intuitive experience of mystics and prophets—direct perceptions or intimations of what appears to them to be absolute truth or reality, and incapable of explicit statement in rational terms because dealing with something outside the reach and scope of human reason.

It is not our purpose here to enter into any discussion of the Church, or of any other organized religion, but simply to make enough of an identification of the institution and its activities so as to be able to see why it has concerned itself with morals and standards of conduct. Our present interest is in its effectiveness as a teacher of attitudes and standards.

There has always been a wide gap between the actual condition in which men find themselves and what they feel would be right for them. This estrangement of men from the ideal, the gap between the fact and the goal, occurs all along the line of human experience. It takes place in the happenings and events in the world around men, and in their own characters, powers, and perceptions. With changing times and differing circumstances, different aspects of this gap—different threats to men's welfare—have assumed special importance. Religion in all communities has addressed itself to the closing of this gap.

If the gap between fact and ideal should appear in the form of a threat of disease and destitution, religious practices may be found mainly concerned with hymns, rites, and observances directed towards intercession in behalf of a flourishing physical and social life.

This gap between fact and ideal may appear in a fearful belief that all the living creation is caught in an ever-recurring cycle of rebirth and reincarnation, a belief which springs from an impersonative attribution to the universe of ultimate concern with making the punishment fit the crime and the reward fit the good deed, all in human terms. Then the religious practices—adjusted to the capabilities of the varied talents and abilities of different types of believers—are directed towards an escape from the wheel of rebirth. For those of a mystical bent this escape, or a foretaste or guarantee of it, may be sought by a way—for instance, as described in the Yoga Aphorisms of Patanjali— of discipline and exercises which result in the direct and unalloyed realization of the ultimate self.

The approach of religion to closing the gap between fact and ideal, this threat to men's welfare, has been varied. A principal route usually present in the approach has been by way of justifying men in the eyes of the supernatural powers and by squaring them with those powers, a process made necessary by inadvertent errors or deliberate misconduct on the part of individuals. The errors or misconduct have brought about a situation in which the men or the group to which they belong will undergo some kind of penalty unless squared with the external powers.

As the knowledge and techniques of the community are improved and it becomes able with the efforts of its own human membership to deal with some threatening aspect of the environment, the intercession of religion with regard to that aspect may become less significant, and the method of intercession become entirely different.

For an instance of a primitive method of religious intercession let us go back to a case we have mentioned earlier, where the particular gap between the fact and the ideal happened to be in the form of a three-year famine in the days of King David. The method adopted for termination of the famine consisted of trying to square the Israelites with the Lord by their delivering to the Gibeonites for hanging seven Israelite descendants of Saul—he having broken an oath to the Gibeonites. This action was supplemented by the transfer of the bones of Saul and Jonathan from Gilead and burying them, along with the collected bones of the seven, in the land of Benjamin.

Today in similar circumstances the religious cure for famine might not be the only recourse of the community, and the religious method would itself be different. To the extent, let us say, that physical means of producing rain might be successful, the gap between fact and ideal would be closed in that manner, perhaps by seeding the clouds with silver iodide, or by use of some more efficient technique. In such an event there would be no need of religious intercession at all. If religious intercession were to be made in our own country today, it would not likely be by way of hanging seven sons of a treaty violator and the reburial of two national heroes. But we too would have our own crudenesses of practice, based on the knowledge and misconceptions of our own time. Our priests and worshipers might be no nearer than those of old to the true core of religious reliance and devotion.

The main offices of religion seem then to have been to discover for men their relation to the power that creates and sustains the whole drama of appearance and existence, and to help men gain contact with that power, and to intercede with that power to close the ever-present gap between fact and ideal and thus to save men from threats to their welfare. That being so, how did religion, including the Christian Church, come to get its intense interest in ethics and the rules of conduct and in private morals?

One area in which the ever-present gap between fact and ideal is evident to each of us is in our own failure or inability to observe the standards we feel to be right for us. The gap between fact and ideal in this field of our conduct—our removal or estrangement from our ideal—may be felt as our own fault, as the result of our own wrong choices. Here the need for a good self-estimate comes into play. That need is so powerful, planted so deep in us and so inescapable, that we are distressed and baffled at our departure from our standards. We feel that somehow due to our own dereliction we are in the wrong, and that something must be done to put us right again. We know as a matter of fact and from experience that we or our group has to pay for our mistakes and errors, even when inadvertently and innocently made, as pneumonia may follow physical exposure. But here we feel we are no longer dealing with mistake or error that is innocent or inadvertent but with deliberately and willfully incurred mistake and error. We feel—whether by processes of impersonation or otherwise we do not here stop to inquire—that God's intention for us has received a setback at our hands and that the payment which we or our group will have to make is in the nature of punishment or retribution for our wrongdoing. The situation can be cured only by our proceeding to do what is right, or else by becoming squared with or being forgiven for our wrongdoing by the power in control of our life and its events.

Religion takes our moral conduct in charge on the ground that doing what we believe to be right is an essential part of the purpose of our lives, part of our ideal attainment. Religion says that we must obey the voice of our conscience. Here again is a recognition of how deep-going and fundamental is the need for a good self-estimate, the need of being worthy in one's own eyes. Religion relies confidently on the sense of guilt arising on departure from our standards. It intercedes to rescue us from the possible consequences of this guilt—from what we fear in the way of a just recompense for our willful wrongdoing.

Religion, and we too, by an almost inevitable impersonation of a part of our nature, attribute goodness and rightness, justice and honesty, to the God who has us in charge. To do otherwise would be to make a grim and tragic joke of our needs for security and a worthwhile role—needs in that case planted in us only to meet final and humanly unjust frustration. God's will towards men as well as for them is taken to be rightness and goodness, else why did he constitute men in such a way as to feel such distress on departure from their conscience and their accepted standards of what is right and good? Men, too, in fairness owe a good and right will towards a God whose will is good and right towards them. So religion tries to direct our conduct aright in the belief that right conduct is in accord with this righteous and good God's will.

Religion should, for the sake of its own future usefulness and mankind's hope of a free order, steadily apply itself to a growing discovery and definition of the true content of good and right, a more accurate determination of what is in fact goodness and rightness.

There is another entirely practical reason why religion concerns itself with standards of conduct. Religion, like any great organized institution taking part in the life of the community, is interested in order and harmony as conditions that further the carrying out of its work. The Christian Church in the Middle Ages thought that the political and social order of the Roman Empire had been providentially established for the work and growth of Christianity. Religion is not blind to the factors of discord, the overreaching and the overgrasping, the intolerances and the inequities that cause disorder and strife and that may even imperil the continued life of the religions, as in the case of the Church in Hitlerian Germany or Soviet Russia. Religion on this account too has always had an understandable concern with ethics, morals, and useful standards of conduct.

Still another, though less tangible basis may exist for the attention of religion to morality and for its belief that when we do what we think is right we are acting in accord with God's will. This belief may be in part a reflection of the experience of the religious mystics, who have discovered it to be impossible even to start upon the course of their devotions if impeded by the presence in themselves of a consciously wrongly directed will. The worldly affections, especially the self-seeking ones, have stood in the way of their gaining their goal. It is of course true that in a nonworldly sense the mystic is engaged in a profound self-seeking.

The concern with wrongdoing and its consequences is a central feature of the Christian religion, as well as of others. In the nomenclature of the Christian Church, the deliberate departure from what is believed to be God's will for us is what constitutes sin. In some, but not all, Christian sects each human baby is regarded as actually born in a state of sin, so-called Original Sin, despite the difficulty of reconciling this opinion with the opinion that sin is deliberately willful.

The closing of the gap between fact and ideal in this particular field of wrong and right consists of rescuing us from the consequences of our sin. The result is what constitutes Salvation. Salvation in its highest form not only saves us from the bonds and consequences of sin, but also sets us so far in the true path that we become directly aware of God's presence, desiring thenceforth only to do his will. Christian salvation is thus *from* sin and *to* God. The happiness of the saved consists in their eternal direct vision of God. The ordinary road to Christian salvation is through membership in the Church and performance of its sacraments. A sacrament is a ceremonial observance (for example, baptism or the Eucharist—the repeating of Jesus' actions at the Last Supper and the re-enactment of the crucifixion) the mere performance of which is held by some sects to convey grace to the recipient. Faith in the revealed truths of the Christian God and certain specified good works are a powerful aid to salvation. If salvation is attained by any of these means or all of them, its attainment is the result of a gift of God's grace.

Volumes could be written—and have been written—about each of the beliefs and observances so cursorily mentioned in the two preceding paragraphs. If the terms have an arbitrary and almost artificial ring, it is because it was many, many years ago that the main theology of the Church was developed and its doctrines cast in a dogmatic form. It is difficult to change the statement of the doctrines and at the same time to preserve organizational discipline and the public appearance of certainty. There is no doubt that this poses a difficult problem for the Church. If it is to retain and increase its influence as a creative force in the community, the Church needs to talk in a language that makes a persuasive appeal to the leaders all along the line who are not clerics and who are without any clerical training. But there is no need for us here to enter any discussion of refinements of doctrines. All we require for our present purposes is the briefest of summaries because, as already stated, we are simply identifying the area and function of organized religion enough to take a look at its influence in the teaching of attitudes and of standards of conduct.

In the Christian Church every possible motive and means is utilized to bring about the conformity of man's will to what is believed to be God's will. The fear of God and God's wrath—his righteous wrath at rebellion to his will—and of the consequences for men of this wrath, is an obviously powerful motive. The love for God, flowing equitably from the recognition of God's love for man, is with a few even more powerful. In our discussion of impersonation and response we saw that love and the influence of the near and dear were powerful factors in setting up ideas of right and wrong in the case of growing children. The same factors are relied upon by religion in its creation of a fidelity to God's will. Love here means closely what it does in human relations—intense attraction and desire, affection, enjoyment, and loyalty. In the operation of such fundamental emotion it is no wonder that a man's whole constitution and being is brought into play, so that in much of the writing of saints and contemplatives there is evident a thinly veiled sexual component in the expression of religious love.

Indeed, religion and religious ritual throughout contain a shadowing, an echo, of powerful constituents in men's minds and emotions—a reflection of their impersonative processes at a deep level and of their elemental feelings towards the mysterious and rationally unknowable influences that lie outside the range of human intelligence or perception.

There are analogies in other fields to this religious effort to reach out towards the perfection that is felt to be God. The painter may try to bring himself and the viewer of his work closer to the feeling and meaning of beauty. So may the musician through rhythm and the organization of sound. Even the philosopher trying to put his finger on a scheme that will let people work out more fully their abilities in the community is engaged in the effort to come closer to what seems right and fitting.

2. EFFECT OF RELIGION ON CONDUCT

The religious teaching of attitudes, like other teaching, is by way of impersonation and response. Religion starts early with the young and reiterates its views and precepts often. Its main difference from other teaching is that the sanctions of love and fear which it invokes gain power from the teacher's—and hence the pupil's—convictions of the awe and might of God. The pupil responds directly to the attitude and emotional set of the religious teacher. He also by impersonation sees himself in the role the teacher is trying to inspire.

The effectiveness of religious teaching is impaired if the clergyman —or the parent as a religious teacher—has himself lost confidence in his own religious belief. The possibility of the growth of such a doubt is again a reason why the terms of religious doctrine and theological statement cannot afford to get too far removed from the body of knowledge and the intellectual temper of the times.

The efficacy of the process of reiteration of religious precept has been recognized for ages. In the Book of Deuteronomy Moses is represented as saying:

"Listen, Israel: 'tis the Eternal, the Eternal alone, is our God. And you must love the Eternal your God with all your mind and all your soul and all your strength." These words you must learn by heart, this charge of mine; you must impress these on your children, you must talk about them when you are sitting at home and when you are on the road, when you lie down and when you rise up. You must tie them on your hands as a memento, and wear them on your forehead as a badge; you must inscribe them on the doorposts of your houses and on your gates.

Religion calls to the aid of its teaching the reiteration and suggestion available in ritual, observances, and memorials. It plants deep its notions of what is right, cultivates and nurses them, and keeps their memory green by continued watering.

Such is the effectiveness of these methods that a man's attitudes acquired through religious teaching may last his lifetime and form the enduring basis of his acceptance of what conduct is right and what wrong.

Let us now look at some specific examples of the effect of religious teaching on conduct.

Religion in China, especially on the doctrinal side, presents a more diverse picture than religion in America. Confucianism, Taoism, and Buddhism have each one had many different beliefs within its own ranks, ranging from highly refined philosophical and religious ideas to crude superstitions. Furthermore, a local temple is likely to adopt features of more than one religion. Chinese worship has been accustomed to local deities of various grades and to an assortment of gods charged with different important aspects of life. The worshiper has not customarily observed hard-and-fast doctrinal lines, like the member of an American Christian sect. When a foreign religion—take the case of Buddhism—has been imported into China, the Chinese have modified its teaching into conformity with their own views and ways. So it is hard to say when it is that the social practice is influencing the religion, and when the religion is influencing the social practice.

In actual Chinese practice, filial piety and loyalty to the family have received a strong religious sanction. The spirit world is close by. The presently living father of a family owes what he is and has to the spirits of his ancestors. And likewise the son owes to the father. The governmental structure reflected the religious belief: the Emperor was the Son of Heaven. The district magistrates were tagged with names specifically appropriate to parents, the "father-mother officials." Proficiency in the understanding of traditional family and social obligation, drilled into the able and promising young and tested by public examinations, was for long years the qualification for public office and a position in the bureaucracy, which thus tended to become a bureaucracy overweighted with scholars. Scholars were a main component of the recognized aristocracy of China. Such a scheme of things was bound to, and did in fact, overemphasize the *status quo*. It was too conservative. The Chinese seemed too much frozen in the traditions of their ancestors, in the old classics, and in forms of art once upon a time creative.

The religious and philosophical leaders of China have never in the past fallen victims to the idea that the world and the people in it and their interrelations can be explained mechanistically, or that tabulated facts can cope with ultimate mysteries. But at the same time, under the influence of their preoccupation with traditional attitudes, this wisdom came up with a harmful corollary: too little attention was paid to mastery over things, too little attention to science for the magnificent results it can in fact achieve. It would be unfair to lay upon religious teaching the entire responsibility for a state of affairs which has other sources as well and which is certainly influenced by the overgreat pressure of Chinese population on Chinese resources. But it may well be fair to call religious leadership to account for failing to turn their attention towards preventing this huge overpopulation. And it is certainly fair to point out the sanction given by Chinese religion to a backward-focusing glorification of ancestors and of tradition.

In any event, the workaday Chinese religion and its too-exclusive preoccupation with traditional family relationships produced results still felt today in the failure of any reasonable scientific control of the environment. For example, consider the following description, in the year 1944, of some problems of hospital maintenance in unoccupied China. Even if we make allowances for the disorganization caused by the Japanese occupation of coastal areas, we get a picture of a culture that has failed to give sufficient attention to knowledge and skills in dealing with things material.

Running a hospital in China consumes 20 to 30 times the effort that it does in the United States. Abundant supplies of water, steam heat, soap, towels and bedding make it relatively easy to keep our hospitals clean. Most of these articles are impossible to obtain in China, or can only be secured by an immense expenditure of money and manpower.

Free China has no water systems, and all water must be carried from wells or nearby rivers. Such water is muddy and must be sterilized, necessitating the use of fuel. The only fuel available to most hospitals is the wood that can be gathered from the countryside. Nearly one-third of all enlisted men attached to a hospital must be detailed to the task of carrying water and fuel to the kitchens and operating rooms. . . .

Bedding is so scarce that a bed has to remain empty while the linen is being laundered. Enamel ware is manufactured exclusively in Occupied China. As 30 per cent of the patients in Chinese hospitals suffer from dysentery the lack of enamel ware is serious, since unpainted wooden pans are difficult to clean. Beds are made of wooden planks laid across two trestles, and their prices mount as the demand for these planks in all kinds of construction work increases.

Most of the hospitals have bamboo walls, straw roofs, paper window panes and mud floors, which during the rainy season resemble muddy football fields.

Religion is but one of the influences at work in the building of standards of conduct, and its particular influence cannot be artificially isolated from that of family, friends, neighbors, and teachers. What is peculiar to religion is that it especially is concerned with the ultimate value of one's role, whether one's life is as a whole worthwhile, and what standards are consistent or inconsistent with a worthwhile life. What religion regards as right standards are likely also to be regarded as right standards by family, friends, neighbors, and school. Therefore in times when a community is not in a period of active change, religion is usually working alongside and in the same direction with other influences that are establishing the rule and role of the rising generation.

When secular leaders of the state are pushing for standards different from those set by religion, and when these leaders have control of the schools, of the press, and of moving pictures and radio, there is an opportunity to test the hold retained, at least on some people, by their religious training and training in their earlier years that may then have been in accord with the religious training. Such a situation occurred in the Nazi Germany of Hitler. It is a matter of history that many of the clergy and pastors and many of those in their congregations stood fast by their old character and against the Nazi frame of mind. They remained honest and fair in the general cruelty, injustice, and claptrap dishonesty of Nazidom. Such an event demonstrates that in the case of some determined men and women the standards that they have come to regard as right stay with them, that a good content of rule and role was in their case successfully taught and acquired, and that their standards persisted against both blandishment and persecution.

Another instance of the efficacy of religion in establishing standards can be found in the feeling of people about certain kinds of offenses which are regarded particularly as violations of right religious attitude. If through religious teaching a substantively insignificant crime is made to seem heinous, a heavy penalty for it is willingly accepted by almost everyone in the community. Take the cases of conversation of witches with the Devil, or Giordano Bruno's heresy that man's perception of the world is relative to the position in space and time from which he views it. Either of these might be the basis for putting the witch or the heretic to death. Here the community accepts just as severe a penalty in the case of an artificially constructed crime as they would in the case of a substantively injurious crime such as horse stealing on the wilderness frontier where a man's horse may be the condition of his life.

Surely if anyone were inclined to deny the power of religion to establish attitudes controlling behavior, this fact of the acceptance of punishment for artificial crime, like heresy, on an equal basis with that for substantive crime, like horse stealing, is an answer that shows in fact that religion can create working standards of right and wrong.

3. RELIGION'S RELATIONS WITH GOVERNMENT

While religion as a teacher of standards influences the practical conduct of contemporary institutions such as the government of the organized state, it is in turn influenced by secular standards and itself reflects them in the development of its own standards. Every institution reflects the contemporary scene.

The church has often tried to utilize the state to further its position and its teaching. Similarly the state has often tried and sometimes succeeded in making use of the church to further the state's aims and strength.

It is said that a by-product of the Reformation was a reduction in the demand for fish. The government of England was disturbed on grounds of national defense, lest the fishing industry should cease to be an adequate supplier of seamen to the Navy. Edward VI ordered fish to be eaten on Fridays and Saturdays in Lent and Elizabeth added Wednesdays. Lord Cecil declared: "Let the old course of fishing be maintained by the straitest observation of fish days for policy's sake: so the seacoasts shall be strong with men and habitations, and the fleet flourish more than ever."

The modern Roman Catholic Church believes as a matter of principle and of doctrine in the value of each individual man and woman. It also as an institution is certain to be aroused by the hostility of rival systems of belief attempting to get control of men's minds and allegiance. Such a rival system is the basically anti-religious and anti-individualistic totalitarian Communism promoted by Russia. In such circumstances, the Church is obviously a bulwark of a political state, like the United States, which finds itself in competition and conflict with Communist Russia. On the domestic scene, within the United States the Church can be expected to look with favor on candidates for political office who take an uncompromising stand against Communism.

When Japan was engaged in the twentieth century in expansion at the expense of China, and then in attempted expansion at the expense of England and the United States, the aims of the government were aided by the doctrine of Japanese religion that the Japanese emperor was an incarnate deity and the Japanese people were culture carriers divinely destined to rule the world. A device had been adopted in the late nineteenth century which verbally observed the principle of freedom of religion but practically denied it. The official cult or state Shinto, with its own shrines, government-supervised and -supported, conducted worship in which everyone, irrespective of conscientious objection, was required to do obeisance to Amaterasu, the sun-goddess, and to the divine emperor. This was said to be a matter of political loyalty, not of religion, and to fail so to worship was subversive and disloyal. Thus, if by any chance the sectarian Shinto churches should for any reason waver in holding believers in line in a faith in emperor worship or the glories of Japanese destiny, the state shrines as a practical matter could influence the minds of all through the compulsory ceremonial at the shrines for emperor worship.

A church subservient to a political goverment can be useful to the government. The church in its process of teaching a man or a child his place in the real and final world and his conduct here in this present world consonant with his welfare in that final world could teach that obedience to lawful authority was part of the divinely ordained scheme of things, and that the present rulers of the state constituted lawful authority in the sight of God. Indeed, it may well be that some such process as this is a part of the true explanation for the long duration and stability of the theocratic regimes of ancient Egypt.

When governments or political leaders have felt that religion is hostile to them, they have sometimes tried to get rid of religion. This seems to be an effort headed for long-term failure. The fact is that men refuse to have their life interpreted as finally meaningless. They will turn to religion, not to the political government, for their assurance. If old religion has been suppressed or has died off, a new one will arise. This is a field in which political government is incompetent, despite the temporary successes of secular leaders in persuading some for a time that some worldly idol, like the German *Volk,* will do in place of God.

In theory it would seem that if the places of worship were closed and the priesthood or ministry outlawed for a period of two generations, an organized religion could be completely suppressed. At least two generations would be necessary, because parents would hand on to their children their own form of religious belief, and the children would be capable of restoring the organization. Presumably religious emissaries and missionaries from abroad would also keep alive the forms and would always be potentially ready to aid in the restoration. Discord and challenge to the government authority would be sure to arise at the start of the program of suppression, and continue for many years.

A government might succeed in breaking the power of a contemporary priesthood—a specific religious hierarchy of a church hostile to the government and its measures. Then when the religious need of the community reasserted itself, the government might well hope that the new priesthood of the restored or new religious organization would no longer be one still hostile to the government and its authority. The most that a government, in addition to attempts to oppose and cure church abuses, can realistically hope is that its own practices will be sufficiently satisfactory to a just religious leadership in the long run. For the leaders of the state—the community in its aspects of political organization—permanently to overthrow and altogether get rid of religious leaders and followers—the community in its aspects of religious organization—is most unlikely because the state cannot provide men with the sense of an ultimately worthwhile role.

For two centuries preceding the Russian Revolution of 1917 the Orthodox Eastern Church, the official Russian church, was dependent on the political authority. Its affairs were supervised by a Holy Synod, itself subservient to the government power. The government officer charged with seeing that the Holy Synod remained in line was described by Peter the Great as the "Czar's eye." Priests must disclose to the government secrets of the confessional where the interests of the state were involved. In such circumstances, truly religious-minded Russians at the leadership level were anything but heart-and-soul loyal to the official church, but were rather an opposition wanting to achieve church independence. Political reformers hated the church as an arm of the political regime and the government they wanted to reform.

The Bolsheviks who came into power in Russia in 1918 were completely antireligious and held to Lenin's view that religion is the "opiate of the masses," a capitalistic device to keep the public drugged and quiescent. They struck at the organized church, being aided in their efforts by the fact that the church in Russia had in fact been the tool of the recent Czars. The Bolsheviks prohibited religious instruction outside the home. All church property was nationalized. Worship was not forbidden and places of worship could be leased by congregations from the government. Religion was ridiculed; courses designed to show that religion was a delusion were taught in the schools; religious belief was belittled by a line of propaganda to the effect that religion today was no more than an interesting anachronism out of keeping with modern times and modern knowledge.

Still, Russians stayed with their religion and its ministers. When the Second World War came, and Russia was under severe German military pressure, the government could no longer afford to alienate religion. So the hostility, which had been a device to strengthen the Russian government, was dropped in order to save both government and people from German conquest. The church was restored, the church hierarchy restored, schools for the ministry again set up. The Stalin government, dedicated to the preservation of Russia—obviously a condition of its own perpetuation as well—saw two things plainly enough. The first and most important was that religion, rather than appearing an anachronism, was such a vital thing to so many Russian people that loyalty to Russia on the part of its religious leaders was essential if a tight and close war was to be won by the hard-pressed state. The second was what we have just indicated: that Christians abroad would make better allies for Russia if the Russian government piped down in its atheistic whistling.

4. THE SEAT OF RELIGIOUS POWER

As in the case of other institutions, the church is subject to internal struggles for control of the seat of power within the church. The character of those who constitute the effective church leadership affects the teaching function of the church, especially in matters of honesty and political morality. If the bishops and higher clergy are generally cynical, grasping, and more attentive to preferment in office and power than to their spiritual duties—as we saw in the case of the Roman Catholic Church before the Reformation—this discourages and unsettles the local priests and tends to the disrepute of the church in everyone's eyes, including those of the parents of the rising generation. The mechanics of impersonation and response require for the most effective church teaching that there be an atmosphere from youth up of respect and reverence for the priest, and this may be jeopardized by the all-too-human jockeyings for places of power in the church.

The prayer and aim of the clergy in its intercession with God on behalf of the church and in its address to God is "Thy will be done." The internal power struggle in the church consists of the process of settling who is to be the official determiner of the content of "Thy will." The whole church body is to be reconciled to a particular group of interpreters of God's will.

Just as the Republican and Democratic leaders in the United States contest with one another over who is the real custodian and interpreter of American democracy, or as a Tito group and a Stalin group contest over who is the true expositor of Communism, so the religious groups and their leaders contest over who is the true spokesman of Christianity.

In the case of Christianity, this process has gone on from the earliest times. Doctrine is originally likely to be uncertain. It takes form in educational groups, discussion in what in the political field we would call "cells" and the like. The process is well set out in the *Acts of the Apostles* and in the New Testament *Letters*.

Then as the doctrine comes to take form and gain acceptance, there begins the contest to determine who is the official interpreter and custodian of the doctrine, with power to tell people what to do and believe for salvation. Again, the *Acts of the Apostles* describes the commencement of this contest in early Christianity. Thereafter the whole history of Christianity and its sects witnesses the carrying on of the contest.

In connection with our present inquiry, this contest for power needs to be noted. This is because the character of the actual church leadership that from time to time comes into control of the church influences the effectiveness of the religious teaching of standards and attitudes. To be sure, a wise and spiritually minded local pastor will in any event be a useful teacher of his congregation, but his effectiveness will be greatly enhanced if the church leadership and the church position is itself held in respect and reverence by all. If the local pastor is not wise and spiritually minded, and if the church organization itself has lost standing and respect, the sanction of the local teaching withers.

5. ANCIENT DOCTRINE

We have noted that the original direct revelation, the primary faith of a religious leader, as soon as he comes to the point of telling some-one else about it, has to be stated in language understood by himself and his contemporaries. The absolute nature of God cannot be stated by a human mind, limited as such a mind is by its incomplete percep-tions and powers. So the religious leader and his followers do the best they can in making statements that convey a representation of the mystical revelation. God is a father. The kingdom of heaven is a place where one can eat and drink. It belongs to the children of God. It is both here and there. It is present and it is to come. It is a house with many rooms. Then the church tries to organize and systematize the statements of the founder and of those close to him. It all has to be done in the light of the knowledge of the time. So we get doctrines of Heaven and Hell, angels, principalities, powers of light and of dark-ness, bodily removals to Heaven, three persons and one God, and other formulas enshrining—and freezing—the doctrine of the church. This kind of statement then is perpetuated by being handed down through generations of priests, who are regarded as custodians of the religious truth, and, as we have said, intermediaries necessary to our salvation.

There is a danger for the effective teaching of the church and the acceptance of that teaching at leadership levels when the knowledge of the times has undergone so much change that the old forms of state-ment no longer convey a contemporary representation of the revela-tion that is the heart of the religion. Adults, and students of mature years, begin to feel doubts about the formulas. The doubts can hardly escape being felt by ordinarily responsive and impersonative youth. The authority of the church as a teacher then suffers. Although the young go to church and Sunday school, they shed what they hear as they feel that their parents do.

If the church statement of its mysteries can be couched in sufficiently modern terms, if its ancient paraphernalia can be modified enough to cease to be so much of a stumbling block to the one who wants to believe, the teaching function of the church will be liberated from the deadweight handicap to which it subjects itself by clinging so long to the old formulas. A theological formula should help and aid a believer; it should not stand in his way so that he and pastor alike have to spend their time in laboriously reconciling it to contemporary ideas and knowledge.

While useful attitudes learned in youth tend to persist, it is well that the persistence should be fortified by continued confidence in the teaching agencies. In the case of the church as such an agency this confidence is shaken by the ancient trappings of the church authority. The church may still possess the kernel of truth, but it is so overlain with forbidding doctrinal husks that it takes a willing and determined young man or woman to make his way through. Most people do not have either the necessary will or the determination, and for them the church teaching may cease to come with authentic power. They may come to doubt the basic sanction, the basic authority, that lies behind the church as a teacher.

Our concern here is with the church as a teacher of standards of conduct and habits of attitude as they affect political order. But it is worthwhile to point out that the same handicap of ancient doctrinal paraphernalia that hampers the church as a teacher of standards also impedes her in a still more vital function. It jeopardizes the authority with which the church fulfills the essential religious function of showing men and women where they stand in relation to the final powers and the ultimate scheme of things, the meaning to them of God and their own lives.

6. A BASIS OF FAITH

We find ourselves today—as men have found themselves from time immemorial—in a world that cannot be understood. Life is not amenable to our wishes; we are subject to painful and disabling disease; catastrophe occurs from time to time; and there is no evident pattern of justice in the treatment accorded this man or that, in health, in intelligence, or in any matters of native equipment most vital to him as a man. Something is missing from our experience to render even the fact of this experience likely or self-explanatory. Our mere being here at all is a stupendous mystery for which we can in no wise account.

Yet in this perplexing and inexplicable world we find ourselves driven on by a host of urgent motives. What sense is there in it? How shall we answer our need to know where we stand and our need for a worthwhile role?

The answer becomes harder rather than easier to discover with the acquisition of more knowledge with passing time. The aspects of the world seem more impersonal and less subject to explanation by primitive impersonation, as more and more inquiry is made into facts. The enormous forces of nature in the revealed universe of the stars and in the binding power within the smallest inferable organizations of matter alike do not readily fit any scheme of a reality concerned with human interests or human fate.

The answer is obviously not going to lie in any demonstrable statement, because the factors of the process that institutes the whole human scene—if there is anything that can truthfully be called a process—are unknown to us. The process is a mystery, and the answer to the human question will be incomplete. In an inquiry where the basic factors are hidden and likely forever impossible to know—why is life, what is energy, what and why is time, what and why are the other modes of human perception that put a barrier between our understanding and what we would understand?—no question about the organization or meaning of the hidden and unknown factors can receive a complete, demonstrated, and proved answer.

We have an intuitive conviction that there is something real—something that if we could perceive it we would place in the class of things we call real—that is somehow hidden within the phenomena of experience, something beyond the reach of the measurements and entities of the mathematicians, physicists, and philosophers. We feel that there is some kind of ground or explanation of things and events, though we have no rational notion what it might be. We refuse to admit—we are unable to admit—that we could perceive things or events at all if there were not something to account for them.

The reality and existence that we see and use every day, we investigate and analyze in order to make still better use of it. But however far investigated or analyzed, we always in the end, despite our learning and our science and our mathematics, are balked. Something is missing and we don't know what. The key to the final door is never there. So we posit this key, and talk about an unseen and inexperienced reality, the philosophically disreputable thing-in-itself. This amounts to an assertion of our faith, our intuition, that if confronted by that unseen and unexperienced whatnot, with perceptions no longer too limited but instead adequate, we would (if we could still remember human terminology and human experience and were willing to descend again to the use of human terminology for a description of something beyond its scope) label this newly perceived whatnot by calling it "reality."

It is hard for us to believe that something can spring from nothing. It is equally hard to believe in an everlasting scheme without beginning or end. A timeless world is harder still, constitutionally disposed as we are to perceive events in terms of time. We are left to a stubborn belief that there is an explanation for the world and what goes on in it, even though we can see that the explanation is beyond the grasp of our reason.

The dog does pretty well in a world of smells, sights, and sounds. The man does pretty well in a world of electrons, protons, waves, and particles. Some other being does better still—but alas, we are not such a being—in a world perceived by means of still less limited perceptions.

Neither in the whole or in any part of the active, striving, knowing, problem-solving, synthesizing individual organism that a man comes to regard as himself is there any localization of the mind or knowledge of what it finally is. We know that if we knock a man on the head hard enough his mind stops functioning as far as any usual communication with others is concerned. We know that drugs alter the normal performance of a man's mind, conditioned as it appears to be in its day-to-day human operations by the physical structure of the brain. But of the physical brain we have no more final knowledge than we have of any other objective thing. There are some data, some appearances, that we can investigate and experiment with, but the investigator himself has those inevitable basic limitations that balk final demonstration or final understanding.

We can find out and apply useful relationships in the data presented to us. We can design bridges that will stand when built according to the design, and nuclear reactors that will perform approximately as predicted. But we cannot by reason grasp entire any single one of these items or events we use or experience, much less the whole scheme of things. No one by the exercise of reason has ever been able to light upon any self-demonstrating or self-authenticating final truth. Something essential is missing. We can say here what has been said about the equations of the mathematicians: the descriptions of the quarry of reality are more revealing about the limitations of the hunter than of the true aspect of the quarry, which is likely to remain untouched as far as the human hunter is concerned.

All we have available to us to aid our understanding are the powers with which we are endowed. We cannot transcend them, and if they have been given to us limited and imperfect, that is that.

Since reason is unable to discover a demonstrable or provable final truth, a man must rely on something other than reason or else be satisfied without any self-authenticating truth, without any key to the significance of our existence and that of the world. We need to know where we stand. Reason cannot tell us. We look elsewhere for our answer, and find it only in hints, not certainties. We have to choose what we will believe.

In choosing what we will believe about our place in the world and the meaning of our life, we have at hand the teaching and practice, as we have seen, of organized religion. The Church says it has the answer, the necessary key, for a good life in a humanly meaningful world, and it tries early and late to put its answer across. It claims to be the one authentic transmitter of the revelation of its founder and of the prophets and saints. From our youth onward, the Church applies itself to get us set to choose to follow the Church's choice of belief, the Church's hint of reality. The Church in addressing to God the prayer "Thy will be done" seeks to define for us not only the content of "Thy will" but also the content of the "Thou," the nature of God himself.

This route to belief, the acceptance of the authority and teaching of organized religion, is the route we most of us follow. We thereby find the certainty we need, our truth in the light of which we make sense of our lives in hope and faith rather than nonsense of our lives in frustration and hopelessness.

But to some the Church's antiquely phrased message of truth fails to carry conviction or authenticate itself. Through organized religion they may gain help, and yet without something further they fail to attain a satisfying belief in a God who means something vital to them or who is in any way concerned with men's efforts to reach after what is fair and right.

Some people have an intuitive conviction of the final worth of what is most meaningful to them in their lives. They just think it unlikely in the light of their whole make-up and experience that their love, or their delight in what is good and beautiful, their powerful, deep-going sentiments are ephemeral, a kind of disappearing froth on the wave of existence. How or why this conviction may be true they cannot say.

Is this belief that what means most to a man in his life has final worth, just an impersonative error? Is it simply another attribution to nature of a human trait, describing the powers of nature as acting like men? We have seen that men have been prone to constructing a god in their own image, who controls this or that aspect of nature, acts as humans act, and is appealed to and humored and placated as if a man.

The men who constructed these impersonative gods did so as an early scientific hypothesis. They imagined a god of thunder and of lightning to account for the thunderstorm. They were looking for a cause of the storm—a cause that they might hope to influence or control.

The case is different with the intuitive conviction of the worth of a man's life. Here the man is well aware of something extremely significant to him, say the love for his children and theirs for him. It is indisputably there. He is not constructing a cause for it. He is not saying a god like a man put it there. He is saying that it seems so significant he chooses to believe that it has an ultimate significance, an imperishable meaning. He does not attempt to say how or why this may be, or how this thing so significant to him fits the entire scheme of things.

The mystery of how anything at all exists—yet here we are and here in fact things do seem to be—is stupendous, intractable, and beyond our human powers to understand. This primary mystery we are obliged to acknowledge whether we want to or not. Perhaps we are justified in not balking at the secondary, lesser mystery of how some aspects of life are recognizable as of final significance. We believe because we can't help it or because we choose to believe. And in either case it is hard to see how anyone can make a successful challenge of our belief.

There are times when some object or some act seems so strikingly beautiful, or so strikingly good, as to awaken in the one who is looking at it, or hearing or perhaps otherwise sensing it, a conviction that here is something wholly valuable, a final and self-explanatory and self-justifying perfection. Perhaps what has happened is that a depth of the person has been touched that ordinarily lies beyond awareness and that now emerges to speak with authority. The core rock outcrops through the overlying sediments. In what unknown fires and by what unknown events was the core formed?

Then there are the more strictly mystical moments of illumination, in which a man seems to come upon a principle that explains and justifies the world, but in a rationally unverifiable way, so that it is hard for him to state the content of the illumination to one who has not himself had a similar experience.

As common an example as any of this relatively uncommon kind of event may be that of the lover who in what seems to him a clear-headed moment suddenly sees that his love is an adequate reason for the existence of the world, for night and day, for the long ages of geologic history, and for the whole activity of nature and of mankind.

He has the same feeling of certainty and of satisfactory discovery that he would have if he had solved a problem on which he had been working and suddenly come upon the correct answer. Or as if he had completed a demonstration and the facts fitted together so that the result was plain and evident. Or as if he had been trying to get into true perspective facts he was studying, and had suddenly succeeded.

But in this particular case he has been through no kind of reasoning process at all. He has been devoted to his loved one. All his powers have been focused, at least in the sense that everything extraneous to his love has been put aside. Then came the illumination and the conviction that the love made sense of things. But he can't say how it is, or put the factors of his experience together in a statement for someone else so that the other says that he too recognizes and feels the same certainty.

Such a revelation of the worth of love is striking and certainly authenticates itself as disclosing to the lover that love meant more to him than even the immense amount we all of us know it to mean without benefit of any such illumination. In his concentration and devotion he has laid hold of a depth of perception ordinarily outside his ken. He thinks he has received a hint of the place of love in the real and final scheme of things. But neither he nor anyone else can demonstrate that in fact love explains the world.

The difficulty is that concentration is known to play such peculiar tricks. In the Yoga Aphorisms of Patanjali are prescriptions for exercises of breathing and of attention as a result of which one is said to see the principle of reality disclosed in this or that particular thing by the process of single-minded concentration upon it. A saint has even been said to have had as a result of concentration thereon and devotion thereto a direct revelation of the Holy Trinity as an explanatory principle of reality.

The mystic, like the prestidigitator, gets out of the hat what he first put into it; but unlike the prestidigitator he may sometimes have put into the hat more than he or anyone else knew, and what he put in may in some cases have been reaches and capacities of the mind and spirit of which he, and everyone else, was ordinarily unaware. Perhaps then in his subsequent illumination there is an authentic hint of a theretofore undisclosed reality about himself. And if what he put into the hat was profound love with his whole being, what he drew out of the hat was a discovery that profound love was even more than met the eye, the senses, or the intelligence.

It may be that the mystic receives a valid hint of a unifying principle of which the ordinary intelligence is unaware, but which the object of his concentration and devotion somehow serves to represent and the process of his concentration and devotion somehow discloses.

How is the rational intelligence to deal with the essentially irrational mystical experience? No experimental testing and checking of the validity of the mystical hint seems to be possible. It is not like the truth of an engineering formula which can be verified by whether the suspension bridge built in accordance with it stands or collapses. We don't feel as solidly based as we would like in the absence of the same kind of tests and checks with which we are familiar in the world of scientific hypothesis and physical experiment.

One thing that reason can do is to separate out and identify experiences that appear to be in the nature of reasoning outside the field of consciousness rather than mystical intuition. This kind of reasoning perhaps took place when Saint Joan's voices gave her sound military advice, or when Isaiah in visions was called to prophesy. The process supplying the content of the voices and visions may not be far removed from that which produced Kekulé's dozing dream of snakelike formations of atoms which disclosed to him the structure of the benzene ring, one of his brilliant contributions to the science of chemistry. It is akin to the sudden rising into Sir William Rowan Hamilton's conscious mind of the essentials of his mathematical concept of quaternions, of whose origin he wrote:

They started into life, or light, full grown, on the 16th of October, 1843, as I was walking with Lady Hamilton to Dublin, and came up to Brougham Bridge, which my boys have since called the Quaternion Bridge. That is to say, I then and there felt the galvanic circuit of thought close; and the sparks which fell from it were the fundamental equations in i, j, k; exactly such as I have used them ever since.

In these cases the mind has been at work outside the field of conscious attention, and then comes through into consciousness with a useful result, sometimes with the accompaniment of visions, sometimes without, depending perhaps on the temperament of the individual who happens to receive the insight.

The rational intelligence can identify, and if need be remove, accretions which have become grafted upon an original mystical experience in the historical course of its interpretation. As we have pointed out, religious leaders are engaged in closing the gap between the imperfect daily scheme of things and some more ideal scheme. The desire of everyone for a worthwhile role, a meaningful life, reaches out for assurance. When the priests or their equivalent seek to provide this assurance through religious belief, they avail themselves of the intuitions and revelations of mystics in establishing the core of belief. The mystical insights and even the dreams and the visions are thus the basis of the organized belief of organized religion. The priests interpret, transmit, and institutionalize the message of the primary religious individual. Even the originator himself can do no more than try to state what his religious experience means in terms of his own time and environment. "There are many rooms in my Father's house; if there were not I would have told you, for I am going away to make ready a place for you."

The interpretations and explanations of mystical experience are the work of the intelligence—mostly that of priests and theologians—and are accordingly subject to rational review as new facts are discovered and as the knowledge of new times and places has changed and increased beyond that of other or earlier times and places. A judgment about things ultimate, if it is to be made at all, has to be made by intuition in light of all available evidence and with what aid reason can give.

In reaching a rational belief, different people weight different parts of the available evidence differently. Some pay much attention to their feelings; others to a supposed orderly mechanism in the world around them; others to the apparent absence of human notions of justice in the way nature treats different individuals; others to their own sense of justice and the demands of their impersonation and response.

If the intelligence—along with its science and knowledge—were able to deal with ultimates, hope and fear would have no place in the formation of religious belief. But since the intelligence is in fact incapable, hope and fear do play a part. The choice of belief that the real world is in harmony with the deepest hopes that he has may seem to a man more reasonable than any other choice.

By whatever route attained, through organized religion or individual insight, a faith that human life is finally worthwhile and that its experiences are ultimately significant will mean for a man that he can go about his work in a spirit of cheerfulness rather than in a spirit of discouragement or at best grim determination.

All of us—atheists, agnostics, skeptics, or believers—look at the same facts, see the same divided community with its discord, secession, and separation. We see alike the misery and hate brought about through intolerance, unfairness, dishonesty, and stupidity. We see the distress and sorrow caused by disease and too hard conditions. It then might be that each of us alike would, if he could, do something to make both political and individual life more harmonious and satisfactory. But the unbeliever—the man looking upon life as essentially and finally meaningless—would go about it as one making the best of a bad job, as one pessimistically cleaning up a sad mess in which he and mankind had been pitched without hope of anything better than easing an undeserved misery.

If we are overwhelmed by sorrow at the death of someone young in battle, we can only get a chilling comfort from an idea that as the whole of life is without any permanent meaning, the death of the young really makes no great difference. But if we believe that the whole of life has a permanent meaning for man, then it is a temporary tragedy, but in the timeless and final world no tragedy.

The world is brighter for one who believes that the motives, needs, loves, and hopes of men are significant, that what is worthwhile to a man has a relation to what is worthwhile in the ultimate scheme of things, and that if he could comprehend the ultimate scheme, he would assent to it as humanly good. He tries to remedy discord and distress, confident that it is finally and truly good for men to exercise their powers freely and fully. In trying to see how impersonation and response can be used so as to lead us into ways of tolerance, honesty, fairness, and wisdom, he may come up with the same answer as the man who is trying to make the best of a bad job. But the belief that life is finally good produces optimism in what he is doing. The whole effort ceases to be a senseless burden. His belief lends him heart and courage in his effort to discover, and then to realize, what is right.

PART III. THE RULE OF A FREE ORDER

XVIII. Tolerance

WE have seen that it is necessary for a community to have an obeyed rule if it is to have order, and that it is necessary for it to have order if it is to make any co-operative achievement as a community. As a crude instance of this we pointed out that the people of a city know—from experience with transport or shipping interruptions—that order is the condition for their obtaining the necessities of life. It is meaningless to talk of a choice between freedom and order, because in human society order is the condition of freedom and—more than freedom—of any significant community accomplishment and even of life itself.

As it is necessary to have a rule for any political order, free or unfree, what we are looking for is the rule that makes for a free order willingly accepted, the rule believed in as part of a worthwhile role. We are trying to avoid the kind of rule characteristic of discord or of an imposed, unfree order. We wish to establish the rule and role that will enlist the energies, powers, and courage of the citizens and direct the motives of reform along lines such as to realize and then maintain a free order.

In this part of the book, The Rule of a Free Order, we examine the political attitudes and habits which can in fact direct the motives of reform and the ambitions of groups and their leaders along the lines of a free order rather than in the historically more usual lines of discord, secession, and separation. We also examine what practical institutional means there may be for maintaining and fortifying a free order.

In our discussion of the divided community we saw the destructive political results of intolerance under both ancient and modern conditions, and under every kind of formal political organization. Intolerance obviously operated in a different environment in the third century of our era from that of the twentieth. In the days of a Roman emperor there were no ways of either conveying instructions quickly to a distance or dispatching troops or political police forces almost at once to a disturbed spot within the empire; nor was there an overwhelming disparity between the kind of weapons available to the government and those available to the governed. In the days of a Hitler every one of those conditions had changed. Yet the attitude and frame of mind and actions of intolerance produced political discord in the one period just as in the other. The resentments and hatred stirred then were the same as those now or in the future. Intolerance bred further intolerance then as now and as in the future. As political and industrial organization becomes larger-scale, and communications more rapid, and armaments more effective, the effects of intolerance by the central government of a large state have perhaps become more oppressive in modern times than in ancient; but the evil has been of the same kind, and predictable in every case as following from the inherent relationships of intolerance and the characteristic behavior of the intolerant.

Now that we come to look at tolerance, we are again looking at an attitude, a frame of mind, and a way of action—along with its appropriate organization and institutional bases—that expresses itself in very different environments in a far-off yesterday, a present today, and a far-off tomorrow. In ancient times one test of a tolerant imperial government might have been how well it recognized and promoted the autonomy of provincial cities; but there was no possible test in its recognition of the autonomy of large-scale industrial corporations, because there was no large-scale industry. As a useful method for us today in studying tolerance, or any other political attitude or way of action, it is best to look at events in our own time today and immediately at hand. It is our own times in which we are most critically interested, and which we want to have right for a good and worthwhile life. We can bring the first-hand test of our own experience to a description of tolerance under the conditions of our own times—what it looks like, the kinds of organization and institutions which promote it, and other conditions favorable to it. We can see whether tolerance and its institutions and organization make for a satisfactory modern community and avoid the seeds of discord.

1. MANY LOCI OF POWER

A tolerant community is characterized by many powerful groups and associations with independence of action. These groupings are found in the various fields important to the life of the community. They are pushing their own interests in accordance with the usual motives of reform which we described in the first part of this book. But, unlike the situations of discord, no one group—governmental or otherwise—or few groups are overreaching and oppressing the rest.

In the economic field the community includes and tolerates independent organizations. Industrial workers are organized in labor unions, with a voice both in industry and politics, on the lookout that the pay of workers is sufficient and their working conditions good. Farmers have their associations and alliances to protect and push their interests. Separate industries have their associations and spokesmen; and there are over-all associations of manufacturers, bankers, or merchants. There are local and nationwide Chambers of Commerce. In the tolerant community all are pressure groups in their own interest. None are agents of a government which centralizes economic power, as in the totalitarian states. All from time to time in fact act unwisely, yet all are operating under such rules of the game—which we are now engaged in investigating—as to preserve a balance and to maintain a reasonably harmonious rather than a discordant, unjust community.

As a specific example of one kind of grouping in a tolerantly organized community, take the case of a manufacturing corporation with 250,000 employees. We have already pointed out that these latter will have their union to speak for some of their vital interests. But in addition to that there is the fact of their tie-in to the manufacturer and the manufacturer's success because their livelihood is involved with the success of the manufacturer. A significant part of the picture is the many smaller suppliers of the big manufacturer, also interested in its welfare, and the similarly interested smaller outfits whose livelihood is involved in the distribution of the manufacturer's products. All alike have their role and their security caught up in the success of the whole venture. If, as is likely, there are capable and forceful leaders and spokesmen within this interrelated enterprise promoting and defending its interests, they will have a political influence.

A source of individual and public opinion which can exert a check on government and on the pushing too hard or holding too tight of some overzealous segment of the community, is an independent religious organization, a church. So much so, in fact, that it has sometimes in history been the other way round: there has been need of strong enough governments to serve as a check on a too potent church. One aspect of a tolerant modern community is churches speaking for themselves and their own views, and not acting as agents of the government or of any other special secular clique within the community.

A church thus stands as an example in the doctrinal field of a politically independent group, just as a manufacturing corporation, with its suppliers and distributors, does in the economic field.

By virtue of their function as experts in the statutory and traditional court-enforced rules in the conduct of business, as, for example, those governing the validity and interpretation of contracts, and as experts in the legal relations between individuals and groups in every aspect of the activities of a modern community, lawyers hold an important placc. Due to their training, the scope of their profession, and the kind of talents which make for success in it, they also hold in the United States a disproportionately high number of political offices, including memberships in the national legislative bodies as well as in those of the several states.

Independent associations of lawyers representing the interests of the profession will be among the opinion-forming groups in a tolerantly organized community. Such is the fact in the United States, where the bar associations, city, county, state, and nationwide, exert an effective political influence—well capable of exerting pressure on a government. The pressure may or may not in a particular case be for the best or wisest course of action. But its existence serves as a check on government power and is evidence that the government has not gained total power in the community. Illustrations of the political power of the bar associations and their leaders are seen in their successful resistance to the proposed reform of the United States Supreme Court enthusiastically sponsored by President Franklin D. Roosevelt with a view to adding to the court additional justices of his own political persuasion, and in their important part in the successful effort to repeal the Eighteenth Amendment to the United States Constitution which had prohibited the manufacture, sale, or transportation of intoxicating liquors.

Discord was characterized by some particular group—sometimes one in control of the government—bringing about in its own interest an inequitable rule that was hard to reform peaceably. The way to avoid this phase of discord is for the community to have many strong, independent groups—the very groups that no totalitarian ruler, as we saw in the *discord* cases, will tolerate. Enough powerful and determined groups in enough important lines are a practical support of continued freedom as well as evidence that such freedom already exists.

There are relatively few outstandingly able people in any line of activity. A tolerantly organized community gives them the opportunity to do what they are capable of doing and to acquire a personal following.

In the economic line a man who is able to organize an industry gets his chance to do so with a minimum of interference as long as he is not injuring others. In his resulting position of personal power he will be a leader in the community with many followers who take their cue from him. Those whose livelihood and security are bound up with his success will certainly treat his views with respect, and his influence in the community, for better or worse, will be great. Such individuals with their following, their publicity, and the support of those in other fields who are attracted by their achievement, exert a check on the growth of any all-too-powerful group in the community which could lay down too great restraints on their initiative and activity.

Similarly in a tolerantly organized community the conspicuously brilliant scientist will be given his scope. Today's equivalent of Giordano Bruno, challenging all dogmatism, whether governmental, ecclesiastical, or scientific, will be welcomed rather then persecuted. If unpopular with most of his contemporaries and with the government, he will nevertheless find refuge and support at the hands of some one or other of the independent powerful individuals or groups that are found in the tolerant community and that have the wealth and means to give him the support he needs.

In the tolerant community there is a balance of abilities. We have mentioned the scientist, who has an unusual quota of curiosity plus intelligence. There are those with an unusually fine sense of proportion or beauty who can attain more than others in some fields of art. There are those who combine with an unusual degree of desire to be the boss some degree of intelligence and they will be leaders in this or that line of acquisitive endeavor, or perhaps successful politicians. There are any number of combinations, and all get their chance to play their part in accord with their capacities.

It is made as easy as possible for new people to move up the ladder. Ownership in independent business corporations is wide. Everything

is done to strengthen and give power to those capable of leadership in
the various lines of activity in the community. And there is a constantly broadening base of a healthy and economically wholesome
people.

This tolerant picture is the opposite of what has occurred when
some particular group has been too strong and has established its own
power so completely as to rule the community for the benefit of the
particular group itself. In the *discord* cases we saw that very thing
occur. In Prussia a conservative aristocracy, the Junkers, became too
strong. Later, in Germany, the middle-class businessmen got too
strong. They in their turn got more than they bargained for when they
put Hitler into power, as he was a political demon rather than the tool
for whom they had mistaken him. In Russia the party of urban workers and their leader Lenin got too exclusively strong at a time of exceptional disorganization and weakness of other Russian groups.

Today in the United States and in England neither a conservative
aristocracy, nor middle-class businessmen, nor a proletarian organization, nor the leaders of any one of these groups, have been strong
enough to monopolize power and rule the community. There is no
quiescently obedient class. Everyone is looking out for a chance to
better his group's position and at the same time tolerating others who
are doing the same thing. It is always true that people do in fact fall
into a rough kind of classification depending on the kind of work they
are doing and the various limitations nature has placed on their native
capabilities. But there is no hard-and-fast drawing of class lines. Especially there is no one class in control of a too-powerful government.
There are groups fulfilling their function among other groups, and
sometimes there will be a class fulfilling its function among other
classes. But in a tolerant community there is complete mobility between these functional classes, and rigid class lines do not exist.

A tolerant society is a complicated relationship between those going
their own way subject to a set of acceptable rules of the game—the
rule of a free order. An arbitrary society is a much simpler, more primitive, less-differentiated organization, where the citizen obeys or gets
knocked on the head. As we saw in the *discord* cases, it is this knocking on the head, or the fear of it, that keeps an arbitrary society for the
time being from flying apart.

One principle of tolerance stated in the most general terms is this:
It is better to give scope to motives than to police them. As we go on in
our discussion of tolerance we shall see many examples of this principle

in actual operation, and the principle will be substantiated in detail. Where abilities are about equal, those closest to the scene of action are the ones who know the facts best and are best able in the exercise of their own judgment to get the most out of what they are trying to do. A man who is given scope to run his organization in his own way gets more satisfaction in working than if he is subject to orders from a bureaucracy. It is the local freedom at the particular point of organized effort that counts.

This principle that it is better to give scope to motives than to police them is the principle which is denied in practice by authoritarian governments. The results of the denial, as we saw in the *discord* cases, are likely to be inefficiency, burdensome interferences, local bad feeling, and actual frustration in trying to do many of the things that need to be done in and for the community.

If a central political committee should try to organize the painting of pictures, or the composing of music, or the development of pure theory in mathematics, and to say exactly what course should be followed in any of these lines, everyone except the committee would see the absurdity of it. This extreme case concerns unusual kinds of individual talent, but it nevertheless points the moral applicable to other cases. While great individual ability is not common throughout the community, it is certainly never concentrated at one spot of political control. Whether in trade, banking, manufacturing, law, engineering, or any essential activtiy in a modern community, the competent abilities are found widely distributed. If the community is to get the full benefit of the man who knows the task at the spot where it is being done, he has to be given his scope at the scene of action.

More motives are involved than a man's desire to do well by himself and his family in an economic way, though that is important at all levels, and obviously must be so at an economically insecure level. A conspicuous example of this last is the fact that on the Russian bureaucratically controlled farms, the small farmers have been much more productive on the plots allowed them for their own produce for their own and their family's use and disposition, than on the state farm when producing for the use of the state. The same economic urge also applies to the owner or to the head of a large business. But here there are more reasons for giving him his scope. When a man has built a business and a business organization, why, other than for greater acquisitive gain, does he want to run it himself? Is it that he wants to be the boss? to give the lead? Is it akin to the enjoyment of the exercise of skill in something he knows how to do? Is it because the business has become part of his worthwhile role, and he looks at it as peculiarly his own on that account? Is it because he thinks he sees others as doing it less well? All of these factors are involved, and every one of them points to why he will do better, be more productive, and take more pride and responsibility in what he is doing if he is given his head and his scope.

European critics have sometimes eyed askance what they regarded as an American preoccupation with the production of bigger and better material things—bathtubs, refrigerators, or our many labor-saving household appliances. Stalin, like Hitler, talked about our pluto-democracy. But the truth is that our material productivity has been only one phase of what the tolerant organization of our community made possible all along the line. It is the normal result in the economic field of the independence and the independent groupings which we have had in all significant fields of community life. Of course it is possible to get too exclusively occupied with materialistic standards. But that does not alter the truth that material productivity of things which make for health and reasonable leisure is entirely good, and a worthwhile aim. The tolerance which has permitted and fostered such productivity has been useful to us and to others.

There is nothing new in all this. The same principle which in recent times has been one of the main causes of the productivity of the American business enterpreneurs and the American corporations has been tried before—unfortunately not sufficiently often—and has shown like usefulness in other times and places. It is the principle which in the great days of the Roman Empire—order being established, burdens light, and local autonomy recognized—saw the blossoming of the provincial municipalities and the productivity of their leaders, the competition to adorn their cities with buildings, baths, and aqueducts—an accomplishment which was of an amazing order in the light of the meager technical means then available for utilizing natural resources. It is the principle reflected in the Old Testament praise of Cyrus as the Messiah because he let local peoples worship in their own way rather than in his. It is the principle of tapping a vast source of achievement by having the community with an organization and set of convictions, a rule and role—especially at the leadership level—such as to let the capable do their do under their own motive power and in accord with their own ideas. It is the principle of tolerance.

2. A TOLERANT GOVERNMENT

We saw in the *discord* cases that a common type of discord was characterized by a government too strong in relation to other groups within the community. The totalitarian governments of our own day, with their imposed order based on excessive threat and use of force, have offered conspicuous examples.

Even in a tolerant community the government in order to carry out necessary government functions has to be so strong that there is the possibility for it to go on to too great a monopoly of power. The government has to have adequate power to defend the community, and this alone involves the economic power that comes through the huge monetary expenditures necessary to provide a modern army, navy, and air force, with their manpower, weapons, and equipment, their land vehicles, ships, and air vehicles. The control of this military and naval and air establishment, so long as the government is able to command its obedience, gives the government an overwhelming physical power which it can if need be exert in maintaining political control and order within the community. The government at the center of a great modern state also disposes of the power of a political police force useful to ferret out subversion by the agents of hostile, or potentially hostile, foreign communities; but also usable on the domestic scene to track down those regarded by the government as undesirable for any reason. The government, also, at either the national or local level has to maintain and fortify those institutions—for example, police forces and criminal and civil courts—which are necessary for the preservation of order against those who refuse to observe the reasonable rules of the community—who refuse or think themselves unable to abide within the rules of tolerance, honesty, and equity to the degree essential to a free order.

For these reasons among others, a strong government is a necessity. But in a tolerant community the institutions and the tradition—the rule to go by—and the disposition at leadership levels is such that the government will neither wish nor dare to risk exerting its strength so as to suppress the many independent loci of power—the associations, corporations, groups, and individuals we have described—with their own followings and their own control of economic power. And these many loci of power are diligent in the defense and preservation of their own positions of strength, and have such support at leadership levels all along the line as to be able successfully to challenge a government leadership that sought to take away their independence.

A tolerant government does not suppress criticism of itself, does not forcibly silence its critics or expel competent members of minority groups. It thereby avoids well-known historical causes of decline. Spain went into decline at the height of its power due to that Catholic zeal which suppressed or expelled the very people who would have enabled Spain to hold its own against England in the rivalry for colonies and overseas trade. France made the same error when she expelled the Huguenots, probably her most competent people industrially. At one and the same time she thereby injured herself, and greatly benefited Prussia, England, and the American colonies who harbored these exiles. In America to this day the contributions of the descendants of the Huguenots are outstanding in usefulness to the community. A tolerant government avoids the kind of catastrophe that overwhelmed Germany for want of powerful critics of the Hitlerian regime who might have saved it from incurring the hatred of all the rest of the world and from a blind pushing on to national disaster. Tolerance could have kept at home in Germany and in Italy the exiled scientists who played such a part in the development of American military weapons in the Second World War.

The truth is that when unity in the community is purchased by the suppression of dissent, the price paid is too high for the community to bear. There are those who say that suppression cannot succeed even in the limited aim of suppression. But that is doubtful. The Roman power, had it been sufficiently intolerant and alarmed, could have snuffed out the life of Christ at the start of his ministry. France did achieve a certain degree of unity by throwing out the Huguenots. Hitler did achieve a certain degree of unity by his persecution of the Jews. But in every case the price paid for this kind of unity is bound to be too high. The community needs ability wherever it can find it. There is a substantive shortage of competent people, and persecuting them is on its face a poor way of utilizing a great potential asset. It is much better to have a scheme of political order sufficiently just to win the loyalty of the competent, so as to be able to tolerate their self-directed energies and gain the good of their creativeness.

We remember from the *discord* cases that the government group is no exception to the rule that groups in the community push their own interests. The government by virtue of its law-making and law-enforcing powers is already in a powerful position, and if to these powers is added a monopoly in large areas of business life employing large segments of the population, the government bureaucracy becomes too readily able to protect itself from the consequences of its own mistakes and errors of business judgment. It loses the correctives supplied by competition and a market of free purchasers and sellers.

An analogous situation of too great concentration of power occurred when the rulers of the Church became the wielders of power in the ruling of the state. There was a pushing of Church secular power to the detriment of her proper spiritual functions. In the same way, if modern government adds monopolistic powers in the field of economic production to its necessary political and economic regulatory powers, either or both of two results will take place. Preoccupation with economic power will interfere with the correct exercise of political powers such as those of defense, or the other way round, as in Russia today, where all the rest of community production suffers except in the area of defense, to which the government subordinates all else. Still another result will be that reform is made too difficult, because a government group disposing of economic as well as military and police power is all too able to resist reform and to suppress reformers.

It is not the size of centralized government which is mainly to be feared, unwieldy though that may become when operating in its many useful and necessary spheres of activity. What is to be feared is the monopoly powers which the government may gain over man's livelihood and opportunities and places of work. It is this monopoly which permits the government leaders of totalitarian states to perpetuate their mistakes and to stay in power uncorrected.

In the economic field, then, the important positions of leadership should be dispersed and in the hands of independent individuals and groups. The useful function of government in this field is to curb the excesses of any of these individuals and groups who start pushing their own interests unfairly and to the detriment of the rest of the community. Our thesis is not that the independent individuals and groups in pushing their own interests do no wrong and make no mistakes. They frequently do in fact do wrong and make egregious mistakes, as, for example, the overextensions of credit in 1929 Wall Street, which set in motion the great depression of the thirties. A finer illustration of greed and its penalties would be hard to find. Our thesis is that a government group in pushing its own interest will, like any other group in a position of power and uncurbed privilege, do wrong and make mistakes and that if the government is possessed of overgreat power the mistakes will be too difficult to correct. The history of authoritarian states, ancient and modern, amply proves this thesis.

In a tolerantly organized community the government is in a position to curb the excesses of individuals and groups; but even more important and significant, many individuals and groups are in positions of power and influence enabling them to curb the excesses of government. One sound element in conscious American government policy has been the effort to check monopoly and maintain competition. The point where monopoly can obviously do the greatest harm through mistakes and inertia is where it is least subject to check, and that is in the case of a monopoly of the government itself. The government therefore should have no monopoly in widespread areas of business vital to the welfare and productiveness of the community.

The government can appear usefully as a preserver of order for producers and distributors as well as the protagonist for the long-range interests of an unorganized public of consumers. The government is regulator and servant, not master. In a totalitarian, intolerant community, on the other hand, the government outweighs everyone else and is mainly the protagonist of its own increase of prestige and power, despite its protestations of good intentions for the community. Such is the historical fact.

The strength of the community is not in any one group but in the capable people all along the line. There is not room or scope in a government bureaucracy for the talent of the nation. That talent frets and deteriorates when it has to work mainly by taking orders instead of by exercising its independent ability.

3. FREE INQUIRY AND FREE SPEECH

Cutting Short Mistakes of Fact

Free inquiry and free speech can be sovereign correctors of error. The Nazi government for want of these fell victim to its own propaganda on the "softness of the plutodemocracies." Free inquiry and free speech could have avoided this error in perspective. The self-glorification of the Nazi *Herrenvolk* and the cruel persecution of the Jews both could have been lessened by a candid presentation of the fact that the Jews had contributed at least as much as the Germans to the world's welfare.

A citizen of Hitler's Germany, had the matter been pointed out to him, could have seen the absurdity of attributing the spread of the plague in the Middle Ages to the poisoning of wells by the Jews. He could have been brought to ask whether the Nazi accusations against the Jews were not a chip off this old medieval block. He might have been brought to see that the Jew-baiters of the Middle Ages would have spent their time better in leaving off Jew-baiting and trying to learn something about the actual conditions of the plague; and it might have occurred to him that the Jew-baiters of his own day would do better to uncover the real causes of Germany's economic and political difficulties. But in the absence of free speech there was no hope of any such curative Nazi eye-opening. The leaders pushed on in their mistakes of fact, and brought upon their people the fears and wrath of the world.

The United States has its faults; but lack of free inquiry and free speech is not one of them. Consider the treatment which would be received in the United States by a leader, whether statesman, churchman, or United States Senator, who should try—as some have—to whip up race or group prejudice as a means of advancing his own power and finding a scapegoat for the troubles of the community. At once his ideas and methods are subjected to the attack of critics. Various organizations interested in the protection of minorities, as well as organizations for the persecuted group, by means of newspaper articles, books, speeches, and appeals on radio and television, afford a check on the attempted promotion of fanatical hatred.

Assume for the moment that a dispassionate inquiry would reveal that the ideals and practice of Russian totalitarianism are inconsistent with the decentralization and local initiative necessary for efficiency in agricultural and industrial production of consumer goods. No Russian citizen would be allowed to demonstrate this fact, or to challenge the party line of the leaders. In the absence of free inquiry and free speech the government has no check in following a mistaken line or perpetuating an error. The community continues to suffer the consequences of overgovernment, until such time as, maybe after a period of many years, the totalitarian apparatus becomes so burdensome as to be discarded.

In a tolerant community, free speech exerts its criticism through many channels. Large organized agencies like some of the great metropolitan newspapers and magazines with national circulation express their opinions. Commentators on the radio have their influence and their followings. Individual writers set forth their views in books and articles. No one is obliged to hew to a party line or to espouse an official governmental view. A corrective is thus provided to the type of discord arising from a government or a church holding too tight to a mistaken line of action or deceiving the public in the interest of staying in office or in a position of privilege. Government by scapegoat —the process of blaming, removing from office, and punishing subordinate officials for community hardship in fact due to the policies of the top leadership—can hardly succeed in a state where free and independent critics point out and hammer home their views as to where the fault and the blame really lie. Where free speech prevails, the government and other standard-setting segments of the community get an overhauling from the organized agencies of free speech when they do a conspicuously bad job or get off on a seriously wrong tack. It is hard to succeed with the cover-up and the fraud upon the public characteristic of those states where the top political officeholders are in control of press, radio, and all sources of public information.

A free teaching profession is also a source of useful criticism of the policies and practices of a current ruling regime. In early grades and with younger and uncritical students, every community will think it best to teach the traditional views of the going concern. Otherwise the young will not know where they stand, and will be ill fitted for the scheme of the community where they are going to live; they will be unsettled, like unassimilated foreigners. But at higher levels of education and experience the presentation of all views should be allowed. If the traditional views have been in fact right and are well presented and defended they can hold their own; and if in fact wrong they ought to be upset.

Many members of the teaching profession are slow in sensing changes that have taken place, and this results in their tilting today against the ogres of yesterday, who are no longer the ogres of today. For example, there was a time in the United States when in fact the big financiers and industrial owners were a group with too great power subject to abuse. But when this situation changed and government leaders and those close to them became the holders of the dangerous power, professional teachers too often failed to note the change, and continued to tilt against the old opponents. Despite this slowness, the community has a better chance of striking down too great concentrations of power if the universities and colleges are thoroughly independent, and the professors can speak out from their academic platform and say what they believe.

Popular Confidence

In a tolerant community the free inquiry and free speech are a source of confidence. They allow a citizen to know to the extent of his capacity the true facts of the current situation. He does not fear that the government is concealing from him community problems and difficulties that the government does not know how to solve. He knows that alert critics of those in power can and will disclose the shortcomings of those in power. Loyal critics are not turned into bitter, underground enemies of the regime. Their views can be stated and met on their merits in the open.

The contrary is the case in a totalitarian state. As the shortcomings of the government are concealed for the benefit of those in power, the citizen has no means of knowing the true state of affairs. When Stalin is the head of the single party apparatus, all is praise of Stalin and his wisdom. The citizen may suspect that there will be starvation next year partly because of bad crops and partly because of government mismanagement of farming and distribution. He may suspect from the sudden disappearance to concentration camp of critics and enemies of Stalin, that Stalin fears the truth. He lives in an atmosphere of uncertainty. This lack of confidence is confirmed when, upon Stalin's death, the new head of government denounces Stalin's crimes and errors, and himself succeeds Stalin as the infallible fount of all wisdom and the unerring guide of the people's good.

In the American Civil War, President Lincoln from time to time exercised extraordinary powers to deal with the emergency. Yet he acted within the fundamental American constitutional scheme of individual liberties and rights. Freedom of inquiry, freedom of speech, freedom of the press, free assembly—all were permitted. He regarded neither the government nor himself as sacrosanct. The competent citizens of the North had no reason to fear that truth was being concealed from them, or that if they gave voice to criticism their persons would be in jeopardy.

If a government suppresses opinion that is critical of the government, and allows publication of only its own war communiqués, people get fearful of what they are not hearing. Today they are vulnerable to foreign radio news broadcasts which may confirm their fears.

Tolerance avoids the discords both of party-line bigotry and of indifference—the excesses of too much conviction and too little conviction. Tolerance has conviction and standards, but does not think itself the sole repository of truth. Bigotry and indifference are alike afraid of the truth because of its consequences for each of them. Tolerance welcomes the truth and the confidence that comes with the truth.

Free Speech and Consent of the Governed

The best quick test of the general satisfaction afforded by a regime is the amount of criticism it can tolerate and, in tolerating, overcome. On the contrary, when a regime suppresses views, it is because it knows there is real cause of major dissatisfaction and it is therefore afraid of hostile criticism in an open and free debate. Although the Roman emperors of the second century had absolute power, their regime was giving general satisfaction for the time being, and they did not as a rule persecute their critics. The political intelligentsia of that day, unlike that in the day of Hitler or of Stalin—could say their say. The southern states in the United States before the Civil War suppressed criticism of slavery. The Nazis suppressed views of ordinary humaneness. The Soviet suppresses views in favor of individual ownership of means of production. The Tennessee Fundamentalists —literal interpreters of the words of the Bible—suppressed the views of geologists. In every case the regime—the going concern—was afraid of the power of the suppressed views.

When powerful groups and their leaders can express views critical of the government, the government is put under pressure to alter its practices for the better and towards a more generally satisfactory rule. Free speech and criticism not only evidence the existence of tolerance, but they perpetuate tolerance by keeping the government tolerant in practice. The United States government today can permit the existence of many independent concentrations of power and permit free speech to all, because on the whole the regime is generally satisfactory, and the government need not fear the hostility of the powerful independent groups within the community. On the other hand, neither the Hitler government nor the Stalin government allowed independent power groups to exist within their states. Nor did they permit free speech, because either independent groups or free speech, and most certainly a combination of both, would have meant the downfall of the unsatisfactory rulers.

The Russian governmental attitude against the publication within Russia of foreign news and foreign views, as well as the Russian governmental hesitation to permit unlicensed export of descriptions of Russian life, alike clearly indicate an official lack of confidence, a fear to expose the people to views and descriptions of a system of life and economics that the intermediate leadership and people might conclude was more satisfactory than their own.

In short, the existence of free inquiry and free speech within a community, along with the presence of active independent powerful groups, characterizes a political community that is genuinely confident that its regime is approximating something fair and just.

Technique of Peaceful Change

A political community needs a technique of peaceful change rather than to have change brought about by violence or the threat of violence. Tolerance of free inquiry and free speech provides such a technique. A determined group seeking reform does not need to strike a blow. In the United States, for example, reformers may put across their idea by persuasion, thereby gaining a following of voters who will use the ballot to elect representatives favorable to their view. Thus, in a particular field, wage earners succeed in gaining statutory protection from unsafe or unwholesome working conditions. Or in a much more general field, people of similar opinion—even if the opinion consists mainly of discontent with the powers that be—can build up their numbers sufficiently to form a major new political alignment and upset the nationwide balance of political power, as in the leadership and fusion of popular elements by Andrew Jackson, or later by Franklin D. Roosevelt. Such a major shift in political control could not take place peacefully in an authoritarianly organized community with an all-powerful single-party government in control of press and other media of communication, no matter how badly the community was in need of major political change.

A reformer of true creative genius—consider the case of Jesus—should be allowed to say what he has to say and discover his following, not be persecuted and killed. At any particular actual historical moment, the overlay of conventions and institutions may result in a failure by the powers that be and the dominant opinion of the time and place to recognize this creative man—painter or religious leader or social reformer, whatever his line may be. Unless there is tolerance in the community to let him speak out and do his work, his message may be extinguished.

The desire to hold too tight to a privileged position being as strong as it is, the community needs all the devices it can muster to keep those in authority alert to the need of change. In the *discord* cases we considered the history of the Junkers in Germany, and their too long and too strong political hold. If such a group is to be brought to see the need of reform, it requires not only the efforts of individual critics to demonstrate the Junker errors, but also powerful organized opinion-forming agencies, such as independent newspapers and journals.

While free speech is necessary to peaceful reform, free speech alone is not sufficient to produce such reform. There was plenty of expression of opinion and a *de facto* free speech in France in the days before the French Revolution. The reform then universally recognized as necessary was mismanaged and the extreme disorder of the French Revolution followed. More than free speech had been needed and was lacking, notably a realistic grasp of the principles of good administration, and a sense of equity or fairness which has usually been conspicuously absent in modern French history.

In the *discord* cases we described the method of government by scapegoat, with particular illustration of it in Czechoslovakia, where local officials were blamed for the shortcomings inherent in Communism itself with its system of overgovernment. The beating of propaganda gongs and the blowing up of false and fraudulent issues of personal treachery and alleged defections from the infallible Communist line would be rendered ineffectual in a state tolerating powerful free agencies of inquiry and speech. The sham would be shown up and the blame put not on a scapegoat but where it really belonged. The top-level government would be under heavy pressure to cure the flaws of overcentralized Communism, rather than supported in covering them up.

To combat secret, subversive political activities may require a political police. The danger to the community from a political police is that it may be diverted to the searching out and suppressing of those who though not enemy agents or advocates of violence are making radical criticism of the state. The result of an authoritarian hunting down and weeding out of those who challenge a traditional prejudice is to destroy straight thinking with its truthfully directed effort to see things as they in fact are.

Authoritarian governments try to avoid the appearance on the surface of the ever-present deep unreconciled differences. The attempt is made to compel everyone to adhere to one political line and to state one political opinion. But the suppression of dissent does nothing to cure the causes of the dissent or the need for a better regime. No matter how much the government plays down the fact that it is overreaching the farm for the benefit of Moscow, or that it is subordinating the legitimate demands of the people for better food to its own schemes for power, the facts themselves of the overreaching and of the shortages remain as factors of inherent political instability.

It is otherwise in a tolerantly organized and governed community. The overreaching is curbed and the shortages are remedied by the better methods and organization promoted by the free discovery and free speaking out of truth. The dissenters are given the chance to get their grievance first aired and then cured. There comes about the reality rather than the pretense of a reconciliation of interests.

4. THINGS TOLERANCE DOES NOT MEAN

Tolerance is inconsistent with indifference. The indifferent man has no firm conviction of right or wrong or of what are good rules of personal or social conduct, and he does not care what takes place in the community as long as he himself is comfortable. The tolerant man, on the contrary, has firm convictions of right and wrong, but is willing to put them to the test of inquiry and has a mind open for improvement of what he believes to be good rules.

Tolerance does not mean that the executive, legislative, or judicial branches of government are required to hire or to retain in employment those with radical revolutionary views. Any such requirement would ruin the *esprit de corps* of the particular governmental unit involved, and be injurious both to its tradition and its effectiveness. Free speech is justified as a technique for peaceful change and requires that dissidents be allowed to present their views; but not from a governmental or any other specific platform. There is no reason why an atheist should think he has a right to promulgate his doctrines as a teacher in the faculty of a church school. If they choose to let him, because they think they can soundly defeat him and his arguments, that is sound. But otherwise he must choose some other time and place to expound his views; and this he is allowed to do in a tolerantly organized community.

Free speech is not to be tolerated when inciting to violence. Free speech is protected because it is a method for peaceable reform. When the means itself defeats its own goal—which is what happens when free speech advocates violence—it puts itself outside the law. A government must suppress incitement to violence.

There is a corollary to the proposition that free speech is for the purpose of keeping routes open for a better political community, an opportunity to air grievances within the body politic so that they can be cured. That corollary is that activities outside the field for which free speech principally exists do not have any politically sound reason for asserting a right to free speech. Thus a publisher who wishes to make money by selling crime comics or to shield his sources of information in the libel of an actress is outside the field for which free speech exists, and should not be able to avail himself of a constitutional protection of free speech. The danger in this kind of case is that assertion of the right to free speech in fields where it is not rightly applicable may set opinion-forming people against free speech in its entirety, and thereby jeopardize the institution of free speech and the necessary technique of peaceful change which it provides.

5. CONDITIONS OF TOLERANCE

Mutuality

Tolerance is dependent on mutuality. If any powerful segment of the community pushes its rights too far, it will no longer be tolerated by the rest of the community.

In the event of a strike in a sensitive spot in the public utilities, such as supply of water or electricity, or the transport of food to a great city, and if the effect of the strike was actually to cut off water, food, or electricity, such a strike could not be tolerated. Were the government itself not unduly weak, the strike would be suppressed, if necessary by force of arms and removing recalcitrant leaders. Similar suppression would occur in the case of a refusal of coal miners to work at a time which might hamper an entire community effort—as in war against a foreigner—or if the coal were critically needed for heat in wintertime. The continuance of tolerance as a political method in cases of this kind depends on enough sense of equity in the leaders of the workers to see their due place in the whole community, or enough sense of truth to fact to see that they cannot push too hard too long.

The case is still clearer when a powerful minority group—for example, the Sudeten Germans in Czechoslovakia, whose activities we discussed in *discord*—owe allegiance not to the political order where they find themselves but to an alien regime. Such a minority cannot be tolerated in its violent interference with community order and in its disobedience aimed at overthrow of the government. If the government is strong enough it must suppress such a minority or else lose its own authority. No community government could adopt a policy of autonomy for minority groups within its necessary defense lines if a powerful minority group insisted on loyalty to the enemy's institutions and an alien nationalism.

It is true that the community is most free when its rules have the willing consent of its various groups of citizens, which requires tolerance. It is true that orderly change is most likely to be made possible by letting minorities put forward their views, which also requires tolerance. But when a strategically placed minority attempts to coerce the community, as, for example, in the ways we have just been discussing, all these reasons for tolerance fall by the wayside on account of the intolerance—the failure of mutuality of tolerance—on the part of the minority. Freedom to advocate changes in the current scheme of things presupposes that this be done without disruption of the necessary degree of order for effective community life and without physical violence to the community or to the authorities charged with the preservation of essential order. Otherwise the authorities will deprive the minority of freedom and will be backed by public sentiment.

It is said that in the reign of Edward VI of England the Protector Somerset tried to allow free discussion of religious differences, with the result that religious parties engaged in brawls, rival crowds being led on by fanatic leaders. In such a failure of mutuality of tolerance, freedom is likely to be taken away.

In the United States, for about a decade in the first quarter of the twentieth century there was established a new Ku Klux Klan—with less justification than in the case of the old Reconstruction Ku Klux Klan, which was formed primarily to try to preserve the South from political chaos. This new Ku Klux Klan was designed to promote native, white, Protestant supremacy and to beat down people and ideas it didn't like. The special human objects of its hatred were Roman Catholics, Negroes, and Jews. Among ideas it opposed were internationalism, Darwinism, birth control, and the repeal of prohibition of alcoholic beverages. Its membership is said to have exceeded four million. Fortunately for the United States, the effects of the disapproval of the leading opinion makers of the nation and the fear and perhaps revulsion of the Klan majority itself upon exposure of certain cases of murder and torture perpetrated by its members, as well as the exposure of the corrupt administration of officials elected in certain states by the Klan vote, together were such that the Klan lost ground, its activities shrank, and its membership dwindled. Otherwise the organization could not have been long tolerated by the community, if the community was to preserve order.

If the government itself is intolerant there is obviously no mutuality of tolerance and no tolerance. Only the strongest—the individuals who are able to control the government machinery and police—are free. That is clear.

Even though tolerance is seen to be at the mercy of powerful intolerant groups who render tolerance impossible for want of the necessary mutuality, nevertheless tolerance is still the best method for heading off the growth of such intolerant groups, because, as we have seen, it keeps alive as long as possible the chance for a peaceful reconciliation of differences, and of preventing irreconcilable differences from arising. Even after a severe cleavage of opinion or of interest has occurred, tolerance—accompanied by fairness and truth to fact—is still the best method of eliminating the cleavage. Suppression may maintain an imposed order, but it does not reconcile the disruptive differences.

Responsibility

To the degree that people abuse the scope that tolerance gives them, the community has to put aside tolerance. There has to be an increase of restrictions and the order shifts to a lesser or greater degree away from a free order towards an imposed order.

If the manfacturers of drugs, due to a failure of equity and honesty, and unduly motivated by greed, make false claims for their product, they thereby abuse free speech and subsequently are deprived of it by pure food and drug legislation which requires them to describe their drugs truthfully.

The excesses of commercialism—again an example of greed at work —offend the artistic, the literary, and the truthful. Such an excess, for example, is the prostitution of admirable means of communication, entertainment, and instruction—the radio and television—to advertisers' devices for selling this or that article. The "singing commercials" are one form of such a device. The artistic, the literary, and the truthful are important formers of opinion. It is foolish by excesses of commercialism to build up in these opinion formers a discontent with the American scene. Continued abuse of great media of communication will presumably be reformed by government regulation. It would be better, and better consonant with maximum freedom and tolerance, if a sense of fairness and equity in the advertisers worked a self-cure.

In our discussion of *discord* we saw that the Wall Street group brought restrictive legislative down upon itself when its greed in the nineteen-twenties caused it to lose sight of the fact that its position of influence called upon it in equity to maintain a sound credit structure and a sound securities market. In a community organized with a universal democratic franchise, it is specially incumbent upon the economically powerful—if only for their own good—to observe the rules of equity and honesty, because such a community is prone to "soak the rich" even when they don't deserve it, let alone when they do. However useful the institution of private property may be compared with other methods of economic control, it is possible for private owners by their inequity and dishonesty to dig their own graves and that of private property as well.

The competitive co-operation of the market place is an effective form of economic co-operation, more effective for the community as consumers, as we have seen, than the regimented co-operation of authoritarian communities. But market-place co-operation has its vulnerable spot, which is the centrifugal components which follow from the nature of the accepted aim in the market place. The main factor in the aim is the separate good of each competing individual, and the common good of all is accidental. And unfortunately this accidental good to all is not inevitable or universal, as has been conclusively shown from time to time, noteworthily in the American economic debacle of the nineteen-twenties and early nineteen-thirties, brought on by the shortsighted greed of business leaders. The freedom of the market place—with its undeniable economic advantages—can be best assured over the long term if those having leadership in the market place temper their competition with a sense of equity, seeing their due place in the whole picture and what they owe to others. This is responsibility. In its absence there is a failure of mutuality of tolerance, and the intolerant free marketeers may no longer be tolerated by the whole community.

One reason that Fascism or Communism or any other form of authoritarian rule appeals to a country where selfish leaders of selfish groups have gone too far in their selfishness, is that it looks like the remedy for the resulting distresses and overreachings. And it is a remedy of sorts, but one that, as we have seen, historically has meant unjust order imposed by a government leadership bent mainly on the preservation of its own power and office.

Effects of Hatred and of Envy

Hatred at leadership levels reduces the chance of tolerance. Hatred is itself a natural result of existing intolerance, and often a sign of intolerance, as the hatred in a family toward the authority which has injured or killed a loved one, or the hatred in a citizen resulting from the injustice done him by an official or even from the snub of a privileged boor. Such feelings, when harbored by enough of the capable, may produce a leadership—some of the leaders in the French Revolution illustrate the fact—disposed towards violent reform. Here again, tolerance by those in the places of power and authority is likely to avoid in the first place the growth of this politically potent hatred.

Envy is a threat to tolerance. Envy sometimes serves as the basis of an appeal—although not expressly stated in terms of envy—to the have-nots against the haves, and in that way is a force in the hands of an ambitious leader for intolerant measures injuring the haves, promoted for the purpose of realizing his own ambitions for power.

Effects of an Unaccepted Regime

When a predominant majority of the leaders all along the line, governmental and other, are functioning within a well-established tradition to which they accede and are basically confident that the current political order is in fact satisfactory for the community, and when the community has enough to eat and enough creature comforts, the government is likely to be tolerant. Critics will be allowed to say their say and urge their reforms. Those in political power, being confident of the general consent of the governed, are not afraid of dissenting views. There is a political flexibility favorable to such political changes and adjustments as are needed. Such on the whole has been the case in the United States since Reconstruction days, and tolerance has come fairly easily.

On the other hand, tolerance is much harder for a government when the people are dissatisfied and there are critical and determined leaders ready to organize and speak for large minority groups. In such circumstances if the government has doubts about the soundness of its beliefs and practices, it is afraid to permit open hostile criticism. Yet this is the very time when tolerance of such criticism is most necessary if peaceful political change for the better is to be realized, and either imposed order or disorder are to be avoided. Even in such cases tolerance can be maintained, as we shall see later, if there is a sufficiently powerful ingrained conviction on the part of leaders all along the line in tolerance, honesty, truth to fact, and equity as the political rule which must be faithfully observed.

Effects of Shortage of Resources

Tolerance becomes increasingly more difficult with the increase of shortages within the community. If rainfall is deficient, water has to be carefully allocated, and a system of legally enforced rights to water has to be put into effect. Just to that extent freedom is curtailed as compared with a community where water is plentiful and anyone can dig his own well anywhere and take water from it for either domestic or industrial use. If there are not enough physical assets of a kind essential for some uneconomic purpose that has to be met—for example, military defense of the community—then truth to fact compels the recognition that tolerance cannot be extended to consuming those assets in ways not related to defense. The government may have to segregate some part of domestic production for sale abroad in order to get the means of exchange to import articles necessary for defense. Tolerance and freedom to do as one will with one's manufactures are thereby curtailed.

In cases of this kind, where scope to individuals and to business organizations is cut down by natural resource limitations, still within these limitations the aim of the community should always be to give as much leeway as possible to those doing the work of the community. Tolerance, with its many benefits and its wide distribution of political and economic power, is preferable to regimentation, with its inefficiencies and burdens. When regimentation for some narrow well-defined purpose, like making war, becomes necessary, the previous presence of tolerance in the community has historically resulted in a wider base of self-reliant leaders on whom the community can draw for its temporary narrowly defined effort.

The size of the population relative to the available resources affects the likelihood of tolerance within the community. If the community is so overcrowded that the food supply is insufficient to give all a diet sufficient for health, the organization and laws of the community will be such as to deny equal opportunity to many and to give a sufficiency to certain groups and poverty to others. This is a better result than near-starvation for all, because there is a chance for some kind of constructive, substantive achievement by the favored groups, possibly even resulting in the discovery of a way out of the too great population pressure. Near-starvation for all, on the other hand, would mean a community without any likely prospect of self-improvement, a drab level of poverty-struck ill health all along the line.

Today, looking at the world community as a whole, the pressure of population on assets is causing gloomy predictions as to the possibility of a world decently fed and with decent creature comforts, if the degree of population increase that seems to be in the offing in fact materializes. The prospects for tolerance on the world scene would be dimmed by any such population increases. The increases are not certain to take place, as population control may be achieved by design, or by change of circumstance having nothing to do with human design, or by catastrophe, as in the event of plague or perhaps atomic warfare.

Temperament of People

Where assets and elbow room are sufficient, the leaders of the community by native endowment and by training must be capable of equity and truth to fact, if tolerance and its benefits are to be realized. For example, in North America there were plenty of assets and plenty of elbow room, yet governmental and popular tolerance failed at the times of the American Revolution and the United States Civil War.

Tolerance presupposes enough people willing to do, and capable of doing, the necessary kinds of work that have to be done in the community. Failing this, some degree of compulsion is required. For example, were a farm population, a peasantry, too inept or too tradition-bound to adopt improved methods of farming, a certain degree of regimentation might help to raise farming standards.

The right solution is to have capable farmers themselves determined to do well and to learn. The history of the development of the Great Plains region—despite incidents of man-made erosion and man-promoted dust bowls and disregard of the necessary limitations of freedom due to water shortage—illustrate what a resourceful people can do in adapting themselves to the environment and the environment to themselves. The development and use of farm machinery, the overthrow of the government ideal of 160-acre homesteads (carried over from the Old Northwest Territory, where it had been so successful, in part because there had been enough water) were tributes to the inhabitants of the Plains and to their capacity to benefit from free scope.

XIX. Organization and Institutions in Aid of Tolerance

EVEN if the community has enough leaders and standard setters capable of exercising tolerance and disposed towards it, and even if resources are sufficient to favor it, this is not enough to bring about tolerance in actual practice. No rule can prevail in the community unless fortified by institutional organization which furthers the following of the rule. Without the powerful organization and institutionalized practices of the Church, the beliefs of Christianity would have failed in competition with those of some other religion, had that itself been well organized.

Tolerance will fail unless it is embodied in the daily fabric of the working rules we live by. It needs to be institutionalized in laws and constitutions enforced by courts of law, as well as observed in the practices and standards of our businesses and other occupations. Tolerance becomes part of our accepted rule to go by when it is realized in customs, attitudes, and agencies that have themselves become part of the rule to go by and that we know we have to take into account as well as count upon.

To impose a rule of tolerance is a contradiction in terms. Yet if tolerance is to be preserved, it has to be enforced against a recalcitrant minority. For example, if most of our leaders are convinced of the value of free speech as a method for peaceable change, then attempts to suppress free speech can be dealt with by a provision in the fundamental law of the land forbidding interference with free speech, and a system of law courts and enforcement officers such that interferences with free speech are in fact defeated. Without this institutional protection of the rule of free speech, the rule would be lost. There would be too many exceptions and violations. Some officials of local or general governments, in the interest of holding on to their offices, would silence their critics. The legal institution and restraint is needed to hold in line the man under such pressure from his motives of immediate self-interest that he will not stay in line of his own accord. If he and others like him are not kept in line with the help of the institution—the organized system of free speech—the rule is lost, no longer anything that people can count upon, no longer a functioning object of loyalty.

If a recalcitrant man is compelled by a law court and the law-enforcing agencies to act tolerantly when he doesn't want to, of course he is not free. Freedom, as we shall later see, comes about from a man's unfettered belief in the rule which he follows and by which he is governed, having the rule as part of his worthwhile role. But this compulsion, this institutional fortification of the rule of tolerance against the intolerant maximizes freedom for everyone else and sustains the free order.

If enough of the leaders and standard setters in the community do not believe in the rule of tolerance, then for the time being there is no chance of a tolerant community, or of an organizational or institutional system which will secure present tolerance.

1. ORGANIZATION AND INSTITUTIONS IN AID OF MANY LOCI OF POWER

We have seen that the best chance for the community to avoid arbitrary government lies in the independent power of many individuals and groups.

One way to build up powerful individuals and groups—a way proved effective both by present and past history—is by means of the institution of private property. This is because private property is likely to result in a widespread number of people and associations of people having economic independence and the independence of view that can go with it, along with a numerically sizable set of backers and followers. The principle of private property, roughly stated, is that the possession, use, and transfer of things and relations that have value are recognized as in the control, as far as possible, of individuals and independent associations of individuals rather than in the control of the officials of the politically organized community, the state.

If the barons in England had had no property and no following, they could not have obtained Magna Carta, the great charter of subsequent political liberties. If the great industrialists and business corporations of today had no property and no following, they could not maintain their freedom from the domination of a government which monopolized industrial property.

In the United States it is private property which has given producers the independence to control the processes of production and to bring forth a large surplus over what is necessary for the satisfaction of basic needs. On such a surplus depends the possibility of feeding, clothing, and housing of those engaged in literature and the arts and sciences, and those who staff hospitals, colleges, libraries. Industrialists who have proved themselves capable of producing and distributing articles useful to the community and wanted by it, have, as a result of the relatively impersonal rules of private property and a free market, come into control of the instruments of production. In countries where there is no institution of private property, it is the politically tough who come into control of production; it is those who survive in the cutthroat competition of political power—a competition bearing no relation to competence in economic production—who gain authority over the instruments of production and their use.

Men are so inefficient that they need constant stimuli to work with maximum effectiveness. Any organization of men engaged in producing economic goods ought for the good of the community to put out in value of product more than it uses up in value of labor and materials. This requires good management of the enterprise. The spur of having to make both ends meet financially and something left over is an effective spur in stimulating good management. Success in making both ends meet plus a profit is directly related to capacity to manage efficiently the instruments of production.

The motives of prestige and personal power operate in every political and industrial system. But a bare desire for prestige and power served by a ruthless disposition does not make for as desirable leadership of the work of the community, as a desire for prestige and power served by the ability to produce efficiently, which last is necessary for survival of a business leader under a system of private property, because if he produces inefficiently and at a loss, he will have to go out of business.

The motives of those seeking political power are no more gentle in action than the motives of those seeking economic power. The industrially competent are likely to make better directors of industry than the politically tough.

Private property cannot think of itself as the be-all and end-all of community life. It must be tempered with truth to fact, and the leaders of the community must have their eyes open to see other vital community necessities—those of defense, for example. A wide base of competent industrialists—developed in a regime of private property —will not make up for a failure to prepare to meet real threats to the community. The relatively poverty-struck and despotically directed Hitler Germany might well have defeated in war the economically broader-based, freer, and immeasurably wealthier, but ill-prepared and blindly led Britain and France.

A free economy, with its free market and with private owners in charge of production and distribution, has proved itself in meeting the day-to-day material needs of the public and providing for an amenable day-to-day life. But it is no guarantee of victory in war against some belt-tightening challenger, concentrated and intent on the means of overthrowing his rich neighbor. A totalitarian regime might succeed in selecting the best and most competent men to head up the lines of production required for the specific purpose of military conquest and give these men their head for the necessary effort. Such a regime might well overcome—by utilizing this very principle of freedom to the competent—the leadership of a much more powerful community which mobilized inefficiently its potentially greater available strength.

We have already mentioned the great business corporations in the United States, as groups exerting independent economic power and as a significant part of the structure of the many loci of power within the community. These corporations, authorized by statute law, are highly important among the institutionalized aids to tolerance. The business corporation structure has made it possible to gather under the control of corporate managements the huge financial resources contributed by stockholders and creditors, which are necessary in large-scale business activity—for example, in the production and distribution of electric power, in transportation, in many branches of manufacturing, and in banking. The growth of the business corporation has gone hand in hand in the United States with the growth of our unprecedentedly great productive assets.

Unlicensed scope cannot be allowed to these corporate creatures of statute. Here, as always, tolerance has to be tempered with truth to fact—in this case the fact of the temptation of powerful individuals or powerful groups to grasp too much and to overreach their neighbors. In the institutional fortification of tolerance so as to give maximum freedom all along the line, we have to guard against abuses of freedom. President Theodore Roosevelt found it nesessary to take measures against those he described as "malefactors of great wealth" and to engage in "busting the trusts." Institutional protection has to be given to organizations of workers—labor unions—to set up a locus of power against possible overreaching of workers by stockholders and management. And then in turn safeguards have to be erected against abuse of union power, as in irresponsibility in observing contracts, or the misuse of funds taken from a not-too-intelligent membership by financially corrupt union leaders.

Antitrust acts are enacted by legislatures in order to avoid too great concentration of industrial power in too few hands, on the same principle that checks and balances are constitutionally maintained between government agencies to prevent, for example, too much concentration of power in the executive part of government.

For purposes of determining the political health and degree of freedom in two countries whose institutions of economic ownership and control are being compared, we have to look at the results in actual practice, rather than at theoretical statements, and have to balance the bad against the good.

In the United States, our kind of free economic and free market organization on the whole works out so that those demonstrated competent in industrial and other economically productive or serviceable fields, direct the economic processes of the country. Along with this good we have to admit the bad—that too often these competent leaders have as their main aim taking care of themselves and letting the Devil take care of the hindmost. Success in selling is their ideal good, the modern golden calf that rules their lives.

In the Soviet Union, on the other hand, the communistic, centrally controlled economic and market organization in practice means that the political leaders direct the agricultural and industrial processes of the Soviet Union for the benefit of the leaders and the maintenance of their own power, and in the interests of industrial workers at the expense of farmers. Along with this bad, we have to admit the good— that the Russian leaders maintain a realistic scheme of national defense, and the necessary production of armament and equipment to make it effective.

The present economic problems of the Soviet Union and of the United States are very different. In the Soviet Union the main problems are those of shortages of consumer goods, including a sufficient diet, and those of transportation. As yet the centralized and bureaucratized methods of economic control in Russia seem to have proved inordinately slow in solving the problems. In the United States the problems are more in the field of unbalances. When existing consumers have at a given moment about all the new and not-so-new automobiles they need for everyone except those newly reaching adult years, what is going to keep consumers buying (and should they keep buying) new automobiles at a rate which will keep the workers in the automobile industry fully employed? Or again, if there has been a burst of buying (and producing) consumer goods all along the line stimulated by borrowing all along the line and a large consumer debt, what will happen when the consumers decide to go slow in incurring new debt and instead to use a larger proportion of their current earnings in paying off the old? The answer is likely to be a falling-off in buying, partial layoff of workers, and a consequent further reduction in consumer buying power and further hesitation in incurring new debt. Obviously we are far from a solution of the problem of maintaining evenly spread, evenly balanced production and distribution.

The Marxians mistakenly assert that a system of property ownership in which private owners compete with one another and are required to show a profit if they are to stay in business, means that the workers are gradually impoverished and deprived of the use of the output of their labor, which is appropriated by the owners in their profits, the workers being correspondingly expropriated. Practice has demonstrated the error of this Marxian assertion. The workers in the United States have in fact had an ever-higher standard of living and an ever-increasing command of real wealth. Profits are invested in capital equipment, which is just a way of saying that they are paid to workmen for producing capital goods, such as machinery and equipment, which are "consumed" by nobody, being instead consumed in the process of making consumers' goods or other producers' goods. The shoes, food, and clothing, and other useful consumable articles are bought not only by those who make or process them, as when the farmer or the worker in a grocery buys a suit of clothes, and the worker in the clothing establishment buys groceries. The consumables are also bought by those workers engaged in producing the capital equipment that is consumed by nobody, as well as by those engaged in services, such as garage attendants and government workers, and also by those managing the various phases and processes of the economy.

The question at issue is not at all one of expropriating the working class of what it produces; but rather of what is the best way to achieve the most efficient production and distribution of goods, and whose are the best hands to have control of this production and distribution. The only way workers could be in fact expropriated would be by having such unbalances in production that the goods would not clear in exchange, or by having actual shortages in the amount of goods produced, or by having a distribution system so bad that it backed goods up with an ensuing failure to keep the workers producing. Any of these results would be more likely to occur in more serious form under a control directed by political leaders selected for their ruthlessness or for their political persuasiveness and promises, or for their subservience to a political overlord, rather than under a control directed by those proved competent in business by success in competition in the very processes of production and distribution.

The strictly economic purpose of economic organization and institutions is to further: first, the production and distribution of what is needed for a healthful life and a good and wholesome standard of living; and second, the provision by those engaged in production and distribution of more than enough to provide for themselves so that there will be the surplus necessary to sustain the arts, letters, and sciences, the universities, museums, hospitals, churches, the varied activities and lines of inquiry, and those engaged in them, which advance knowledge and the ability of men to control their environment and themselves. It is this surplus which furnishes food, clothing, and shelter to intelligent researchers and to other people endeavoring to find methods for the rational use of renewable resources, for example, fresh water and crops, and attempting to discover new economic resources and new types of useful materials and fuels. It is these researchers and students who can lay the foundation for a new technology that is mankind's best hope for avoiding an eventual evil day when shortages of resources, perhaps notably the metals and food, would otherwise bring about a world, which if not actually poverty-struck, would at least have to live by standards of a good life far less dependent on material possessions than the present-day American standard.

The best and most influential positions in the community will come into the hands of the ambitious and the energetic; and this is true of the economic field as of others. Our problem is to have our organizational and institutional set-up such that these positions will be as widely distributed as possible, so that we can tap the abilities of as many of the ambitious and energetic as possible, and not have the livelihood and activity of all subject to the control of a very few leaders of a government with monopolistic economic power.

When equalitarians are distressed because too few of the people own too much of the wealth, as if one one-hundredth of the people owned one-fifth of the wealth, the remedy they are likely to propose is socialism or Communism, which in practice means that not one one-hundredth, but one one-millionth of the people will control the wealth, this one one-millionth being the leaders of the political government. The fact that the political leaders may be changed from time to time by popular election, or, as is the case in many countries, by palace revolution, does not alter the fact of overcentralized bureaucratic control and its liability to mistakes which are hard to correct for want of the existence of any location of correcting power, or any institutional correcting mechanism.

The "wealth"—the land, the natural resources, and the productive equipment of the country—should certainly, in any well-ordered modern community, in the course of a few years, produce several times over its own present value. The interest of the community is in seeing this annual product sufficient and well distributed. No matter what the physical possibilities of production or even overproduction may be at a given moment in present or future history, it is a waste of the community effort to produce and distribute inefficiently, to have too many people engaged in any economic effort that could be equally well or better performed by fewer people. The economic question to be asked in determining what institutions—what methods of ownership and control—are best, is the question, What methods will bring into being and distribute most satisfactorily this annual product? The answer is indicated by the facts that a method such as that of private property, which gets the control into a relatively large group of leaders selected because of their proved success in production and distribution, is going to be better than a method such as government ownership, which gets control into too few hands, and those few selected for abilities having nothing to do with skill in economic production or distribution.

Decentralization and wide dissemination of economic control throughout the community go hand in hand with—it is almost another aspect of—the many loci of independent political power in the community, which we have seen to be necessary to avoid the *discord* that has invariably characterized communities subject to overpowerful government. Important as the institution of private property has been historically in the stimulation of economic productivity, it has been even more important as a source of independent, self-reliant leaders within the community and as a means of maintaining within the community politically powerful individuals, groups, and associations, all of whom serve as bulwarks against a too-powerful concentration of power in one spot, notably in a government officialdom which controls the means of livelihood of all.

Well-laid Taxes

Taxes are compulsory contributions for the maintenance of government officials, employees, and the activities carried on or supported by government. In the United States today tax contributions are made in money payments. At various other times or places they are or have been made in kind, that is to say, in the form of goods and services, or in forced labor.

The inescapable reason for the laying of taxes in an organized community is that they are needed to provide supplies or revenue to maintain essential government functions, for example, defense or the administration of justice. Taxes are also used, either deliberately or inadvertently, for the regulation of the conduct of business in the community. Taxes are also laid in aid of social reform along lines that can be influenced by the incidence of taxation.

Even on the narrowest construction of necessary government authority, the taxes which have to be laid and collected to support the essential legislative, judicial, and executive functions within a complex modern community run to an extremely large amount. The fact-finding preliminary to legislation or regulation, the maintenance of legislatures and their necessary ancillary personnel, the exercise of police powers in aid of health and public order, the establishment and support of public education, the maintenance of judges, clerks, and other personnel of courts of law, and, beyond all else in costliness, the maintenance of armed forces with their equipment, means of transportation, and their weapons, land, sea, and air—all these must be provided by taxation. If additional undertakings—for example, old-age benefits and unemployment insurance—are regarded by the community as government functions, these too require the imposition of some form of taxes to cover the costs.

Well-known regulatory taxes in the United States have been among others tariffs on imports to put foreign producers at a disadvantage in competing with American producers, and taxes on oleomargarine or its sales to put oleomargarine producers at a disadvantage in competing with the dairymen who produce butter. The federal government in 1866 levied a prohibitive 10 per cent tax on state bank notes in order to force banks into the national banking system. It would be possible, if federal government officials and legislators should become convinced that there are cancer-provoking qualities in the tars in cigarette smoke, for a graduated tax to be laid related to the quantity of tars in cigarettes in interstate commerce, which would result in regulation of the content of cigarettes available to the public.

Sometimes there have been important accidental regulatory effects of taxation, as in the injury to good forestry practices and tree conservation, brought about in some areas by a general property tax falling equally on all lands of equal value. This injury is due to the fact that trees take a long time to mature, so that a general property tax with current, present-day, undelayed incidence may make it difficult for the forester to let his trees, or enough of them, grow to maturity, and make it impossible for him to put his forest on a permanent yield basis as opposed to a present-day clean-sweep cutting.

In the laying of taxes for essential government functions or for purposes of regulation or for social improvement, two areas of principle —one economic and the other political—have to be observed to insure that the impact of the taxes on the community will not prove harmful.

The first principle is strictly economic: taxes are to be laid in such a way as not to hinder the ability of the community to produce the greatest amount of useful and usable goods of which it is capable. Farm and industrial organizations, individual farmers and workers, and individual farm and industrial leaders must not have their ability to produce to meet the community needs cut down by taxation. The impact of taxes must not impede the construction of new equipment and new factories. The way must be left open for innovators in commerce and industry to get started and to get ahead.

Under the system of control and management of industry in the United States today, our great corporations produce a large proportion of the manufacturing and industrial output that serves the economic needs of the community. Taxation should be laid so as not to impair the productive strength of such corporations.

In the area of production of economic goods a great corporation has an advantage over a small one in the size and arrangement of its plants. It can afford to build, for example, for maximum efficiency in producing heavy and relatively heavy equipment and appliances.

Yet individuals and managers of small corporations may have unorthodox or radical production ideas superior to those of the management of the great corporations. These ideas, inventions, or innovations very likely represent an economic threat to established equipment and machinery, perhaps to a huge capital investment. In that case the current dominant corporations in whatever line is threatened by the new ideas may be mainly interested in slowing down the impact of the innovations by buying them out or by resisting in some other way the upsetting effect of the innovations. Taxes must be laid in such a way as to permit the innovator to amass the necessary purchasing power to compete with the established corporations.

Taxation to raise large amounts has to be broadly based, laid on widespread business exchanges and transactions, or if laid on income then laid all along the line, because it is the entire working effort of the whole community which alone throws off enough product or brings in enough income to sustain large taxation. The truth of this is easily illustrated in the case of income taxes in the United States by the figures on distribution of individual incomes. According to the United States Treasury Department, of the total adjusted gross income of $268 billion reported in the year 1956 on federal individual income tax returns, over $200 billion fell in income classes of under $10,000, and only $27 billion dollars in income classes of over $20,000. The federal individual income tax liability in that year amounted to about $33 billion.

It is hard to tell when the point is being approached at which the capable leadership level of the community will have their performance cut down by too heavy or badly laid taxes. It is easy enough in retrospect to see when the thing has happened. In Rome the economic strength of the empire was due to the ambitions and energy of the leading citizens of the municipalities. We remember that the creative activity of these leaders was crushed by taxes and by the imposition of personal liability for the taxes laid upon their communities. We also reviewed the political and economic effects of the irrationally laid taxes in France in the days just before the French Revolution.

If the general standard of living in an industrialized community is improving, if food is in plentiful supply, if capital equipment is being maintained and enlarged to keep pace with enlarging needs for the goods turned out by it, if better methods of production are being developed and put into use, if education and the arts and sciences are flourishing, and if public health services, transportation, and other public utilities are in good and improving condition, then, whatever else may be right or wrong in the community, the evidence is persuasive that the tax impact is not too burdensome in an economic sense.

More than strictly economic considerations need to be observed in taxation. There is a political consideration of equal importance—namely, that taxes be laid and their burden fall in such a way as to foster the many loci of economic and political power necessary to a free order and its preservation.

This principle of preservation of many loci of power is generally well observed in the laying of taxes in the United States today. Routes are left open to places of independent economic and political power both for organizations and individuals.

Corporation taxes have not been so high as to injure corporations or their shareholders. The federal corporate income tax has been treated by corporations as if it were an item of cost in their operations, and its economic impact has fallen on the users and consumers of the corporate product. The corporations have an independent influence as centers of economic power. Able men find scope for their energies and ambitions within the corporate structure. The officers of the corporations are recognized as leaders in their communities.

The fact that capital gains are taxed at a relatively low rate means that individuals who are shareholders, but do not otherwise function within the corporate structure, can attain economic independence if the corporation itself prospers. Such individual owners of capital can also participate in the building of new corporate or other ventures, and thereby increase their economic independence and perhaps gain a following for their ideas.

Taxation could obviously be used to cut down the possibility of gaining this individual economic independence. It is obvious that if 90 per cent of a taxpayer's income over $100,000 including capital gains should be taxed away, the nine-tenths would no longer be available to him for investment in business. To the extent that new investment is needed for improving or enlarging the plant—the productive equipment—of the community, it can be obtained in other ways: for example, from small investments by a great number of investors, or, in the case of already established corporations, by the use of their own retained earnings for betterment or increase of their plant, or by investment by the government in the necessary new plant.

The question involved is not mainly economic, despite the fact that the intelligent initiative of some large investors might be lost to the community. The question is mainly political and relates to the wisdom of reducing the economic and political power of the large independent investors by cutting down their wealth and with it their position of influence in the community. Thereby their effectiveness as possible critics of government policy is reduced and also their ability to act as checks on the growth of arbitrary government. Along with this—the other side of the same coin—is the increased trend towards a substantial government monopoly of both economic and political power, which we have seen to be the essential condition of the kinds of *discord* characteristic of too-great government power.

In the United States today there are no discriminatory taxes against the organized agencies of free speech and criticism, such as the newspapers, or publishers of books or magazines, the radio and television stations, or the theater. Private educational institutions, which can be a great force for the expression and teaching of independent opinion, are exempt from tax on their educational property and activities.

It may be that the present American tax structure has too great an impact on those of middle income—perhaps the doctor, or teacher, or other practitioner of a profession or the proprietor of a useful small business. There may be an impairment of their chance as independent-minded citizens to build enough economic security to participate as much as they might in the growth of a large body of self-reliant individuals, and the avoidance of a political power too concentrated and representing too few facets of interest.

If the broad-based taxation necessary to raise the large amounts of revenue required for basic government purposes—such as defense, for example—were in the form of transaction taxes, as on sales all along the line from raw materials to finished product, or other taxes relatively easy to understand, administer, and collect, the income tax could then be used positively so as to strengthen local leadership and local organization.

The income tax could be reserved for those purposes which have traditionally been carried on to a large degree locally by public-spirited citizens, as in the fields of higher education, scientific and medical research and development, museums, privately endowed schools and colleges with their advantages of relative freedom from political control and consequent freedom to experiment, and the like local activities pushing forward men's understanding of a complicated and baffling world.

It would be possible in this use of the income tax to get the benefits of both a central over-all look at the needs of health and education and also of the principle of money applied directly at the scene and under the local control of those familiar with the local work and the local problem. The central over-all look as of a given date might indicate, let us say, that $1 billion is needed to be spent each year for the next five years in the improvement of medical education. Income tax would be laid to include this amount. A credit against the tax for the entire amount due from any given taxpayer would be allowed to the taxpayer upon his contributing the amount directly to medical education. Such a tax would have at least two effects: first, it would assure the spending on medical education of the amount thought desirable by the central over-all look; second, it would assure the spending locally at the scene under decentralized initiative and control of the amounts contributed by the taxpayers. There would of course be nothing to prevent contributions in excess of the amount of the strict income tax liability. The many loci of power necessary to the free order would be strengthened. The central bureaucracy would be unwound by no longer having to have a large personnel concerned with the handling and administrations of funds for medical education or with that degree of substantive control of medical education that follows along with financial control.

Were such a principle of income taxation as this applied in the fields of science, health, and in the less static branches of education, as well as in the development of the arts and letters in schools, colleges, museums, and libraries, we could expect such a blossoming in these fields as has hitherto been unknown.

2. INSTITUTIONS IN AID OF FREE INQUIRY AND FREE SPEECH

We have seen that free inquiry and free speech provide a useful method of checking mistaken courses of action from being carried too far, of keeping the government tolerant in actual practice, and thereby aiding the maintenance of many loci of power. They also provide the best technique yet discovered for peaceful rather than violent political change. But how can free inquiry and free speech themselves be best fortified by the organization and institutions of the community so as to enable those who believe in them to preserve them against overzealous reformers and other intolerant pushers of particular interests?

The written Constitution of the United States has contained since

December 1791 a provision guaranteeing the right of free speech against abridgment by statute enacted by the federal legislature. There are also state constitutional provisions imposing like restrictions on state legislatures. The protection of freedom of speech against abridgment by state legislatures and governments has been strengthened by federal constitutional provisions in existence since July 1868. The pertinent provisions of the federal constitution are in Amendment I and Section 1 of Amendment XIV. Amendment I reads:

Congress shall make no law respecting an establishment of religion, or prohibiting the free exercise thereof; or abridging the freedom of speech, or of the press; or the right of the people peaceably to assemble, and to petition the government for a redress of grievances.

Section I of Amendment XIV reads:

All persons born or naturalized in the United States, and subject to the jurisdiction thereof, are citizens of the United States and of the State wherein they reside. No State shall make or enforce any law which shall abridge the privileges or immunities of citizens of the United States; nor shall any State deprive any person of life, liberty, or property, without due process of law; nor deny to any person within its jurisdiction the equal protection of the laws.

At the present time in the United States freedom of speech and of the press, freedom of religion, and the right of peaceable assembly are among the fundamental personal rights shielded by the Fourteenth Amendment against attack by the States. That is to say, the liberties and immunities of the citizens protected by the First Amendment against impairment by the national government, have in effect received like protection by the Fourteenth Amendment against State governments.

An observer from another land, or a skeptic at home, might be doubtful about the efficacy of paper barriers such as these—words in a written constitution—to stand in the way of the desires of officials to retain their offices by silencing criticism, or to keep the powers that be from cutting off the voice of those pressing for unpalatable reform, or to act as a curb on political leaders of temporary political majorities in their efforts to use all available methods to assert their own position against that of unpopular minorities. Yet the fact is that such barriers, when incorporated in the traditional structure of community life and protected by a functioning organization of law courts and enforcement agencies, become a living part of that "rule to go by" to which leaders and people adhere. The written Constitution and the appropriate institutions and rules for its maintenance are something to which people can and do rally as the familiar protectors of their familiar rule and role. The fact that you and I will not know where we stand or what we can do or what we can expect and count upon, if our established rules and agencies are upset, makes in actual practice a powerful opinion and feeling in favor of the written Constitution and the institutional enforcement of its provisions.

The history of the decisions of the law courts in the United States, feeling their way to a rule which protects free speech as a technique for peaceful change, and yet warding off the danger of free speech as an inciter of violent change, affords a practical illustration of a right political rule—in this case the rule of tolerance—receiving the organizational and institutional embodiment necessary to its preservation as the rule of the community.

We know that a technique for political change is essential. Violence, either in denying change or as a technique for change, is wasteful, destructive, and prone to excess, as we saw in the *discord* cases. Free speech, on the other hand, is a useful and constructive technique for change. It is for this reason that we try to fortify and institutionalize free speech.

Those opposed to freedom of speech hold that the state can be undermined by subversive ideas as well as by subversive violence, and that just as the powers that be are justified in suppressing the latter, so they are in suppressing the former. The answer we have already indicated. There must be a technique for change. We outlaw violence because destructive. We accept free speech because possibly constructive. We know that suppression or violence mean either imposed order or disorder. We cut off free speech when it directly incites to violence and disorder, because our principal political reason for protecting free speech is that it alone can be a nonviolent and relatively orderly agent of change. In the absence of incitement to violence, we protect free speech.

When we do not permit free speech to incite to violence, we are maintaining order because we know that order is itself the first condition of any freedom or security. We hope that the order we are protecting is in fact the only kind of order that can be maintained over the long term without discord—a free order changing by way of peaceful growth, an order characterized by tolerance, honesty, truth to fact, and equity. Any other order is an imposed order.

Revolutionists, who by experience know the power of free speech, are likely to be the first to suppress it when they become the government. Since they got their own start through the power of the word, they fear the power of the word in the mouth of their opponent. In the *discord* cases, both Mussolini and Hitler provided demonstrations of this. The former, who rose by way of newspaper editing, bit the hand that fed him.

Let the would-be radical reformers say their say—short of incitement to violence, which must be firmly suppressed. Those advocating violence must expect violence to be used against them. Then, if our own order is reasonably just, we can defend it more easily and persuasively than the reformer can attack it. We can succeed in this defense, because we have on our side all the primitive desire of people for security, for a familiar rule to go by.

Free speech might be made more responsible and less liable to abuse if we required publishers of political pamphlets, broadsides, and radio broadcasts to state the actual interests behind the publication. For example, each publication could be required to state those who have financed it and their political affiliations. Such a requirement would naturally lead to a fear on the part of a reforming writer or speaker or his supporters that they might be persecuted if the authorities knew just who they were and what were their interests. The way to obviate such a fear is to have the institutionalized rules such that a speaker or writer knows certainly and reliably that he will invariably be protected from persecution. In that event, to require a statement of the backing and affiliations of a political utterance would not hamper free speech. It would render it more communicative and truthful. We all know that in the ordinary concerns of life we listen to our neighbor with better understanding when we are aware of his background and interests. What the man is, and what he is after, are parts of his expression just as much as his words, and enable us better to understand the words and the intent with which they are stated.

The conditions for the maintenance of free speech over the long term are: that enough of the leaders and the able of the community strongly believe in tolerance as a political rule; that the political institutions which we have just been talking about—the constitutions, laws, and their organized agencies—are appropriate to the maintenance of free speech; and that on the whole the affairs and situation of the community are satisfactory enough so that most of the capable all along the line are willing to be tolerant both of free speech by others and in their own use of free speech, so that there is present that mutuality which we have seen to be a basic condition of tolerance. If any of these conditions fail for long, free speech will fall before the threat of force or the use of force.

3. INSTITUTIONS IN AID OF SCOPE TO MOVE AHEAD

In describing the characteristics of a free community we noted that there was mobility between classes. Those who were competent, no matter from what level of social standing or prestige they took their origin, were able to move to a place commensurate with their abilities.

It is true that in any large complex community people arc to a certain extent sorted out by the facts of geography as well as by their abilities into the kinds of work they will be found doing. In that sense there is bound to be a classification of function, so that there are, for example, more or less well-defined classes such as those of farm labor, mining labor, factory workers, clerical workers, managers at various levels, and those controlling the uses of property—land and productive equipment—either as private owners or as political committees. Any of these classes can as a class move in esteem and in position in the social scale as, for example, if its work becomes better paid, better mechanized and so less physically burdensome.

If those within the several classes are performing their respective functions well, there is nothing harmful in the presence of these classes based on function—indeed their presence is unavoidable as a result of the necessary division of work of an effective community. What is harmful and what should as far as possible be avoided is that these classes become fixed to such a degree that there is not free movement of individuals between classes. Those of ability should not be too much hindered from going up the ladder, or those without ability too much bolstered from going down. Anyone capable of making a real contribution to the good of the community should be given the chance to get into a position where he can do so.

Barriers to free mobility between open classes are raised in various ways: by statute, by custom, often fortified by organized religion. Barriers often involve the prohibition of marriage across class lines. Classes as defined by ancient custom—as a priestly class, a warrior class, a farmer and merchant class, a laboring class—may after the lapse of time no longer parallel at all accurately the main interests of the community or be in agreement with current economic techniques. As a result, the marriage rules, and class and sub-class boundaries, become enormously complex, as in the caste system in India. Whatever caste may have done in the way of letting a man know where he stood in some aspects of his social and economic life, and to that extent providing him with a rule to go by, none the less it became a burden which the community much needed to change.

A modern example of class plus caste—with its legacy of problems still unresolved—was that of the relations between white and Negro in the United States in the days of Negro slavery. After the ending of slavery the caste line still remained, with its usual differentiation of social and economic standing.

There are institutions that inherently work against rigid class lines. We can see at least three that are conspicuous in the United States. One is a free market, which gives anyone, or any business organization, a chance for economic improvement by producing and bringing to the market what people want to buy. If I offer a good salable article at a lower price than my competitor, I can sell it, irrespective of who I am. Another is the vertical arrangement of our industrial units, our corporations, which cut across any horizontal class lines that might be historically present, and in which efficiency requires active co-operation from top to bottom of the organization, everyone being a useful part of the useful whole. The third institution we have that tends to break down class lines and which is notably effective in doing so is the universal franchise for the electing of political officeholders. As we have seen, the normal officeholder wants to get and perpetuate his office more than he wants almost anything else, and this requires him, in a community like ours where there is more than just a single political party, to cater to the vote of any large block in the electorate. Such catering is incompatible with his supporting customs or traditions which are oppressive to any large group of voters in his constituency. This means that if the members of any large class in the community have the right to vote and the intelligence to organize for their own betterment, and if they are allowed to vote and to organize, the officeholders will propose measures favorable to bettering the position of the class and its members.

This very virtue of the universal franchise in other than a single-party political system, the fact that it almost compels officeholders to look out for the interests of large blocks in the electorate, has its accompanying weakness which we have already mentioned—that is, that the officeholders come to represent too much and to be too much influenced by the standards, opinions, desires, and envies of the unconstructive. Possible ways of dealing with this weakness of the universal franchise we consider later.

The leaders of those groups which hold the position of prestige and political dominance in the community should see to it that members of other groups get an opportunity for an education as good as they are capable of acquiring. A dominant group should not humiliate the members of other groups. A dominant group should give fair business opportunities to the members of other groups. If these rules were observed, the members of the groups not yet assimilated to the tradition of the going concern would have their chance to prove what they had in them to contribute to the community. If they in fact had the capabilities to do well by themselves and by the community, they would make their way and gain their standing in a free order.

In various past times of history as well as today, there have been groups under severe degrees of oppression, segregation, and hostile prejudice who have none the less continued generation after generation to produce their fair share of great and very great men. Continued hostile prejudice against such a group is not justifiable, even though difficulties of assimilation may still remain. The dominant groups of the community may still correctly feel that this group—perhaps as a result of the very excellence of its own tradition—does not easily become assimilated to the ways of the going concern. The best prospect of assimilation of such a group lies in the increasing justice and attractiveness of the going concern.

Institutions giving people their chance to get ahead should not be confused with institutions catering to the less capable at the expense of the more capable. Such a confusion has at times certainly taken place in American schools, when equalitarian standards have been allowed to outweigh the fact that the good of the community and the advances in its health, welfare, knowledge, control over natural resources, and achievement in the arts and letters are all dependent on the excellent. Education appropriate to varying degrees of intelligence and varying temperaments is needed, always with an eye to the achievement, preservation, and defense of a free order.

4. INSTITUTIONS IN AID OF TOLERANT GOVERNMENT

When discussing the need in a modern community for a government strong enough to perform even the minimum of essential government functions, we saw that this meant a very powerful government indeed. We then pointed out the possibility that such a necessarily powerful government would, by the fact of taking on additional functions, be self-aggrandized to overgovernment. In Communist Russia the control of army and police has been in the same hands that controlled other great segments of community activity, as its industry, its transportation, and a great part of its agriculture. The problem is an old as well as a modern one. The relatively flexible rule of the early empire by the Roman imperial government, characterized by the self-government of the cities throughout the empire, gave way to overgovernment and overtaxation as the central government later overrode the freedom of the cities. It is as though in the United States today the relative self-government of the great private corporations were supplanted by a central government ownership and management of industry. In each case, ancient and modern alike, a fairly free and creative, but complex, form of order would have given way to a more primitive, simple, cumbersome, and arbitrary form of order.

One historical way to keep a government from exerting too-extensive powers has been to have it so organized that it cannot exert them. This means more than just a written constitution limiting the powers of government, and more than a paper organization of courts to preserve the constitutional limitations. It means the temper and disposition of the local leadership throughout the community. It means loyalty to the courts which preserve the constitution. The picture is such that if government executive officials attempt to extend their power beyond constitutional limitations, they are at the moment restrained from doing so by other organized agencies of the community, the courts and the legislature, and are then shortly removed from office by organized elective procedures giving effect to the views of the community leadership all along the line.

In the United States there are several principles of governmental organization designed to preserve the community against too great power in the hands of government officials. These principles are strictly concerned with the distribution of powers within the government itself. They are different from other institutional principles we have so far discussed, for example, that of private property, which fortifies the many loci of power and limits the field of government by its customarily recognized occupation of areas of activity that might otherwise belong to government. Two of these principles of government organization are explicitly reflected in our written constitution: one is the separation of government powers—the distribution of government powers into different branches of the total central government organization. The other is the federal organization, distributing powers between the central government and local or state governments. Within our local governments there is also observed the first principle—that of separation of powers.

The constitutional separation of powers in the United States is such that legislative, executive, and judicial functions of the government are vested in different officials in separate legislative, executive, and judicial departments. The legislature enacts statutory rules of law and has the power of the purse. The executive administers the statutes, enforces law and and order, generally carries out the mandates of the courts, collects, by tax gathering or by borrowing, and spends the amounts authorized by the legislature, has charge of foreign relations, and wages war. The judiciary in the course of deciding cases brought before it by litigants determines the meaning of statutes, reconciling them with the written constitution, and determines the boundaries of the powers of the separate branches of government.

Such a separation of powers lessens the probability of the rise to absolute authority of a Hitler or a Stalin, who vests in himself and his circle the totality of government powers. It might be thought that the separation of powers had obvious defects in the probability of a paralysis of government through unreconciled conflicts between the legislature and the executive. In the United States the chance of this is diminished by the fact that both legislature and executive are likely to have been elected by the same political party and, on the occasions when that is not the case, by the fact that our political officeholders have been brought up in a school of compromise and give-and-take, itself partly the result of this same separation of government powers.

Our system of competing political parties, which makes the likelihood that legislature and executive will have been elected as candidates of the same party, is sometimes referred to as extra-constitutional, and it is so in the sense that the federal constitution made no mention of parties. But a written constitution which provided for periodic elections by secret ballot and which protected freedom of speech and of the press, and freedom of assembly, supplied an environment in which competing political parties were almost certain to arise, and did in fact arise.

In the actual working out of the relations between the institutional separation of government powers and the existence of a free order, we find ourselves in a self-perpetuating cycle with results directly opposite to those of the self-perpetuating cycles of arbitrary government and imposed order which we saw in the *discord* cases. The separation of powers preserves the free order against acquisition of arbitrary power by a clique of government officials, and the factual satisfactions of a free order in turn make people loyal to the separation of powers as the political rule with which they are familiar and which they trust.

In times of crisis, as in foreign war or threat of war, the power of the executive is greatly expanded as a result of the necessity of focusing the nation's energies on the limited aim of successful war. In the United States these crises have not yet existed in such intensity, or for so long a time, as to have led us to abandon permanently the separation of governmental powers. We have as yet always returned from a state of emergency executive power to our traditional constitutional scheme.

The second principle of governmental organization in the United States, that of federalism, has a dual purpose. It aims to put in the hands of local state and municipal governments, familiar with local attitudes and living conditions, the governmental control of local affairs and the maintenance of local order. It aims to put in the hands of the central federal government the powers which it can exercise effectively and well, and which state governments could either not do at all or only do ineffectively or in a way likely to be harmful to the whole federated community. Accordingly the federal government is given control of affairs affecting the nation as a whole, such as the conduct of international relations and diplomacy, the maintenance of the armed services, regulation of interstate and foreign commerce, and control of the currency.

Such a federal organization gives general regulatory power over local life and local business to a number of organized and independent governments close to the scene, governments each of which can serve as a rallying point and a spokesman for local interests. These independent units of political power and influence, responsive to the opinions of the local constituencies and jealous of their own prerogatives, are a practical set of agencies inconsistent with the building up of an all-powerful central government. At the same time the local governments, as a result of the federal powers and controls, are prevented from hurting the good of the whole nationwide community by blindly selfish short-term measures in the supposed interest of the local community. For example, state governments are unable to raise tariff barriers against the products of producers in other states, or to levy duties on goods in transit through their borders, actions which if allowed by the political institutions would probably be taken and would result in cramping and restricting the necessary trade of the country.

The functioning of the federal system in the United States has shown a trend towards relative increase of influence and power in the central government and a decrease in the state governments. This is partly due to the fact that changing industrial techniques and the growth of rapid transport and communications have brought more and more local activities within the scope of the constitutional federal government power to regulate interstate commerce. Federal law now deals with working conditions in local factories either because they are producing goods destined for interstate commerce, or because their production in some way affects the functioning of interstate commerce. A New Jersey or a Delaware corporation may affect interstate commerce because it owns the shares of other corporations operating in many states and thereby controls them. Agriculture, though a local activity, has an obvious impact on both interstate commerce and the national health and strength. The criminal moving by automobile across state lines can escape effective law enforcement by a given state.

Another factor which has greatly expanded the federal area of control of local activities is less a matter of principle than of the location of a wide taxing and spending power in the federal government. The federal government has the financial strength and constitutional power to make grants of money to a state to aid in construction of public buildings or housing, or highways, or in the establishment of hospitals, or in the control of cancer. Grants may be made for insurance for the aged, or for school lunches for the young. Any such grant can be made upon conditions which involve a greater or lesser degree of federal control or regulation of the activity for which the grant is made. There is no question that such grants are frequently made for things which need to be done, and if individuals can't or won't do them, and if state and local governments can't or won't do them, then if they need to be done and the community can substantively afford them, the federal government is likely to see that they are done.

In order that the federal government do well what it alone can do, and in order that the loci of power essential to a free order be maintained with their dispersed political rallying points, it is necessary to organize state and local governments in such a way and with such revenue-raising powers that those things which individuals and private organizations will not do well, and which the federal government should not do—both for the sake of its own efficiency and for the preservation of a free order—will be done by state and local governments.

We have already suggested one reform which would result in funds necessary for health, education, and the arts and sciences, being made available locally for local administration. That reform was the laying of income tax for amounts needed in these fields and the allowing of direct credit against the tax for the contribution of these amounts locally. Similar in principle would be the allocation to state and local governments of adequate areas of tax jurisdiction so as to make available the necessary sources of revenue for state and local government activities—as today, for example, taxes upon real estate are generally reserved for county, town, and school district revenue.

Even after an adequate allocation of areas of taxation between federal government on the one hand, and state and local governments on the other, and even after a well-conceived stimulus to local giving as well, some states or some districts might nevertheless be so poor or so unable to appeal to donors in their own and other states, as to have, let us say, substandard education and substandard hospitals. In such cases, if any there might be, the present and future good of the whole national community might well require federal aid, that is to say, the federal government decree of compulsory support by the inhabitants of other states and districts for such a poverty-struck state or district.

The context in which we are presently looking at the principles of separation of powers and of federal organization within governments chosen in free elections is the context of institutional aids to the promotion and preservation of tolerance. Volumes have been written about these principles, largely in other contexts. Our cursory look is to point out and stress this most important area of all—the institutional fortification of tolerant government.

The answer to the question whether government is to be based on an enthusiastic doctrinaire minority irrespective of public consent— as in Soviet Russia—or on a general consent—as in the United States—depends largely on the historical scheme in which the community finds itself, the actually existing political beliefs and rules and the institutions through which these beliefs and rules are expressed. The energetic and ambitious are going to be the motive power in any case. What is important is whether they operate tolerantly and under a generally acceptable law and tradition, or whether they have to rely on terror and force to support an arbitrary power and order.

Should all present-day governments disappear from the scene—including our own republicanism, our particular brand of representative democracy—the same perennial issues of tolerant government would still have to be met and solved. There will always be both in the separate nations, and on the world scene of international relations and world order, the same need for a free order and institutions to preserve it and to minimize the chance of imposed order, tyranny, or disorder. There will always be the need of aiding and fostering tolerance, honesty, truth to fact, and equity, without which there can be no just political order, small or great.

XX. Honesty

1. HONESTY IN INTENT AND IN ACT

When a man gives his word intending it to be relied upon, intending to keep his word and in fact keeping it, he is honest. When he takes an action intending it to be relied upon, and himself intending to fulfill the plain promise of his action, and in fact fulfilling it, he is honest. The honest man's ostensible purpose, as expressed in word or deed, is his real purpose; and all those having to do with him can rely upon his word and deed.

Honesty is a condition of effective co-operative effort. When a man wants to produce the maximum constructive result with the aid of other equals, honesty is required of him. Otherwise the others have to divert their time and energies and resources from the substantive work that is to be performed into protecting themselves against deceit.

In a modern diversified community there are many positions of influence and leadership. A bishop in the church, the president of a great bank, or a government minister—as a member of the President's cabinet in the United States—can be taken as examples. The nature of the official position in such cases proclaims or states its proper function, and when a man takes the office he thereby joins in that statement as a statement of his own function, and holds himself out as someone who can be relied upon to carry out the duties of his office faithfully. If he deliberately fails to perform the function and fulfill the duties, he is deliberately dishonest. He is not entitled to the perquisites or pay of his office. Examples of this kind of dishonesty we saw in the *discord* cases, in government, in business, and in religion.

The schemer, often lacking confidence in his own substantive ability, who sets person against person within the organization of which he is a member and to which he purports to owe his loyalty, is dishonest in that his intent and actions belie the obligation of membership in the organization. He hopes by his scheming to profit and gain advancement from the ill feeling he creates between other members of the organization. Whether successful or not in his schemes, he injures the organization.

Dishonesty and deceit are the rule for dealing with enemies, either pretended or real, as in games or war. When the diplomat lies to the representative of a foreign country, or the boxer feints to open up his opponent's defense, at least two conclusions are justified. One is that the man is engaged in conflict and not in co-operation. The other is that people are disposed to rely on the words and actions of those with whom they are dealing. Honesty in word and act is the norm. Otherwise there would be no possible effectiveness in deception.

A modern governmental practice which undermines honesty at the source, and one which we have already had occasion to describe, is the practice of those totalitarian regimes which encourage children to spy on their parents, using schoolteachers as reporters of what children have heard in the home about their parents' attitude towards the governmental regime. If the home, and the relation between parents and children, cannot be one of candor, if there is not an atmosphere of honesty and trust, it is hard to see how the children coming from such a home can have acquired by example a wholehearted habit of honesty, rather than a cautious watching of one's own step as well as that of the other fellow.

Honesty liberates us for constructive activity freed from the burden of having to protect ourselves from our associates. Each can go ahead confidently in reliance on his neighbors and his government. All are unleashed for whatever creativeness or productivity they are capable of showing. As a free order is an order in which people can pursue their self-determined lines of work towards their ends without too much interference or frustration, honesty is one condition of a free order.

2. HONESTY AND PRIVATE PROPERTY

The realization in practice of basic useful rules of conduct—as tolerance, honesty, truth to fact, and equity, without which no community is a fit place in which to live—and also the satisfaction in fact of basic human needs—as those for food, drink, shelter, and health —are obviously goals in the light of which any particular procedures and institutions in the service of these goals are to be evaluated. Institutions and procedures have to be corrected and adjusted to what is substantively useful to the community, not the other way round.

When we were discussing the institution of private property, we saw that it was inherently—by its very nature—well fitted to serve and foster the many loci of power that are essential to, and the mark of, a tolerant community. Unfortunately private property has no such direct, inherently beneficial influence in the promotion of honesty. Dishonesty can flourish almost as well in a regime of private ownership as in a totalitarian Communist regime. Therefore we have to be alert to correcting and adjusting the institution of private property so that along with its undeniable advantages to the existence of many loci of power in a free order it will be made equally advantageous to the growth of honesty, which is also essential to a free order.

An illustration of statutory compulsion towards conduct approximating honesty is furnished by the pure Food and Drug Acts in the United States. The general purpose of such statutes is to prevent the adulteration or misbranding of foods or drugs. In the case of drugs, for example, the statute overcomes the propensity of competing producers or distributors of drugs to misstate the attributes of their wares. The label must not claim that the drug will cure baldness when in fact it is quite inert as to the growth or nongrowth of hair. Such a statute is useful in letting the purchaser of a drug know what he is really getting. Of course the community would be a more wholesome and orderly and free community if such a statute were unnecessary because of the honesty of all producers and distributors of drugs. But the community is still sound and on the whole honest if the need for such a statute is to protect most of its producers and distributors—honest if left to their own intent and practices—from the unscrupulous competition of a minority (the smaller, the better) of rascals.

An enforceable code of ethics in the advertising trade requiring truth in advertising would be useful. It is not only that the purchaser of goods would be protected from misleading representations and claims. Still more important would be the effect on the youth of the country. Dishonesty in advertising in press, radio, and television subjects youth to a continuous demonstration that to some of their respected elders what brings in the dollar is of more practical significance than truthfulness. This is an educational example of which the country would be well rid.

It is because private property is so useful in the preservation of tolerance by means of its many loci of independent power in a free order, that those who believe in private property must be alert to cure its serious shortcomings and defects. They must not close their eyes to these defects or forget that competition of private owners, while making a useful pressure for efficiency, can make a harmful pressure for dishonesty and overreaching. They must be clear about what is bad as well as what is good. They must themselves get rid of the bad, lest sincere, determined, and mistaken reformers throw out the whole institution of private property, the bad and the good together. This last has happened in some countries in our own times.

3. HONESTY AND THE RULE OF LAW

The characteristic of a modern totalitarian chief of state is that he is in practice above the constitutional and statute law. There are no rights of his subjects that are binding upon him. As we saw in the *discord* cases, his government is unreliable and given to unpredictable administrative shifts which make its policies and its promises something that cannot be counted upon. It is, as the saying goes, a government of men rather than of laws. It is in effect dishonest, as no one can act in confidence that he has rights of working subject to clear and known rules of law. Continuity of long-term effort is mainly possible to those working on something vital to the regime—as some aspects of national defense. Those who offend the regime by actual act, or by way of suspected act, are liable to sudden search, seizure, and disappearance. In the *discord* cases we saw the fear and uncertainty of the ruled under arbitrary and fraudulent governments—*dishonest* governments.

A government of laws rather than of men—a government of law-abiding rather than of lawless men—is by way of contrast honest. The citizens have laws they can count upon as controlling their ruler as well as themselves. They have a rule to go by, a rule preferable to one alterable with the changing ideas of expediency of the ruler.

The function of the rule of law is that the rule of law, like every species of honesty, allows a man to predict the conduct of others in a way that he can count upon. The law by giving all concerned a rule to go by becomes thereby an institutionalized aspect of honesty.

The law of contract is a good example of the rule of law in action. The law of contract is an acknowledgment in civil institutions that honest declarations of intent are so useful that they are to be publicly promoted and sanctioned. A discovery that must have been made in time immemorial by people working together was the advantage gained by each when one said: "I will do this, if you will do that," to which the other agreed, and then both performed in accordance with their word and agreement. The obvious utility of such an agreement would tend to establish the making and observing of promises as the right rule of conduct, the right way of dealing between people. The law of contract has come through a long development since the original discovery of the value of making promises and keeping them.

The law of contract is not primarily to keep the would-be fraudulent in line, although it has its uses for that. It is primarily to give people a more certain rule to rely on. The intent of honesty is to state a position, an attitude, or a promise clearly and reliably. The law perfects honesty by making honesty's statements more definite than would be possible without the law's progressively developing formulation of rules of interpretation based on the law's historical experience with those making and performing promises. Although this is the main function of contract law, it does undeniably also serve a purpose in keeping the fraudulent and dishonest from compelling better-minded people to descend to the dishonest level of trickery and deceit. As long as the dishonest are in a distinct minority, the law can more or less successfully make their behavior approximate what is honest.

Honesty between nations as well as the rule of the law are both wanting on the world scene. There is as yet no sufficient foundation of generally accepted aims to serve as basis for a rule of law, and too many of the nations regard one another as enemies or potential enemies. Honesty will not arrive on the world scene until, as a very minimum, truth to fact has made clear to all the grievousness of the continued hostilities of separation, and at the same time discovered institutional and other means for dissipating hostility. Equity, too, will pave the way for honesty on the world scene. Equity desires to see each man and each group of men receive their due. Equity is aware that all men of all nations find themselves willy-nilly on the same voyage of life, their hopes humanly alike and alike frustrated.

XXI. Truth to Fact

1. COMMUNITY RULES RIGHT FOR BOTH
PRESENT AND FUTURE

The community in the course of its ordinary activities establishes rules for the everyday conduct of its business and the carrying on and pursuit of its many interests. The rules are often established through formalized organizations—as the branches of government or the religious organizations—or as a result of the actions of leaders in the many lines of activity. It is important that these community rules—these rules of the game—serve not only as satisfactory present ways of doing things, but that they also are such as to meet the needs of the community for continuing right growth.

In the early days of the United States, in the year 1807, Robert Fulton launched the steamboat *Clermont* and in August of that year made a trip in her from New York to Albany. Fulton had the backing of a leading American statesman and financier, Robert Livingston. The two of them had been granted a monopoly by the legislature of New York giving them the exclusive privilege of navigating all boats propelled by steam on all water within the state of New York. A few years later a licensee under this monopoly, one Aaron Ogden, to protect his monopoly and abolish competition, brought suit in the courts of New York to prevent and restrain one Thomas Gibbons, who held a coasting license of the United States Government under a federal statute regulating coastal trade but who had no New York license, from operating steamboats on the Hudson River between New Jersey and New York. The highest court in New York State decided in favor of Ogden and his monopoly. Gibbons appealed to the Supreme Court of the United States, which reversed and annulled the New York decree and dismissed Ogden's suit. Chief Justice Marshall delivered the opinion of the court holding that the constitutional power of the United

States federal government "to regulate Commerce . . . among the several states" included the control of interstate navigation, and that as the constitution was by its terms the supreme law of the land, "the acts of New York must yield to the law of Congress; and the decision sustaining the privilege they confer against a right given by a law of the Union, must be erroneous."

In establishing this rule for the case before it, the Supreme Court accomplished a result satisfactory both for the present and the future needs of the community. As far as the rule for the present was concerned, a decision the other way would have given a rule to go by with which those concerned could have continued to do business, by getting New York and New Jersey licenses. That would have been feasible. But the rule of the Supreme Court decision was simpler for those engaged in navigation because thenceforth they did not have to busy themselves about acquiring licenses and paying fees to jealous and competing jurisdictions, and had but one law instead of several with which to comply.

The most significant service rendered by the decision in *Gibbons v. Ogden* was its provision of a rule for the future which permitted the healthy growth of commerce within the whole United States. A complexity of local trade barriers and local tariffs (an inefficient friction like that characteristic of pre-Revolutionary France, with its impediments to businessmen and travelers) would have followed a decision confirming exclusive New York jurisdiction over New York waters, Connecticut jurisdiction over Connecticut waters, and so on. Instead, a rule was provided which made the whole United States a free-trade area for interstate commerce. The rationale of the rule covered transportation by road as well as by water, and later by railroad and by air. The rule of *Gibbons v. Ogden,* in short, met the needs of the future development of the whole country along useful economic lines.

A major change in European historical development took place when the strength of tradesmen and businessmen of city and town working in the interests of improving their position in the community began to push against the difficulties caused to trade and business by feudal disorganization. At length feudalism and the feudal nobility were overthrown as the ruling system—or lack of system—in Europe. This overthrow of feudalism not only improved the immediate situation of those who engaged in trade, but it was a step in the direction of giving more scope to the capable for the long future, a step in the direction of meeting better the long-term needs of the community.

There was a new and more useful distribution of political power, the loci of power coming into more constructive hands than those of the feudal landlords. In the course of this development, at some times and places, the king and his bureaucracy, seeking to strengthen the monarchy against the nobility, took an effective part in building up the middle-class groups and breaking down the feudal restraints.

When the great financiers in the United States, the so-called "robber barons," around the turn into the twentieth century, were pushing their own financial power by gathering the funds for the organization of the American railroads, local and transcontinental, their activities in fact resulted in meeting the needs of the community for the future in the shape of better means of transportation of the necessities and amenities of life. Here again those mainly motivated by their own self-interest had at the same time a view of what the community needed.

In many of the historical cases when the long-term needs of the community have in fact been met, luck has played a large part in that result, as when the capable pushing their own interests happened to be on what was indeed the right track for the future.

Luck also plays a part in putting community leaders on the wrong track. For example, who could have foreseen that the discovery of the cotton gin, by making slavery profitable, would put the American South into an economic rut, the whole South itself a slave to King Cotton and unable to break away from this economic servitude, while at the same time the American North, no abler and no more intelligent, was building up a flourishing, diversified economic life. The South had a rule to go by, but it was a rule harmful to its own future.

We saw in our discussion of the *Motives of Reform* that a political change which may be good as a corrective may or may not continue to serve as a good long-term new rule. When the middle-class leaders, the tradesmen, supplanted the feudal leaders, the community rule did in fact change for the better, and there was a continuing growth in the direction of free order. On the other hand, when the leaders of the urban proletariat came into power in Russia, supplanting the ineffective old regime and the very brief interlude of power of something more like the middle-class leaders in the rest of Europe, the new rule appeared to set itself definitely away from a free order, as the political power of the Bolsheviks became entrenched.

In the *discord* cases we saw that for the time being a rule to go by can be followed and have the consent of a great part of the leaders all along the line, and yet be a rule bad for the future of the community, because out of keeping with the realities of the situation and the actual needs of the community. Such a rule, for instance, was that provided by Hitler. It satisfied the need of the Nazi leaders to know where they stood, it flattered their pride and gave them for the time being a mistaken sense of worthwhile role, but it misjudged the Nazi and German strength and the temper and feeling of the rest of the western world, and brought Germany to a crashing defeat. Hitler, realist though he purported to be, failed to see the facts as they actually were.

In the absence of leaders who see the change that needs to be made in some community rule if the community is to prosper, there may be a failure to change the rule. An illustration of this kind of carry-over of a rule is to be found in the religious requirement that Moslem women were to be veiled—covered from the top of head to toe—when in public. This rule, which was harmless in the weather conditions of Arabian oases, became harmful to health in a new environment with hot and excessively humid summers.

More than a thosuand years ago in China the system of qualifying for a position as a government official through competitive literary examination came to full development. The Chinese written language is said to be so complicated that only those who had much leisure— which meant in this case the landlords or the sons of landlords—would be likely to qualify, as no one else would have time to master the intricacies and involved refinements of the language or to memorize sufficiently long passages from the classics. The kind of semi-hereditary bureaucracy that resulted from this method of selecting officials characterized China to the twentieth century. Over this long period China lost ground from as advanced a country as any in the world to one extremely backward in its mastery over the technical utilization of materials. The old rule for selecting leaders, with its emphasis on recondite literary learning, meant that China was to stand still technologically while the Western World, with a leadership no more intelligent than the Chinese but with less damaging institutional methods of selecting them, improved its techniques and with them its possibilities for wealth, health, and power.

We have already mentioned the effect on practical tolerance in America that came from having plenty of elbow room and a vast land in which independent-minded people could find new opportunities in the westward-moving frontier. The process of reduction of the frontier and the qualities required for it were aided by the luck of the Puritan tradition of hard work as ethically and religiously desirable—the conditions of the new world having early modified the pure Puritan doctrine of salvation solely by faith.

This industrious conquest of the land and the rule of each man on his own, pushing his own immediate interest, came to have its serious drawbacks. The wish to get profits off the land sometimes led to serious injury to the land. In the nineteen-thirties, and notably in the spring of 1934, this injury to the land had a dramatic demonstration in the dust storms which blackened the skies in the Southwest High Plains in the United States, the national "Dust Bowl" calamity. Choking blizzards of powdery soil brought night in midday, the drifts of dust piled up on buildings and halted traffic. Silt was in the air all the way to the Atlantic Seaboard. What had happened was the climax and the reward of a process of overtilling, overfarming, and overgrazing the grasslands which extended from the 100th meridian westward to about the Rocky Mountains, an area of low rainfall. The "Dust Bowl" incident illustrated what may occur when a technique useful in one set of circumstances—that of adequate rainfall east of the 100th meridian—is applied in a different set—that of a dryland area.

In the matter of conservation of renewable resources, so as to preserve our grasslands and our forests in such a condition as to be of maximum present and future use, the element of luck again has played an important part. Organizations of those people who enjoy forests, wildlife, the headwater areas of streams, and those who take pleasure in natural beauty, have been powerful supporters of statutes for the protection of forest and field. It is for the most part purely accidental that their enjoyment of nature has happened to be in line with the needs of the community for conservation, as, for example, in the preservation of the habitat of birds which eat insects destructive to crops, or in the preservation of watershed areas in the hills so essential to a good year-round flow of streams and the continuing supply of water necessary to life and to industry.

The interest of these conservation-minded people, motivated by an enjoyment of natural beauty, has by way of luck been at least as hard-headed and in accord with real facts and real needs as the interest of the farmers, herdsmen, and lumbermen. The conservationists have been of benefit to the United States as a corrective for the exclusively profit-minded people whose shortsightedness would injure the long-term welfare of the community, including their own welfare.

We may conclude that even when the people of a community are free and feel that they are free, two further conditions are necessary

—good luck aside—for the maintenance and growth of a free order. The first condition is that the community leaders and standard setters are aware of what in fact are the real needs of the community. The second is that the activities of these leaders and standard setters are in accord with these real needs of the community rather than injurious to its long-term prospects. These two conditions can only be fulfilled if the leaders and standard setters make a determined effort, with freedom from bias and prejudice, to lay in all the facts pertinent to the solution of any problem with which the community is faced, and to draw from the facts as truthfully as they can the right and appropriate conclusion. Then they must act upon the conclusion. This effort to see things actually as they are, followed by action in the light of the facts to meet the real needs of the community, I call *truth to fact*. It is a political virtue essential to the growth of a free order.

2. SOME CONDITIONS OF THE RULE OF TRUTH TO FACT

As in the case of other political virtues, it is necessary that enough of the leadership level in the community are capable by native endowment and by education to exercise the virtue of truth to fact. Education can perhaps help to instill the technique necessary to get at the real facts and to put two and two together. If temperament and disposition should make it impossible for a sufficient proportion of top and intermediate leaders to gain the discipline and intelligence required for truth to fact, a free order would be unlikely in the community.

The events of *discord* and of *secession* offer a historical record of the failure of truth to fact—the failure to see the real needs of the community and to act so as to meet these needs. This failure has historically been due to excesses of the ordinary motives that spur leaders and their groups to improve their position or to maintain a favored position in the community. These excesses meant—they were the other side of one and the same coin—intolerance, dishonesty, and unfairness, and led to the failure to reconcile reform efforts as a result of what we called pushing too hard and holding too tight. Particular motives were too much in the ascendant to allow of truth to fact.

Strong partisanship may interfere with truth to fact in a way dangerous to the community. For instance, before the United States' entry into the Second World War, it was early evident that Britain and France were in desperate danger from the German onslaught, the danger for Britain shortly becoming mortal upon the military and political fall of France. At the same time we in the United States were on notice of a Japan acutely hostile to us. Our political leaders, Republican and Democratic, had to decide what to do to protect our country against the growing threat to us—which later materialized—represented by Germany and Japan. The creation of an adequate army of our own and the support of England as our first line of defense were logical courses to adopt. The country's defense was under the administration of the Democratic executive, President Franklin D. Roosevelt. In Congress there was a Democratic majority in both the Senate and the House of Representatives. Measures enacted by Congress and then carried into execution by the President would in these circumstances be regarded by the people of the country as primarily achievements of the Democratic party. The members of both major political parties were patriotic, all had the same facts available to be seen by their eyes, differences of opinion ran deep, and the members of neither party voted unanimously for one side or the other on a particular question.

The influence of partisanship was nevertheless clear. To take the Republican votes on three vital measures: On the repeal of the arms embargo, which repeal (act of November 4, 1939), by its "cash and carry" provisions, allowed the export of munitions to Britain and France, the Republican vote in the Senate was 8 in favor, 15 against; in the House 21 in favor, 143 against. On the organization of an adequate army through the adoption of compulsory military service, the Selective Training and Service Act of September 16, 1940, which provided for the registration of all men between twenty-one and thirty-five and for the training over a one-year period of 1,200,000 troops and 800,000 reserves, the Republican vote was in the Senate 8 in favor, 10 against; in the House 52 in favor, 112 against. Not quite a year later, and only four months before the Japanese attack on Pearl Harbor and the declaration of war by Germany and Italy on the United States, selective service was before Congress for extension, the question being whether our new army was to be broken up or maintained. On the selective service extension (act of August 18, 1941) the Republican vote was in the Senate 7 in favor, 13 against; in the House 21 in favor, 133 against. (The over-all House vote—on August 12—was 203 to 202.)

When a country is politically organized with a constitutionally strong executive, as in the United States, there is not invariably present the danger of governmental paralysis in an emergency, as is the case in a government organized with a weak executive, for example, the governments of the Third and Fourth Republics in France. The constitutional strength of the American executive is well suited to crisis government, allowing in effect an emergency dictatorship to deal with acute threats of outside pressure in peace and the actualities of outside pressure in war. Yet it is not hard to visualize circumstances in which the legislative branch of the government might fail to appropriate funds or to make other statutory enactments needed to meet a critical threat. In such case, what should a law-abiding executive do? What is the right course for him when the duly enacted statutes forbid the action that needs to be taken and the duly constituted lawmakers are too shortsighted to change the statutes? The answer is that there is more than statute law to be observed. The statutes exist for the good of the country, and not the other way round. The executive—the administrative arm of government—has to see the whole picture and do what needs to be done if he can. In a severe crisis, if the legislators are unable to rise to the actual occasion (as was almost the case in the House vote of 203 to 202 for the extension of selective service), the executive in meeting the crisis may have to evade, or even to abandon, the constitutional form of government; and the leaders in the various community lines will, if the country is still capable of survival, accept this evasion or abandonment. The continuance of an existing form of government may therefore come to depend on the truth to fact of the members of a particular legislature.

Strongly evoked emotions and desires may make it difficult to practice truth to fact and make accurate use of the intelligence in its service. At the time of the secession of the southern states in the United States Civil War, the wishful thinking of the planter aristocracy led them to close their eyes to the much greater potential stength of the North and to overrate their own southern prospects, military and economic.

Fear and hatred for a political opponent interfere with truth to fact so much as to bring about gross exaggeration of his faults and blindness to his strengths. In the United States the right-wing fear and hatred of President F. D. Roosevelt prevented the right-wingers from seeing the useful results of his "tinkering with money" and experimenting with the effects on the economy of large uneconomic expenditures. It took the vast uneconomic expenditures of the Second World War, with its issues of money and credit for armaments and for services which had no exchange value, to show that the domestic economy might benefit in more normal times from expansion of the money supply to employ people in activities with no economic exchange value. Uneconomic peacetime expenditures, of course, need not involve the immense wastefulness of substantive materials and effort that is characteristic of wartime production for destruction.

The things which people are in a position to do to serve some particular motive, on the one hand, or what they are afraid may be done to them, on the other, may so affect truth to fact as to turn right around their notions of what is morally acceptable. This is well illustrated by the change of attitude in the United States in regard to the wartime bombing of civilians. In 1939, when we were unable to take part in such bombing or perhaps to make an adequate defense against it, it seemed outrageous to us. By 1945 our potential had changed in both respects, and we bombed civilians on a scale theretofore unknown without those qualms of conscious conscience that might have been expected by one familiar with our earlier attitude and utterances.

Even in the investigation of matters which would appear to be strictly in the scientific field, investigators sometimes find themselves running foul of strongly held preconceived political principles which try to bend truth away from its own pursuit of the actual evidence. We remember that Galileo's investigations of the motions of the earth ran foul of some of what the Church regarded as its revealed body of truth. We remember that the Soviet geneticists have had the political heat on them to emphasize the effects of environment and economics on individual development and to de-emphasize the effects of hereditary capacity, quite irrespective of which way the evidence may ultimately point. In a convention of Soviet statisticians in the early nineteen-fifties, reference was made to bourgeois statistics, on the one hand, as against Marx-Lenin-Stalinist statistics, on the other, as if it were taken for granted that the Soviet party line established the truth and that the function of statistics was to bolster this party line rather than to make a nonpartisan disclosure of facts.

We know how strong particular motives are—how often men's desires, ambitions, fears, envies, and hatreds rule them to such an extent as to bring about discord. These motives sometimes make use of the intelligence in their service, sometimes they push on towards their goal impulsively without regard to consequences other than attainment of some immediate aim. An example of this failure to use intelligence was provided by the French Communists calling a general strike at the time when General De Gaulle was making a bid for strong executive power. In the actual circumstances of relative political strength of De Gaulle followers and of Communists, the Communists' call, whether successful or unsuccessful, could only strengthen the hands of the hated De Gaulle: if successful, because it would make the French see the need of a powerful executive to deal with the crisis and restore order; if unsuccessful, because it would demonstrate the lack of following of the Communist leadership.

The powerful particular motives are so strong as to raise the question whether there is a substantial hope of bringing them under the control of truth to fact exercised by enough leaders of the community so that the rule of truth to fact will prevail in community decisions. The community needs to attain the use of the intelligence in the service of truth to fact. The community needs to escape the use of the intelligence in the service of particular motives in excess or no use of the intelligence at all.

Intelligence in the political and social world is like vision in the physical world. It does not determine our ultimate goals, but it lets us see what some assumed goals really look like. It lets us compare, refine, and make more precise prospective goals so that we see better what we really want. It lets us see ways to reach the goals. Truth to fact and intelligence in its service may, on many particular occasions and between leaders of groups in the heat of some particular controversy, be weaker than the narrow partisan desires, ambitions, fears, envies, and hatreds. But for other leaders and groups in the community who are not in the heat of the particular controversy, and even for those who are if they can attain to it, truth to fact and intelligence are the best hope for the community to find the right solution of the controversy and to put the solution into effect. In our discussion of motives of reform we saw the great influence exerted by those leaders of opinion not themselves involved directly in the push of this or that particular group to improve its position.

It is neither necessary nor possible that all leaders exercise truth to fact; but it is necessary that enough of them do, if the community is to avoid discord and reach solutions and compromises of its controversies consonant with the maintenance and growth of a free order. It is encouraging that truth to fact and the use of intelligence in its service have existed over considerable periods of time in communities where there has been tolerance, freedom of speech, and many loci of independent power, as in much of the modern history both of Britain and the United States.

XXII. Truth to Fact and Political Institutions

1. THE TEST OF INSTITUTIONS

The degree of growth to a free order in both freedom and the acceptance of the order by the community is measured by the increase of tolerance, honesty, truth to fact, and equity and by the strengthening of the belief in the rule of these political virtues. It is these virtues in actual operation that spell political justice.

The degree of the increase of discord and of departure from a free order parallels and accompanies the falling off in the community of tolerance, honesty, truth to fact, and equity, and the lessening of belief in them as the right rule and role.

It follows that for a growing free order it is necessary that the statutes, the organizations, and the various institutional practices promote and foster and do nothing to injure the rule of tolerance, honesty, truth to fact, and equity. This is the most important requirement of those which have to be fulfilled for the long-term good of the community. It is even more important than the obviously important requirement that these same statutes, organizations, and institutions function effectively to attain their more specific objectives.

In the heat of political controversy over specific political issues—the more or less normal atmosphere of politics—we get easily interested in the mechanical aspects of a statute and whether it will achieve the technical goals for which we are designing it. A statute must attain its specific aim—as parity prices for farmers to preserve their purchasing power relative to workers in industry, or a functioning governmental authority in the development of a river valley for flood control, navigation, and electric power and as a standard for costs of producing electric power, or a tax statute to bring in needed revenue. We easily forget what is even more significant for all of us for the long term—namely, the effect the statute will have on tolerance, honesty, truth to fact, and equity, which alone can preserve justice and avert discord.

Thus, in case of the development of the river valley, the legislation and the administrative machinery which it sets up must build dams which are technically effective and which are not too wasteful in terms of other ways of providing flood control, navigation, and power— these are what we have been referring to as the specific mechanical requirements that should be met. But still more important is the fact that the statute and its administration promote tolerance, so as to bring out and increase local and individual initiative of the people in the valley and elsewhere; honesty, in being an accurate rather than a questionable yardstick of hydroelectric costs; equity, in fair dealing with those in the valley whose business is substantially affected by the impact and results of the new development.

In a going political concern, such as the United States today, we get so accustomed to the political rules, to the methods of our organization and institutions for the carrying on of our day-to-day social and business lives, that we take the rules, the organization, and the institutions more or less for granted. We forget both their artificiality— that they might have developed to be quite other than they are—and their necessity—that no political or social aim or idea would be realized without appropriate organization or institutions.

The necessity of organization is seen by us more clearly when we look at unfamiliar situations. For example, in the *discord* cases we saw the organization of Jacobin Clubs to bring into realization the aims and ideas of the French Revolutionary leaders, or of Communist cells to further the aims and ideas of Communist revolutionaries. We saw the Committees of Correspondence essential to our own American Revolution.

The ordinary sequence in the development of any organization or institution is that first a need is felt, then an idea or reaching after a method for meeting the need, and then the organization and the institutions for actually meeting the need, the realization of the idea. In some cases the process is simple. The people of a state have need of better communications. Better roads will meet part of the need, and this obvious aim is realized by the organized institution of the State Highway Department. So also in the fields of realizing the ideas for meeting other obvious needs, like municipal fire departments or municipal sanitation departments.

In a much more complex situation, there are the various economic needs, the ideas or reaching after methods for meeting them, and the huge organizations and institutions of the markets, and of industry, which render the realization of the aim possible.

In a totally different area we can see the same sequence. We know that people have the need of a worthwhile role. We know they feel this need very strongly in the ultimate sense of needing to make sense of their lives here on earth, so as not to be purposeless and abandoned in a world essentially alien, indifferent, or hostile to them. Then, as we have seen in our discussion of religion, a prophet or religious leader turns up with a revelation of man's place in the universe, of how he can achieve salvation, a route which brings him release from homelessness and a hope of final satisfaction of his need for a worthwhile role. Then there comes the activity of the disciples of the religious leader or prophet, the organization and institutionalizing of the body of his followers, and the missionary and proselytizing activity that results in growth of the organization and the further development of the institution that makes possible the realization of the religious idea of the prophet. Such an institution with which we are all familiar would be one of the great Christian churches, with its hierarchy of officials, its body of doctrine, and its ritual and articles of belief—its rules to go by.

The pamphleteers and the American political leaders at the time of the American Revolution had a true idea for meeting a real need when they promoted the notion of American independence as the means for fulfilling American possibilities, and this true idea was finally realized in our organization and our institutions for war and then for peace.

In the United States today there is the demonstrable need for better education of those capable of taking it. There is, or should be, the idea of how the schools and colleges if rightly set up and administered can provide the education. Then there is the actual organization, the effective institutionalized education in practice, which should realize the idea of what education ought to be achieving.

The mechanics of organization and institutions, whether in the field of health, education, government, or anywhere else, however built up and imposing, cannot take the place of right goals. For example, no matter how beautiful the buildings of a university or of a school, or how imposing its plant, or how large its expenditures, if the university or the school doesn't know what it is doing, and is moving along an educational line in fact not right for the times and the actual conditions, the idea that it is realizing in practice will be a specious idea. There will be a lot of motion but no worthwhile meeting of the actual educational needs of the community.

If mechanics of institutions and institutional activity cannot take the place of right ideas, it is equally true that the ideas cannot be realized without the institutions and institutional activity. The idea has to be a true idea for meeting the need—not a specious idea of gadgetry that will leave the need still unmet—and then over and above that the organization and the institutions have to be in fact capable of realizing, bringing into actual effect in practice, the true idea.

Today in Russia, governmental and political institutions are judged to be right and good if they promote communism and the Russian brand of Marxism. In the United States, governmental and political institutions are judged to be right and good if they promote democracy and our brand of republican government. In Russia the question would be: Do tolerance, honesty, truth to fact, and equity promote Russian communism? In the United States the question would be: Do tolerance, honesty, truth to fact, and equity promote American democracy? But this is putting the cart before the horse. The substantive conditions of political justice and of a free order are tolerance, honesty, truth to fact, and equity. We do not judge this substance, these political virtues, by how well they promote democracy or communism. On the contrary, we judge democracy or communism by how well it promotes the political virtues, the substance of a just political state.

2. DIFFERING SOLUTIONS OF SIMILAR PROBLEMS

It is thought by some that the effect of the Wars of the Roses in England was of unpredictable benefit to England. They point out that the warfare consisted of rival nobles and their bands of retainers fighting and robbing one another, with no great injury to the rest of the community—townsman or farmer. The benefit lay in the fact that the nobles and their bands, even though they did not succeed in totally killing one another off, none the less went far enough in that direction to hurt their own chance of continued domination in the community. This loss of position spared England the kind of burdensome political and economic privileges of the nobility which for so many years so disorganized the governmental structure in France.

Whatever the truth of this theory may or may not be, it is certainly true that the subsequent development over the years of the representative governmental institutions of England and the growth of the power of Parliament resulted in a more efficient and just scheme of government than came to exist in France. If we wish briefly to state in what this greater effectiveness and justice consisted, it was that the British institutions to a large degree, and despite backsliding, exhibited in practice the rule of tolerance and equity, and the French did not. In England there was more scope for talent to do its do and more practical recognition of the worth and the rights of those outside the nobility. This difference facilitated a greater growth of trade in England than in France, and a more just and equitable tax structure which in turn, under the conditions then existing, increased the practical degree of tolerance and equity.

In the *discord* cases we saw that the old republican government of Rome proved to be incapable of dealing with the problems of the widespread territory that had come under the military domination of Rome by the beginning of the Christian Era. There is no need of reviewing the story here. For our present purposes it is sufficient to point out that the inefficiencies of senatorial rule had made the exercise of truth to fact impossible. Even if some leader saw the facts as they were, the inefficiencies of the governmental organization were such that the action called for by the facts was not forthcoming. The block was removed and the disorganization corrected by the reforms of Augustus.

A situation similar in principle has been evident in our own times in the case of the Fourth French Republic, formed in 1946 and ended in 1958. European France throughout a long and creative history has been and is today blessed by nature with an unusual completeness in the resources necessary for a balanced, prosperous economy. By the spring of 1958 France, according to French official statistics, had so far recovered from her losses in the Second World War that the real standard of living of her people had increased by one-third per capita over what it was in 1938 just prior to the war. This is impressive even if we allow that a statistical figure like this obscures the misery of annuitants, pensioners, and others living on fixed incomes who had suffered cruelly from monetary inflation, and also obscures the fact that French housing was dilapidated due to rent ceilings so low that landlords could not afford a decent maintenance of their properties and were afraid to build anew. But despite France being on the way towards substantive economic improvement, there was a flaw in her governmental institutions which seemed to render her incapable of taking the external action necessary to save her empire, or to adopt any long-term coherent military policy—a failure that was bleeding France in her colonies, and even more vitally in Algeria. It was a flaw which prevented France's neighbors and friends from being able to rely on her intent or position, and made it impossible to achieve a sound monetary system necessary for her strength at home as well as abroad.

The unavoidable substantive problems of France were great. Among them was the need to maintain enough military strength in Europe as well as abroad, with the financial burden thereby involved. There was also a psychological hurdle in the way of France participating in a rational Western European economic market and trade grouping, or a co-ordinated defense scheme against the Russian threat—this hurdle being the old and historically justified fear of an economically strong and rearmed Germany.

Such problems would have been difficult enough for even the most effective government. But France had added to these problems a man-made, artificial, institutional inefficiency which rendered her incapable of solving the problems.

This failure in the French institutions was a paralyzing discontinuity in the executive arm of government, a cripplingly rapid turnover in French government leadership. France has often tried, but never been able, to copy successfully the British parliamentary system of an executive—the Prime Minister and cabinet—responsible to the legislature and going out of power on loss of confidence by the legislature. The successful functioning of such a system depends on two major political parties with a tradition of compromise and a necessary minimum degree of political discipline and common sense in the party leaderships. France has had a multiplicity of parties represented in the legislature. The legislature of the Fourth Republic consisted of a National Assembly—the principal legislative power—and an indirectly elected Council of the Republic. The National Assembly which was elected on January 2, 1956, for five years, had at the year end of 1957, a membership of 596 deputies belonging to fourteen different parties, the largest eight of which were 142, 97, 91, 75, 43, 30, 21 and 21 in numbers respectively. The relatively well-disciplined minority Communist party had the 142 delegates.

As the Premier and his Cabinet fell from power on a vote of no confidence or a vote of censure in the National Assembly, and as the Assembly was never able to get together a majority coalition that could hold solidly for more than a few months at most, the make-up of the executive arm of the Fourth Republic shifted in a kaleidoscopic manner. The only permanent officer, the President of the Republic, elected by the legislature for a term of seven years, was despite his nominal title of chief of the armed forces, a ceremonial figure without substantial authority. The result of the rapid changes of Premier and Cabinet and lack of continuity in policy was to render the French executive leadership unwilling or unable to discipline the nation into the work and taxes at home, and the effort abroad, necessary to meet the civil and military demands on France, because any Cabinet which should take these needed steps would at once be voted out of office in the National Assembly.

The two aspects of truth to fact are determination to see things as they are—the real needs—and thereupon action so as to meet these real needs. The institutions of the Fourth Republic had made it close to impossible for any Premier and Cabinet to measure up to the first aspect and impossible to measure up to the second. France was without any effective executive power of government.

In this juncture of crisis the French military, basing their activity in and from Algeria, were about to attempt to take Paris by force and to overthrow the Republic.

France was saved a disorderly revolution by the leadership—backed by popular sentiment—of Charles De Gaulle. The frightened National Assembly chose him as Premier, after consultations between De Gaulle and the various party leaders. His minimum conditions were six months of what in effect would be emergency dictatorship with power to rule by decree, special powers in Algeria, and authority to prepare a reformed constitution to be presented directly to the people in a popular referendum, bypassing the Assembly. The last demand was, of course, the hardest to take, because it was the handwriting on the wall for the Deputies, indicating that the old political ropes they knew how to manipulate were going to be cut, and that they were likely to lose their offices under a new system of elections. However, they swallowed hard and France was saved from probable profound disorder.

The constitutional reforms proposed by De Gaulle, and overwhelmingly adopted by the French people, were such as to make truth to fact once more possible in France's internal and external politics. The President, instead of being a mainly ceremonial figure, was vested with authority. He had power to name the Premier (formerly parliamentary approval was required); to name on the Premier's proposal the other members of the "government"—i.e., the Cabinet of Ministers who head the executive branches; to promulgate law enacted by the legislature or to send back a law or parts of it to the legislature for new reading; to submit to a popular referendum certain kinds of important law, for example, laws dealing with the organization of public powers (such submission to a referendum would normally be on proposal of the "government"); to dissolve the National Assembly, but not within a year after its election; to preside over the higher councils and committees of national defense as chief of the armies; to exercise a constitutional dictatorship "when the institutions of the Republic, the independence of the nation, the integrity of its territory, or the execution of its international commitments are threatened in a grave and immediate manner and the regular functioning of the public powers is interrupted"; to communicate with the legislature by messages which are not debated.

The reforms of the relations of the houses of the legislature and its relations to the Premier and Ministers made for greater continuity in the executive power. It was made harder for the National Assembly to turn a government out of office; the National Assembly had over its head the threat of dissolution—and likely loss of office—at the hands of the President. The field of the law within the scope of the legislature was defined as the "rules" concerning broad fields of legislation and the "fundamental principles" of organization of defense, local administration, education, property, employment, unions, and social security. Matters not within this field of rules and principles were within the jurisdiction of the "government" ruling by decree. As to whether a bill was or was not in the domain of the "law" was to be decided by a Constitutional Council. No bill or amendment formulated by members of the legislature was receivable in the National Assembly—which had the first jurisdiction of financial bills—if it would have as a consequence either a diminution of resources or the creation or increase of public debt (a provision which would appear to have taken the spending power from the Assembly and put it in the executive).

The Constitutional Council consisted of nine members (one-third renewed every three years), three named by the President of the Republic, three by the president of the National Assembly, and three by the president of the Senate, and in addition former Presidents of the Republic, who are members of the Constitutional Council for life.

Laws dealing with the organization of public powers before promulgation, and regulations of the parliamentary assemblies before becoming effective, must be determined to be constitutional by this Council. Any law prior to promulgation might be submitted to the Constitutional Council by the President of the Republic, the Premier, or the president of the Assembly or Senate. A provision declared unconstitutional could not be promulgated or put in force. The decisions of the Constitutional Council could not be appealed.

A constitutional framework such as this, plus electoral reforms reducing the chance of representation in the legislature of many splinter parties, held out promise of improvement of the legislative and executive chaos which had characterized too much of the history of the Fourth Republic. Now there was a hope that France might set her fiscal and military activities in order. The differences between European France and Algeria might still prove too difficult for resolution in such a way as to result in a reasonably just arrangement embracing both in a community of interest; but even here there was now hope.

3. EXERCISING THE POWER OF THE PURSE

Central governments today are likely to have constitutional control of the currency and the power to issue money, and combined with this the practical power to spend in any field that concerns the public welfare. Many of these expenditures are uneconomic in the sense that they do not represent a corresponding putting on the market of present or future goods or services that have a sale value or that anyone wants to buy or can buy—for an extreme example, expenditures on a battleship. There is an historical tendency to pay for a great part of these uneconomic expenditures by issues of new money or new credit, rather than by taxes. In the United States such issues of new purchasing power take the form of the establishment of bank deposits for the account of the government against the issue of government bonds, these deposits being spendable money. If bank credit is at the time tight, the banks can borrow federal funds from the Federal Reserve Banks against these same bonds, thereby creating the money reserves to support the deposit liability. This is in essence printing press money.

The effect of uneconomic expenditures and the creation of new credit to pay them is, in an economy operating somewhere near full productive capacity, to make money too plentiful in relation to economic goods and services and thereby to force prices up. Carried to an extreme the process represents runaway inflation and destroys the people's medium of exchange, rendering the purchasing power of everyone's wages or salaries uncertain, and making hazardous to sellers any business contracts requiring future money payments. Old people—pensioners, for example—and other people or groups receiving fixed income, such as colleges or hospitals relying on income from endowment, find that prices have risen too fast for them, and they are hurt either in their ability to buy the necessities of life in the case of individuals, or to carry on their work in the case of the colleges or hospitals.

In the United States—as in any other country with desirable assets —there is obviously one vital spot where it must not have a failure. That is in adequate defense and all that it takes to have an adequate defense. The maintenance and development of an adequate defense brings in its train the very necessity we are now talking about, which is of paying for the uneconomic defense expenditures without needlessly harming our community by spoiling our medium of exchange. The defense is essential.

One thing that has made the Russians such a tough opponent on the world scene is that they maintain a first-class military establishment in the charge—on the military and scientific sides—of as good leaders as they can find. They have no notions of individual rights or equality or hesitancy to require community sacrifice. The total annual military expenditure of Russia in the mid-nineteen-fifties was about of the same order as that of the United States; but it represented about a quarter of their whole income as compared with about one-twelfth of ours. There was no reason at all why we could not maintain a defense establishment stronger than Russia's, while we felt the pinch less and paid for it as we went along. We have never been in the substantive situation where our military necessities were more than we could carry with relative ease.

For keeping our fiscal house in order and preserving the value of everybody's purchasing power, our institutional set-up relied on the truth to fact of our popularly elected House of Representatives and Senate, and to a lesser extent on the legislative veto power of the President. The Russians for keeping their fiscal house in order and preserving the value of their currency—in economic circumstances which were substantively much more difficult than ours—relied on the radically different institutional set-up of imposed control by a self-perpetuating party leadership.

We can do much institutionally to avoid the danger of overissues of money. Good personnel in the committees of the legislature, as the House and Senate both have a part in authorizing expenditures and appropriating amounts to be spent and in the incurring of debt, is important. A system of selection of these committees and their chairmen from those with appropriate experience and character is necessary if the committees are to do their work well. The main protection is to have the legislative and the executive arm of government manned with officials capable of truth to fact, able both to see the facts and to act in accord with them in the best public interest. And this on the institutional side requires a sound system of nominating candidates for public office and a sound system of elections—matters which we will look at later.

The reason the matter is so important is that a breakdown at a single fundamental spot like this can bring about a radical overhauling of a form of government. Historians often look about for broad changes in sentiment and attitude as bringing about sudden political change; but the fact is that sudden change—and even the broad sentiment that is likely to accompany it—are likely to stem from some particular failure at a critical and sensitive spot in the community scene. We have reviewed some of these failures in earlier parts of this book, and the radical changes precipitated by them.

XXIII. Current Institutions and Principles of Reform

1. TWO-PARTY SYSTEM AND UNIVERSAL FRANCHISE

The institutional method of selecting the chief executive—the President—of the United States as it actually functions in the mid-twentieth century is on the whole well suited to obtaining a capable President. The procedure for nominating candidates for the office is more significant than the procedure of actual popular election. It is the nomination that chooses the candidates, one of whom will be President. The electorate is of importance indirectly through its influence on the nominators—in that the characteristics of the multitude of voters who constitute the electorate make some particular potential candidate seem to the nominators likely to poll a large popular vote. This influence affects the kind of candidates who will be in fact nominated.

Our two great nationwide political parties—which in the mid-twentieth century were sufficiently close together in strength of numbers so that no election could be regarded as a sure thing—each hold a presidential nominating convention. The members of a convention are those active in practical party politics in the various states of the United States. They represent, on a geographical basis, a mixed population, urban and rural, and are charged with finding a candidate who will run well in all the states. They are under the necessity of compromising any extreme views in order to hit upon a nominee who will appeal to the whole electorate. They are under the strongest pressure to nominate someone who can beat the candidate of the other party. This means someone who will hold his own party vote as well as appeal to independents and to independent-minded voters of the other party.

In finding a candidate who is likely to run well, the nominating convention is aided by the fact that in our federal system there are many well-tried and experienced officeholders—notably governors of states—well known to the electorate, which is the whole adult public. The convention of neither party dares nominate a man mainly notable for his subservience or amenability to the bosses of his own party, as such a candidate could be beaten by any one of several well-known public figures. The convention is therefore likely to nominate someone who has made his mark in state administration, or someone so distinguished and famous for other achievement as to be a strong vote-getter. In either case the candidate is likely to make an able President if elected.

No doubt much of the pressure to find an able candidate is due to the fact that the two parties are fairly well balanced in numbers. There have been times in the past where one party was relatively so much the stronger that its leaders have been able to nominate a candidate mainly for his usability by the party bosses, and elect him.

Even when one party has been for some years stronger than its rival, there is a valuable practical advantage in a two-party system, in that there is a loyal opposition, openly organized and functioning, ready to take over the national administration if the party in power appears to have made some kind of public failure. So, for example, the Democratic candidate Franklin D. Roosevelt took over from the Republicans in 1932 at the depth of the great economic depression.

In a one-party state such as Russia, a similar crisis of economic depression would have meant that various leaders in industry and banking would have been "liquidated." As the party is all-powerful and responsible for everything that happens, it would have been necessary to find some scapegoats in the party associated with the industrial and banking phases of the bureaucracy, and have them publicly condemned as party traitors and backsliders whose antiparty activities were responsible for the economic difficulties. Were the crisis severe enough, the leader of the party might get his throat cut figuratively or literally, and the leadership be taken over by a plotter within the party. Of course a leader so coming to power may be an able one; he is certain to be tough and hard-boiled—good and useful qualities as far as they go.

Our two-party system seems more likely to come up with a constructive chief executive, certainly one more law-abiding and less given to violence as the means of rule. A two-party system is more likely to get a Grover Cleveland than a Commodus or a Stalin. No paper prescriptions are able to insure the selection of a good ruler. It is a functioning institutional combination that turns the trick.

A two-party system, with its organized opposition ready to take over, plus free speech and free press, plus universal franchise and secret ballot, all together provide such a combination. This institutional combination makes wholesome use of the strong desire of candidates and officeholders to get and hold office. If an official is to retain office or a candidate to get office he has really to show the likelihood of doing well by all large groupings whose members make up the electorate. Those with extremist or too one-sided programs are not likely to succeed. A Hitler cannot retain office, nor a Stalin get office.

In a one-party system, on the other hand, even with nominal universal franchise but with no organized opposition and without benefit of free public criticism and inquiry, the keen desire for office of officials and their rivals is not utilized for the good of the community. Instead it takes itself out in palace plots and cutthroat competition. The press and the radio are used, not to develop the truth through free criticism but to deceive the public with slogans of party infallibility.

As no one knows the answers to the ever-present specific political and economic problems, the important thing in a chief executive is that he be reasonably intelligent and fair-minded, willing to take likely looking chances while at the same time recognizing the importance of everyone along the line knowing the ropes well for the sake of getting the work of the country efficiently done. Our method of selecting our President seems under present conditions as likely as any now in existence anywhere of getting such a man in office.

Despite these advantages of the two-party system in the United States, circumstances might well occur which would require a reform in our method of selecting our chief executive, as well as of our national legislature.

We might run into a real difference of opinion, a real conflict, between groups in the community. At present, despite economic differences of interest, as between farmer and city man, or between employer and employee, we still none of us—possibly excepting a few gangster-ridden unions and the violence they both exhibit themselves and generate in others—regard groups other than our own as hated opponents to be beaten down at all costs and to be deprived of traditional rights. We still believe in private property and the idea that it is best for all of us to let the capable get ahead. We work in practice on the theory that the various interests in the community are reconcilable, rather than on the theory that one group has to hold another down. As our two political parties both profess the same view in these basic matters, our elections do not arouse excessive bitterness, and we are all more or less satisfied—or able to get along—with the politically victorious party.

England in the mid-twentieth century may be testing whether a two-party system can continue to function over the long term when there is a real difference of opinion. In England in recent times there has been a basic difference between those believing in socialization and government ownership of industry on the one hand, and those believing in individual decentralized control on the other. But the British leaders and intermediate leaders are by tradition a tolerant, compromising lot, and not given to taking such differences to heart as religiously or logically as the leaders of most other countries; and that is a safety factor. Perhaps they are capable of trying socialism, and still, despite the practical and mechanical difficulties of scrambling and unscrambling methods of ownership and control, of turning around and throwing it out in its ineffective and cumbersome aspects.

Were we in the United States to develop a multiplicity of political parties, representing this and that particular opinion, we could—as France has done—lose the practical utility of the two-party system, and, unless extensive modification was made in our method of election, get a President with whom too many of the voters would be dissatisfied, as well as a legislature so fragmented as to be unable to pull itself together to meet the real needs of the country.

As matters of scientific competence and technical mastery become more and more significant to the welfare and growth of a modern industrial community, and to its survival in time of war, there might come the day—particularly as to our national legislature and its committees—when there was simply a failing of the minimum of understanding necessary to give the go-ahead to the scientists and technicians best qualified either in peace or war to produce the needed equipment or armament. In peace the problem might not be critical as long as we have a competitive industry locally owned and controlled, and dependent for survival in a free market only to the extent it is progressive, research-minded, and alert to improved techniques. But in war, when control is in the hands of officeholders and the final decisions are made by elected officials—whether legislative or executive—a failure to appoint sufficiently competent technical heads for vital segments of national defense or a failure to choose rightly between this and that scientific judgment are both possibilities that unfortunately seem too easy of realization. An imminent prospect of failure at this spot might require a reform of significant aspects of our political methods.

If the intermediate leadership of the United States should no longer give a reasonably intelligent steer to the electorate, or if the quality of the electorate should become such that it could no longer take and follow such a steer, we might repeat in modern conditions the situation which occurred in Rome when candidates for the imperial office were put up for office by the legions, and in consequence their capabilities and ideas about the needs of Rome tended to deteriorate towards those of the soldiers, who knew nothing of the real needs. We would find ourselves in a like situation today if it came about that a candidate for the Presidency could succeed only if his ideas approximated the ideas of a relatively ignorant electorate. We know already that it is an advantage to a candidate to make promises pleasing to this and that group in the electorate, irrespective of whether the promises can be performed or are even mutually inconsistent. Other things being equal a candidate of reasonably good character can make such promises more convincingly if he himself does not see the impossibility of performance or the mutual inconsistency. The candidate, like the electorate, might get too far away from the real existing conditions, because a candidate who saw the truth and stated it could not get elected.

To ascertain public opinion in order to learn the actual conditions which will hamper or help an officeholder who is trying to push on with the ever-necessary changes and improvements needed for a growing free order, is a sound and necessary procedure. But to ascertain public opinion in order to follow its notions is, except as a means of getting into office, unsound and represents a danger to the future of the universal democratic franchise.

It is still too early to tell whether the universal free franchise is going to prove a right political development over the long term. It is much to be desired that it will prove to be so, because as we have seen it has undeniable advantages, particularly in its peaceful removal from office of an unsatisfactory government. A gradual broadening of the base of political power has taken place in western countries in progressive stages, through extension of the franchise and otherwise, from monarch to nobility to a middle class, and then from the middle class to everyone. This could prove to be a passage from relatively bad through relatively good to relatively bad. The reason is that the location of power in a middle class may over the long term give greater scope to the competent than is possible for ancient or modern equivalents of the other stages. The community needs not only to have capable people within its numbers but also an institutional framework which taps and frees their abilities to the benefit of the community.

2. GUIDES IN MAKING REFORMS

When reform of a going concern becomes necessary, the attempt should be made to preserve what has in practice been proved good in the going concern, and at the same time to foster tolerance, honesty, truth to fact, and equity, as the necessary conditions of a growing free order.

In modifying a method of electing representatives to a legislature, one guide should be the proven good of a two-party system. In modern times in Western Europe there has been ample demonstration that many real divisions and differences of view in a legislative body mean that it can accomplish little. It is caught by a multiparty paralysis. The practice of truth to fact and tolerant compromise becomes impossible. Therefore in any reform it would be a step in the wrong direction to make representation based on competing groups, or professions, or industries, or agriculture, or specific interests. It is better to elect on a diversified geographical basis. For the same reason proportional representation is to be avoided, because it too emphasizes overrepresentation of minorities—overrepresentation in the sense that a representative body so selected is likely to be too divided for effectiveness.

Although careful to preserve a two-party system, it would be an error to try to choke off the creation of new parties. A new party, if successful, would probably make its first success locally and thereafter nationally, although circumstances might arise—as they have in the past in the United States—which could make a new national alignment promptly successful. In an election for a local legislature a new party might well come off with the winning majority. If in a national election, such a party, let us say in State XYZ of the United States, should poll a majority vote, but on a nationwide basis was not one of the two parties obtaining the largest nationwide votes, its representation from State XYZ would not be seated in the national legislature. Instead, the candidates from XYZ who had polled the largest plurality as candidates of one of the two nationwide largest parties would be seated. Such a procedure would have the merit of putting pressure on both local and national politicians of the two major parties to keep their parties flexible enough in doctrine to make an extremely wide appeal to voters throughout the country. It would also make splinter party politicians try to reconcile their views and candidacies with those of a major party. The man's desire to get and hold national office or national patronage would put heavy pressure on him to tie up with a major party.

Where representation is on a broad geographical basis, the representative, if he wants to hold office, has to be generally acceptable to most principal real interests in his constituency and he cannot afford to overoffend any of them. This state of affairs offers the best chance of getting reasonable compromise and a working reconciliation in the proceedings of a representative body.

A community needs to discover and develop the elite or elites that will do best for its welfare and to put them in charge of its affairs. We have already pointed out that in modern conditions a defense establishment able to function well immediately is unlikely in the absence of an able political leadership. A representative democracy with free universal franchise must justify itself by discovering and developing a political leadership more effective than that produced by any other form of political organization.

We have explained why in the United States the selection of candidates for the Presidency by conventions of experienced politicians is likely to come up with good candidates. We have also pointed out the danger of our election procedures taking a turn such that the ideas of candidates for office would gravitate towards those of a relatively less well-informed public as problems become relatively more complex. When and if we find we must alter our institutions for the selection of candidates and their election to office, we would do well to avoid direct democracy in the selection. Selection should take place through some kind of machinery that, like our present Presidential nominating conventions within our two-party system, puts the nomination in the hands of a group chosen from those with practical political experience and under automatic pressure to come up with a reasonably good candidate.

Some have suggested that a system of multiple voting would increase the likelihood of election of capable public officials. Every voter would have a single basic vote, and some would be allowed additional votes on the basis of degree of education, achievement in this or that line of community activity, and the like. The purpose of such a reform would be to put pressure on a candidate to make his appeal to the electorate on something other than a basis of counting the most noses in his favor, which, as we have seen, tends to an inferior order of political campaigning and of political promises. A practical difficulty with such a reform is seen in the actual motives which in the past have sometimes led to an extension of the franchise: the Conservation party widens the franchise to extend it to women, because it thinks it will benefit most from the women's vote; the Progression party wishes to extend the franchise to eighteen-year-olds, because it thinks it will benefit most from the youthful vote. It is likely that the basis for awarding multiple votes would be the subject of political manipulation of this kind, so that it would be hard to make such a system politically sound.

The loyalty of citizens and subjects to their ruler except in extreme discord or outright rebellion is very strong, stemming as it does from men's need to know where they stand—the need of a rule to go by. We recall that back in the Roman days, the populace of Italy and of the provinces alike regarded the Emperor—whose regime in reality was the cause of their troubles—as the likely savior from their troubles. Hereditary monarchy has been a relatively stable feature of government on account of this public devotion to the public figurehead. In recent times we have seen peoples loyal to despots who were undeserving of any loyalty and who were harming their subjects. The problem in selecting a head of government is not to get someone to whom the people will rally but someone who is worth rallying to. What is needed is that the figurehead and his sponsors and colleagues really stand for and practice tolerance, honesty, truth to fact, and equity. The best system of selection of a ruler is the one that is most likely to produce this result.

What a political regime or system calls itself doesn't determine what it really is or its appropriateness to a growing free order. In England over the years the name and the forms of an unlimited monarchy were preserved while the substance changed to a limited monarchy controlled by the people's representatives. In the Rome of Augustus the name and the forms of a republic were retained while the substance changed to an absolute monarchy. Russia today calls itself a people's democracy, but the substance is that of a despotism of the party bosses. No matter what the changes of form, the political truth remains that when the many loci of power are lost, and the intermediate local leadership no longer forms local opinion, and the independent quality of representatives fails, the days of free order are numbered.

If the national legislature in a modern representative democracy should prove incapable of performing its functions in a way requisite for the safety of the country—we remember the one vote by which our House maintained the army on the eve of our enemies attacking us and forcing our entry into the Second World War—some sort of reform would be necessary. The minimum reform, still preserving the good and the familiar of a known system, would be to restrict the powers of the house in such vital areas as it had proved itself incapable. This is the rationale of the reform that was made in 1958 in connection with defense and fiscal powers of the French House of Deputies.

If a body of representatives, due to failure of the qualities of its members, had to be generally deprived of legislative powers, there still should be recognition of the value of a parliament as a place for expressing the opinion of different sections of the country, and for investigative functions and inquiries, and bringing the pressure of public opinion and free criticism to bear on the executive branch of government. A reform which might produce this result would be the vesting of both legislative and executive power in the executive and his office, with a legislative veto power in the representative body. Then if the executive's legislative program were vetoed, the country would still function under the old familiar legislation until such time as the executive was able to bring, through clear proof of necessity plus public opinion aroused by the intermediate leadership, such pressure on the representatives as to allow the passage of the new legislation.

Faced with a specific problem, experts differ greatly on what specific measures are advisable. For instance, in the economic field they differ on whether some degree of monetary inflation is good or bad for business generally. Or what balance should be kept between building more capital equipment as compared with more production of consumer goods through use of the current stock of capital equipment, and what is the right principle of relationship between the two. The thing of which we can be sure is that the political virtues of tolerance, honesty, truth to fact, and equity let us keep experimenting and improving, steering clear of stagnation on the one hand and of mistaken reform on the other. In the United States in 1932, when the country faced a breakdown in its credit machinery and in providing a decent opportunity of livelihood to many of its good citizens, political wisdom lay in extensive reform, holding fast only to the main principles of a free order.

If the country's business leaders wish to forestall extensive reform at the hands of the political government, it is for these leaders themselves competently to work out sound and satisfactory methods of growth within the current tradition. For example, in the United States if we are to avoid socialization and overcentralized control of our industry, the business leaders themselves need to work out a development of the present economic system that will cure its defects in a less radical manner. If they are to preserve the good in the many loci of power of private control, they will need to be creative enough to cure the specific ills, such as unemployment, to which we are presently liable.

3. CHANGED CIRCUMSTANCES REQUIRE CHANGED INSTITUTIONS

From time to time in history there occur changes of circumstances so great that old institutions are no longer adequate in the changed environment. Then major changes of institutions take place. The aim of political leaders and statesmen at such a time should be to see that the institutional changes are both appropriate to the new developments and to the rule of tolerance, honesty, truth to fact, and equity.

Prior to the Industrial Revolution and the development of steam power, as a general rule the ownership of broad acreage of land was the basis for wealth and economic power. There were exceptions, as when wealth arose in some cases from trade and commerce. But it is fair to say that land was wealth, and that when wealth changed hands it was between one landholder and another.

With the coming of steam power a little land could be the site for a plant producing great wealth. As more power in new applications improved communications and transport, it was no longer exceptional for fortunes to be won in trade by land or sea. This change meant the eventual breakdown of any monopoly of economic power in the members of a landed aristocracy. Institutions needed to be developed to reflect and to make politically useful this fact of changing location of economic power. As we saw in the *discord* cases, the change of institutions was usually to the tune of intolerance, dishonesty, mistake, and unfairness, though it need not have been, and in England on the whole, despite the "dark Satanic mills," was not.

When the American colonies had newly won their independence from England, the institutional problem was whether it would be possible to devise a framework by which the separate colonies could be made into a viable united strong community. The institutional device which solved the problem was the United States Constitution, with its division of state and federal powers, which we have already discussed. A specific institutional invention which made the Constitution acceptable to the less populous colonies was the so-called Connecticut Compromise, which provided for equal representation in the United States Senate of each state, large or small. This offered protection against the unqualified majority rule that would have resulted if legislative power had been exclusively centered in the House of Representatives, where relative size of population in electoral districts was the basis of representation. This invention made it possible for the erstwhile colonies to get together in a governmental scheme that was institutionally favorable to tolerance and equity in the treatment of regional minorities.

The unrestrained individualism of many small landholders—which had worked so well in the development of the well-watered American old Northwest—was not appropriate to the later settlements west of the 100th meridian, where there was a shortage of rainfall. Here the institutional problem was to find a method of ownership and control suitable for what has been called a dryland democracy. It was only after a good many years and a good many blunders that the United States House and Senate worked out a statutory answer on a feasible basis.

To invoke *laissez faire* in order to break loose from cramping governmental restrictions, as was the position of Adam Smith, is one thing; to invoke *laissez faire* in order to ward off needed reform of economic abuse is quite another. In the former case truth to fact is trying to find out how to modify the going concern so as to achieve greater productivity. In the latter case truth to fact is suppressed and desirable change is thwarted.

In the United States today we are working under a financial system which grew by means of trial and error—or what has perhaps been more accurately called blunder and success—through a long period of years here and abroad when the principal economic problems were those of overcoming ever-present shortages. We still have, and always will, a problem of efficient production. But we also now have a new problem by which the evolution of our financial institutions over the years has not been significantly influenced. That is the problem of equitable and efficient distribution of the plenty we are capable of producing. Here our institutional task—the task to which our business leaders need to address themselves—is the discovery of a means of keeping production balanced on a reasonably high operating basis, with smooth distribution to a fully employed working population.

The amount of what the United States is able currently to produce can properly be cut back on account of conservation requirements, as in the use of crops—such as timber—that can only renew themselves at a rate set by nature. It is also rational to conserve the use of metals, although here events may prove that technologically we will learn how to mine the mineral resources of the sea, or to produce new substances which will do the work of the metals.

But the volume of feasible production of what needs to be consumed for a good level of life should not be cut down by an artificial financial overlay, by any cherished institutional setup of debt and credit. These are institutional means of facilitating substantive production and distribution, and should be adjusted to our substantive ability and capacity, not the other way round.

There is a backwardness in being dependent, as we sometimes seem to be, on military expenditures for continued full employment and so-called good times. Issues of money for employment of people in useful though uneconomic lines of work would serve the purpose better than issues of the same size for building military equipment for the most part destined for destruction or the scrap heap.

Our wartime experience, when we produce immense armaments for our own use, give away huge amounts of the same to our allies, and at the same time have ample food, clothing, housing, and transportation available, demonstrates at least one thing. It is that we are substantively able to effect this huge production and distribution. But our financial rules are such as to saddle us with a great debt in the process. Debt has its place in the economic process and as one form of tool in control of the money supply—but not the kind or size of debt associated with the deficit financing of the United States federal government.

Our current financial methods try to make a future generation pay for present war. Yet it is today that all the work of the war is done, all the fighting, all the construction, all the waste. It is impossible to do any of this tomorrow; it has to be today in today's war. And yet institutionally we purport to pay for it tomorrow. We let our financial overlay act as a damper to our substantive abilities. Anything that we have produced or built through the instrumentality of deficit financing in our present institutional setup certainly demonstrates that the building or production is a thing within our substantive capability. The bad monetary results of our federal deficit financing should be avoidable with better financial institutions and methods than our traditional system of debt creation. Among the bad monetary results of deficit financing and a national debt one-third the size of the whole national wealth is the loss suffered by individual holders of national savings bonds who are paid back in dollars bearing less purchasing power than those with which they paid for their bonds.

One feature of monetary reform might be grants of money for needed uneconomic production which we now finance through the machinery of our federal government debt. In times when business was booming, excess purchasing power would be taken off the market by widely levied transaction taxes, so as to avoid runaway prices and to preserve a reliable currency of steady purchasing power. Taxation would be largely concerned with maintaining the correct amount of available purchasing power, by preventing money becoming so out of line with the amount of economic goods as to inflate prices. A reform along lines such as this would avoid the excessive debt structure and the consequent debt manipulation which ride us in our present federal methods of financing necessary uneconomic production.

In connection with a technology which may someday—assuming there is not a too-great growth of population—be such as to be capable of providing ample supplies of any needed resources, there will be an institutional question as to how to make the provision of the resources compatible with the continuing existence of the many loci of independent power which are necessary to a free order.

Suppose that in the United States it was found physically and economically practicable to produce ample quantities of fresh water from the sea, and that the process for doing this was managed by a government agency, either because of the interstate aspects involved or because of reasons analogous to those which have led to municipal, rather than private, ownership and management of the present New York City water supply. Suppose further that this production of fresh water was combined with the recovery of industrially useful and valuable minerals (as even today certain industrial minerals are recovered from the sea). Then arises the problem of how to get the most effective utilization of these minerals. The traditional way in the United States would be to sell them to private entrepreneurs. Perhaps some other method could be devised to decentralize the process of their use. To the extent any method of decentralization was complete enough to give independent control and exercise of judgment to those close to the actual utilization of the minerals, according to their local initiative and with the absence of overmuch political direction, the method would probably approximate private property in its political results.

In the United States the large base of material assets, plus the inherited structure of decentralized control and management of the assets, puts our economic problems in a context more favorable to their solution within the framework of a free order than would otherwise be the case.

The British Isles suffer from a shortage of physical assets. We have already discussed the benefits that accrued to England when she was the workshop of the world and led the world in industrial technology and mechanization. Her trade with the rest of the world flourished, and she became the great creditor nation and world financier. But when other parts of the world caught up with her or surpassed her in manufacturing techniques and capacity, the situation changed. She now has a harder task to preserve a free order with its many loci of power and its tolerance.

It will be difficult for England to compenstate for this lack of the natural resources that provide a national basis of strength. Nuclear energy might solve the problem of sufficient mechanical power. But nuclear energy will be available everywhere and to those with more and better other assets. England's puzzle is a hard one; and only a high order of political intelligence or unforeseeable luck will resolve it favorably to her and the preservation of a free order.

The problem comes to Russia in a different way. She has adequate material resources, except for deficient rainfall and a present shortage of water, and except for a too-brief growing season over much of her territory. But she has a tradition, in the past as well as in recent years, of a bureaucratic, overcentralized control of her economy, which makes it hard to visualize the growth of a free order. And yet if, under the pressure of needing to develop an efficiently managed industry, she is forced to decentralize control and should thereby happen upon something approximating many loci of real economic power, she might be well set for a freer future. She would have grafted individualism upon a tradition of strong, taken-for-granted, obedience to the organized community. Conceivably she might thus hit upon the answer to the ever-present political question of how to combine the necessary degree of central control and over-all direction and obedience with the equally necessary—more necessary to a decent life—local initiative and local control of the actual work of the country.

In the United States, we have to approach the goal from the other side: we have to graft loyalty and obedience to the good of the whole community upon a highly individualistic tradition, and to rid ourselves of the overcommercialization of our ideas and ideals. Russia might possibly reach the goal by accident through pressures for decentralization for economic efficiency, despite the resistance of doctrinaire Marxists and stubborn officials. We will have to see our way to it.

If a free order is to be maintained in the course of changing institutions as circumstances and techniques change, all, no matter what their line of work, will need to lend a hand. Those engaged in education—in our schools and colleges—have a major part to play in establishing the necessary active belief in tolerance, honesty, truth to fact, and equity. What should be the right attitude of businessmen and the professions can be illustrated by the profession of law. Lawyers have a hand in the drafting of our statutes—federal, state, and municipal—and a hand in the drawing of contracts governing our business and our labor relations. The duty of the lawyer is to his client. But that duty can be performed in consciousness of another duty, vital to the good of his client and his country alike, which is the duty of fostering a growing free order and the condition upon which it depends—the rule of tolerance, honesty, truth to fact, and equity.

XXIV. Equity

1. A DEFINITION

In the discussion of *discord* in the first part of this book we saw that violent disorder has occurred when a privileged group blocked the advance of some other group or groups who were capable of functioning better in the interest of greater welfare and strength for the whole community. For example, in Europe the feudal nobility stood obstinately in the way of the rising power of the merchants and the city leaders. A parallel situation came about in Russia as a result of the Czarist regime holding too tight to privilege while failing to tap or to liberate the leadership abilities within the community, and suppressing them instead. We also saw that unjust, imposed order resulted when a community leadership (like that of the Nazis) succeeded through force and fraud in arousing for the time being a consensus of opinion in favor of suppressing minorities and minority leaders who did not have the strength to strike back.

The cure for such discord, whether of disorder or of unjust order, arising from what we called holding too tight to privilege or pushing too hard for power, lies in the attitude and practice of fairness by enough community leaders—the political virtue of equity. A leader can be possessed of a good degree of truth to fact, and see things more or less as they in fact are, and still push too hard his own or his group's particular interests or hold his own or his group's particular privileges too tight for the good of the community. The many loci of power that we know to be necessary for a free order can push too hard or hold too tight unless governed by equity as their rule.

Ambition—the will to power—is necessary to community progress, as without it the community, for better or worse, would lack the motive power essential to produce social change. The stressing by leaders of the rights of their respective groups is a condition of constructive activity in the community. The difficulty comes when the rights are overstressed at the expense of others, when the ambition is out of bounds. Group leaders should stand up for the position and autonomy of their group; but should at the same time see what that position and autonomy have rightly to contribute to the community, the right place of the group as part of the whole going concern. Each group while pushing its own aims and interests is also to see the right aims and interests of the whole and of other groups. The intent thus to see and to realize the fair place of others as well as one's own fair place is equity.

We have observed before that the creative energies and qualities— as, for example, determination and courage—while good in and for themselves are nevertheless neutral as to their good or bad direction and purpose because they can equally well serve wrong causes as well as right. Their usefulness in the results they in fact produce depends on how they are directed. Equity, which intends to find what people's abilities and rightful goals may be and then to give them the chance to realize those goals, is thereby a factor in providing the right direction.

In the internal activities of a free community, tolerance gives the creative abilities their head, equity their rein, but not a cramping rein, rather the rein of spontaneous right direction.

2. EQUITY IN RELATION TO THE OTHER POLITICAL VIRTUES

Just as truth to fact alone will not solve difficult community problems, neither will equity alone. Both are needed. Without equity the calculation of truth to fact would too often be mistaken because misled by bias and partisanship. For example, when a problem is presented like that of the western American farmer who had to sell at prices determined by a world market but had to buy from eastern manufacturers whose wage rates and prices were protected by a tariff on imports, equity is needed and also truth to fact to find a solution. If in such a conflict of interest the East is in control of the national legislature, equity is needed or else the overreaching of the farmer will continue because no attempt will be made to apply truth to fact to finding a fair solution. If the West is in control of the national legislature, truth to fact is needed or there may be a harmful solution in the form of subsidizing farm crops with the result of huge overproduction and expensive federal purchase and warehousing of a glut of produce. Equity on the part of the farm leader will recognize that this particular solution has to be done away with in the interest of the community as a whole.

Equity prevents overreaching and the consequent necessity of over-reacting against the overreaching. American labor had historically in the nineteenth century to make such a hard fight for its rights against ownership that a legacy of bitterness was left on both sides. Intolerance bred intolerance. The equity on the part of industrial leaders which alone would have prevented the original intolerance simply was not there. An underdog can hardly be tolerant towards a snarling top dog. The cure is for men to cease to act like dogs.

As a community becomes more crowded, equity becomes more necessary. In the old days in the United States when there was an unoccupied physical frontier for expansion, if a man's neighbors or employers were inequitable and unjust he could and did move along into new fields. Anybody with a healthy body and hands was needed somewhere. There was ample living space where he could make his own way. There was plenty of that elbow room which we saw was such a practical protection against intolerance. Today the situation has changed. Tolerance is no longer made easy by wide elbow room. Equity is needed if tolerance is to be our working rule.

In equity each sees his place in the community and what it calls for in duty to his fellows. For example, the owners and editors of a great newspaper in the United States must report public affairs significantly and truthfully so as to inform the reader of actual important facts. They must see to it that the reporters and correspondents in Washington put their emphasis on what really looks to them like the important activities on the executive, legislative, and judicial sides of the government, rather than on relatively frivolous but perhaps picturesque witchhunts and inquisitions of one kind and another. For another example, the merchandiser in his advertising must be substantially honest, as this is what fairness to the community requires. What stands in the way in the case of both the newspaper and the merchandiser is Dante's old wolf, the vice of greed—in our particular society the profit motive out of bounds.

A man's equitable right to something which he claims as his position or his property depends on the degree to which he is in fact performing the function of the position or making right use of the property with respect to which he is asserting his claim. In the case of an office which he holds, this means that he is doing what a holder of that office ought, in the light of all the circumstances, to be doing. In the case of a claim which he is making to property or service, it means that he is using the property or service in a way consistent with the good of the community whose rules permit him to have or to control the property or service.

Take the specific case of a business corporation which receives income for providing amusement to the public in an extensive way— say as the owner or licensee of a television broadcasting station or a network of such stations. Suppose the amusement is of a character in fact bad for the young people of the community and debasing to their standards of behavior or their civic and social standards. The business corporation is not entitled to the income. A sense of equity would prevent such a wrong use from ever developing, and would insure that a powerful medium of communication was used for communicating something worthwhile and valuable.

In Western Europe and the United States we pride ourselves on a historical growth that has brought us out of a society of status, where everyone has his place assigned to him, perhaps even from birth, and is told by the ruling regimes his social limits and his social function. We assert the superiority of a tolerant society of contract where one can make his own way and his own agreements and arrangements, and find his own place; and we rightfully decry the totalitarian regimes where the committee tells people what to do and fixes their status.

And yet, if we wish to remain a society of contract without sooner or later running into *discord,* the condition is that our leaders all along the line be governed by equity. For instance, if the community is to continue to tolerate the business leader going his own way with as little restriction as possible, then the business leader must have a sense of equity and recognize the needs for the social and cultural growth of his fellow citizens in an improving free order, and see himself as his brother's keeper rather than as his brother's exploiter.

It is fortunate that the natural influence of imitative response and impersonation is, in the absence of some special intervening interest, benevolent and equitable in its trend. The sense of equity accordingly has at least a double basis—one in this primitive trend of response and impersonation and the other in the conclusion of truth to fact that equity is necessary for a just society and a free order.

3. INSTITUTIONS PRODUCING EQUITABLE RESULTS

An institutional fortification of equity may be needed to protect an equitable majority from injury by the activities of an inequitable minority, and to set a public rule of conduct along equitable lines.

Examples of this institutional support of equity are seen in those statutes which forbid the sweating of labor in bad working conditions or unconscionable hours of work, or which forbid the keepers of saloons to furnish hard drinks to the youthful or to be open at all hours or on all days, or in general to promote maximum drunkenness. In each case the restraint is on excesses of the urge for profit, in the former on the baker, the clothier, or other manufacturer, in the latter on the makers and purveyors of strong drink. Statutes providing for the conservation of assets for both present and future, as in regulations preventing the pollution of water supplies and streams—so as to promote public health, public recreation, and the supply of fish—or in regulations of forest practices in the harvesting of timber so as to provide a sustained yield, are examples of the institutional promotion of equitable results.

Statutory measures for producing equitable results have a further significance in that they prove the existence of equity in community leaders to a degree sufficient to have brought into being these institutional aids to equity. By setting a practical, working example for all in the community of the results of equity, they also play a part in establishing equity as the taken-for-granted rule of community conduct.

The fact that statutory restraints on particular interests are sometimes needed should not be allowed to obscure the much more widespread area in which equity is voluntarily practiced by the majority throughout a good community.

As it is particular interests of individuals and groups that are likely to be the principal threats to an equitable attitude on their part, there is a line of institutional approach to equitable results which depends on bringing these particular interests into line with an equitable aim. An example of this kind of institution is the secret universal franchise which brings pressure to bear on officeholders to be solicitous, as if motivated by equity, of the welfare of any large group of voters. Otherwise they fear they will be turned out of office.

Institutional arrangements can also be made which will remove the likelihood of particular interest coming into conflict with the effort to do equity. An instance is the constitutional provision for life tenure during good behavior of the judges of federal law courts in the United States. As a result of life tenure the judge is removed from the temptation to cater to the persons who have the power of reappointing or re-electing him to office or of removing him. On the other hand, if a judge is periodically up for popular re-election to office he may find it harder to apply the law impartially in a contest, let us say, between a hospital management which has very few votes and a labor union which has a great many votes.

The failure to neutralize particular interests so as to prevent their interfering with equity is seen in the one-party totalitarian states. Here men are judges in their own cause, as the party leaders are the determiners of what is justice in a particular case and of what is in accord with the needs of the state. They naturally lean towards what happens to accord with their own particular interests and needs. There is no impartial judge. Injustices and inequities are the result, discord rather than free order.

4. ASSIMILATION OF NEWCOMERS TO A FREE ORDER

We wish to bring up our children to be good and useful members of a good community, a free order. A sense of fairness towards them requires us to make the effort both to provide a free order fit for them and also to see to it that they are fit for a free order.

We saw in our discussion of the sources of the ideas of what is right, that the young acquire their practical working belief about what is right from the attitude and conduct of those around them and especially those with whom they are in close contact. The process is largely through imitative response to and impersonation of their parents and teachers, and later of community leaders in all the many lines of activity of which they hear and see. Equity requires of these leaders all along the line that they follow in practice the rules which are right for a free order, which means among other things the practice of tolerance, honesty, and truth to fact.

Equity requires that each man should have the chance to find what is best for him. This in turn requires that his circumstances—as enough food, enough health, and enough freedom from the grindstone —are such as to let him gain the worthwhile experiences of life, including the beauty and the love of which he is capable. Whether or not a particular man gets the result—realizes on his chance—depends mostly on himself and his maker. Some people turn the trick under difficult and unlikely conditions. Others just don't have it in them, and miss though the conditions look right. But equity aims to give each his chance.

It was the tolerance, honesty, truth to fact, and equity of enough of our predecessors that have given the present working generation of Americans a good community in which to live, and a community capable, if it will, of defending itself against and surpassing all comers both militarily and in the great fields of science and the satisfaction of creative curiosity and the attainment of substantive achievement along the many lines worthy of a great people. Fairness to the young requires that our leaders all along the line retain and practice these great political virtues. We do not wish to lose for ourselves or our children the key to what has made us a good community, and so repeat—under our modern conditions—the old Roman experience of gradual deterioration and disappearance as a creative influence on the world scene.

What is true of the assimilation of the rising generation of native youth to the ideas and attitudes and practices that constitute and preserve a free order is in principle true of the assimilation of other newcomers also, as the immigrant alien, or the member of a group physically within the community but as yet a minority group imperfectly assimilated, and especially the children born to immigrant or minority-group parents. As it is harder to impersonate and to have a spontaneous fellow feeling for strangers with strange ways, it is necessary that a deliberate effort be made to be fair to them in the process of their adjustment to the life of the community.

The antithesis of equity in this sense was exemplified by the Nazi leadership. The Nazi leader in the effort to instill in those he regarded as Germans—however dull and stupid many of them might be—a pride in themselves and a jingoistic sense of superiority and standing, taught them to despise alien national and racial groups—as the Poles and the Jews, who were justly to be oppressed due to their inherent inferiority as aliens and strangers.

In a population containing groups of differing national origin, or of differing racial origin, the aim of equity is to give to each group its fair chance and to expect to get from each group the best contribution it can make to the community. This fair chance, just as in the case of the simon-pure native of native majority ancestry, means good and healthful living conditions, as good an education for the children and the young as they are capable of taking, a chance to get ahead, as in business—all with the aim that each group will thus be enabled to show what it and its members are actually good for. These requirements of fairness are always obligatory, irrespective of questions of marriage across group lines, or the correctness or incorrectness of a caste solution to problems posed by interracial relations. Equity of course does not require the forsaking of truth to fact in the effort to find out what is really the best arrangement of race relationships in the interest of a growing free order, or to find out how to have a population with the greatest feasible number of members constitutionally and temperamentally capable of tolerance, honesty, truth to fact, and equity.

5. EQUITY ON THE WORLD SCENE

We know that political communities, the separate states of the world, have often fought international wars, either for purposes of aggrandizement or to avoid subjugation by a would-be conqueror. In our discussion of *separation* we saw that war, quite aside from its cruelties and destructiveness, did not set the stage for a better or more just world scene than existed before the war, because war was wholly directed to conquest or defense, and not in the least directed to or concerned with a just and free world order. It was only by accident and on a few occasions that a victorious group with much superior ways to those of the vanquished had succeeded, after the hatreds of war had worn off and been forgotten, in establishing an order to which the vanquished became assimilated as willing participants. We saw that it was true of the First and Second World Wars in the twentieth century that neither had made any lessening of separation on the world scene and had in fact set the stage for new critical fears and hatreds.

If within a particular organized community a man wants to have freedom, that means—in the field of his community relationships—that he wants to be allowed to do what he believes in and thinks worthwhile. We know that a condition of his being allowed on a peaceful basis to do what he believes in, is that he believes in what in fact somewhere nearly approximates what the rest of the community is going to find beneficial or at least not positively harmful to it. If he is not sufficiently governed by equity and the intent to find a good and due place in the community picture, he may well light on a course of action that deprives him of freedom rather than makes him free.

The same thing is true of the various political communities in their relationships with one another on the world scene. Unless the leaders of a community are governed by equity, the intent to find the due and right place of their community in a whole just and free order, they will not light on a course of action that is acceptable to the balance of peoples. Instead, like Hitler or like Stalin or like other national leaders in an era of intense nationalism, they push the freedom of action of their own community too hard, and intensify the ills and conflicts of separation.

The educational scheme from earliest childhood to latest adulthood needs to be aimed so as to produce in capable children, and thereafter to maintain in their maturity, a fair-minded *habit*. This would be the opposite of that prejudice against strangers as strangers that stands in the way of equity on the world scene. The fair-minded and equitable habit could go hand in hand with strong convictions, but the convictions would be subject to review in the light of the actual facts. Equity utilizes truth to fact. While it may have a connection with softheartedness, it has nothing to do with softheadedness. It is not blind or foolish. It knows that if the process of impersonation of other people's needs and attitudes is to be sufficiently accurate so that equity will not miss its mark, events and people must be seen as they really are.

What makes it hard for a community and its leaders to get at the actual truth about the people and purposes of some other community is prejudice. Prejudice in relations between countries takes the form of a convinced and preconceived assumption about the facts—whether in actuality supportable or unsupportable by the true facts—which is present on the part of the members of one well-defined and self-conscious political group towards outsiders. The terms used from ancient times to modern, and the tone and color of the terms, bear witness to this attitude towards outsiders: the barbarians, the gentiles, the frogs, the wops, and the like. Now in some of these cases the outsiders have in fact perhaps been as a group inferior, in others superior, to the group exhibiting the prejudice. The point to remember is that the prejudice is itself no evidence of the fact. Neither is the opposition to the prejudice evidence of the fact. Equity, the intent to find each one's due and true scope in a right whole order, is the clue to an escape from the labyrinth of prejudice, because it makes a man want to find the facts and apply truth to fact in the situation at hand.

Equity breeds equity. Therefore if those who are today fair maintain their physical power and push on in fairness in their relations with others, the attitude may be catching and a progression set under way on the world scene towards supplanting intolerance with tolerance, and dishonesty with honesty.

XXV. Towards a Free Order on the World Scene

1. OBSTACLES

When we were discussing the *divided community* we described the present condition of political separation on the world scene—the separate states of the world at sword's point. There is no need to spell out the facts again. But a summary in general terms may serve to recall the salient features.

We saw the absence of a free order and of the conditions for free order. There was no tolerance between nations: the leaders of each painted and preached the others as hostile strangers; there was no spirit of co-operative compromise, no attitude of peaceful give-and-take. There was no honesty: the foreign country was to be deceived whenever that looked likely to produce a short- or long-term advantage at home. Deceit and threat of violence were the two approaches to actual or potential enemies among the powerful foreign states. There was no equity: the leaders of each separate state were concerned solely with its own aggrandizement. No attempt was made to see the place of other states in a just world scheme. In dealings between the separate states there was no familiar rule to go by, except the rule of suspicion. There was a fear on the part of each community of the unfamiliar ways of other communities, often compounded by feelings of racial hostility towards those abroad. Each country wished to push its own interests by its own methods.

In this world community—really a world disunity—of separate states, there was nothing analogous to the consensus of disinterested leadership opinion not directly involved in a specific dispute that is so important in the case of a particular country in bringing about pressure for the equitable settlement of differences between competing groups within the country. There was no orderly way of curing the situation when a naturally privileged state overreached a less fortunate neighbor. Nor was there any institutional machinery for peaceful adjustment of conflicts when conflict arose because the people of some state or region needed, or thought they needed, to improve their position. There was nothing in common upon which to base such institutions.

The absence both of common recognized need and of any base in tolerance, honesty, or equity for institutions for the peaceable adjustment of particular needs, as, for example, the need to control a food supply or the need of access to a better climate or better living conditions or more useful assets, has meant that there are no adequate institutions and no serviceable way of peacefully satisfying these critical needs when they arise. The usual historical method of attempted adjustment has been by violence—attempted wars of conquest or of defense. The separate states, when faced with the need of improving position, have fought one another to achieve their aims.

We have spoken earlier of the internal discord in a community where too great a population is pressing too hard on too small a food supply and too few material assets. We may emphasize here that penury and shortages within a country produce extremist leaders who are longer on promises than on possibility of performance. Hungry young men without work to provide them a living—a condition always too common in the world and intensified today in some areas by falling death rates without a corresponding fall in birth rates—make local distress. The foreigner, the alien, is blamed by the extremist local leader for the distress. Blaming the foreigner is no route to a free order embracing the whole world scene.

A community may be working its way out of relative poverty and may at this particular point in its history be able to exert great military strength by putting a very large share of its growing productivity into armies and military equipment, while its population generally has an unduly low standard of living. The leaders of such a community, for their own self-preservation as leaders, are under pressure to erect barriers—iron curtains—to hide from their own people true comparisons of their living conditions with the much better living conditions of other communities. This necessity of relying on concealment and fraud at home makes these leaders a poor risk for openness and honesty abroad.

Enormous increases of food and industrial materials would have to be presently produced to provide a comfortable standard of living for the present peoples of the world, let alone the even greater increases needed in the near future to care for growing populations. Mere density of a local population is not itself of too great significance. If the dense local population is manufacturing and performing services for a great area on which it can draw for food and supplies of raw material, it is a sign of developed economic organization. The relation that has to be rightly maintained is the productivity of the producing people and areas to the entire community by which the production is used and consumed. The solution of the problem of pressure of population on resources can be worked at from both ends: from one end, the increase and better utilization of resources; from the other, the control of population so as to have a right relation of productive areas and productive equipment to the populations dependent upon them. There is nothing inevitable about shortage of resources. We may learn to mine the oceans for metals, and we may devise substitutes for metals, which do not themselves require metals for their fabrication. Nor is there anything inevitable about growth and overdensity of population, or even maintaining present densities.

Unfortunately there does in fact at present exist on the world scene a wrong relation of numbers of people to presently available production. This is an underlying obstacle to the chance of a free order embracing the whole world scene, and apparently this wrong relation is likely to worsen before ways of improvement are devised.

It is in the light of these various obstacles to a free order on the present world scene of *separation* that we survey prospects for a growing free order on the world scene and possible practical steps to take in that direction.

2. LEARNING THE HARD WAY

Our goal on the world scene is the supplanting of disorder and unjust order by a free order. As the world scene at present is not one of either a good or free order, the task is even more difficult than that of altering a good order for the better. The task is displacing a bad, long-standing disorder by a new free order.

In our earlier discussion of separation we saw that the recent world-wide wars had resulted in no improvement of order on the world scene. The victors did nothing useful or constructive with their victory. The Americans in vain tried to relapse into the precise state of affairs existing before the war. The Russians proceeded with the construction of an unfree and imposed order. Nowhere was there any solid aim or purpose—far less any solid action—towards the growth of a free order on a world basis.

It is true that in the history of the world to date, improvement as well as deterioration of order have usually been to an accompaniment of violence. Conquest has at times resulted in an improved order holding greater possibility for a greater degree of consent of the governed and over greater regions than had been the case before the conquest. Today, therefore, in looking for a peaceful way of improving world order and in trying to devise a way of bypassing the violence, we have to try to learn what we can from the good that has been produced in the violent course of history.

When one state has conquered another, or when a state has succeeded in overcoming an attempted seccession by one or more of its regions, or when a revolutionary party has succeeded in its revolutionary attempt, if a free order is to be thereafter established, the problem of the victorious leaders is in each case the same. Force must be tapered off, and the enmities and hatreds which are the legacy of force must be dispelled. This will take more than a single generation. Then, if the rule of tolerance, honesty, equity, and truth to fact can sooner or later be established, there will be a free order with the likelihood of maximum consent of the governed and minimum need of governmental force and threat of force.

In ancient times the Persians discovered the use of tolerance towards subject populations, and allowed local religions their accustomed ways, thereby gaining the friendship of local leaders. Witness the naming in the Book of Isaiah of Cyrus as the Messiah—the Lord's Anointed:

Thus the Eternal, the true God, hails Cyrus whom he consecrates—for 'tis I the Eternal who call you by name. I the God of Israel . . . I called you by your name; you know me not, but I delight in you.

The Romans brought to conquered regions a more equitable government and more useful customs and laws, fairly administered, than they had known before. Thus, after the lapse of time, Gaul became a loyal province, proud of its place in the Roman scheme, and a powerful defense to the Empire.

The Norman conquerors in England provided an order superior to what had existed before. Much later in the history of England, the leaders of that country supplanted disorder in India with a much improved degree of relatively just order.

The American Revolution, despite the torn feelings between loyalists and revolutionaries, supplanted an imposed order with a growing free order. And the violence of the Civil War in the United States, which still leaves its legacy of bitterness, kept in being the possibility of a wider free order in the violently preserved United States than could have existed in the two separate national states which would have resulted from successful secession.

Were there to be established today a world government for the limited purpose of maintaining peace and commanding an international police force for that purpose, the resulting peaceful order—assuming the force should be successful in keeping peace—would be an imposed order. This is because in the absence of any satisfactory method of making radical changes in the present international situation, the unsatisfied claims and desires of people in many regions of the world would still be as insistent and as thwarted as ever. There is nothing in the continuance of an unjust state of affairs—which is the present going concern on the world scene—that is made any more just by the forceful suppression of resort to international war.

It can of course be persuasively argued that international war is now so horrible that its prevention at even the cost of prolonging an unjust order on the world scene is the lesser of two terrible evils. But advocates of a world government with powers limited to the preservation of peace should realize that they are advocating the threat of force to maintain what will likely be an unjust order. They are also running the risk of palace revolutions and coups to get control of the world police force, should an effective police force be established. All this may be better than international war; but it is far from a free order on the world scene, which is what the world needs.

It is only as the rule of tolerance, honesty, equity, and truth to fact becomes more widely established as the international rule of a group of effectively powerful states of the world or of a single dominantly powerful state too strong to be successfully challenged (perhaps a world conqueror) that there can be real hope of a free order on the world scene.

No one wants a world conqueror today. One thing we want to avoid is the dreadful pain and injustice of war and the possibility of any world conqueror at all—even a just one. But whether world conqueror or not, or international police force or not, or world government or not, what practical steps can be taken that will increase the prospect of growth of a free world order and the consent of the governed on the world scene? If there are such steps, they should be taken at once in the hope thereby of lessening the chance of recourse to such war as might now prove almost inconceivably destructive. There is nothing in such steps that could interfere with the simultaneous development of other institutional means of trying to avoid war. On the contrary, our hope is to take such steps as themselves are the condition of long-term avoidance of war or of unjust world government—steps which will provide a sound foundation for improved world relations and a possible just and free order on the world scene.

3. AVAILABLE PEACEFUL STEPS

In making a better world scene we obviously have to start off from the base of the world scene of separation as it actually exists today. We may hope eventually to come up with something like a world commonwealth of states devoted to the general over-all aim of the development of the maximum possibilities of individual men and women everywhere, yet with local diversity, local concentrations of real political power, and local administration of the work actually being done. We know that the condition of such a just regime—or of any other actual, realized embodiment of a free world order—is the rule of tolerance, honesty, truth to fact, and equity. We also know that in the absence of a decent livelihood for all, there will be *discord* and no chance of realizing this rule that is the condition of free order.

This is all stated in the most general terms and does not get us forward very far in the way of actual steps towards a free world order. But we need to be aware of the general nature of the goal we are after in order to see whether particular steps we may propose are really in the direction we are trying to take.

We have seen that in a country like the United States there are a large number of associations whose interests cross state lines: great business corporations, farm granges, churches, labor unions, for example. An individual may belong to several of these great groups, owing loyalty to each of those in which he belongs. They are focuses of economic and social interest and of political power. We can see that if similar associations could cross international lines effectively, they would in the same way command loyalty and be one means of softening the present hard lines of separation between the politically organized separate nations, the separate states of the world.

It follows that we should aim to have citizens and nationals of one country take part in as many activities as possible across state lines, together with the citizens and nationals of other countries. The common enterprises thus created would aid the understanding of one group for the other—would increase on all sides the possibilities of more accurate impersonation—and provide a basis for the building of further mutual interests and mutual involvement in the attacking and solution of common problems. We should particularly aim to have as many economic interests of individuals and groups across state lines as possible. Where a man's treasure is, there his heart is also; and a leading and capable industrialist with a large stake in a foreign country will do everything he can to preserve and further his interest, and to avoid the kind of modern war which would destroy it.

At geographical border zones where differing national customs are in contact, the usual practice today as in the past is for nationalistic leaders to intensify national loyalties in a feverish promotion of national prestige. Yet it is at exactly these border zones, where the possibility of conflict is great, that there is also the greatest opportunity for one tradition to gain familiarity—and thereby the hope of possible friendship—with another. Here leaders and people could learn that what they could have in common is more significant for their lives than the prejudices of continued national hostility and its all too obvious dangers. But the learning process requires tolerance, honesty, truth to fact, and equity.

Utilizing Common Interests

The fear of what would happen in a modern war is a motive that puts pressure on governments to try to find practical steps to better relations between countries in the hope of maintaining peace. If, in the hope of a quick victory or in a desperate effort to avoid defeat, recourse was had to the use of hydrogen bombs, the destruction of life and of material goods and plant would be on a stupendous scale. As this fear is present in the minds of all sane leaders in every country, its very horror spurs these leaders to find some way of establishing better international relations. The fear acts as a deterrent to the making of war by one great power on another, and may provide the necessary time and breathing space for tentative tries at better relations.

There have been times when the members of tribes engaged in desert warfare against one another have been obligated by custom to give protection to an enemy starving on the desert, because starvation was so great a common threat to all living on the desert as to override a particular tribal loyalty. The institutional device which sanctioned this custom was the death penalty. A similar recognition of the common threat of hydrogen bombs to mankind might come to override particular national loyalties. The sanction against violation would lie in the conviction that the violating nation would itself suffer destruction.

Although there is a divisive interest between national groups for a greater share and greater control of what the world produces, there is a common interest in a production large enough to meet everyone's needs. Such increased production can be realized only as a result of better application of knowledge and techniques to the actual existing environments in the various countries. As the achievement of such goals is to be effected by education and better science and its application, there is here a field for the formation of educational and scientific groups which cross national lines. As much information should be pooled as possible. Conventions of domestic and foreign teachers, scientists, and other workers and leaders should be held at frequent intervals in the countries concerned. The fact of such conventions, and other like assemblies of nationals from both sides of state lines, and agreements across state lines for putting their practical ideas in practice, would increase understanding of local problems by the nationals of the different countries at the leadership level, and provide a likely step towards lessening hostility.

In the advance towards scientific goals the development of a new line of inquiry, the solution of a new problem, is furthered by a full and free distribution of information. Those of the necessary intelligence and qualifications to push the work forward should be free to observe anywhere. Agreements between the several countries should be such as to make this possible. The institutional setup should be such that whenever the nationals of one country make a significant advance, they could immediately become mentors of it to nationals of other countries. All should be willing to copy the achievements of others and to say that they do so.

As health is obviously dependent, among other more elusive factors, on enough to eat, the attention of those seeking international results in the field of health would have in part to be turned to the discovery of practical ways of utilizing temporary or permanent surpluses in one country by the inhabitants of another. The actual carrying out of the distribution or exchanges involved should be made by such methods, accompanied by truthful information, as to promote the maximum possible international goodwill.

International committees of nationals of the different countries involved in exchanges of goods, like those involved in exchanges of ideas, would become accustomed to working together on a common problem. It is perhaps not too much to hope that when this kind of activity had taken place successfully on a sufficient scale, similar—or in appropriate cases the same—committees could apply themselves to ironing out specific difficulties in relations between countries in areas where the committee members knew the facts and were used to working together. All this would require a departure from the present custom of conducting international negotiations in the presence of overmuch publicity and the resulting temptation to use meetings as sounding boards for loud speech and national self-aggrandizement.

Were one of the world's great religious faiths to undergo such a rejuvenation as to make a convincing appeal at leadership levels everywhere, or were a new religious faith to succeed in universal appeal, the organization—the Church—which became the active embodiment of such a religion could be a source making for a powerful common interest across state lines.

Removal of Government Barriers

In view of the control that the government of a modern state can exercise over its citizens and other inhabitants, those who form opinion in the community should set themselves to persuade the leaders of government that barriers to the creation of interests which cross state lines must be broken down as an essential step towards international peace. Otherwise international business, scientific, cultural, and religious groups and associations will be thwarted in their development.

The leaders of national governments are to see their nations on the world scene as analogous to the independent groups and associations within a nation. That is to say, while a nation may have its own identity and independence, it is nevertheless a part of a whole world scene, and of the adventure and drama of mankind.

From current and past history it looks as though one of the least promising ways to approach world peace is by the absolute self-determination of states along racial and national lines. One plausible way of lessening the rigid drawing of such lines would be free emigration and immigration between countries. Yet we have seen in our study of *discord* that emigration and immigration without restriction would mean that the receiving country would be unable to assimilate the newcomers into its own political tradition. It would have enclaves of essentially alien ways in its midst. If the sending country were over-populated it would, in the absence of birth control, make up the numbers lost in emigration, and would remain under too great population pressure on its resources.

Great human community achievements are likely, as we have seen, to be the result of the lead given to the community by some particular group whose goals and ideas are right in fact. What would free immigration mean to such a community, either directly as a result of the influx of alien newcomers or by way of alteration of the political ideals and traditions of the native leaders of the community and their followers? If the immigrants were sufficiently able and of a character adaptable to the ways of the community, well and good. But if of a totally different tradition from that of the state to which they come, or incapable of adapting to its tradition, or if to any degree subversive agents owing primary loyalty to the state from which they come, then free migration would be inimical both to world peace and to domestic free order.

What, then, should the rule of a government be towards those who wish to enter its state as newcomers, or what should it do to attract or repel inhabitants of other states as prospective immigrants?

Any community has to build on the basis of circumstances as it actually finds them as a result of past history. That platform of fact is the only one from which a government can launch out on a useful program. Suppose then that today the people of one or more great states find themselves in a good climate, with comparative plenty in the way of physical assets, and a technological base allowing such productivity that the people are not in danger of famine or want. The leaders of such a country will in its own interest want to have as large a proportion of capable people as possible doing the work of the country. The country should make itself attractive to newcomers, but only admit those of good health, good intelligence, and of a character adapted to membership in a free order—qualities susceptible with greater or less degrees of accuracy to test. In times of political stress in other countries, circumstances may themselves provide a test of fitness, as in the case of some subject to political persecution, as we saw in the case of the Huguenots.

Countries less favored by nature should also enter the competition for making themselves attractive to newcomers, applying the same tests of ability, health, and fitness for a free order.

This policy of competition across state borders for the acquisition of desirable citizens should prove out as a factor in breaking down the rigid racial and nationalistic barriers that are often a dangerous aspect of international relations. Minority cultural groups could then work out a reconciliation one with another in a great state—a great political unit with an already good dominant political tradition. If that great state should achieve a true free order, all would be willing to be assimilated to it in the main rule necessary to a free order—namely, the rule of tolerance, honesty, truth to fact, and equity—and the institutions suitable to that rule.

A country with too heavy pressure of people on its resources should not just because of that fact be looked upon as entitled to free migration to greener pastures. Such free migration would work against getting as large a proportion as possible of the capable in the best climate with the best assets—which presumably would be the most likely way to get the maximum production of useful goods and food to satisfy the demands on the world scene. From each according to his abilities; to each according to what he is able to do with it. This should be in the best interest of everyone everywhere.

If poverty exists in some region because of too dense population, before the cure is adopted of letting the people emigrate without restriction to relatively roomier foreign territories, the government and people of that region should be induced to achieve a better ratio at home of population to resources and production. Appropriate help should be supplied from abroad to aid in gaining that object. Foreign countries should be expected to accept as immigrants only those, both in number and in potentiality, who are likely to be assimilable to a good political order.

Economic Co-operation

Circumstances at times exist—they do today—when the leaders of opinion in neighboring states, even though historical enemies in peace and in war, see that their respective countries are mutually dependent on one another's giving up rigid economic barriers if all are to achieve an improvement in productivity such as to maintain and then increase their weight and their voice in world councils, and to improve their standard of living. An incentive is thereby provided for the governments of the states to draw together in a program and its statutory implementation which will provide enough basis of political agreement to allow a mutual development of trade and industry beneficial to the participants. Then as this program is realized in actual practice, there will be a hopeful solid beginning of a gradual overcoming of the historical fear, suspicion, and hate that are the legacy from previous years of hostility and war.

We are not here concerned with that economic aid in the way of food and goods, or grants of money to purchase food and goods, which ought sometimes to be extended by one community to another. Such aid may be a work of justice and mercy, or it may be aid to strengthen a potential friend as against a potential enemy. We are here concerned with more permanent arrangements of trade and economic cooperation, such as may lead to sound, strong, and peaceful political relationships.

In the process of uniting for mutually beneficial economic development, the measures taken must—if the scheme is to be permanently useful—preserve and foster the conditions of a free order. For example, if the participating states are all well industrialized, care must be taken through preservation of competition and avoidance of monopoly to promote the many loci of power we know to be essential to the growth of a tolerant free order. Where a vital natural resource, such as a great deposit of metallic ore, is located within the boundaries of one of the states, ownership by the citizens of all the states should be permitted and encouraged, so as to escape the fear that the produce of the mine is being sold in such a way as to unduly benefit the country where it is located, at the expense of the other countries. Ownership by one of the states itself is an insecure base for confidence and reliance on the keeping of agreements.

In establishing institutional provisions to permit the smooth functioning of increased trade and exchange across state lines, and then in making the institutions actually work, close acquaintance and perhaps close ties will come into being between citizens of the different states which, together with individual investment across state lines, will all work in the direction of doing away with the hostility that is fostered by too rigid national lines of separation. These institutions have among other things to provide for satisfactory land, water, and air transport, the more or less rapid removal of frontier dues and barriers, the statutory right of nationals of one participating country to carry on business in the others, the financial and balance of trade measures to keep currencies sound and exchangeable (perhaps leading to a single union currency), the financing of capital requirements by banks operating across state lines, and the regulations governing their procedures, the protection of labor, and its right to work anywhere in the participating states—assuming that these states are enough alike in custom, tradition, and inheritance so that racial friction will not thereby be produced—as well as provisions to protect farmers from the effects of temporary glut of this or that particular item of produce. The logical requirements for successful functioning of such an economic union themselves tend to the superseding of the unrestricted political authority of the participating states by the necessary authority of the interstate economic agencies. The relations of those within the growing economic union to those outside involve matters of adjustment, in the course of which those within the union will tend to come closer together and to diminish their old attitudes of hostility and suspicion.

We have already seen that when a man feels that he has become part of a great group or widespread community that gives him fair scope for his talents, he can then hold less intensely a fighting loyalty to some smaller entity which earlier bound him. For a time the two loyalties go on side by side. Then change and growth make one predominate over the others. The citizen of Connecticut who also is a citizen of the United States does not feel that Connecticut and its citizens must make war on New York and its citizens. He still acknowledges loyalty to Connecticut but it is within a larger scheme of loyalty to the United States—a scheme within which he finds his satisfactory role. Economic union is a practical step to such a larger scheme of loyalty on the world scene, a step in the direction of a world free order.

The leaders of such an international economic union should in time find ways to permit others to become affiliated with the growing union, so as to entrain new participants, and to gain a wider base of good international and supernational relations.

If in such a growing economic union one or more of the powerful states should come to achieve a good and just free order, the example would exert a powerful influence on all others in the group, and in course of time outside the group as well. A light would be lit that even iron curtains would find it hard to shut out.

Extensions of Law and Legal Process

We saw on the domestic scene that the law of contract, and courts to interpret and enforce the carrying out of agreements by providing damages and penalties for failure to do so, were necessary even in a business community where almost all were honest and wanting to abide by their agreements. Such legal procedures were needed to protect the honest from the dishonest and unscrupulous minority, and to relieve the honest themselves from pressure to adopt short cuts and sharp practices, contrary either to the letter or spirit of agreements, through fear that the other party was planning to do so. Similarly the criminal law and the law-enforcement agencies make it unnecessary for the honest and law-abiding citizen to jump the gun in his own behalf for fear that his neighbor will do so first. Each person is aware of the advantage of this rule that makes it no longer necessary to jump the gun.

Between the separate states of the world there is the same fear on the part of one state of sudden hostile action by another, and the same pressure to jump the gun, and consequently pressure to be armed to the teeth for self-defense. While there is also the same need for a reliable interpretation and enforcement of international agreements, there is no judge or arbiter on whom a competitive state is willing to rely in matters which it regards as essential to its safety or welfare.

Legal justice requires a judge without a particular interest in the dispute at hand. At present there is no way of finding such a judge in cases involving national security or ambitions, racial pride, claims of superiority of one group of people over another.

Legal justice also requires a predominant public opinion which stands back of the enforcement of legal decision and supports the determination of the judge. This condition too is absent in the case of international disputes and their settlement.

A still more fundamental stumbling block is that in the case of major substantive political differences, such as rights to good living room and access to good assets, there are no principles of law to apply. On the domestic scene the law represents the mandate to obey the working rules which the community by custom, often aided or extended by statutes, has found to be good for furthering the orderly carrying on of life and its activities within the community. Between the separate states of the world there are no such generally accepted working rules.

And yet, when all this has been admitted, there is in this field the possibility of taking a first step, which may lead to other more solid steps in the direction of more peaceful international relations. This step follows the principle of laying hold of anything useful at hand—building on something, even though not as extensive a foundation as you might like to have. The step is increasing the jurisdiction of international courts of justice.

When political leaders of two countries have made an agreement or a treaty on political matters, there is no reason—other than dishonesty of intent on the part of one set of leaders or the other—to refuse to provide that a tribunal of disinterested judges should decide what the agreement means in the case of a falling out about it. This interpretation is a judicial function, as opposed to the making of the agreement, which may have involved factors mainly in the realm of policy.

One area in which the extension of legal process is practicable is in the interpretation of treaties or statutes which set up an interstate economic union such as we have just discussed. A uniform interpretation of the treaties and statutes is necessary within all of the participating member states. A court of law whose function is this interpretation and whose decisions are to be recognized and binding in each of the several jurisdictions, marks a definite step in the direction of enforcement of rights and duties which have a supernational basis.

As the decisions of such a tribunal prove satisfactory as a means of smoothing out friction over disputes about treaty observance, the leaders of the separate states of the world may feel their way to more and more situations where they are prepared to be bound by law. Here again, the progress would be slow except as leaders of the respective states and their citizens through other activities across state lines begin to feel more interests in common than has been the case hitherto and historically.

4. ALLIANCE IN WAR

Communities theretofore suspicious of one another and potentially hostile may be thrown together—as in military alliance—by the common interest of dealing with a common feared threat. That this has not in the past proved a good basis for steps to permanent peace between the allies is common knowledge. To cite the falling out amongst allies following World Wars One and Two demonstrates this sufficiently.

Yet the allies are thrown together by a common powerful interest during the time of threat. Every effort should be made by statesmen to try to build upon this base something better than the old *status quo* of separation and hostility temporarily put in abeyance to meet the common military threat. A model for this kind of action was the successful steps taken by the leaders of the American colonies to frame the United States and the United States Constitution following the successful American Revolution. They did not fall back into either the condition of separate communities or the relatively impotent national regime represented by the earlier Articles of Confederation between the revolting American states.

5. AN INTERNATIONAL CONFERENCE

The United States federal government—the central government at Washington—has direct taxing power, administered by its own agents, over the citizens of the several states. In addition it has the power of spending for substantially anything for which the federal Congress—the House and Senate—see fit to appropriate. This spending power is aided by the constitutional lodging of control of the currency in Congress. One result of the combined taxing and spending powers has been a trend towards equalization of purchasing power of consumers throughout the United States. In the states which are today more poorly endowed than some of their neighbor states, there is much federal aid and assistance. It is not just a one-way benefit, as these less prosperous states all contribute to the nation's total economy and varied social life, as well as to the industrial profits of the richer states in the Union.

By way of analogy one might imagine a world federation of the hitherto separate states of the world, with a supergovernment which had direct taxing power and the power by spending, and a consequent power of lifting the living level of poorer parts of the world without injury to the more productive parts. However, in the present state of world resources and technology, such a prospect is out of the question. It has been estimated that if all the people presently living in the world were to consume nonrenewable resources (metals and coal and oil, for example) at the rate per person now consumed in the United States, this would mean a tenfold increase of such consumption annually. The amount of factory and equipment which would be required to produce an annual flood of consumer goods at the per capita level of that of the United States would itself represent a spectacular increase in the use of these dwindling resources. No one suggests that this, or anything like it, is attainable over the near term even if desirable.

Leaders of a country that is in possession of relatively good assets, like Russia or the United States, would not participate in any such federation. They would fear forcible attempts at equalization or taking from their country assets which it needed for itself. Russia or the United States would be likely to resist a supergovernment even with the limited power of maintaining an army to keep peace, unless it were in control of the army, or certain that the army would not fall under the control of others. This is because an army strong enough to keep peace between powerful nations would, as we have already pointed out, be strong enough to help those who controlled it dominate the world.

Yet here again, while recognizing the fact that building any kind of a just and free order on the world scene will be a long process, we should not give up in despair and balk at the effort to take what practical steps we can in that direction.

Among these steps is a world forum, a conference of representatives of the separate states of the world, where a world consensus of opinion can be formed. In such a forum pressure can be brought to bear against those seeking to enlarge their own power and influence by way of imposition of an unjust order upon others. In such a forum measures can be devised and opinion marshaled in their behalf, which can promote the taking of those useful steps across state lines in the fields of health, trade, production of food and consumer goods, and all constructive activities for the peaceful improvement of international relations.

The delegates to such a conference will be well aware of the true comparison between freedom and the lack of it in the several countries; and their judgment gradually inclined towards the desirability of a free order ruled by tolerance, honesty, truth to fact, and equity. The example of free order, when attained in particular states, would be persuasive.

It is also possible that an opinion-forming international conference of this kind, as it proved useful and successful in its actions and recommendations, would gradually enhance its own prestige and become itself an object of loyalty of leaders in the various regions of the world. By a course of growth as a useful institution—the growth in England of the power of Parliament offers an analogy in much less difficult circumstances—such a conference might acquire political power. In the future, as the leaders of the several countries in the world were actually engaged in international activities on a greater, more friendly scale, such an international conference might feel its way to more power, be trusted with more power, as some kind of world representative congress. Needless to say, the problems of representation in such a congress if it were to have actual power would have to be carefully worked out so that all countries would feel their interests to be sufficiently protected. The problems would be far more difficult than those which confronted the founding fathers of the United States when they hit upon the Connecticut Compromise for different bases of representation in national House and Senate which made agreement upon the present form of the United States possible.

XXVI. Friends and Enemies
on the World Scene

1. ONCE AN ENEMY NOT ALWAYS AN ENEMY

We remember that many medieval towns regarded one another as enemies. But when the leaders of these towns came to recognize that they could do better in common peaceful relations of trade and commerce, the towns became amicable neighbors in a new, wider, national focus of interests. A new category of enemies was thenceforth found to be more meaningful. We remember the traders in France allying themselves with the King—utilizing the King, and he them—as against various mutually hostile feudal nobles, whose conflicts with one another were interfering with the good development of town and country alike.

From the point of view of the world as a whole, today's quarreling nations and national leaders are analogous to the separate independent quarreling feudal jurisdictions and their noble leaders. In those days the capable people were looking for some way to avoid the local conflicts in the interest of realizing the constructive possibilities with which the conflicts were interfering. So today capable leaders are looking for a way to avoid the international conflicts of today.

Between nations with evident possibilities of co-operative action along certain lines—as the economic improvement of production and trade in the nations of Western Europe—steps have been taken in our own time towards getting together and building a wider integration of interests across state lines. But what of the case between avowed enemies with profound differences in doctrinal belief—as the Communist totalitarian states with their centralized controls and the private property states with their decentralized controls? In this kind of conflict it is hard to see the new focus of wider interest which will bring the present enemies together. How, for example, is a political leader of the United States or a political leader of Russia really to come to see and believe that his country will do better in a new regime where it is only a part of the going concern, than either in the old regime where it is master in its own house, or in a new regime, established by way of violence, where it might hope still to be master?

We might summarize in the most general terms what we have already seen to be the reasons why two conflicting communities either get together or else stay apart. What has brought two sides together has been the advantages both can see in peaceful relations. What keeps two sides apart has been the disadvantages they can see in any kind of closer union—particularly falling under the control of someone with a repugnant doctrine of some kind, or running too big a risk of long-term inferior status and position (as, for example, in a geographically unfavorable climate) on the part of an ambitious component group.

As for the incentives for hostile contemporary leaders and their states to get together, we have named the fear of destruction as most significant. It is clear that the nation as an object of its citizen John Smith's loyalty is not serving him as well as it might, if it throws him into a mid-twentieth-century war. We know that the failure to serve interests, especially vital ones, is a potent factor in the start of the breakdown of a traditional loyalty. John Smith and his fellows, with a greater or less degree of awareness, begin feeling their way to something better. So that if any leader can light on the steps, or on institutions that look reasonably promising, towards an orderly way out of *separation,* there will be a great potential following ready to try the steps and be loyal to the institutions.

Once an enemy not always an enemy. History indicates that the change from enemy to friend is likely to come about because old enemies see some new threat on the horizon which they get together to defeat. The world in that case is not more peaceful. There is just a realignment of who are friends and who enemies. For example, after the Second World War the United States gets together with its former enemies Japan and West Germany to oppose its former ally the Soviet Union.

Changes may take place that remove part of the reason for enmity. A nation that has not had sufficient control of a good food supply or of land with climate, resources, and area adequate for producing needed industrial equipment as well as needed food, may have come into control of sufficient new good land and resources. This may have been either by way of conquest of a neighbor or by way of agreement and some kind of effective and reliable economic union. In either case—though conquest of a neighbor gives rise to uneasiness on the part of others—such a nation would be a better prospect in the future as a peaceful partner on the world scene because better satisfied along the lines of fundamental need.

Unfortunately climatic changes have been slow, measured on a time scale of millennia rather than decades, so the fact that Russia's growing season is too short, her temperatures too cold, her harbors too ice-bound, and her rainfall too little for the kind of growing country she is, puts pressure on her for political expansion. At the same time, Russia's political regime, as we have seen, seems to be one resented and feared by strangers. This combination of physical and political facts makes making a friend of Russia basically difficult at the moment, and increases the danger of attempts at violent conquest on her part. Her enemies, as a condition of their own defense or more hopefully of a solution of her problem as a member of the world community, must see Russia's problem for what it is.

Once an enemy on grounds of doctrinal belief not always so. We have earlier pointed out that the intermediate leadership levels of Russia in the first quarter of the twentieth century were generally willing to take their chance on a new form of centralized government and property control with which they were unfamiliar, as against a government and a control by landlords with which they were all too familiar and knew to be overreaching. It is possible for a revolution to take place the other way round—from a too familiar overreaching by an overcentralized government to a system of decentralization, many real loci of power, and the conditions of a free order.

2. UNWELCOME CHANGES IN CURRENT REGIMES

As the best prospects for peace on the world scene lie in the doing away with iron curtains and the attainment of free order in the various regions of the world, we would do best to try to find our friends in those countries whose leaders are aiming over the long term for a free order. But this must not blind us to the fact that in countries where there is not a sufficient proportion of people ready for it, a free order is not possible. If, in some backward country, progress is to be made from subsistence farming in closed village units to a better-balanced economy with more industrialization, it is likely that for the time being political compulsion will have to be brought to bear by the leaders of such a country. An illiterate poverty-struck people may need a despotic government to direct its first steps in improvement.

The United States, if it wishes to make friends of the leaders of a backward country who are trying to get some industrialization, must determine what group of hardheaded leaders are likely to be realistic enough to succeed and then back them, perhaps with direct grants of aid, preferably with agreements of and in exchange for raw materials which they may have and which we need. We of course are also right to hold out the true good to be found in eventual decentralized free order; and this we do best by being an example of that good. But to think that such a backward country is soon, if ever, to have democratic procedures along the lines of our own model, or to expect them shortly to have decentralized production of consumer goods is unrealistic in the extreme. For such a decentralized scheme to succeed there needs first to be good education available to those capable of receiving it, and then self-reliance on the part of many intermediate leaders within the community. This takes time.

The leaders of the Russian Soviet Communist regime try to make allies of the backward countries by promising them technological aid, just as we do. If industrialization is to be brought to an illiterate agrarian country whose people would like its benefits because it looks like the only way out of poverty and plague, there have to be unwelcome changes in local administration, education, and in the old traditional features of a way of life incompatible with industrialization. The Russians may be more ready than we to back a friendly local potentate in knocking together the heads of recalcitrant village leaders.

3. BE POWERFUL, AND PUSH TOWARDS AN EQUITABLE SCHEME

It is easy to recognize some institutions that will *not* make for a better world order—for example, an iron curtain erected against the presentation of full facts about one country to another. If the leaders of any country profess they are for peace, but maintain an iron curtain against full and truthful information from outside, they are in actual practice against peace. They have outlawed the prospect of setting impersonation to work in the understanding by one people of other peoples' ways, problems, successes, and hopes.

The question rises whether it is inevitable that some differences between enemies should be too deep for peaceful reconciliation. On the answer depends the possibility of change by nonviolent growth towards a free order on the world scene. If the differences are too deep, even if international war were to be avoided—which would be doubtful—there would certainly be attempts at internal subversion and palace revolution in the effort of leaders of hostile interests or regions to gain the upper hand.

Our hope must be that a free order which stays strong will show that its rule of tolerance, honesty, truth to fact, and equity provides a model and a means for reconciling even the deepest practical differences. It is likely that more than one set of institutions can be found to be compatible with free order. Two regions, or states, or nations, each organized with a true free order, need not fight one another. They can work out their differences equitably and tolerantly.

It is possible to draw up a statement which, in the light of present-day techniques and known useful natural resources, sets out what a modern community needs in the way of climate, rainfall, soil, mineral resources, access to the sea, and so on, in order to have the base for the standard of life attainable by a modern community in present-day circumstances. It is also possible to see which of the present separate states of the world approximately have such resources, and which are in real want of them.

When a state is in want of the necessary resources, it is very likely not strong enough to take them from some other state by force, and in that case, in the absence of trade, will remain a have-not state, its inhabitants unhappy and in relative poverty. But if well-endowed and well-developed neighbors are fair-minded and equitable, a system of exchanges can be worked out to supply wanting materials and equipment—always subject to the conditions that those receiving the equipment become capable of using it, and that population pressures are not too great for the currently available resources on the world scene.

The burden of establishing a peaceable and just world community is upon those who are in the good climates and have the plentiful resources. The others are only in a position to claim more than they have at present, and if thwarted, to try to correct their position by force or by emigration and the gaining of influence within a well-endowed state.

The setting-up of peace plans or the making of nonaggression pacts, in the absence of a positive effort for interstate justice and equity, is nothing but a disguised form of holding too tight to a privileged position.

The sanction in equity against gangsterism within a particular functioning community, let us say the United States of America, is that the community provides other better methods by which individuals and groups can acquire a livelihood and standing within the community—methods which, unlike gangsterism, are consonant with domestic peace and a free order. There is no equivalent sanction against gangsterism in the case of the separate states of the world. Consequently in the world community there is no moral ground for condemning aggressive war other than the horror of war itself.

It follows that if peace is to be prosecuted with sincerity by the well-endowed communities, it is essential that while pushing their own rights, interests, and positions, they at the same time see what an equitable world picture would look like, and recognize their own place within such a picture. If they wish to eliminate international gangsterism, they will need to provide means by which the several have-not states of the world can better their positions peacefully.

It is only by an attempt to see the possible good and value rather than the strangeness of foreign ways of doing things, at the same time maintaining a critical and skeptical attitude at home so as to distinguish truthfully between what is useful and what is harmful in its own way of doing things, that a community can escape intolerance towards the foreigner. Only in this way, for example, is there a way out of the hostilities of excessive nationalism.

A man will, and very likely should, love his own neighborhood and its ways more than he does those of strangers. But this does not justify a failure to attempt a rational judgment as to those respects in which his people's ways are inferior to those of the stranger.

It should be possible in the United States for schools and colleges to present truthfully views about foreign history. To the extent that a foreign community is in fact a real threat to us, that of course has to be recognized for the sake of survival. But as a practical means of building up tolerance and equity, show truthfully what the foreigner's problems are and why he is adopting the solutions—mistaken though they may be—that he is in fact adopting. By giving this kind of accurate information to our capable young men and women, we would begin to allow the natural tendencies of impersonation to make for friendliness—tendencies all too easily overridden by hostility and suspicion. Such teaching would diminish some of the more irrational fears and hatreds.

National leaders are afraid of an education which teaches friendship for foreigners, because they think this may make for a pacifism that will render their nation defenseless against some other warlike nation—let us say one with a *Herrenvolk* philosophy and education. Yet the main hope that present-day nations, the separate states of the world, will progress peacefully to some more inclusive kind of grouping lies in the growth of the feeling of friendship and common cause with the foreigner.

Things must be seen as they are. Leaders must have a view of what makes a good and right community at home and on the world scene, a free order and the conditions of a free order. Then there will be hostility to the foreigner only as he is in fact overreaching his place or is trying to set up a community wherein to exert an imposed and unjust dominion over others. The creation of an eventual free order on the world scene will be rendered more likely if the rulers of the several states apply the same thoroughgoing corrections in their community practices and attitudes towards neighbors that would be promoted over the long term by a hypothetical just world conqueror.

A just peace within a community—and this is as true of the world community as any other—is on a secure basis only as long as the competent members of the community are trying to find their right place in the entire picture. Equity is therefore a necessary condition of a just and peaceful world scene.

Truth to fact lets us see that we must be powerful if we wish to survive in the present world, where in fact those with power lay down the law to those without power or without powerful supporters to speak for them. That is to say, that while working towards a free order on the world scene and equitably taking every available step towards just peace, we must still see things as they are in a presently unjust world and be guided thereby. A country working towards justice and itself trying to realize a free order at home at the same time that it is trying to allay world suspicion and hatred, must be so powerful that no one will take the chance of using force against it.

Equity and truth to fact are the hope for making a start towards free order and just peace on the world scene. Tolerance and honesty will have to come later, because without equity and truth to fact—and particularly equity—there will be no will to tolerance and honesty, no desire for them.

XXVII. Rule as Role

1. UNFETTERED BELIEF IN RULE

The government of any politically organized community is stronger if the people who are subject to its control believe rather than disbelieve in the regime and the rule by which they are being governed. This is because a rule that is thoroughly believed in by a member of the community and accepted by him as part of his worthwhile role is willingly followed. Every government group is aware of this and does all it can to instill into its citizens and subjects a belief in its rule.

So we saw in our discussion of *discord* that the Nazi government in Hitlerian Germany and the government of Stalin in Russia aimed to induce a belief in the infallibility of their respective regimes. This they attempted by various forms of deception, including false assertions of fact, concealments of fact, and making scapegoats of lesser officials for the mistakes of the top officials or for unavoidable disasters.

A belief in a regime induced by such means, or a belief eventually brought about in a man through fear of punishment or demotion if he fails to profess belief, is not a free or unfettered belief. A follower of Hitler, or of Stalin, may have in many cases come more than halfway to think that he was living and functioning under the good rules of a good game. But he was blinded, or blinded himself through fanaticism, to what a real look at the actual facts would have shown.

Compare in terms of freedom the convinced Nazi with an oppressed German opposed to the Nazi regime. The convinced Nazi at best could have been said to be free in the sense that he believed in the rule and felt free from unwanted external restraint. But he was unfree because blinded to many of the significant facts bearing upon his conduct and that of his country, and because his choice was therefore fettered, being made by a mind shackled by misinformation. The oppressed German, on the other hand, someone of the dissident Christian ministry, for example, was obviously unfree in that he hated the regime and political rule to which he was subject and was keenly aware of external restraint. He was free in that his mind was not yet corrupted or deceived, but still independent and trying to look at all the facts.

Fettered, unfree beliefs have been common enough in history. In ancient days the believers in Moloch had their system of human sacrifice to placate the deity—a belief induced by who knows what dark fears and tragic mistakes of fact. Or more recently there is that tribe in Siberia which is said to have believed that a man's condition through a future life after death would be the same as his condition at the time of death. So the son of some aged father would be torn between natural love of his parent and the mistakenly induced sense of duty to kill him in a comparatively comfortable moment for the sake of his long future. Such beliefs are not such a far cry as we might wish from today's irrational beliefs that also run counter to the demands of natural response and impersonation—for instance, the harsh Nazi racial beliefs. Such beliefs require a blind, unquestioning acceptance, because free inquiry, like a fresh breeze, would clear the air of them.

For a free order, an unfettered belief in the rule is requisite rather than a belief which is the result of force, fraud, fear, concealment, or mistake of fact. Such an unfettered belief characterizes a whole, free man.

The word freedom and the word free are used in many contexts and with many variations of meaning. But in every case, from the most superficial definitions to the most accurate, there is present the idea of absence of compulsion. This means more than the absence of physical compulsion. A man would not be free if he were having to make his choices of action without benefit of knowing the pertinent facts where the facts had been deliberately concealed from him or he was the victim of deception or fraud.

In this book we are interested in a free order in a politically organized community, and not in any theoretical or abstract idea of perfect individual freedom divorced from the realities of actual life of the individual as a member of a real community. Nevertheless, for the sake of a whole look at the picture of practical political freedom, it is worthwhile to state summarily, and without further discussion, what this abstract and ideal freedom might be. A man could perhaps be said to be completely free if the internal factors of his native temperament and acquired disposition (including his beliefs) and the external conditions of his environment were such that all his actions were in line with his conscious desires and needs, and his conscious desires and needs were in line with his basic desires and needs, and if in addition his desires and needs were in harmony with one another without any conflict between desire and need.

With any such perfect freedom, or the possibility of it, we are not here concerned, other than as a perhaps useful reminder that actual approaches to freedom in human affairs are not to be condemned because not matching a theoretical ideal. And if we are not concerned with freedom in the abstract, still less are we concerned with those metaphysical problems of free will and of who and what is a free agent—matters with which the human intelligence, subject as it is to inherent limitations of perception and insufficient powers of understanding, has proven unable to cope.

Here we leave this short digression on abstract freedom and shall not return to it. Our interest is in freedom in a free political order.

2. TWO ASPECTS OF FREEDOM

Two significant aspects of freedom for a man who is a member of a politically organized community are: living by a rule that gives maximum scope to his talents and his choices, and living by a rule that gives maximum likelihood of unfettered belief in the rule.

As to maximum scope to the individual, we have shown that this is provided by the rule of tolerance, honesty, truth to fact, and equity, and that departures from this rule bring about discord, imposed order, or disorder, with their accompanying restraints and frustrations.

We have reviewed the authoritarian view of government as the provider of scope to the people. This view is that the wisdom of a tight, self-perpetuating governmental group is necessary to provide an imposed social order and framework within which the government controls and directs in detail the activities of the rest of the community. The authoritarian political leaders purport to believe that only in this way can individuals and associations be prevented from working at cross purposes in a wasteful and disorganized manner. We have shown by actual historical examples, mainly from modern times, that in practice an authoritarian government group is unable to direct either equitably or efficiently a complex contemporary community, and that instead it pursues the ordinary group motive of protecting its own position, power, and prestige by any means available, including dissimulation, failure to admit error, and what we have called government by scapegoat.

As to living by a rule that gives maximum likelihood of unfettered belief in the rule, we have shown that the authoritarian theory is that the whole people—leaders in the various lines of community activity, intermediate leaders, and followers—are incapable of unfettered belief in a right rule. Accordingly a rule, a party line, is laid down by the authoritarian government and fortified once again by refusal to admit error, by fraud, and by force or threats of force, and by rigid censorship of ideas and the means of public communication and information. We saw that the rule of such a government was characterized by a ratio of a large amount of force or threat of force on the one hand to a small amount of consent of the governed and free belief in the regime on the other.

The modern authoritarian state with its long-armed, sharp-eared, and prying-eyed single-party government is not a fit abode for a fair-minded man who wants to live a life where he and his friends can be free of intimidation, get honest answers to their questions, and come to a wholehearted belief in the rule of their community and the worthwhileness of their role as citizens.

In a free order, on the other hand, with its many loci of independent power and its rule of tolerance, honesty, truth to fact, and equity, the leaders all along the line and the good and capable people can come to an unfettered belief in the rule by which they live. The more facts the citizen knows accurately and the more diligently he pushes his inquiry—an inquiry, for example, like that we have made in this book—the stronger the rule of the free order will stand. Dissimulation and fraud are not needed to bolster such a rule. We have seen that free inquiry discloses the weaknesses and the fallacious elements inherent in authoritarian rule. That is why free inquiry cannot be tolerated by an authoritarian regime. But under free and intelligent questioning the free order and its rule emerge as something clearly desirable, and the object of the citizen's unfettered belief as the rule of a free order and a good community. The belief is as we have seen well based in the actual historical facts of political life. Consequently, the better these facts are known, the more evident is the desirability of the rule of a free order as the alternative to discord, which is the absence of free order.

The two aspects—the two requirements—of political freedom are thus satisfied for the citizen governed by the rule of the free order, the rule of tolerance, honesty, truth to fact, and equity. He has maximum scope within the rule, and it is a rule which can gain his unfettered belief. He can take an active hand and self-reliant part in the growth of ever more satisfactory free order in his community.

3. RULE OF A FREE ORDER TAKEN TO HEART

Some of the most serious of the *discord* cases, with a bad prognosis for the near future and for the distant future if not cured, were those characterized by apathy and indifference at leadership and other levels in the community. No community effort or individual effort on behalf of the community seemed worthwhile. Apathy in some cases resulted from too great substantive burden, as in prolonged war, or from too hard circumstances, as disease. But the most striking cases—as that of France before the Second World War—were those of loss of any sense of worthwhile role or any conviction of valuable purpose. The French leaders did not believe in their political order enough to make it worthwhile to get ready to defend it. We recall that in such cases each man is for himself to get what he can out of the current situation, but without heart in anything like a truly satisfactory role for himself as a member of a great community.

Laissez-faire, leaving each to his own devices, is a good principle when the ambitious people in the community have a sense of group discipline and of loyalties to the community which they take for granted and which thus temper *laissez-faire,* so that the benefit of both the individual initiative and the loyalty to the group is gained. But when the group loyalty is gone, the individual initiative degenerates into a rat race and into indifference to any good community aims or achievement.

We remember that historically a softening process has often taken place in the leaders of those dwelling in good climates, in the "fertile crescents," with good assets and relative plenty. This softening process has resulted in a loss of will to see that the community gets ahead. So it is that the relatively well-to-do communities have succumbed periodically to conquerors from a relatively harsher environment and less easy circumstances. Those living a comfortable existence have sometimes not been willing to go out of their way in the direction of real discomfort, such as might be involved in a belt-tightening and the sacrifice of present comforts because of necessary preparation for defense. Not so those who are hungry, but not so hungry as to have lost their strength and ambition. To them the simple and worthwhile purpose of satisfying their hunger at the expense of their soft neighbors is natural enough.

In the United States at mid-twentieth century there appeared to have been a lessening of belief in the worthwhileness of the community aims and ideals. Some of our officers and soldiers in the Second World War, and notably in Korea, were not imbued with the same belief in their country and its ways as was true of officers and soldiers in either the Civil War or the First World War. In this they may have only been reflecting a like loss of belief by leaders of community opinion.

The indifferent and the apathetic are not free. Their full powers are in abeyance. They do not have an unfettered belief in a cause and the conviction that it is worthwhile. Often they know this, but do not see the way out of their indifference. Dedication to a worthwhile role is the cure.

A potent factor in bringing about change in the organization and control of the community has always been the determination, conviction, and loyalty to a cause of some leader or leaders. In ancient times the Hebrew prophets and their faithfulness to a religious conviction strongly taken to heart demonstrated the power of a cause taken to heart. We remember in much more modern times, in the early history of our own country, the driving force of the Puritan leaders. A little later the determination of the American Revolutionary leaders to be free of arbitrary government had a long-term political result in the state and federal bills of individual rights in state and federal constitutions.

Taking a cause to heart has power for evil accomplishment as well as good, as we saw all too well demonstrated in our own times by the leadership of the Nazi party in Germany. The fact important for our purposes here is that the determination and conviction of the Nazis and their erroneous *Herrenvolk* ideal was enough to have enabled them to overpower, had it not been for the intervention of others, the potentially much stronger France and Britain, the leaders of the former being afflicted with indifference because scarcely believing in their own political order as worthwhile, and the leaders of the latter with blindness.

In our own times we have seen the Russian party chiefs attempt to make use of the political effectiveness of a cause taken to heart by trying to instill in a large number of intermediate leaders the kind of conviction and belief which was so powerful in the small group of Revolutionary leaders who overthrew the Kerensky regime and established the present Soviet State.

In Russia the location of centralized political power is in the top leaders of the present-day Communist party, and it is these leaders who wield ultimate authority and are the makers of policy. The formal government officials can be in effect viewed as executive, legislative, and judicial arms which carry out and fulfill the policies of the party leadership. The party itself is so organized as to have offices of party officials more or less paralleling those of the officials in the formal governmental structure, in the interests of preserving political orthodoxy all along the line.

In the effort to get as broad a base as possible of orthodox party believers, the Russian leadership had taken into the Communist party of the Soviet Union members who in 1960 were reported to amount to about one out of every twenty-five of the population. Only those were admitted to the Party who, as a result of trials of belief, character, and energy, appeared to be convinced Communists, prepared to hew strictly to the line of the party leadership. The leaders thus hoped to have a sufficiently large politically reliable elite, who could be counted upon as loyal supporters of the leaders and program because they had demonstrated in word and deed that they had taken the Russian brand of Communism to heart. In its own words, the Party was described as *"a voluntary militant union of like-minded Communists consisting of people from the working class, the working peasants, and working intelligentsia."*

Causes taken to heart for the short term are to be distinguished in their political effects from those taken to heart over the long term.

One common cause which commands short-term belief is defense of the community of which a man is a part. People rally to the defense of their community and its ways when the community is under open attack; and if, unlike the France of the Second World War, they have not previously been too long asleep may defeat the attack. But when the pressure is off, the obvious need for unity in defense is no longer present, and the unifying cause in which to believe in gone.

Another cause which commands short-term community belief is the push for more assets, better natural resources, and greater wealth. In ancient and modern times, as we saw in our discussion of *separation,* wars of conquest or attempted conquest have been frequent. But unless a conqueror has a better idea of political order than the conquered, there will be no advance in the life of the new community, no cause worthy of its long-term belief. The conqueror will not have a good place in history, except such histories as he himself writes.

Another cause which can gain belief is that which we have seen at work historically in the United States with its store of natural resources and its space for expansion. Every American believed that American wealth and American economic achievement could be bigger and better than that anywhere else, and that all could partake in this wealth—better material possessions, better food, better housing. Such a belief constitutes a cause that enlists men's energies, and is far preferable to political and social indifference. But when reasonable wealth has been obtained and when the limitless frontier has become limited, the cause as a factor for avoiding discord loses its effectiveness, because the specific motive power of economic pioneering has lost its urgency for many, and the plenitude of land and space has been cut down for all.

Such are short-term causes taken to heart. While they may hold a community together in working for a particular obvious goal, their power to continue to do so does not last. There is no holdover that makes people work for permanent improvement in the community. No better world community and no better local communities came about as a result of the First and Second World Wars, because the aims of the belligerents had been nothing more than either aggrandizement or defense. Although each of these provided a cause taken to heart, each was a short-term cause without the motive power necessary to long-term reform.

It is otherwise with those causes taken to heart which consist of an idea of a right and better way for the conduct of community life. If the ideal is in fact right, and not spurious like the Nazi aim of an order lorded over by a synthetic *Herrenvolk,* the community or group which promotes the idea may be forever after held in high regard. The Roman political order, more equitable than other orders of its day, still makes us look upon the Romans as politically great. The Hebrew religious ideal, persistently held, meant a long-term advance in their own community and in other communities on the world scene. The American tolerance and fair play for each citizen, which have characterized the United States in most of its community life and been institutionalized in its Bill of Rights, have been causes of long-term loyalty and features of political greatness.

The rule of a free order—the rule of tolerance, honesty, truth to fact, and equity—if taken to heart and seen by the community leaders as a worthwhile role and aim now and for the future will render the community politically great and useful over the long term both for itself and others. The progressive realization of the rule of a free order is an aim, a compass, to hold in good times and bad, no matter what other substantive aims or goals the community is for the time being pursuing. The greatness and honor of our own community will be realization of the rule of justice, the rule of a free order.

4. RULE OF A FREE ORDER AS SECOND NATURE

We know as a matter of practical experience that men and women tend to cling to the religious attitudes and beliefs they have learned when young. If these attitudes and beliefs are then and thereafter fostered by a professional priesthood and in addition do not run head on into conflict and inconsistency with the subsequent experience and knowledge of the believers, they are held for life.

Even if beliefs learned when young and then intensively cultivated fail to bring practical satisfaction to the believer, they may still maintain a hold on him. For instance, in our own times refugees from the arbitrary injustices, harshness, and terror of the Soviet regime in Russia think their difficulties have been due to the shortcomings of particular officials who have fallen away from the ideal party rule. In most cases they continue to take for granted the rightness of authoritarian government and the centralized control of activity and thought. They have half come to take such a rule for granted as the right kind of rule, as a result of themselves having had to assert such a belief for many years and having heard reiterated over and over again the slogans of such a belief. They cling to the familiar tenets of the totalitarian system and do not clearly see that the injustice and terror from which they have fled necessarily stem from the system itself. They do not see that people being what they are, arbitrary and harsh government is bound to follow when a party committee wielding the effective power of government, and motivated by the invariable desire to protect itself and its position of power, does not have the check of other loci of power in the community.

If fallacious tenets and false beliefs hammered into the minds of the young and then and thereafter perpetuated by diligent propaganda maintain such a hold in continuing belief and require a thoroughgoing new education for their eradication, how much more effective would be the true tenets and true beliefs of the rule of the free order if hammered into the minds of the young. In such a case the more inquiry in late years, the more education, the more free investigation, the stronger the beliefs and tenets would appear. There would be no need, as in the case of Soviet Russia, for erecting barriers against free inquiry and free exchange of ideas, because such inquiry and exchange would only serve to strengthen rather than weaken confirmation in the rightness of the belief in the rule of the free order.

One generation should not default in teaching the next generation whatever it has learned through experience to be good and useful. If the elders have discovered, maybe painfully, what works and what doesn't, what is good and what is bad, they must give the young the benefit of what they have learned. In our formal school courses, such as those in current affairs, or in history, or in the social sciences, and certainly also to a great extent in literature, there is an opportunity for teachers to show that tolerance, honesty, truth to fact, and equity are conditions of a decent community of which one would wish to be a member. In the conduct of the classroom the rule of the free order can be taught by example, by discipline, and by reward for practical observance. In games the principle of the observance of good rules of a good game can become second nature along with ingrained practical understanding that without willing observance of the good rules the game itself deteriorates and ceases to be good.

The conditions of a free order—what makes a just and good community—are not self-evident. If the conditions are to be learned and understood, it is necessary that they be convincingly taught. But though not self-evident, these conditions of a free order are fortunately not abstruse or recondite. They can be understood by anyone of reasonable intelligence. So the process of learning the rule of the free order as second nature can go ahead on two levels in our schools, starting at once where we are today. These two levels are those of intelligent understanding of the rule and actual practice of the rule, in work and on the playground. No organizational change in the schools is needed, nor would mere organizational change suffice. What is needed are school principals and teachers who have a realistic grasp of why a free order is essential to a good community and a clear understanding of the conditions, the rule, essential to a free order.

Deception need not and should not be used in teaching a rule which is right and which can gain unfettered belief. The reasons for this are several. One of the elements of the rule of a free order is honesty. Example is just as strong as precept, if not stronger, in the teaching of a rule as second nature. Therefore dishonesty in teaching cannot be effectively used to teach honesty. Also when the dishonesty comes to be recognized by the pupil, either at the time or later, his confidence in his teacher, whether parent or schoolteacher, will be weakened, and the teaching distrusted.

The fact that teaching the rule of a free order must be honest does not prevent the use of all possible arts of persuasion in an upbringing and education designed to fortify the rule and to establish it as second nature in the young. Honesty does not mean a lazy failure to train and to convince the rising generation.

Propaganda and its devices for persuasion have fallen under suspicion, because they have been so extensively used by doctrinaire authoritarian rulers to bolster regimes which would be undermined if the capable citizens had free access to all available political facts at home and abroad. But it is sensible and wise to use propaganda and its devices, including the hammering in of truthful slogans, in the training of useful citizenship. At the same time free access is allowed to all the facts, as this will strengthen the lesson of the propaganda.

It is true that a good regime and a free order will gain strength and the belief of its citizens the more thoroughly the citizens can grasp the meaning and the lessons taught by historical fact. But this does not mean that the lessons teach themselves or that the leaders of a free order can afford to lie back and yield the field of active persuasion to the Devil and his political agents.

It is right to use every formal and informal means possible to establish the rule of tolerance, honesty, truth to fact, and equity as habitual second nature.

Calculation under the stress of events, the operation of enlightened self-interest under the pressure of particularistic motives, is subject to mistake and error which will result in discord. The cure is to have the rule of tolerance, honesty, truth to fact, and equity so ingrained as to govern and control the special interests and intense motives that otherwise lead to discord. This cure will more likely be seen in fact, if the young have been brought up with the rule of the free order as their taken-for-granted, second-nature rule.

5. BELIEF IN THE RULE OF A FREE ORDER ON THE WORLD SCENE

On the domestic scene within a modern state a free order is dependent on this: that a preponderance of those at opinion-forming and standard-setting levels believe in and act substantially in accord with the rule of tolerance, honesty, truth to fact, and equity, taking it for granted as their rule of action. It is this which makes it possible for appropriate institutions—legal, statutory, and customary—to come into being and to continue to function so as to fortify and maintain the rule. The many independent groups and loci of power within the community, necessary as a counterbalance to too strong and arbitrary government and necessary also for efficient economic productivity and social experiment, are kept from flying apart in *discord* by this same acceptance of the rule of a free order as the rule for adjusting and compromising conflicting group interests.

On the world scene there is presently no corresponding belief in or acceptance of the rule of a free order. The independent loci of power on the world scene are the separate countries, the separate states of the world, which are independent to such a degree that their political leaders and rulers acknowledge no rule of tolerance, honesty, truth to fact, and equity as between these separate states. Those citizens of the separate states who constitute the opinion-forming and standard-setting levels have not awakened to the fact that the rule of a free order is the only practical condition of a community life at home and abroad free from the danger of destruction. There is present neither the belief in the rule nor its acceptance as a taken-for-granted rule of action which makes possible the design and functioning on the world scene of institutions appropriate for the existence and maintenance of a free order. On the contrary, some political leaders frankly assume that imposed order, rather than free order, is the only alternative to disorder and continued separation on the world scene. If they are right, the future likely prospect for a large part of mankind is at best a prospect of unhappiness and of life subject to the control of force, fraud, and fear.

On the domestic scene the groups within the community—the various organizations, associations, corporations, unions, and the like—which carry on the varied activities of community life are not any one of them regionally self-sufficient. For necessities such as food or the materials for shelter they are dependent on transportation and exchange with one another. They therefore are under the pressure of necessity to get and stay together in some kind of orderly regime where the rules are understood, so that production, distribution, and exchange are not fatally interrupted.

On the world scene, in contrast, some at least of the great separate states are regionally self-sufficient to such an extent that they are not under a like compulsion to get together with one another in an over-all working international community.

Yet in our own day there is a new compulsion at work in the direction of at least a minimum of world order. This is the fear everywhere of the possibilities of destruction that lie in weapons like the hydrogen bomb. This constitutes an immediate pressure for some kind of world arrangement, some kind of world relationship or order, which will not be subject to universally lethal warfare. Consequently citizens and leaders at the opinion-forming and standard-setting levels are looking for a way of escape from the excessive dangers of international separation and violent rivalry.

We may well be at a juncture in world history where and when the necessities of the actual circumstances are making a compulsory pressure for at least enough world order to avoid the chance of war with nuclear weapons. It is a pressure which is bound to overcome obstacles for the sake of the actual physical survival of the world's inhabitants. The minimum essential degree of order would seem to be a disarmament or control agreement designed to avoid war with nuclear weapons, and so policed as to provide general confidence that the agreement would achieve its end.

Even this minimum necessary degree of international order might well pave the way, through successful experience with its mutual working arrangements and superintendence, to additional international agreement in other fields where agreement would benefit all concerned.

Just as in the case of domestic legislation and the executive measures to carry it out, so also in the case of any international agreement and its actual operative arrangements one of our aims should be to see that the growth of tolerance, honesty, truth to fact, and equity—in this case on the world scene—are promoted as much as possible on every occasion. We know that if an actual free order with its appropriate institutions is finally to be realized for the world community, rather than imposed order or disorder, it is necessary first that enough of the leaders all along the line in the powerful countries come to believe in the rule of a free order.

One established type of institution already existing nearly everywhere on the world scene, which could take an effective part in promoting the rule of tolerance, honesty, truth to fact, and equity, is a religious organization which crosses national lines. We know that in addition to the strict religious function of helping a man find his relation to reality or God, churches have historically also concerned themselves with the teaching of ethics and of trying to close the gap between what man at the moment is and what he might and ought to be. A church, as an international ethical and religious group, can, if its leaders have sufficient vigor and conviction, set itself to creating a climate of opinion favorable to the rule of a free order. It could be an organized source of moral opinion and pressure, along with other proponents of free order in the community, too strong to be disregarded by political leaders. For the time being a government hostile to the church might force church teaching to go underground. The teaching of determined religious leaders—like that of leaders of reforming political cells—has historically often survived such suppression and been carried on to later victory.

If we in the United States wish to convince leaders of other countries that the rule of a free order is the only route to a just and humane world community, we have to begin where we now find ourselves and go on from there. We must work with and through those of our own people who are in closest contact with people abroad and with foreign visitors to our own country. Here one difficulty is that even when our leaders in many lines of activity in fact observe the rule of tolerance, honesty, truth to fact, and equity, they fail to understand the need for the rule and why it provides the one alternative to discord or unjust order. This means that they are inarticulate in promoting the rule.

In our relations with countries which do not allow free speech and where contacts of our citizens with theirs are both limited and policed, the difficulties are at a maximum. As things stand there is less chance that those of our leaders who do presently understand the rule of the free order and the need for it will make any effective contact with the leaders of the foreign countries. This makes it all the more important that our education and formation of opinion at home should not fail to teach the rule of the free order, its need and its reasons, to those who are going to be in contact with the citizens who live under the restrictive and imposed order of these countries. Among our people who will almost surely be in contact with these foreigners are our diplomats and state representatives, visitors to scientific or legal or other international conferences and congresses (which even an authoritarian ruler dare not completely forbid for fear of alienating his own intelligent people), and our political representatives and their staffs at political conferences, such, for example, as meetings at an international assembly, or special meetings for particular political purposes or mixed technical and political purposes, as rules for exploration and control of relations in interplanetary space.

In these activities many of those involved will be technical specialists, engineers, and others with scientific training. It is essential that all these should also have a thoroughgoing understanding of the rule of a free order and the need for it. Yet in our country, those with technical and scientific training have been notoriously deficient both on the teaching and on the learning side of any training in doctrine or in political values, good or bad. Granted that there are historical reasons for this, as, for instance, the legacy of the so-called long war between science and theology, it is nevertheless today a lapse and failure in our means for promoting an understanding abroad of the need of the rule of a free order if there is to be a just world.

In the world there are communities of people living in a primitive state of economic development, and largely illiterate. The political organization of their countries is either in the hands of foreigners, or where it is in their own hands is as likely to be disorganization as organization. These countries, if only for want of sufficient economic and military power, will not in the near future be calling the turn on the establishment of a world pattern, good or bad, for the relations of countries of greater power, wealth, and education. In such countries, as we have noted, a government which would be likely to promote their advance and to satisfy their hopes for better human fulfillment would very likely be for the time being authoritarian. This we cannot balk at. But here too the only right long-term aim is for a free order. And, at a time when leaders of these people are trying to break new political ground and find a new place in the world community, it is important for them to see that a free order is their best aim and purpose. We must devote ourselves to convincing them that an authoritarian regime is only justified as an intermediate step towards free order, and not as a step towards the getting and keeping of power by this or that clique or clan. Here again, it is by the understanding and intelligence of our technicians, missionaries, and representatives— and by our example at home—that we can hope to persuade these newly emerging political states and their leaders of the need of free order and its rule if life is to be decent and just.

No community leadership, advanced or primitive, ought to give up the aim of free order, or settle forever for unfree and imposed order, with its inevitable discord, force, and deception. We have seen that it is possible to demonstrate that without the rule of tolerance, honesty, truth to fact, and equity, either disorder or imposed order is bound to hold the field. Every intelligent American citizen should be able to make this demonstration.

In our relations with other countries our example, as well as our words, must be that of a true free order, fair rather than unfair. Unfortunately in our existing relations with some of these countries, particularly those dependent on foreign skills and materials for their economic development, our American and Western European system of private ownership of industry has at times looked to their people like a mechanism of economic exploitation rather than what it should be, a better means of production and distribution, and a bulwark against arbitrary government.

Most people dread war and fear arbitrary government. It follows that if they once clearly see that what produces war and what characterizes arbitrary government is in each case the same set of evils— intolerance, dishonesty, untruthfulness, and unfairness—they will want to get rid of the evil rule and to gain instead a rule of tolerance, honesty, truth to fact, and equity. This is our opportunity.

In the first part of this book we saw that in any community there are those who are alive to the injustices around them and ready to try a cure. For example, in the United States between the First World War and the end of the Second there were many at opinion-forming levels—writers, teachers, scientists, and preachers—who, struck by American injustices, were ready to jump from the frying pan of these injustices which they knew into the fire of Communist authoritarianism and its much greater injustices, of which they knew nothing.

In a community which is in fact marked by great injustice and a governmental regime characterized by the use of too much force and reliance on dishonesty and deception towards its citizens, some of the latter are intelligent enough and good-willed enough to be ready to follow a scheme in fact better and to come to believe in a free order and its rule. They can visualize a regime of tolerance, honesty, and fairness as preferable to a continuance of the intolerance, unfairness, force and fraud with which they are all too familiar at home. We must do all we can to further their chance of belief in a free order and to strengthen their hands.

In a modern community, even one exhibiting a politically aloof and iron-curtained state organization such as that of Russia, there is bound to be within the schools and universities, within the churches, and in the literary, artistic, scientific, and business circles a leaven of those who know or who can be brought to see that a just world cannot be built upon imposed order with its force, fraud, and fear, and that such a regime is a hateful thing at home and abroad. From time to time, even in a world of separation and strong international barriers we will be in contact with some of these independent-minded people. Then is when we need to have a firm and understanding belief in the rule of a free order, so as to be able then and there to take part in communicating ideas across national barriers.

In the difficult days of our own time we are obliged to spend much of our effort in building armaments and constructing a system of defense so powerful as to be invincible, lest our own country and community be overthrown by those who believe in imposed order. Yet at this very time, throughout this period, no matter how long the interval of international discord and separation, we must promote, explain, and show the need on the world scene of a free order and the rule of a free order in the world community. We must ourselves achieve a true free order at home. The precept and the example would together be irresistible.

Concluding Remarks

IN this book we have set before ourselves a standard by which to test the goodness and justice of a politically organized community. That standard is a free order. The closer a community comes to observing and exhibiting in practice the rule of a free order and the greater the degree in which its leaders accept that rule as their working and worthwhile role, the better that community will be both for its own people and the people of the rest of the world.

Although we have given an account of various institutions favorable to the maintenance and growth of a free order, we have not attempted to describe the customs or set out the political constitution of an ideal community, because changing circumstances would shortly change the features of any such community. What we have done is to describe, in the course of a review of the facts of our divided world, the rule and role, that set of political attitudes and political virtues, failing which no country, whatever its physical assets or wealth, would be a just or good place in which to live.

We have described a goal that is really right for which to strive, a purpose and role that we can see to be excellent. If our own country can itself attain a free order at home and promote a free order on the world scene it will justify its existence and its power in the sight of all good men at home and abroad, and have a place of honor in history.

REFERENCES AND ACKNOWLEDGMENTS

References and Acknowledgments

For the facts recited in *A Free Order* I have mainly made use of standard reference works, histories, and other secondary sources which appeared reliable. Many of these sources are named in the following list of References and Acknowledgments. What I have done in the book is to set generally accessible facts in a perspective which permits conclusions as to what are the causes and signs of free order and of unjust order.

Page

3   Acts 19:24 *et seq.*, E. J. Goodspeed, translator, from *The Bible, An American Translation* (copyright 1935 by The University of Chicago).

6   *Vision of Piers Plowman* (Arthur Burrell version), p. 117, Everyman ed.

18   Folkish state. *Mein Kampf,* vol. 2, ch. 2 (translation sponsored by an editorial committee), Reynal & Hitchcock, by arr. with Houghton, Mifflin, 1939, at p. 606.

23   *Unam Sanctam,* papal bull of Boniface VIII, 1302. The translation is from Ernest F. Henderson, *Select Historical Documents of the Middle Ages* (London, Geo. Bell & Sons, 1892).

29   Proclamation of Duke of Brunswick. Translation is from Document #411, in Vol. 2, J. H. Robinson, *Readings in European History,* 443–4–5 (Ginn & Co., 1904/6).

37   Carlsbad Resolutions. Translation is from Document #461 in Vol. 2, J. H. Robinson, *op. cit.,* at 548, 9.

41f.   Emperor Henry IV and Pope Gregory VII. Translations are from Documents 112 (Henry) and 113 (Gregory) in Vol. I, J. H. Robinson, *op. cit.,* 279 at 280, and 281 at 281–2, respectively.

43f.   Peter of Aragon's vassalage to Pope. S. R. Packard, in *Europe and the Church Under Innocent III* (Holt, 1927), at 47, says, "The thirteenth century did not think in the nationalistic terms dear to the twentieth and many persons undoubtedly considered such an event entirely honorable for the prince concerned, but it was certainly a striking example of the power and prestige of Rome."

47f.   Dante and Pope Nicholas III. The translation from Canto XIX of the *Inferno* is from H. R. Huse, *The Divine Comedy, a New Prose Translation* (Rinehart & Co. Inc. 1954, Holt, Rinehart & Winston, Inc., successors).

501

Page

48f.   Nicholas Clamanges on the mercenary church. Translation is from Document 212 in Vol. I, J. H. Robinson, *op. cit.,* 508 at 509.

50   Dietrich Vrie on sale of ordination. Translation is from Document 213 in Vol. I, J. H. Robinson, *op. cit.,* 510.

53   Capito, writing to Luther, Sept. 4, 1518. Translation from Document 241 in Vol. II, J. H. Robinson, *op. cit.,* 62.

56   Instructions for proclaiming indulgences. Translation from Document 239 in Vol. II, J. H. Robinson, *op. cit.,* 54, 55, 56, 57.

57   Effect of coin clinking in chest. The quotation is from article on Johann Tetzel in 21 *Encyc. Brit.* (14th ed.), 980 at 981.

57f.   Extracts from Luther's 95 Theses. Translation is from Document 240 in Vol. II, J. H. Robinson, *op. cit.,* 58 *et seq.* In Thesis 28 I have changed the word "rattles" to "clinks" to point up the reference to Tetzel's statement, above.

61   Erasmus letter to Melanchthon. The quotation is from article on Erasmus in 8 *Encyc. Brit.* (14th ed.), 676 at 679.

61   Milton on new presbyter and old priest. Sonnet "On the new forcers of Conscience under the Long Parliament." In the *Poetical Works of John Milton* (Oxford Complete Edition, 1904), 86, this appears as the last line of a sonnet not yet completed in sonnet form.

62   Council of Trent on knowledge of faith and freedom from inquisitiveness. Quoted in J. H. Randall, Jr., *The Making of the Modern Mind* (Houghton Mifflin, 1926), 166.

63   The ingredients of the German Folk. The quotation is from *Vom deutschen Volk und seinem Lebensraum,* translated by H. L. Childs under title *The Nazi Primer* (Harper & Brothers, 1938, Harper & Row, Publishers, Inc., successors), 34–5.

64   The tall and slender Nordic, *id.,* 17–8.

64f.   Nazi statutes against Jews, *id.,* 77–9.

67   Lincoln's Plan of Reconstruction. Document 230 in 1 Commager, *Documents of American History* (6th ed., Appleton-Century-Crofts, 1958), at p. 431.

68   Stevens on punishment of South. Walter L. Fleming, *Sequel of Appomattox* (Yale, 1919), 59.

69   Gerrit Smith on character of Negroes. *Ibid.,* 60.

70   Wade Hampton on attitude of South. *Ibid.,* 31.

72f.   First Reconstruction Act (March 2, 1867). For text see 2 Commager, *op. cit.,* Doc. 260.

75   Result of 1868 election. Figures are from *Historical Statistics of the United States, 1789–1945* (U.S. Govt. Printing Office, 1949).

76   South Carolina legislature. Figures are from 2 S. E. Morison, *The Oxford History of the United States* (Oxford U.P., 1927) 341.

80   Spanish Constitution of December 1931. The provisions of this constitution are outlined in the 1936 *World Almanac,* at p. 697.

82   The Cortes elected in November 1933. Figures are from the 1935 *World Almanac. The Political Handbook of the World,* 1934 (Council

Page

      on Foreign Relations) enumerates the parties of Right, Center, and Left as 212, 162, and 98, respectively, for a total of 472 instead of 473.

84f.   Cortes elected in February 1936. Figures are from 1937 *World Almanac. The Political Handbook of the World,* 1937 enumerates the parties of Left, Center, and Right as 248, 50, and 175, respectively, for the same total of 473.

87   Hymn to Aton. Translation by Robert Hillyer, *The Coming Forth by Day* (B. J. Brimmer, 1923) 67–8, reprinted in *Anthology of World Poetry* (ed., Mark Van Doren, Reynal & Hitchcock, 1934, 1936), 250.

91   The French nobility. The estimate of 140,000 out of a total population of 26,000,000 is from Taine, *The Ancien Régime* (transl. Durand, N.Y., 1931). Brinton, Christopher, and Wolff in Vol. 2 of *A History of Civilization* (Prentice-Hall, 1955) at p. 97 estimate the nobles as roughly 400,000 out of a population of around 26,500,000, and as holding about one-fourth of the land. The Abbé Sièyes in his pamphlet *What Is the Third Estate?* (February 1789) refers to "the 25,000,000 or 26,000,000 individuals who constitute the nation with the exception of about 200,-000 nobles or priests." J. H. Stewart, *A Documentary Survey of the French Revolution* (Macmillan, 1951), 52.

101   Comte de Provence on his brother the King. Quoted in 8 *The Cambridge Modern History* (14 vols., Macmillan, 1902–1936), 79.

101f.   Turgot's letter to Louis XVI. Quoted in E. J. Lowell, *Eve of the French Revolution* (1892, Houghton Mifflin, 40th Impression, 1942), 238.

102   Proportion of officers to enlisted men. 8 *Camb. Mod. Hist.,* 51.

103f.   On Turgot's reforms at Limoges and as Controller of the Finances see Paul Harsin art. on *Turgot in Encyc. Soc. Sci.,* also 8 *Camb. Mod. Hist.,* 84 *et seq.;* E. J. Lowell, *op. cit.,* 235 *et seq.*

105   Malouet's advice to the King's ministers, 8 *Camb. Mod. Hist.,* 124 and 132.

106   Mirabeau's written advice to the King. Quoted in 2 Robinson, *op. cit.,* Doc. No. 399, 412 at 415.

107   On the comparatively light taxes of the early empire see Tenney Frank, *A History of Rome* (Holt, 1923), 519; Rostovtzeff, *Social and Economic History of the Roman Empire* (Oxford, 1926), 54.

112   Sale of war supplies to U.S. Steel Export Corporation. W. L. Langer and S. E. Gleason, *The Challenge to Isolation* (Harper, for Council on Foreign Relations, 1952), 512. Exchange of destroyers for bases, H. L. Stimson and McG. Bundy, *On Active Service in Peace and War* (Harper, 1947, 1948), 356 *et seq.;* Langer and Gleason, *op. cit.,* ch. 22, "The Destroyer Deal."

113   Leaders of Congress of opinion that extension of service would not be authorized. H. L. Stimson and McG. Bundy, *op. cit.,* 377. Vote of 203 to 202 in House of Representatives, *World Almanac* (1942), 70.

123f.   Jacobins and Bolsheviks. The Jacobins arose contemporaneously with the French Revolution and their membership as well as their views were changing with the changing revolutionary situation. The Bolsheviks had

Page

a more established revolutionary doctrine and a history antedating the Russian revolution. J. H. Stewart, in *A Documentary Survey of the French Revolution* (Oxford U.P., 1951), has a note concerning the followers of the communistic Babeuf and their "creed," in which he observes (at p. 656): "It indicates how one group was endeavoring to transform some of the ideas of the philosophes and the early revolutionaries into a workable social and economic pattern, and how it anticipated the socialism of the nineteenth century."

129   Unemployment in Czechoslovakia, 1929 and 1934. Figures are from 1935 *World Almanac.*

130   May election results. *The Political Handbook of the World,* 1936 (Council on Foreign Relations).

132   May 1946 election results. *New York Times,* Feb. 29, 1948. Membership of cabinet, *The Political Handbook of the World,* 1947.

132ff.   Daily events in Communist take-over in Czechoslovakia. Account taken mainly from contemporaneous daily and Sunday issues of *New York Times.*

151   Contribution of Huguenots to America. See article *Huguenots in America,* 3 *Dictionary of American History* (Charles Scribner's Sons, 6 volumes, 1940), 57.

151   Nazi-instigated murder of young Italian leaders. Foreign Policy Association *Bulletin,* July 14, 1944.

159   Philip the Fair on priority of king to priest. Philip is quoted in W. A. Dunning, *A History of Political Theories: Ancient and Mediaeval* (Macmillan, 1902), 224.

162   Parties in French National Assembly. *The Political Handbook of the World,* 1958 (Council on Foreign Relations), 69.

169   Right to import slaves. U.S. Constitution, Art. I, Sec. 9, Clause 1, and Art. V. Relative voting strength of South. *Ibid.,* Art. 1, Sec. 2, Clause 3.

170f.   George Fitzhugh of Virginia. Quoted from Fitzhugh's *Cannibals All!* in Craven, Johnson, and Dunn, *A Documentary History of the American People* (Ginn, 1951), 370.

171   Republican Platform of 1860. 1 Commager, *op. cit.,* Doc. 192.

171f.   Lincoln to Stephens. Craven et al., *op. cit.,* 398f.

172f.   Charleston *Mercury* of Oct. 11, 1860. Craven et al., *op. cit.,* 394f.

173   Montgomery Convention was on Feb. 4. R. B. Morris, *Encyclopedia of American History* (1961 edition), 228. For text of the permanent constitution of March 11, 1861, see 1 Commager, *op. cit.,* Doc. 201.

173   Lincoln's Second Inaugural Address. 1 Commager, *op. cit.,* Doc. 238.

176   Declaration of Independence. Every American home has a copy of this. Some newspapers publish a facsimile each July 4th. Each annual issue of the *World Almanac* contains a copy.

180   Japanese resources. Guy-Harold Smith and Dorothy Good, *Japan, A Geographical View* (American Geographical Society, Special Publication No. 28, 1943). (The ratio of fish consumption to meat appears in Table VI, p. 26.)

Page

182   Hidejiro Nagata and Teiichi Muto. Quoted in Otto D. Tolischus, *Through Japanese Eyes* (Reynal & Hitchcock, 1945, Harcourt, Brace & World, Inc., successors), 82, 81.

190f.   On Congress of Vienna see art. under that title by Charles K. Webster in 23 *Encyc. Britannica* (14th ed., 1929), 143. March 25, 1815, alliance of Austria, England, Prussia, and Russia, W. L. Langer, ed., *Encyc. of World History* (rev. 1948), 602.

192f.   Hitler's aims as disclosed in *Mein Kampf*. See particularly Vol. I, ch. 4, and Vol. II, ch. 14, in complete edition (Reynal & Hitchcock, by arr. with Houghton Mifflin, 1939. English translation).

203   The line of division between Slav and German 1,000 years ago and today. For the history of this line, illustrated with maps, see Werner J. Cahnman, "Frontiers between East and West in Europe." 39 *The Geographical Review* (American Geographical Society, October 1949), 605–624.

210   The "dark Satanic mills." William Blake, *Milton,* preface.

218f.   Joseph's plan of approach to the Pharaoh. Genesis 46:31–34, *The Bible,* a new translation, by James Moffatt, (Harper & Brothers, 1935, Harper & Row, Publishers, Inc., successors).

219   Sulla's proletarian followers. M. Rostovtzeff, *Social and Economic History of the Roman Empire* (Oxford, 1926), 26–7.

219f.   Müller's statement. U.S. Dept. of State Publ. No. 1864 (1943), *National Socialism,* 9. Woltmann's *ibid.,* 11.

220   O'Sullivan on "our manifest destiny." Quoted in 3 *Dict. Am. Hist.* at p. 332.

223f.   Arnold Gesell, M.D., *Wolf Child and Human Child* (Harper, 1941).

225f.   For an interesting parallel to a child's need for parental affection, see Harlow and Harlow, "A Study of Animal Affection," in *Natural History,* December, 1961, 48 *et seq.*

229   Sanction for equity to slaves and aliens. Deuteronomy 5:15; 15:15; 16:12; 24:8, 22, Moffatt translation.

230   Cure of famine as recounted in 2 Samuel 21. Moffatt translation.

231   Psalm 29. Moffatt translation.

232   David Hume on Cause and Effect. See especially Section IV, Sceptical Doubts Concerning the Operations of the Understanding, in his *Enquiry Concerning the Human Understanding.* (Several editions.)

235   Japan's brilliant history about to be smeared by devils. *New York Times,* March 22, 1944.

235f.   Submerged nature personified in dreams. C. G. Jung reports such dreams. Cf. his *Psychology and Religion* (Yale, 1938), esp. pp. 26–52.

238   It is perhaps hardly necessary to document the need of a child for affection and the results of affection in his life. A modern view is briefly stated in Witmer and Kotinsky, editors, *Personality in the Making;* The Fact-Finding Report of the Midcentury White House Conference on Children and Youth (Harper, 1952), esp. chs. 4, 9 at p. 178, and 11 at pp. 252–255.

Page

251 "Please," begged the victim, "let me go." This stanza is quoted in Gregor Ziemer, *Education for Death* (1941, Oxford), 67.

252 Micah 6:6–8, Moffatt translation.

257 Exports from The New World. *Historical Statistics of the U.S., Colonial Times to 1957* (U.S. Bureau of the Census, 1960), 551, Series U 116–127, gives statistics of value of U.S. exports to Europe (U.K., France, Germany, other) from 1790 on.

259 Sacred Harlotry. Cf. art. "Baalism" in Ferm, ed., *An Encyclopedia of Religion* (Philosophical Library, 1945). See also art. "Harlot" in Funk and Wagnalls, *New Standard Bible Dictionary* (3d rev. ed., 1936, The Blakiston Co.). A story involving a pretended temple prostitute is recounted in Genesis 38.

259f. Ahura Mazda on treatment of the dog. Zend Avesta quoted in Ballou, ed., *World Bible* (Viking, 1944), 196, 198, from *The Sacred Books of the East*. Vol. 4 (Oxford, 1880) of this series is a translation by James Darmesteter of the Zend Avesta.

266 Phoenician achievement. H. S. Lucas, *A Short History of Civilization* (McGraw-Hill, 1943), 81–85. See also article "Phoenician Civilization" in *Columbia Encyclopedia* (2d ed., 1950).

269 See Ser. Z, 1–8, in *Historical Statistics of United States* for estimate of the population of the colonies by decades from 1610 to 1790; and Ser. Z, 20, for per cent distribution of whites by nationality in 1790. In 1780, the two most heavily populated of the New England colonies, Massachusetts and Connecticut, had in round numbers, respectively, 235,300 and 183,800 inhabitants. Of the "assigned" nationalities in the 1790 estimate, 82 per cent of Massachusetts was English, 8.4 per cent was unassigned, and the balance other "assigned." In Connecticut the corresponding percentages were 67 per cent English, 26.4 per cent unassigned, and the balance other "assigned."

269f. Massachusetts Bay Company charter. 1 Commager, *Documents of American History* (6th ed., 1958), Doc. No. 12.

270f. Rightness of religion for those in political authority. The arguments of the Massachusetts leaders are quoted in Craven et al., *op. cit.*, 35.

271 Growth of Massachusetts Bay Colony in decade 1630–1640. C. M. Andrews, *The Fathers of New England* (Yale, 1919), 34 *et seq.*

274 German immigration into middle colonies. 2 *Dict. Am. Hist.*, art. "German immigration," by G. M. Stephenson.

274 Franklin's estimate of German population in Pennsylvania. J. T. Adams, *The American* (Charles Scribner's Sons, 1943), 141. German newspapers, *id.*, 123.

275 George Washington on the "Dutch"-speaking Germans. D. S. Freeman, 1 *George Washington: Young Washington* (Charles Scribner's Sons, 1948), 221.

275 John Wesley and the Moravians. R. M. Cameron in art. "John Wesley" in 23 *Collier's Encyclopedia* (1962). A small colony of Moravians was in Georgia from 1735 to 1740. 4 *Dict. Am. Hist.*, art. "Moravians."

Page

275   5 *Dict. Am. Hist.*, art. "Scotch–Irish," estimates their numbers in the colonies in 1790 at about 225,000. For their migration, see Michael Kraus, *The United States to 1865* (U. of Michigan, 1959), 106ff.

275f.   Walloons and Huguenots. Articles under those titles in 5 and 3 *Dict. Am. Hist.*

276   Colonial seagoing trade. E. B. Greene, *Provincial America* (1690–1740), (Harper, 1905), esp. ch. XVII. For the Molasses Act of 1733, see art. under that title in *Dict. Am. Hist.*

276   Passages from Peckham's *Discourse of the Necessitie and Commoditie of Planting English Colonies upon the North Partes of America* (1583) are quoted from Hakluyt in Craven, Johnson, Dunn, *op. cit.*, 5 *et seq.*

277   Captain John Smith on the effects of feeding from a common store is quoted in J. T. Adams, *op. cit.*, 24.

277f.   The unpopular Sir Thomas Smith, his government. Craven, Johnson, Dunn, *op. cit.*, 16–17. For the dates in which Smith held office, see biog. sub. tit. "Smythe, Sir Thomas" in *Webster's Biographical Dictionary* (Merriam, 1943).

278   Effect of geography of tidewater region. J. T. Adams, *op. cit.*, 26.

279f.   Conflict between those up country and "old tidewater aristocracy," Harry F. Byrd, art. "Virginia," 23 *Encyc. Brit.* (14th ed.), 188; see also art. "Tidewater" in *Dict. Am. Hist.*, by Alfred P. James.

279   Population of Virginia in 1700, 1740, and 1756. Harry F. Byrd, *loc. cit.*

281   Proclamation of 1763. 1 Commager, *Docs. Am. Hist.*, Doc. No. 33.

282   New England Confederation. R. B. Morris, ed., *op. cit.*, 36. Text of Articles of Confederation. 1 Commager, *op. cit.*, Doc. No. 18.

282f.   1754 plan for colonial union. 1 Commager, *op. cit.*, Doc. No. 31. R. B. Morris, ed., *op. cit.*, 67.

284   Galloway's Plan of Union. 2 *Dict. Am. Hist.* art. Text of plan, 1 Commager, *Docs. Am. Hist.*, No. 55.

285   Washington's statement on the unpredictability of the militia is quoted in Senate Doc. 274 (1940) at p. 10.

285   Articles of Confederation, Allan Nevins, art. in 1 *Dict. Am. Hist.* Text, 1 Commager, *Docs. Am. Hist.*, No. 72.

285f.   Wyoming Valley. See arts. in 5 *Dict. Am. Hist.* under titles Wyoming Valley, Settlement of; Wyoming Massacre; and Yankee-Pennamite Wars; by M. E. Case, Frances Dorrance, and J. P. Boyd, respectively.

287   James Madison on weakness of Confederacy, quoted in 1 Morison, *The Oxford History of the United States* (Oxford, 1927), 77.

287ff. Jedidiah Morse on defects in the Confederacy and iniquity of Rhode Island. Quotations from his *The American Geography* (1792, 2d ed.) in Craven, Johnson and Dunn, *op. cit.*, at 176 and 178f.

289   Shays' Rebellion. R. B. Morris, ed., *Encyc. Am. Hist.* (2d ed., 1961), 115f. For a contemporary view, Jedidiah Morse, quoted in Craven *et al.*, *op. cit.*, 177.

290   General Washington on combustibles in every state. 1 Morison, *op. cit.*, 81.

Page

290f.   A short treatment of the Constitutional Convention is Max Farrand, *The Framing of the Constitution of the United States* (Yale, 1913), based on the author's 3-volume *The Records of the Federal Convention* (Yale, 1911). (There is a 4-volume, revised edition of *The Records,* 1937.)

292ff.   For a survey of Rome in first third of fourth century, Tenney Frank, *A History of Rome* (Holt, 1923), ch. XXX. For a bleak picture of the situation faced by the fourth-century emperors and their failure to find a solution, M. Rostovtzeff, *The Social and Economic History of the Roman Empire* (Oxford, 1926), 454 to 478. See also the Introduction by C. D. Williams to Clyde Pharr's *The Theodosian Code and Novels* (Princeton, 1952).

296   Stilicho, "generally regarded as one of the greatest statesmen and generals of the late empire." Art. Flavius Stilicho, *Columbia Encyc.* (2d ed., 1950).

296f.   Ataulf's ambition, as quoted by Orosius. Henri Pirenne, *Mohammed and Charlemagne* (tr. by B. Miall, Norton, 1939), 26.

297   Athanaric as reported by Jordanes. Quoted in J. F. Scott, A. Hyma, A. H. Noyes, *Readings in Medieval History* (Appleton-Century-Crofts, 1933), 34.

298   Gallo-Gothic political alliance. Dill, *Roman Society in the Last Century of the Western Empire* (Macmillan, 1910), 328f. Avitus reigned only fourteen months. Art. "Marcus Maecilius Avitus" 1 *New Century Cyclopedia of Names* (Appleton-Century-Crofts, 1954).

298   Odovakar western emperor. This was in 476, a traditional, but as Tenney Frank observes, a rather meaningless date for marking the end of the Roman Empire of the West. *Op. cit.,* 581f.

299   Romans and Goths as conquerors of Gaul. On the difference in effects of a conquest by civilized of uncivilized and vice versa, James Hadley, *Introduction to Roman Law* (Appleton, 1873, reissued Yale, 1931), 26f.

300   The lines from Juvenal's Third Satire are from the translation by William Gifford (1756–1826), reprinted in Godolphin, ed., *The Latin Poets* (Modern Library, 1949).

310   Those interested in a psychologist's view of some of the early factors influencing the development of an individual's way of meeting the world might look at H. A. Murray's ch. V in *Explorations in Personality,* by the workers at the Harvard Psychological Clinic (Oxford, 1938).

311f.   Polybius lived in the second century B.C. Tenney Frank, *op. cit.,* 191–193, quotes from him on Roman republican character.

315f.   The lines from Sophocles' *Antigone* are from E. F. Watling's translation of *The Theban Plays* (Penguin, 1947), 138f.

316   Medical corpsman's heroism. A. L. Wilson at Besange la Petite. *New York Times,* June 26, 1945.

316   "Even if there are religious taboos about eating fish, it should not be too difficult for chemists to impregnate tapioca flour with the required

Page

quantity of proteins." George Kuriyan, "India's Population Problem," in *Focus* (V. 5, No. 2, Oct. 1954), American Geographical Society.

316f.   Greased cartridges. 11 *Camb. Mod. Hist.* (1909), 745f.

317   Sacred water and spread of disease. Jacques May in 40 *Geographical Review,* 1950, No. 1.

318   Translation of *Piers Plowman* by H. W. Wells (Sheed and Ward, 1945), Passus VII, lines 109 *et seq.*

319   Feeling of guilt on retreat. Jack Belden in *Time,* Jan. 1, 1945.

320   Fear paralysis in combat. F. P. Matthews, art. "Hysteria" in 12 *Collier's Encyclopedia* (1962). William Sargant, *Battle for the Mind* (rev. ed., Penguin, 1961), 26.

323   Numbers of those of foreign or mixed parentage in U.S. *Statistical Abstract of the United States: 1955* (U.S. Govt. Printing Office), Table No. 30.

324   12 per cent of Americans competent on Bill of Rights. N.Y. State Bar Assn. Circular No. 45, Jan. 29, 1951.

328   The Yoga Aphorisms of Patanjali. Translated by Swami Vivekananda. *The Wisdom of China and India* (Lin Yutang, ed., Random House, 1942), 115–132.

329   Cure of a famine. 2 Samuel 21. Moffatt translation.

334   Deuteronomy 6:4–9, Moffatt translation.

334f.   The Chinese family. K. S. Latourette, *A Short History of the Far East* (1947, Macmillan), ch. 5, "Chinese Civilization" at 158ff. F. L. K. Hsu, art. "China" in *Most of the World* (Ralph Linton, ed., Columbia, 1949), 731–813 at 761ff.

335f.   Running a hospital in China. American Bureau for Medical Aid to China, *Bulletin,* May–June, 1944.

337f.   Fish days for policy's sake. Herbert Heaton, *Economic History of Europe* (Harper, 1936), 393.

338   State Shinto and state policy. A. E. Haydon, *Biography of the Gods* (Macmillan, 1942), 214.

340   The "Czar's eye." Sir Bernard Pares, "Religion Under the Czars and the Soviets," in *U.S.S.R.: A Concise Handbook* (E. J. Simmons, ed., Cornell, 1947), 339.

349   A translation of Kekulé's account of his dream may be found in O. J. Walker, "August Kekulé and the Benzene Problem" in *Annals of Science* (vol. 4, no. 1, Jan. 15, 1939), 34–46 at 40.

349   Sir William Rowan Hamilton's discovery. Hamilton is quoted in Louis Brand, *Vector and Tensor Analysis* (Wiley, 1947), 408fn.

360   Cyrus the Messiah. Isaiah 45:1.

367   Khrushchev's exposure of Stalin. Text in Dan N. Jacobs, ed., *The New Communist Manifesto and Related Documents* (2d ed., Harper Torchbooks, 1962), 78 to 130.

373   Religious brawling in reign of Edward VI. G. M. Trevelyan, *History of England* (Longmans, Green, 1927), 314f.

Page

373f. Ku Klux Klan (twentieth century). R. A. Billington, art. under that title in 3 *Dict. Am. Hist.*

374 Pure Food and Drug Laws. H. G. Singer, art. under that title in 19 *Collier's Encyc.*, 1962.

386 Wealth producing more than own value in few years. Total national wealth in 1958 estimated at about $1,683 billion. *Statistical Abstract of U.S., 1962,* Table 457. Gross national product in same year slightly more than a quarter of this figure, at $444.5 billion. *Id.,* Table 420.

389 Distribution of individual income in U.S.A. in 1956. *Facts and Figures on Government Finance* (10th ed., 1958–1959, Tax Foundation, Inc. 1958), Table 87.

393 Liberties and immunities of citizens protected against state governments as well as federal. *The Constitution of the United States of America, Analysis and Interpretation,* prepared by Legislative Reference Service, Library of Congress, E. S. Corwin, ed. (U.S. Govt. Printing Office, 1958), 757 *et seq.*

410f. *Gibbons v. Ogden* (1824), 9 Wheaton 1.

413 Harmless custom in dress becoming harmful. Ellsworth Huntington, *Mainsprings of Civilization* (Wiley, 1945), 296f.

413 Social effects of difficult Chinese written language. O. and E. Lattimore, *The Making of Modern China* (Norton, 1944), 79ff.

414 Dust Bowl calamity. Bliss Isely, art. "Dust Bowl" in 2 *Dict. Am. Hist.*

416 Figures on votes, from *New York Times,* Sept. 25, 1944, and *World Almanac,* 1942, 70. Dates of acts, R. B. Morris, ed., *Encyc. Am. Hist.*

418 Bourgeois statistics and Marx-Leninist statistics. Translation in *Scientific Monthly* (August 1952) of official Soviet account of convention.

418f. Call by Communist-led General Confederation of Labor for general strike, May 27, 1958. *World Almanac,* 1959, 103.

423 Characteristics of the Wars of the Roses. H. A. L. Fisher, *A History of Europe* (rev. ed., Houghton Mifflin, 1939), 342.

424 *France from Reconstruction to Expansion, 1948–1958* (Ambassade de France-Service de Presse et d'Information, N.Y., April 1958, p. 48), gives comparative figures for prewar and postwar France.

425 Membership of National Assembly. *Polit. Hdbk. of World 1958,* 69.

426ff. Constitution of Fifth Republic. Text in *New York Times,* Sept. 5, 1958.

429 U.S.S.R. and U.S.A. military expenditures. *New York Times,* June 16, 1958.

441 The so-called Connecticut Compromise. Max Farrand, *The Framing of the Constitution of the United States* (Yale, 1913), ch. VII, "The Great Compromise."

458 Isaiah 45:1, 3, 4. Moffatt translation.

461f. Hospitality to stranger on the desert. Ellsworth Huntington, *Mainsprings of Civilization* (Wiley, 1945), 173f; to an enemy raider, *ibid.,* 178. Cf. W. G. Sumner, *Folkways* (Ginn, 1906), Sec. 551. On death penalty for breach of hospitality to one not an enemy. Judges 20:13.

466f. Contemporary instances of economic communities functioning across

Page

national barriers are the European Coal and Steel Community (1951 treaty) and the European Economic Community (1957 treaty).

469   Court of law for interstate economic union. Cf. The Honorable A. M. Donner, "The Court of Justice of the European Communities," *The Record of the Assn. of the Bar of the City of New York*, vol. 17, no. 5, May 1962, 232–243.

470   Estimate of increase of consumption of nonrenewable resources to provide per capita use like that in U.S.A. Karl Sax, *The Population Explosion* (Foreign Policy Assn. Headline Series, No. 120, Nov.–Dec. 1956), 38.

475   On U.S.S.R. climate and some of its effects. Chauncy D. Harris, "U.S.S.R. Resources: Agriculture," *Focus*, vol. 13, no. 5, Jan. 1963 (American Geographical Society).

481   Conflict between natural love and filial duty. Franz Boas, *Race and Democratic Society* (Augustin, 1945), 134f.

486   Communist party membership. *The Statesman's Year-Book, 1960–1961*, estimates the party membership at 8,708,000 out of a total population of about 208,800,000. Page 1450.

486   Self-description of Communist party. Quoted, *ibid.*, 1449, from rules adopted by the 19th Congress of the party, Oct. 13, 1952.

INDEX

Index